UNIVERSITY OF
STRATHCLYDE LIBRARIES

D0243855

Ceserani and Kinton's

The Theory
of Catering

11ᵗʰ Edition

Professor David Foskett

and Victor Ceserani

Hodder Arnold

A MEMBER OF THE HODDER HEADLINE GROUP

ANDERSONIAN LIBRARY
★
WITHDRAWN
FROM
LIBRARY
STOCK
★
UNIVERSITY OF STRATHCLYDE

Your Partner for Success

KNORR, PG tips, FLORA, HELLMANN'S, CARTE D'OR and Unilever Foodsolutions are registered trademarks.

Unilever Foodsolutions Unilever *UK* Brooke House Manor Royal Crawley West Sussex RH10 9RQ

Internet www.unileverfoodsolutions.co.uk

D642.47 KIN 05183 7/08

Orders: please contact Bookpoint Ltd, 130 Milton Park, Abingdon, Oxon OX14 4SB. Telephone: +44 (0)1235 827720. Fax: 144 (0)1235 400454. Lines are open from 9.00–5.00, Monday to Saturday, with a 24-hour message-answering service. You can also order through our website www.hoddereducation.co.uk.

British Library Cataloguing in Publication Data
A catalogue record for this title is available from the British Library

ISBN 978 0 340 93926 0

First published 2007
Impression number   10 9 8 7 6 5 4 3 2 1
Year   2012 2011 2010 2009 2008 2007

Copyright © 2007 David Foskett and Victor Ceserani
Chapter 12 © Hodder Arnold
Chapter 12 of this textbook is written by Unilever Foodsolutions and reproduced with kind permission. Colman's, Flora, Carte D'Or, Hellmann's, Lipton, Knorr, PG Tips and Unilever Foodsolutions are registered trademarks of Unilever.
Chapter 17 © Paul Hambleton

All rights reserved. No part of this publication may be reproduced or transmitted in any form or by any means, electronic or mechanical, including photocopy, recording, or any information storage and retrieval system, without permission in writing from the publisher or under licence from the Copyright Licensing Agency Limited. Further details of such licences (for reprographic reproduction) may be obtained from the Copyright Licensing Agency Limited, Saffron House, 6–10 Kirby Street, London EC1N 8TS.

Cover photo by Sam Bailey
Illustrations by Barking Dog Art
Original photography by Sam Bailey
Typeset by Fakenham Photosetting Limited, Norfolk.
Printed by CPI Bath for Hodder Arnold, an imprint of Hodder Education, a member of the Hodder Headline Group, An Hachette Livre UK Company, 338 Euston Road, London NW1 3BH.

CONTENTS

ACKNOWLEDGEMENTS

We are greatly indebted to the following people and organisations for their helpful advice and contributions to this edition.

Lionel Benjamin for cost control; John Cousins for an overview of food and beverage service; Romilly Edelmann for hygiene nutrition and food science; Richard Fagan of Ebex; Edward Griffiths for planning a function; Paul Hambleton, Thames Valley University, for Chapter 17, on ICT; Michael Stapleton, UK Corporate Affairs Director, Compass Group UK; British Egg Information Services; British Hospitality Association; Dairy Council; Food Service Intelligence; Sea Fish Authority.

Russums Catering Clothing and Equipment
Bill Graney, Manager Client Services, Harrison Catering
Alexia Chan, Rick Jackman, Deborah Edwards, Lynn Brown and Laura DeGrasse at Hodder Arnold
Colin Fisher, hygiene consultant
John Campbell, Executive Chef, and all the staff at The Vineyard at Stockcross
Sam Bailey, photographer
Barry Gregory, Chef Lecturer, Halesowen College
Gary Hunter, Head of Culinary Arts, Westminster Kingsway College
Steve Thorpe, Programme Manager Food and Beverage Curriculum, City College Norwich
Tony Taylor, Deputy Director, Academy of Service Industries, Bournemouth and Poole College
Baxter Storey

Crown copyright material is reproduced by permission of the controller of the Controller of HMSO.

The authors and publisher would like to thank the following for permission to reproduce copyright illustrative material:
All-Clad, fig 6.34; Aramark Catering UK, fig 2.1; Charvet Premier Ranges Ltd, fig 6.4; Compass Group UK, figs 1.8-1.12, 1.15, 2.1-2.4, 4.122, 5.9, 6.9, 6.11, 6.23, 6.24, 6.29, 7.9, 7.18–7.21, 10.1, 10.2, 10.6, 10.8, 11.4, 14.3, 14.4, 15.10, 16.2, 16.5–16.10, 16.12, 16.13, 16.19, 16.26, 17.1; Ingram Publishing, fig 4.96; Meat and Livestock Commission, figs 4.3-4.12, 4.14-4.16, 4.18-4.25, 4.27, 4.28, 4.30-4.43; Photodisc, figs 10.3, 10.5, 10.7, 10.13; The Ritz London, figs 8.9, 10.4, 10.9, 10.10, 10.12; Russums Catering Clothing and Equipment, figs 6.12, 6.13, 6.15, 6.16, 6.21, 6.22, 6.26, 6.28, 6.40, 6.41, 7.8, 7.12, 15.8, 15.11, 16.20, 16.21, 16.25; Unilever Foodsolutions, fig 12.4

The authors and publisher would like to thank the following, whose expertise and kind help were instrumental in the making of the film clips which accompany this book: John Campbell and the staff at The Vineyard at Stockcross; Andie Way, Robert Perry, Janet Rowson, Sue Montgomery, Sibel Roller and Elaine O'Sullivan at Thames Valley University; Helen Evans, Gary Marshall and the Covent Garden Market Authority; Adam Hands, Marigold Keylock and Winchcombe Abbey Primary School; Andy Hazell, Mike Anthony and Gloucester RFC; Dipna Anand and the staff at The BrilliantRestaurant, Southall; Dr Claire Mills at IFR, Norwich; The Loon Fung Superstore, Alperton; and Russ Timpson at The Fire Strategy Company. The films were produced and created by Adrian Moss of Instructional Design Ltd. Cheltenham.

FOREWORD

The Theory of Catering is a must-read. I remember in my university days reading textbooks by *the* authorities in their field – but that's all they are, memories. They, too, were must-reads at the time, but invariably grew dusty on the shelves after graduation.

The Theory of Catering, however, is a true necessity for any student of catering and hospitality anywhere in the world. It is a book you will keep with you throughout your career. Most importantly, it not only covers the theory of catering, but also the practice. It is a comprehensive, authoritative book for everyone in the field. Whether back-of-house or front-of-house, this book is essential.

I know, having started a business from scratch, that ideas are useless on their own. It is ideas combined with action that make things happen. *The Theory of Catering* bridges the gap between idea and application, between theory and practice.

It is a privilege to work with Professor David Foskett MBE in my capacity as Chancellor of Thames Valley University (TVU). David is truly one of the titans of the hospitality industry, and as Associate Dean of the London School of Tourism, Hospitality and Leisure at TVU he has helped create a beacon of excellence, renowned not just across the UK but worldwide.

And with *The Theory of Catering*, David and Victor Ceserani have produced a book that is itself a beacon of the industry – a work that is clear, and clearly useful, to people at all levels. Whether a student or a practitioner, this book is indispensable.

Lord Bilimoria of Chelsea CBE DL
Founder and Chief Executive, Cobra Beer; Chancellor, Thames Valley University

INTRODUCTION TO THE 11TH EDITION

As travel, tourism, recreation and hospitality become increasingly important in the economic life of the vast majority of countries, so the need for well-trained operatives and managers continues to grow.

This book is designed to meet the needs of those training for, or involved in, the catering industry (often referred to as the hospitality industry).

This 11th edition has been revised and updated to keep in line with the continuing changes both in industry and catering education. As in previous editions we have not attempted to write a completely comprehensive book, but rather have set out an outline as a basis for further study. In this way we hope to assist students at all levels and, for those who wish to study at great length, further references and websites are suggested where appropriate.

HOW TO USE THIS BOOK AND CD-ROM

A single-user licence CD-ROM is enclosed in the back of this book. Insert the CD-ROM into your computer and it will run automatically. You must be connected to the Internet to use this resource and you will need to follow the on-screen instructions to install the Dynamic Learning Player the first time you use it.

When you start using the CD-ROM for the first time, it may be helpful to click on 'DL tutorial' at the top of the screen. This will provide you with a step-by-step introduction to accessing and using the different features of Dynamic Learning.

If you get stuck at any time, click 'Help' at the top of the screen.

The CD-ROM has several features, which are arranged in sections that correspond to the chapters in this book. These features include:

- **Knowledge quiz:** there is an on-screen quiz for each chapter. Answer ten multiple-choice questions about what you have read, and print out your results page as a record of your achievement.
- **Video clips:** these short videos about the hospitality and related industries star real people who work in the field.
- **Useful websites:** these useful links will take you to other websites related to each particular topic. If you are connected to the Internet, simply clicking on each link will open the website in a new web browser window. *Please note: all weblinks contain live content and information, and as such this content is liable to change. Hodder & Stoughton Ltd are not responsible for the content of any external website.*
- **Interactive activities:** these on-screen exercises will test your understanding. They relate to the material on commodities in Chapter 4.
- **Images and other resources:** many of the images and tables from the book are included on

the CD-ROM. You can download these and use them in your coursework, presentations, etc. The CD-ROM also includes some extra material which does not appear in the book.

A network version of the CD-ROM is also available (ISBN 9780340941768). In addition to the features listed above, this version includes worksheets relating to each chapter in the book. These are only accessible to teachers with a password. Visit www.hoddereducation.co.uk to purchase this resource.

Whenever you see this icon in the book, it means that there is some material on the CD-ROM, or on the network version, which relates to what you are reading.

OBTAINING EMPLOYMENT AND BUILDING A CAREER

With the decision made to come into catering, it is to be hoped that prior to or during the course, students will have worked in the industry and seen some of the different types of work available. If possible, they will have obtained experience in a variety of different establishments (hotels, hospitals, industrial, restaurants, etc.). People do best at that which interests them most, so try to find out what appeals to you.

Having got on the ladder, you need to consider the following points when trying to progress up it.

- Do not get off one rung until you have got onto another one – in other words, make certain you have a job to go to before leaving your present employment.
- It is generally advisable to stay with your first employer for at least a year, and to spend at least a year in each subsequent job.
- It is desirable to keep in continuous employment; gaps do not present employers with a view of a stable employee.
- Advancement is more likely if you keep within one area of catering (contract, hospital, restaurants, etc.) so that experience gained can be of benefit to employers. However, some careers, such as teaching, need people experienced in several aspects of the industry.
- Know where you are going and have attainable goals. However, if a real mistake has been made and a move has been wrong then a change may be for the best.

In evaluating the need to progress, the following factors need to be considered apart from the money: value of the new experience, the establishment's reputation, conditions and hours of work, opportunities for advancement in existing establishment, facilities offered for self-development (further courses, overseas experience, etc.).

If possible, when leaving college or any employment, endeavour to leave in such a way that you can return at any time. The catering industry needs people who are loyal, prepared to work hard and to enjoy their work together as a team.

LIST OF ABBREVIATIONS

ACAS	Advisory Conciliation and Arbitration Service
ASC	Assured Safe Catering
BEd	Bachelor of Education – (Hons) = Honours
BEPA	British Egg Producers Association
BHA	British Hospitality Association
BHT	butylated hydroxytoluene
BSc	Bachelor of Science
BSE	bovine spongiform encephalopathy
CAD	computer-aided design
CAP	Common Agricultural Policy
CCP	critical control points
CCTV	closed-circuit television
CEMA	Catering Equipment Manufacturers Association
CJD	Creutzfeldt-Jakob disease
CO_2	carbon dioxide
COSHH	Control of Substances Hazardous to Health
CPA	Chevalier Dans L'ordre des Palmes Académique
DEFRA	Department for Environment, Food and Rural Affairs
DfES	Department for Education and Skills
DMS	Diploma in Management Studies
DNA	deoxyribonucleic acid
DSO	direct service organisation
ECA	European Catering Association
EFTA	European Free Trade Association
EHO	Environmental Health officer
EPOS	electronic point of sale
ETSU	energy technology support unit
EU	European Union
F&B	food and beverage
GDS	global distribution system
GMO	genetically modified organisms
GMS	glycerol monostearate
GNP	gross national product
HACCP	hazard analysis and critical control point
HCIMA	Hotel and Catering International Management Association (now the Institute of Hospitality)
HMSO	Her Majesty's Stationery Office
HSE	Health & Safety Executive
HSEO	Health and Safety Enforcement Officer
HTF	Hospitality Training Foundation
ICT	information and communication technology
IT	information technology
JIT	just-in-time
KFC	Kentucky Fried Chicken
MAP	modified atmosphere packaging
MBA	Master of Business Administration
MBE	Member of the Order of the British Empire
NHS	National Health Service
P&O	Peninsular and Orient
PC (i)	personal computer
PC (ii)	practical cookery
PDA	personal digital assistant
pH	a measurement of acidity, alkalinity (potenz Hydrogen)
PMS	property management systems
PPE	personal protective equipment
QUID	Quantitative Ingredients Declaration
RAM	random access memory
RIDDOR	Reporting Injuries, Diseases & Dangerous Occurrences
SWOT	strengths, weaknesses, opportunities, threats
TVP	texturised vegetable protein
UK	United Kingdom
VAT	value added tax
VDU	visual display unit
WTTC	World Travel and Tourism Council
YM	yield management

QUALIFICATION MAPPING GRIDS

CHAPTER	NVQ LEVEL 1 FOOD AND DRINK	VRQ LEVEL 1 DIPLOMA IN INTRODUCTION TO PROFESSIONAL COOKERY	NVQ LEVEL 1 FOOD PREPARATION AND COOKING	NVQ 1 MULTI SKILLS
1. An overview of the UK and global hospitality industry		Unit 101		
2. Employment in the hospitality industry				
3 Food and society				
4 Food commodities			1FP1, 1FP2, 1FP3, 1FC1, 1FPC1, 1FPC2, 1FPC3, 1FPC4, 1FPC5, 1FPC6, 1FPC7	Background knowledge: 1FPC1, 1FPC2, 1FC1, 1FPC1, 1FPC2, 1FPC3, 1FPC4, 1FPC5, 1FPC6
5 Elementary nutrition, food science, diet and health		Unit 104		
6 Kitchen planning, equipment, services and energy conservation		Unit 105		
7 Production systems				
8 Menu planning, development and structure				
9 Food purchasing, storage and control				
10 An overview of food and beverage service				
11 Chemistry in the kitchen, and product development				
12 Product development and manufacturing to deliver convenience in the kitchen				
13 Managing resources	1GEN4	Unit 106	1GEN4	1GEN4
14 Marketing, sales and customer care	1GEN3			1GEN3
15 Health, safety and security	1GEN1	Unit 103	1GEN1	
16 Hygiene and food legislation	2GEN4 1GEN1	Unit 202	2GEN3 1GEN1	2GEN3, 2GEN4, 1GEN1
17 Information and communication technology in the hospitality industry				

CHAPTER	NVQ LEVEL 2 FOOD AND DRINK	NVQ LEVEL 2 PROFESSIONAL COOKERY	VRQ LEVEL 2 DIPLOMA IN PROFESSIONAL COOKERY	NVQ LEVEL 2 FOOD PROCESSING AND COOKING	NVQ LEVEL 2 IN HOSPITALITY
1. An overview of the UK and global hospitality industry			Unit 201		
2. Employment in the hospitality industry					
3 Food and society					
4 Food commodities		Background knowledge: 2FC1, 2FP3, 2FC3, 2FP4, 2FC4, 2FP7, 2FC7, 2FC2, 2FC1, 2FC3, 2FC4, 2FC7, 2FC2, 2FC5, 2FC6, 2FP2, 2FP5, 2FP6, 2FPC8	Background knowledge: Unit 208, Unit 209, Unit 210, Unit 211, Unit 212.	Background knowledge: 2FC1, 2FC3, 2FC4, 2FC7, 2FPC8	Background knowledge: 1FP1, 2FPC8, 1FPC1, 1FPC2, 2FP1, 2FP2, 2FP3, 2FP4, 2FP5, 2FP6, 2FP7, 2FC1, 2FC2, 2FC3, 2FC4, 2FC5, 2FC6, 2FC7
5 Elementary nutrition, food science, diet and health		2FPC13	Unit 204	2FPC13	2FC13
6 Kitchen planning, equipment, services and energy conservation				HS1	2DS8, HS1
7 Production systems		2FC8, 2FC9		2FC8, 2FC9	2FC8, 2FC9
8 Menu planning, development and structure			Unit 205		
9 Food purchasing, storage and control		2P&C1, 2GEN2	Unit 205	2GEN2, 2P&C1	2GEN2
10 An overview of food and beverage service					
11 Chemistry in the kitchen, and product development					
12 Product development and manufacturing to deliver convenience in the kitchen					
13 Managing resources	1GEN4	1GEN4		1GEN4	1GEN4
14 Marketing, sales and customer care	1GEN3				2R9
15 Health, safety and security	1GEN1	1GEN1	Unit 203	1GEN1	1GEN1
16 Hygiene and food legislation	2GEN4 1GEN1	2GEN3	Unit 202	2GEN3 1GEN1	2GEN3 2GEN4
17 Information and communication technology in the hospitality industry					

CHAPTER	NVQ LEVEL 3 HOSPITALITY SUPERVISION	NVQ LEVEL 3 PROFESSIONAL COOKERY
1. An overview of the UK and global hospitality industry		
2. Employment in the hospitality industry		
3 Food and society		
4 Food commodities		Background information: 3FP1, 3FP2, 3FP3, 3FP4, 3FP5, 3FC1, 3FC2, 3FC3, 3FC4, 3FC5, 3FC6
5 Elementary nutrition, food science, diet and health		2FPC13
6 Kitchen planning, equipment, services and energy conservation	HS1, HS3, HS7, HS8	HS3
7 Production systems		
8 Menu planning, development and structure	HS9	HS9
9 Food purchasing, storage and control		
10 An overview of food and beverage service		
11 Chemistry in the kitchen, and product development		
12 Product development and manufacturing to deliver convenience in the kitchen		
13 Managing resources	HS2, HS3, HAS5	HS2, HS3
14 Marketing, sales and customer care	H519, H523, HS5	
15 Health, safety and security	HS4	HS4
16 Hygiene and food legislation	HS4	2GEN3, 3GEN1
17 Information and communication technology in the hospitality industry		

PART 1

THE HOSPITALITY INDUSTRY

Chapter 1 AN OVERVIEW OF THE UK AND GLOBAL HOSPITALITY INDUSTRY

THE UK HOSPITALITY INDUSTRY

The largest sectors in the UK hospitality industry, in terms of numbers of outlets, are hotels and pubs – a microcosm of the catering industry itself since it comprises a wide variety of outlets, from sports clubs and stadia to theme parks, historic properties, cinemas and beyond. Indeed, many researchers are unsure whether to include the leisure sector within the catering market, since it consists of a large number of outlets, each of which serves only small quantities of food. However, this sector will be among those showing the fastest growth over the next few years.

Like hospitality and tourism, all leisure markets benefit from improving economic conditions. For many people, real disposable income has grown and the forecasts are that it will continue to grow. On average, people were approximately a third more wealthy at the end of the 1990s than they were at the beginning. In wealthy markets, the leisure and pleasure sectors outperform the economy in general. It is usually the case that, as people become wealthier, their incremental income is not usually spent on upgrading the essentials but on pleasure and luxury items. However, whenever there is a downturn in the economy, the leisure sectors suffer disproportionately.

The leisure industry has been described as the biggest, fastest-growing industry in the UK. Within the leisure sector, some areas have slowed down, while others are consolidating and concentrating on core businesses. One of the most useful ways of categorising the leisure sector is to separate it into popular leisure activities – for example, theatre, ten-pin bowling and cue sports, casinos, bingo, and health and fitness.

In terms of meals served, the most significant sectors are food service, followed by pubs, staff catering and health care. An expected rise in household incomes of 3.4 per cent per annum in real terms between 1999 and 2009 will result in a rise of 3.7 per cent in money spent on eating out. This means that spending on catering will account for a slightly greater share of personal disposable income by 2009.

Traditionally, catering activity has been divided into either profit or cost sector markets. The profit sector includes such establishments as restaurants, fast-food outlets, cafés, takeaways, pubs, and leisure and travel catering outlets; the cost sector refers to catering outlets for business and industry, education and health care. Recent developments have blurred the division between profit- and cost-orientated establishments.

The food service management industry

Food and service management covers feeding people at work in business and industry, catering in schools, colleges and universities, hospitals and health care, welfare and local authority catering, and other non-profit-making outlets.

Despite its complexity, catering represents one of the largest sectors of the UK economy and is fifth in size behind retail food, cars, insurance and clothing. It is also an essential support to tourism, another major part of the economy, and one of the largest employers in the country.

Table 1.1 Total number of outlets in UK business and industry 1990, 2001–2005

The total number of outlets in business and industry is estimated by Horizons as follows:

	2005		2004		2002		2002		2001		1990	
	OUTLETS	%	OUTLETS	%	OUTLETS	%	OUTLETS	%	OUTLETS	%	OUTLETS	%
Contracted outlets	8973		9975	50	8939	51	9078	51	9002	51	7056	31
Self-operated outlets	8786		8841	50	8776	49	8755	49	8821	49	15,922	69
TOTAL outlets	17,759		17,816		17,715		17,833		17,823		22,978	

Source: British Hospitality Association (BHA), Food and Service Management Survey, 2006

Table **1.2** Number of outlets and meals served, 2005

TYPE OF OUTLET	OUTLETS	%	MEALS SERVED (m)	%
Business and industry	8214		553	
Department store staff	597		22	
Prison and prison shops	162		70	
	8973	51.0	645	41.2
Health care				
NHS and Trust hospitals	369		175	
Private hospitals	50		4	
Private and state nursing homes	420		25	
	839	4.8	204	13.0
Education				
State schools	3960		105	
Further education/higher education/universities	546		160	
	4506	25.5	265	16.9
Independent schools and private nurseries	754	4.3	100	6.4
Local authorities				
Courts	75		3	
Police and fire service	157		16	
Town hall	40		2	
Welfare	19		1	
	291	1.7	22	1.4
Ministry of Defence	490	2.8	105	6.7
Oil rigs, construction sites and training centres	202	1.1	16	1.0
Catering for the public*	1553	8.8	210	13.4
Total	17,608		1567	

*Excluding all events
Source: BHA, Food and Service Management Survey, 2006

Figure 1.1 Number of outlets

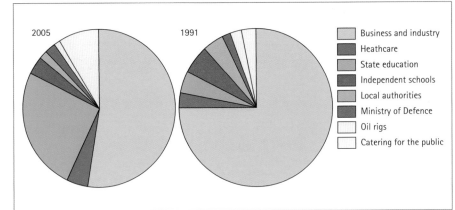

Source: BHA, Food and Service Management Survey, 2006

Figure 1.2 Number of meals

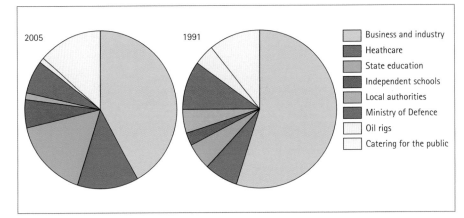

Source: BHA, Food and Service Management Survey, 2006

Figure 1.3 Contracted outlets vs self-operated outlets

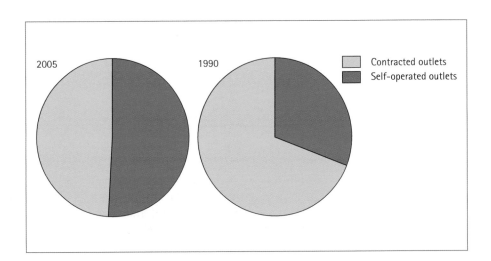

Source: BHA, Food and Service Management Survey, 2006

Figure 1.4 Meals served by food and service management companies, 1990 and 2005 (business and industry)

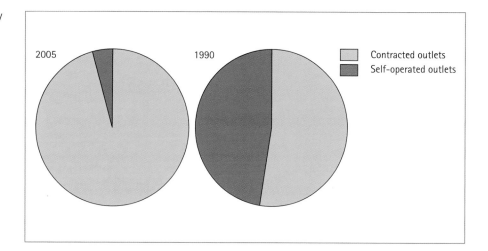

Source: BHA, Food and Service Management Survey, 2006

Figure 1.5 Types of catering contract, 1994 and 2005

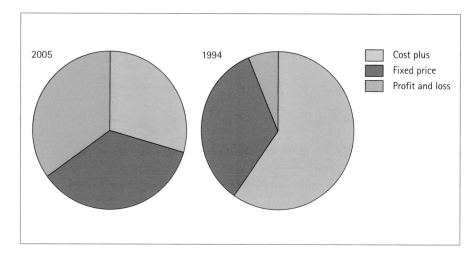

Source: BHA, Food and Service Management Survey, 2006

The UK tourism, hospitality and leisure industry

The UK tourism, hospitality and leisure industry is estimated by the government to have been worth £75 billion in 2004. Including all business expenditure, the total market is worth £81.5 billion. Expenditure on accommodation is more difficult to pin down. It is estimated at £10.3 billion (after excluding categories such as camp sites and youth hostels). UK Travel Survey reports a figure of £7.5 billion, but this excludes business expenditure, food and beverage, expenditure by overseas visitors (business and non-business), functions, conferences, and other activities such as health clubs.

Table 1.3 The UK hospitality and catering industry, 2001–2004

	2001	2002	2003	2004
Outlets	262,511	262,971	262,910	262,948
Meals (m)	8439	8471	8488	8583
Food purchases (£m)	8783	88,896	8848	9004
Food sales (£m)	24,939	25,232	25,162	25,687
Food and drink sales (£m)	33,475	33,890	33,824	34,549

Source: BHA, British Hospitality: Trends and Statistics, 2005

Table 1.4 Countries of origin of overseas visitors to the UK, 2000 and 2002–2004

RANK	COUNTRY	VISITS (000S)				SPENDING (£M)*			
		2000	2002	2003	2004	2000	2002	2003	2004
1	USA	4097	3611	3346	3623	2752	2443	2658	2882
2	France	3087	3077	3073	3252	684	733	694	770
3	Germany	2757	2556	2611	2958	887	743	820	822
4	Irish Republic	2087	2439	2488	2559	570	674	681	749
5	Netherlands	1439	1419	1549	1619	374	384	446	463
6	Spain	849	1010	1203	1462	409	444	518	617
7	Italy	949	977	1168	1346	472	406	502	521
8	Belgium/ Luxembourg	1048	1010	978	1159	234	196	204	232
9	Australia	777	702	723	788	517	531	528	709
10	Canada	773	660	652	742	445	338	343	477

* At current prices
Source: National Statistics website: www.statistics.gov.uk

Table 1.5 UK accommodation industry registered with national tourist boards, 2004: size by unit and no. of bedrooms. *Source: BHA, British Hospitality: Trends and Statistics, 2005*

	HOTELS AND INNS		GUEST HOUSES		BED & BREAKFAST		OTHERS	
	UNITS	BEDROOMS	UNITS	BEDROOMS	UNITS	BEDROOMS	UNITS	BEDROOMS
England	12,520	377,203	7,306	70,774	14,492	62,416	2,252	116,314
Scotland	1,269	41,557	847	5,611	1,968	5,314	22	4,420
Wales	689	14,690	338	1,956	571	1,688	408	2,473
Northern Ireland	131	6,075	140	1,057	666	2,456	7	2,228
Total	14,609	439,525	8,631	79,398	17,697	71,874	2,689	125,435

Table 1.6 Value of UK tourism and leisure industry (£bn), 2004

	TOTAL	ALL TOURISM – INBOUND TOURISTS	DOMESTIC HOLIDAYS – UK RESIDENTS	LEISURE/ BUSINESS – UK RESIDENTS
Overnight accommodation	9.9	2.0	7.9	–
Eating out of home	20.1	1.0	4.1	15.1
Drinking out of home	15.9	0.3	3.0	12.6
Rail, car, coach, taxi, cab travel for leisure, tourism	4.5	1.0	2.1	1.3
Air travel within UK, and from start points outside UK to destinations within UK	3.3	1.1	2.2	–
Cinemas, theatres, museums, zoos, historical properties, theme parks, gardens	2.8	0.7	–	2.1
Social clubs, leisure classes, bingo, dances, discos, social events	4.9	–	–	4.9
Sports – spectating	0.8	0.2	–	0.6
Sports – participating	1.2	–	–	1.2
Shopping on holiday, shopping by overseas visitors	3.1	3.1	–	–
Gambling	4.9	–	–	4.9
Business-related expenditure	10.2	3.7	–	6.5
Total	81.5	13.0	19.3	49.1

Source: BHA, British Hospitality: Trends and Statistics, 2005

Almost 70 per cent of visitors to the UK come from western Europe. The number of visitors from North America increased each year between 1990 and 2000. Following 9/11, arrivals in 2001 from North American and from other markets declined sharply, but they recovered in 2002 and, in 2004, reached record highs.

While there is a clear overlap with tourism, the hospitality industry consists of all those business operations that provide for their customers any combinations of the three core services of food, drink and accommodation. There are, however, a number of sectors within the hospitality industry that can be regarded as separate from tourism – for example, industrial catering and those aspects of hospitality that attract only the local community.

Restaurants in the UK have approximately 40 per cent of the commercial market, while small establishments employing fewer than ten staff form the majority of the industry. The south-east of England has the highest concentration of catering and hospitality outlets. Rapid expansion took place in the hospitality industry during the 1980s, throughout all sectors. Within the hotel sector, room stocks have increased by some 40 per cent. This period of growth has been fuelled by the need for the large companies to maintain competitive advantage and by the provision of a suitable environment for growth. However, the key feature of the UK hospitality industry is the extent of the fragmentation of ownership. The hotel sector is predominantly independently owned. These properties come in all shapes, sizes and locations. More than three-quarters of them have fewer than 20 rooms and are invariably family-run.

The hotel sector, despite its disparate nature, can be divided into distinct categories, such as luxury, business, resort, town house and budget properties. Each category has its own characteristics. Business hotels, as the name suggests, are geared to the corporate traveller; the emphasis therefore tends to be on functionality. These hotels will usually have a dedicated business centre, up-to-date communication technology in the rooms, and ample conference and meeting facilities. Business hotels are more likely to be chain operated, often with a strong brand element. Town houses, meanwhile, are notable for their individuality, intimacy and emphasis on service. These hotels are invariably small and, as the name suggests, located in converted town houses with a domestic feel that is emphasised by their decor. The fastest-growing sector is budget hotels (e.g. Travel Lodge, Travel Inn), where the accommodation units are co-located with a food source operation such as Little Chef.

Clearly the provision of food and beverage (F&B) varies greatly between establishments, e.g. formal dining and buffet set-ups, traditional fare and theme restaurants, room service and public bars. Again, some general differences can be discerned between the various hotel categories. Upmarket hotels are likely to provide a full range of F&B services, usually with at least one à la carte restaurant, 24-hour room service and a well-stocked bar. Town house properties, in contrast, generally provide little or no food, while budget hotels are characterised by the presence of a family restaurant. This is often a stand-alone, branded outlet that also draws custom from the surrounding area.

Recently many hotels have been re-examining the place of F&B in their operations. While many town houses open with no restaurant at all, other hotels believe that F&B provision is an essential guest service. This has led them to consider alternative methods of running a restaurant, such as contracting out to a third party or introducing a franchise operation.

The economics of running a restaurant in a hotel show why this has taken place. While F&B receipts traditionally provide about 20–30 per cent of a hotel's total revenue, over three-quarters of this will be absorbed by departmental expenses, including payroll costs of approximately a third. A hotel's room department typically provides

50–60 per cent of revenue, but departmental costs account for only 25–30 per cent of this.

Food tourism

The experience of food and taste is an important element in tourism. In defining food tourism there is a need to differentiate between those tourists who consume food as a part of the travel experience and those whose activities, behaviours and even choice of destination are influenced by their interest in the food. Similar to these people are those who are interested in wine and visit the noted wine-producing areas of the world. For such people, vineyards, wineries, wine festivals, wine shows, wine tasting and/or experiencing the attributes of a wine region are the prime motivating factors. Similarly, food tourism refers to visits to food producers, food festivals, restaurants and specific locations renowned for a particular food, as well as food tasting and/or experiencing the attributes of specialist food production regions, or even visiting a restaurant to taste the dishes of a well-known chef; for food tourists, such factors provide the motivation for them to travel to a certain area. (Some people, for example, travel to Perigord in France to taste the foie gras and truffles, and sample the local Bergerac wine for which the area is renowned.)

The globalisation of the hospitality and tourism industries

Businesses today find themselves competing in a world economy for survival, growth and profitability. Managers working in the industry have to learn to adjust to change in line with market demands for quality and value for money, and increased organisational attention must be devoted to profitability and professionalism.

The globalisation of the hospitality and tourism industries has advanced under the pressures of increased technology, communication, transportation, deregulation, elimination of political barriers, sociocultural changes and global economic development, together with growing competition in a global economy. An international hospitality company must perform successfully in the *world's* business environment. There are a vast number of influences in the external international environment that greatly affect the multinational organisation. Some of these are as follows.

- Monetary and fiscal policies and exchange controls: some countries may limit the amount of money that can be withdrawn from their country, as well as impose large payments for international transactions (e.g. joint ventures, entry to the country).
- Financial and investment markets, individual consumer and corporate interest rates, the availability of credit, exchanges, and so on.

- Taxation and tariffs: taxes on individuals, corporations and imported goods, imposed by the host country/government.
- Trade/industrial factors: import/export measures of activity in commerce, and so on. These can serve as indices in determining the state of the economy (e.g. prosperity, depression, recession, recovery).
- Labour markets: the level of unemployment, welfare spending, and so on.

Travel, tourism and hospitality together make up the world's largest industry. According to the World Travel and Tourism Council (WTTC), the annual gross output of the industry is greater than the gross national product (GNP) of all countries except the United States and Japan. Worldwide, the industry employs over 112 million people. In many countries, especially in emerging tourism destinations, the hospitality and tourism industry plays a very important role in the national economy, being the major foreign currency earner.

As the world economy continues to become more interdependent, this will give rise to increasing amounts of business travel. With this in mind, it is clear that the global economic environment plays a significant role in the internationalisation opportunities available to hospitality and tourism companies, and that global economic policies and developments play a critical role in the hospitality and tourism industry.

One of the principal challenges confronting the industry of the future will result from the ongoing transition to the 'information age'. The convergence of computing, telecommunications and content will shape the way and pace at which people live and work. Above all, it will change the nature of the exchange process between providers and their customers – the latter will have more choice. The information superhighway will offer numerous ways to find out whether a hospitality company or restaurant, say, delivers on its promises. Dissatisfied clients will be able to vent their feelings to an Internet-connected community of millions. Companies will in turn be expected to systematically accumulate information about their customers.

The effects of international tourism

By 2010 there will be approximately one billion tourist journeys a year, if annual increases match the World Tourism Organization's (WTO's) long-term predictions of a 4.1 per cent average annual growth rate. However, the signs are that international tourist arrivals will overshoot these forecasts by some distance, creating dynamic opportunities for companies in the hospitality industry.

By 2010, it is estimated that there will be approximately 791 million intra-regional travellers and 216 million long-haul travellers, as emerging markets such as China and India continue to grow and people with disposable income keen to spend it on travel will make the most of low-cost carriers and the easing of visa restrictions. While massive growth is

Figure 1.6 Regional market share of international tourist arrivals, 1995 and 2010 (%)

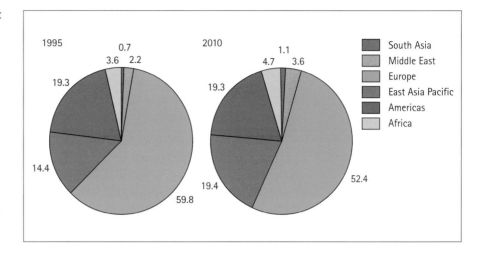

Source: UN World Tourism Organization, Tourism 2020 Vision, volume 5, Middle East

forecast for these emerging markets, other regions around the world, particularly Europe and America, will remain among the most visited destinations (see Figure 1.6).

China is investing heavily in travel and tourism. India's buoyant economy and its boom in business and leisure travel are driving a strong growth in tourism. To reduce the region's economic reliance on oil, many countries of the Gulf States are now focusing on tourism, capitalising on their natural assets, historic cultures and Islamic traditions: the Middle East is now the fourth most visited region in the world.

Investment in tourism in the Middle East is highest in the United Arab Emirates (UAE), followed by Saudi Arabia. Dubai's hotel market currently ranks among the world's best. International tourism is part of the wider move towards globalisation.

Airlines

Many people reach the hotel reception desk via an airline. Today, more than 1.6 billion passengers a year use the world's airlines for business and leisure travel. By 2010 this figure is likely to be around 2.3 billion.

People choose to fly for both business and leisure reasons. Some airlines, such as Aer Lingus, have only one class on all UK and European services. Food and drink has to be purchased on these flights as the carrier is trying to minimise the low-cost formula – so much so that Aer Lingus is leaving the One World Alliance to pursue its own low-cost strategy. (It does, however, offer business class on its transatlantic and Dubai services.) The use of in-flight entertainment is slowly making its way to the low-cost sector.

Tier systems are used by airlines to describe the prestige of a passenger based on their frequent flyer programmes. A first, platinum or premium tier traveller will normally have travelled hundreds of thousands of miles with the carrier and will have access to its lounges and lots of other goodies. Fierce competition between low-cost and traditional carriers, as well as cost-cutting by both airlines and corporate travel managers, have triggered this trend.

The major carriers are now offering all-business-class flights and are investing heavily to improve their products. According to the report, 'Hospitality 2010' (Deloitte/NYU, 2006), this upward market segmentation is illustrated by the airlines' marketing, which highlights:

- increased comfort on board the aircraft, and the availability of gyms, shower facilities and massages
- increased technology – e.g. broadband, videoconferencing
- mood lighting to aid jet lag and assist sleep
- on-board entertainment, online gaming, etc.
- a range of reading materials, menu items, wines, etc.
- door-to-door service rather than gate to gate.

THE HOSPITALITY INDUSTRY: PRODUCT AND SERVICE

The hospitality product consists of tangible and intangible elements of food, drink and accommodation, together with the service, atmosphere and image that surround and contribute to the product.

The hospitality industry contains many of the characteristics of service industries with the added complications of the production process. It is the production process that is the complicated element as it focuses on production and delivery, often within a set period of time.

The need to provide the appropriate environment within which hospitality can be delivered means that most hospitality businesses need a substantial amount of investment in plant and premises. This creates a high fixed cost/low variable cost structure. The variable costs in servicing a room are minimal, although the hotel itself – particularly in the luxury hotel market – has a high fixed cost. In general, the financial break-even point for hospitality businesses is often fairly high. Exceeding this level will result in high profits, but low volumes will result in substantial losses.

Hospitality services suffer from fluctuations in demand: demand fluctuates over time and by type of customer. Forecasting business is therefore often difficult because of the mixture of patterns and variables that can affect demand, making planning, resourcing and scheduling difficult. Hospitality cannot be delivered without customers, who are involved in many aspects of the delivery of the hospitality service.

Achieving a satisfactory balance between demand patterns, resource scheduling and operational capacity is a difficult task for managers in hospitality. Managing customer demand to achieve optimum volume at maximum value is extremely complex. Too few customers could spell financial ruin; too many customers without the required capacity or resources, often means that the customers' experience suffers, leading to dissatisfaction. Scheduling of resources is also difficult, if too many staff are on duty to cover the forecast demand, then profitability suffers. Insufficient staffing creates problems – with servicing and staff morale. Forecasting is therefore a crucial function, which contributes to the successful operation of the hospitality business.

The ability to deliver a consistent product to every customer is also an important consideration. Staff must be trained in teams to deliver a consistent standard of product and service. This means being able to cater not just for individual customers but to the needs of many different groups of customers, all with slightly different requirements. The success of any customer experience will be determined at the interaction point between the customer and the service provider.

The service staff have an additional part to play in serving the customer: they are important in the future selling process, and therefore should be trained to use the opportunity to generate additional revenue.

From this analysis we are able to identify four characteristics of the hospitality industry that make it a unique operation.

1 Hospitality cannot be delivered without customers who provide the source of revenue for the continued financial viability of the operation. The customer is directly involved in many aspects of the delivery of the hospitality service, and is the judge of the quality of the hospitality provided.
2 Achieving a satisfactory balance between demand patterns, resource scheduling and operations is a particularly difficult task in the hospitality industry.
3 All hospitality operations require a combination of manufacturing expertise and service skill, in many cases 24 hours a day. To deliver a consistent product to each individual customer requires teams of people well trained to deliver to a set standard every time.
4 No matter how well planned the operation, how good the design and environment, if the interaction between customer and service provider is not right this will have a detrimental effect on the customer experience of the total product, and a missed opportunity to sell future products. Good interaction between customers and service providers can also increase present sales – for example, a waiter can 'up sell' by suggesting in a positive way additions to the meal, perhaps items the customer may not even have considered but is delighted by the recommendation or subtle persuasion.

Hotel catering

Hotel food and beverage strategy

Unlike in the past, when hotels typically operated food and beverage facilities merely to satisfy the demands of their guests, today's hoteliers are increasingly adopting a more proactive approach by using their food and beverage outlets as a means to generate not only profitability but also publicity, as well as to cultivate a loyal following. Traditionally, hotel restaurants have not been profitable enterprises for hotels, given that they were often considered to be only an essential value-added service for guests.

Mintel has identified four hotel catering formats, as follows.

1 **General:** hotels featuring restaurants that cater primarily for residents of the hotel and, second, for walk-in guests who are not residents. These often take the form of casual, all-day dining facilities. The most enterprising of these are attempting to attract different consumers at different times of the day. For example, the Harrington Hotel in London aims to attract residents in the morning for breakfast, conference and banqueting clients for lunch, and walk-in customers for evening meals.

2 **Signature:** hotels that have developed a restaurant as a brand that stands alone from the hotel, and is therefore primarily aimed at walk-in customers. Most of these restaurants are located in luxury or upscale establishments, a number of which are managed by celebrity chefs such as Giorgio Locatelli, Gary Rhodes, Gordon Ramsay, Brian Turner, Angela Harnett and Marcus Wareing. Signature restaurants tend to operate independently of the hotel they are attached to. Establishments that fall into this category include Nobu (Metropolitan Hotel, London), Chino Latino (Park Plaza, Leeds and Nottingham) and Locanda Locatelli (Hyatt Churchill, London).

3 **Outsourced:** hotels that outsource the management and operation of their catering provision to a third party. The outsourcing of a hotel's food and beverage operations can take several forms: a lease contract, management contract or an agreement with a contracted caterer. An example of an outsourced food and beverage hotel operation is the Cumberland Hotel, London, which contracted Restaurant Associates, a division of the contract catering giant Compass plc, in early 2005 to operate all its bars and restaurants.

4 **Budget:** hotels that provide only a limited catering service, and sometimes no catering at all other than food from vending machines. The budget hotel sector in the UK is rapidly expanding, and consequently the vast majority of new hotels do not have any food and beverage facilities at all – in part this is due to lenders providing limited capital to developers in the accommodation sector.

Recently, there have been a number of other developments, which are blurring the lines between signature and outsourced restaurants.

- Parallel, the restaurant operations division of the contract caterer Aramark, announced in February 2004 that Refettorio, the upscale restaurant at the Crowne Plaza – London The City, will be run as a joint venture with Giorgio Locatelli, a celebrity chef and Crowne Plaza (part of the Intercontinental Hotel Group). Each partner is anticipated to take a share of the profits.

- Gary Rhodes, another celebrity chef, is set to manage the brasserie and fine dining operation at a major London hotel, in partnership with Restaurant Associates (at the time of writing, details had not been finalised, although the name Rhodes at Hyde Park has been suggested).
- Furthermore, many hotel chains that have come to rely upon the strength of their brand names have resorted to developing sub-brands designed to appeal to both guests and non-residents. For example, Thistle introduced three branded catering concepts in its hotels in 2001: CoMotion is marketed as a deli-style café; the Faya brand offers Mediterranean food; the third brand, Gengis, offers a range of Mediterranean and Asian food.

Conferences and banqueting

Spend on hotel catering by the conference and banqueting segment was £808 million in 2004 and, at the time of writing, was expected to have increased by 5 per cent in 2005 to £851 million. Overall, spend by this segment is expected to account for 21 per cent of total catering expenditure in 2005. TRI Hospitality Consulting reports that conferences accounted for 10 per cent of the market mix in UK hotels in 2004, thus implying that those in this market are above-average spenders on hotel catering.

The trend for one-day conferences (i.e. conferences that do not require an overnight stay) remains, as well as the demand for smaller conference facilities. According to the Meetings and Incentive Association's (MIA) UK Conference Market Survey 2004, the average duration of meetings and conferences in the UK was 1.4 days for the corporate sector and 1.6 days for associations. The survey also found that 84 per cent of corporate meetings or conference delegates visited city-centre hotels and 21 per cent had attended meetings or conferences at out-of-town hotels.

However, the MIA survey identified that food was the top bone of contention for both association and corporate delegates. Food quality is certainly an issue and it is apparent that there is a clear need for hotels to look for innovative ways to enhance existing catering facilities and services.

Outsourcing: a growing trend

The contracting-out of food and beverage services to third parties will continue to be a major trend in the hotel catering sector over the next few years, although this will be much stronger in London than in the provinces. As many hotels continue to remain sluggish owing to evolving consumer demand for food and beverages and intense competition from the high street, the attraction of outsourcing food and beverage services will become increasingly appealing.

Vertical integration between many hotel and restaurant groups has meant that the outsourcing decision is often not such a radical step to take for many hoteliers, as costs and revenues remain within the group. Most outsourcing is agreed on either a flat fee or percentage basis and this is expected to remain unchanged.

Figure 1.7 The UK eating-out market, 2005

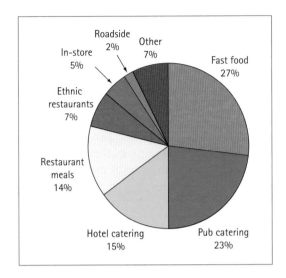

Source: Mintel

Outsourcing is not always a straightforward option for hotels, however. To attract walk-in customers, a hotel ideally needs to be located where there is easy access to the restaurant itself, and the location of the hotel itself (city centre, countryside, etc.) needs to fit with the clientele that are being targeted – that is, the product must be attractive to the passing trade. Despite these constraints, the number of outsourced restaurants is expected to increase considerably over the next three years.

In-house catering development

With increased consumer interest in food and eating out, hotels are becoming more focused on developing attractive food and beverage facilities in-house. The success of in-house catering development will depend on the willingness of hotels to deliver a product that will be attractive to the outside market, and to maintain this product so that it evolves with changing consumer tastes and trends. According to human resource specialists within the hotel sector, key factors holding back further development are that food and beverage managers in hotels tend to be hoteliers rather than restaurateurs, as well as the shortage of experienced culinary and service staff.

For the majority of the population, pub restaurants and gastropubs remain the most popular places to eat out (see Figure 1.7).

TYPES OF CATERING ESTABLISHMENT

Commercial catering

Hotels and restaurants

The exact number of hotels in the UK is uncertain but there are approximately 22,000 registered with tourist boards (BHA, 2000). Their turnover makes up about 1 per cent of UK GDP (BHA, 1999) and they employ about 220,000 people, or about 13 per cent of those employed in the hospitality industry (HTF, 2000). There are around 7000 rooms available in five-star hotels in the UK and 43,000 in four-star hotels. The majority (over 80 per cent) of these are in group-owned hotels. The presence of international chains is high in the five-star market. In the UK there are more hotel bedrooms (74,000) in the mid-market three-star category than in any other category (BHA, 2000). The independent hotelier traditionally dominates this market.

In some cases special types of meal service – such as grill rooms or speciality restaurants, some with high-profile chefs – may limit the type of foods served (e.g. smörgasbord or steaks will be provided).

Wine bars, fast foods, takeaway: quick service

Customer demand has resulted in the rapid growth of a variety of establishments offering a limited choice of popular foods at a reasonable price, with little or no waiting time, to be consumed either on the premises or taken away.

Delicatessens and salad bars

These offer a service (usually lunch) based on a wide variety of bread and rolls (e.g. panini, focaccia, pitta, baguettes and tortilla wraps). Fresh salads, home-made soups and one hot 'chef's dish of the day' may be available.

A chilled food selection, from which customers can pick and mix, can provide the basis for a day-long service, including breakfast. A 'made to order' sandwich counter and a baked jacket potato bar with a good variety of fillings are very popular components of some of these establishments.

Private clubs

These are usually administered by a manager appointed by a management committee formed from club members. Good food and drink with an informal service in the 'old English' style are required in most clubs, particularly in the St James's area of London.

Nightclubs and casinos usually offer the type of service associated with the restaurant trade.

Chain catering organisations

There are many establishments with chains spread over wide areas and in some cases overseas. Prospects for promotion and opportunities are often considerable, whether in a chain of hotels or restaurants. These are the well-known hotel companies and restaurant chains, the popular type of restaurant, chain stores and shops with restaurants, which often serve lunches, teas and morning coffee, and have snack bars and cafeterias.

Licensed house (pub) catering

There are approximately 61,000 licensed houses in the UK and almost all of them offer food in some form. To many people the food served in public houses is ideal for what they want – that is, often simple, moderate in price and quickly served in a congenial atmosphere.

There is great variety of food on offer in such places, from the ham and cheese roll operation to the exclusive à la carte restaurant. Public-house catering can be divided into the following categories:

- the luxury-type restaurant
- gastropubs – there is a growing trend for well-qualified chefs to work in pubs and develop the menu according to their own specialities, making good use of local produce
- the speciality restaurant – e.g. steak bar, fish restaurant, carvery, theme
- 'fork dishes' served from the bar counter, where the food is consumed in the drinking areas
- finger snacks – e.g. rolls, sandwiches.

Beer and pub facts

Beer

- Around 90 per cent of the beer sold in the UK is produced in the UK.
- In the UK 28 million pints of beer are consumed every day, which equates to 100 litres per head each year – compared to 20 litres of wine per head.
- Beer is a traditional and wholesome produce made from natural ingredients.
- Over one-third of the UK barley crop is bought by UK brewers, who are also major users of English hops.
- There are over 2000 different beer brands available in the UK, and over 1.5 million pints a day are exported to over 120 different countries.
- UK brewers are industry leaders on environmental issues. Since 1976, energy usage per pint of beer produced has been reduced by 45 per cent, water consumption reduced by 40 per cent, and carbon dioxide (greenhouse gas) emissions reduced by over 40 per cent.

Pubs

- Eight out of ten adults count themselves pub-goers, and over 15 million people drink in a pub at least once a week.
- Over 900,000 people rely on beer and pubs for their employment.
- Over 80 per cent of pubs are small businesses run by tenants, licensees and owners.
- The average pub spends over £70,000 per annum on locally sourced goods and services.
- The pub food market continues to thrive; UK pubs now serve over one billion meals per year.

Licensed retailing is a vast sector of the hospitality industry and is experiencing rapid change. Movements in organisations' structures and size, mergers and divestment ownerships, and management skills have been driven by two macro influences. First, the impact of 'Beer Orders', forcing restrictions on the linkages between brewing and licensed retail

Further information
To find out more about the licensed trade, contact: The British Institute of Innkeeping, Wessex House, 80 Park Street, Camberley, Surrey GU15 3PT, or visit www.bii.org.

outlet ownership, has brought about substantial restructuring of the industry. Five types of pub operators or retailers have emerged as a result of Beer Orders:

1 national retailer with brewing interest
2 national retailer with no brewing interests (either demerged or fully independent)
3 regional or local retailer with brewing interests
4 regional or local retailer with no brewing interests
5 totally independent operator or free houses.

Second, pub food is the fastest-growing source of pub revenue and accounts for approximately 20 per cent of total sales.

Beer remains the cornerstone of the pub, but different beers, such as cask and speciality draught ales, stout and premium lagers, are driving sales. Sales of soft drinks, wines, tea and coffee continue to grow.

Successful pubs are now diversifying to become significant leisure and retail outlets using sophisticated management controls, technological systems and marketing skills. A wider range of customer needs will be catered for, alcohol will continue to play an important part but food, entertainment and leisure facilities will become an increasing trend. Many pubs will specialise in particular markets by developing brands or concepts to attract target groups.

Speciality restaurants

Moderately priced speciality eating houses are in great demand and have seen a tremendous growth in recent years. In order to ensure a successful operation it is essential to assess customers' requirements accurately and to plan a menu that will attract sufficient customers to give adequate profit. A successful caterer is the one that gives customers what they want and not what she/he *thinks* the customers want. The most successful catering establishments are those that offer the type of food they can sell, which is not necessarily the type of food they would like to sell.

Country hotels

Country house hotels have been and are being developed in many tourist areas. Many are listed buildings, stately homes or manor houses. They normally have a reputation for good food, wine and service.

Consortia

A consortium is a group of independent hotels that purchase products and services such as marketing from specialist companies providing members of the consortium with access to international reservation systems. This enables the group to compete against the larger chains.

Motels/travel lodges

These establishments are sited near motorways and arterial routes. They

Table 1.7 The evolution of the pub

PERIOD	CHARACTER OF A PUB	CONSUMER GROUP	PRODUCTS	PUB IMPLEMENTATIONS
Up to late 1960s	Drinking place	Men	Bitter (mainly cask) Spirits Basic food	Downmarket Basic facilities of the community Home-grown entertainment 'Ordinary' to working-class men, not to other groups in society
Late 1960s to mid-1970s	The themed pub	Men Youth	Bitter Loss of cask Lager Spirits Basic food	Youth market Mass market Insensitive developments High-tech entertainment Jukeboxes Fruit machines Sound/light One-bar pubs
Mid-1970s to 1990	Targeted concept	Men Youth Women	Bitter Growth of cask Lager Soft drinks Wine Substantial growth in food	Retailing revolution Pub is the hero Targeted concepts Introduction of service standards
1990s on	Leisure experience	Men Youth Women Families Older people	Increasing low/non-alcohol products: beers wines spirits soft drinks coffee Increasing food sales Increasing premium/special products Greater range of packaged products More premium cask ales More premium lagers Increasing leisure facilities – games and accommodation	Signage/branding revolution Concept types will crystallise Greater customer recognition Opportunity to sign and label pubs better More open retail format The term pub will become less relevant 'Pubs' will become more ordinary to society as a whole

Source: Whitbread Market Research

focus on the business person who requires an overnight stop or the tourist who is on a driving holiday. These properties are reasonably priced, they consist of a room only with tea- and coffee-making facilities. Staffing is minimal and there is no restaurant. However, there will be other services close by, often managed by the same company. The growth and success of the budget hotel sector has been one of the biggest changes to affect the hospitality industry in recent years.

Timeshare villas/apartments

A timeshare owner purchases the right to occupy a self-catering apartment, a room or a suite in a hotel or leisure club for a specified number of weeks per year over a set period of years, or indefinitely.

Health farms

The health farm often takes the form of a luxury hotel where the client is able to access a number of specialist health treatments for those who are stressed, overworked or wish to lose weight.

Guest houses

Guest houses are to be found all over the UK. The owners usually live on the premises and let their bedrooms to passing customers. Many have regular clients. Guest houses usually offer bed, breakfast and evening meal, and are small privately owned operations.

Farms

Farmers, recognising the importance of the tourism industry in the countryside, formed a national organisation called the Farm Holiday Bureau. Most members have invested to transform basic bedrooms to meet the required standards. The National Tourist Board inspects every member property to ensure good value and quality accommodation. In most cases the accommodation is on or close to working farms.

Youth hostels

The Youth Hostels Association (YHA) runs hostels in various locations in England and Wales. These establishments cater mainly for single people and for those groups travelling on a tight budget. In some locations they also offer a number of sports facilities.

Sea ferries

Ferries cross the English Channel and Irish Sea. As they fight it out with the airlines in a competitive travel market, and in the case of the English Channel, Eurostar and Le Shuttle, they have invested in the total travel experience, offering very good restaurant and leisure facilities, fast-food restaurants, shopping, bars and lounges. These services are often run by contract caterers (often known as contract food service providers) on behalf of the ferry operator.

Airline services

Airline catering is a specialist operation (see Chapter 7, pages 343–347).

Airports

Airports offer a range of hospitality services catering for millions of people every year. They operate 24 hours a day, every day of the year. Services include themed restaurants, speciality restaurants, coffee bars and seafood bars, as well as food courts, often supplemented with a general shopping arcade.

Public-sector catering (cost sector)

This sector covers hospitals, universities, colleges, schools, prisons, the armed forces, police and ambulance services, local authority buildings, Meals on Wheels, and the like. It has been known for many years as 'welfare catering' and characterised by its non-profit-making focus, minimising cost by achieving maximum efficiency. However, with the introduction of competitive tendering, many public-sector operations have been won by contract caterers (often known as contract food service providers), which have introduced new concepts and commercialism to the public sector. This sector is more commonly known as the cost sector.

Prisons

Prison catering may be run by contract caterers or by the Prison Service. The food is usually prepared by prison officers and inmates. The kitchens are also used to train inmates in food production, to encourage them to seek employment on release. Prisons have now lost their Crown Immunity, which prevented prosecution for poor hygiene and negligence. There are also usually staff food service facilities in prisons for all the personnel who work there, such as administrative staff, prison officers and management.

The armed forces

Services here include feeding armed service staff in barracks, in the mess, and in the field or on ships. Much of the work involved is specialist, especially field cookery. However, the forces – like every other section of the public sector – are looking to reduce costs and increase efficiency. Consequently they too have initiated market testing and competitive tendering through the Ministry of Defence, resulting in contract caterers taking over many service operations at all the aforementioned locations.

Public catering

The fundamental difference between public catering and the catering in hotels and restaurants is that the hotel or restaurant is run to make a profit and provide a return on the investment capital. The aim of public

Figure 1.8 Contract catering in a police canteen

Figure 1.9 Armed forces canteen

catering is to minimise cost and cover overheads by achieving maximum efficiency. The standards of cooking should be equally good, though the types of menu may be different because of the specific nutritional needs of some parties, such as school children and soldiers. Hospital catering is classified as 'welfare catering', its objective being to assist the nursing staff to get the patient well as soon as possible. To do this it is necessary to provide good-quality food that has been carefully prepared and cooked to retain the maximum nutritional value, and present it to the patient in an appetising manner and with hygiene of utmost importance.

The National Health Service

NHS Trusts have a duty of care to ensure that best value and cost effectiveness is achieved for the catering operation. The scale of catering services in the NHS is enormous. Over 300 million meals are served each year in more than 300 NHS Trusts across approximately 1200 hospitals. The NHS spends in the region of £500 million per annum on food.

The staffing structure of the catering department depends on the size of the hospital and who runs the catering services. However, the normal approach may include the following.

- **Catering managers** plan menus, obtain supplies, recruit and develop personnel, and generally deal with day-to-day operational issues and liaise with the hospital administrators and management. Responsibility for training, safety and hygiene is also part of their duties. They visit the wards to advise on the service of food to the patients, and control the provision of the catering facilities for the doctors, nurses and other hospital employees. Visitor feeding and coffee shop facilities, and convenience shops and general vending facilities across these sites, are also part of their responsibility.
- **Operations managers** assist and deputise for catering managers, but are primarily concerned with the preparation and service of food and drink to all stakeholders, or they may be responsible for a small specialist unit within the complex or a satellite production unit away from the main building area.
- **Kitchen or production managers** are responsible to the catering manager or the operations manager for the running of one or more hospital kitchens. Chefs are graded according to experience and technical qualifications. In larger hospitals, a **head chef** would be in charge of a kitchen under the control of the operations or production manager.
- **Dining room supervisors** are in charge of the staff serving in the staff and visitor restaurants; these are often combined these days, but reflect a different pricing structure to each of these stakeholders because food is often part of an employee's employment contract and hence there is an element of subsidy in their meal price.

Figure 1.10 Hospital catering

People interested in being of service to the community and gaining job satisfaction do find this aspect of catering rewarding. Conditions, hours of work and pay as well as promotion prospects are factors that contribute to making this a worthwhile career.

All NHS hospitals are managed by Trust Boards, some of which have chosen to appoint a hotel services manager, who has responsibility for the management of catering, domestic, portering and other services; this provides an extended career path and an opportunity to develop new skills. Contract catering firms now often provide these wider hospital services in addition to food service, and career development, for this reason, can be extremely wide-ranging and opportunistic.

In July 2000 the NHS plan set out a work programme for the NHS to improve standards of food. This is seen as essential in enabling the NHS to deliver a quality service, and to put patients at the heart of health care.

Catering systems within the NHS
There are many different methods of providing catering services within the NHS. Some hospitals cook food in traditional kitchens and send it to the wards to be served to patients or staff and visitor feeding areas. Some buy in chilled or frozen foods that are regenerated (reheated) in mobile trolleys and some have ward kitchens in which a certain amount of preparation and finishing is undertaken adjacent to the wards themselves. Some new patented technologies are now appearing whereby chilled food freshly prepared outside the hospital grounds is generated by pressurised cooking in the ward kitchens; this clearly saves valuable kitchen space that can be turned over to provide more hospital beds for needy patients. One such modern method is called Steamplicity, and has served to reduce costs considerably while increasing the choice, quality, presentation and nutritional elements of the food.

The NHS Menu Group included experienced NHS catering and dietetic professionals, along with nurses and representatives of the private-sector caterers nominated by the Hospital Caterers Association, dieticians by the British Dietetic Association, and nurses nominated by the Chief Nursing Officer.

It sets out a long-term strategy for modernising and improving health services around the needs and expectations of patients. The Better Hospital Food programme attempts to improve standards for patients in the following ways.

Figure 1.11 Hospital catering dieticians

- Providing a 24-hour NHS catering service. This covers breakfast, drinks and snacks, light lunchtime meals and an improved two-course evening dinner.
- A national franchise for NHS catering aims to ensure hospital food is provided by organisations with a national reputation for high quality and customer satisfaction.
- Hospitals are to have ward housekeepers 'to ensure that the quality, presentation and portion size of meals meets patients' needs; that patients, particularly the elderly, are able to eat the meals on offer; and that the service patients receive is genuinely available around the clock'.

- Dieticians advise and check on nutritional values in hospital food. Patients' views should be measured as part of the Performance Assessment Framework, and the quality of food will be subject to inspections.

Patients who are able, are encouraged to eat at normal meal times and the normal mealtime service caters for the needs of the majority of patients. The NHS plan recognises the need to provide meals outside normal periods for patients who cannot eat at the usual mealtimes or are prevented from eating at the breakfast, lunch and/or dinner services.

The 24-hour catering service comprises three elements:

1 the Ward Kitchen Service
2 the Snack Box
3 the Light Bite.

These are all available on request (subject to certain clinical considerations). They represent the minimum level of service required.

- **The Ward Kitchen Service:** a ward-based kitchen service from which patients can obtain light refreshments such as tea/coffee/cold drinks, toast/preserves, biscuits and fruit, at any time of the day or night.
- **The Snack Box:** this offers a number of items presented in a box, making up a replacement meal for patients who have missed a meal, or where patients would prefer a lighter alternative to the meals on offer throughout the Mealtime Service. There should be at least three alternative boxes on offer:
  (a) a children's box
  (b) a snack box
  (c) a sandwich snack box.
- **The Light Bite:** some patients may want a more substantial hot alternative and the Light Bite should be offered in these circumstances. These meals are designed to be quick and easy to prepare and serve to patients at ward level, and are likely to be of the pre-prepared microwaveable type. This means patients should be able to get nutritious, tasty hot food at any time of the day or night.

Dieticians
In many hospitals a qualified dietician is responsible for:

- collaborating with the catering manager on the planning of meals
- drawing up and supervising special diets
- instructing diet cooks on the preparation of special dishes
- advising the catering manager and assisting in the training of cooks with regard to nutritional aspects
- advising patients.

In some hospitals the food for special diets will be prepared in a diet bay by diet cooks.

Diets

Information about the type of meal or diet to be given to each patient is supplied daily to the kitchen. This information will give the number of full, light, fluid and special diets, and with each special diet will be given the name of the patient and the type of diet required.

Modern developments

As with all catering services, the health care sector seeks to continually improve the food and drink services to all stakeholders on hospital premises, whether they be patients, the personnel directly or indirectly dealing with them, or patients' visitors.

The education sector school meals service

School meals play an important part in the lives of many children, often providing them with their only hot meal of the day. This was recognised as early as 1879 when a formal school meals service was first introduced; it came under government control in 1906. By 1944 the Education Act, which regarded the midday meal as the main meal of the day, required all maintained schools to provide a meal, conforming to strict nutritional and price guidelines, to anybody who wanted one. The school meals service continued to serve the community, without substantial change until 1980, when government policies sought to change the rationale and organisation of the service by way of the Education Act 1980. This Act removed the obligation to provide school meals except where children were entitled to a free meal. At the same time minimum nutritional standards were abolished, along with the fixed charge, allowing those schools that continued with a service to serve and charge what they liked.

In April 2001, for the first time in over 20 years, minimum nutritional regulations were re-introduced by the DFES (see www.dfes.gov.uk), designed to bring all schools up to a measurable standard set down in legislation. From this date, Local Education Authorities (LEAs) and all schools with delegated budgets for the provision of school meals, were responsible for seeing that the compulsory minimum nutritional standards for school lunches were met. From this date there was also a duty to provide a paid-for meal, where parents requested one, except where children are under five years old and part-time. (This does not affect the LEA's or the school's duty to provide a free meal to those children who qualify for one.)

In 2006 the UK Government announced new standards (see box) for school food. There are three parts, to be phased in by September 2009. Together they cover all food sold or served in schools: breakfast, lunch and after-school meals, and tuck, vending, mid-morning break and after-school clubs.

School meals are generally organised in one of three ways: by a direct service organisation (DSO), which is the catering arm of a local authority; by a private contractor; or by in-house provision controlled by individual

Further information
To find out more about NHS and hospital catering, visit the following websites.
- NHS Estates Information Centre: www.nhsestates.gov.uk
- Hospital Caterers Association: www.hospitalcaterers.org
- British Dietetic Association: www.bda.uk.com

The new standards

1 Interim food-based standards for school lunches – all schools by September 2006.
2 Food-based standards for school food other than lunch – all schools by September 2007 (schools are recommended to adopt these from September 2006).
3 Nutrient-based standards and new food-based standards (i.e. not interim) for school lunches – primary schools by September 2008 at the latest and secondary schools by September 2009 at the latest.

The new standards are shown in the following tables.

Table 1.8 Interim food-based standards for school lunches from September 2006 (primary, secondary and special schools)

Fruit and vegetables – these include fruit and vegetables in all forms (whether fresh, frozen, canned, dried or in the form of juice)	Not less than two portions per day per child, at least one of which should be salad or vegetables, and at least one should be fresh fruit, fruit tinned in juice or fruit salad (fresh or tinned in juice). A fruit-based dessert shall be available at least twice per week in primary schools.
Meat, fish and other non-dairy sources of protein – these include meat (including ham and bacon) and fish (whether fresh, frozen, canned or dried); eggs; nuts; pulses; and beans (other than green beans)	A food from this group should be available on a daily basis. Red meat shall be available twice per week in primary schools, and three times per week in secondary schools. Fish shall be available twice per week in primary schools and twice per week in secondary schools. Of that fish, oily fish shall be available at least once every three weeks. For the purposes of lunches for registered pupils at primary schools, sources of protein in this group can include dairy sources of protein.
Manufactured meat products	Manufactured meat products may be served occasionally as part of school lunches, provided that they meet the legal minimum meat content levels set out in the Meat Products (England) Regulations 2003. Products not specifically covered by these legal minima must meet the same minimum meat content levels prescribed for burgers, are not 'economy burgers' as described in the Meat Products (England) Regulations 2003, and containing none of the following list of offal, except that mammalian large or small intestine may be used as a sausage skin (including chipolatas, frankfurters, salami, links and similar products): brains, lungs, rectum, stomach, feet, oesophagus, spinal cord, testicles, large intestine, small intestine, spleen, udder.
Starchy foods (also see additional requirement on deep frying below) – these include all bread (e.g. chapattis), pasta, noodles, rice, potatoes, sweet potatoes, yams, millet and cornmeal	A food from this group should be available on a daily basis. Fat or oil shall not be used in the cooking process of starchy foods on more than three days in any week. On every day that a fat or oil is used in the cooking process of starchy foods, a starchy food for which fat or oils is not used in the cooking process should also be available. In addition, bread should be available on a daily basis.

Deep-fried foods	Meals should not contain more than two deep-fried items in a single week. This includes products that are deep-fried in the manufacturing process.
Milk and dairy foods – includes milk, cheese, yoghurt (including frozen and drinking yoghurt), fromage frais and custard	A food from this group should be available on a daily basis.
Drinks	The only drinks available should be: • plain water (still or fizzy) • milk (skimmed or semi-skimmed) • pure fruit juices • yoghurt or milk drinks (with less than 5% added sugar) • drinks made from combinations of those in bullet points 1 to 4 of this list (e.g. smoothies) • low-calorie hot chocolate • tea, and • coffee. NB: artificial sweeteners could be used only in yoghurt and milk drinks; or combinations containing yoghurt or milk.
Water	There should be easy access at all times to free, fresh drinking water.
Salt and condiments	Table salt should not be made available. If made available, condiments should be available only in sachets.
Confectionery and savoury snacks	Confectionery, chocolate and chocolate-coated products (excluding cocoa powder used in chocolate cakes, or low-calorie hot drinking chocolate) shall not be available throughout the lunch time. The only savoury snacks available should be nuts and seeds with no added salt or sugar.

Table 1.9 Nutrient-based standards for school lunches from September 2008 (primary schools) or September 2009 (secondary and special schools)*

Energy	30% of the estimated average requirement (EAR)
Protein	Not less than 30% of reference nutrient intake (RNI)
Total carbohydrate	Not less than 50% of food energy
Non-milk extrinsic sugars	Not more than 11% of food energy
Fat	Not more than 35% of food energy
Saturated fat	Not more than 11% of food energy
Fibre	Not less than 30% of the calculated reference value (Note: calculated as non starch polysaccharides)
Sodium	Not more than 30% of the SACN recommendation
Vitamin A	Not less than 40% of the RNI
Vitamin C	Not less than 40% of the RNI
Folate/folic acid	Not less than 40% of the RNI
Calcium	Not less than 40% of the RNI
Iron	Not less than 40% of the RNI
Zinc	Not less than 40% of the RNI

This table summarises the proportion of nutrients that children and young people should receive from a school lunch. The figures are for the required nutrient content of an average lunch over five consecutive school days. Nutrient values, except for sodium, are based on Department of Health (1991), and those for sodium on Scientific Advisory Committee on Nutrition (2003).

Notes

EAR = estimated average requirement – the average amount of energy or nutrients needed by a group of people. Half the population will have needs greater than this, and half will have needs below this amount.

RNI = reference nutrient intake – the amount of nutrient that is enough to meet the dietary requirements of about 97% of a group of people.

SACN = Scientific Advisory Committee on Nutrition – for details of figures for the dietary reference values and derived amounts of nutrients for children and young people see Crawley (2005), with the exception that the derived reference value for fibre for boys aged 15–18 years should be capped at 18 g.

Table 1.10 Food-based standards for school lunches from September 2008 (primary schools) or September 2009 (secondary and special schools)

Fruit and vegetables – these include fruit and vegetables in all forms (whether fresh, frozen, canned, dried or in the form of juice)	Not less than two portions per day per child, at least one of which should be salad or vegetables, and at least one should be fresh fruit, fruit tinned in juice or fruit salad (fresh or tinned in juice).
Oily fish	Oily fish shall be available at least once every three weeks.
Manufactured meat products	Manufactured meat products may be served occasionally as part of school lunches, provided that they meet the legal minimum meat content levels set out in the Meat Products (England) Regulations 2003. Products not specifically covered by these legal minima must meet the same minimum meat content levels prescribed for burgers, are not 'economy burgers' as described in the Meat Products (England) Regulations 2003, and contain none of the following list of offal, except that mammalian large or small intestine may be used as a sausage skin (including chipolatas, frankfurters, salami, links and similar products): brains, lungs, rectum, stomach, feet, oesophagus, spinal cord, testicles, large intestine, small intestine, spleen, udder.
Bread	Bread should be available on a daily basis.
Deep-fried foods	Meals should not contain more than two deep-fried items in a single week. This includes products that are deep-fried in the manufacturing process.
Milk and dairy foods – includes milk, cheese, yoghurt (including frozen and drinking yoghurt), fromage frais and custard	A food from this group should be available on a daily basis.
Drinks	The only drinks available should be: • plain water (still or fizzy) • milk (skimmed or semi-skimmed) • pure fruit juices • yoghurt or milk drinks (with less than 5% added sugar) • drinks made from combinations of those in bullet points 1 to 4 of this list (e.g. smoothies) • low-calorie hot chocolate • tea, and • coffee. NB: artificial sweeteners could be used only in yoghurt and milk drinks; or combinations containing yoghurt or milk.

Water	There should be easy access at all times to free, fresh drinking water.
Salt and condiments	Table salt should not be made available. If made available, condiments should be available only in sachets.
Confectionery and savoury snacks	Confectionery, chocolate and chocolate-coated products (excluding cocoa powder used in chocolate cakes, or low-calorie hot drinking chocolate) shall not be available throughout the lunch time. The only savoury snacks available should be nuts and seeds with no added salt or sugar.

Source: School Food Trust

Information and guidance is available on www.dfes.gov.uk/ schoollunches and www.schoolfoodtrust.org.uk/school-lunch.php.

schools. Each of these providers must be responsible for all aspects of the catering service, including: control of finances; menu planning; food purchasing; kitchen planning; monitoring of the nutritional regulations; and general administration. Supervision of the individual units is undertaken by catering managers, cook-supervisors or, in the case of smaller units, a cook-in-charge. The service is mainly staffed by part-time female operatives, who find that working in the school meals service can be fitted in with their domestic responsibilities. Due to the increased complexity of nutritional, hygiene, and health and safety regulations, the traditional role of 'school cook' has been replaced by a more professional approach to the catering function. All staff receive some form of training, often to a high level, so that the strictest standards of personal and kitchen hygiene can be maintained.

Many schools should offer a multi-choice menu taking into consideration the wide-ranging needs of children from various cultural and religious backgrounds. In addition to these main meals a range of healthy snacks, drinks, fresh fruit, yoghurts, confectionery, and a selection of freshly prepared rolls, sandwiches, pastries and salads can also be purchased. As well as the set menu, many senior schools offer coffee shop-style operations and also supplement out-of-hours food provision with a vending service providing water, fruit, smoothies and a range of other similar products. A breakfast service (often referred to as 'breakfast clubs') can also be found in many schools where there is a need, to provide for children who go to school without any breakfast.

Because standards of living of general households are high today, the demands of school children are high too, as they try to replicate their food provision at home. Consequently the amount of produce choice, and different types and styles of food service have increased dramatically in recent years, and many LEAs have contracted food provision to contract caterers in order to deliver this high degree of choice and more topical and contemporary foods to meet demand from pupils.

Figure 1.12 School meals

School lunches are seen as part of a whole-school approach to healthy lifestyles and social training, and the correlation between pupils' behaviour and their diet at school has long been established. Concentration levels, brain activity and metabolic functions are highly dependent on diet and nutrition, and therefore accentuate the case for good nutrition and a healthy lifestyle.

The further and higher education systems (colleges and universities) also offer extensive food service provisions; many of these are contracted out to contract caterers, often for both residential and non-residential students. These reflect the provisions described for schools above. However, in this sector, even greater demands are placed by students on product ranges, choice and sophistication in service style. The coffee shop, food takeaway, convenience store and food court principles are well established here, and often replicate the provision made in airports, railway stations and shopping malls of wide-ranging food and outlet types catering for diverse ethnic cultures, client time constraints and differing client budgets. Staff dining facilities regularly feature in all educational establishments, sometimes as separate facilities to those of the students, but often combined with them, particularly in the further and higher education sectors.

The private school sector is often a hybrid of the public school and higher and further education markets, and thus reflects all the aforementioned trends. This market is also prolifically serviced by the private contract caterer, albeit that many of these schools maintain their own personnel to provide the service.

Sample menus
Sample menu for primary schools
The sample menu in Table 1.11 is based on one produced by the School Meals Review Panel (SMRP), and meets the interim food-based standards (see box). It will give you some idea of what a lunch service that meets the standards might look like.

Menus can be produced and tailored to meet the individual needs of a school. At least one vegetarian option is included every day.

Table 1.11 Sample menu for primary schools

	MONDAY	TUESDAY	WEDNESDAY	THURSDAY	FRIDAY
Main dishes	Cheese and tomato pizza Vegeburger	Chicken and broccoli lasagne Vegetable risotto	Roast lamb with minted gravy Vegetable curry	Savoury minced beef Vegetable bolognese	Salmon fishcakes Mexican beans
Starchy dishes	Jacket wedges Soft noodles	Baguette	Roast potatoes Basmati rice Chapatti	Spaghetti Jacket potato	Boiled new potatoes Tortilla wrap
Daily selection of breads					
Vegetables	Sweetcorn and peas Cucumber and carrot sticks	Carrots Cherry tomatoes and coleslaw	Lentil dahl French beans	Mixed salad Broccoli florets	Baked beans Roasted vegetables
Fruit and desserts	Daily selection of fresh fruits and yoghurts				
	Fruit salad Banana and chocolate brownie	Ice cream and fruit Oat cookies	Apple and blackberry crumble Greek yoghurt Pears	Apricot rice pudding Jellied fruit salad	Fruit squares Orange and lemon rice
Drinks	Water and a choice of semi-skimmed milk and flavoured milks				

Source: School Food Trust

Further information
Further information on school meals policy may be obtained from the DfES, Sanctuary Buildings, Great Smith Street, Westminster, London SW10 3BT, Pupil Welfare and Opportunities Division Area 4E8. www.dfes.gov.uk/ schoollunches.

Sample menu for secondary schools
Table 1.12 shows a sample menu for use in secondary schools. Remember that manufactured meat products may be served only occasionally.

Residential establishments
Under this heading are included schools, colleges, universities, halls of residence, nursing homes, homes for the elderly and hostels, where all meals are provided. It is essential in these establishments that the nutritional balance of food is considered (see Figure 1.13), and it should satisfy all the residents' nutritional needs, as in all probability the people eating here will have no other food provision. Since many of these establishments cater for students, and the age group that leads a very energetic life, these people usually have large appetites and are growing fast. All the more reason that the food should be well prepared from good ingredients, nutritious, varied and attractive.

The contract food service sector
Contract food service management (often referred to as contract catering) covers such areas as feeding people at work in business and industry,

Table 1.12 Sample menu for secondary schools

	MONDAY	TUESDAY	WEDNESDAY	THURSDAY	FRIDAY
Main dishes	Beef curry	Pork calypso	Spicy chicken risotto	Lamb and pasta medley	Salmon fishcakes
	Vegetable and bean curry	Lentil and tomato quiche	Vegetable lasagne	Caribbean casserole	Spicy vegetable burgers
Daily choices	Lamb burgers, Quorn burgers, chicken fajitas, cheese and tomato pizza, chilli tortillas				
Starchy dishes	Brown rice Chapatti	Jacket wedges Pasta twirls	Ciabatta rolls Rice and peas	Boiled new potatoes Couscous	Chips
Vegetables	Lentil dahl Vegetable curry Mixed salads	Baked beans Peas Mixed salads	French beans Mixed salads Broccoli florets	Roasted vegetables Mixed salads	Coleslaw Cauliflower gratin Mixed salads
Jacket potatoes	Jacket potato with choice of tuna, baked beans or Cheddar cheese				
Choice of breads, rolls and fillings	Choice of bagels, pitta bread, granary, ciabatta and crusty brown rolls, tortilla wraps, burger buns Choice of fillings: egg and cress, tuna and cucumber, smoked mackerel, ham and tomato, chicken tikka				
Fresh fruit, yoghurt and desserts	Daily selection of fresh fruits and yoghurts				
	Apricot oat bars Banana custard	Jelly yoghurt whip Apple brown Betty	Apple and blackberry crumble and custard Rice pudding with sultanas	Spiced apple cake Pineapple and crème fraîche	Ice cream and fruit Banana and chocolate brownie

Source: School Food Trust

catering in schools, college and universities, private and public health care establishments, public and local authority catering, and other non-profit-making outlets such as the armed forces, police and ambulance services, or the remote sector such as oil and gas exploration rigs. There is also a large market in this sector for catering in the executive dining rooms of many corporations and providing all their corporate hospitality needs.

Work in the traditional sectors – called cost or non-profit-making catering – continues but, because contractors are readily developing their interests in more commercial catering arenas such as stadia, general leisure venues and the like, the term food service management describes more accurately the total contract catering industry.

Definitions in this sector are becoming increasingly blurred as contract catering enterprises move into other areas, including catering for members of the public in such outlets as leisure centres, department stores and DIY stores, supermarket restaurants and cafés, airports and

Figure 1.13 The balance of
good health

railway stations, as well as at public events and places of entertainment.
Contractors are also providing a range of other support services such as
housekeeping and maintenance, reception, security, laundry, bar and
retail shops.

Catering for business and industry

The provision of staff dining rooms for industrial or business settings has
allowed many catering workers employment in first-class conditions.
Apart from the main meal services, beverage services, retail shops,
franchise outlets and/or vending machines may be part of the service. In
some cases a 24-hour, seven-day service is necessary, but generally the
hours are more streamlined than in other sectors of the hospitality
industry. Food and drink is provided for all employees, sometimes
separately but increasingly together in high-quality restaurants and
dining rooms. Training and career development potential is
excellent, with an emphasis on personnel retention and people
development.

Many industries have realised that output is related to the welfare of
their employees. Satisfied workers produce more and better work, and
because of this a great deal of money is spent on providing first-class
kitchens and dining rooms, and improving the dining experience. This
can also mean that the workers receive their food at a price lower than
its actual cost, the rest of the cost being borne by the company. This is
called a subsidy and contributes to the overall employment benefits of an
employee.

Further information
Information on catering
for business and industry
can be obtained from
the Association of
Catering Excellence,
Bourne House, Horsell
Park, Woking, Surrey
GU21 4HY, or by visiting
www.acegb.org

However, many companies are increasingly competing within a global economy. Competition is fierce, and this has led them to cut costs, meaning that many organisations are moving towards a nil subsidy for meals consumed at the place of work.

Criteria for establishing a catering operation
A company is not committed to providing any catering facility if:

- there are suitable facilities available within easy access of the employee's place of work
- these facilities offer a reasonable choice of food
- the times of opening are suitable to employer and employees.

If the above criteria are not met and the demand for catering services exists then a catering facility should be established. Often, employers will provide a facility even if the above criteria exist, in order to provide better welfare and amenities for their people, so hoping to retain them as employees for longer.

Holiday centres

Holiday centres around the UK provide leisure and hospitality facilities for families, single people and groups. Many companies have invested large sums of money in an effort to increase the quality of the holiday experience. Center Parcs, for example, has developed subtropical pools and also offers other sporting facilities. Included in its complexes are a range of different restaurant experiences and food courts, bars and coffee shops. These centres are examples of year-round holiday centres, encouraging people to take breaks from home, weekend breaks, and so on.

Motoring services

Many motoring services areas provide food court-type facilities for travellers, offering a comprehensive range of meals on a 24-hour, seven-day basis. These are becoming increasingly sophisticated, with baby changing, infant and pet feeding facilities, bathrooms and showers, extensive ranges of branded food outlets and often accommodation, fuel, convenience shops, and car washing and maintenance facilities. MOTO is one such an example; it operates across the country and makes most of the provisions above available in all of its outlets.

Drive-thru restaurants

Drive-thru restaurants are a relatively new concept in the UK. Drive-thrus are an American import – the most notable of these being the McDonald's Drive-thrus located in many parts of the UK. Customers stay in their vehicles and drive up to a microphone in order to place a request. This is then relayed to a fast-food service point and, as the car moves forward in the queue, the order is prepared and then presented to the driver at the service window. This type of facility is often part of the provision made in centres such as the motoring services described above.

Transport catering

Railway

Meals on trains may be served in restaurant cars and snacks from buffet cars. The space in a restaurant car kitchen is very limited and there is considerable movement of the train, which causes difficulty for the staff.

Two train services run by separate companies are running through the Channel Tunnel. One is Euro Tunnel's Le Shuttle train, which transports drivers and their vehicles between Folkestone and Calais in 35 minutes. Food and drink is limited to that bought on dry land before the train departs.

Foot passengers wishing to travel from Waterloo to Paris or Brussels travel on Eurostar trains. Eurostar sees the airlines as its direct competition; therefore it provides airline catering standards on board the train for first- and premier-class passengers. Meals are served by uniformed stewards and stewardesses in an environment similar to an airline's club class. This food is included in the ticket price. Provision for economy travellers is usually via buffet carriages or trolley services along the aisles of the train. This is another area into which contract food service providers have expanded.

Marine

The large liner's catering is of a similar standard to that of the big first-class hotels, and many shipping companies are noted for the excellence of their cuisine. The kitchens on board ship are usually oil-fired, and extra precautions have to be taken in the kitchen in rough weather. Catering at sea includes the smaller ship, which has both cargo and passengers, and the cargo vessels, which include the giant tankers of up to 100,000 tonnes. Cross-Channel ferries tend to feature an extensive range of modern branded food outlets, some of a food court nature and others in a buffet or carvery style, and usually supplemented by a fine dining concept, bars, pub-type outlets and retail convenience shops.

Other aspects of catering

The services

Catering for the armed services is specialised and they have their own training centre; details of catering facilities and career opportunities can be obtained from career information offices. Contract caterers (contract food service management operators) are increasingly being used throughout the armed services.

Contract catering

Often known as contract food service management, this hospitality sector has expanded rapidly as a result of targeting new markets such as leisure and public services, as described previously, but also as a result of the industrial trend to contract out non-core business activities (BT, for example, had run its own catering services nationally for many years but has subsequently contracted out all its many UK locations to the Compass Group).

A recent Eurest lunchtime survey suggested that the time taken by employees to eat at work is reducing annually and currently stands at a little over 20 minutes. Contract catering operators such as Compass have had to respond to this changing demand, and therefore branded retail outlets have become a growth area, which also reflects the commercial influence of contracting.

There are many catering concerns that are prepared to undertake catering for businesses, schools or hospitals, leaving these establishments free to concentrate on the business of educating, nursing, and so on. By employing contract caterers and using the services of people who have specialised in catering, organisations can thus relieve themselves of the worry of entering a field outside their province. Contract caterers are used by nearly every type of organisation, including the armed forces, business and industry in general, supermarkets, department stores and DIY chains, leisure centres, museums and galleries, and at sporting fixtures and events.

Contracts will vary considerably, but popular options are fixed price, cost plus, concession and profit and loss arrangements, or a mixture of these. Some arrangements will be subsidised and others won't. Contract permutations can be endless, but need to serve the interests of all stakeholders.

Contracts

No two services or clients' requirements are the same. For this reason, contracts differ from company to company. Some examples of the types of contract available are as follows.

- **Executive lease:** the contractor provides a senior executive who will direct the client's catering operation. Normally the whole operation remains the responsibility of the client and the staff are employed by the client. The aim is for the contractor and the executive to bring a level of expertise, which the client is unable to provide. The senior executive will be involved in implementing the systems managers and in the policy making. The contractor will provide a manager for the unit; all staff are employed by the client on their terms and conditions.
- **Management:** the client employs the contractor to supply a total catering service using the contractor's own on-site management and staff. The client also provides all the facilities and equipment. The contractor submits a monthly account to the client, which identifies all the expenditure and income associated with the operation. The difference between the expenditure and income, including the contractor's fee, will be payable to or from the contractor.
- **Fixed price:** the contractor works to an annual budget fixed with the

client. If the contractor overspends, she/he pays. However, if she/he underspends she/he retains the difference.

• **Concession:** the contractor undertakes to manage an operation and rely for profit on his or her ability to maintain income levels over expenditure levels.

Contractor's charges

Contractors generally offset their administration costs, and they gain their profits from the following three sources:

1 fees charged
2 cash spent by customers
3 discounts from food and materials supplied to the client's operation.

The fees can be made up in a number of ways:

• a set annual figure charged on a weekly or monthly basis
• a percentage of takings or costs
• a combination of both with different percentages applying to various sections of costs
• a per capita or per meal charge.

With over 60 companies registered in the UK, contract catering is one of the biggest and most diverse sectors in the industry. Compass (mentioned above in connection with BT) and Sodexho are two of the largest food organisations in the UK, with 8400 locations. These include Little Chef, Travelodge and motorway service stations.

Table 1.13 Types of catering contract, 2002, 2004–2005

	2005		2004		2002	
	NUMBER	%	NUMBER	%	NUMBER	%
Cost plus/management fee (the client is billed for the cost of the operation plus a management fee)	5182	29.4	4898	27.2	5585	29.4
Fixed price/performance guarantee (the client agrees a total subsidy and costs cannot rise above that figure)	6262	35.6	9335	51.8	10,091	53.2
Profit and loss concession contracts and total risk contracts (the caterer and the client share the profit (or the loss); in total risk contracts the caterer invests in the facility and earns all the revenue)	6164	35.0	3685	20.4	3250	17.1
TOTAL	17,608*		18,028**		18,979**	

*Excludes 118 purchasing contracts
**Includes 55 purchasing contracts in 2004 (0.3%), and 53 purchasing contracts in 2002 (0.3%)

Partnership

This describes the situation where the client and customer are partners in the operations and share the costs and revenues.

Outside catering

When functions are held where there is no catering or where the function is not within the scope of the normal catering routine, then certain firms will take over completely. Considerable variety is offered to people employed on these undertakings and often the standard will be of the very highest order. A certain amount of adaptability, ingenuity and specialist equipment is required, especially for some outdoor jobs, but there is less chance of repetitive work. Greater flexibility is necessary on behalf of the personnel, often involving considerable travel, remote locations and outdoor venues. The types of function will include garden parties, agricultural and horticultural shows, the opening of new buildings, banquets, parties in private houses, military pageants and tattoos, and sporting fixtures such as horse racing, motor racing, football and rugby.

Franchising

Franchising is an agreement whereby one pays a fee and some set-up costs in exchange for the use of an established name or brand that is well known by potential purchasers and therefore likely to generate more business than an unknown or start-up brand. An example of this would be where the contract caterer Compass Group franchises the Burger King brand from its owner in exchange for a fee and a proportion of the turnover. There are normally strict guidelines, or 'brand standards', laid down for the franchisee (franchise user) to perform to, and these will govern which ingredients and raw materials are used and where they come from, together with portion sizes and the general product and service 'offer'. The franchisor (the franchise provider) will 'mystery shop' or check on the brand standards regularly to ensure that the brand's reputation is not being jeopardised. The franchisor will normally also provide advertising and marketing support, accounting processes, help with staff training and development, and design provision for merchandising and display materials.

A form of franchising is also practised in the pub business in addition to other systems like the managed pub.

Many companies that supply caterers with products like soft drinks, ice cream and coffee distribute their products by means of purchased operators. Some suppliers providing food and drink to caterers have 'brand franchises', sometimes backing their product with appropriate equipment and advertising material to ensure that caterers prepare, present and promote the products in a consistent way.

Operating styles vary considerably, from pizzas, hamburgers and baked croissants to full-menu restaurants, coffee shops and pancake houses. Despite all the differences, all the franchise schemes work on the same basic principle: an established catering company offers a complete

Figure 1.14 The Purser's Department.

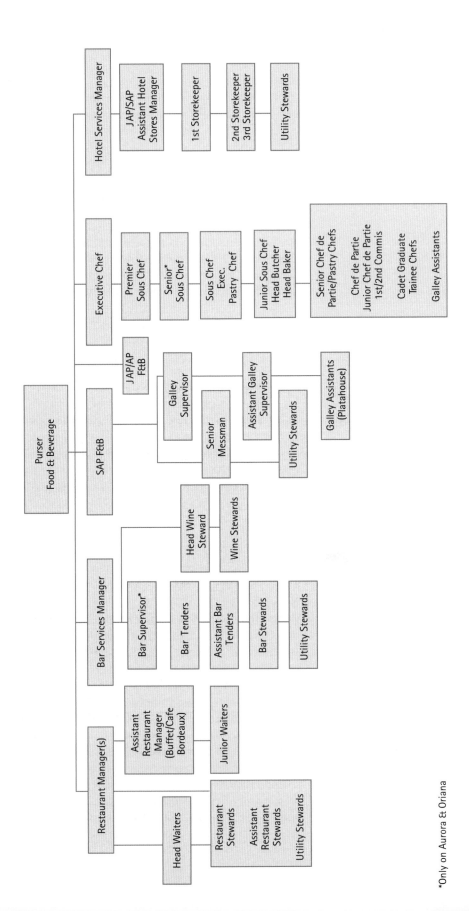

*Only on Aurora & Oriana

package of experience, operating systems and ongoing marketing support sufficient to enable outside operators to set up and operate their own units within the chain. The investor makes an initial franchise payment and then pays a continuing royalty or commission, which is often expressed as a percentage of gross turnover. All investment in property, buildings and equipment is borne by the franchise; in some cases the franchise might play some part in securing the property and assisting with design, building and fitting out so that a consistent look and feel is established.

Franchising has several advantages.

- First, it allows for many outlets to be set up nationally and, by doing so, maximises on economies of scale in purchasing promotional material in the development of the brand image.
- The franchisee gains because the opportunity is shared to invest in a pre-tested catering concept, backed by advertising, research and development, training and other resources that may otherwise be beyond their financial parameters.
- The banks also show an interest in franchising – in many ways they see it as a reasonably safe investment because of its established, tried-and-tested nature.
- The oldest franchising schemes in the UK are Wimpy, established in the mid-1950s and KFC, which started in the early 1960s. Many of the most active franchise schemes are based on a fast-food style of menu and operating system. Now there is a growing market involving wider menus and medium-spend restaurants, mainly licensed. Examples include Pizza Hut, Delice de France, Marks & Spencer Simply Food, Krispy Kreme bakery products, TGI Friday's, and many others.

Catering at sea

Cruise companies are rapidly increasing their number of cruise liners and the size of their ships. This means the job opportunities and promotion prospects are excellent, and training is also provided. The benefits of travel all over the world, producing food and serving customers at the very highest standards in hygienic conditions makes it a most interesting and worthwhile career. As an example of working conditions, staff may work for three months and then have, say, two months off. On-board hours of work could be ten hours a day, seven days a week. This appeals to many people who wish to be producing food at its best in excellent conditions. Figure 1.14 illustrates a Purser's Department F&B.

Cruise ships are floating luxury hotels, and more and more people are becoming interested in cruising as a lifestyle.

Food and beverage purchases on cruise liners
On cruises where the quality of the food is of paramount importance, other factors such as the dining room's ambience of refinement and elegance are also of great significance. Ship designers generally want to

avoid Las Vegas-type glittery dining rooms, but also those that are too austere. Interestingly enough, the success of the dining operation is tied to the design of the ship.

Ship architects design cruise liners to provide quick and easy access to the kitchen areas, where food is prepared. In a sense, these architects design the ship around the galley and dining rooms. The food on most cruises can be described as excellent, quality banquet-style cuisine. Ships must be designed with easy access to the galley so waiters are able to get food quickly and with as little traffic as possible. If waiters or assistant waiters are reluctant to take long trips to the galley to get something a passenger requests, there will be problems. A distinction can be made between dining and eating on cruises, as shown in Table 1.14.

This set of polarities doesn't apply as much to the new giant ships that have many different dining rooms. On such ships passengers can eat in the dining room of their choice, more or less whenever they want, at tables of various sizes. This gives passengers maximum freedom, but they lose the opportunity to get to know people at their table.

Dining is one of the most important – and selling – points for cruise lines. People who take cruises want to dine well and generally they do, though cooking dinner for 800 people per sitting and giving people what they want takes skill and management.

Table 1.14 The differences between dining and eating on cruises

DINING	EATING
Dining room	Buffet line
Set times	Any time
Assigned tables	Choice of seating
Elegance	Cafeteria-like ambience
Elaborate table settings	Formica-topped tables
Menus	See what is available
Waiters	Self-serve
Sociability	Separation

Figure 1.15 Self-service

Cruise ship staff

The purser is much like a hotel front-desk manager or assistant manager. Unlike the hotel manager – who tends to larger operational issues – the purser administers day-to-day affairs. Some examples include management of passenger accounts, mail, messages, printing, the storing of valuables and immigration and customs requirements. On larger vessels, the purser has two assistants: the crew purser (who treats crew issues) and the hotel purser (who tends to passenger matters). The purser may have a large team of assistants who staff the purser's desk, coordinate publications, deliver messages and handle other concerns.

The shore excursion manager orchestrates the operation and booking of port-based packages. On certain lines, he or she is sometimes called the concierge, with broader responsibilities such as booking customised port experiences, changing flights, and so on. On larger ships a team of people attends to shore excursions, including an on-board travel agent who can book a passenger's future cruise needs. (If a sale is made, the passenger's travel agent will usually get the commission for that sale.)

The cruise director coordinates all entertainment and informational activities that take place as part of the cruise experience. Part host, part entertainer, gregarious and always gracious, the cruise director serves as a critical link between passengers and crew. He or she presides over many functions, including passenger orientation and disembarkation meetings. The cruise director also manages the musicians, entertainers, on-board lecturers (experts who provide their services in exchange for a free cruise), social hosts (who converse and dance with single women on board), health club staff, photographers and, in some cases, the shore excursion manager.

The executive chef controls the preparation and serving of all food and beverages. He or she supervises the assistant or sous chef, the pastry chef, food preparers and other kitchen staff.

The head housekeeper or chief steward manages all stateroom, public space and other shipboard cleaning. He or she supervises a squad of cabin or room stewards, who tend to the passengers' stateroom needs. (Cabin stewards have a much more active, personal and round-the-clock relationship with guests than do maids at hotels.)

The food and beverage manager oversees the serving of meals and drinks. (On smaller ships this may be handled by the executive chef.) The food and beverage manager watches over the dining room maitre d', table captains, waiters and busboys. The food and beverage manager also oversees the bartenders, drink servers and wine steward.

Corporate hospitality

The purpose of corporate hospitality is to build business relationships and to raise corporate awareness. Corporate entertaining is also used as a means of thanking or rewarding loyal customers.

Companies are increasingly recognising the increasing importance of relationship marketing and corporate reputation.

Reasons for spending money on corporate hospitality include:

- building relationships with potential customers
- to reward customers/thank them for loyalty
- as a marketing tool/raise company or product profile
- increase business/sales
- to achieve closer informal contact in a relaxed environment
- to raise and keep up the company's profile/public relations
- repeat business/retention of clients or customers
- keep the customers happy/to entertain them, act as a sweetener
- to talk about business/networking
- to achieve better communication interaction/improved understanding
- expected to do it
- to reward/boost staff or team morale
- social benefits/opportunity to relax.

Eventia is the professional association for the corporate and events industry. This industry is considered to be worth more than £700 million a year. A major new industry report commissioned by the World Tourism Organization (UNWTO), Meeting Professionals International (MPI) and Reed travel Exhibitions (RTE) strongly recommends adopting a form of 'tourism satellite accounting' to measure the economic global importance of the meetings industry, which is an important economic contributor.

The main reasons for the growth of this sector are company expansion and increased budgets for corporate hospitality. Those companies with increased budgets are generally committing to bigger or more superior events and increased spending per head, or holding events more frequently.

An emerging trend is for companies to use corporate hospitality in a more targeted way rather than taking a broad-brush approach. Companies are therefore being more selective about invitees and matching them to appropriate events.

A total of 90 per cent of corporate hospitality is aimed at current customers or clients. There is also a trend towards using corporate hospitality to motivate employees, in an increasingly competitive corporate environment that encourages companies to invest in their own workforce.

Recipients of corporate hospitality are more likely to accept invitations from current suppliers rather than from potential suppliers.

Using the Internet as a business tool
As in all areas of business, the Internet is playing an increasingly important role in corporate hospitality. It is used to source information, and bookings can also be made online.

Websites detail comprehensive corporate hospitality information on events throughout the year. Online services allow customers to book an event directly, offering real benefits to the customer. These include:

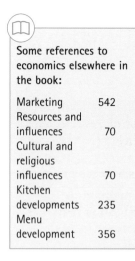

Some references to economics elsewhere in the book:

- official hospitality in official locations
- cost efficient by booking direct from source
- time efficient
- one-stop shop service from initial enquiry through the event
- for many caterers, access to any established name, with the attendant back-up of media, advertising and merchandising material, is a strong argument for franchising.

REFERENCES

Crawley, H. (2005) *Nutrition-Based Standards for School Food*. British Nutrition Foundation (also available at www.cwt.org.uk).

Deloitte/NYU (2006) 'Hospitality 2010'. New York, NY: Deloitte Services/New York University (downloadable at www.nyu.edu/public.affairs/releases/detail/1116).

Department of Health (1991) *Dietary Reference Values for Food Energy and Nutrients for the United Kingdom*. London: HMSO.

Mancini, M. (2004) *Cruising: A Guide to the Cruise Industry*, 2nd edition. Florence, KY: Thomson Delmar Learning.

Scientific Advisory Committee on Nutrition (2003) *Salt and Health*. London: The Stationery Office.

TOPICS FOR DISCUSSION

1 Give your impressions of the food that was served at your previous schools, with suggestions for improvement.

2 Explain the importance of food for the hospital patient, with suggestions for the types of food to be offered.

3 Industrial catering is an important aspect of the catering industry; discuss why this is so and give examples of menus for three different dining rooms.

4 Discuss what you think persons travelling on aircraft would like to eat and explain how it may, or may not, be feasible to provide it.

5 How do you think changes in the industry will occur over the next ten years? Explain why you think they will happen.

6 Each student in the group to obtain a number of menus from each type of catering and pool for group discussion.

7 What impact, if any, do you think organic foods will have on menus?

8 What essential differences attract staff to the various aspects of the industry (consider, for example, pay, conditions of work, career prospects)?

9 Establishments such as motorway facilities should meet special needs; explain what they are and how they are met, then select another area of catering and state what those needs are and how they are achieved.

Chapter 2 EMPLOYMENT IN THE HOSPITALITY INDUSTRY

EMPLOYMENT OPPORTUNITIES

Further information
To find out about jobs in the hospitality industry visit:
www.chefjobs.co.uk
www.hospitality
recruitment.co.uk
www.hoteljobs.co.uk

For those employed in the hospitality industry it is important to understand that there is a considerable amount of legislation that regulates both the industry itself and employment in the industry. Employers who contravene the law or attempt to undermine the statutory rights of their workers – for example, paying less than the national minimum wage or by denying them their right to paid annual holidays – are not only liable to prosecution and fines but could be ordered by tribunals and courts to pay substantial amounts of compensation.

Workers and employees

An employee is a person who is employed under a contract of employment or service. An essential feature of a contract of employment is the 'mutuality of obligation'. The employer undertakes to provide the employee with work on specified days of the week for specified hours, and, if employed under a limited-term contract, during an agreed number of weeks or months; while the employee undertakes to carry out the work in turn for an agreed wage or salary.

Workers

Workers that are not necessarily employees have certain levels of protection. A worker is an individual who works under a contract of employment where the individual undertakes any work or services for another party to the contract whose status is not that of a client or customer.

Workers who are not employees nonetheless enjoy the protection afforded by:

- Health & Safety legislation
- anti-discriminatory laws
- National Minimum Wage Act 1998
- Part-time Workers (Prevention of Less Favourable Treatment) Regulations.
- Working Time Regulations 1998
- Public Interest Disclosure Act 1998

Recruitment and selection

When advertising for new staff it is important to be aware of the following legislation:

- Children and Young Persons Act 1933
- Licensing Act 1964
- Rehabilitation of Offenders Act 1974
- Data Protection Act 1988
- Asylum and Immigration Act 1996
- National Minimum Wage Act 1998
- Working Time Regulations 1998
- Sex Discrimination Act 1975
- Race Relations Act 1976
- Disability Discrimination Act 1995
- Human Rights Act 1998

Job advertisements

It is unlawful to discriminate against job applicants on grounds of:

- sex, marital status or gender
- colour, race, nationality, or national or ethnic origins
- disability
- sexual orientation
- religion or beliefs
- trades union membership or non-membership.

The following words should be avoided in a job advertisement:

- pleasing appearance
- strong personality
- energetic
- articulate
- dynamic
- no family commitments.

These could be construed, or misconstrued, as indicating an intention to discriminate on grounds of sex, race or disability.

Use of job titles with a sexual connotation (e.g. 'waiter', 'barmaid', 'manageress') will likewise be taken to indicate an intention to discriminate on the grounds of a person's sex, unless the advertisement contains an indication or is accompanied by an illustration to the contrary.

Job applications

Job application forms must be designed with care. A form should explain the need, if necessary, for 'sensitive personal information', to reassure the candidate that such data will be held in the strictest confidence and in keeping with the provisions of the Data Protection Act 1998.

Human Rights Act

Candidates must be informed at interview and when the application is sent out that they have to wear uniforms on duty, or protective clothing.

Any surveillance monitoring the company is likely to carry out must also be disclosed to applicants.

Asylum and Immigration Act

It is an offence under the Asylum and Immigration Act 1996 to employ a foreign national subject to immigration control who does not have the valid and subsisting right to enter or remain in the UK, or to take up employment while in the UK. Job application forms should caution future employees that they will be required, if shortlisted, to produce documents confirming their right to be in, and to take up employment in, the UK.

Job interviews

The purpose of the job interview is to assess the suitability of a particular applicant for the vacancy under consideration. The interviewer should ask questions designed to test the applicant's suitability for the job, covering qualifications, training and experience, and to elicit information about the individual's personal qualities, character, development, motivation, strengths and weaknesses.

If a job applicant resigned or was dismissed from previous employment, the interviewer may need to know why. Admitted health problems, injuries and disabilities may also need to be discussed in order to determine the applicant's suitability for employment – for example, in a high-risk working environment.

Employers may lawfully ask a job applicant if he or she has been convicted of any criminal offence, but must be aware of the right of job applicants, under the Rehabilitation of Offenders Act 1974, not to disclose details of any criminal convictions that have since become 'spent'.

The interview should not ask questions about sexuality or religion. Questions on religion may be asked if, for example, aspects of the job may directly affect the beliefs of an individual – an example would be the handling of alcoholic drinks.

Job offers

An offer of employment should be made or confirmed in writing and is often conditional on the receipt of satisfactory references from former employers. Withdrawing an offer of employment once it has been accepted could result in a civil action for damages.

Written statement of employment particulars

Every employee, whether full-time, part-time, casual, seasonal or temporary, has a legal right to be provided with a written statement outlining the principal terms and conditions of his or her employment. This must be issued within two months of the date on which the employee first starts work, but ideally on the employee's first day at work.

Any employee who is *not* provided with a written statement of employment particulars may refer the matter to an employment tribunal.

If the employee's complaint is upheld the employer will be ordered either to provide the statement or accept a statement written by the tribunal. An employer who presumes to discipline, dismiss or otherwise punish an employee for asserting his or her statutory rights, before an employment tribunal, may be ordered to pay that employee compensation.

Employment of school-age children

The employment of school-age children in hotels, restaurants and public houses at weekends and during the school holidays is regulated by the Children and Young Persons Act 1933 and by local authority by-laws. As a rule no child may be employed:

- if under age 14
- during school hours
- before 7.00 am or after 7.00 pm on any day
- for more than two hours in a school day or on a Sunday
- for more than eight hours (or, if under 15, for more than five hours) on any one day (other than a Sunday) that is not a school day
- for more than 12 hours in any week that is a normal school week
- for more than 35 hours (or, if under 15, for more than 25 hours) in any week in which the child is not required to be at school
- for more than four hours on any day without a rest break of at least one hour
- at any time in a year unless, at that time, he or she has had, or could still have, during school holidays, at least two consecutive weeks without employment
- to do any work other than light work (i.e. work of a kind that is unlikely to affect the safety, health or development of a school-age child or to interfere with the child's education, or regular and punctual attendance at school).

Before employing a school-age child, (or within seven days of doing so) an employer must apply to the relevant Local Education Authority for an Employment Certificate.

Prohibited occupations

Most local authority by-laws prohibit the employment of school-age children in:

- hotel kitchens
- cook shops
- fish and chip shops
- restaurants
- snack bars and cafeterias
- any premises in connection with the sale of alcohol, except where alcohol is sold exclusively in sealed containers.

Figure 2.1 Outdoor catering

Employment legislation

Equal pay

Under the Equal Pay Act 1970, a woman engaged in like work, or work of a basically similar nature, or in work rated as equivalent, or in work of equal value to that undertaken by a man in the same employment is entitled to be paid the same as that man, and to enjoy equivalent terms and conditions of employment. The same rule applies if a woman is appointed or promoted to a job previously occupied by a man. In the absence of any express term, every contract of employment (and every collective agreement imported with an employee's contract) will be treated in law as containing an implied equality clause.

National minimum wage

Every worker aged 16 and over, who is no longer of compulsory school age, must be paid no less than the appropriate national minimum wage. The rate varies with age, and there are three levels of minimum wage. As of 1 October 2006 the rates are:

- £5.35 per hour for workers aged 22 years and older
- a development rate of £4.45 per hour for workers aged 18–21 years inclusive
- £3.30 per hour, which applies to all workers under the age of 18 who are no longer of compulsory school age (this varies in England and Wales, Scotland, and Northern Ireland; check www.hmrc.gov.uk/nmw/ for further information and up-to-date details).

Statutory Sick Pay

Employers in Great Britain are liable to pay up to 28 weeks' Statutory Sick Pay to any qualified employee who is incapable of work because of illness of injury.

Employers who operate their own occupational sick pay schemes may opt out of the Statutory Sick Pay scheme, so long as the payments available to their employees under such schemes are equal to or greater than payments to which they would otherwise be entitled under Statutory

Sick Pay, and so long as these employees are not required to contribute towards the cost of funding such a scheme. Payments made under Statutory Sick Pay may be offset against contractual sick pay, and vice versa.

Meaning of 'incapacity for work'

An employee is incapacitated for work if he or she is incapable, because of disease or bodily or mental disablement, of doing work that he or she can reasonably be expected to do under the contract of employment. Under the Food Safety (General Food Hygiene) Regulations 1995, food handlers suffering from (or carriers of) a disease likely to be transmitted through food or while afflicted with infected wounds, skin infections, sores or diarrhoea must not be allowed to work in any food handling, even in any capacity in which there is a likelihood of directly or indirectly contaminating food with pathogenic micro-organisms. In these circumstances, the worker is deemed to be incapacitated for work and, subject to the usual qualifying conditions, entitled to be paid Statutory Sick Pay until such time as the risk has passed.

Working Time Regulations

The Working Time Regulations apply not only to employees but also to every worker (part-time, temporary, seasonal or casual) who undertakes to do or perform work or service for an employer.

The 1998 Regulations are policed and enforced by employment tribunals (in relation to a worker's statutory rights to rest breaks, rest periods and paid annual holidays) and by local authority Environmental Health Officers.

Restrictions on working hours

The 1998 Regulations (as amended from 6 April 2003) impose a number of restrictions on working hours and periods of employment for workers aged 18 and over.

- Adult workers have the right not to be employed for more than an average of 48 hours a week.
- Adolescent workers may not lawfully be employed for more than eight hours a day or for more than 40 hours a week.
- Adult workers may not lawfully be employed at night for more than an average eight hours in any 24-hour period.
- Adolescent workers may not lawfully be employed at night between the hours of 10.00 pm and 6.00 am (or between 11.00 pm and 7.00 am if their contracts require them to work after 10.00 pm).
- Every worker is entitled to a minimum weekly rest period of 24 hours (or 48 hours in every fortnight); or, if under the age of 18, a minimum weekly rest period of 48 consecutive hours.
- Every worker is entitled to a daily rest period of a minimum 11 consecutive hours or, under the age of 18, a daily rest period of a minimum 12 consecutive hours.

- Every worker is entitled to a minimum 20-minute rest break during the course of any working day or shift lasting or expected to last for more than six hours or, if under the age of 18, a minimum 30-minute break during the course of any working day or shift lasting, or expected to last, for more than 4.5 hours.
- Every worker is entitled to a minimum four weeks' paid holiday in every holiday year.
- If an adult worker is content to work more than an average 48 hours a week, he or she must sign an agreement to that effect.

Parental leave

Under the Maternity and Parental Leave Regulations 1999, the employed parents of a child who is under the age of five (or under the age of 18, if adopted) have the legal right to take up to 13 weeks' unpaid parental leave during the first five years of the child's life or, if adopted, until the fifth anniversary of adoption or the child's 18th birthday.

Statutory Maternity Pay

A pregnant employee who has worked for her employer for a minimum period of 26 weeks into the 15th week before her expected week of childbirth will normally qualify to be paid up to 26 weeks' Statutory Maternity Pay during her ordinary maternity leave period.

Paternity leave and pay

Under the Paternity and Adoptive Leave Regulations 2002, complemented by the Paternity and Adoption Leave Regulations 2003, which came into force, respectively, on 8 December 2002 and 6 April 2003, an eligible employee is entitled to either one week's or two consecutive weeks' paternity leave in respect of a child born or expected to be born in or after 6 April 2003, if he is the child's biological father or the current spouse or partner of the child's mother.

Flexible working

Under the Flexible Working (Eligibility, Complaints and Remedies) Regulations 2002, eligible employees who are the parents (or adoptive parents) of children under the age of six, or of disabled children under the age of 18, and who wish to spend more time with their children, have the legal right to apply to their employers for a more flexible pattern of working hours.

The meaning of flexible working

Flexible working could involve shorter working hours or a shorter working week, a system of staggered or annualised hours, flexi-time, job-sharing, part-time work, term-time working, self-rostering, and so on.

Time off work

Employees have the legal right to be permitted a reasonable amount of paid or unpaid time off work to enable them to carry out their functions as public officials, shop stewards, members of recognised independent trades unions, safety representatives, pension schemes, trustees, and so on.

The legislation does not specify what constitutes a 'reasonable' amount of time off. A great deal will depend on the particular circumstances and a degree of common sense.

Unlawful discrimination

It is unlawful for employers to discriminate against job applicants or existing workers by denying them access to opportunities for employment, promotion, transfer or tracking, or by victimising them, harassing them or subjecting to any other detriment because of their race, colour, nationality, national or ethnic origins, sex, disability, sexual orientation, religion or beliefs. It is also unlawful for employers – as the providers of goods, facilities and services to members of the public – to discriminate against would-be or existing customers or guests on any of the above grounds, either by denying them access to these facilities and services, or by treating them less favourably than they treat or would treat other members of the public.

Sex Discrimination Act 1975

Under this Act it is unlawful to discriminate against a woman by refusing to interview her or offer her a job regardless of qualifications, skills or experience simply because she is a woman, or to treat her less favourably than a man.

Sexual harassment is prohibited under amendments to the 1975 Act. The amended Act states that a person subjects a woman to harassment if, on the grounds of her sex, he engages in unwanted conduct that violates her dignity or creates an intimidating, hostile, degrading, humiliating or offensive environment for her.

Racial discrimination

Under the Race Relations Act 1976, as amended in July 2003 by the Race Relations Act 1976 Amendment Regulations 2003, it is unlawful for any employer, regardless of the size of his or her business or undertaking, to discriminate against any person (job applicant, customer or member of the public) by denying that person access to employment, goods, facilities or services because of his or her colour, race, nationality, or national or ethnic origins.

The 1976 Act (as amended in 2003) identifies four types of discrimination in the field of employment that (unless shown to be justified irrespective of the colour, race, nationality, or national or ethnic origins of any person affected by such discrimination) could prompt a complaint to an employment tribunal or attract the attention of the Commission for Racial Equality (CRE). These are: direct discrimination; indirect discrimination; discrimination by way of victimisation; and discrimination by way of harassment.

1 **Direct discrimination:** this occurs when an employer discriminates against job applicants and existing employees on racial grounds by:
   - denying job interviews
   - refusing them access to employment
   - offering them less favourable terms and conditions of employment
   - withholding opportunities for promotion or transfer (or access to other benefits such as overtime or shift work)
   - segregating them from other members of staff
   - victimising or harassing them (or permitting others to do so)
   - dismissing them, selecting them for redundancy or subjecting them to any other detriment (or, in the case of an employee on a fixed- or limited-term contract, refusing to renew that contract when it expires).

   By 'racial grounds' is meant by any of the following:
   - colour
   - race
   - nationality
   - national or ethnic origins.

2 **Indirect discrimination:** there is indirect racial discrimination when an employer deliberately or inadvertently applies a requirement or conditions to a candidate for employment, promotion or transfer etc., which although applied equally to every candidate competing for the same job, nonetheless puts a candidate of a particular racial group at a disadvantage relative to other candidates who are not of the same racial group. Such discrimination is unlawful:
   - if the proportion of persons of the same racial group as that candidate who can comply with that requirement or condition is considerably smaller than the proportion of persons not of that racial group who can comply with it
   - if the employer cannot show that requirement or condition to be justifiable irrespective of the colour, race, nationality or ethnic origins of the person to whom it is applied, and which is to the detriment of that other candidate because he or she cannot comply with it.

3 **Discrimination by way of victimisation:** an employer is guilty of unlawful racial discrimination by way of victimisation if he or she treats (or would treat) other employees more favourably, and does so because the employee in question:
   - has brought (or is contemplating bringing) legal proceedings against the employer (or some other person acting on the employer's behalf) alleging a breach of his or her statutory rights under the 1976 Act
   - has given (or proposes to give) evidence or information to the CRE or an employment tribunal in connection with proceedings brought by some other person (such as a fellow employee) under the 1976 Act, or has alleged (in good faith) that his or her employer (or some other person, such as a manager, supervisor, or member of the

workforce) has committed an act that amounts to a contravention of the 1976 Act.

4 **Discrimination by way of harassment:** under the 1976 Act, as amended by the Race Relations Act 1976 Amendment Regulations 2003, employers are guilty of unlawful racial discrimination if they harass any existing or prospective employees for reasons connected with their race or ethnic or national origins. By 'harass' is meant engaging in unwanted conduct, which, in the perception of the employee in question, has the purpose or effect (or should reasonably be considered as having the effect) of violating his or her dignity, or creating for that person an intimidating, hostile, degrading, humiliating or offensive working environment.

Employers who fail to take steps to eliminate harassment in the workplace will, in most situations, be held vicariously liable for the activities of managers, supervisors and other members who themselves engage (or encourage others to engage) in such conduct.

Disability discrimination

The Disability Discrimination Act 1995 cautions employers that it is unlawful to discriminate against disabled job applicants and existing employees either by refusing to contemplate employing, promoting or transferring any person who admits to being disabled (regardless of that person's suitability for appointment, promotion or transfer to the vacancy under consideration), or by offering any such candidate or employee less favourable terms and conditions than those offered to able-bodied persons appointed to (or already doing) the same job. By the same token, employers are not required to treat disabled job applicants more favourably than employees competing with them for appointment, promotion or transfer to the same job.

The meaning of 'disability'

For the purposes of the 1995 Act, a person has a disability if he (or she) has a physical or mental impairment that has a substantial and long-term adverse effect on his (or her) ability to carry out normal day-to-day activities. The term 'mental impairment' includes an impairment resulting from, or consisting of, a mental illness, but only if the illness is clinically well recognised.

An impairment is to be taken to affect a person's ability to carry out normal day-to-day activities if it has an effect on his or her mobility, manual dexterity, physical coordination, continence, concentration, perception of danger, speech, hearing or sight, or the ability to lift, carry or move everyday objects.

Any job advertisement that indicates, or might reasonably be understood to indicate, an intention to discriminate against disabled job applicants or that suggests a reluctance or inability on the employer's part to make appropriate adjustments to the workplace to accommodate the needs of people with particular disabilities, is admissible as evidence in any subsequent tribunal.

The employer's duty to make adjustments

Employers must take appropriate steps to accommodate a disabled person who might otherwise be at a disadvantage relative to able-bodied persons doing (or applying for) the same or similar work. These would include making adjustments to the premises, allocating some of the disabled person's duties to another person, altering his or her working hours, requiring or modifying equipment, providing supervision, and so on.

An employer's refusal to appoint a disabled person to a particular job may be justifiable on health and safety grounds, or because it is self-evident that the applicant would be quite incapable of doing that job – given the nature and extent of the applicant's disability, the type of work to be done and the conditions in which that work is to be carried out.

Chronically sick and disabled persons

The Chronically Sick and Disabled Persons Act 1970 (amended by the Chronically Sick and Disabled Persons (Amendment) Act 1976) imposes a duty on the owners and developers of new commercial premises (hotels, pubs, restaurants) to consider the needs of disabled persons when designing the means of access to (and within) these premises, including the means of access to parking facilities, toilets, cloakrooms and washing facilities.

Discrimination on grounds of sexual orientation

The Employment Equality (Sexual Orientation) Regulations 2003 state that it is unlawful for employers, regardless of the number of people they employ, to discriminate against job applicants and existing employees on grounds of their sexual orientation. This includes homosexuality, heterosexuality and bisexuality. The regulations envisage four types of discrimination on such grounds: direct discrimination; indirect discrimination; harassment; and victimisation.

Figure 2.2 Restaurant with disability access

Figure 2.3 Disability access in different environments

Discrimination on grounds of religion or belief

The Employment Equality (Religion or Belief) Regulations 2003 state that it is unlawful for any employer to discriminate against a job applicant or existing employee because of that applicant's or employee's religion or beliefs. The regulations prohibit discrimination, victimisation or harassment occurring after an employment relationship has come to an end.

The term 'religion or belief' means any religion, religious belief or similar philosophical belief.

Exceptions for genuine occupational requirements

The regulations allow that it is permissible in certain circumstances for an employer to discriminate against a job applicant (or a candidate for promotion or transfer) on the grounds of his or her religion or belief if being of a particular religion or having certain beliefs is a genuine and determining occupation or requirement for the vacancy in question.

A restaurant serving kosher or halal foods, for example, may be justified in its refusal to engage the services of cooks or waiting staff who are not of the Jewish or Islamic faiths, if certain foods have to be treated and prepared in a particular way before being served to customers.

Dress codes

People applying for work in establishments with particular dress codes should be given to understand that their employment would be dependent on their adhering to these codes. The Equal Opportunities Commission (EOC) is unhappy about dress codes that require female workers to wear short or revealing skirts or low-cut blouses while at

Figure 2.4 A modern staff restaurant

work. However, its view is that there is no breach of the Sex Discrimination Act 1975 or the Human Rights Act 1998 so long as the employer's policy on dress and appearance is made known to job applicants at employment interviews and employees are willing to accept it as part of their terms and conditions of employment.

Employers are not obliged to allow members of staff, whose religions require them to pray at certain intervals during the day, to take time off in order to comply with their religion's obligations.

Disciplining and grievance procedure

The written statement of initial employment particulars necessarily issued to all employees must include a note explaining the employer's disciplinary rules and procedures, or refer the employee to some other reasonably accessible document that explains them.

Although employers are under no strict obligation to develop their own rules and procedures for dealing with disciplinary issues within the workplace, the reasonableness of an employer's decision to dismiss an employee, for whatever reason, might very well be challenged before an employment tribunal, especially if the evidence before the tribunal reveals that the employer had failed to follow the best practice guidelines laid down in ACAS Code of Practice on Disciplinary and Grievance Procedures (see box).

The ACAS Code of Practice

ACAS Code of Practice on Disciplinary and Grievance Procedures

The ACAS Code of Practice on Disciplinary and Grievance Procedures provides practical guidance for employers on the development and implementation of disciplinary rules and procedures, and on the statutory right of employees and other workers to be accompanied at any formal disciplinary or grievance hearing by a fellow worker or full-time trades union official.

ACAS Advisory, Conciliation and Arbitration Service

ACAS staff are employment relations experts. Their job is to help people to work together effectively. This ranges from setting up the right structures and systems to finding a way of settling disputes when things go wrong.

ACAS has a wealth of experience working with employers, employees, trades unions and other representatives.

ACAS was founded in 1974. It is a publicly funded body, run by a council of 12 members from business, unions and the independent sector.

Employing staff

- Summary of regulatory requirements
- Equal opportunities
- Race, sex, sexual orientation, religious belief

Jobs, training and promotion must be open to all, regardless of colour, race, nationality, ethnic or national origin, sex including gender reassignment, marital status, sexual orientation, religion or belief.

Disability

You must not discriminate against disabled people (for example, in recruitment or promotion procedures) and may have to make reasonable adjustments for disabled staff (for example, to their employment conditions or workplace). Exemptions apply if you have fewer than 15 employees but from 1 October 2004 these rules apply to businesses of all sizes.

Employee rights

• Terms and conditions of employment

If employed for one month or more, an employee must receive (within the first two months) a written statement of their main employment particulars. The statement must include the main terms and conditions, including details of pay, holidays, details of notice and disciplinary procedures.

You must treat part-time workers the same as comparable full-time workers in their terms and conditions, including pay, pensions, holidays and training.

Transfer of an undertaking

Employees terms and conditions are preserved when a business or an undertaking (or part of one) transfers to a new employer. Employers are required to consult either representatives of an appropriate recognised trades union or elected representatives of any employees affected by the transfer.

Fair and unfair dismissal

To claim unfair dismissal, employees must generally have completed a year's service but no qualifying service is needed if the dismissal is for certain reasons (e.g. pregnancy).

Period of notice

For continuous employment of at least one month but less than two years, one week's notice must be given unless a longer period is stated in the employment contract. For continuous employment of two years of more, at least two weeks' notice must be given, unless a longer period is stated in the contract. After two years' continuous employment, one additional week's notice for each further complete year is required. After 12 years' continuous employment a minimum of 12 weeks' notice is required.

Unions

Employees have the right to belong or not to belong to a union, and the right not to be refused employment on the grounds of trades union membership or non-membership. Workers also have a statutory right to be accompanied by a fellow worker or a trades union official during disciplinary and grievance hearings.

Redundancy

• Under 20 employees
There is no obligation to notify of redundancy. If the employee has at least two years' continuous service since the age of 18, they have a redundancy entitlement. This varies according to age, length of service and pay rate.
• 20–99 employees
Must give at least 30 days' notification. If you are going to make at least 20 employees at one establishment redundant over a period of 90 days or less you must consult either representatives of a recognised independent

trades union or other elected representatives of affected employees.

- More than 99 employees
Must give at least 90 days' notification.

Illegal working

Employers risk prosecution if they employ illegal workers. You can avoid this risk by making simple checks on all new employees before they start working for you. Ask to see their passport or other documents listed by the Home Office as acceptable evidence of their right to work in the UK. You need to keep copies of the documents you have checked.

Maternity, parental leave and time off for dependants

Employees expecting babies are entitled to 26 weeks' ordinary maternity leave. If they have worked for at least 26 continuous weeks by the beginning of the 15th week before the baby is due to be born they can also take up to 26 weeks' additional maternity leave. Employees with at least one year's continuous service are entitled to 13 weeks' parental leave for each child up until the child's fifth birthday (similar rights apply to adoption). Employees are entitled to reasonable time off to deal with an emergency involving a dependant.

Flexible work

Parents with children under six or disabled children aged under 18 have the right to request a flexible working pattern, and their employers have a duty to consider their applications seriously.

Stakeholder pensions

If you have five or more employees, and are not exempt, you must give access to a stakeholder pension scheme to those employees entitled to join it. You must make payroll deductions of an employee's contribution into their stakeholder pension if they ask you to.

Pay and tax, tax credits and student loan deductions

- Equal pay
Men and women must get the same pay for the same or like work, and for work of equal value.

- PAYE
When you take on your first employee, inform the New Employers Helpline on 0845 60 70 143. They will arrange for a PAYE scheme to be set up and send you a New Employer's Starter Pack. This contains the forms and guidance you will need to make deductions for tax and National Insurance Contributions (NICs).
    Depending on your employees' circumstances you may have to make payments of tax credits and make student loan deductions; the Inland Revenue will tell you if you have to do this.

- Itemised pay
All employees must be given itemised pay statements showing deductions, tax credits and student loan deductions.

National minimum wage

There is a minimum wage of £5.35 per hour for those aged 22 years and over, a 'development rate' of £4.45 per hour for workers aged 18–21 years inclusive, and £3.30 per hour, which applies to all workers under the age of 18 who are no longer of compulsory school age. For agricultural workers, minimum rates of pay set by the Agricultural Wages Board apply.

National Insurance

For employees aged 16 or over, employer and employee NICs become payable once earnings exceed the 'earnings threshold' (£91/week from April 2004). If you are a limited company there are special NIC rules for the directors.

Statutory Sick Pay (SSP)

If the employee is sick for less than four consecutive days no SSP action is needed. If the employee is sick for four consecutive days or more:

- if the employee is entitled to SSP – pay SSP in the same way as wages, and keep records of payments made and dates of sickness absence lasting four consecutive days
- if the employee is not entitled to SSP they may claim State Incapacity Benefit instead – issue Form SSP1.

Statutory Maternity Pay (SMP)

Tell employees how you wish to be informed about maternity absence and:
- if the employee is entitled to SMP – pay SMP and keep a record of payments made
- if the employee is not entitled to SMP she should claim State Maternity Allowance instead – issue Form SMP1.

Hours

- Limits on working time
Employees have rights on average weekly working hours and night working. They are also entitled to rest periods, breaks and paid annual leave. The law gives adolescent workers extra protection.

- Shops
If the floor area is less than 280 metres square there are no restrictions on small shops' Sunday opening hours. Larger shops may open for any six continuous hours between 10.00 am and 6.00 pm.
  Shop and betting shop workers have statutory rights related to Sunday working.

- Driving
There are limitations on driving hours within certain periods.

Insurance health and safety

Employers must take out Employers Liability Insurance and display the certificate.
  Check your responsibility regarding the health and safety of employees with the Health & Safety Executive (HSE). You must also register your business with either the HSE (most factories, workshops, etc.) or your local authority (most offices, shops, catering businesses, etc.).

TOPICS FOR DISCUSSION

1 Outline the function of an employment tribunal.
2 Discuss the reasons why the hospitality industry is poorly represented by trades unions.
3 Discuss some of the legislation that protects people from employment discrimination.
4 Why is it important to any organisation to develop good industrial relations?
5 Do you believe that the current employment legislation is adequate, inadequate or prohibits the development of the hospitality industry?

Chapter 3 FOOD AND SOCIETY

WORLD FOOD SUPPLY AND FOOD SECURITY

Obtaining sufficient food is an important concern for every nation in the world, and in some countries food shortage is an extremely serious problem. Worldwide about 840 million people, or about 14 per cent of the total population, do not have adequate food. These people suffer from under-nutrition, a condition of nutrient deficiency that causes general weakness and fatigue, stunts mental and physical development in children, and makes people susceptible to potentially fatal diseases such as dysentery and tuberculosis.

Creating an adequate food supply poses two challenges. The first is to provide enough food to meet the needs of the earth's expanding population without destroying the natural resources needed to continue producing food. The second challenge is to ensure food security – that is, to make sure all people have access to enough food to live active, healthy lives. Just producing enough food does not guarantee that the people who need it are able to get it.

Some people do not have enough money to buy food, or to buy land, seeds and tools to farm food. Natural or human-made disasters, such as drought or war, prevent people from obtaining food, so they are put at risk of suffering under-nutrition. In industrialised countries poverty prevents people from obtaining food; in developing countries, the circumstances that cause food insecurity include poverty, low crop yields and unproductive economic policies.

Factors affecting food production

The number of farmers worldwide has been decreasing since the 1950s as they migrate to cities to find other work. Farmers are sometimes forced to give up uneconomical farms (e.g. those that are too small) and move to the cities to take up employment in order to earn a better income. Some farms have been taken over for the development of industry and roads. The presence of fewer farmers, and the loss of knowledge passed down through generations of farming families about the most productive agricultural practices for a region, affect the variety, quality and quantity of food produced.

Food production requires water, arable land, energy to operate machinery, and the human and animal labour needed to work the land. These vital resources are distributed unevenly around the world, and many have been depleted or damaged by modern agricultural techniques. Scientists estimate that, since 1945, about 17 per cent of the earth's vegetated surface, or 2 billion hectares (4.9 million acres), have been degraded, or made less productive, by human mismanagement. Poor agricultural practices, such as overgrazing and irrigation without proper drainage, have degraded about 552 million hectares (13.6 million acres) – 38 per cent of the world's total cultivated area.

Water, essential for the growth of all crops, is the natural resource in shortest supply. More than 20 countries lack sufficient water to grow enough food for their populations. Over half of these people live in the arid, or dry, regions of Africa and the Middle East, where periodic droughts and water scarcity lasting months, sometimes years, contribute to food shortages. By 2025, if current population trends continue, about 75 per cent of Africans will live in regions where water shortages limit food production. The increasing costs of irrigation, the greater fluctuations in drought, and the floods anticipated with global climate change and population growth are all pushing in the direction of more pressure on water resources.

One of the main causes of water depletion is irrigation – the artificial use of water for crops that makes unproductive lands fertile. Too much irrigation depletes fresh water supplies, seriously damages the environment and creates serious problems for human populations. Arable land is another disappearing agricultural resource. The amount of arable land per person has been shrinking since 1981. An estimated 8 million hectares (20 million acres) of farmland is replaced each year by homes, shopping centres, industries and roads built to accommodate growing populations. Modern farming practices also contribute to the decline of arable land by causing the wearing away, or erosion, of topsoil (the upper layer of soil that provides the nutrients plants need). Erosion leaves only nutrient-poor subsoil, which cannot support plants.

Farming techniques, particularly irrigation, also contribute to salinisation (the accumulation of salt in soils). Salinisation stunts plant growth, decreasing harvests and eventually making soils unusable. According to the United Nations Food and Agriculture Organization

(FAO), salinisation has degraded an estimated 7–10 per cent of the world's 250 million hectares (618 million acres) or irrigated lands.

Modern farming techniques depend on extensive use of fossil fuels – oil, gasoline and natural gas – for a variety of functions. Extensive use of fossil fuels damages the environment, contributing to air, soil and water pollution, ozone depletion and global warming.

Factors affecting food security

The world population is projected to reach 8 billion by 2025. Food production must keep pace with the increasing number of people living in the world. Since 1960, world food production has grown faster than population, mainly because of the 'green revolution': the effort to increase and diversify crop yields in agriculturally less advanced regions of the world.

The introduction of irrigation, fertilisers, pesticides and new seed varieties resulted in increased yields of rice, wheat and corn in many countries. In most countries, however, added water and fertiliser do not increase yields as much as they did in the past, and in the future food production may not match population growth.

Although the control of population growth rates is an important aspect of achieving food security, a low population growth rate does not guarantee food security, nor does a high growth rate create food insecurity. Population growth negatively affects food security only when other food-related variables are impaired. For instance, a country may not have enough water or available land to support more people, or agricultural techniques may not produce enough food for a growing population.

Food availability depends on physical access – this means there are adequate markets, and good road and transport links, storage and distribution systems. A lack of any of these can cause a food crisis. War and political strife also disrupt access to food, resulting in famines and food shortages.

Grain and cereal production plays a significant role in the world's food security. Grains such as rice, wheat and corn provide about 30 per cent of the calories people consume each day. Grain supplies may be threatened, however, by the world's reliance on a small number of crop varieties. Throughout history, farmers planted many varieties of rice, wheat, corn, millet and other grains, selected for how well they grew in local soils, how they withstood local insects and diseases, and how they adapted to the climate.

In the twentieth century most of the regional varieties have been replaced by new varieties of rice, wheat and corn that produce more grain but are vulnerable to unpredictable diseases or insect infestations. To provide a stable food supply, agriculture needs diverse crop varieties so that the failure of one or two crops is less likely to cause famine.

To ensure food security, an adequate diet must include not only calories but also the full range of nutrients that humans need. Of particular importance is protein, which is essential for muscles, bones, the antibodies that prevent infection and the many enzymes that regulate all the body's systems. Grains, beans and seeds are common sources of protein in developing countries. Meat, milk, cheese and eggs are more likely to be consumed in industrialised countries. The demand for these products is high, despite the inefficient use of land required to produce them.

To raise chickens and pigs, it takes an estimated 2–4 kg of grain to produce 1 kg of meat, and for cows the figure is estimated at 7 kg of grain per 1 kg of meat. In contrast, direct consumption of grains by humans is far more efficient.

In 2002 about 70 per cent of marine fish stocks were being harvested faster than they could reproduce, according to a report by the United Nations Environment Program (UNEP). The UNEP also noted that major changes were needed in the use and management of marine fisheries to avoid the commercial extinction of many fisheries.

Fish farming (known as aquaculture) is expanding rapidly, especially in developing countries, where it contributes towards efforts to secure food supplies. Between 1970 and 2000, aquaculture increased from 3.9 per cent to 27.3 per cent of the total volume of fish raised or captured.

Salmon, scallops and trout are common farmed products. Fisheries exports earn more money worldwide than sugar, coffee, tea and cocoa combined – crops traditionally raised for export by developing countries.

Crops grown for sale to other countries also influence food security. Export crops can include staple foods such as rice, or luxury foods such as strawberries. Export sales provide income for farmers, enabling them to purchase food, and exports help countries reduce debts owed to other countries for imports.

To ensure food security in times of low crop yields, natural disasters or famine, nations must use stored foods. Global cereal reserves, also known as world carry-over stocks, are an indicator of work food security. By the beginning of the twenty-first century, stores had dropped to their lowest level in 20 years. The decrease in grain stores is the result of cutbacks in grain production in Europe and the USA, lower yields due to regional weather problems, and soil erosion resulting from poor farming practices. As yields have decreased, many countries have dipped deeper into carry-over stocks to feed their growing populations.

Countries that cannot grow or buy enough food to feed their people, or that experience natural disasters or political disruption, are dependent on wealthier countries.

GLOBALISATION

Globalisation is the rapid integration of trade and culture between the world's nations. With a more open market, goods – and, by association, cash – can travel across the globe much more freely. This greater global trade has been able to happen for the following reasons.

- Governments have changed laws that in the past restricted economic trade.
- New technologies have enabled faster communication.
- Travel and transport costs have reduced.
- Foreign (western) companies have looked abroad for investment.

International bodies such as the World Trade Organization (WTO) and the European Union were partly created to help reduce barriers to trade and investment, and allow the global marketplace to flourish.

Economic 'globalisation' generally means the integration of national economies with the global economy, the increasing flow of money around the world and the growth of multinational companies; many of these companies are food manufacturing companies and supermarket chains. This is also known as 'corporate globalisation'.

The WTO is the body that makes and enforces the laws and rules that control international trade. The aim of the WTO is to make trade run as 'freely' as possible so that companies can buy and sell products and services without any barriers in their way. Barriers to trade can include things like environmental standards and levels, and safety rules, as these can get in the way of making cheap products and low-cost services. For example, if the UK consumer demands tough standards on toxic pollution, this would be considered a barrier to foreign companies, which may not be able to meet these standards as quickly as domestic companies.

The WTO can overrule national laws that might make trade run less freely. These might be laws to protect the environment, or health or tax benefits to support local businesses. The WTO can use fines and sanctions to force countries to get rid of such protective measures. As a result, governments should hold back from policies that might conflict with WTO rules.

Free trade, fair trade and ethical trade

Free trade means that governments have to treat local and foreign producers in the same way – for example, by not creating barriers against importing goods, services or people from other countries, or giving national businesses and farmers an advantage over foreign firms by offering them financial support. In practice free trade has never existed, and reducing trade barriers is always subject to intense political negotiation between countries of unequal power.

Fair trade encourages small-scale producers to play a stronger role in managing their relationship with buyers, guaranteeing them a fair financial return for their work.

Ethical trade involves companies finding ways to buy their products from suppliers who provide good working conditions, and respect the environment and human rights.

The World Trade Organization

The WTO was created in 1994 to liberalise world trade through international agreements. Based in Geneva, it has 140 member countries, some having more power than others.

The International Monetary Fund (IMF)

The IMF was set up in 1944, along with the World Bank (see below), to maintain a stable international trading system. It monitors countries' economies, and gives out loans to help the international economic system function smoothly.

The World Bank

The World Bank is the main organisation providing financial help for development. It was originally established to help Europe recover after the Second World War.

TASTE

Why do we eat what we eat, select one dish from the menu in preference to another, choose one particular kind of restaurant or use a takeaway? Why are these dishes on the menu in the first place? Is it because the chef likes them, the customer or consumer wants them, or is this the only food available? What dictates what we eat?

Catering reflects the eating habits, history, customs and taboos of society, but it also develops and creates them. You have only to compare the variety of eating facilities available on any major high street today with those of a short while ago.

Taste affects food choice, and is based on biological, social and cultural perspectives. The perception of taste results from the stimulation of the taste cells that make up the taste buds. Taste is not specific to individual foods, but to the balance between four main types of chemical compound. These compounds correspond to four sensations (see pages 488–493).

Some factors that affect what we eat

The individual

Everyone has needs, and wishes these to be met according to his or her own satisfaction.

- Tastes and habits in eating are influenced by three main factors: upbringing, peer group behaviour and social background. For example, children's tastes are developed at home according to the eating patterns of their family, as is their expectation of when to eat meals; teenagers may frequent hamburger or other fast-food outlets; and adults may eat out once a week at an ethnic or high-class restaurant, steakhouse or pub.

- Degree of hunger will affect what is to be eaten, when and how much to eat – although some people in the western world overeat and food shortages cause under-nourishment in poorer countries. Everyone ought to eat enough to enable body and mind to function efficiently; if you are hungry or thirsty it is difficult to work or study effectively.
- Health considerations may influence choice of food, either because a special diet is required for medical reasons, or (as the current emphasis on healthy eating shows) because everyone needs a nutritionally balanced diet. Many people nowadays feel it is more healthy not to eat meat or dairy products. Others are vegetarian or vegan for moral or religious reasons.

Relationships

Eating is a necessity, but it is also a means of developing social relationships. The needs and preferences of the people you eat with should be considered. This applies in the family or at the place of study or work. School meals can be a means of developing good eating habits, both by the provision of suitable foods and dishes, and by creating an appropriate environment to foster social relationships. Canteens, dining rooms and restaurants for people at work can be places where relationships develop.

Often the purpose of eating, either in the home or outside it, is to be sociable and to meet people, or to renew acquaintances or provide the opportunity for people to meet each other. Frequently there is a reason for the occasion (such as birthday, anniversary, wedding or awards ceremony), requiring a special party or banquet menu, or it may just be for a few friends to have a meal at a restaurant.

Business is often conducted over a meal, usually at lunchtime but also at breakfast and dinner. Eating and drinking help to make work more enjoyable and effective.

Emotional needs

Sometimes we eat not because we need food but to meet an emotional requirement:

- for sadness or depression – eating a meal can give comfort to oneself or to someone else; after a funeral people eat together to comfort one another
- for a reward or a treat, or to give encouragement to oneself or to someone else; an invitation to a meal is a good way of showing appreciation.

IDEAS ABOUT FOOD

People's ideas about food and meals, and about what is and what is not acceptable, vary according to where and how they were raised, the area in which they live and its social customs.

Different societies and cultures have had in the past, and still have, conflicting ideas about what constitutes good cooking and a good chef, and about the sort of food a good chef should provide. The French tradition of producing fine food and highly respected chefs continues to this day – whereas other countries may traditionally have less interest in the art of cooking, and less esteem for chefs.

What constitutes people's idea of a snack, a proper meal or a celebration will depend on their backgrounds, as will their interpretation of terms such as lunch or dinner. One person's idea of a snack may be another person's idea of a main meal; a celebration for some will be a visit to a hamburger bar; for others, a meal at a fashionable restaurant.

The idea of what is 'the right thing to do' regarding eating varies with age, social class and religion. To certain people it is right to eat with the fingers, others use only a fork; some will have cheese before the sweet course, others will have cheese after it; it is accepted that children and, sometimes, elderly people need food to be cut up into small pieces, and that people of some religions do not eat certain foods. The ideas usually originate from practical and hygiene reasons, although sometimes the origin is obscure.

IMAGES OF FOOD

Fashions, fads and fancies affect foods and it is not always clear if catering creates or copies these trends.

Nutritionists inform us what foods are good and necessary in the diet, what the effect of particular foods will be on the figure and how much of each food we require. This helps to produce an 'image' of food. This image changes according to research, availability of food and what is considered to constitute healthy eating.

What people choose to eat says something about them as a person – it creates an image. We are what we eat, but why do we choose to eat what we do when there is choice? One person will perhaps avoid trying snails because of ignorance of how to eat them, or because the idea is repulsive, while another will select them deliberately to show off to other diners. One person will select a dish because it is a new experience, another will choose it because it was enjoyed when eaten before. The quantity eaten may indicate a glutton or a gourmand; the quality selected, a gourmet.

The food itself

Crop failure or distribution problems may make food scarce or not available at all. Foods in season are now supplemented by imported foods, so that foods out of season at home are now available much of the time. This means that there is a wide choice of food for the caterer and the customer.

Food is available through shops, supermarkets, cash and carry, wholesalers and direct suppliers. People at home and caterers are able to purchase, prepare, cook and present almost every food imaginable due to rapid air transport and food preservation. Food spoilage and wastage are minimised; variety and quality are maximised.

It is essential that food looks attractive, has a pleasing smell and tastes good. Food that is nutritious but that does not look, smell or taste nice is less likely to be eaten. With cooking, these points must be considered, but it should be remembered that people's views as to what is attractive and appealing will vary according to their background and experience.

RESOURCES

Money, time and facilities affect what people eat – the economics of eating affects everyone.

How much money an individual is able, or decides to spend on food is crucial to what is eaten. Some people will not be able to afford to eat out, others will be able to eat out only occasionally, but for others eating out will be a frequent event. The money that individuals allocate for food will determine whether they cook and eat at home, use a takeaway (e.g. fish and chips, Chinese), go to a pub, eat at a pancake house, or at an ethnic or other restaurant.

The amount of time people have to eat at work will affect whether they use any facilities provided, go out for a snack or meal, or bring in their own food.

The ease of obtaining food, the use of convenience and frozen food, and the facility for storing foods, has meant that in the home and in catering establishments the range of foods available is wide. Foods in season can be frozen and used throughout the year, so if there is a glut then spoilage can be eliminated.

INFLUENCES

The media influences what we eat – television, radio, newspapers, magazines and literature of all kinds have an effect on our eating habits (see Table 3.1).

Healthy eating, nutrition, hygiene and outbreaks of food poisoning are publicised; experts in all aspects of health, including those extolling exercise, diet and environmental health, state what should and should not be eaten.

Information regarding the content of food packets and the advertising of food influences our choice. Knowledge about eating and foods is

Table 3.1 Influences on what people eat

MEDIA	TRANSPORT	RELIGIOUS
TV Books Newspapers Journals	Transport of foods by sea, rail, air, Transport of people	Taboos Festivals
GEOGRAPHICAL	HISTORICAL	ECONOMIC
Climate Indigenous fish, birds, animals, plant life	Explorations Invasions Establishment of trade routes	Money to purchase Goods to exchange
SOCIOLOGICAL	POLITICAL	CULTURAL
Family School Workplace Leisure Fashion and trends	Tax on food Policies on 'food mountains' Export and import restrictions	Ethnic Tribal Celebrations
PSYCHOLOGICAL	PHYSIOLOGICAL	SCIENTIFIC
Appearance of food Smell Taste Aesthetics Reaction to new foods	Nutritional Healthy eating Illness Additives	Preservation Technology

learnt from the family, through teachers, at school meals, at college, through the media, and through the experience of eating at home and abroad.

The influences listed in Table 3.1 are separated for convenience, but in reality they overlap. Only when sufficient food is available for survival can pleasure from food develop.

Cultural influences

Cultural variety

The races and nations of the world represent a great variety of cultures, each with their own ways of cooking. Knowledge of this is essential in catering because:

- there has been a rapid spread of tourism, creating a demand for a broader culinary experiences
- many people from overseas have opened restaurants using their own foods and styles of cooking
- the development of air cargo means perishable foods from distant places are readily available
- the media, particularly television, have stimulated an interest in worldwide cooking.

A few years ago it was necessary for a caterer to be knowledgeable about traditional classical French cooking; today they must also be aware of the foods and dishes of many other races. It is not within the scope of this book to deal in depth with gastronomy, but it is hoped that this brief introduction will stimulate an interest in the terms and foods associated with ethnic cooking.

Religious influences

Throughout the world religion always has, and still does, affect what many people eat. Some people's diets are restricted daily by their religion; others are influenced by what they eat on special occasions. Fasts, feasts, celebrations and anniversaries are important happenings in many people's lives. It is necessary for those involved in catering to have some basic knowledge of the requirements and restrictions associated with religions.

Christianity

For most Christians, eating habits are not affected – though some will be vegetarians, usually for moral reasons, and some may refrain from eating meat on Fridays. Some sects (for instance, Mormons) have many rules and restrictions regarding eating and drinking – for example, complete abstinence from tea, coffee and alcohol, and an emphasis on wholesome eating. Many Christians refrain from eating certain foods during Lent, usually choosing to cut out something they like very much. Other religious days often observed are as follows.

- Shrove Tuesday: the day before the start of Lent, when pancakes are on many menus, traditionally to use up ingredients prior to Lent.
- Good Friday: hot cross buns are often eaten as a reminder of Christ's crucifixion.
- Easter Sunday: simnel cakes are made with marzipan and chocolate, and Easter eggs (decorated boiled or chocolate eggs) are eaten as a symbol of new life and the Resurrection.
- Christmas Day (25 December): celebrated with feasting, with roast turkey today often replacing the traditional roast beef and boar's head, followed by Christmas pudding and mince pies.

Islam

Muslims celebrate the birth of Mohammed at the end of February or early in March. Alcohol and pork are traditionally forbidden in their diet. Only meat that has been prepared according to Muslim custom by a halal butcher is permitted. During Ramadan, which lasts for one month and is the ninth month of the Muslim calendar, Muslims do not eat or drink anything from dawn to sunset. The end of the fast is celebrated with a feast called Idd-ul-Fitar, with special foods. Muslims from Middle Eastern countries would favour a dish like lamb stew with okra; those from the Far East, curry and rice.

Hinduism

Most Hindus do not eat meat (strict Hindus are vegetarians) and none eats beef since the cow is considered sacred. Holi is the festival that celebrates the end of winter and the arrival of spring. Raksha Bandha celebrates the ties between brothers and sisters at the end of July or in August, and Janam Ashtami celebrates the birth of Krishna, also in August. Dussehra is the festival of good over evil; Diwali is the festival of light, celebrating light over darkness, held in October or November. Samosas (triangles of pastry containing vegetables), banana fudge and vegetable dishes of all kinds, as well as favourite foods, are eaten to celebrate.

Sikhism

The Sikhs do not have strict rules regarding food but many are vegetarians. Baisakhi day in April celebrates the new year and is the day Sikhs are baptised into their faith. Diwali and Guru Nana K's birthday are also days of celebration.

Buddhism

Strict Buddhists are vegetarians and their dishes vary since most live in India and China, where the available foods will differ. Vesak in May is the festival to celebrate the life of the Buddha.

Judaism

The religion of the Jews has strict dietary laws. Shellfish, pork and birds of prey are forbidden. Acceptable foods are fish with scales and fins, animals that have 'cloven hoofs' and birds killed according to the law. Strict Jews eat only meat that has been specially slaughtered, known as kosher meat.

Milk and meat must neither be used together in cooking nor served at the same meal, and three hours should elapse between eating food containing milk and food containing meat.

The Jewish Sabbath, from sunset on Friday to sunset on Saturday, is traditionally a day of rest. In the evening plaited bread called chollah is broken into pieces and eaten. Matzo, an unleavened crispbread, is served at Passover as a reminder of the exodus of the Jews from Egypt. Pentecost celebrates the giving of the Ten Commandments to Moses on Mount Sinai; cheesecake is now a traditional dish served at this celebration. Hanukkah, the Jewish Festival of Lights in December, is a time of dedication, when pancakes and a potato dish, potato latkes, are usually eaten.

FUSION CUISINE

Fusion or eclectic cuisine is the mix of modern national styles and flavourings from different countries that has developed over recent years.

Its origins can be traced to Australian chefs who have been influenced by ideas from countries of the Pacific Rim. These various styles, ideas and methods are today drawn from a variety of sources throughout the world.

Transportation has greatly assisted the development of fusion cuisine. Further development on this theme has been the introduction of matching serving dishes and plates to the food with the effect of enhancing the overall presentation. Such a concept stretches the chef's creativity and imagination, pioneering new dimensions of food presentation, making the dishes ever more attractive, adding colour, flair and fashion to dining out.

Modern restaurants place great emphasis on decor, space, fashion and overall design. The chef's role is to match the food's style and presentation to this new era of food styles. Examples of these styles are:
- French Thai
- Indian with French presentation
- American Japanese
- Australian/Pacific Rim.

TOPICS FOR DISCUSSION

1 The effects of religion on the eating habits of certain cultures.
2 The most popular British foods; why they are the most popular.
3 The benefits of having a wide variety of ethnic restaurants in the country.
4 The effects of people's eating habits, other than cultural or religious.
5 Examine the origins of, and why and how Welsh, Scottish, Irish and/or English styles of cooking have developed.
6 What has developed as 'American food'; explain why this has become a worldwide phenomenon.
7 Why have oriental and Asian foods become popular in Britain?
8 The American fast-food industry and its effect on Britain.

Chapter 4 FOOD COMMODITIES

Figure 4.1 Purchasing fruit and vegetables

THE STUDY OF COMMODITIES

When studying commodities, students are recommended to explore the markets to get to know both fresh foods and all possible substitutes such as convenience or ready-prepared foods. Comparison should be made between various brands of foods, and between convenience and fresh unprepared foods. Factors to be considered when comparing should include quality, price, hygiene, labour, cost, time, space required and disposal of waste.

Students are advised to be cost conscious from the outset in all their studies and to form the habit of keeping up to date with the current prices of all commodities, equipment, labour and overheads. An in-built awareness of costs is an important asset to any successful caterer.

Further information
Further information about meat, poultry, fish, fruit and vegetables can be found in *Practical Cookery* and *Advanced Practical Cookery*.

Seasonality

The following are some of the reasons why eating seasonally is a good idea.

- Food tastes better in season.
- Food is better for you in season. Seasonal food is more likely to be local; and local food will have spent the minimum time in transit. So, sometimes, seasonal food is healthier.
- Seasonal food is better for the environment. If you believe that human activity contributes to climate change then buying air-freighted French beans from Kenya in the winter is foolhardy, given the vast amount of greenhouse gas produced by such unnecessary trade – and especially when there are so much great local vegetables around in winter. Seasonal food fits into traditional systems of farming, which don't need the same energy-intensive inputs of pesticides, herbicides and artificial fertiliser as intensive systems.
- Seasonal food is cheaper. Crop permitting, almost anything that's in season will be plentiful and therefore cheaper.
- Seasonal food supports local agriculture. Whether it's from the farm down the road or a specialist producer a few hours away, seasonal food that suits our climate is more likely to have been grown closer to home. Buying locally offers another market for beleaguered food producers, who are often squeezed between the impossible demands of the supermarket buyers and cut-price competition from overseas.
- Seasonal food makes you think about preserving. Jams, chutneys, jellies, pickles preserves ... all of these were invented as ways of preserving a seasonal surplus.
- Finally, seasonal food brings variety into our lives. Who wants to eat the same things all year round? There is always a seasonal treat to look forward to in Britain, and once you know what they are, it will change the way you eat and shop – even the way you order in restaurants – and turn each month, even each week, into a gastronomic adventure.

Organic foods

Consumers are gradually becoming more interested in organic foods and more environmentally friendly. Although there are no nutritional reasons for using organic produce, organic foods are said to contain fewer contaminants. They have a lower content of pesticides, or none at all; however, global sources of contamination cannot be avoided by the organic farmer. Food inspection, particularly by the Department of Environment, Food and Rural Affairs (Defra), keeps a good check on the content of undesirable substances in conventional produce. The prospect of contamination, therefore, is not a good reason for using organically grown produce either. The main argument for using organic produce is that it supports environmentally sustainable development in farming. Caterers may thus consider using organic produce as a social priority. Some caterers have started using organic produce as they become more environmentally conscious.

Today's consumers, whether guests in a restaurant, staff in firms' restaurants or hospital patients, have a natural expectation that insensitive use of the environment or resources should be avoided. Staff in catering have a natural expectation with regard to a sensible working environment.

One of the problems for the organic market is the lack of a good distribution network. It is difficult to establish a distribution network as long as there are only a few catering kitchens that use organic vegetables. The solution to the problem is to distribute organic produce through traditional distribution channels, and this is being developed. The quality of organic produce is variable. The majority of caterers and food manufacturers at present take organic produce seriously. The trend for the future is likely to be towards environmentally friendly food products rather than organic food products.

'Organic' is a term defined by European law, and all organic food production and processing is governed by strict legislative standards. Catering operations preparing and selling organic menus must be certified with a UK certification body – for example, Soil Association Certification Ltd.

Environmentally friendly food products

These are foods that are produced under conditions that save on electricity and water as well as other environmental factors, or they can be products made using environmentally friendly technology. Products may be packed in environmentally friendly packaging and produce grown with a limited use of fertilisers and crop sprays, but not necessarily totally organic. In this way a trend may be expected in which industry slowly takes on the idea of organic production and increasingly begins to market environmentally friendly food products to the catering industry.

MEAT

Cattle, sheep and pigs are reared for fresh meat. Tenderness and flavour are increased in beef and lamb if hung after slaughter. Pork and veal are hung for three to seven days, according to the temperature. Meat is generally hung at a temperature of 1°C (34°F).

Conversion of muscle to meat

Glycogen is a carbohydrate energy reserve stored in the muscle of animals. It is used to provide energy in the living animal, and is broken down to water and carbon dioxide. In muscle after slaughter there is no supply of oxygen and therefore the glycogen is converted to lactic acid. The build-up of lactic acid reduces the pH from about 7.0 to 5.6 (i.e. it makes the meat more acidic). This natural acidity is important for the keeping quality of meat.

Under some conditions this process cannot follow the normal pattern. In particular, if there is insufficient glycogen present in the muscle at slaughter the pH does not fall to the same extent and dark, firm, dry meat results. This is caused by insufficient feed prior to slaughter or a prolonged period of stress. Another condition, known as PSE (pale soft exudative), results if animals (especially pigs) are subjected to a period of acute stress prior to slaughter. This results in the pH fall occurring too rapidly, which gives rise to denaturation of the muscle protein.

Carcass hanging

The method of carcass hanging used can give rise to marked differences in eating quality. Hanging the carcase by the hip bone (aitch bone) instead of the traditional Achilles tendon, puts tension on the important muscles of the hindquarter. This 'stretching' effect in some muscles makes them more tender. Traditionally carcasses were 'hung' (held as carcasses) for a period of several days. In fact, boning can take place as soon as 12 hours (pigs), 24 hours (sheep) or 48 hours (cattle) after slaughter, provided a period of ageing is allowed following butchery.

Ageing of meat

Like cheese and wine, meat benefits from a period of ageing, or maturation, before it is consumed. This gives an increase in both the tenderness and flavour. The increase in tenderness occurs as enzymes, naturally present within the meat, break down key proteins. The so-called calpain enzymes are important for the development of tenderness. Flavour may be increased by the release of small protein fragments with strong flavour. Minimum ageing periods of seven days from slaughter to consumption are often recommended for beef, lamb and pork. The flavour of meat is also dependent on the animal's diet, and the fat content dependent on species.

Storage

Meat should be stored at its appropriate temperature, usually between 1 and 5°C (34–41°F). Raw meat should be stored separately from cooked meat or meat products. Chilled meat must be used by the 'use by' date.

Temperatures of chillers and freezers should be measured regularly. Chilled cooked meat must generally be stored below 8°C (46.4°F) but if it has been prepared for consumption without further cooking or reheating the temperature must be at or below 5°C (41°F). Cut or sliced, smoked or cured meats must be stored at or below 5°C (41°F), and vacuum-packed meat below 3°C.

Cuts and joints

For economic reasons of saving on both labour and storage space, very many caterers purchase meat by joints or cuts rather than by the carcass.

The Meat Buyer's Guide is a manual that has been designed to assist caterers who wish to simplify and facilitate their meat purchasing, and provides information and cutting guides.

Food value

Meat, having a high protein content, is valuable for the growth and repair of the body and as a source of energy. It is an important source of several vitamins, minerals and other nutrients (e.g. vitamins B, A and D, zinc and iron).

Preservation

- **Salting:** meat can be pickled in brine; this method of preservation may be applied to silverside, brisket and ox tongues. Salting is also used in the production of bacon, before the sides of pork are smoked. This also applies to hams.
- **Chilling:** this means that meat is kept at a temperature just above freezing point in a controlled atmosphere.
- **Freezing:** small carcasses, such as lamb and mutton, can be frozen; their quality is not affected by freezing. They can be kept frozen until required and then thawed out before use. Some beef is frozen, but it is inferior in quality to chilled beef.
- **Canning:** large quantities of meat are canned; corned beef is of importance since it has a very high protein content. Pork is used for tinned luncheon meat and in canned hams.

(i) **Further information**
For further information about meat contact the Institute of Meat, Third Floor, 50–60 St John St, London EC1M 4DT; the Meat and Livestock Commission, PO Box 44, Winterhill House, Snowdon Drive, Milton Keynes MK6 1AX or visit www.meatandhealth.co.uk. See also *Practical Cookery* and *Advanced Practical Cookery*, and *The Meat Buyer's Guide* (for full details see the 'References' section on page 179).

Beef

The hanging or maturing of beef at a chill temperature of 1°C (34°F) for up to 14 days has the effect of increasing its tenderness and flavour and is essential as animals are generally slaughtered around the age of 18 to 24 months. Also, a short time after death, an animal's muscles stiffen – a condition known as rigor mortis. After a time chemical actions caused by enzymes and increasing acidity relax the muscles and the meat becomes soft and pliable. As meat continues to hang in storage rigor mortis dissipates, and tenderness and flavour increase. (Pork, lamb and veal are obtained from young animals, so toughness is not a significant factor.)

Large quantities of beef are prepared as chilled boneless prime cuts, vacuum packed in film. This process has the following advantages: it extends the storage life of the cuts; the cuts are boned and fully trimmed, thus reducing labour costs and storage space.

It is essential to store and handle vacuum-packed meat correctly. The storage temperature should be 0°C (32°F) with the cartons the correct way up so that the drips cannot stain the fatty surface. A good circulation of air should be allowed between cartons.

When required for use, the vacuum film should be punctured in order to drain away any blood before the film is removed. On opening the film a slight odour is usually discernible, but this should quickly disappear on exposure to the air. The vacuum-packed beef has a deep-red colour, but when the film is broken the colour should change to its normal characteristic red within 20–30 minutes. Once the film has been punctured the meat should be used as soon as possible.

Quality

Lean meat should be bright red, with small flecks of white fat (marbled). The fat should be firm, brittle in texture, creamy white in colour and odourless. Meat of traceable origin is best.

Figure 4.2 Side of beef

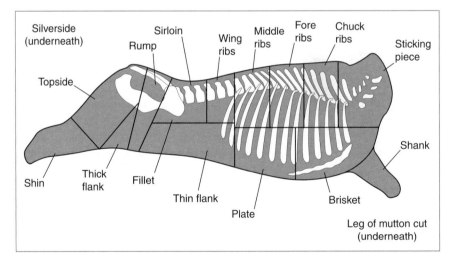

Figure 4.3 Beef, silverside (rolled)

Figure 4.4 Rolled topside of beef

Figure 4.5 Boned shin of beef

Figure 4.6 Fillet and loin of beef

Figure 4.7 Forerib of beef

Figure 4.8 Beef, chuck steaks

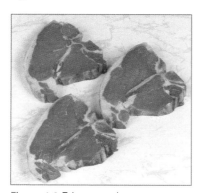

Figure 4.9 T-bone steaks

Figure 4.10 Sirloin steaks

Figure 4.11 Fillet steaks

Figure 4.12 Rib eye steaks

Veal

Originally, most top-quality veal came from Holland, but as the Dutch methods of production are now used extensively in Britain, supplies of home-produced veal are available all year round. Good-quality carcasses weighing around 100 kg can be produced from calves slaughtered at 12–24 weeks. This quality of veal is necessary for first-class cookery.

The flesh of veal should be pale pink and firm, not soft or flabby. Cut surfaces must not be dry, but moist. Bones in young animals should be pinkish white, porous and with a small amount of blood in their structure. The fat should be firm and pinkish white. The kidney ought to be firm and well covered with fat.

Welfare veal comes from calves that are loosely penned. The colour of the meat as a consequence is a deeper shade of pink.

Figure 4.13 Side of veal

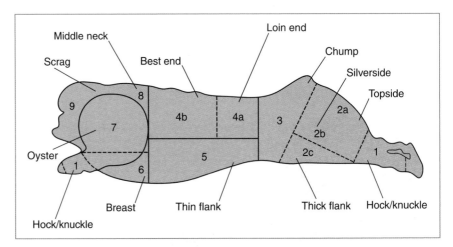

Figure 4.14 Veal kidneys

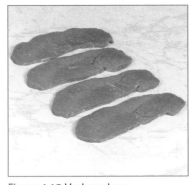

Figure 4.15 Veal escalopes

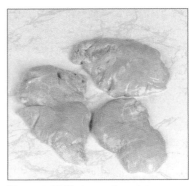

Figure 4.16 Veal sweetbreads

Pork

Lean flesh of pork is usually pale pink. The fat usually is white, firm, smooth and not excessive. Bones are usually small, fine and pinkish. The quality of the skin or rind depends on the breed. Suckling pigs weigh 5–9 kg dressed and are usually roasted whole. Boars are wild or uncastrated male pigs. The meat of wild boars is available from specialist farms (see below).

Figure 4.17 Side of pork

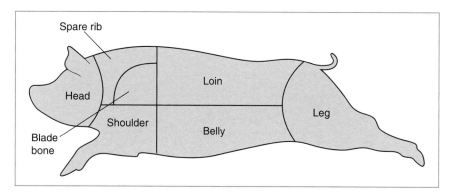

Figure 4.18 Leg of pork, boned and rolled

Figure 4.19 Boned leg of pork

Figure 4.20 Loin of pork

Figure 4.21 Pork chops

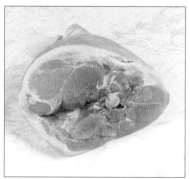

Figure 4.22 Gammon

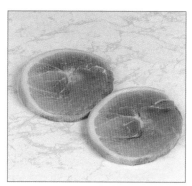

Figure 4.23 Gammon steaks

Figure 4.24 Suckling pig

Figure 4.25 Pig's trotters

Boars

Boars are uncastrated male pigs. The meat of boars is available from specialist farms. It is better to obtain good-quality animals from suppliers using as near as possible 100 per cent pure breeding stock. Animals that are free to roam and forage for food may have a better flavour than farm-reared ones that have been penned and fed. Animals are best between 12 and 18 months old, and weighing 70–75 kg on the hoof. Slaughtering is best done during late summer when the fat content is lower. Recommended hanging time is between seven and ten days at a temperature of between 1 and 4°C. Marinating before cooking greatly improves the taste and texture of boar meat.

Bacon

Bacon is the cured flesh of a pig (60–75 kg dead weight) specifically reared for bacon because its shape and size yield economic bacon joints.

The curing process consists of salting either by a dry method and smoking, or by soaking in brine followed by smoking. Unsmoked bacon is brine cured but not smoked; it has a milder flavour but does not keep as long as smoked bacon.

There should be no sign of stickiness. There must be no unpleasant smell. The rind should be thin and smooth. The fat ought to be white, smooth and not excessive in proportion to the lean. The lean meat of the bacon should be deep pink in colour and firm, depending on the cure.

Bacon should be kept in a well-ventilated, preferably cold, room. Joints of bacon should be wrapped in muslin. Sides of bacon are also hung on hooks. Cut bacon is kept on trays in the refrigerator or cold room. Bacon can also be vacuum packed ('vac packed').

Pancetta are rolled slices of cured pork belly. Pancetta is salt cured, flavoured with herbs and spices and air dried. Lardo is an extremely fatty Italian bacon.

Figure 4.26 Side of bacon

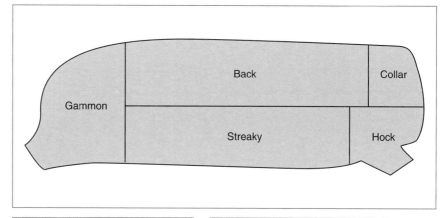

Figure 4.26 Side of bacon

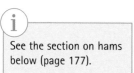
See the section on hams below (page 177).

Figure 4.27 Back bacon

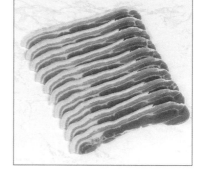

Figure 4.28 Streaky bacon

Lamb and mutton

In Britain, more lamb and mutton is eaten than in any other European country. Lamb is generally meat from animals under one year old; mutton is the term for older animals.

The carcass should be compact and evenly fleshed. The lean flesh of lamb ought to be firm and of a pleasing dull-red colour, and of a fine texture or grain. The fat should be evenly distributed, hard, brittle, flaky and clear white in colour. The bones should be porous in young animals.

The factors influencing lamb composition, quality and value are essentially similar to those described above for beef.

Figure 4.29 Carcass of lamb

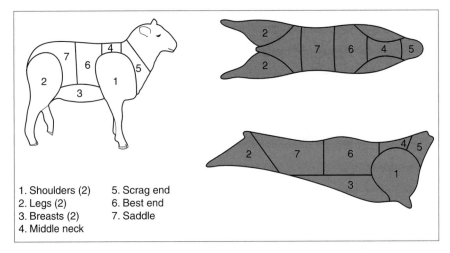

1. Shoulders (2)
2. Legs (2)
3. Breasts (2)
4. Middle neck
5. Scrag end
6. Best end
7. Saddle

Figure 4.30 Saddle of lamb

Figure 4.31 Pair of best ends of lamb

Figure 4.32 Boned and rolled lamb shoulder

Figure 4.33 Shoulder of lamb

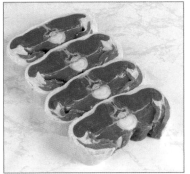

Figure 4.34 Double loin chops of lamb

Figure 4.35 Lamb loin chops

Figure 4.36 Lamb cutlets

Figure 4.37 Best ends of lamb (racks, French trimmed)

Figure 4.38 Valentines of lamb

Figure 4.39 Leg chops

Figure 4.40 Lamb rosettes

Figure 4.41 Lamb hearts

Figure 4.42 Lamb kidneys

Offal and other edible parts of the carcass

Offal is the name given to the parts taken from the inside of the carcass: edible offal includes liver, kidney, heart and sweetbread. Tripe, brains, oxtail, tongue and head are sometimes included under this term. Fresh offal (unfrozen) should be purchased as required and can be refrigerated under hygienic conditions at a temperature of -1°C (30°F), at relative humidity of 90 per cent for up to seven days. Frozen offal should be kept frozen until required.

Tripe

Tripe is the stomach lining or white muscle of beef cattle. Honeycomb tripe is from the second compartment of the stomach and considered the best. Smooth tripe is from the first compartment of the stomach and is not considered to be as good as honeycomb tripe. Sheep tripe, darker in colour, is obtainable in some areas. Tripe may be boiled or braised.

Oxtail

Oxtails should be 1.5–1.75 kg, lean and with no signs of stickiness. They are usually braised or used for soup.

Suet

Beef suet should be creamy white, brittle and dry. It is used for suet paste. Other fat should be fresh and not sticky. Suet and fat may be rendered down for dripping.

Bones

Bones must be fresh, not sticky; they are used for stock, which is the base for soups and sauces.

Liver

Calves' liver is the most expensive and is considered the best in terms of tenderness and delicacy of flavour and colour. Lambs' liver is mild in flavour, tender and light in colour. Ox or beef liver is the cheapest and, if taken from an older animal, can be coarse in texture and strong in flavour. Pigs' liver is full flavoured and used in many pâté recipes.

Figure 4.43 Calves' liver

Quality

Liver should appear fresh and have an attractive colour. It must not be dry or contain tubes. It should be smooth in texture.

Food value

Liver is valuable as a protective food; it consists chiefly of protein and contains useful amounts of vitamin A and iron.

> **i**
>
> **Further information**
> Further information on meats and offal can be found in *Practical Cookery* and *Advanced Practical Cookery*, and *The Meat Buyer's Guide* (for full details see the 'References' section on page 179).

Kidney

Lambs' kidney is light in colour, delicate in flavour, and ideal for grilling and frying. Calves' kidney is light in colour, delicate in flavour and can be used in a wide variety of dishes. Ox kidney is dark in colour, strong in flavour and is generally used mixed with beef, for steak and kidney pie or pudding. Pigs' kidney is smooth, long and flat by comparison with sheep's kidney; it has a strong flavour.

Quality

Ox kidney should be fresh and deep red in colour. Lambs' kidney should be covered in fat, which is removed just before use; the fat should be crisp and the kidney moist.

Food value

Kidneys are a rich source of vitamin A and iron.

Heart

Ox or beef hearts are the largest used for cooking. They are dark coloured, solid, and tend to be dry and tough. Calves' heart, coming from a younger animal, is lighter in colour and more tender. Lambs' heart is smaller and lighter, and normally served whole. Larger hearts are normally sliced before serving.

Quality

Hearts should not be too fatty and should not contain too many tubes. When cut they should be moist.

Food value

Hearts have a high protein content and are valuable for growth and repair of the body.

Tongue

Tongues must be fresh. They should not have an excessive amount of waste at the root end. Ox tongues may be used fresh or salted. Sheep's tongues are used unsalted.

Sweetbreads

Sweetbreads is the name given to two glands, one is the pancreas, and is undoubtedly the best as it is round, flat and plump; the other is the elongated sausage-shaped thymus gland.

Quality

Sweetbreads should be fleshy, large and creamy white in colour.

Food value

Sweetbreads are valuable foods, particularly for hospital diets. They are very easily digested and useful for building body tissues.

Meat substitutes

Textured vegetable protein (TVP)

This is a meat substitute manufactured from protein derived from wheat, oats, cottonseed, soya beans and other sources. The main source of TVP is the soya bean, due to its high protein content.

TVP is used chiefly as a meat extender, varying from 10–60 per cent replacement of fresh meat. Some caterers on very tight budgets make use of it, but its main use is in food manufacturing.

By partially replacing the meat in certain dishes – such as casseroles, stews, pies, pasties, sausage rolls, hamburgers, meat loaf and pâté – it is possible to reduce costs, provide nutrition and serve food that is acceptable in appearance.

Myco-protein

This meat substitute is produced from a plant that is a distant relative of the mushroom. Myco-protein contains protein and fibre, and is the result of a fermentation process similar to that used in the production of yoghurt. It may be used as an alternative to chicken or beef, or in vegetarian dishes.

Quorn is the brand name for myco-protein (see above).

i

Further information
For information on quality, types of poultry and their use see *Practical Cookery* and *Advanced Practical Cookery*. For further information on poultry in general, contact the British Poultry Council: www.poultry.uk.com.

POULTRY

Poultry is the name given to domestic birds specially bred to be eaten and for their eggs. Poultry is Britain's most popular meat: almost twice as much poultry is consumed as beef.

Season

Owing to present-day methods of poultry breeding and growing, poultry is available all the year round either chilled or frozen.

Food value

The flesh of poultry is more easily digested than that of butchers' meat. It contains protein and is therefore useful for building and repairing body tissues, and providing heat and energy. Its fat content is low and it contains a high percentage of unsaturated acids.

Storage

Fresh poultry must be hung by the legs under chilled conditions, otherwise it will not be tender; the innards are removed as soon as possible after slaughter.

Frozen birds must be kept in a deep-freeze cabinet below -5°C until required. To reduce the risk of food poisoning, it is essential that frozen birds be completely thawed, preferably in a refrigerator, before they are cooked. Chilled birds should be kept at between 3 and 5°C.

Chicken

Chicken is probably the most popular type of poultry dish. It comes in various types, with different uses:

- spring chickens (poussin) – four to six weeks old
- broiler chickens – three to four months old
- medium and large roasting chickens
- capons (castrated cock birds)
- old hens – used in soups and sauces.

Quality
Fresh chicken should have a plump breast, a pliable breast bone and firm flesh. The skin should be white with a faint bluish tint and unbroken. The legs should be smooth with small scales and spurs.

Figure 4.44 Chicken: whole and prepared for cooking

Figure 4.45 Corn-fed chicken

Figure 4.46 Poussin

Duck/duckling and goose/gosling

Goose is traditionally in season from Michaelmas (29 September) until Christmas.

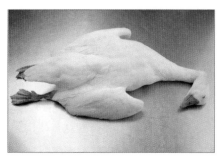

Figure 4.47 Goose

Figure 4.48 Goose prepared for cooking

Quality

The feet and bills should be bright yellow. The upper bill should break easily. The webbed feet must be easy to tear. Ducks and geese may be roasted or braised.

Turkey

Quality

The breast should be large, the skin undamaged and with no signs of stickiness. The legs of young birds are black and smooth, the feet supple with a short spur. As the bird ages the legs turn reddish grey and become scaly. The feet become hard.

Turkeys are usually roasted and served hot or cold. Turkey meat is also used in a variety of other dishes.

Figure 4.49 Turkey

Figure 4.50 Turkey prepared for cooking

Guinea fowl

When plucked these grey and white feathered birds resemble a chicken with darker flesh. The young birds are known as squabs. The quality points relating to chicken (see page 91) also apply to guinea fowl.

Figure 4.51 Guinea fowl: whole and prepared for cooking

Pigeon

Pigeon should be plump, the flesh mauve-red in colour and the claws pinkish. Tame pigeons are smaller than wood pigeons. Squabs are young, specially reared pigeons.

Figure 4.52 Wood pigeon: whole and prepared for cooking

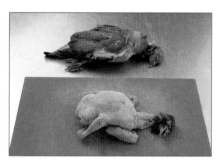

Figure 4.53 Squab: whole and prepared for cooking

Ostrich

Ostrich is usually sold as a fillet (taken from the thigh) or leg steak. The neck or offal is also available and is cheaper. It is often compared to beef, but it has a slightly coarser texture with less fat and lower cholesterol.

GAME

Game is the name given to certain wild birds and animals that are eaten; there are two kinds of game:

1 feathered
2 furred.

Food value

As it is less fatty than poultry or meat, game is more easily digested, with the exception of water fowl, which has oily flesh. Game is useful for building and repairing body tissues, and for energy.

Storage

Hanging is essential for all game. It drains the flesh of blood and begins the process of disintegration that is vital to make the flesh soft and edible, and also to develop flavour. The hanging time is determined by the type, condition and age of the game, and the storage temperature. Old birds need to hang for a longer time than young birds. Game birds are not plucked or drawn before hanging. Venison and hare are hung with the skin on. Game must be hung in a well-ventilated, dry, cold storeroom; this need not be refrigerated. Game birds should be hung by the neck with the feet down.

Availability

Game is available fresh in season between the dates shown in Table 4.1, and frozen for the remainder of the year:

Table 4.1 Game in season*

Grouse	12 August–10 December
Snipe	12 August–31 January
Partridge	1 September–1 February
Wild duck	1 September–31 January
Pheasant	1 October–1 February
Woodcock	31 October–1 February

* Venison, hares, rabbits and pigeons are available throughout the year

Venison

Venison is the flesh from any member of the deer family, which includes elk, moose, reindeer, caribou and antelope. Red deer meat is a dark, blood-red colour; the flesh of the roe deer is paler and the fallow deer is considered to have the best flavour.

Meat from animals over 18 months in age tends to be tough and dry, and is usually marinated to counteract this. Young animals up to 18 months produce delicate, tender meat that does not require marinating. Nowadays, venison is extensively farmed in the UK.

Venison contains 207 calories per 100 g, and young venison has only about 6 per cent fat (compared to beef, lamb and pork at around 20 per cent fat). It has the highest protein content of the major meats.

Venison is very suitable for a low-cholesterol diet because the fat is mainly polyunsaturated. The carcass has little intramuscular fat; the lean meat contains only low levels of marbling fat.

Figure 4.54 Venison

Both farmed and wild venison are available. Joints should be well fleshed and a dark brownish-red colour. Venison is usually roasted or braised in joints, served hot or cold with a peppery/sweet type sauce. Small cuts may be fried and served in a variety of ways. Venison is available as: shoulder, boned and rolled; haunch, boned and rolled; prepared saddles and steaks; also as pâté, in sausages and burgers; and smoked.

Other meats

- **Alligator** is a white meat, with a veal-like texture and a shellfish-like flavour.
- **Bison** should be treated like a gamey, well-hung version of beef. However, because it is so lean it needs to be cooked quickly and served rare or medium rare.
- **Camel** is available as fillet, steak or diced. It comes in frozen from Africa.
- **Crocodile** has a firm-textured, light-coloured meat with a delicate fishy taste, similar to monkfish, that absorbs other flavours well. It is surprisingly fatty.
- **European wild boar** has been reintroduced to British farms. It produces rich, dark-red meat with a dense texture.
- **Kangaroo** is similar to venison in flavour. It has a fine-grained meat that, once cooked, is similar in texture to liver; it is best served rare or medium rare.
- **Kid** usually comes from goats bred for their milk. However, the South African Boer goat, which is bred for its meat, has recently been introduced into this country. It has a rich, yet delicate flavour with very little fat.
- **Kudu** is a breed of wild African antelope that is culled in a controlled way. The animals are very large and the meat has a stronger flavour than wild venison. It needs to be tenderised by marinating and cooking.

Hare and rabbit

The ears of hares and rabbits should tear easily. In old hares the lip is more pronounced than in young animals. The rabbit is distinguished from the hare by its shorter ears, feet and body.

Hare may be cooked as a red wine stew thickened with its own blood, called jugged hare, and the saddle can be roasted.

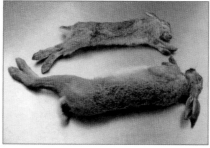

Figure 4.55 Rabbit and hare: furred

Figure 4.56 Rabbit and hare: skinned

Game birds

The beak should break easily. The breast plumage should be soft. The breast should be plump. Quill feathers should be pointed, not rounded. The legs should be smooth.

- **Pheasant:** This is one of the most common game birds. Average weight is 1.5–2 kg. Young birds have a pliable breast bone and soft pliable feet. They should be hung for five to eight days, and can be used for roasting, braising or pot roasting.

Figure 4.57 Male and female pheasants and one prepared for cooking

Figure 4.58 Red-legged and English partridge: whole and prepared for cooking

- **Partridge:** The most common varieties are the grey-legged and the red-legged partridge. Average weight is 200–400 g. Hang for three to five days. Use for roasting or braising.
- **Grouse:** A particularly famous and popular game bird is the red grouse, which is shot in Scotland and Yorkshire. Average weight is 300 g. Young birds have pointed wings and rounded soft spurs. Hang for five to seven days. Use for roasting.
- **Snipe:** Weight is about 100 g. Hang for three to four days. The heads and neck are skinned, the eyes removed; birds are then trussed with their own beaks. When drawing the birds, only the gizzard, gallbladder and intestines are removed. The birds are then roasted with the liver and heart left inside.
- **Woodcock:** These are small birds with long, thin beaks. Average weight is 200–300 g. Prepare as for snipe. Usually roasted.
- **Quail:** These are small birds weighing 50–75 g, produced on farms and usually packed in boxes of 12. Quails are not hung. They are usually served roasted, grilled, spatchcock or braised.
- **Wild duck:** Wild duck include mallard and widgeon. Average weight is 1–1.5 kg. Hang for one or two days. Usually roasted or braised.
- **Teal:** The smallest duck, weighing 400–600 g. Hang for one to two days. Usually roasted or braised. Young birds have small pinkish legs and soft down under the wings. Teal and wild duck must be eaten in season otherwise the flesh is coarse and has a fishy flavour. Usually roasted or braised.

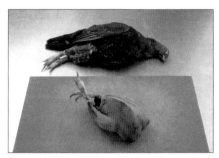

Figure 4.59 Grouse: whole and prepared for cooking

Figure 4.60 Snipe: whole

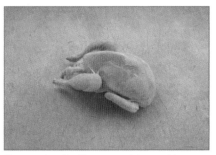

Figure 4.61 Quail: prepared for cooking

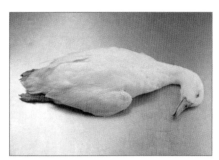

Figure 4.62 Duck: whole

Figure 4.63 Gressingham duck: prepared for cooking

Figure 4.64 Wild duck: prepared for cooking

FISH

Fish have always made up a large proportion of the food we consume because of their abundance and relative ease of harvesting. However, because the fish supply is not unlimited, due to overfishing, fish farms (e.g. for trout, salmon, cod, halibut and turbot) have been established to supplement the natural sources. Overfishing is not the only problem: due to contamination by man, the seas and rivers are increasingly polluted, thus affecting both the supply and suitability of fish, particularly shellfish, for human consumption.

Fish are valuable, not only because they are a good source of protein,

Table 4.2 Kinds of fish: seasons and purchasing units

FISH	SEASON	PURCHASING UNIT
Oily		
Anchovy	Imported occasionally June to December (home waters)	Number and weight
Common eel	All year, best in autumn	Number and weight
Conger eel	March to October	Weight
Herring	All year except spring	Number and weight
Kingfish	Check with supplier	Weigh with fillets
Mackerel	September to July	Number and weight or fillets
Pilchard (mature sardine)	All year	Number and weight
Salmon (farmed)	All year	Number and weight
Salmon (wild)	February to August	Number and weight
Salmon trout	February to August	Number and weight
Salmon (Pacific)	July to November	Number and weight
Sprat	September to March	Number and weight
Sardines	All year	Number and weight
Trout	February to September	Number and weight
Trout (farmed)	All year	Number and weight
Tuna	All year	Steaks or pieces
Whitebait	When available	Weight
White, flat		
Brill	June to February	Number and weight
Dab	March to December	Number and weight
Flounder	May to February, best in winter	Number and weight
Halibut	June to March	Number and weight or steaks
Megrim	April to February	Number and weight
Plaice	May to February	Number and weight or fillets
Skate	May to February	Wings, number and weight
Sole, Dover	May to March	Number and weight or fillets
Sole, lemon	All year, best in spring	Number and weight or fillets

Table **4.2** continued

FISH	SEASON	PURCHASING UNIT
Turbot	All year	Number and weight or fillets
Turbot (farmed)	When available	Number and weight
Witch	All year, best in spring	Number and weight or fillets
Round		
Barracuda	Check with supplier	Number and weight of fillets
Bass (wild/farmed)	June to September	Number and weight or fillets
Bream, fresh water	August to April	Number and weight or fillets
Bream, sea	June to December	Number and weight or fillets
Carp (mostly farmed)	Fluctuates throughout year	Number and weight or fillets
Cod	All year, not at best in spring	Number and weight or fillets
Dogfish (huss, flake, rigg)	All year, best in autumn	Steaks or fillets
Grey mullet	May to February, best autumn and winter	Number and weight
Grouper	Check with supplier	Number and weight or fillets
Haddock	All year, best autumn and winter	Number and weight or fillets
Hake	June to February	Number and weight or fillets
John Dory	September to May	Number and weight or fillets
Ling	September to July	Number and weight or fillets
Monkfish (anglerfish)	All year, best in winter	Number and weight or tails
Pike	All year	Number and weight
Perch	May to February	Number and weight
Pollack (yellow, green)	May to December	Number and weight
Redfish	All year	Number and weight or fillets
Red gurnard	All year, best from July to April	Number or weight
Red mullet	Imported best in summer, UK autumn	Number and weight and fillets
Sea bream	June to February	Number and weight
Smelt	Occasionally	Number and weight

Table 4.2 continued

FISH	SEASON	PURCHASING UNIT
Shark (porbeagle)	Occasionally	Steaks or pieces
Snapper, red snapper	Check with supplier	
Whiting	All year, best in winter	Number and weight or fillets

but because they are suitable for all types of menus, and can be cooked and presented in a wide variety of ways. The range of different types of fish of varying texture, taste and appearance is indispensable to the creative chef.

Types or varieties

Oily fish are round in shape (e.g. herring, mackerel, salmon). White fish can be round (cod, whiting, hake) or flat (plaice, sole, turbot). Shellfish and cephalopods are discussed on pages 109–113.

Purchasing unit

Fresh fish is bought by the kilogram, by the number of fillets or by whole fish of the weight required. For example, 30 kg of salmon could be ordered as 2 × 15 kg, 3 × 10 kg or 6 × 5 kg. Frozen fish can be purchased in 15 kg blocks. Fish may be bought on the bone or filleted in steaks or supremes. (The approximate loss from boning and waste is 50 per cent for flat fish, 60 per cent for round fish.) Fillets of plaice and sole can be purchased according to weight. They are graded from 45 g to 180 g per fillet, and go up in weight by 15 g.

Storage

Fresh fish are stored in a fish box containing ice, in a separate refrigerator or part of a refrigerator used only for fish at a temperature of 1–2°C (34–36°F). The temperature must be maintained just above freezing point.

Frozen fish must be stored in a deep-freeze cabinet or compartment at −18°C (0°F).

Smoked fish should be kept in a refrigerator.

Food value

Fish is as useful a source of animal protein as meat. The oily fish, such as sardines, mackerel, herrings and salmon, contain vitamins A and D in their flesh; in white fish, such as halibut and cod, these vitamins are present in the liver. Since all fish contains protein it is a good body-building food, and oily fish is useful for energy and as a protective food because of the vitamins it contains.

The bones of sardines, whitebait and tinned salmon, which can be eaten, provide calcium and phosphorus.

Owing to its fat content, oily fish is not so digestible as white fish and is not suitable for use in cookery for invalids.

Oily fish

- **Anchovies:** Anchovies are small, round fish used mainly tinned in this country; they are supplied in 60 g and 390 g tins. They are filleted and packed in oil. They are used for making anchovy butter and anchovy sauce, for garnishing dishes and for savouries, snacks and salads.
- **Common eel:** Eels live in fresh water and are also farmed, and can grow up to 1 m in length. They are found in many British rivers and considerable quantities are imported from Holland. Eels must be kept alive until the last minute before cooking and are generally used in fish stews.
- **Conger eel:** The conger eel is a dark-grey sea fish with white flesh, which grows up to 3 m in length. It may be used in the same way as eels, or it may be smoked.
- **Herring:** Fresh herrings are used for breakfast and lunch menus; they may be grilled, fried or soused. Kippers (which are split, salted, dried and smoked herrings) are served for breakfast and also as a savoury. Average weight is 250 g.

  King fish come from the Spanish mackerel family; their flesh is orangey-pink coloured.

Figure 4.65 Herring

Figure 4.66 Kipper

- **Mackerel:** Mackerel are grilled, shallow-fried, smoked or soused, and may be used on breakfast and lunch menus. They must be used fresh because the flesh deteriorates very quickly. Average weight is 360 g.

Figure 4.67 Mackerel

- **Pilchards:** These are mature sardines and can grow up to 24 cm. They have a good, distinctive flavour.
- **Salmon:** Salmon is perhaps the most famous river fish; it is caught in British rivers like the Dee, Tay, Severn, Avon, Wye and Spey. It is also extensively farmed in Scotland and Norway. A considerable number are imported from Scandinavia, Canada, Germany and Japan. Apart from using it fresh, salmon is tinned or smoked. When fresh, it is used in a wide variety of dishes.

Figure 4.68 Side of fresh salmon

Figure 4.69 Salmon

Figure 4.70 Side of smoked salmon

Figure 4.71 Sardine

- **Salmon trout (sea trout):** Salmon trout are a sea fish similar in appearance to salmon, but smaller, and are used in a similar way. Average weight is 1.5–2 kg.
- **Sardines:** Sardines are small fish of the pilchard family, which are usually tinned and used for hors d'oeuvre, sandwiches and as a savoury. Fresh sardines are also available and may be cooked by grilling or frying.
- **Sprats:** Sprats are small fish fried whole; they can also be smoked and served as an hors d'oeuvre.
- **Trout:** Trout live in rivers and lakes in the UK; they are cultivated on trout farms. Trout may be poached and served grilled or shallow-fried, and may also be smoked and served as an hors d'oeuvre. Average weight is 200 g.

Figure 4.72 Trout

Figure 4.73 Smoked trout

- **Tuna:** Tuna has dark reddish-brown flesh that, when cooked, turns a lighter colour. It has a thin texture and a mild flavour. If overcooked it dries out, so is best cooked medium rare. It is used fresh for a variety of dishes or tinned in oil and used mainly as an hors d'oeuvre and in salads.
- **Whitebait:** Whitebait are the fry, or young, of herring; they are 2–4 cm long and are usually deep-fried.

Figure 4.74 Whitebait

White flat fish

- **Brill:** Brill is a large flat fish, which is sometimes confused with turbot. Brill is oval in shape; the mottled brown skin is smooth with small scales. It can be distinguished from turbot by its lesser breadth in proportion to length; average weight is 3–4 kg. It is usually served in the same way as turbot.
- **Dab:** Dab is an oval-bodied fish with sandy brown upper skin and green freckles. Usual size is 20–30 cm. It has a pleasant flavour when fresh, and may be cooked by all methods.
- **Flounder:** This is oval, with dull brown upper skin (or sometimes dull green with orange freckles). Usual size is 30 cm. Flesh is rather watery and lacks flavour, needing good seasoning. It can be cooked by all methods.
- **Halibut:** Halibut is a long and narrow fish, brown, with some darker mottling on the upper side; it can be 3 m in length and weigh around 20–50 kg. Halibut is much valued for its flavour. It is poached, boiled, grilled or shallow-fried. It is also smoked.

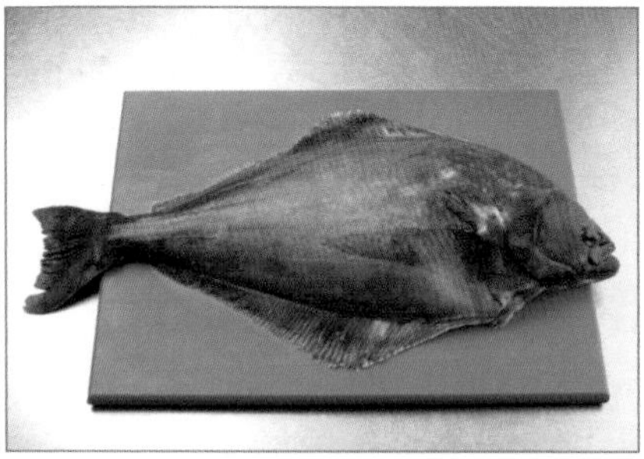

Figure 4.75 Halibut

Figure 4.76 Smoked halibut

- **Megrim:** Megrim has a very long slender body, sandy-brown coloured with dark blotches. Usual size is 20–30 cm. It has a softish flesh and an unexceptional flavour, so needs good flavouring. It is best breadcrumbed and shallow-fried.
- **Plaice:** Plaice are oval in shape, with dark-brown colouring and orange spots on the upper side. Used on all types of menus, they are usually deep-fried or grilled. Average weight is 360–450 g.

Figure 4.77 Plaice

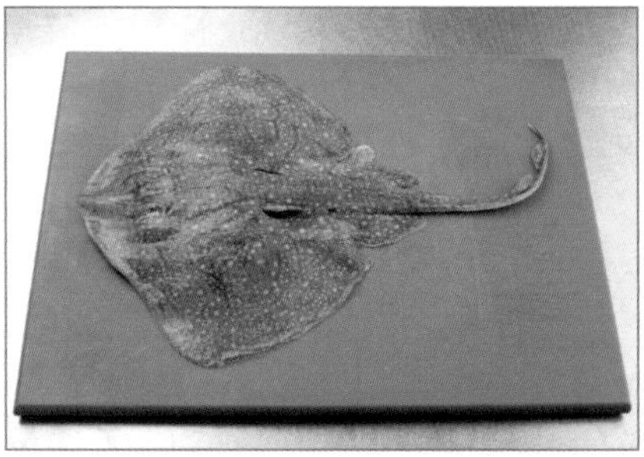

Figure 4.78 Skate

- **Skate:** Skate, a member of the ray family, is a very large fish and only the wings are used. It is usually served on the bone and either poached, shallow- or deep-fried, or cooked in a court bouillon and served with black butter.
- **Sole:** Sole is considered to be the best of the flat fish. The quality of Dover sole is well known to be excellent. Sole is cooked by poaching, grilling or frying (both shallow and deep). It is served whole or can be filleted and garnished in a great many ways.

Figure 4.79 Dover sole

Figure 4.80 Lemon sole

- **Lemon sole:** This is related to Dover sole, but is broader in shape, and its upper skin is warm, yellowy-brown and mottled with darker brown. It can weigh up to 600 g, and may be cooked by all methods.
- **Turbot:** Turbot has no scales and is roughly diamond in shape; it has knobs known as tubercles on its dark skin. In proportion to its length it is wider than brill; 3.5–4 kg is the average weight. Turbot may be cooked whole, filleted or cut into portions on the bone. It may be boiled, poached, grilled or shallow-fried.
- **Witch:** This is similar in appearance and weight to lemon sole, with sandy-brown upper skin. It is best fried, poached, grilled or steamed.

Figure 4.81 Brill

Figure 4.82 Turbot

Round fish

- **Barracuda:** A game fish with reddish flesh that, when cooked, turns pastel white. A mild-flavoured fish, it should be cooked as a supreme with the skin left on to prevent drying out.
- **Bass:** Bass have silvery grey backs and white bellies; small ones may have black spots. They have an excellent flavour, with white, lean, softish flesh (which must be very fresh). Bass can be steamed, poached, stuffed and baked, or grilled in steaks. Usual length is 30 cm but they can grow to 60 cm. Bass is usually farmed but sea bass is available (also called wild or natural) off the south coast of Britain. Farmed bass is also available from France and Greece.
- **Bream:** Sea bream is a short, oval-bodied, plump, reddish fish, with large scales and a dark patch behind the head. It is used on many less expensive menus; it is usually filleted and deep-fried, or stuffed and baked, but other methods of cooking are also employed. Average weight is 0.5–1 kg, size 28–30 cm. Bream are caught fresh or farmed.
- **Carp:** This is a freshwater fish, usually farmed. The flesh is white with a good flavour, and is best poached in fillets or stuffed and baked. The usual size is 1–2 kg.
- **Cod:** Cod varies in colour but is mostly greenish, brownish or olive grey. It can measure up to 1.5 m in length. Cod is cut into steaks or filleted and cut into portions; it can be deep- or shallow-fried or poached. Small cod are known as codling. Average weight of cod is 2.5–3.5 kg.

Figure 4.83 Cod

Figure 4.84 Gurnard

- **Coley (saith, coalfish, blackjack):** Coley is dark greenish-brown or blackish in colour, but the flesh turns white when cooked. It has a coarse texture and a dry undistinctive flavour, so is best used in mixed fish stews, soups or pies. Average size is 40–80 cm.
- **Dogfish (huss, flake, rigg):** These are slender, elongated small sharks. The non-bony white or pink flesh is versatile, and is usually served shallow- or deep-fried. It has a good flavour when very fresh. Length is usually 60 cm and weight 1.25 kg.
- **Grey mullet:** This has a scaly, streamlined body, which is silver-grey or blue-green. Deep-sea or offshore mullet has a fine flavour, with firm, moist flesh. It may be stuffed and baked or grilled in steaks. Some people believe that flavour is improved if the fish is kept in a refrigerator for two to three days, without being cleaned. Length is usually about 30 cm, weight 500 g.
- **Grouper:** Types include brown, brown spotted, golden strawberry and red speckled. Grouper has a light pinkish flesh that cooks to a greyish-white, with a pleasant mild flavour.
- **Gudgeon:** Gudgeon are small fish found in continental lakes and rivers. They may be deep-fried whole. On menus in this country the French term 'en goujon' refers to other fish such as sole or turbot, cut into pieces the size of gudgeon.
- **Gurnard:** A large family of tasty fish with many culinary uses.
- **Haddock:** Haddock is distinguished from cod by the 'thumb mark' on its side and by its lighter colour. Every method of cooking is suitable

Figure 4.85 Smoked haddock

Figure 4.86 Arbroath smokie (haddock smoked over hardwood)

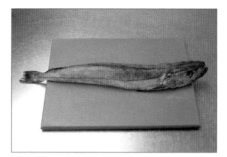

Figure 4.87 Hake

Figure 4.88 John Dory

for haddock, and it appears on all kinds of menus. Apart from fresh haddock, smoked haddock may be served for breakfast, lunch and as a savoury. Average weight is 0.5–2 kg.

- **Hake:** Owing to overfishing, hake is not plentiful. It is usually poached and is easy to digest. The flesh is very white and has a delicate flavour.
- **John Dory:** John Dory has a thin distinctive body, flattened from side to side, which is sandy-beige in colour and tinged with yellow, with a blue/silver-grey belly. There is a blotch on each side, referred to as the 'thumbprint of St Peter'. It has very tough sharp spikes. The flavour is considered superb, and the fish may be cooked by all methods, but is best poached, baked or steamed. The large bony head accounts for two-thirds of the weight. Usual size is 36 cm.
- **Ling:** This is the largest member of the cod family; it is mottled brown or green with a bronze sheen, and the fins have white edges. Size can be up to 90 cm. Ling has a good flavour and texture, and is generally used in fillets or cutlets, as for cod.
- **Monkfish:** Monkfish has a huge flattened head, with a normal fish-shaped tail. It is brown with dark blotches. The tail can be up to 180 cm, weight 1–10 kg. It may be cooked by all methods, and is a firm, close-textured white fish with excellent flavour.
- **Pike:** Pike has a long body, usually 60 cm, which is greeny-brown, flecked with lighter green, with long toothy jaws. The traditional fish for quenelles, it may also be braised or steamed.
- **Perch:** Perch has a deep body, marked with about five shadowy vertical

Figure 4.89 Monkfish

Figure 4.90 Monkfish tail, prepared

Figure 4.91 Red mullet

Figure 4.92 Snapper

bars, and the fins are vivid orange or red. Usual size 15–30 cm. It is generally considered to have an excellent flavour, and may be shallow-fried, grilled, baked, braised or steamed.

- **Pollack:** This is a member of the cod family, and has a similar shape and variable colours. Its usual size is 45 cm. It is drier than cod, and can be poached, shallow-fried or used for soups and stews.
- **Redfish:** This is bright red or orange-red, with a rosy belly and dusky gills. Usual size is 45 cm. It may be poached, baked or used in soups.
- **Red gurnard (grey and yellow gurnard may also be available):** This has a large 'mail-checked', tapering body with very spiky fins. Usual size is 20–30 cm. It is good for stews, braising and baking.
- **Red mullet:** Red mullet is on occasion cooked with the liver left in, as it is thought that this helps impart a better flavour to the fish. Mullet may be filleted or cooked whole, and the average weight is 360 g.
- **Rockfish:** Rockfish is the fishmonger's term for catfish, coalfish, dogfish, conger eel and the like, after cleaning and skinning. It is usually deep-fried in batter.
- **Shark:** The porbeagle shark, mako or hammerhead, fished off the British coast, gives the best-quality food. It is bluish-grey above with a white belly and matt skin. Size is up to 3 m. It may be cooked by all methods, but grilling in steaks or as kebabs are particularly suitable.
- **Smelt:** Smelts are small fish found in river estuaries and imported from Holland; they are usually deep-fried or grilled. Before grilling they are split open. The weight of a smelt is 60–90 g.
- **Snapper:** There are several kinds of snapper, all of which are brightly coloured. Deep-red or medium-sized ones give the best flavour. Snapper may be steamed, fried, grilled, baked or smoked.
- **Swordfish:** Swordfish is popular grilled, barbecued, roasted or shallow-fried.
- **Whiting:** Whiting is very easy to digest and is therefore suitable for use in cookery for invalids. It may be poached, grilled or deep-fried and used in the making of fish stuffing. Average weight is 360 g.
- **Wrasse:** Fish of variable colours, but usually tinged with red and blue, covered in white and green spots. Wrasse has a variety of culinary uses and can be baked and steamed.

Further information
For further information on fish, visit: www.seafish.org or contact the Seafish Industry Authority, 18 Logie Mill, Logie Green Road, Edinburgh EH7 4HG.

Shellfish

Shellfish are of two types:

1 crustaceans (lobster, crabs)
2 molluscs (oysters, mussels).

Crabs are used in hors d'oeuvre, cocktails, salads, dressed crab, sandwiches and bouchées. Soft-shelled crabs are eaten in their entirety. They are considered to have an excellent flavour and may be deep- or shallow-fried or grilled.

Shellfish is a good body-building food. As the flesh is coarse and therefore indigestible a little vinegar may be used in cooking to soften the fibres.

Figure 4.93 Crab

Figure 4.94 Crayfish

- **Crawfish:** Crawfish are like large lobsters without claws, but with long antennae. They are brick-red in colour when cooked. Owing to their size and appearance they are used mostly on cold buffets but they can be served hot. The best size is 1.5–2 kg. Menu examples include langouste parisienne (dressed crawfish Paris-style).
- **Crayfish:** Crayfish are a type of small freshwater lobster used for salads, garnishing cold buffet dishes and for recipes using lobster. They are dark brown or grey, turning pink when cooked. Average size is 8 cm.
- **Lobster:** Lobsters are served cold in cocktails, hors d'oeuvre, salads, sandwiches and on buffets. They are used hot for soup, grilled and served in numerous dishes with various sauces.
- **Prawns:** Prawns are larger than shrimps; they may be used for garnishing and decorating fish dishes, for cocktails, canapés, salads, hors d'oeuvre and for hot dishes, such as curried prawns. Prawns are also popular served cold with a mayonnaise-type sauce.
- **Scampi, Dublin Bay prawns:** Scampi are found in the Mediterranean. The Dublin Bay prawn, which is from the same family, is caught around the Scottish coast. These shellfish resemble small lobsters, about 20 cm long, and only the tail flesh is used for a variety of fish dishes, garnishing and salads.

Figure 4.95 Lobster, raw

Figure 4.96 Lobster, cooked

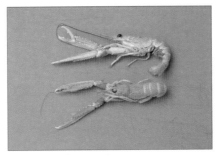

Figure 4.97 Langoustine

- **Shrimps:** Shrimps are used for garnishes, decorating fish dishes, in cocktails, sauces, salads, hors d'oeuvre, potted shrimps, omelettes and savouries.

Molluscs

- **Clams:** There are many varieties; the soft or long-neck clams, such as razor and Ipswich, and small hard-shell clams such as cherrystones, can be eaten raw. Large clams can be steamed, fried or grilled and used for soups (chowders) and sauces.
- **Cockles:** These are enclosed in pretty cream-coloured shells of 2–3 cm. Cockles are soaked in salt water to purge and then steamed or boiled. They may be used in soups, salads and fish dishes, or served as a dish by themselves.
- **Mussels:** Mussels are extensively cultivated on wooden hurdles in the sea, producing tender, delicately flavoured, plump fish. British mussels are considered good; French mussels are smaller; Dutch and Belgian mussels are plumper. All vary in quality from season to season. Mussels are kept in boxes, covered with a damp sack and stored in a cold room. They may be served hot or cold or as a garnish.
- **Oysters:** Oysters are produced from centres in England, Scotland, Ireland and Wales. Since the majority of oysters are eaten raw it is essential that they are thoroughly cleaned before hotels and restaurants receive them. Oysters must be alive; this is indicated by their firmly

Table 4.3 Shellfish: seasons and purchasing units

SHELLFISH	SEASON	PURCHASING UNIT
Clams	All year	Number and weight
Cockles	All year, best in summer	Weight
Common crab	All year, best April to December	Number and weight
Spider crab	All year	Number and weight
Swimming crab	All year	Number and weight
King crab, red crab	Check with supplier	Imported frozen, shelled, prepared
Soft-shelled crab	Check with supplier	Number and weight
Crawfish	April to October	Number and weight
Dublin Bay prawn	All year	Number and weight
Freshwater crayfish	Mainly imported, some farmed in the UK, wild have short season	Number, weight and by case
Lobster	April to November	Number and weight
Mussels	September to March	Weight
Oysters	May to August	By the dozen
Prawn and shrimp	All year	Number and weight
Scallop	Best December to March	Number and weight
Sea urchin	All year	Number and by case

closed shells. They are graded in sizes, and the price varies accordingly. Oysters should smell fresh. They should be purchased daily. Oysters are in season in the UK from September to April (i.e. whenever there is an 'r' in the month). During the summer months oysters are imported from France, Holland and Portugal.

Oysters are stored in barrels or boxes, covered with damp sacks and kept in a cold room to keep them moist and alive. The shells should be

Figure 4.98 Clams

Figure 4.99 Mussels

Figure 4.100 Scallops

tightly closed; if they are open, tap them sharply and, if they do not shut at once, discard them.

The popular way of eating oysters is in the raw state. They may also be served in soups, hot cocktail savouries, fish garnishes, as a fish dish, and in meat puddings and savouries.

- **Scallops:** Great scallops are up to 15 cm in size, bay scallops up to 8 cm, queen scallops are small-cockle sized, and are also known as 'queenies'. Scallops may be steamed, poached, fried or grilled.
- **Sea urchin or sea hedgehog:** The sea urchin has a spine-covered spherical shell. Only the orange and yellow roe is eaten, either raw out of the shell or removed with a teaspoon and used in soups, sauces, scrambled eggs, and so on; 10 to 20 urchins provide approximately 200 g roe.
- **Winkles:** Winkles are small sea snails with a delicious flavour. They may be boiled for three minutes and served with garlic butter or on a dish of assorted shellfish.

Cephalopods and fish offal

Cuttlefish
Cuttlefish are usually dark with attractive pale stripes, and their size can be up to 24 cm. They are available all year by number and weight. Cuttlefish are prepared like squid and may be stewed or gently grilled.

Octopus
Octopus is available all year by number and weight. Large species are tough and need to be tenderised; they are then prepared as for squid. Small octopi can be boiled, then cut up for grilling or frying. When stewing, a long cooking time is needed.

Squid
The common squid has mottled skin and white flesh, two tentacles, eight arms and flap-like fins. Usual size is 15–30 cm. Careful, correct preparation (see below) is important if the fish is to be tender. It may be stir-fried, fried, baked, grilled or braised.

Figure 4.101 Octopus

Figure 4.102 Squid

Preparation
- Pull head away from the body together with the innards.
- Cut off the tentacles just below the eye.
- Remove the small, round cartilage at the base of the tentacles.
- Discard the head, innards and pieces of cartilage.
- Scrape or peel off the reddish membrane that covers the pouch

Liver

An oil rich in vitamins A and D is obtained from the liver of cod and halibut. This is used medicinally.

Roe

Those used are the soft and hard roes of herring, cod, sturgeon and the coral from lobster. Soft herring roes are used to garnish fish dishes and as a savoury. Cod's roe is smoked and served as an hors d'oeuvre. The roe of the sturgeon is salted and served raw as caviar, and the coral of lobster is used for colouring lobster butter and lobster dishes, and also as a decoration for fish dishes.

Figure 4.103 Cod roe

VEGETABLES

Fresh vegetables and fruits are important foods, both from an economic and nutritional point of view. On average, each person consumes 125–150 kg per year of fruit and vegetables.

The purchasing of these commodities is difficult because the products are highly perishable, and supply and demand varies. The high perishability of fresh vegetables and fruits causes problems not encountered in other markets. Fresh vegetables and fruits are living organisms and will lose quality quickly if not properly stored and handled. Improved transportation and storage facilities can help prevent loss of quality. For more information on organic vegetables see page 76.

Automation in harvesting and packaging speeds the handling process and helps retain quality. Vacuum cooling – a process whereby fresh produce is moved into huge chambers, where, for about half an hour, a low vacuum is maintained, inducing rapid evaporation, which quickly reduces field heat – has been highly successful in improving quality.

Experience and sound judgement are essential for the efficient buying and storage of all commodities, but none probably more so than fresh vegetables and fruit.

The grading of fresh fruit and vegetables within the EU

There are four main quality classes for produce:

1 Extra Class – for produce of top quality
2 Class I – for produce of good quality
3 Class II – for produce of reasonably good quality
4 Class III – for produce of low marketable quality.

Food value

- **Root vegetables:** useful in the diet because they contain starch or sugar for energy, a small but valuable amount of protein, some mineral salts and vitamins; also useful sources of cellulose and water.
- **Green vegetables:** no food is stored in the leaves, it is only produced there; therefore little protein or carbohydrate is found in green vegetables; they are rich in mineral salts and vitamins, particularly vitamin C and carotene; the greener the leaf, the larger the quantity of vitamin present; chief mineral salts are calcium and iron.

Preservation

- **Canning:** certain vegetables are preserved in tins – artichokes, asparagus, carrots, celery, beans, peas (fine, garden, processed), tomatoes (whole, purée), mushrooms, truffles.
- **Dehydration:** onions, carrots, potatoes and cabbage are shredded and quickly dried until they contain only 5 per cent water.
- **Drying:** the seeds of legumes (peas and beans) have their moisture content reduced to 10 per cent.
- **Pickling:** onions and red cabbage are examples of vegetables preserved in spiced vinegar.
- **Salting:** French and runner beans may be sliced and preserved in dry salt.
- **Freezing:** many vegetables, such as peas, beans, sprouts, spinach and cauliflower, are deep frozen.

Types of vegetables

Roots
- **Beetroot** – two main types, round and long; used for soups, salads and as a vegetable.

- **Carrots** – grown in numerous varieties and sizes; used extensively for soups, sauces, stocks, stews, salads and as a vegetable.
- **Celeriac** – large, light-brown, celery-flavoured root, used in soups, salads and as a vegetable.
- **Horseradish** – long, light-brown, narrow root, grated and used for horseradish sauce.
- **Mooli** – long, white, thick member of radish family, used for soups, salads or as a vegetable.
- **Parsnips** – long, white root, tapering to a point; unique nut-like flavour; used in soups, added to casseroles and as a vegetable (roasted, purée, etc.).
- **Radishes** – small summer variety, round or oval, served with dips, in salads or as a vegetable in white or cheese sauce.
- **Salsify** – also called oyster plant because of similarity of taste; long, narrow root used in soups, salads and as a vegetable.
- **Scorzonera** – long, narrow root, slightly astringent in flavour; used in soups, salads and as a vegetable.
- **Swede** – large root with yellow flesh; generally used as a vegetable, mashed or parboiled and roasted; may be added to stews.
- **Turnip** – two main varieties, long and round; used in soups, stews and as a vegetable.

Figure 4.104 Root vegetables (left to right: parsnip, carrots, celeriac, horseradish, radishes, mooli)

Figure 4.105 Tubers (left to right: yam, sweet potato, potatoes, new potatoes, Jerusalem artichokes)

Tubers

- **Artichokes, Jerusalem** – potato-like tuber with a bitter-sweet flavour; used in soups, salads and as a vegetable.
- **Potatoes** – many varieties are grown but all potatoes should be sold by name (King Edward, Desirée, Maris Piper); this is important as the caterer needs to know which varieties are best suited for specific cooking purposes. The various varieties fall into four categories: floury, firm, waxy or salad potatoes. Jersey royals are specially grown, highly regarded new potatoes. Purple Congo are a blue potato. Truffle de Chine are a deep-purple potato grown in France. Turo/Eddo are two basic varieties found in tropical areas. A large barrel-shaped tuber and a smaller variety, which is often called eddo of dashheen. They are all a dark mahogany-brown with a shaggy skin, looking like a cross between a beetroot and a swede.

- **Sweet potatoes** – long tubers with purple or sand-coloured skins and orange flesh; flavour is sweet and aromatic; used as a vegetable (fried, puréed, creamed, candied) or made into a sweet pudding.
- **Yams** – similar to sweet potatoes, usually cylindrical, often knobbly in shape; can be used in the same way as sweet potatoes.

Bulbs

- **Fennel** – the bulb is the swollen leaf base and has a pronounced flavour. Used raw in salads and cooked.
- **Garlic** – an onion-like bulb with a papery skin inside of which are small individually wrapped cloves; used extensively in many forms of cookery; garlic has a pungent distinctive flavour and should be used sparingly.
- **Leeks** – summer leeks have long white stems, bright green leaves and a milder flavour than winter leeks; these have a stockier stem and a stronger flavour; used extensively in stocks, soups, sauces, stews, hors d'oeuvre and as a vegetable.
- **Onions** – there are numerous varieties with different-coloured skins and varying strengths; after salt, the onion is probably the most frequently used flavouring in cookery; can be used in almost every type of food except sweet dishes.
- **Shallots** – have a similar but more refined flavour than the onion and are therefore more often used in top-class cookery.
- **Spring onions** – are slim and tiny, like miniature leeks; used in soups, salads and Chinese and Japanese cookery. Ramp looks like a spring onion but is stronger.

Figure 4.106 Bulbs (left to right: leek, garlic, onion, shallots, spring onions)

Figure 4.107 Leafy vegetables (clockwise from top: cabbage, pak choi, spinach, watercress)

Leafy

- **Chicory** – a lettuce with coarse, crisp leaves and a sharp, bitter taste in the outside leaves; inner leaves are milder.
- **Chinese leaves** – long white, densely packed leaves with a mild flavour resembling celery; make a good substitute for lettuce and can be boiled, braised or stir-fried as a vegetable.
- **Corn salad** – sometimes called lamb's lettuce; small, tender, dark leaves with a tangy nutty taste.

- **Cress** – there are 15 varieties of cress with different flavours, suitable for a large range of foods.
- **Culaboo** are leaves of the tero plant, poisonous if eaten raw, but widely used in Asian and Caribbean cookery.
- **Lettuce** – many varieties including cabbage, cos, little gem, iceberg, oakleaf, Webb's; used chiefly for salads, or used as a wrapping for other foods, e.g. fish fillets.
- **Mustard and cress** – embryonic leaves of mustard and garden cress with a sharp warm flavour; used mainly in, or as a garnish to, sandwiches and salads.
- **Nettles** – once cooked the sting disappears; should be picked young, used in soups.
- **Radicchio** – round, deep-red variety of chicory with white ribs and a distinctive bitter taste.
- **Red salanova** – a neat, tasty lettuce; very suitable for garnish.
- **Rocket** – a type of cress with larger leaves and a peppery taste.
- **Sorrel** – bright-green sour leaves, which can be overpowering if used on their own; best when tender and young; used in salad and soups.
- **Spinach** – tender dark-green leaves with a mild musky flavour; used for soups, garnishing egg and fish dishes, as a vegetable and raw in salads.
- **Swiss chard** – has large, ribbed, slightly curly leaves with a flavour similar to but milder than spinach; used as for spinach.
- **Vine leaves** – all leaves from grape vines can be eaten when young.
- **Watercress** – long stems with round, dark, tender green leaves and a pungent peppery flavour; used for soups, salads, and for garnishing roasts and grills of meat and poultry.

Brassicas

- **Broccoflower** – a cross between broccoli and cauliflower. Chinese broccoli is a leafy vegetable with slender heads of flowers.
- **Broccoli** – various types including calabrese white, green, purple sprouting; delicate vegetable with a gentle flavour used in soups, salads, stir-fry dishes, and cooked and served in many ways as a vegetable.
- **Brussels sprouts** – small green buds growing on thick stems; can be used for soup but are mainly used as a vegetable, and can be cooked and served in a variety of ways.
- **Cabbage** – three main types including green, white and red; many varieties of green cabbage available at different seasons of the year; early green cabbage is deep green and loosely formed; later in the season they firm up, with solid hearts; Savoy is considered the best of the winter green cabbage; white cabbage is used for coleslaw; green and red as a vegetable, boiled, braised or stir-fried.
- **Cauliflower** – heads of creamy-white florets with a distinctive flavour; used for soup, and cooked and served in various ways as a vegetable.
- **Chinese mustard greens** – deep green and mustard flavoured.

Figure 4.108 Brassicas (clockwise from top left: kale, broccoli, cauliflower, Brussels sprouts, kohlrabi)

Figure 4.109 Pods and seeds (clockwise from top left: okra, sweetcorn, runner beans, mange tout, peas, bean sprouts)

- **Kale and curly kale** – thick green leaves. The curly variety is the most popular.
- **Pak choi** – Chinese cabbage with many varieties.
- **Romanescue** – pretty green or white cross between broccoli and cauliflower.

Pods and seeds

- **Broad beans** – pale-green, oval-shaped beans contained in a thick fleshy pod; young broad beans can be removed from the pods, cooked in their shells and served as a vegetable in various ways; old broad beans will toughen and, when removed from the pods, will have to be shelled before being served.
- **Butter or lima beans** – butter beans are white, large, flattish and oval-shaped; lima beans are smaller; both are used as a vegetable or salad, stew or casserole ingredient.
- **Mangetout** – also called snow peas or sugar peas; flat pea pod with immature seeds that, after topping, tailing and stringing, may be eaten in their entirety; used as a vegetable, in salads and for stir-fry dishes.
- **Okra** – curved and pointed seed pods with a flavour similar to aubergines; cooked as a vegetable or in creole-type stews.
- **Peas** – garden peas are normal size, petits pois are a dwarf variety; marrowfat peas are dried; popular as a vegetable, peas are also used for soups, salads, stews and stir-fry dishes.
- **Runner beans** – popular vegetable that must be used when young; bright-green colour and a pliable velvety feel; if coarse, wilted or older beans are used they will be stringy and tough.
- **Sweetcorn** – also known as maize or Sudan corn; available 'on the cob', fresh or frozen or in kernels, canned or frozen; a versatile commodity and used as a first course, in soups, salads, casseroles and as a vegetable.

Stems and shoots

- **Asparagus** – the three main types are white, with creamy white stems and a mild flavour; French, with violet or bluish tips and a stronger more astringent flavour; and green, with what is considered a delicious

aromatic flavour; used on every course of the menu, except the sweet course.
- **Bean sprouts** – slender young sprouts of the germinating soya or mung bean, used as a vegetable accompaniment, in stir-fry dishes and salads.
- **Cardoon** – longish plant with root and fleshy ribbed stalk similar to celery, but leaves are grey-green in colour; used cooked as a vegetable or raw in salads.
- **Celery** – long-stemmed bundles of fleshy, ribbed stalks, white to light green in colour; used in soups, stocks, sauces, cooked as a vegetable and raw in salads and dips.
- **Chicory** – also known as Belgian endive; conical heads of crisp white, faintly bitter leaves used cooked as a vegetable and raw in salads and dips.
- **Fallow wax beans** – similar to French beans.
- **Fiddlecoke fern** – also called ostrich fern; 5 cm long, a bit like asparagus and used in oriental dishes.
- **Globe artichokes** – resemble fat pine cones with overlapping fleshy, green, inedible leaves, all connected to an edible fleshy base or bottom; used as a first course, hot or cold; as a vegetable, boiled, stuffed, baked, fried or in casseroles.
- **Kohlrabi** – stem that swells to turnip shape above the ground; those about the size of a large egg are best for cookery purposes (other than soup or purées); may be cooked as a vegetable, stuffed and baked and added to stews and casseroles.
- **Palm hearts** – the buds of cabbage palm trees.
- **Samphire** – the two types are marsh samphire, which grows in estuaries and salt marshes, and white rock samphire (sometimes called sea fennel), which grows on rocky shores. Marsh samphire is also known as glass wort and sometimes sea asparagus.
- **Sea kale** – delicate white leaves with yellow frills edged with purple; can be boiled or braised, or served raw like celery.
- **Thai beans** – similar to French beans.
- **Water chestnuts** – common name for a number of aquatic herbs and their nut-like fruit; the best-known type is the Chinese water chestnut, sometimes known as the Chinese sedge.

Figure 4.110 Stems and shoots (left to right: globe artichoke, celery, fennel)

Figure 4.111 Fruiting vegetables (clockwise from top left: avocado, Italian aubergine, red pepper, yellow pepper, tomatoes)

Fruiting

- **Aubergine** – firm, elongated, varying in size with smooth shiny skins ranging in colour from purple-red to purple-black; inner flesh is white with tiny soft seeds; almost without flavour, it requires other seasonings, e.g. garlic, lemon juice, herbs, to enhance its taste; may be sliced and fried or baked, steamed or stuffed. Varieties include baby, Japanese, white, striped, Thai.
- **Avocado** – fruit that is mainly used as a vegetable because of its bland, mild, nutty flavour; two main types are the summer variety, which is green when unripe and purple-black when ripe, with golden-yellow flesh; the winter ones are more pear-shaped with smooth green skin and pale green to yellow flesh; eaten as first courses and used in soups, salads, dips and as garnishes to other dishes, hot and cold.
- **Courgette** – baby marrow, light to dark green in colour, with a delicate flavour becoming stronger when cooked with other ingredients, e.g. herbs, garlic, spices; may be boiled, steamed, fried, baked, stuffed and stir-fried.
- **Cucumber** – a long, smooth-skinned fruiting vegetable, ridged and dark green in colour; used in salads, soups, sandwiches, garnishes and as a vegetable.
- **Gourds (exotic)** – include bottle gourds, chayotes (chow-chow), Chinese butter lemons.
- **Marrow** – long, oval-shaped edible gourds with ridged green skins and a bland flavour; may be cooked as for courgettes.
- **Peppers** – available in three colours, green peppers are unripened and they turn yellow to orange and then red (they must remain on the plant to do this); used raw and cooked in salads, vegetable dishes, stuffed and baked, casseroles and stir-fry dishes.
- **Pumpkins** – vary in size and can weigh up to 50 kg; associated with Halloween as a decoration but may be used in soups or pumpkin pie.
- **Squash** – many varieties e.g. acorn, butternut, summer crookneck, delicate, hubbond, kuboche, onion. Flesh firm and glowing; can be boiled, baked, steamed or puréed.
- **Tomatoes** – along with onions, probably the most frequently used 'vegetable' in cookery; several varieties, including cherry, yellow, globe, large ridged (beef) and plum; used in soups, sauces, stews, salads, sandwiches and as a vegetable. Tomatoes are also sundried for use when fresh tomatoes lack flavour.

Plantains

- **Ackee** – tropical fruit used in Caribbean-style savoury dishes.
- **Breadfruit** – fruit from a tropical tree found in the Islands of the South Pacific Ocean.

Mushrooms and fungi

All mushrooms, both wild and cultivated, have a great many uses in cookery, in soups, stocks, salads, vegetables, savouries and garnishes. Wild mushrooms are also available in dried form.

Table 4.4 Seasons for home-grown vegetables

SPRING		
Asparagus	Broccoli – white and	New turnips
Cauliflower	purple	New potatoes
	New carrots	Greens

SUMMER		
Artichokes, globe	Cos lettuce	Carrots
Turnips	Beans, broad	Sea kale
Asparagus	Peas	Sweetcorn
Cauliflower	Radishes	
Aubergine	Beans, French	

AUTUMN		
Artichokes, globe	Beans, runner	Salsify
Parsnips	Cauliflower	Swedes
Field mushrooms	Red cabbage	Marrow
Artichokes, Jerusalem	Broccoli	Celeriac
Aubergine	Celery	Turnips
Peppers	Shallots	

WINTER		
Brussels sprouts	Parsnips	Celeriac
Chicory	Cauliflower	Swedes
Cabbage	Broccoli	Turnips
Kale	Red cabbage	
Celery	Savoy cabbage	

ALL YEAR ROUND		
Although the following vegetables are available all year round, nevertheless at certain times – owing to bad weather, heavy demand or other circumstances – supplies may be temporarily curtailed. However, owing to air transport, most vegetables are now available all year round.		
Beetroot	Mushrooms	Cucumber
Tomatoes	Leeks	Carrots
Spinach	Watercress	Cabbage
Onions	Lettuce	Potatoes

- **Mushrooms** – field mushrooms found in meadows from late summer to autumn; creamy white cap and stalk and a strong earthy flavour.
- **Cultivated mushrooms** – available in three types: button (small, succulent, weak in flavour), cap and open or flat mushrooms.
- **Ceps** – wild mushrooms with short, stout stalks with slightly raised veins and tubes underneath the cap in which the brown spores are produced.
- **Chanterelles or girolles** – wild, funnel-shaped, yellow-capped mushrooms with a slightly ribbed stalk that runs up under the edge of the cap.

Figure 4.112 Mushrooms and fungi
(clockwise from top left: girolles, chestnut,
pieds du moutons, flat, button, chanterelle,
shiitake)

- **Horns of plenty** – trumpet-shaped, shaggy, almost black wild mushrooms.
- **Morels** – delicate, wild mushrooms varying in colour from pale beige to dark brown-black with a flavour that suggests meat.
- **Oyster mushrooms** – creamy gills and firm flesh; delicate with shorter storage life than regular mushrooms.
- **Shiitake mushrooms** – solid texture with a strong, slightly meaty flavour.
- **Truffles** – black (French) and white (Italian) are rare, expensive but highly esteemed for the unique flavour they can give to so many dishes; black truffles from France are sold fresh, canned or bottled; white truffles from Italy are never cooked, but grated or finely sliced over certain foods (e.g. pasta, risotto).

FRUIT

For culinary purposes fruit can be divided into various groups:
stone fruits, hard fruits, soft fruits, citrus fruits, tropical fruits and melons.

Food value

The nutritive value of fruit depends on its vitamin content, especially vitamin C; it is therefore valuable as a protective food. The cellulose in fruit is useful as roughage.

Storage

- **Hard fruits,** such as apples, are left in boxes and kept in a cool store.
- **Soft fruits,** such as raspberries and strawberries, should be left in their punnets or baskets in a cold room.

- **Stone fruits** are best placed in trays so that any damaged fruit can be seen and discarded.
- **Peaches and citrus fruits** are left in their delivery trays or boxes.
- **Bananas** should not be stored in too cold a place because the skins will turn black.

Quality and purchasing points

Soft fruits deteriorate quickly, especially if not sound. Care must be taken to see that they are not damaged or too ripe when bought. They should appear fresh; there should be no shrinking, wilting or signs of mould. The colour of certain soft fruits is an indication of ripeness (e.g. strawberries, dessert gooseberries).

Hard fruits should not be bruised. Pears should not be overripe.

Preservation

- **Drying** – apples, pears, apricots, dates, peaches, bananas and figs are dried; plums when dried are called prunes, and currants, sultanas and raisins are produced by drying grapes.
- **Canning** – almost all fruits may be canned; apples are packed in water and known as solid packed apples; other fruits are canned in syrup.
- **Bottling** – bottling is used domestically, but very little fruit is commercially preserved in this way; cherries are bottled in maraschino.
- **Candied, glacé and crystallised fruits** are mainly imported from France.
- **Jam** – some stone fruits and all soft fruits can be used.
- **Jelly** – jellies are produced from fruit juice.
- **Quick freezing** – strawberries, raspberries, loganberries, apples, blackberries, gooseberries, grapefruit and plums are frozen and must be kept below 0°C (32°F).
- **Cold storage** – apples are stored at temperatures of between 1–4°C (34–39°F), depending on the variety of apple.
- **Gas storage** – fruit can be kept in a sealed storeroom where the atmosphere is controlled; the amount of air is limited, the oxygen content of the air is decreased and the carbon dioxide increased, which controls the respiration rate of the fruit.

Fruit juices, syrups and drinks

Fruit juices such as orange, lemon and blackcurrant are canned. Syrups such as rosehip and orange are bottled. Fruit drinks are also bottled; they include orange, lime and lemon.

Table 4.5 Different fruits and their seasons*

FRUIT	SEASON	FRUIT	SEASON
Apple	All year round	Greengage	August
Apricot	May to September	Lemon	All year round
Avocado pear	All year round	Mandarin	November to June
Banana	All year round	Melon	All year round
Blackberry	September to October	Orange	All year round
Blackcurrants	July to September	Peach	September
Cherry	June to August	Pear	September to March
Clementine	Winter	Pineapple	All year round
Cranberries	November to January	Plum	July to October
Damson	September to October	Raspberry	June to August
Date	Winter	Redcurrants	July to September
Fig	July to September	Rhubarb	December to June
Gooseberry	July to September	Strawberry	June to August
Grapefruit	All year round	Tangerine	Winter
Grapes	All year round		

* Because of modern storage methods and air transport the majority of these fruits may be available all year round

Uses

With the exception of certain fruits (lemon, rhubarb, cranberries) fruit can be eaten as a dessert or in its raw state. Some fruits have dessert and cooking varieties (e.g. apples, pears, cherries and gooseberries).

Stone fruits

Damsons, plums, greengages, cherries, apricots, peaches and nectarines are used as a dessert; stewed (compote) for jam, pies, puddings and in various sweet dishes and some meat and poultry dishes. Peaches are also used to garnish certain meat dishes. Varieties of plums include Dessert, Victoria, Gamota, Mayoris, Burbank; for cooking, Angelina, Stanley, Beech Cherry and Reeves Seedling.

Hard fruits

The popular English dessert apple varieties include Beauty of Bath, Discovery, Spartan, Worcester Pearmain, Cox's Orange Pippin, Blenheim Orange, Laxton's Superb and James Grieve; imported apples include Golden Delicious, Braeburn and Gala. The Bramley is the most popular

Figure 4.113 Stone fruits (clockwise from top: mango, plums, nectarines, dates)

Figure 4.114 Hard fruits (clockwise from top left: Comice pears, quinces, William pears, Braeburn apples, crab apples, Red Delicious apples)

cooking apple. The William, Conference and Doyenne du Comice are among the best-known pears. Other varieties of Pear include: Anjou, Beurre-Beth, Beurre-Bose, Beurre-Hardi, Beurre-Supersin, Forelle, Morton Poirde, Onwaide, Rocha, Housi and Perry Tieatsin.

Apples and pears are used in many pastry dishes. Apples are also used for garnishing meat dishes and for sauce served with roast pork and duck.

Soft fruits

Raspberries, strawberries, loganberries and gooseberries are used as a dessert. Gooseberries, blackcurrants, redcurrants and blackberries are stewed, used in pies and puddings. They are used for jam and flavourings, and in certain sauces for sweet, meat and poultry dishes. Other varieties of soft fruit include: dewberries, jam berries, young berries, boysenberries, sunberries, wineberries, blueberries and elderberries. Varieties of gooseberries include: Leveller, London and Golden Drop.

Figure 4.115 Soft fruits (clockwise from top: redcurrants, raspberries, blackberries, strawberries)

Figure 4.116 Citrus fruits (clockwise from top left: pink grapefruit, orange, lemons, limes, satsuma, white grapefruit)

Citrus fruits

Oranges, lemons, limes and grapefruit are not usually cooked, except for use in marmalade. Lemons and limes are used for flavouring and garnishing, particularly fish dishes. Oranges are used mainly for flavouring and in fruit salads, also to garnish certain poultry dishes. Grapefruit are served at breakfast and as a first course generally for luncheon. Mandarins, clementines and satsumas are eaten as a dessert or used in sweet dishes. Kumquats look and taste like tiny oranges and are eaten with the skin on. Tangelos are a cross between tangerines and grapefruit, and are sometimes called uglis. Pomelos are the largest of the citrus fruits, predominantly round but with a slightly flattened base and pointed top.

Tropical and other fruits

- **Banana** – as well as being used as a dessert, bananas are grilled for a fish garnish, fried as fritters and served as a garnish to poultry (Maryland); they are used in fruit salad and other sweet dishes.
- **Bubaco** – hybrid of the papaya.
- **Cape gooseberry** – a sharp, pleasant-flavoured small round fruit, sometimes dipped in fondant and served as a type of petit four.
- **Carambola** – also known as starfruit, has a yellowish-green skin with a waxy sheen; the fruit is long and narrow and has a delicate lemon flavour.
- **Cranberry** – these hard red berries are used for cranberry sauce, which is served with roast turkey.
- **Curuba** – also known as banana passion fruit; soft yellowish skin.
- **Custard apple** – heart-shaped or oval light tan or greenish quilted skin; soursops (prickly custard apples) have dark-green skins covered in short spines.
- **Date** – whole dates are served as a dessert; stoned dates are used in various sweet dishes and petits fours.
- **Dragon fruit** – yellow or pink; pink are large, about 10 cm long and covered with pointed green-tipped scales.
- **Durian** – large fruit that can weigh up to 4.5 kg; round or oval, have a woolly olive-green outer layer covered with stubby, sharp pikes, which turn yellow as they ripen; contains creamy white flesh with the texture of rich custard.
- **Feijon** – member of the guava family, resemble small slightly pear-shaped passion fruit, with a dark-green skin that yellows as the fruit ripens.
- **Fig** – fresh figs may be served as a first course or dessert; dried figs may be used for fig puddings and other sweet dishes.
- **Granadilla** – largest members of the passion fruit family; like an orange in shape and colour, light in weight and similar to a passion fruit in flavour.

- **Grape** – black and white grapes are used as a dessert, in fruit salad, as a sweetmeat and also as a fish garnish.
- **Guava** – vary in size between that of a walnut to that of an apple; ripe guavas have a sweet pink flesh and can be eaten with cream or mixed with other fruits.
- **Jackfruit** – related to breadfruit; the large, irregularly shaped oval fruits can weigh up to 20 kg; they have a rough spiny skin, which ripens from green to brown.
- **Jujube** – also known as Chinese jujubes, apples or dates; small greeny-brown fruit.
- **Kiwano** – also known as horned melon, horned cucumber or jelly melon; the oval fruits have thick, bright golden-orange skin covered with sharp spikes. The skin conceals a bright green, jelly-like flesh, encasing edible seeds, rather like a passion fruit.
- **Kiwi fruit** – have a brown furry skin; the flesh is green with edible black seeds that, when thinly sliced, gives a pleasant decorative appearance.
- **Loquat** – native to China and South Japan, also known as Japanese medlar. They have a sweet scent and a delicate mango-like flavour.
- **Lychee** – a Chinese fruit with a delicate flavour, obtainable tinned in syrup and also fresh.
- **Mango** – can be as large as a melon or as small as an apple; ripe mangoes have smooth pinky-golden flesh with a pleasing flavour; they may be served in halves sprinkled with lemon juice, sugar, rum or ginger; mangoes can also be used in fruit salads and for sorbets.
- **Mangostine** – apple-shaped with tough reddish-brown skin, which turns purple as the fruit ripens; they have juicy creamy flesh.
- **Maracoya** – also known as yellow passion fruit. Vibrant green with a thick shiny skin, which turns yellow as it ripens. Inside orange pulp enclosing hard grey seeds.
- **Passion fruit** – the name comes from the flower of the plant, which is meant to represent the Passion of Christ; size and shape of an egg with

i

Further information
For further information, visit the website of the Fresh Produce Consortium (website: www.freshproduce.org.uk).

Figure 4.117 Tropical fruits (clockwise from top left: pineapple, papaya, coconut, kiwis, passion fruit)

Figure 4.118 Melons (clockwise from top: watermelon, cantaloupe, honeydew, ogen)

crinkled purple-brown skin when ripe; flesh and seeds are all edible. Has many uses in pastry work.
- **Pawpaw (papaya)** – green to golden skin, orangey flesh with a sweet subtle flavour and black seeds; eaten raw sprinkled with lime or lemon juice. Served with crab or prawns and mayonnaise as a first course.
- **Pepino** – smooth golden skin heavily streaked with purple, sometimes called a tree melon. Native to Peru.
- **Persimmon** – a round orange-red fruit with a tough skin, which can be cut when the fruit is ripe; when under-ripe they have an unpleasant acid-like taste of tannin.
- **Pineapple** – served as a dessert; also used in many sweet dishes and as a garnish to certain meat dishes.
- **Pomegranate** – apple-shaped fruit with leathery reddish-brown skin, and a large calyx or crown. Inside is a mass of creamy-white edible seeds, each encased in a tiny translucent juice sac.
- **Prickly pear** – also known as 'Indian fig'. Fruit of the cactus. Skin is covered in prickles. Greenish-orange skin and orangey-pink flesh with a melon-like texture.
- **Rambutan** – related to the lychee, sometimes known as hairy lychees.
- **Rhubarb** – forced or early rhubarb is obtainable from January; natural rhubarb from April–June; used for pies, puddings, fools and compotes.
- **Sapodilla** – oval fruit from central America. Light brown skin, the flesh is sweet, with inedible hard black pips.
- **Sharon fruit** – a seedless persimmon tasting like a sweet exotic peach.
- **Snake fruit** – large member of the lychee family, the creamy flesh is divided into four segments each encasing a very large inedible brown stone.
- **Tamarillo** – known as the 'tree tomato', large egg-shaped fruits with thick, smooth wine-red skins. Each fruit has two lobes containing a multitude of black seeds.
- **Tamarind** – red, egg-shaped, flavour a mix of tomato, apricot and coconut, used in sweet dishes and salads.

Melons

There are several types of melon. The most popular are listed below.
- **Honeydew** – long, oval-shaped melons with dark green skins; the flesh is white with a greenish tinge.
- **Charentais** – small and round with a mottled green and yellow skin; the flesh is orange coloured.
- **Cantaloupe** – large round melons with regular indentations; the rough skin is mottled orange and yellow and the flesh is light orange in colour.
- **Ogen** – small round mottled green skins, each suitable for one portion (depending on size); mainly used as a dessert, hors d'oeuvre or in sweet dishes.

Care must be taken when buying as melons should not be over- or under-ripe. This can be assessed by carefully pressing the top or bottom of the fruit and smelling the outside skin for sweetness. There should be a slight degree of softness to the cantaloupe and charentais melons. The stalk should be attached, otherwise the melon deteriorates quickly.

NUTS

Nuts are the reproductive kernel (seed) of the plant or tree from which they come. Nuts are perishable and may easily become rancid or infested with insects. Some people have an allergy to nuts, which can cause severe illness and possibly death.

Season

Dessert nuts are in season during the autumn and winter.

Food value

Nuts are highly nutritious because of their protein, fat and mineral salts. They are of considerable importance to vegetarians, who may use nuts in place of meat; they are therefore a food that builds, repairs and provides energy. Nuts are difficult to digest.

Storage

Dessert nuts, those with the shell on, are kept in a dry, ventilated store. Nuts without shells, whether ground, nibbed, flaked or whole, are kept in airtight containers.

Quality and purchasing points

Nuts should be of good size. They should be heavy for their size. There must be no sign of mildew.

Uses

Nuts are used extensively in pastry and confectionery work and vegetarian cookery, and also for decorating and flavouring. They are used whole or halved, and almonds are used ground, nibbed and flaked.

Types

- **Almonds:** Salted almonds are served at cocktail parties and in bars. Ground, flaked or nibbed almonds are used in sweet dishes and for decorating cakes.

Marzipan (almond paste) has many uses in pastry work.

- **Brazil nuts:** Brazil nuts are served with fresh fruit as dessert and are also used in confectionery.
- **Chestnuts:** Chestnuts are used in certain stews, with vegetables (e.g. Brussels sprouts) and as stuffing for turkey. Chestnut flour is used for soup, and as a garnish for ice cream. Chestnut purée is used in pastries and gâteaux. Chestnuts are also available dried.
- **Coconut:** Coconut is used in desiccated form for curry preparations, and in many types of cakes and confectionery. Coconut cream and milk are also made and used in West Indian, Malaysian and Thai cookery.
- **Cob or hazel nuts:** These nuts are used as a dessert and in praline. Chopped or ground, they have many uses in pastry work.
- **Macadamia nuts:** These expensive nuts have a rich, delicate, sweetish flavour. They can be used in pasta dishes, savoury sauces for meat, game and poultry, and in ice cream, sorbets and puddings.
- **Pecans:** Pecan nuts are usually roasted and may be salted. Also used for desserts, various sweets and ice cream.
- **Peanuts and cashew nuts:** These may be salted and used as bar snacks. Also used in some stir-fry dishes. Peanuts are also used for oil and peanut butter.
- **Pine nuts:** Seeds of the stone pine, a native of the Mediterranean region. An important ingredient in pesto sauce.
- **Pistachios:** These small green nuts, grown mainly in France and Italy, are used for decorating galantines, small and large cakes and petits fours. They are also used in ice cream.
- **Walnuts:** Walnuts, imported mainly from France and Italy, are used as a dessert, in salads and for decorating cakes and sweet dishes. They are also pickled while green and unripe, and used for making oil.

EGGS

The term egg applies not only to those of the hen, but also to the edible eggs of other birds, such as turkeys, geese, ducks, guinea fowl, quails and gulls. Around 26 million hens' eggs are consumed each day in the UK and approximately 85 per cent of these are produced in the UK.

The British Egg Industry Council set up the British Egg Information Service in 1986. The British Egg Products Association (BEPA) introduced a strict Code of Practice in 1993, which covers all stages of production, from the sourcing of raw materials to packaging and finished production standards. Members of the BEPA can qualify to show a date stamp on their products, which signifies that the products have been produced to standards higher than those demanded by UK and European law. The aim of the date stamp is to reduce the risk of infection in hens, to monitor and take remedial action where necessary, and to ensure that eggs are held and distributed under the best conditions.

Figure 4.119 The quality of eggs

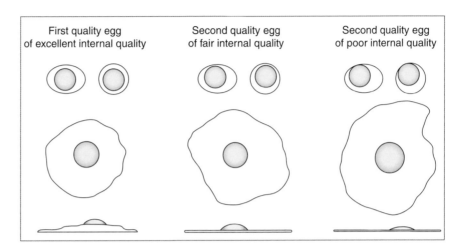

Food value

Eggs contain most nutrients and are low in calories: two large eggs contain 180 calories. Egg protein is complete and easily digestible, therefore it is useful for balancing meals. Eggs may also be used as a main dish; they are a protective food and provide energy and material for growth and repair of the body.

Production

Hens' eggs are graded in four sizes:

1 small – 53 g or under
2 medium – 53–63 g
3 large – 63–73 g
4 very large – 73 g and over.

The size of an egg does not affect the quality but does affect the price. The eggs are tested for quality, then weighed and graded under European law, as follows.

- Grade A – naturally clean, fresh eggs, internally perfect with intact shells and an air cell not exceeding 6 mm in depth.
- Grade B – eggs that have been downgraded because they have been cleaned or preserved, or because they are internally imperfect, cracked or have an air cell exceeding 6 mm but not more than 9 mm in depth.
- Grade C – eggs that are fit for breaking for manufacturing purposes but cannot be sold in their shells to the public.

They are then packed into boxes containing 360 (or 180). The wholesale price of eggs is quoted per 'long hundred' (120). All egg boxes leaving the packing station are dated. The 'Lion' quality mark on eggs and egg boxes means that the eggs have been produced to the highest standards of food safety in the world. Always buy eggs from a reputable retailer where they will have been transported and stored at the correct temperature (below 20°C)

Raw eggs and salmonella

In a number of salmonella food poisoning cases, raw eggs have been suspected as being the cause. Most infections cause only mild stomach upsets but the effects can be serious in vulnerable people such as the elderly, the infirm, pregnant women and young children. Consumers, particularly the more vulnerable, are advised to avoid eating raw and lightly cooked eggs, uncooked foods made from raw eggs, and products such as mayonnaise, mousses and ice creams. Caterers are advised to use pasteurised eggs. Dishes with an obvious risk of passing on contamination also include soft-boiled eggs, scrambled eggs and omelettes. The Department of Health has issued the following guidelines, which apply to raw eggs.

Table 4.6 Egg constituents and their usage

Usage of egg products	FROZEN			LIQUID			DRIED		
	Whole egg	Yolk	Whites	Whole egg	Yolk	Whites	Whole egg	Yolk	Whites
Ready meals	*	*	*	*	*	*	*	*	*
Pies/flans	*	*	*	*	*	*	*	*	*
Baked goods	*	*	*	*	*	*	*	*	*
Cakes	*	*	*	*	*	*	*	*	*
Dairy products	*	*		*	*		*	*	
Desserts	*	*	*	*	*	*			*
Biscuits	*	*	*	*	*	*	*	*	*
Drinks	*	*	*	*	*	*			
Baby food	*	*		*	*		*		
Soup		*			*			*	
Salad dressing		*			*		*	*	
Noodles	*	*		*	*		*	*	
Meat binder			*			*			*
Pet foods	*	*		*	*		*	*	

- Grade B eggs are broken out and pasteurised.
- Look for the Lion quality mark on the egg shell and egg box – it shows that the eggs have been produced to the highest standards of food safety in the world, including a programme of vaccination against salmonella enteritidis.
- There does not appear to be a similar risk with eggs that are cooked thoroughly.
- Eggs should be stored in a cool dry place, preferably under refrigeration.
- Eggs should be stored away from possible contaminants such as raw meat.
- Stocks should be rotated: first in, first out.
- Hands should be washed before and after handling eggs.
- Cracked eggs should not be used.
- Preparation surfaces, utensils and containers should be cleaned regularly and always cleaned between the preparation of different dishes.
- Egg dishes should be consumed as soon as possible after preparation or, if not for immediate use, refrigerated.

Egg products

Most egg products are available in liquid, frozen or spray-dried form. Whole egg is used primarily for cake production, where its foaming and coagulation properties are required. Egg whites are used for meringues and light sponges where their foaming property is crucial.

Table 4.7 Composition of eggs (approximate percentages)

	WHOLE EGG	WHITE	YOLK
Water	73	87	47
Protein	12	10	15
Fat	11		33
Minerals	1	0.5	2
Vitamins			

Uses of fresh eggs

Eggs are used extensively in:

- hors d'oeuvre
- meat and poultry dishes
- soups
- pasta
- egg dishes
- salads
- fish dishes
- sweets and pastries
- sauces
- savouries.

Table 4.8 Uses of egg products

Pasteurised whole egg*†‡	Hard-boiled eggs*
Salted whole egg*†	Pickled eggs
Sugared whole egg*†‡	Chopped hard-boiled egg with mayonnaise*
Pasteurised yolk*†‡	Scrambled egg*†
Salted yolk*†	Omelettes†
Sugared yolk*†‡	Egg custard blend*†
Pasteurised albumen*†‡	Quiche blend*†
Sugared albumen*	Egg/milk blends*†‡
Egg granules†	

* Chilled
† Frozen
‡ Dried

Other types of eggs

Turkeys' and guinea fowls' eggs may be used in place of hens' eggs. The eggs of the goose or duck may be used only if they are thoroughly cooked. Quails' eggs are used in some establishments as a garnish, or as an hors d'oeuvre.

Availability

Further information
For further information on British Eggs, visit: www.britegg.co.uk.

Table 4.8 shows the many egg products carrying the date stamp (see above) that are currently available. If you would like something a little different, it's worth talking to your supplier as he may be able to tailor the product to meet your specific needs.

DAIRY PRODUCTS

Milk

Milk is a white, nutritious liquid produced by female mammals for feeding their young. The milk most used in this country is that obtained from cows. Goats' milk and ewes' milk can also be used.

Food value

Milk can make a valuable contribution to our daily eating pattern and can help to meet our nutritional needs as part of a balanced, varied diet. Milk is one of the most nutritionally complete foods available, containing a wide range of nutrients, which are essential for the proper functioning of the body. In particular, milk is a good source of protein, calcium and B group vitamins, and whole milk is a good source of vitamin A.

Storage

Milk is a perishable product and therefore must be stored with care. It will keep for four to five days in refrigerated conditions. Milk can easily be contaminated and therefore stringent precautions are taken to ensure a safe and good-quality product for the consumer.

- Fresh milk should be kept in the container in which it is delivered.
- Milk must be stored in the refrigerator (four to five days).
- Milk should be kept covered as it easily absorbs smells from other foods, such as onion and fish.
- Fresh milk should be ordered daily.
- Tinned milk should be stored in cool, dry, ventilated rooms.
- Dried milk is packaged in airtight tins and should be kept in a dry store.
- Sterilised milk will keep for two to three months if unopened, but once opened must be treated in the same way as pasteurised milk.
- UHT (ultra-heat-treated) milk will keep unrefrigerated for several months. Before using, always check the date stamp, which expires six months after processing, and make sure to rotate stocks. Once opened it must be refrigerated and will keep for four to five days.

Packaging

Bulk fresh milk can be supplied in a variety of types of packaging. These come in the form of a plastic bag-in-box, which holds a capacity of between 12 and 20 litres. This should be placed in the appropriate refrigerated unit and the contents can be drawn off as required by fitting the correct tap device.

All packs contain fresh pasteurised homogenised milk and can be obtained in either whole, semi-skimmed or skimmed varieties.

Other types of packaging include:

- polybottles (large plastic bottles) of fresh milk available in 1-litre, 2-litre and 3-litre sizes
- bottles of fresh milk available in 0.5-litre size
- cartons of fresh milk available in 0.5-litre and 1-litre sizes.

All the above milks are pasteurised and come in whole, homogenised whole, semi-skimmed and skimmed varieties; in addition milk in cartons is available as UHT (ultra-heat-treated) and milk in bottles is available in UHT and sterilised varieties.

Milk heat treatment and types of milk

Milk is heat treated in one of several ways to kill any harmful bacteria that may be present.

- Approximately 99 per cent of milk sold in the UK is **heat treated**.
- **Pasteurised milk** – the milk is heated to a temperature of at least 71.7°C (161°F) for 15 seconds and then cooled quickly to less than 10°C (50°F).

- **UHT (ultra-heat-treated) milk** – milk is homogenised (see below) and then heated to a temperature of at least 135°C for 1 second, the milk is then packed under sterile conditions.
- **Sterilised milk** – milk is pre-heated to 50°C, separated and standardised to produce whole, semi-skimmed or skimmed milk. Filled bottles are then passed through a steam pressure chamber at temperatures of between 110°C and 130°C for 10–30 minutes, and then cooled in a cold water tank.
- **Homogenised milk** – milk is forced through a fine aperture that breaks up the fat globules to an even size so that they stay evenly distributed throughout the milk and therefore do not form a cream line.
- **Whole milk (blue cap)** – comes as pasteurised or pasteurised homogenised, and has a fat content of an average 3.9 per cent.
- **Semi-skimmed milk (green cap)** – comes as pasteurised and has a fat content of between 1.5 and 1.8 per cent.
- **Skimmed milk (red cap)** – comes as pasteurised and UHT, and contains just 0.1 per cent fat.
- **Channel Islands milk** – milk that comes from the Jersey and Guernsey breeds of cow, and has a particularly rich and creamy taste and distinct cream line; it contains, on average, 5.1 per cent fat.
- **Evaporated milk** – a concentrated sterilised product with a final concentration about twice that of the original milk.
- **Condensed milk** – concentrated in the same way as evaporated milk but with the addition of sugar; this product is not sterilised but is preserved by the high concentration of sugar it contains.
- **Dried milk powder** – milk produced by the evaporation of water from the milk by heat, or other means, to produce solids containing 5 per cent or less moisture; available as a whole or skimmed product; dried milk is skimmed milk powder to which vegetable fat has been added.
- **Soya milk** – can be offered as an alternative to vegans and people with intolerance to cows' milk.
- **Goats' milk** – nutritionally similar to cows' milk and can be useful for people with lactose intolerance.
- **Rice milk** – an alternative to dairy milk for vegans and those with an intolerance to lactose. It is heat stable, which makes it a good replacement for cows' milk in cooking although it tends to have a sweeter taste.
- **Coconut milk** – is high in saturated fat but low in calories. It can be served as a drink but is more often used as a marinade and in cooking.

Uses of milk
Milk is used in:

- soups and sauces
- the making of puddings, cakes and sweet dishes
- the cooking of fish and vegetables
- hot and cold drinks.

Cream

Cream is the lighter-weight portion of milk, which still contains all the main constituents of milk but in different proportions. The fat content of cream is higher than that of milk, and the water content and other constituents are lower. Cream is separated from the milk and heat treated. Cream is that part of cows' milk rich in fat that has been separated from the milk.

Table 4.9 Types of cream and their fat content

DESCRIPTION	MINIMUM BUTTERFAT CONTENT PER CENT BY WEIGHT
Clotted cream	55
Double cream	48
Whipping cream	35
Whipped cream	35
Sterilised cream	23
Cream or single cream	18
Sterilised half cream	12
Half cream	12

Other creams available include:

- extra thick double cream (48 per cent) homogenised and pasteurised – will not whip
- spooning cream or extra thick textured cream (30 per cent)
- frozen cream (single, whipping or double)
- aerosol cream – heat treated by UHT method to give a whipped cream
- soured cream (18 per cent) cream soured by addition of a 'starter'
- crème fraîche – is a similar product with a higher fat content.

Whipping of cream

For cream to be whipped it must have fat content of 38-42 per cent. If the fat content is too low there will not be enough fat to enclose the air bubbles and form the foam. Conversely, if the fat content is too high, the fat globules come into contact too easily, move against each other and form butter granules before the air can be incorporated to form the foam.

The addition of stabilisers to cream prevents seepage (particularly important when cream is used in flour confectionery). Cream substitutes are, in the main, based on vegetable fats or oils, which are emulsified in water with other permitted substances.

Storage

- Fresh cream should be kept in the container in which it is delivered.
- Fresh cream must be stored in the refrigeration until required.

i

Further information
For further information, contact the Ice Cream Alliance – Tel: 01332 203333, Email: info @ice-cream.org

- Cream should be kept covered as it easily absorbs smells from other foods, such as onion and fish.
- Fresh cream should be ordered daily.
- Tinned cream should be stored in cool, dry, ventilated rooms.
- Frozen cream should be thawed only as required and not refrozen.
- Artificial cream should be kept in the refrigerator.

Ice cream and other frozen dairy products

Ice cream is made by stirring, while freezing, a pasteurised mix of one or more dairy ingredients – milk, concentrated fat-free milk, cream, condensed milk – sweetening agents, flavourings, stabilisers, emulsifiers, and optional egg or egg yolk solids or other ingredients.

Frozen custard (French ice cream, French custard ice cream) is similar to ice cream but contains a higher content of egg yolk solids.

Reduced-fat ice cream, low-fat ice cream, light (lite) ice cream and fat-free ice cream all contain less fat per serving.

Sherbet contains 1 to 2 per cent milk fat and 2 to 5 per cent total milk solids. Water, flavouring (e.g. fruit, chocolate, spices), sweetener and stabilisers are added. Sherbet has more sugar than ice cream.

Frozen yoghurt is made by freezing a mixture of pasteurised milk, with or without other milk products, flavourings, seasonings, stabilisers, emulsifiers and lactic acid cultures.

Nutritional information

Ice cream and frozen yoghurt are nutritious foods providing high-quality protein, riboflavin (B2), calcium and other essential vitamins and minerals, The calorie and fat contents of these dairy foods vary depending on the type of milk used and the addition of cream, egg yolk solids or sweetening agents.

Yoghurt

Yoghurt is a cultured milk product made from cows', ewes', goats' or buffalo milk. Differences in the taste and texture of the product depend on the type of milk used and the activity of the micro-organisms involved. A bacterial 'starter culture' is added to the milk, which causes the natural sugar 'lactose' to ferment and produce lactic acid. There are two types of yoghurt:

1 stirred yoghurt, which has a smooth fluid consistency
2 set yoghurt, which is more solid and has a firmer texture.

All yoghurt is 'live' and contains live bacteria that remain dormant when kept at low temperatures, unless it clearly states on the packaging that it has been pasteurised, sterilised or ultra-heat-treated. If stored at room temperature or above, the dormant bacteria become active again and produce more acid. Too high an acidity kills the bacteria, impairs the flavour and causes the yoghurt to separate.

Yoghurt is available plain (natural) or in a wide variety of flavours; it often has pieces of fruit added during manufacture. Yoghurt beverages are available in a variety of flavours.

Food value
Yoghurt is rich in nutrients containing protein and a range of vitamins and minerals. It is particularly useful as a source of calcium.

Table 4.10 Yoghurt

TYPE	% FAT CONTENT PER 150 G POT	STORAGE AND CHARACTERISTICS
Very low fat – plain (natural)/fruit	0.3	14 days if refrigerated
Low fat – plain (natural)/fruit	1.1–1.2	14 days if refrigerated
Whole milk/creamy	4.2	14 days if refrigerated
Greek, Greek style	13.7	14 days if refrigerated
Bio or BA	percentage fat content as for very low fat, low fat and whole milk yoghurts	14 days if refrigerated; has a less tart flavour and is said to aid digestion

Other fermented milk products

- **Cultured buttermilk** – this product is made from skimmed milk with a culture added to give it a slightly thickened consistency and a sharp taste; it contains less than 0.5 per cent fat and should be kept refrigerated.
- **Smetana** – this is a cultured product containing 10 per cent fat; it has a slightly sharp flavour and can be served chilled as a drink or used as an alternative to soured cream in recipes.

i

Further information
To find out more, visit the Dairy Council's website at:
www.milk.co.uk

CHEESE, FATS AND OILS

Cheese

Cheese is made from milk protein coagulated by an enzyme such as rennet (an animal product). For vegetarian cheese a non-animal enzyme is used

Cheese is made worldwide from cows', ewes' or goats' milk; it takes approximately 5 litres of milk to produce 0.5 kg of cheese.

There are many hundreds of varieties, and most countries manufacture their own special cheeses.

Quality
The skin or rind of cheese should not show spots of mildew, as this is a sign of damp storage. Cheese, when cut, should not give off an over-

strong smell or any indication of ammonia. Hard, semi-hard and blue-vein cheese, when cut, should not be dry. Soft cheese, when cut, should not appear runny, but should have a delicate creamy consistency.

Hygiene

Cheese is a living product and should be handled carefully. It should always be wrapped in greaseproof or waxed paper or foil, or put in a closed container. Cheese stored in a refrigerator should have plenty of air circulating around it.

Natural rind can be exposed to air, so it can breathe, but cut surfaces should be covered with film to prevent drying out. Mould-ripened cheeses should be separated from other cheeses. Remove cheese from the refrigerator about an hour before serving to allow it to return to room temperature.

Recent scares about food poisoning included soft unpasteurised cheeses – this is because listeria can grow and multiply at a lower temperature than most bacteria; at 10°C (50°F) or warmer, growth is rapid.

Storage

All cheese should be kept in a cool, dry, well-ventilated store and whole cheeses should be turned occasionally if being kept for any length of time. Cheese should be kept away from other foods that may be spoilt by the smell.

Food value

Cheese is a highly concentrated form of food. Fat, protein, mineral salts and vitamins are all present. Therefore it is an excellent body-building, energy-producing, protective food.

Preservation

Certain cheeses may be further preserved by processing. A hard cheese is usually employed, ground to a fine powder, melted, mixed with pasteurised milk, poured into moulds then wrapped in lacquered tinfoil (e.g. processed Gruyère, Kraft, Primula).

Figure 4.120 Soft cheeses

Uses

Soups, pasta, egg, fish and vegetable dishes, savouries.

Types

British cheese: some examples

- **Cheddar** – golden colour with a close texture and a fresh mellow, nutty flavour.
- **Cheshire** – orange-red or white, loose crumbly texture and a mild mellow, slightly salty flavour.
- **Double Gloucester** – orange-red, a buttery open texture with a delicate creamy flavour.
- **Dunlop** – a Scottish equivalent of Cheddar, milder and lighter in colour and texture.
- **Leicester** – red in colour with a buttery open texture; a mellow medium strength.
- **Caerphilly** – a Welsh cheese, white in colour and flaky, with a fresh, mild, slightly salty flavour.
- **Lancashire** – white in colour, soft and crumbly with a fresh mild flavour.
- **Wensleydale** – white in colour, moderately close texture with a fresh, mild, slightly salty flavour; excellent with crisp apples or apple pie.
- **Stilton** – white with blue veins, soft and close texture, and a strong flavour.

French cheese: some examples

- **Brie** – white, round cheese with close, soft, creamy texture and delicate flavour.
- **Camembert** – white, round with soft, close, creamy texture and full flavour.
- **Chevre** – a generic name for a wide range of goats' cheeses.
- **Fourme d'Ambert** – sometimes called a French stilton; salty, full flavour.
- **Roquefort** – blue cheese made from ewes' milk; rich, sharp flavour with salty aftertaste.

Italian cheese: some examples

- **Bel Paese** – round, firm, pearly-white texture and a fresh, creamy taste.
- **Gorgonzola** – blue vein with a rich, sharp flavour; Dolcelatte is a milder version.
- **Mascarpone** – rich, creamy, slightly acrid, used mainly in desserts.
- **Mozzarella** – traditionally made from buffalo milk; pale and plastic looking, sweet flavour with a little bite.
- **Parmesan** – hard, low-fat cheese; grated and used extensively in cooking.
- **Ricotta** – fresh, white, crumbly and slightly sweet, similar to cottage cheese.

i

Further information
To find out more, visit the Dairy Council's website at:
www.milk.co.uk

Other cheeses: some examples
- Ireland – **Cashel blue**: a creamy rich blue cheese.
- Netherlands – **Edam**: round, full-flavoured with low-fat content; covered in red skin.
- Switzerland – **Gruyère**: firm, creamy-white with a full fruity flavour.
- Greece – **Feta**: white, moist, crumbly with a refreshing salty-sour taste.

Soft curd cheeses
- **Curd cheese** – made from pasteurised milk soured by the addition of a milk-souring culture and rennet; produce a soft, milk-flavoured, low-fat (11 per cent) cheese; made from either skimmed or medium-fat milk.
- **Cottage cheese** – a low-fat, high-protein product made from pasteurised skimmed milk; also available are very low-fat, sweet and savoury varieties.
- **Fromage frais** – (fresh cheese) or fromage blanc is a fat-free soft curd cheese to which cream can be added to give richer varieties; also available in low-fat, medium-fat, savoury and fruit flavours.
- **Quark** – a salt-free, fat-free soft cheese made from skimmed milk.

Low-fat hard cheese
There is a range of hard cheese with half the fat of traditional cheese.

Vegetarian cheese
Traditional hard cheeses made using a non-animal rennet are also available.

Fats

Storage of all fats
Fats should be kept in a cold store, and in a refrigerator in warm weather.

Butter
Butter is a natural dairy product made by churning fresh cream. During the churning process, the butterfat globules in the cream coalesce to form butter, and the excess liquid – known as buttermilk – is drained off. A little salt is added, between 1 and 2.5 per cent, depending on the type of butter, to enhance its flavour and keeping qualities.

Food value
Butter contains 80–82 per cent fat and is therefore a high-energy food. The remaining constituents are water (approximately 16 per cent) and milk proteins. The fat-soluble vitamins A and D are present in butter, and there is a small amount of calcium. Each 100 g of butter supplies 733 kilocalories (3014 kilojoules).

Quality
The flavour of butter is rich, creamy and mellow. The colour of butter varies from a delicate pale yellow to a rich, bright colour; both are entirely natural, as explained below. Butter's texture is smooth and creamy, and remains firm when chilled. It should be kept refrigerated, below 5°C (41°F) for optimum quality, where it can be kept for up to six weeks. Butter kept at room temperature soon deteriorates and exposure to light causes rancidity. As a recommendation, butter should be kept covered in a cool, dark place, away from strong flavours or smells that could taint its delicate taste.

Production
Essentially, there are two types of butter: lactic and sweetcream.

In lactic, or 'continental taste', butter, the pasteurised cream is ripened before churning with a lactobacillus culture to produce a mildly acidic flavour. This mild acidity enhances the keeping properties, meaning that this type of butter can be purchased as unsalted or slightly salted, where 1–1.5 per cent salt is added.

In sweetcream butter – traditionally produced in the UK and the Republic of Ireland, and imported from New Zealand – the cream is not ripened before churning and therefore the salt content needs to be a little higher (between 1.5 and 2.5 per cent) to assist keeping qualities.

Apart from the salt, there are no additives in butter. The colour of butter is entirely natural, and varies slightly according to the type of butter, the breed of cow and the pastures on which they feed. Seasonal variations affect the colour of the butter slightly, as the cow's diet changes during the year.

Uses
The unique taste and texture of butter means that it is ideal for spreading and using in all types of cooking, both professionally and in the domestic kitchen. It is the foundation of many classic recipes, as it improves the flavour and appearance of a great many foods.

Butter is used as a base for making soups, sauces, compound butters and for hard butter sauces like brandy butter. It is also used for making cakes and pastries, butter icings and frostings. Sometimes unsalted butter is chosen for these recipes.

Butter is ideal for shallow-frying foods, but it is not suitable for stir-frying or deep-frying, where higher temperatures would cause the butter to burn. Melted butter makes an ideal baste for brushing grilled foods, and can be combined with chopped fresh herbs, spices, grated citrus rind, and so on, to vary the flavour.

For finishing cooked foods, butter can be used as a glaze.

In sandwiches, butter acts as a protective layer, preventing moist foods from permeating the bread. The butter also gives the finished sandwich a delicious flavour.

Clarified butter can be made by gently heating butter until it has melted and separated. The milk solids can then be strained off. The resultant clarified butter can be used at higher temperatures. Ghee is a type of clarified butter, widely used as the basis of Indian cooking. A type of clarified butter known as concentrated butter is made by removing most of the water and milk solids. It is suitable for cooking and baking, but not for spreading or finishing foods.

Margarine

Margarine is produced from milk and a blend of vegetable oils emulsified with lecithin, flavouring, salt, colouring, and vitamins A and D.

Food value

Margarine is an energy-giving and protective food. With the exception of palm oil, the oils used in the manufacture of margarine do not contain vitamins A and D; these are added during production. Margarine is not inferior to butter from a nutritional point of view.

Quality

There are several grades of margarine: block (hard or semi-hard); soft (butter substitute); semi-hard for making pastry; and cake margarine, which creams easily and absorbs egg. Some margarines are blended with butter. Taste is the best guide to quality.

Uses

Margarine can be used in place of butter, the difference being that the smell is not so pleasant, and nut brown (beurre noisette) or black butter (beurre noir) cannot satisfactorily be produced from margarine. The flavour of margarine when used in the kitchen is inferior to butter – it is therefore not so suitable for finishing sauces and dishes. It should be remembered, however, that it is equally nutritious and may be cheaper than butter.

Vegetable shortening and high-ratio fat are available. They are used extensively in bakery products.

Animal fats

- **Lard:** Lard is the rendered fat from pigs. It has almost 100 per cent fat content. It may be used in hot water paste and with margarine to make short paste. It can also be used for deep- or shallow-frying.
- **Suet:** Suet is the hard solid fat deposits in the kidney region of animals. Beef suet is the best, and is used for suet paste and mincemeat.
- **Dripping:** Dripping is obtained from clarified animal fats (usually beef) and is used for deep- or shallow-frying.

ⓘ

Further information
To find out more, contact Unilever Ltd, Unilever House, Blackfriars, London EC4 or visit www.unilever.co.uk.

Polyunsaturated fats and monounsaturated fats

Polyunsaturates, and to a lesser extent monounsaturates, have been shown to lower blood cholesterol levels and therefore help in reducing the risk of heart disease.

It is better to eat foods rich in monounsaturates (olive oil and rapeseed oil) and polyunsaturates (sunflower oil and soya oil), than foods rich in saturates.

Rapeseed oil, which, like olive oil, contains mostly monounsaturated fat, is a good and cheaper alternative to olive oil. Sunflower, soya bean and corn oil all contain mostly polyunsaturated fat so are also good choices.

Some oils are labelled as vegetable oil or blended oils. All of these are also low in saturated fat and are generally cheaper.

Oils

Choice of oil

The choice of an oil as a food ingredient or for cooking will usually involve a compromise. The factors that will need to be taken into account may include:

- price – variations will occur according to supply and demand
- intended use – some oils are versatile others are of limited use
- durability – in use and in storage
- nutritional and health concerns
- flash point – for frying purposes an oil must, when heated, reach a high temperature without smoking; food being fried will absorb the oil if the oil smokes at a low temperature; as oils are combustibles they can catch fire (known as the flash point); in some cases the margin between smoking and the flash point may be narrow (see *Practical Cookery* for further information).

Types of oil include:

- peanut (groundnut)
- cotton seed
- palm
- rapeseed
- olive
- coconut
- soya bean
- sunflower
- palm
- corn
- speciality (e.g. almond, grapeseed, hazelnut, walnut).

Herbal oils are available or can be made by adding chopped fresh herbs (e.g. tarragon, thyme, basil) to olive oil and keeping refrigerated in screw-top jars for about three weeks, then strained and rebottled. If fresh green herbs are used, blanching and refreshing them will enhance the colour of the oil.

Food value

As oil has a very high fat content it is useful as an energy food.

ⓘ

Further information
To find out more, contact the National Edible Oils Distribution Association, see: www.neoda.org.uk.

Storage:
Oil should be kept in a cool place. If refrigerated some oils congeal but will return to a fluid state when removed from the refrigerator. Oils keep for a fairly long time but may go rancid if not kept cool.

Uses
- Mayonnaise, vinaigrette and hors d'oeuvre dishes.
- Pasta, certain doughs and breads use olive oil.
- Deep-frying, lubrication of utensils and slabs.

CEREALS

Cereals are cultivated grasses, but the term is broadened to include sago, rice and arrowroot. All cereal products contain starch. The following are the important cereals used in catering: wheat, oats, rye, barley, maize, rice, tapioca, sago and arrowroot. A wide variety of cereals are processed into breakfast foods (barley, wheat, rice, bran and corn).

Wheat

Source
Wheat is the most common cereal produced in the western world; it is grown in most temperate regions. Large quantities are home-grown and a great deal, particularly in the form of strong flour, is imported from Canada.

Food value
Cereals are one of the best energy foods. Wholegrain cereals provide vitamin B and are therefore protective foods.

Wheat and flour quality
Flours vary in their composition and, broadly speaking, are defined by the quality of wheats used in the grist prior to milling, and by their rate of extraction. The extraction is the percentage of whole cleaned wheatgrain that is present in the flour. A typical mill will produce hundreds of different types of flour using a wide range of home-grown and imported wheats.

Storage
Keep in airtight containers in a cool, dark, dry place. Whole grains can be stored for up to two years; flaked, cracked grains and flours should be used within two to three months of purchase.

Sprouting
Whole grains (e.g. wheat grains, raw buckwheat and barley) can be sprouted, which greatly enhances their nutritional value.

Cooking

Cereals can be used in other ways, besides being ground into flour for bread, cakes, and so on. Whole grains can be added to stews and casseroles, or cooked until soft. Cracked or kibbled grains are cut or broken pieces of whole grains (e.g. kibbled wheat and bulgar wheat). Meal, a coarse kind of flour, can be used to make porridge or thicken soups, or mixed with wheat flour to add interesting flavours and textures to ordinary breads, biscuits, muffins, etc.

Whole grains should be washed thoroughly. Boil the required amount of water, add the washed grain, stir once, put a tight-fitting lid on the pan and simmer for the required cooking time or until the liquid is absorbed. Turn off the heat and leave to stand for five minutes before removing the lid.

Flour

Flour is probably the most common commodity in daily use. It forms the foundation of bread, pastry and cakes, and is also used in soups, sauces, batters and other foods.

- White flour contains 72 to 85 per cent of the whole grain (the endosperm only).
- Wholemeal flour contains 100 per cent of the whole grain.
- Brown flour contains 85–95 per cent of the whole grain.
- High-ratio or patent flour contains 40 per cent of the whole grain.
- Self-raising flour is white flour with the addition of baking powder.
- Semolina is granulated hard flour prepared from the central part of the wheat grain. White or wholemeal semolina is available. Semolina is used for couscous.
- Bulgar (cracked wheat) is used in tabbouleh.

Further information
To find out more, visit the Flour Advisory Bureau's website: www.fabflour.co.uk.

Storage of flour

- The storeroom must be dry and well ventilated.
- Flour should be removed from the sacks and kept in wheeled bins with lids.
- Flour bins should be of a type that can easily be cleaned.

Uses of flour products

- **Soft flour** – cakes, biscuits, all pastes except puff and flaky, thickening soups and sauces, batters and coating various foods.
- **Strong flour** – bread, puff and flaky pastry, and pasta.
- **Wholemeal flour** – wholemeal bread and rolls.
- **Gnocchi** and **milk puddings**.

Rye

Rye flour is obtained from the cereal rye and is the most important European cereal after wheat.

Rye is the only cereal apart from wheat that contains gluten proteins.

However, these gluten proteins are not of the same quality or quantity as those in flour produced from wheat. Dough produced from rye flour has a sticky, dense consistency. The baked product has a low volume. Rye flour is available as light, medium and dark rye. Likewise the colour and flavour of rye bread can range from light and mild to dark and strong, depending on the type of rye flour used. It should be stored in dry conditions at 10–16°C (50–61°F).

Rye flour must be weighed accurately to ensure that:

- the recipe remains balanced
- the correct yield is obtained
- a uniform product is obtained
- faults are prevented.

Oats

Oats are either rolled into flakes or ground into three grades of oatmeal: coarse, medium and fine.

Source
Oats are one of the hardiest cereals, and are grown in large quantities in Scotland and the north of England.

Food value
Oats have the highest food value of any of the cereals. They contain a good proportion of protein and fat.

Storage
Because of the fat content, the keeping quality of oat products needs extra care. They should be kept in containers with tight-fitting lids, and stored in a cool, well-ventilated storeroom.

Uses
- **Rolled oats** – porridge.
- **Oatmeal** – porridge, thickening soups, coating foods, cakes and biscuits, haggis.
- **Patent rolled oats** – nowadays largely displace oatmeal and have the advantage of being already heat treated, and consequently more quickly and easily cooked.

Barley

The whole grain of barley is known as pot or Scotch barley and requires soaking overnight. Pearl barley has most of the bran and germ removed, and it is then polished. These products are used for making barley water for thickening soups and certain stews.

Barley when roasted, is changed into malt and as such is used extensively in the brewing and distilling of vinegar. Barley needs the same care in storage as oats.

Buckwheat is the seed of the plant 'bran buckwheat'. The grain is usually roasted before cooking, and is also ground into a strong savoury flour for pancakes and baking.

Maize

Maize is also known as corn, sweetcorn or corn on the cob, and besides being served as a vegetable is processed into cornflakes and cornflour. Maize yields a good oil suitable for cooking.

Cornflour

Cornflour is produced from maize and is the crushed endosperm of the grain, which has the fat and protein washed out so that it is practically pure starch.

Cornflour is used for making custard and blancmange powders, because it thickens very easily with a liquid, and sets when cold into a smooth paste that cannot be made from other starches.

Custard powder consists of cornflour, colouring and flavouring.

Cornflour is used for thickening soups, sauces, and custards, and also in the making of certain small and large cakes.

Rice

Rice is the staple food of half the world's population and is second only to wheat as the world's most important food grain.

Three main types of rice are used in this country:

- **long grain** – a narrow, pointed grain, best suited for savoury dishes and plain boiled rice because of its firm structure, which helps to keep the rice grains separate (e.g. basmati, patna)
- **medium grain** – an all-purpose rice suitable for sweet and savoury dishes (e.g. carolina, arborio)
- **short grain** – a short, rounded grain, best suited for milk puddings and sweet dishes because of its soft texture (e.g. arborio).

Types
- **Brown rice** – any rice that has had the outer covering removed but retains its bran and as a result is more nutritious.
- **Wholegrain rice** – whole and unprocessed rice.
- **Wild rice** – seed of an aquatic plant related to the rice family. It has a nutty flavour and a firm texture.
- **Ground rice** – used for milk puddings.
- **Rice flour** – used for thickening certain soups (e.g. cream soups).

Further information
To find out more about
cereals, see
www.vegsoc.org/info/
cereals.html.

- **Rice paper** – a thin, edible paper produced from rice, used in the preparation of macaroons and nougat.
- Precooked instant rice, par-boiled, ready-cooked and boil-in-the-bag rice is also available.

Storage

Rice should be kept in tight-fitting containers in a cool, well-ventilated store.

Tapioca

Tapioca is obtained from the roots of a tropical plant called cassava. Flake (rough) and seed (fine) are available. Tapioca may be used for garnishing soups and milk puddings.

Sago

Sago is produced in small pellets from the pith of the sago palm. It may be used for garnishing soups and for making milk puddings.

Arrowroot

Arrowroot is obtained from the roots of a West Indian plant called maranta. It is used for thickening sauces and is particularly suitable when a clear sauce is required as it becomes transparent when boiled. Arrowroot is also used in certain cakes and puddings, and is particularly useful for invalids as it is easily digested. It is easily contaminated by strong-smelling foods, therefore it must be stored in airtight tins.

Potato flour

Potato flour is a preparation from potatoes, suitable for thickening certain soups and sauces.

RAISING AGENTS

The method of making mixtures light or aerated may be effected in several ways.

Baking powder

Baking powder may be made from one part sodium bicarbonate to two parts of cream of tartar. In commercial baking the powdered cream of tartar may be replaced by another acid product (e.g. acidulated calcium phosphate).

When used under the right conditions it produces carbon dioxide gas;

to produce gas, a liquid and heat are needed. As the acid has a delayed action, only a small amount being given off when the liquid is added, the majority of the gas is released when the mixture is heated. Therefore cakes and puddings when mixed do not lose the property of the baking powder if they are not cooked right away.

Uses
Baking powder is used in sponge puddings, cakes and scones, and in suet puddings and dumplings.

Yeast

Yeast is a fungus form of plant life available as a fresh or dried product.

Storage and quality points
- Yeast should be wrapped and stored in a cold place.
- It should have a pleasant smell.
- It should be ordered only as required.
- It should crumble easily.
- It must be perfectly fresh and moist.

Food value
Yeast is rich in protein and vitamin B. It therefore helps towards building and repairing the body, and provides protection.

Uses
Yeast is used in bread and bun doughs, cakes and batters.

SUGAR

Sugar is produced from sugar cane grown in a number of tropical and subtropical countries and from sugar beet, which is grown in parts of Europe, including the UK. Syrups and treacle (for cooking and spreading) are liquid forms of sugar. It is also possible to buy organic sugar.

Food value

As sugar contains 99.9 per cent pure sugar, it is invaluable for producing energy.

Sugar in cooking

Sugar is not just a sweetener; it can be used in a number of different ways.

- As a preservative: at the right concentration sugar helps to stop micro-organisms growing and so prevents food spoilage (for example, in jams

Further information
To find out more, visit the website of British Sugar plc:
www.britishsugar.co.uk.

and other preserves). This is why reduced-sugar jams spoil much more quickly than traditional jams.
- It helps to produce subtle changes in flavour. Sugar offsets the acidity and sour flavour of many foods such as mayonnaise, tomato products, and tart fruits like gooseberries and grapefruit.
- As a bulking agent: sugar gives the characteristic texture to a variety of foods – including jams, ice cream and cakes.
- To raise the boiling point or lower the freezing point. This is essential in some recipes (for example, making ice cream).
- To speed up the process of fermentation (by yeast) in baking. This makes the dough rise (for example, bread and tea cakes).
- It makes cakes light and open-textured when it is beaten with butter or eggs in a recipe.

Types

- Refined white sugars: granulated, caster; cube; icing.
- Unrefined sugar: brown sugar.
- Partially refined sugar: demerara.
- Syrups and treacle.

Storage

Sugar should be stored in a dry, cool place. When purchased by the sack, the sugar is stored in covered bins.

BEVERAGES (DRINKS)

The simplest, cheapest drink of all is water, which varies from place to place in taste and character according to the substances dissolved or suspended in it. Soft water has a low content of lime. Hard water has an abundance of lime (if the flavour of lime is too strong, the water may have to be softened to remove the excess of lime).

Water that has been artificially softened should not be used for coffee or tea making. The mineral content of water used for brewing can significantly affect the final taste of the coffee or tea. A blend of coffee or tea brewed in the very hard water of London has a completely different taste to the same blend brewed in Edinburgh, where the water is very soft. Water can also contain varying degrees of other substances (e.g. iron and sulphur), which in some instances are considered to be beneficial to health, and these are known as mineral waters.

Drink can be broadly classified into two categories: alcoholic and non-alcoholic (beverage or soft drink). Although the word beverage means a drink the generally accepted definition is a non-alcoholic liquid, e.g. chocolate, coffee, tea, cocoa, fruit drinks, mineral waters, milk.

Alcoholic drinks include cocktails, aperitifs, fancy drinks, wines, fortified wines, spirits, beers, cider, perry. Low-alcohol drinks are also available.

Non-alcoholic drinks

Coffee

Coffee is produced from the beans of the coffee tree, and is grown and exported from regions such as South America, India, the Middle East, the West Indies, Africa, Java and Sumatra. The varieties of coffee are named after the areas where they are grown, such as Mysore, Kenya, Brazil, Mocha and Java.

Purchasing units

Coffee beans – either unroasted, roasted or ground – are sold by weight. Coffee essence is obtained in bottles of various sizes.

Food value

It is the milk and sugar served with coffee that have food value. Coffee has no value as a food by itself.

Types of coffee

- **Espresso** – steam under pressure is forced through powdered coffee.
- **Cappuccino** – strong filtered coffee with whisked hot milk added.
- **French coffee** – usually contains chicory; the root is washed, dried, roasted and ground. The addition of chicory gives a particular flavour and appearance to the coffee.
- **Coffee essence** – a concentrated form of liquid coffee, which may contain chicory.
- **Instant coffee** – liquid coffee that has been dried into powder form.
- **Decaffeinated coffee** – has had most of the caffeine removed and is, therefore, less of a stimulant.

Arab or Turkish coffee

Although the coffee bean spread from Arabia (the Middle East) to the rest of the world, the Arab method of making coffee did not. There is a fundamental difference between the Arab and other methods: the Arabs boil their coffee, traditionally, three times. Boiling coffee boils away the most delicate flavours, but it is a romantic way to make strong-tasting coffee. Arab coffee is made in an *ibriq*, a small copper pot with a long handle. Two teaspoons of finely ground coffee plus one of sugar are added to a cup of water and the mixture is brought to the boil. The *ibriq* is taken off the heat as it comes to the boil, usually three times, and then it is poured out and drunk. A cardamom seed can also be added for flavour.

The filter method

The drip, or filter, method is possibly the most widely used method today. Finely ground coffee is placed in a paper or reusable cone-shaped unit and nearly boiling water poured on top. For best results, a small quantity of water should be poured on first to wet the grounds and speed up the release of caffeol. The resulting brew filters through the unit into a pot or mug and is ready to drink. The coffee grounds remain in the cone. There are electric versions that automate this process, including heating the water, and in general make a better or more consistent cup of coffee than the manual versions. The filter method is particularly prevalent in Germany and the USA.

The plunger/cafetière

The plunger method, said to have been invented in 1933, extracts the most flavour from the ground beans. The pot is warmed, coarsely ground coffee is placed in the bottom, hot water is added to the grounds and stirred, then it is allowed to steep for three to five minutes before the plunger is pushed down to separate the coffee grounds from the coffee infusion. This method is only slightly less convenient than the filter method and is today one of the two fastest-growing ways to make fresh ground coffee. Cheaper pot models have nylon rather than stainless steel mesh to separate the grounds from the infusion, but they do not last as long.

The jug

The jug method of making coffee is the simplest of all. The coffee should be quite coarsely ground and then the hot water added. It is somewhat like the cafetière method, but without the convenience of the cafetière's plunger to separate the coffee grounds from the infusion. The jug is not now widely used, although it is always a serviceable stop-gap method.

Espresso and cappuccino

Today, espresso and cappuccino, which were invented in Italy, are the fastest-growing methods of making coffee. All the other methods involve a 'natural' form of infusion, and for a small cost you can have a system that will make acceptable coffee. But not with espresso. Espresso machines force the hot water through very finely ground and compacted coffee and then into the cups below. Good espresso is expensive to make because in order to extract the greatest amount of flavour from the coffee, a high level of pressure is required and thus a high-specification machine. Yet when making espresso, it is important not to 'over-extract' the coffee, which means the machine should be switched off sooner rather than later. While the coffee is still coming out as a golden-brown liquid it is perfect. This liquid is the 'crema', which lies on top of the black coffee underneath. The crema will dissipate a few minutes after the coffee is made, but in those few minutes it will tell you everything about

Figure 4.121 Cafetière and filter machine

Figure 4.122 A modern coffee machine

the quality of the espresso. Too light or too thick or too thin … all mean that the espresso is sub-standard. Espresso can become like a religion to some people. And there certainly is a big difference between a really good espresso and a not so good one. How much we spend in terms of money or energy in seeking out the best is one of those lifestyle choices we all make for ourselves.

Espresso is the foundation of cappuccino; it is the coffee upon which a luxuriant structure of frothed and foamed milk is ladled and poured. A good espresso is less obvious under its head of frothed milk, but the quality of the coffee underneath is still an important factor. The milk, ideally semi-skimmed, is poured into a jug, into which a steam spout is placed. The steam control should not be turned on until the nozzle of the steam spout is under the surface of the milk. Once the steam is gurgling and bubbling under the milk, the jug should be moved around or the milk will spoil. The aim is to aerate the milk and give it the consistency of whipped cream without burning it. It is essential that the cups are warm when the milk is poured in or the froth will deflate. They are normally stored upside-down on top of the espresso machine. The combination of frothed and steamed milk is then poured and ladled onto the coffee in the cup, gently as though folding it in. The small amount of remaining milk is poured too. And there you have the perfect cappuccino!

The Moka-Napoletana
No Italian home is without one or more mocha jugs of varying sizes, and no matter what you think of the coffee, their visual appeal is undeniable. Wonderfully designed double-beaded stove-top pots, they combine the

characteristics of espresso and percolator coffee. They force the water, which has come to the boil in the lower chamber, up through a tube and then down through the finely ground coffee. Handled expertly they can satisfy coffee cravings and produce an adequate 'espresso-type' coffee in under a minute.

The percolator

The coffee percolator was a civilising influence in the American wild west; it was certainly widely used throughout the USA, where, until the recent coffee 'revolution', it was a standard piece of equipment in most homes. The percolator heats the coarsely ground coffee and cold water so that it boils and bubbles up into the top of the unit. It is an excellent way to have the relaxing sound of the coffee liquid burbling and gurgling, and to waft the aroma of coffee through the home, as all the volatile, wonderful flavours go out of the percolator and into the air. There is possibly no worse way to make fresh coffee than this.

Soluble, or instant, coffee

The first soluble 'instant' coffee was invented in 1901 by the Japanese-American chemist Satori Kato, of Chicago. It was not marketed commercially until the launch of Nescafé in 1938. The quality and diversity of instant coffee have grown dramatically over the years, and we can make a good cup of coffee from today's products. Instant coffee has a number of advantages over fresh brewed coffee, including ease and convenience. It stays fresher longer, it is hard to damage the flavour, however hard you try, and most of all it is fast, cheap and clean. Instant coffee is manufactured, just like any other coffee, from ground beans. The first stage involves the preparation of a coffee concentrate from which the water is removed, either by heat, known as spray dried, or by freezing, to produce a soluble powder or granules. During the process of dehydration, the coffee essences may be lost, but these are captured and returned to the processed coffee.

Flavoured coffees

An interesting and fast growing area of the market is flavoured coffees. Today there are over 100 different flavoured varieties available. While coffee connoisseurs may turn up their noses at the idea of spoiling the flavour of their sacred brew, there are definitely moments when a chocolate or cinnamon flavoured coffee is just right. Coffee is a wonderful taste itself, but also acts very well as the platform for many other flavours. Flavouring coffee is actually an old trick. In the Middle East it is traditional to add cardamom to coffee, while the practice of adding cinnamon has been widespread in Mexico for many years. The growth in popularity of flavoured coffee is proof of coffee's versatility and strength. The flavours are added directly to the beans by roasting them, then spraying them with a carrier oil and then the particular flavouring. Another way to make a cup of flavoured coffee is to add a syrup to hot brewed coffee. This makes an ideal summer coffee drink, which can be served cold, as can iced coffee: pre-made coffee which has been chilled with either ice cubes or crushed ice added. By far the most important flavouring added to coffee over the world is milk. Although milk is not added to Arabian coffee, and coffee purists tend not to add milk, most people find coffee more palatable with its addition.

Caffeine content

The amount of caffeine in a cup of coffee can vary greatly, depending on its origin or the composition of the blend, the method of brewing and the strength of the brew. Instant, or soluble, coffee generally contains less caffeine than roast and ground coffee, but may be consumed in greater volume. Robusta coffees have about twice as much caffeine as arabicas. A 'cup' is usually understood to contain 150 ml (5 oz in the United States) but an espresso may be as small as 40 ml.

Composition

The composition of coffee is complex, with a large range of compounds including flavanoids, chlorogenic acids, nicotinic acids and caffeine.

Uses

Coffee is mainly used as a beverage, which may be served with milk, cream or as a flavouring for cakes, icings, mousse and ice cream. It can be brewed to suit individual tastes. The many different pure blended and instant (soluble) coffees that can be brewed in a wide selection of different coffee makers, or by various special brewing methods, make it possible to provide a brew to suit everyone. Whatever type of coffee is drunk, and regardless of roasting time, fineness of grind or brewing method, there are basic rules to observe for making a good cup of coffee.

Rules for making coffee

- Use good coffee that is freshly roasted and ground.
- Use ground or vacuum-packed coffee within ten days or the quality will deteriorate. Store in airtight containers in a cool place.
- Use freshly drawn, freshly boiled water cooled to 92–96°C (198–205°F) (to preserve the flavour and aroma of the coffee). Do not use boiling water.
- Measure the quantity of coffee carefully: 300–360 g per 5 litres.
- After the coffee has been made it should be strained off, otherwise it will acquire a bitter taste if kept hot for more than 30 minutes. Do not reheat brewed coffee.
- Milk, if served with coffee, should be hot but not boiled.
- All coffee-making equipment must be kept scrupulously clean, washed thoroughly after each use and rinsed with clean hot water (never use soda).

Further information
To find out more, visit the website of the Roast and Post Coffee Company:
www.realcoffee.co.uk.

- Make coffee in pots that have been thoroughly dried and warmed.

Preparing instant coffee

The majority of people in the UK drink 'instant' coffee. Instant coffee is convenient because it can be made into individual cups by adding water to the coffee and stirring. After the seal is broken on the container of instant, or soluble, coffee it should be stored in an airtight container and kept in a cool place. The flavour of instant coffee is improved if it is made in a pot using approximately one heaped teaspoon for each cup, and according to taste. Fresh water that is below boiling point should be added.

Tea

Tea is an evergreen plant of the camellia family, which is kept to bush size for easy plucking; only the two top leaves and bud on each stalk are plucked. There are more than 1500 blends of tea and tea grows in more than 31 countries.

Use a good quality loose leaf or bagged tea. This must be stored in an airtight container at room temperature. Always use freshly drawn boiling water. In order to draw the best flavour out of the tea the water must contain oxygen; this is reduced if the water is boiled more than once. Measure the tea carefully. Use one tea bag or one rounded teaspoon of loose tea for each cup to be served. Allow the tea to brew for the recommended time before pouring (see Table 4.11).

Blends

Blends of tea provide the widest possible choice of tea with many different characteristics and flavours. A popular brand-leading blend can contain as many as 35 different teas.

Speciality teas take their name from: the area or country in which they are grown; a blend of tea for a particular time of day; a blend of teas known after a person; a blend of teas to which fruit oil, flower petals or blossoms have been added or a 'made' processed tea.

Flavoured teas are real tea blended with fruit, herbs or spices. These should not be confused with tisanes and fruit infusions made from herbs, hibiscus leaves and fruits, which do not contain any real tea. Several varieties of green tea are also available, which research suggests has half the caffeine of black teas.

Buying

Tea comes in either tea bag or loose-leaf packs, which cover a wide variety of catering needs.

Storage

Packs of tea should be stored in a clean, dry and well-ventilated

> **i**
>
> **Further information**
> To find out more, visit the website of the UK Tea Council:
> www.tea.co.uk.

storeroom, away from strong-smelling products. Once a pack is opened, tea should be kept in a dry, clean airtight caddy because it will pick up any nearby aroma or flavour and become tainted.

Food value
Tea is a natural product. It contains no artificial colourings, preservatives or flavourings, is virtually calorie free and has no fat content if taken without milk or sugar. Teas contains caffeine (40 mg per cup), which acts as a gentle stimulant and helps give tea its diuretic effect. It also contains manganese, potassium, fluoride, and vitamins A, B1, B2 and C. The main producing countries are India, Sri Lanka, Kenya, Malawi, Indonesia and China.

Cocoa
Cocoa is a powder produced from the beans of the cacao tree. It is imported mainly from West Africa.

Food value
As cocoa contains some protein and a large proportion of starch it helps to provide the body with energy. Iron is also present in cocoa.

Storage
Cocoa should be kept in airtight containers in a well-ventilated store.

Table 4.11 Recommended brewing times for tea

	TYPE	COUNTRY OF ORIGIN	BREWING TIME	MILK/BLACK/ LEMON	CHARACTERISTICS
Darjeeling	Black	India	3–5 minutes	Black or milk	Delicate, slightly astringent flavour
Assam	Black	India	3–5 minutes	Black or milk	Full-bodied with a rich, smooth, malty flavour
Ceylon blend	Black	Sri Lanka	3–5 minutes	Black or milk	Brisk, full flavour with a bright colour
Kenya	Black	Kenya (Africa)	2–4 minutes	Black or milk	A strong tea with a brisk flavour
Earl Grey	Black	China or India/Darjeeling	3–5 minutes	Black or lemon	Flavoured with the natural oil of citrus bergamot fruit
Lapsang souchong	Black	China	3–5 minutes	Black	Smoky aroma and flavour
China oolong	Oolong	China	5–7 minutes	Black	Subtle, delicate, lightly flavoured tea

Uses

For hot drinks, cocoa is mixed with milk, milk and water, or water. Hot liquid is needed to 'cook' the starch and make it more digestible. Cocoa can be used to flavour puddings, cakes, sauces, icing and ice cream.

Chocolate

Cocoa beans are used to produce chocolate, and over half of the cocoa bean consists of cocoa butter. To produce chocolate, cocoa butter is mixed with crushed cocoa beans and syrup. With baker's chocolate, the cocoa fat (butter) is replaced by vegetable fat thus giving a cheaper product that does not need tempering. For commercial purposes, chocolate is sold in blocks known as couverture. Pure chocolate couverture is made from cocoa mass, highly refined sugar and extracted cocoa butter. It is the additional cocoa butter that gives couverture its qualities for moulding, its flavour and therefore its higher price.

Uses

Chocolate or couverture is used for icings, buttercreams, sauces, dipping chocolates and moulding into shapes.

Drinking chocolate

This is ground cocoa from which less fat has been extracted and to which sugar has been added. It can be obtained in flake or powder form.

Mineral waters and soft drinks

A wide range of mineral waters are available, both home produced and from overseas, and either natural (still or naturally carbonated) in character or treated with gas (carbon dioxide) to give a light sparkle or fizz. Examples of natural mineral waters are Buxton and Malvern. Manufactured soft drinks include grapefruit, lime juice (still) and tonic water, Coca-Cola, ginger beer (sparkling), and so on.

Squashes and cordials are all concentrated fruit extracts, meant to be broken down with fresh or aerated water into a long drink, and to be served hot or iced. Fruit juices are the unfermented juice of fresh fruits such as apple, grape, orange and tomato.

Fruit syrups are concentrated fruit juices preserved with sugar or manufactured from compound colourings and flavours (orange, lime, cherry). A large range of compound flavourings is available.

Milk drinks

Milk can be offered plain, either hot or cold. Other milk drinks include:

- **milkshake** – a mixture of fresh milk, ice cream and a flavouring syrup, rapidly whisked and served in a tall glass
- **ice cream soda** – a combination of fruit syrup and fresh cream in a long glass filled with soda water and topped with ice cream
- **egg nog** – beaten eggs (preferably pasteurised) with fruit syrup and

sugar added, mixed with hot or cold milk in a tall glass and topped with grated nutmeg

- other products from which beverages are made either by the addition of hot water or milk include Bournvita, Bovril, Horlicks and Ovaltine.

Alcoholic drinks

Wine

Wine has been made for over 6000 years and is produced in most parts of the world. It is the fermented juice of the grape and is available in many styles: red, white, rosé, sparkling, organic, alcohol-free, de-alcoholised and low alcohol. Wines may be dry, medium dry, or sweet in character, and according to the type and character they may be drunk while young (within a short time of bottling) or allowed to age (in some cases for many years).

Bottled wines should always be stored on their sides so that the wine remains in contact with the cork. This keeps the cork expanded and prevents air from entering the wine which, if allowed to happen, will turn the wine to vinegar.

Fortified wines

Fortified wines are those that have been strengthened by the addition of alcohol, usually produced from grape juice; the best known are port, sherry and Madeira.

Aromatised wines

Aromatised wines are produced by flavouring a simple basic wine with a blend of ingredients (fruit, roots, bark, peel, flowers, quinine, herbs). Vermouth and Dubonnet are two examples of aromatised wines popular as aperitifs.

Spirits

Spirits are distillations of fermented liquids that are converted into liquid spirit; they include whisky, gin, vodka, brandy and rum.

Liqueurs

Liqueurs are flavoured and sweetened spirits. A wide range of flavouring agents are employed (e.g. aniseed, caraway, peach, raspberry, violet, rose petals, cinnamon, sage, honey, coffee beans). Many different liqueurs are available (e.g. Cointreau, cherry brandy).

Cocktails and mixed drinks

Further information
To find out more see Durkan and Cousins (1995).

Cocktails are usually a mixture of a spirit with one or more ingredients from liqueurs, fruit juices, fortified wines, eggs, cream, etc. Cocktails may be garnished with mint, borage, fresh fruit, olives, and so on.

Mixed drinks have an assortment of names that include flips, fizzes, nogs, sours and cups. Cocktails and mixed drinks can also be made from non-alcoholic ingredients.

Beer

Beer is a term that covers all beer-like drinks such as ale, stouts and lagers. Beer is made from a combination of water, grain (e.g. barley), hops, sugar and yeast. Types of beer include: bitter, mild, strong ale, barley wine, porter and lager. Reduced-alcohol beers are also available.

Beers are good sources of energy; they contain high levels of carbohydrates and protein. Beers are richer in minerals than wines, but lower in alcohol at only 3–5 per cent.

Cider

Cider is fermented apple juice. Also in this category are:

- pomagne – a sparkling cider
- scrumpy – strong, homemade, rough cider.

Perry

Perry is fermented pear juice.

PULSES

Pulses are the dried seeds of plants that form pods.

Types

- **Aduki beans** – small, round, deep-red, shiny beans.
- **Black beans** – glistening black skins and creamy flesh.
- **Black-eyed beans** – white beans with a black blotch.
- **Borlotti beans** – pink-blotched mottled colour.
- **Broad beans** – strongly flavoured beans, sometimes known as fava beans.
- **Butter beans** – available large or small, also known as lima beans.
- **Cannellini** – Italian haricots, slightly fatter than the English.
- **Chickpeas** – look like the kernel of a small hazelnut; the main ingredient of hummus.
- **Dhal** –the Hindi word for dried peas and beans.
- **Dutch brown beans** – light brown in colour.
- **Flageolets** – pale-green, kidney-shaped beans.
- **Ful mesdames or Egyptian brown beans** – small, brown, knobbly beans, also known as the field or broad bean in England.
- **Haricot beans** – white, smooth oval beans.
- **Lentils** – available in bright orange, brown or green.
- **Mung beans** – chiefly used for beansprouts.
- **Pinto beans** – pink-blotched mottled colour.
- **Puy lentils** – grey-coloured; do not require soaking and they hold their shape when cooked. Considered the finest of lentils.
- **Red kidney beans** – used in chilli con carne.

- **Soissons** – the finest haricot beans.
- **Soya beans** – the most nutritious of all beans.
- **Split peas** – available in bright green or golden yellow.

Food value

Pulses are good sources of protein and carbohydrate, and therefore help to provide the body with energy. With the exception of the soya bean, they are completely deficient in fat.

Storage

All pulses should be kept in clean containers in a dry, well-ventilated store.

Uses

Pulses are used extensively for soups, stews, vegetables and salads, as accompaniments to meat dishes and in vegetarian cookery.

HERBS

Of the 30 well-known types of herbs, approximately 12 are generally used in cookery. Herbs may be used fresh, but the majority are dried so as to ensure a continuous supply throughout the year. The leaves of herbs contain an oil that gives the characteristic smell and flavour.

Herbs have no food value but are important from a nutritive point of view in aiding digestion because they stimulate the flow of gastric juices. The most commonly used herbs are described below.

- **Basil:** Basil is a small leaf with a pungent flavour and sweet aroma. Used in raw or cooked tomato dishes or sauces, salads and lamb dishes.

Figure 4.123 Herbs (a) (clockwise from top left: coriander, oregano, parsley, flat-leaf parsley)

Figure 4.124 Herbs (b) (clockwise from top left: rosemary, bay, lemon thyme, thyme)

Figure 4.125 Herbs (c) (clockwise from top left: chives, chervil, tarragon, marjoram)

Figure 4.126 Herbs (d): mint, sage

- **Bay leaves:** Bay leaves are the leaves of the bay laurel or sweet bay trees or shrubs. They may be fresh or dried, and are used for flavouring many soups, sauces, stews, fish and vegetable dishes, in which case they are usually included in a faggot of herbs (bouquet garni).
- **Borage:** This is a plant with furry leaves and blue flowers that produces a flavour similar to cucumber when added to vegetables and salads.
- **Chervil:** Chervil has small, neatly shaped leaves with a delicate aromatic flavour. It is best used fresh, but may also be obtained in dried form. Because of its neat shape it is often used for decorating chaud-froid work. It is also one of the 'fines herbes' (see below) – the mixture of herbs used in many culinary preparations.
- **Chive:** Chive is a bright-green member of the onion family, resembling a coarse grass. It has a delicate onion flavour. It is invaluable for flavouring salads, hors d'oeuvre, fish, poultry and meat dishes, and chopped as a garnish for soups and cooked vegetables. It should be used fresh.
- **Coriander:** A member of the parsley family, coriander is one of the oldest flavourings used by man. It is both a herb and a spice. The leaves have a distinctive pungent flavour.
- **Dill:** Dill has feathery green-grey leaves and is used in fish recipes and pickles.
- **Fennel:** Fennel has feathery bright green leaves, and a slight aniseed flavour, and is used for fish sauces, meat dishes and salads.
- **Lemon grass:** Lemon grass is a tall plant with long, spear-shaped grass-like leaves with a strong lemon flavour. A natural companion to fish, also used in stir-fries and salads.
- **Lovage:** Lovage leaves have a strong celery-like flavour; when finely chopped they can be used in soups, stews, sauces and salads.
- **Marjoram:** Marjoram is a sweet herb that may be used fresh in salads, and in pork, fish, poultry, cheese, egg and vegetable dishes; when dried, it can be used for flavouring soups, sauces, stews and certain stuffings.

- **Mint:** There are many varieties of mint. Fresh sprigs of mint are used to flavour peas and new potatoes. Fresh or dried mint may be used to make mint sauce or mint jelly for serving with roast lamb. Another lesser-known but excellent mint for the kitchen is apple mint. Chopped mint can be used in salads.
- **Oregano:** Oregano has a flavour and aroma similar to marjoram but stronger. It is used in Italian and Greek-style cooking, in meats, salads, soups, stuffings, pasta, sauces, vegetable and egg dishes.
- **Parsley:** Parsley is probably the most common herb in Britain; it has numerous uses for flavouring, garnishing and decorating a large variety of dishes. Flat-leaf, or French, parsley is also available.
- **Rosemary:** Rosemary is a strong fragrant herb that should be used sparingly, and may be used fresh or dried for flavouring sauces, stews, salads and for stuffings. It can also be sprinkled on roasts or grills of meat, poultry and fish during cooking and on roast potatoes.
- **Sage:** Sage is a strong, bitter, pungent herb that helps the stomach to digest rich fatty meat; it is therefore used in stuffings for duck, goose and pork.
- **Samphire:** Samphire is not really a herb, but the leaves of a low, branched bush found on salt flats. It has a mellow grassy sweetness that complements fish and shellfish dishes.
- **Tarragon:** This plant has a bright-green, attractive leaf. It is best used fresh, particularly when decorating chaud-froid dishes. Tarragon has a pleasant flavour and is used in sauces, one well-known example being sauce béarnaise. It is one of the fines herbes and, as such, is used in omelettes, salads, fish and meat dishes.
- **Thyme:** Thyme is a popular herb in the UK; it is used fresh or dried for flavouring soups, sauces, stews, stuffings, salads and vegetables.

Fine herbs (fines herbes)

This is a mixture of fresh herbs – usually chervil, tarragon and parsley – that is referred to in many classical cookery recipes.

Other herbs

Balm, bergamot, fennel, savory, sorrel, tansy, lemon thyme and other herbs are used in cookery, but on a much smaller scale.

SPICES

Spices are natural products obtained from the fruits, seeds, roots, flowers or the bark of a number of different trees or shrubs. They contain oils that aid digestion by stimulating the gastric juices. They also enhance the appearance of food and add a variety of flavours. As spices are

Figure 4.127 Spices (a) (clockwise from top left: tamarind, liquorice, red chilli, ginger, green chilli)

Figure 4.128 Spices (b) (left to right: nutmeg, cloves, star anise)

Figure 4.129 Spices (c) (clockwise from top left: black peppercorns, white peppercorns, juniper berries, pink peppercorns)

Figure 4.130 Spices (d) (clockwise from top left: sesame seeds, cardamom, cumin, caraway seeds, poppy seeds)

concentrated in flavour, they should be used sparingly, otherwise they can make foods unpalatable. Most spices are grown in India, Africa, the West Indies and the Far East.

- **Allspice or pimento:** This is so called because the flavour is like a blend of cloves, cinnamon and nutmeg. It is the unripe fruit of the pimento tree, which grows in the West Indies. Allspice is picked when still green, and dried when the colour turns to reddish brown. Allspice is ground and used as a flavouring in sauces, sausages, cakes, fruit pies and milk puddings. It is one of the spices blended for mixed spice.
- **Anise:** This is also known as sweet cumin, and has a sweet aniseed flavour. It is used for fish, sweets, creams and cakes.
- **Anise (pepper):** A strong, hot-flavoured red pepper.
- **Anise (star):** Stronger than anise, this has a slight liquorice flavour. Used in Chinese cookery with pork and duck.
- **Asafoetida:** This is used in Indian cookery to add flavour to vegetarian dishes. Available in block or powder form.
- **Caraway:** Caraway seeds come from a plant grown in Holland. The seeds are about 0.5 cm long, shaped like a new moon and brown in colour. Caraway seeds are used in seed-cake and certain breads, sauerkraut, cheese and confectionery. Also for flavouring certain liqueurs such as kümmel.

Figure 4.131 Spices (e) (clockwise from top: cinnamon quills, saffron filaments, turmeric, allspice)

- **Cardamom:** Cardamom is frequently used in curry; it has a warm, oily sharp taste, and is also used in some sweets (e.g. rice pudding) and drinks (e.g. coffee and tea).
- **Cassia:** This comes in thicker sticks than cinnamon, is less delicate and more expensive. Used in spiced meats and curries.
- **Celery seed:** Slightly bitter, this should be used sparingly if celery or celery salt is not available.
- **Chillies and capsicums:** These are both from the same family and grow on shrubs. The large, bright-red type are capsicums; these are ground and known as paprika. There are many types of chillies; they vary in taste, colour, piquancy and heat (always test the heat by cutting off a small piece and tasting with the tip of the tongue). The seeds are one of the hottest parts of the chilli and they can be removed by splitting the chilli in half then scooping them out with the point of the knife. Hands should always be washed thoroughly after preparing chillies because the oils are exceptionally strong and will burn the eyes, mouth and other delicate areas of the body. Chillies are used in many dishes: pizzas, pasta and in Indian, Thai and Mexican cookery.
- **Chinese five spice powder:** Usually consists of: powdered anise, fennel, cloves, cinnamon and anise pepper. Used extensively in Chinese cookery.
- **Cinnamon:** Cinnamon is the bark of the small branches of the cinnamon shrub, which grows in China and Sri Lanka. The inner pulp and the outer layer of the bark are removed and the remaining pieces dried. It is a pale-brown colour and is obtained and used in stick or powdered form, mainly by bakeries and for pastry work.
- **Cloves:** Cloves are the unopened flower buds of a tree that grows in Zanzibar, Penang and Madagascar. The buds are picked when green, and dried in the sun until they turn a rich brown colour. They are used for flavouring stocks, sauces, studding roast ham joints and in mulled wine.
- **Coriander:** Coriander is a pleasant spice obtained from the seed of an annual plant grown chiefly in Morocco. It is a yellowish-brown colour and tastes like a mixture of sage and lemon peel. It is used in sauces, curry powder and mixed spice.

- **Cumin:** This is frequently used in curry, is powerful, warm and sweet, and has a slightly oily taste.
- **Dill seeds:** These are used for flavouring fish soups, stews and cakes.
- **Fennel seeds:** Fennel seeds have a sweet aniseed flavour; used in fish dishes and soups.
- **Fenugreek:** Fenugreek is roasted, ground and frequently used in curry; slightly bitter, with a smell of fresh hay.
- **Garam masala:** This literally means 'hot spices'; it is not a standardised recipe, but a typical mixture could include: cardamom seeds, stick cinnamon, cumin seeds, cloves, black peppercorns and nutmeg.
- **Ginger:** Ginger is the rhizome or root of a reed-like plant grown in the Far East. The root is boiled in water and sugar syrup until soft. Ground ginger is used mainly for pastry and bakery work and for mixed spice. Whole root is used for curries, pickles, stir-fry dishes and sauces.
- **Juniper berries:** If these are added to game, red cabbage, pork, rabbit and beef dishes, they give an unusual background flavour.
- **Krachai:** A type of ginger with a slightly strange flavour.
- **Nutmeg and mace:** The tropical nutmeg bears a large fruit like an apricot that, when ripe, splits. Inside is a dark-brown nut with a bright-red net-like covering, which is the part that becomes mace. Inside the nut is the kernel or seed, which is the nutmeg. Although the two spices come from the same fruit, the flavour is different. Mace is more delicate and is used for flavouring sauces and certain meat and fish dishes. Nutmeg is used in sweet dishes (particularly milk puddings), sauces, soups, vegetable and cheese dishes. It is also used for mixed spice.
- **Poppy seeds:** Poppy seeds are used as a topping for bread, cakes, etc.
- **Saffron:** The stigmas from a crocus known as the saffron crocus (grown chiefly in Spain) are dried and form saffron, which is a flavouring and colouring spice. It is used in soups, sauces and particularly in rice dishes, giving them a bright-yellow colour and distinctive flavour. Saffron is very expensive as it takes the stigmas from approximately 4000 crocus flowers to yield just 30 g.
- **Sesame seeds:** These are used as a topping for bread and cakes, and in Chinese and vegetarian cookery.
- **Surmac seeds:** These are used in Middle Eastern cooking for their acidic lemon/peppery flavour. Deep red-maroon colour.
- **Turmeric:** Turmeric grows in the same way as ginger and it is the rhizome that is used. It is without any pronounced flavour and its main use is for colouring curry powder. It is ground into a fine powder, which turns it yellow. Turmeric is also used in pickles, relishes and as a colouring in cakes and rice.

Others

There is a large number of other spices, and spice and herb mixtures available – for example, chermonla, curries, harissa and garam marsala.

Some additional ingredients used in Asian and fusion cuisine

(Fusion cuisine is a mixture of food styles and ingredients from the cookery styles of East and West.)

- **Ajowan:** A native Indian plant used in Indian recipes. An ingredient of Bombay mix, and breads such as parathas, bean and pulse recipes.
- **Annatto:** Shrub indigenous to both the Caribbean and tropical America; has heart-shaped glossy leaves and pink flowers. The seeds are washed and dried separately for culinary use. An orange food colour is made from the husk.
- **Asafoetida:** Indigenous to Iran and Afghanistan and the north of India. Used in vegetable, fish, pulse and pickle ingredients.
- **Bamboo shoots:** Mild-flavoured, tender shoots of the young bamboo. Widely available fresh, or sliced or halved in cans.
- **Bengali five spices:** Bengali in origin, also known as panch phoron. Contains cumin seeds, fennel seeds, mustard seeds, fenugreek seeds and nigella seeds.
- **Berbera:** An Ethiopian blend of spices: dried red chillies, white cardamoms, allspice berries, black peppercorns, cumin seeds, coriander seeds, ajowan seeds, ground ginger, fenugreek seeds, cloves, ground nutmeg and salt.
- **Blackbean sauce:** Made from salted black beans, crushed and mixed with flour and spices (such as ginger, garlic or chilli) to form a paste. Sold in jars and cans.
- **Cajun spice mix:** Spice mixture used for fish, chicken and meat. Contains garlic, dried oregano, white mustard seeds, salt, black peppercorns, chilli powder, cumin seeds, paprika and dried thyme.
- **Cardamom pods:** Available both as small green pods and larger black pods containing seeds. They have a strong aromatic quality.
- **Chillies:** There are over 24 different types of chillies – for example, small green or red, garlic, and so on.
- **Chilli bean sauce:** Made from fermented bean paste mixed with hot chilli and other seasonings.
- **Chilli oil:** Made from fermented bean paste mixed with hot chilli and other seasonings.
- **Chilli powder:** Milder than cayenne pepper and more coarsely ground; prepared from a variety of mild and hot chillies.
- **Chilli sauce:** A very hot sauce made from chillies, vinegar, sugar and salt. Sold in bottles.
- **Chinese chives:** Also known as garlic chives.

- **Chinese rice wine:** Made from glutinous rice, also known as yellow wine huang jin or chiew because of its colour. The best variety is called shuo hsing or shuoxing, and comes from south-east China. Dry sherry may be used as a substitute.
- **Coconut milk and cream:** Not to be confused with the 'milk' or juice found inside the fresh coconut. The coconut milk used for cooking is produced from the white flesh of the coconut. If left to stand, the thick part of the milk will rise to the surface like cream.
- **Curry leaves:** Come from the tropical tree of the citrus-rue family, native to southern India and Sri Lanka. Strong, curry aroma. A classical way of using curry leaves is by frying mustard seeds in hot ghee, then adding a little asafoetida and several curry leaves for a few seconds, before stirring them into a plain dhal dish or dhal-based Indian soup.
- **Dashi:** Light Japanese stock, available in powder form. The flavour derives from kelp seaweed.
- **Dried shrimps and shrimp paste:** Dried shrimps are tiny shrimps that are salted and dried. They are used as a seasoning for stir-fry dishes. Shrimp paste, also known as terasi, is a dark, odorous paste made from fermented shrimps.
- **Galangal:** Fresh galangal, also known as lengkuas, tastes and looks a little like ginger, with a pinkish tinge to its skin.
- **Gram flour:** Made from ground chickpeas, this flour has a unique flavour.
- **Harissa:** Spice mix used in Moroccan, Tunisian and Algerian cooking. Used as a dip or accompaniment. Contains dried red chillies, olive oil, coriander seeds, garlic, cumin seeds and salt.
- **Hoi sin sauce:** A thick, dark brownish-red sauce that is sweet and spicy.
- **Juniper:** Grown in Hungary, southern Europe. An evergreen coniferous tree of the cypress family. The berries are used in the production of gin. A seasoning for some birds, venison, duck, rabbit, pork, ham and lamb.
- **Kaffir lime leaves:** These are used like bay leaves, to give an aromatic lime flavour to dishes.
- **La Kama:** Moroccan spice mix. Black peppercorns, ground ginger, ground turmeric, ground nutmeg, cinnamon stick.
- **Liquorice:** Native of the Middle East and south-east Europe. The root is the most important part; it sends out a deep and extensive network of rhizomes, which are grown for three to five years before they are harvested. The roots and rhizomes are cleaned, pulped, then boiled, and the liquorice extract is then concentrated by evaporation. Liquorice is best known as an ingredient in confectionery, also used in the making of Guinness and to flavour the Italian liquor sambuca.
- **Mahlebi:** Tree found only in the Middle East and Turkey. This ground spice is used in breads and pastries.

- **Mango powder:** The unripe mangoes are sliced, sundried and ground to a powder, then mixed with a little ground turmeric. Used in vegetarian dishes, curries and chutneys.
- **Mirin:** A mild, sweet Japanese rice wine used in cooking.
- **Miso:** A fermented bean paste that adds richness and flavour to Japanese soups.
- **Nigella:** Grown in India. The seeds are held in a seed head similar to a poppy head. Sometimes used as a substitute for pepper. Nigella is one of the five spices in Bengali five spices. It is widely used in Indian cooking, in dhal and vegetable dishes, pickles and chutneys. The seeds are often scattered on naan bread.
- **Noodles:** There are several types of noodles:
  - cellophane noodles – also known as bean thread, transparent or glass noodles, made from ground mung beans
  - egg noodles – made from wheat flour, egg and water
  - rice noodles – made from ground rice and water
  - rice vermicelli – thin brittle noodles that look like white hair
  - somen noodles – delicate, thin white Japanese noodles made from wheat flour
  - udon noodles – Japanese noodles made of wheat flour and water.
- **Nori:** Paper-thin sheets of Japanese seaweed.
- **Oyster sauce:** Made from oyster extract.
- **Pak choi:** Also known as bok choi, this is a leaf vegetable with long, smooth milky-white stems and dark-green foliage.
- **Palm sugar:** Strongly flavoured, hard brown sugar made from the sap of the coconut palm tree.
- **Papaya seeds:** Seeds of the papaya fruit. Can be used fresh or dried. Rich in the enzyme papain, which is an efficient meat tenderiser of commercial value.
- **Pomegranate seeds:** Grown in Mediterranean countries, South America, the USA and parts of Africa. Grenadine is a syrup made from the juice of the pomegranate. Fresh pomegranate seeds are sprinkled on hummus.
- **Ras el hanout:** Moroccan spice mixture. Contains black peppercorns, coriander seeds, cumin seeds, cloves, green cardamoms, ground turmeric, cinnamon stick, ground ginger, salt nutmeg, dried red chillies and dried flowers.
- **Red bean paste:** A reddish-brown paste made from puréed red beans and crystallised sugar.
- **Rice vinegar:** There are two basic types:
  - red vinegar – made from fermented rice, has a distinctive dark colour
  - white vinegar – stronger in flavour, distilled from rice.
- **Sake:** A powerful fortified rice wine from Japan.
- **Sambaar powder:** Also known as sambar, used in south Indian dishes; made from red chillies, coriander seeds, black peppercorns, fenugreek

seeds, urad dhal, channu dhal, mung dhal, ground turmeric and cumin seeds.

- **Sambal keeap:** Indonesian sauce used as an accompaniment or a dip. Dark soy sauce, lemon juice, garlic, red chilli, deep-fried onion slices.
- **Sambals:** Sambals is an accompaniment that is spooned directly on to the plate. Made from seeded red chillies puréed with salt.
- **Soy sauce:** A major seasoning ingredient in Chinese cooking, made from fermented soya beans, combined with yeast, salt and sugar. Chinese soy sauce falls into two main categories: light and dark. Light has more flavour than the sweeter dark sauce, which gives food a rich, reddish colour.
- **Spring roll wrappers:** Paper-thin wrappers made from wheat or rice flour and water.
- **Sumac:** Bush grown in Italy, Sicily and the Middle East. Its red berries are dried. Widely used in Lebanese, Syrian, Turkish and Iranian cuisines.
- **Szechuan peppercorns:** Also known as tarchiew; aromatic, best used roasted and ground. Not as hot as white or black peppercorns.
- **Tamarind:** The brown, sticky pulp of the bean-like seed pod of the tamarind tree. Used in Indian, Thai and Indonesian cooking.
- **Thai fish sauce (nam pla):** The most common flavouring in Thai food, in the same way soy sauce is used in Chinese dishes. It is made from salted anchovies and has a strong, salty flavour.
- **Thai nam prik sauce:** This is the most famous of the Thai sauces, it can be served on its own or used as a dip. Contains brown sugar, lemon juice, fish sauce, fresh red chillies, dried prawns, blanchan, cooked prawns, garlic and fresh coriander.
- **Thai parsley:** Similar in appearance to spring onion but without the bulb.
- **Thai red curry paste (krueng gueng phed):** Used for meat, poultry and vegetable dishes. Contains red chillies, groundnut oil, red onion, blanchan, lemon grass, salt, cumin seeds, citrus peel, garlic, galangal, green chillies, white onion, fresh coriander and coriander seeds.
- **Toey leaves:** Also known as pandanus leaves, these are long, flat blades, bright green in colour.
- **Tofu:** Puréed, pressed soya beans, also known as bean curd. Rich in protein.
- **Wasabi:** Edible root used in Japanese cooking, to make a condiment with a sharp, pungent and fiery flavour. Similar to horseradish.
- **Water chestnuts:** Walnut-sized bulbs from an Asian water plant that looks like sweet chestnuts.
- **Wonton wrappers:** Small, paper-thin squares of wheat flour and egg dough.
- **Yard-long beans:** Long, thin beans similar to French beans but three or four times longer.
- **Yellow bean sauce:** A thick paste made from salted, fermented yellow soya beans crushed with flour and sugar.

• **Zedoury**: A member of the ginger and turmeric family, bright yellow in colour. Has a musky aroma with a hint of camphor.

CONDIMENTS

Salt

Food value
Salt (sodium chloride) is essential for stabilising body fluids and preventing muscular cramp. Salt should always be used in moderation as it has been proved that excess salt in the diet can be harmful to health, causing high blood pressure.

Storage
Salt must be stored in a cool, dry place as it readily absorbs moisture. It should be kept in airtight packets, drums or bins.

Uses
Salt is used for curing fish such as herrings and haddocks, and for cheese and butter making. Salt is also used for the pickling of foods, in the cooking of many dishes and as a condiment on the table.

Pepper

Pepper is obtained from black peppercorns, which are the berries of a tropical shrub. White peppercorns are obtained by removing the skin from the black peppercorn. White pepper is less pungent than black, and both may be obtained in ground form.

Green peppercorns are fresh unripe pepper berries, milder than dried peppercorns, available frozen or in tins. Pink peppercorns are softer and milder than green peppercorns, available preserved in vinegar.

Ground pepper is used for seasoning many dishes and as a condiment at the table.

Cayenne pepper
Cayenne is a red pepper used on savoury dishes and in cheese straws. It is a hot pepper that is obtained from grinding chillies and capsicums.

Paprika
Paprika is a bright-red mild pepper used in Hungarian dishes, e.g. soups, stews (goulash). Smoked paprika is available in sweet, hot and bitter-sweet versions.

Mustard

Mustard is obtained from the seed of the mustard plant. There are three different types of seed: white, brown and black. It is sold in powder form and is diluted with water, milk or vinegar for table use, or sold ready mixed in jars. A large variety of continental mustards are sold as a paste in jars, having been mixed with herbs and wine vinegar.

Vinegar

Malt vinegar is made from malt, which is produced from barley. Artificial, non-brewed, pure or imitation vinegars are chemically produced solutions of acetic acid in water. They are cheaper and inferior to malt vinegar, having a pungent odour and a sharp flavour.

Spirit vinegars are produced from potatoes, grain or starchy vegetables, but they do not have the same flavour as malt vinegar. Red or white wine vinegars are made from grapes; they are more expensive and have a more delicate flavour than the other vinegars.

All vinegars can be distilled; this removes the colour. The colour of vinegar is no indication of its strength as burnt sugar is added to give colour.

Balsamic vinegar is a specially matured vinegar from Italy, with a distinctive flavour that varies in strength according to the age of the vinegar, which can be up to 30 years.

Other vinegars include chilli, sherry, cider, rice, herb (especially tarragon) thyme, oregano, sage, rosemary, and fruit such as raspberry and strawberry.

Uses

Vinegar is used as a preservative for pickles, rollmops and cocktail onions; and as a condiment on its own or with oil as a salad dressing; it is used for flavouring sauces such as mayonnaise and in reductions for sharp sauces (e.g. sauce piquante, sauce diable).

COLOURINGS, FLAVOURINGS, ESSENCES

Colourings

A number of food colourings are obtained in either powder or liquid form. Natural colours include the following.

- **Cochineal:** Cochineal is a red colour, produced from the cochineal beetle, used in pastry and confectionery work.
- **Green colouring:** This can be made by mixing indigo and saffron, but chlorophyll, the natural green colouring of plants, such as in spinach, may also be used.
- **Indigo:** Indigo is a blue colour seldom used on its own but, when mixed with red, it produces shades of mauve.
- **Yellow colouring:** A deep-yellow colour can be obtained from turmeric roots and is prepared in the form of a powder mainly used in curry

and mustard pickles. Yellow colouring is also obtained by using egg yolks or saffron.

- **Brown:** Brown sugar is used to give a deep brown colour in rich fruit cakes; it also adds to the flavour.
- **Blackjack or browning:** Blackjack, or commercial caramel, is a dark-brown, almost black liquid; it is used for colouring soups, sauces, gravies, aspics, and in pastry and confectionery.
- **Chocolate colour:** This can be obtained in liquid or powder form, and is used in pastry and confectionery.
- **Coffee colour:** This is usually made from coffee beans with the addition of chicory.

Other colourings

A large range of artificial colours are also obtainable; they are produced from coal tar and are harmless. Some mineral colours are also used in foodstuffs. All colourings must be pure and there is a list of those permitted for cookery and confectionery use.

Flavourings and essences

Essences are generally produced from a solution of essential oils with alcohol, and are prepared for the use of cooks, bakers and confectioners. Among the many types of essence obtainable are:

- almond
- pineapple
- lemon
- raspberry
- orange
- strawberry
- peppermint
- vanilla.

Essences are available in three categories: natural, artificial and compound. The relative costs vary considerably and it is advisable to try all types of flavouring essence before deciding on which to use for specific purposes.

Natural essences

- Fruit juices pressed out of soft fruits (raspberries or strawberries).
- Citrus fruit peel (lemon, orange).
- Spices, beans, herbs, roots, nuts (caraway seeds, cinnamon, celery, mint, sage, thyme, clove, ginger, coffee beans, nutmeg and vanilla pod).

Artificial essences

Artificial essences (such as vanilla, pineapple, rum, banana and coconut) are produced from various chemicals blended to give a close imitation of the natural flavour.

Compound essences

Compound essences are made by blending natural products with artificial products.

GROCERY, DELICATESSEN

Delicatessen literally means 'provision store', but the name is commonly used to cover the place where a wide range of table delicacies may be bought.

- **Agar agar:** This is obtained from the dried purified stems of a seaweed; it is also known as vegetable gelatine and is used in vegetarian cookery.
- **Anchovy essence:** This is a strong, highly seasoned commodity used for flavouring certain fish sauces and fish preparations such as anchovy sauce or fish cakes.
- **Aspic:** Aspic jelly is a clear savoury jelly, which may be the flavour of meat, game or fish. It may be produced from fresh ingredients (see *Advanced Practical Cookery*) or obtained in dried form. It is used for cold larder work, mainly for coating chaud-froid dishes, and may also be chopped or cut into neat shapes to decorate finished dishes.
- **Charcuterie:** Charcuterie is the name given to cold meat preparations usually pork (e.g. hams), galantines, black puddings, pâtés, salamis and a large variety of continental sausages and cured meats (e.g. bresaola).
- **Caviar:** Caviar is the uncooked roe of the sturgeon, which is prepared by carefully separating the eggs from the membranes of the roe and gently rubbing them through sieves of coarse hemp. It is then soaked in a brine solution, sieved and packed.

  Sturgeon fishing takes place in the estuaries of rivers that run into the Caspian or Black Sea, therefore caviar is Russian or Iranian in origin. The types normally obtainable in Britain are Beluga, Osetrova and Sevruga. These names refer to the type of sturgeon from which the caviar is taken.

  Caviar is extremely expensive, and needs to be handled with great care and understanding. It should be kept at a temperature of 0°C (32°F) but no lower, otherwise the extreme cold will break the eggs down. Caviar must never be deep frozen.

  A red caviar (keta) is obtained from the roe of salmon. From the lumpfish a mock caviar is obtained. These are considerably cheaper than genuine caviar.
- **Extracts (meat and vegetable):** Extracts are highly concentrated forms of flavouring used in some kitchens to strengthen stocks and sauces (Bovril, Marmite, Maggi and Jardox are some examples).
- **Foie gras:** This expensive delicacy is obtained from the livers of specially fattened geese and is produced mainly in Strasbourg. It is available fresh and cooked in a variety of ways (e.g. terrine, pâté).
- **Gelatine:** Gelatine is obtained from the bones and connective tissue (collagen) of certain animals; it is manufactured in leaf or powdered form and used in various sweets, such as bavarois. (See also 'Agar agar', above.)
- **Haggis:** This traditional Scottish dish is made from the heart, lungs

(lights) and liver of the sheep, mixed with suet, onion and oatmeal, and sewn up in a stomach bag. It is boiled and served with mashed potatoes.

- **Hams:** A ham is the hind leg of a pig cured by a special process, which varies according to the type of ham. One of the most famous English hams is the York ham, weighing 6–7 kg, which is cured by salting, drying and sometimes smoking. The Bradenham ham is of coal-black colour and is a sweet-cured ham from Chippenham in Wiltshire. Hams are also imported from Northern Ireland and Denmark. These are all cooked before use. Continental raw hams – Westphalian from Germany, Bayonne and Ardenne from France, Parma from Italy and Serrano from Spain – are cut into thin slices and served raw.
- **Horseradish:** Horseradish is a plant of which only the root is used. It is washed, peeled, grated and used for horseradish sauce and horseradish cream.
- **Panettone:** An Italian light-textured yeast bread containing sultanas and candied fruit.
- **Pickles:** These are vegetables and/or fruits preserved in vinegar or sauce and include red cabbage, gherkins, olives, onions, walnuts and capers. Mango chutney is a sweet chutney that is served as an accompaniment to curried dishes.
- **Smoked herring, anchovies and sardines:** These are preserved in oil and used as hors d'oeuvre.
- **Smoked salmon:** British, Scandinavian or Canadian salmon weighing between 6 and 8 kg are used for smoking. A good-quality side of smoked salmon (see Figure 4.70) should have a bright, deep colour and be moist when lightly pressed with the finger tip at the thickest part of the flesh. A perfectly smoked side of salmon will remain in good condition for not more than seven days when stored at a temperature of 18°C (64°F). This versatile food is used for canapés, hors d'oeuvre, sandwiches, and as a fish course for lunch, dinner or supper.
- **Snails:** Edible snails are raised on the foliage of the vine. They are obtainable in boxes that include the tinned snails and the cleaned shells. The snails are replaced in the shells with a mixture of butter, garlic, lemon juice and parsley, then heated in the oven and served in special dishes. Snails are also farmed in Britain.

CONFECTIONERY AND BAKERY GOODS

- **Cake covering:** This is produced from hardened vegetable fat with the addition of chocolate flavouring and colour.
- **Cape gooseberries:** A tasty, yellow-berried fruit resembling a large cherry. Cape gooseberries are often dipped in fondant and served as a petit four.
- **Chocolate vermicelli:** A ready-made preparation of small fine

chocolate pieces used in the decorating of small and large cakes and some chocolate-flavoured sweets.

- **Cocktail cherries:** Bright-red cherries preserved in a syrup, often flavoured with a liqueur known as maraschino. In addition to being used for cocktails they are also used to give colour to grapefruit and grapefruit cocktails.
- **Fondant:** A soft, white preparation of sugar that has many uses in pastry and confectionery work, chiefly for coating petits fours, pastries and gâteaux.
- **Gum tragacanth:** A soluble gum used for stiffening pastillage; only a very clear white type of gum tragacanth should be used. It is obtained from the shrubs of the genus *Astragalus*.
- **Honey:** A natural sugar produced by bees working upon the nectar of flowers. It is generally used in the form of a preserve and in pastry work.
- **Ice cream:** A frozen preparation of a well-flavoured, sweetened mixture, which can be made in many ways and in many flavours. Ice cream may be bought ready prepared, usually in 5-litre containers that are suitable for deep-freeze storage. The storage temperature for ice cream should not exceed -19°C (-32°F).
- **Jam:** A preserve of fruit and sugar obtainable in 28 g, 0.5 kg and 1 kg jars, and 3 kg tins. Raspberry and apricot jams are those most often used in the pastry.
- **Marmalade:** A preserve of citrus fruits and sugar, which is used mainly for breakfast menus and for certain sweets.
- **Marrons glacés:** Peeled and cooked chestnuts preserved in syrup. They are used in certain large and small cakes, sweet dishes and as a variety of petits fours.
- **Marzipan:** A preparation of ground almonds, sugar and egg yolks used in the making of petits fours, pastries and large cakes. Marzipan may be freshly made and is also obtained as a ready-prepared commodity.
- **Mincemeat:** A mixture of dried fruit, fresh fruit, sugar, spices, nuts, etc., chiefly used for mince pies. It can also be obtained in 0.5 kg and 1 kg jars, and 3 kg tins.
- **Pastillage (gum paste):** A mixture of icing sugar and gum tragacanth, which may be moulded into shapes for set pieces for cold buffets and also for making baskets, caskets, etc., for the serving of petits fours.
- **Piping jelly:** A thick jelly of piping consistency obtainable in different colours and flavours. It is used for decorating pastries and gâteaux and cold sweets. Piping jelly is obtainable in large tins.
- **Redcurrant jelly:** A clear preserve of redcurrants used as a jam as an accompaniment and also in the preparation of sauces.
- **Rennet:** A substance originally obtained from the stomachs of calves, pigs and lambs, but that can now be obtained in synthetic form. Rennet is prepared in powder, extract or essence form, and is used in

the production of cheese and for making junket. Vegetable rennet, for vegetarians, is also available.

- **Vanilla:** This is the dried pod of an orchid used for infusing mild sweet flavour into dishes. After use rinse the vanilla stick, dry and store in a sealed jar of castor sugar ready for reuse.
- **Wafers:** Thin, crisp biscuits of various shapes and sizes usually served with ice cream. They are obtainable in large tins of approximately 1000, and half-tins of approximately 500 wafers.

REFERENCES

Campbell, J., Foskett, D. and Ceserani, V. (2006) *Advanced Practical Cookery* (4th edn). London: Hodder Arnold.

Durkan, A. and Cousins, J.A. (1995) *The Beverage Book*. Hodder & Stoughton.

Foskett, D., Ceserani, V. and Kinton, R. with contributions by Campbell, J. (2004) *Practical Cookery* (10th edn). London: Hodder Arnold.

North American Meat Processors Association (2006) *The Meat Buyer's Guide*. John Wiley & Sons, Inc.

Some references to commodities elsewhere in the book:

TOPICS FOR DISCUSSION

1 Factors that affect the quality of meat.
2 Pros and cons of using meat substitutes such as TVP and Quorn.
3 Purchasing of meat (by carcass, joints or portion-controlled cuts).
4 Much of today's poultry lacks flavour. How can this be remedied?
5 The popularity of fish compared to meat and poultry.
6 The best ways to purchase fish.
7 Buying policy for vegetables and fruit.
8 The importance of vegetables and fruit in the diet.
9 Eggs and the caterer.
10 Compare the uses of butter, margarine or oil in cooking.
11 What is a sensible policy for selling cheese in a restaurant?
12 Is the average caterer sufficiently knowledgeable about the different types of flour and their suitability for specific purposes?
13 Should the caterer be offering a wider range of choice of teas and coffees?
14 The value of using pulses.
15 The value of using herbs and spices.

Chapter 5 ELEMENTARY NUTRITION, FOOD SCIENCE, DIET AND HEALTH

FOOD AND NUTRIENTS

A food is any substance, liquid or solid, that provides the body with materials for:

- heat and energy
- growth and repair
- regulating the body processes.

These materials are known as nutrients. They are:

- proteins
- vitamins
- fats
- minerals
- carbohydrates
- water.

The study of these nutrients is termed nutrition. Only those substances containing nutrients are foods (alcohol is an energy provider but it also has the effects of a drug, so it is not listed under nutrients). Most foods contain several nutrients; a few foods (such as sugar) contain only one nutrient.

For the body to obtain the maximum benefit from food it is essential that everyone concerned with the buying, storage, cooking and serving of food, and the compiling of menus should have some knowledge of nutrition.

Digestion

Digestion is the breaking down of food with the help of enzymes. Enzymes are proteins that speed up (catalyse) the breakdown processes (see Figure 5.1). Digestion takes place:

- in the mouth, where food is mixed with saliva, and starch is broken down by the action of an enzyme in saliva
- in the stomach, where the food is mixed and gastric juices are added, and proteins are broken down

Table 5.1 Foods containing the various nutrients and their use in the body

NUTRIENT	FOOD IN WHICH IT IS FOUND	USE IN BODY
Protein	Meat, fish, poultry, game, milk, cheese, eggs, pulses, cereals	For building and repairing body tissues; some heat and energy
Fat	Butter, margarine, cooking fat, oils, cheese, fat meat, oily fish	Provides heat and energy
Carbohydrate	Flour, flour products and cereals, sugar, syrup, jam, honey, fruit, vegetables	Provides heat and energy
Vitamin A	Oily fish, fish liver oil, dairy foods, carrots, tomatoes, greens	Helps growth; resistance to disease
Vitamin B1 – thiamin	Yeast, pulses, liver, whole grain, cereals, meat and yeast extracts	Helps growth; strengthens nervous system
Vitamin B2 – riboflavin	Yeast, liver, meat, meat extracts, wholegrain cereals	Helps growth, and helps in the production of energy
Nicotinic acid (niacin)	Yeast, meat, liver, meat extracts, wholegrain cereals	Helps growth
Vitamin C – ascorbic acid	Fruits such as strawberries, citrus fruits, green vegetables, root vegetables, salad	Helps growth, promotes health
Vitamin D (sunshine vitamin)	Fish liver oils, oily fish, dairy foods	Helps growth; builds bones and teeth
Iron	Lean meat, offal, egg yolk, wholemeal flour, green vegetables, fish	Building up the blood
Calcium (lime)	Milk and milk products, bones of fish, wholemeal bread	Building bones and teeth, clotting the blood, the working of the muscles
Phosphorus	Liver and kidney, eggs, cheese, bread	Building bones and teeth, regulating body processes
Sodium (salt)	Meat, eggs, fish, bacon, cheese	Prevention of muscular cramp

Table 5.2 The main functions of nutrients

ENERGY	GROWTH AND REPAIR	REGULATION OF BODY PROCESSES
Carbohydrates	Proteins	Vitamins
Fats	Minerals	Minerals
Proteins	Water	Water

- in the small intestine, where proteins, fats and carbohydrates are broken down further and additional juices added.
- in the large intestine, where bacteria attack undigested substances such as dietary fibre.

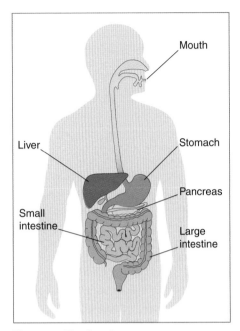

Figure 5.1 The digestive tract

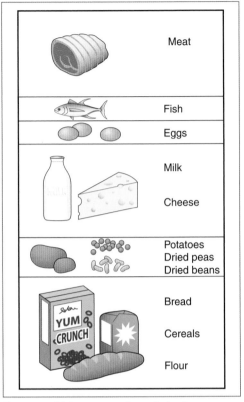

Figure 5.2 Main sources of protein in the average diet

Absorption

To enable the body to benefit from food it must be absorbed into the bloodstream; this absorption occurs after the food has been broken down; the product then passes through the walls of the digestive tract and into the bloodstream. This occurs in:

- the stomach, where simple substances, such as alcohol and glucose, are passed through the stomach lining into the bloodstream
- the small intestine, where more of the absorption of nutrients takes place due to a further breakdown of the food
- the large intestine, where water is reabsorbed from the waste.

Food should smell, look and taste attractive in order to stimulate the flow of saliva and digestive juices. This will help the digestive process and ensure that most food is broken down and absorbed. If digestion and absorption are not efficient this could lead to a deficiency of one or more nutrients and a state of malnutrition.

Protein

Protein is an essential part of all living matter; it is therefore needed for the growth of the body and for the repair of body tissues.

There are two kinds of protein:

1 animal protein
2 vegetable protein.

Animal protein is found in meat, game, poultry, fish, eggs, milk and cheese: myosin, collagen (meat, poultry and fish); albumin, ovovitellin (eggs); casein (milk and cheese).

Vegetable protein is found mainly in the seeds of vegetables. The proportion of protein in green and root vegetables is small. Peas, beans and nuts contain most protein, and the grain of cereals such as wheat has a useful amount because of the large quantity eaten – for example, gliadin and glutenin forming gluten with water (wheat and rye).

What is protein?

Protein is composed of amino acids; so the protein of cheese is different to the protein of meat because the number and arrangement of the acids are not the same. A certain number of these amino acids is essential to the body and must be provided by food. Proteins containing all the essential amino acids in the correct proportion are said to be of high biological value. The human body is capable of converting the other kinds of amino acids to suit its needs.

It is preferable that the body takes in both animal and vegetable protein, so that a complete variety of the necessary amino acids is available.

Table 5.3 The proportion of protein in some common foods

ANIMAL FOODS	PROTEIN (%)	PLANT FOODS	PROTEIN (%)
Cheese, Cheddar	26	Soya flour, low fat	45
Bacon, lean	20	Soya flour, full fat	37
Beef, lean	20	Peanuts	24
Cod	17	Bread, wholemeal	9
Herring	17	Bread, white	8
Eggs	12	Rice	7
Beef, fat	8	Peas, fresh	6
Milk	3	Potatoes, old	2
Cheese, cream	3	Bananas	1
Butter	<1	Apples	<1
		Tapioca	<1

Source: Fox and Cameron, 1995

During digestion, protein is split into amino acids; these are absorbed into the bloodstream and used for building body tissues and to provide some heat and energy.

Table 5.3 shows the proportion of protein in some common foods. It shows that there is no such thing as a pure protein food (i.e. one containing 100 per cent protein). Foods with even the highest content do not contain more than 45 per cent.

It follows that, because protein is needed for growth, growing children and expectant and nursing mothers will need more protein than other adults, whose requirements are mainly for repair. Any spare protein is used for producing heat and energy. In diets where protein intake is minimal, it is important that there is plenty of carbohydrate available so that protein is used for growth and repair, rather than for energy purposes.

Fats

What is fat?

Fats contain essential fatty acids that are essential to the diet. Edible fats are composed of glycerol with three fatty acids attached and are therefore called triglycerides.

There are three types of fatty acid:

1 monounsaturated
2 polyunsaturated
3 saturated.

These different types give different properties to different fats (e.g. butyric acid in butter, oleic acid in most oils, and stearic acid in solid fats such as beef suet).

Hard fats are mainly of animal origin and contain more saturated fatty acids, while, in comparison, oils and soft fats contain more polyunsaturated acids.

To be useful to the body, fats have to be broken down into glycerol and fatty acids so that they can be absorbed; they can then provide heat and energy. The food value of the various kinds of fats is similar, although some animal fats contain fat-soluble vitamins A and D. The function of fat is to protect vital organs of the body and to provide heat and energy; certain fats also provide vitamins and add flavour and texture to food.

There are two main groups of fats: animal and vegetable. Fats can be divided into:

• solid fat
• oils (fat that is liquid at room temperature).

Table 5.4 Percentage of saturated fat in an average diet*

Milk, cheese, cream	16.0
Meat and meat products	25.2
Other oils and fats	30.0
Other sources, including eggs, fish, poultry	7.4
Biscuits and cakes	11.4
The 25.2% for meat and meat products split down into:	
Other meat products	9.1
Beef	4.1
Lamb	3.5
Pork, bacon and ham	5.8
Sausage	2.7

* *A diet high in saturated fat is associated with an increased risk of heart disease*

Fats are obtained from the following foods (see also Table 5.4):

* animal origin – dripping, butter, suet, lard, cheese, cream, bacon, meat fat, oily fish
* vegetable origin – margarine, cooking fat, nuts, soya beans.

Oils are obtained from the following foods:

* animal origin – halibut and cod liver oil
* vegetable origin – from seeds or nuts.

The contribution of animal fat in the western diet is gradually changing as healthy eating policies encourage a reduction in total fat intake, particularly animal fats. There has been a swing towards skimmed milk, leaner cuts of meat, cooking with vegetable oils, and a reduced market for eggs, high-fat cheeses and butter.

Fats should be eaten with other foods such as bread, potatoes, etc., as they can then be more easily digested and utilised in the body.

Certain fish – such as herrings, mackerel, salmon and sardines –

Table 5.5 Sources of saturated and unsaturated fats

High in saturated fats	Dairy products	Butter, cream, milk, cheese
	Meat	Liver, lamb, beef, pork
	Others	Coconut oil, palm kernel oil, palm oil, hard margarine, lard
High in polyunsaturated fats	Vegetable oils	Corn (maize) oil, soya bean oil, safflower seed oil, sunflower seed oil
	Nuts	Most, except coconut and cashew nuts
	Margarines	Many soft varieties especially soya bean and sunflower seed

Source: Fox and Cameron, 1995

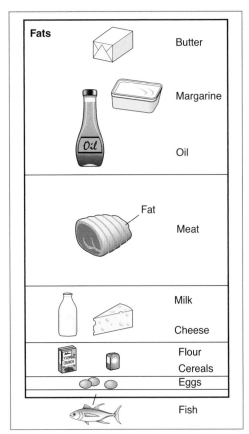

Figure 5.3 Main sources of fat in the average diet

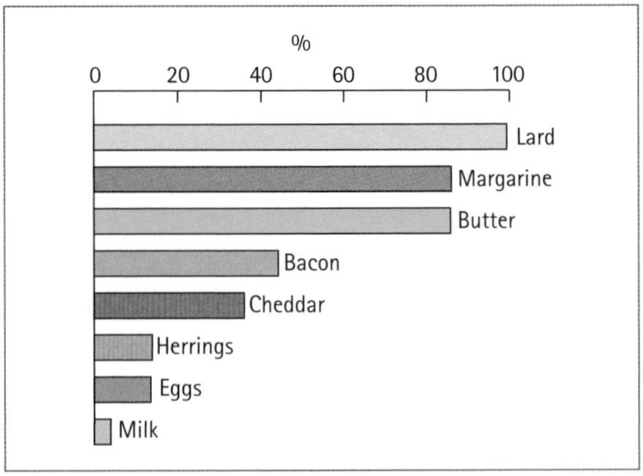

Figure 5.4 Proportion of fat in some foods

contain oil (fat) in the flesh. A type of fat that is increasingly popular as a dietary supplement is omega-3, which can be found in the flesh of oily fish. Other fish, such as cod and halibut, contain the oil in the liver.

Vegetables and fruit contain very little fat, but nuts have a considerable amount.

Carbohydrates

What are carbohydrates?
Carbohydrates are made up by plants and then either used by plants as energy or eaten by animals or humans for energy. Carbohydrates are made up of sugar molecules.

There are three main types of carbohydrate:

1 sugar (saccharide)
2 starch (polysaccharide)
3 cellulose (fibre).

The function of carbohydrates is to provide the body with most of its

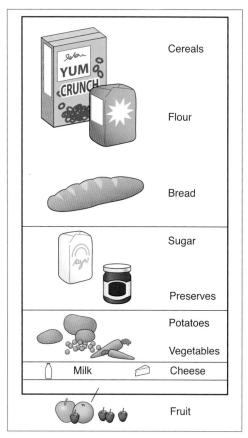

Figure 5.5 Main sources of carbohydrates in the average diet

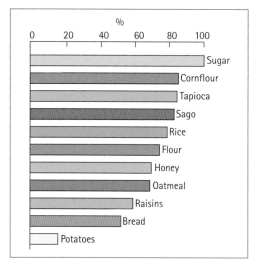

Figure 5.6 Proportion of carbohydrate in some foods

energy. Starch is composed of a number of glucose molecules (particles), and during digestion starch is broken down into glucose.

Sugar

There are several kinds of sugar:

- glucose – found in the blood of animals and in fruit and honey
- fructose – found in fruit, honey and cane sugar
- sucrose – found in beet and cane sugar
- lactose – found in milk
- maltose – produced naturally during the germination of grain.

Sugars are the simplest form of carbohydrate and the end products of the digestion of carbohydrates. They are absorbed in the form of glucose and simple sugars, and used to provide heat and energy.

Starch
Starch is present in the diet through the following foods:

- whole grains – rice, barley, tapioca
- powdered grains – flour, cornflour, ground rice, arrowroot
- vegetables – potatoes, parsnips, peas, beans
- unripe fruit – bananas, apples, cooking pears
- cereals – cornflakes, shredded wheat, etc.
- cooked starch – cakes, biscuits, bread
- pastas – macaroni, spaghetti, vermicelli, etc.

Cellulose
Cellulose is the coarser structure of vegetables and cereals, which is not digested but is used as roughage in the intestine. It is often now referred to as dietary fibre.

Vitamins

What are vitamins?
Vitamins are chemical substances found in small amounts in many foods. They are vital for life, and if the diet is deficient in any vitamin, ill health results. As they are chemical substances they can be produced synthetically.

General function of vitamins
Vitamins assist the regulation of the body processes:

- to help the growth of children
- to protect against disease.

Vitamin A
Vitamin A:

- assists in children's growth
- helps the body to resist infection
- enables people to see better in the dark.

Vitamin A is fat soluble; therefore it is to be found in fatty foods. It can be made in the body from carotene, the yellow substance found in many fruits and vegetables.

Dark-green vegetables are a good source of vitamin A, the green colour masking the yellow of the carotene. Carotene is gradually destroyed by light (hence the fading of orange-coloured spices and vegetables on prolonged storage).

At very high levels, vitamin A can be toxic.

Sources of vitamin A are:

- halibut liver oil
- milk
- butter
- watercress

- cod liver oil
- herrings
- kidney
- carrots
- liver
- spinach
- margarine (to which vitamin A is added)
- tomatoes
- cheese
- apricots
- eggs.

Fish liver oils have the most vitamin A. The amount of vitamin A in dairy produce varies. Because cattle eat fresh grass in summer and stored feedstuffs in winter, the dairy produce contains the highest amount of vitamin A in the summer. Kidney and liver are also useful sources of vitamin A.

Vitamin D

Vitamin D controls the use the body makes of calcium. It is therefore necessary for healthy bones and teeth. Like vitamin A it is fat soluble.

An important source of vitamin D is from the action of sunlight on the deeper layers of the skin (approximately 75 per cent of our vitamin D comes from this source). Other sources include:

- fish liver oils
- oily fish
- egg yolk
- margarine (to which vitamin D is added)
- dairy produce.

Vitamin B

When first discovered vitamin B was thought to be one substance only; it is now known to consist of at least 11 substances, the two main ones being:

1 thiamin (B1)
2 riboflavin (B2).

Others include folic acid and pyridoxine (B6).

Vitamin B is water soluble and can be lost during cooking; it is required to:

- keep the nervous system in good condition
- enable the body to obtain energy from the carbohydrates
- encourage the growth of the body.

Vitamin C (ascorbic acid)

Vitamin C:

- is necessary for the growth of children
- assists in the healing of cuts and the uniting of broken bones
- prevents gums and mouth infection.

Vitamin C is water soluble and can be lost during cooking or soaking in water. It is also lost through poor storage (keeping foods for too long, bruising or storing in a badly ventilated place) and by cutting vegetables into small pieces.

Table 5.6 Sources of vitamin B

THIAMIN (B1)	RIBOFLAVIN (B2)	NICOTINIC ACID
Yeast	Yeast	Meat extract
Bacon	Liver	Brewers' yeast
Oatmeal	Meat extract	Liver
Peas	Cheese	Kidney
Wholemeal bread	Egg	Beef

Sources of vitamin C include:

- blackcurrants
- potatoes
- Brussels sprouts and other greens
- strawberries
- lemons
- oranges
- grapefruit
- tomatoes
- bananas
- fruit juices.

The major sources in the British diet are potatoes and green vegetables.

Figure 5.7 Main sources of vitamins in the average diet

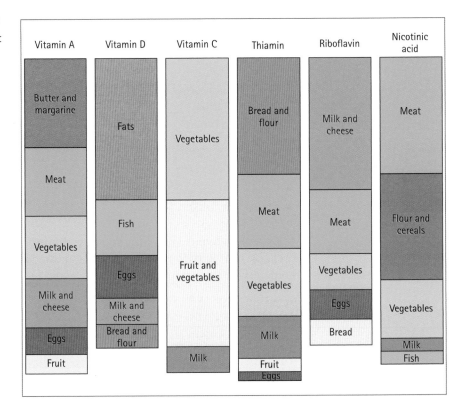

Table 5.7 Cooking times and vitamin C retention for some common foods

COOKING TIME (MINS)	% RETENTION OF VITAMIN C DURING BOILING			
	Brussels sprouts	Cabbage	Carrots	Potatoes
20	49	–	35	–
30	36	70–78	22	53–56
60	–	53–58	–	40–50
90	–	13	–	17

Source: Fox and Cameron, 1995

MINERAL ELEMENTS

What are mineral elements?

There are 19 mineral elements, most of which are required by the body in very small quantities. The body has, at certain times, a greater demand for certain mineral elements and there is a danger then of a deficiency in the diet. Calcium, iron and iodine are those most likely to be deficient.

Calcium
Calcium is required for:

- building bones and teeth
- clotting of the blood
- the working of the muscles.

   The use the body makes of calcium is dependent on the presence of vitamin D.

   Calcium can be found in:

- milk and milk products
- bones of tinned oily fish
- vegetables (greens)
- drinking water
- wholemeal bread and white bread (to which calcium is added).

Note that it is still the practice to add calcium, iron, thiamin and nicotinic acid to flour despite the findings of DHSS Report No. 23 (1981) which recommended that this practice should be discontinued.

   Although calcium is present in certain foods (spinach, cereals) the body is unable to make use of it as it is not in a soluble form and therefore cannot be absorbed.

   Because of the need for growth of bones and teeth, infants, adolescents, expectant and nursing mothers have a greater demand for calcium.

Phosphorus

Phosphorus is required for:

- building bones and teeth (in conjunction with calcium and vitamin D)
- the control of the structure of the brain cells.

Sources of phosphorus include:

- liver
- bread
- cheese

- eggs
- kidney
- fish.

Iron

Iron is required for building haemoglobin in the blood and is therefore necessary for transporting oxygen and carbon dioxide round the body.

Sources of iron include:

- lean meat
- wholemeal flour
- offal

- green vegetables
- egg yolk
- fish.

Iron is most easily absorbed from meat and offal, and its absorption is helped by the presence of vitamin C.

Iron may also be present in drinking water and obtained from iron utensils in which food is prepared.

As the haemoglobin in the blood should be maintained at a constant level, the body requires more iron at certain times than others (e.g. after loss of blood).

Sodium

Sodium is required in all body fluids, and is found in salt (sodium chloride). Excess salt is continually lost from the body in urine. The kidneys control this loss. We also lose sodium in sweating, a loss over which we have no control.

Sodium levels in processed foods have been highlighted in recent years by the government as being too high. Too much salt in the diet can lead to hypertension and heart disease. The Food Standards Agency (FSA) has now set salt targets for processed retail foods in order to control this area of health.

Many foods are cooked with salt or have salt added (bacon and cheese) or contain salt (meat, eggs, fish). Excess sodium can cause hypertension (high blood pressure) in middle age.

Iodine

Iodine is required for the functioning of the thyroid gland which regulates basal metabolism (see page 197).

Sources of iodine include:

- sea foods
- iodised salt
- drinking water obtained near the sea
- vegetables grown near the sea.

Figure 5.8 Main sources of iron and calcium in the average diet

Other minerals
Potassium, magnesium, sulphur and copper are some of the other minerals required by the body.

Water
Water is required for:

- regulation of body temperatures by evaporation of perspiration
- all body fluids
- metabolism
- digestion
- excretion
- absorption
- secretion.

Sources of water include:

- drinks of all kinds
- foods, such as fruits and vegetables, meat, eggs
- combustion or oxidation – when fats, carbohydrates and protein are used for energy, a certain amount of water (metabolic water) is produced within the body.

THE EFFECTS OF COOKING ON NUTRIENTS

Some foods are best eaten when freshly harvested, without further preparation or cooking. Fruit such as bananas, and vegetables such as tomatoes and lettuce fall into this category. Cooking and storage over prolonged periods reduces the nutritional value of these foods.

With the above exceptions, the digestibility of most foods is enhanced through cooking.

Protein

When protein is heated it coagulates and shrinks. Too much cooking can spoil the appearance of the food, such as scrambled eggs, as well as causing destruction of certain vitamins. On being heated, the different proteins in foods set, or coagulate, at different temperatures; above these temperatures shrinkage occurs; this is particularly noticeable in grilling or roasting meat. Moderately cooked protein is the most easy to digest: a lightly cooked egg is more easily digested than a raw egg or a hard-boiled egg.

Carbohydrate

Unless starch is cooked thoroughly it cannot be digested properly (e.g. insufficiently cooked pastry or bread). Foods containing starch have cells with starch granules, covered with a cellulose wall that breaks down when heated or made moist, making the starch digestible (this is called gelatinisation of starch).

When browned – for example, the crust of bread, toast, roast potatoes or the skin of rice pudding – the starch forms dextrins and these taste sweeter. This is known as the caramelisation of sugar.

On heating with water or milk, the starch gelatinises and causes the food to thicken (i.e. thickening of gravy).

Fat

The nutritive value of fat is not affected by cooking. During cooking processes a certain amount of fat may be lost from food when the fat melts, such as in the grilling of meat.

Mineral elements

There is a possibility of some minerals being lost in the cooking liquor, so diminishing the amount available in the food. This applies to soluble minerals, such as salt, but not to calcium or iron compounds, which do not dissolve in the cooking liquor.

Iron
Iron may be acquired from foods cooked in iron utensils. The iron in foods is not affected by cooking.

Calcium
Cooking foods in hard water may very slightly increase the amount of calcium in food.

Vitamins

- Vitamins A and D withstand cooking temperatures, and are not lost in the cooking.
- Vitamin B1 (thiamin) can be destroyed by high temperatures and by the use of bicarbonate of soda. It is soluble in water and can be lost in the cooking.
- Vitamin B2 (riboflavin) is not destroyed easily by heat, but bright sunlight can break it down.
- Vitamin C is lost by cooking and by keeping food warm in a hot place. It is also soluble in water (the soaking of foods for a long time and bruising are the causes of losing vitamin C). It is unstable and therefore easily destroyed in alkaline conditions (bicarbonate of soda must not be used when cooking green vegetables).

FOOD REQUIREMENTS

Energy is required to enable the heart to beat, for the blood to circulate, the lungs and other organs of the body to function, for every activity such as talking, eating, standing, sitting, and for strenuous exercise and muscular activity.

Young and active people require a different amount of food from elderly, inactive people because they expend more energy; this energy is obtained from food during chemical changes taking place in the body.

The energy value of a food is measured by a term called a kilocalorie or Calorie (strictly speaking, this term should be written with a capital C although popularly is often written with a small c). This is the amount of heat required to raise the temperature of 1000 g of water from 15 to 16°C.

A new unit is now gradually replacing the Calorie. This is the joule. Since the joule is too small for practical nutrition, the kilojoule (kJ) is used:

1 Calorie=4.18 kJ

(Both units will be given here and, for ease of conversion, 1 Calorie will be taken to equal 4.0 kJ.)

Foods contain certain amounts of the various nutrients, which are measured in grammes.

Table **5.8** Reference nutrient intakes (RNIs) for protein, vitamins and minerals

AGE	PROTEIN G/DAY	VITAMIN A MG/DAY	THIAMIN MG/DAY	RIBOFLAVIN MG/DAY	
0–3 months	12.5	350	0.2	0.4	
4–6 months	12.7	350	0.2	0.4	
7–9 months	13.7	350	0.2	0.4	
10–12 months	14.9	350	0.3	0.4	
1–3 years	14.5	400	0.5	0.6	
4–6 years	19.7	500	0.7	0.8	
7–10 years	28.3	500	0.7	1.0	
Males					
11–14 years	42.1	600	0.9	1.2	
15–18 years	55.2	700	1.1	1.3	
19–50 years	55.5	700	1.0	1.3	
50+ years	53.3	700	0.9	1.3	
Females					
11–14 years	41.2	600	0.7	1.1	
15–18 years	45.0	600	0.8	1.1	
19–50 years	45.0	600	0.8	1.1	
50+ years	46.5	600	0.8	1.1	
Pregnancy	+6	+100	+0.1*	+0.3	
Lactation	+11	+350	+0.2	+0.5	

= for last three months only
**= 10 μg/day after age 65 years*
Reprinted from The Science of Food (4th edn), P. M. Gaman and K. B. Sherrington, copyright 1998, with permission from Elsevier

The energy value of nutrients is as follows:

- 1 g carbohydrate produces 4 Calories (16 kJ)
- 1 g protein produces 4 Calories (16 kJ)
- 1 g fat produces 9 Calories (36 kJ).

The energy value of a food, diet or menu is calculated from the nutrients it contains; 28 g of food containing:

- 10 g carbohydrate will produce 10 x 4 = 40 Calories (160 kJ)
- 2 g protein will produce 2 x 4 = 8 Calories (32 kJ)
- 5 g fat will produce 5 x 9 = 45 Calories (180 kJ)
- total – 93 Calories (372 kJ).

Foods having a high fat content will have a high energy value; those containing a lot of water, a low energy value. All fats, cheese, bacon and other foods with a high fat content have a high energy value.

	NIACIN MG/DAY	FOLATE MG/DAY	VITAMIN C MG/DAY	VITAMIN D MG/DAY	CALCIUM MG/DAY	IRON MG/DAY
	3	50	25	8.5	525	1.7
	3	50	25	8.5	525	4.3
	4	50	25	7	525	7.8
	5	50	25	7	525	7.8
	8	70	30	7	350	6.9
	11	100	30	–	450	6.1
	12	150	30	–	550	8.7
	15	200	35	–	1000	11.3
	18	200	40	–	1000	11.3
	17	200	40	–	700	8.7
	16	200	40	**	700	8.7
	12	200	35	–	800	14.8
	14	200	40	–	800	14.8
	13	200	40	–	700	14.8
	12	200	40	**	700	8.7
	+0	+100	+10	10	+0	+0
	+2	+60	+30	10	+550	+0

Men require more Calories (kJ) than women; big men and women require more than small men and women; people engaged in energetic work require more Calories (kJ) than those with sedentary occupations.

BASAL METABOLISM

Basal metabolism is the term given to the amount of energy required to maintain the functions of the body, and to keep the body warm when it is still and without food. The number of Calories (kJ) required for basal metabolism is affected by the size, sex and general condition of the body. The number of Calories (kJ) required for basal metabolism is approximately 1700 per day.

In addition to the energy required for basal metabolism, energy is also required for everyday activities, such as getting up, dressing and walking; the amount required will be closely related to a person's occupation.

The approximate energy requirements per day for the following examples are:

- clerk – 2000 Calories (8000 kJ)
- carpenter – 3000 Calories (12,000 kJ)
- labourer – 4000 Calories (16,000 kJ).

VALUE OF FOODS IN THE DIET

Dairy products

Dairy products are a very important group of foods. Not only do they contain protein, carbohydrates and fat, but they are also a good source of calcium and vitamins.

Milk
Milk is designed by nature to be a complete food for young animals and humans. Cows' milk is almost the perfect food for humans due to its nutritional value.

When milk is taken into the body it coagulates in the same way as in the making of junket. This occurs in the stomach, when digestive juices (containing the enzyme rennin) are added. Souring of milk is due to the bacteria feeding on the milk sugar (lactose) and producing lactic acid from it, which brings about curdling.

Composition of milk
The approximate composition of milk is as follows:
- 87 per cent water
- 3–4 per cent proteins (mostly casein)
- 3–4 per cent fat
- 4–5 per cent sugar
- 0.7 per cent minerals (particularly calcium)
- Vitamins A, B and D (the vitamin content varies from season to season, and according to breed of cow and preservation method).

Table 5.9 The nutrient composition of creams per 100 g

TYPE	ENERGY (KJ)	PROTEIN (G)	FAT (G)	CARBOHYDRATE (G)	SODIUM (MG)	CALCIUM (MG)
Half cream	568	2.8	12.3	4.1	55	96
Single cream	813	2.6	19.1	3.9	50	91
Whipping cream	1536	2.0	39.3	3.0	42	62
Double cream	1847	1.7	48.0	2.6	39	50

Source: Fox and Cameron, 1995

In Channel Islands milk (Jersey and Guernsey) the percentage of fat must be 4 per cent; in all other milk the minimum is 3 per cent.

Milk is a body-building food because of its protein content, an energy food because of the fat and sugar it contains, and a protective food as it contains vitamins and minerals. Because of its high water content, while it is a suitable food for infants, it is too bulky to be the main source of protein and other nutrients after the first few months of life. It is also deficient in iron and vitamin C. However, it may be included in everyone's diet as a drink and can be used in a variety of ways.

Skimmed milk, which has had the cream layer removed, is increasing in popularity. Not only does it provide a lower calorie intake for those watching their weight, but also the potentially harmful animal fat has been removed.

Cream

Cream is the fat of milk; the legal minimum fat content of single cream is approximately 18 per cent, for double cream 48 per cent and clotted cream 60 per cent. Cream is therefore an energy-producing food, which also supplies vitamins A and D. It is easily digested because the fat is in a highly emulsified form (i.e. the fat globules are very small).

Butter

Butter is made from the fat of milk and contains vitamins A and D, the amount depending on the season. Like cream, it is easily digested.

Composition of butter
The approximate composition of butter is:

- 84 per cent fat
- 1 per cent salt
- 15 per cent water
- vitamins A and D.

Butter is also an energy-producing food, and a protective food in so far as it provides vitamins A and D.

Cheese

Cheese is made from milk; its composition varies according to whether the cheese has been made from whole milk, skimmed milk or milk to which extra cream has been added.

The composition of Cheddar cheese is approximately:

- 40 per cent fat
- calcium
- 30 per cent water
- vitamins A and D
- 25 per cent protein.

The food value of cheese is exceptional because of the concentration of the various nutrients it contains. The minerals in cheese are useful, particularly calcium and phosphorus. Cheese is also a source of vitamins A and D.

It is a body-building, energy-producing and protective food because of its protein, fat and mineral elements, and vitamin content.

Cheese is easily digested, provided it is eaten with starchy foods and eaten in small pieces as when grated.

Margarine

Margarine, which is made from animal and/or vegetable oils, and skimmed milk, has vitamins A and D added to it. The composition and food value of margarine are similar to those for butter.

Meat, poultry and game

Meat consists of fibres, which may be short, as in a fillet of beef, or long, as in silverside of beef. Generally, the shorter the fibre the more tender and easily digested the meat. However, it is the cooking method that makes the most difference. Meat is carved across the grain to assist mastication and digestion of the fibres.

Hanging the meat helps to make the flesh more tender; this is because acids develop and soften the muscle fibres. Marinating in wine or vinegar prior to cooking also helps to tenderise meat so that it is more digestible. Expensive cuts of meat are not necessarily more nourishing than the cheaper cuts.

Meat is a very good source of protein and has variable amounts of fat, water, iron and thiamin, depending on the species and cut. Meat is a poor provider of calcium and vitamin C. Bacon and pork, in general, are particularly valuable because of their thiamin content. Red meat is a good source of iron, while poultry generally has a lower fat content, especially once the skin has been removed. Meat of all kinds is therefore important as a body-building food.

Fish

Fish is as useful a source of animal protein as meat.

The amount of fat in different fish varies: oily fish contain 5–18 per cent, white fish less than 2 per cent.

When the bones are eaten, calcium is obtained from fish (tinned sardines or salmon).

Oily fish is not so easily digested as white fish because of the fat content; shellfish is not easily digested because of the coarseness of the fibres.

Fish is important for body-building, and certain types of fish (oily fish) supply more energy and are protective because of the fat and vitamins A and D contained in the fish.

Eggs

The egg can store sufficient nutrients to supply a developing embryo with everything required for its growth.

Egg white contains protein called albumin (not to be confused with albumen, which is another name for the white of the egg itself) and the amount of white is approximately twice the amount of yolk.

The white is approximately one-eighth protein and seven-eighths water. In comparison the yolk is about one-third fats, half water, one-sixth protein, and a mixture of vitamins and minerals such as vitamins A and D, thiamin, riboflavin, calcium, iron, sulphur and phosphorus. All these factors make eggs a body-building, protective and energy-producing food. Eggs are also a rich source of cholesterol.

Fruit

The composition of different fruit varies considerably: avocado pears contain about 20 per cent fat, whereas most other fruits contain none. In unripe fruit the carbohydrate is in the form of starch, which changes to sugar as the fruit ripens. The cellulose in fruits acts as a source of dietary fibre.

Fruit is valuable because of the vitamins and minerals it contains. Vitamin C is present in certain fruits, particularly citrus varieties (oranges, grapefruit), blackcurrants and other summer fruits. Dried fruits such as raisins and sultanas are a useful source of energy because of their sugar content, but they contain no vitamin C. The vitamin C in fruit is lost during storage. Frozen fruit maintains its vitamin C content during freezing.

Composition of fruit
The approximate composition of fruit is:

- 85 per cent water
- 0.5 per cent minerals
- 5–10 per cent carbohydrate
- varying amounts of vitamin C
- 2–5 per cent cellulose.

Very small amounts of fat and protein are found in most fruits. Fruit is a protective food because of its mineral and vitamin content.

Nuts

Nuts are highly nutritious because of the protein, fat and minerals they contain. Vegetarians may rely on nuts to provide the protein in their diet.

Nuts are not easily digested because of their fat and cellulose content.

Vegetables

Green vegetables

Green vegetables are particularly valuable because of their vitamin and mineral content; they are therefore protective foods. The most important minerals they contain are iron and calcium. Green vegetables are rich in carotene, which is made into vitamin A in the body.

The greener the vegetable, the greater its nutritional value. Vegetables that are stored for long periods, or that are damaged or bruised, quickly lose their vitamin C value, therefore they should be used as quickly as possible.

Green vegetables also act as a source of dietary fibre in the intestines. Onions and leeks are also green vegetables. The main value of onions is to add flavour rather than any major nutritional benefit.

Root vegetables

Compared with green vegetables most root vegetables contain more starch and sugar; they are therefore a source of energy. Swedes and turnips contain a little vitamin C, and carrots and other yellow-coloured vegetables contain carotene, which is changed into vitamin A in the body.

Potatoes

Potatoes contain a large amount of starch (approximately 20 per cent) and a small amount of protein just under the skin. Because of the large quantities eaten, the small amount of vitamin C they contain is of value in the diet.

Onions

The onion is used extensively and contains some sugar, but its main value is to provide flavour.

Peas and broad beans

These vegetables contain carbohydrate, protein and carotene.

Cereals

Cereals include wheat and wheat products.

Cereals contain from 60 to 80 per cent carbohydrate in the form of starch and are therefore energy foods. They also contain 7–13 per cent protein, depending on the type of cereal, and 1–8 per cent fat.

The vitamin B content is considerable in stoneground and wholemeal flour, and B vitamins are added to other wheat flours, as are calcium and iron salts.

Oats contain good quantities of fat and protein.

Of all cereals in the British diet, bread is by far the most important. The government fortifies flour (not wholemeal) with calcium, iron, thiamin and niacin to improve its nutritional value.

Sugar

There are several kinds of sugar, such as those found in fruit (glucose), milk (lactose), cane and beet sugar (sucrose).

Sugar, with fat, provides the most important part of the body's energy requirements.

Saccharin, although sweet, is chemically produced and has no food value.

Liquids

Water

Certain waters contain mineral salts; hard waters contain soluble salts of calcium. Some spas are known for the mineral salts contained in the local water. Bottled natural mineral waters are sold in many places (particularly supermarkets), and are being used more widely in the catering industry and in the home. Fluoride may be present naturally in some waters, and makes children's teeth more resistant to decay.

Fruit juices

In recent years there has been a tremendous increase in the consumption of fruit juices sold in cartons as a chilled drink or in 'long life' form, which will keep almost indefinitely before being opened. In addition, freshly squeezed orange juice is a popular alternative drink in many places, including airport and rail terminal restaurants.

The nutritional value of fruit juices is very similar to that of whole fruit as they are produced by extracting the juice from fresh fruit. In recent years, there has been a tremendous increase in the consumption of fruit juices sold in the UK because they are an easy source of vitamin C, and the increase in the number of juices sold in individual cartons, either chilled or long life, has made them very convenient.

Tea, coffee and cocoa

Tea and coffee have no food value in themselves, but the caffeine in them acts as a stimulant on the nervous system, therefore helping prevent fatigue.

Cocoa contains some fat, starch and protein, also some vitamin B and mineral elements.

When tea, coffee and cocoa are served with milk and sugar they do have some food value.

Alcoholic beverages

Alcohol must be considered as a foodstuff because it provides the body with energy. The energy value of wine is the same as that of milk, but without the nutritional benefit. Alcohol is a drug and affects the central nervous system. The effect of alcohol can range from mild stimulation to – if consumed in large quantities and over a long period of time – death.

CATERING FOR HEALTH

Practical guidance on healthier catering

Concern that many catering courses include little information about nutrition led to the publication of guidance by the FSA and the Department of Health: *Catering for Health: A Guide to Teaching Healthier Catering Practices* (see the 'References' section on page 233 for details of how to obtain a copy).

Encourage a balanced diet

Food intake needs to provide the vitamins, minerals, protein and fibre the body requires, without too much fat, sugar and salt. Following the widely accepted model of five food groups, 'the balance of good health' (see Figure 1.13), developed in 1994 by the Health Education Authority, the Department of Health and the Department for Environment, Food and Rural Affairs means, for most people:

1 starchy foods (a third of total food intake)
2 fruit and vegetables (a further third of total food intake) – five portions of a variety of fruit and vegetables each day; a portion would be any of the following – half a large grapefruit, a whole apple, orange or banana, two plums, small bunch of grapes, half to one tablespoon of dried fruit, two to three tablespoons of cooked or canned fruit, two tablespoons of raw, cooked, frozen or canned vegetables, a bowl of salad, a glass of fruit juice (not more than one per day)
3 meat, fish and other non-dairy sources of protein (moderate amounts only)
4 milk and dairy foods (moderate amounts only)
5 foods containing fat and foods containing sugar (relatively small amounts only); fats that contain a small proportion of saturates and a high proportion of unsaturates (polyunsaturates or monounsaturates) are better for health.

To follow these guidelines, most people need to increase by half their intake of starchy food, double the amount of fruit and vegetables they eat, and substantially reduce their intake of fat and sugar. Most people also need to cut down the amount of salt in their diet.

Caterers can assist customers to achieve a more balanced diet, within the parameters of their eating-out experience. When the customer base is all or mostly captive – in a home for the elderly, hospital, boarding school, the armed forces, workers on an oil rig, and so on – there are three meals a day, and a menu cycle that can be viewed over a week or fortnight. So, for example, the number of red meat main courses can be limited to two or three days a week, while fish is offered on one or two days a week. A variety of fruit can be included in all meals, with perhaps fruit juice or grapefruit segments at breakfast; so can starchy foods, with cereals and/or porridge at breakfast, and bread rolls.

Vegetables and salads can feature more prominently for midday and evening meals. Dishes relatively high in fat and sugar can be limited to treats, perhaps once a week.

When the customer base is transient – as in most restaurants, pubs, wine bars, hotels, cafés, and so on – the menu choice can be varied to offer, say, a pasta dish, white meat and fish as well as red meat, dishes that are low in fat, interesting vegetables and salads, and imaginative, appealing dishes based on these. Alternatives might be offered to all-time favourites: a baked jacket potato with a salad garnish as an alternative to French fries with the main course.

Healthy catering by stealth has more chance of success than any attempt to corral customers into a better lifestyle, unless you are confident of reaching the quite narrow market segment that wants only healthy dishes. Just as high-street retailers do with sandwiches and snacks aimed at the lunchtime market, it may work well to brand one or two dishes as healthy choices. But this description could deter sales where the customers are eating out for a celebration, leisure or entertainment. Fashion and peer pressure play a powerful role in influencing what is acceptable.

Bear in mind your customers' approach to food

Customers' approach to food is through experience, education, background, sophistication, travel, and so on. Some people enjoy experimenting, others don't. Some enjoy wholegrain pastas, rice and bread, for example, while others won't touch them. Healthy catering should not be introduced in such a way that it alienates people.

Even where there is quite strong customer resistance, subtle changes can be introduced over time, if necessary, to the content, presentation and service of favourite dishes.

Adapt recipes, preparation and cooking methods

With thought and skill, a substantial contribution can be made to a balanced diet without loss of flavour or texture, or restricting customer choice. Nor should it jeopardise operating margins. Indeed the process, by encouraging creativity, could lead to improved profits, with high added value yet less expensive ingredients.

There are many practical changes that can be made to the way food is prepared and cooked, which will lead to a healthier choice for your customers. To get the best results, some trialling and experimentation is recommended.

Possibilities include the following

- **Adapt recipes:** use alternative flavourings to salt and proprietary products high in salt; reduce quantities of fat/oil; replace butter with olive oil or a mixture of butter and olive oil; thicken with purées of vegetables/fruit/pulses, or potatoes in place of a roux; enrich with lower-/reduced-fat products; use natural fruit juice to sweeten; use wholemeal with white flour for pastry.

- **Adjust preparation methods:** trim visible fat, remove poultry skin; leave skin on potatoes, vegetables and fruit (to increase fibre content and reduce vitamin loss); use chunky/thick cuts (to reduce fat absorption/vitamin loss).
- **Selected ingredients:** lean cuts and joints of meat; skinless poultry; fish rich in oils beneficial to health (e.g. salmon, mackerel, herring, trout); white fish (very little fat); prepared dishes that can be oven baked or grilled instead of fried; unsugared breakfast cereals; fruit juices and products in their natural juices/unsweetened; oils, fats and spreads that are high in monounsaturates or polyunsaturates; pre-prepared and convenience products that are low in salt/sugar/fat.
- **Change to low-fat cooking methods:** grill, bake, poach, microwave, stir-fry (quick cooking, minimum oil), shallow-fry in non-stick pans (to use less oil), steam chips to blanch.
- **For vegetables:** favour cooking methods that reduce vitamin loss – steam, microwave or stir-fry, cook in small batches (to reduce hot holding time).

Marketing and presentation

Describe dishes and menu choices in ways that will appeal to your customers. Avoid terms like 'health', 'low in fat', 'low in saturates', especially if your customers are eating out for enjoyment. Emphasise the positive: unusual flavours and combinations, freshly cooked, tasty, satisfying, interesting textures, colourful garnishes, exotic ingredients, associations with foreign travel, ethnic cuisines, and so on.

Feature as dishes of the day, special promotions, house specialities, and in counter and buffet display those dishes that have been prepared and cooked according to healthy catering guidelines.

Expand the choice of accompaniments and sauces to give appealing, healthier alternatives to those that are high in fat or sugar. Choose garnishes that increase the starch, fibre, vegetable and/or fruit content.

Include healthy additions in the price, such as a granary or wholemeal roll with soup, fresh fruit with a sandwich or lunchtime snack, rice or naan bread with a curry. Select healthy choices for promotional offers.

Involve your staff: brief them on the dish content so that descriptions are appealing and accurate, and questions can be answered helpfully.

Take care not to use misleading or false descriptions, or terms that have a specific legal meaning under the food labelling regulations, such as 'low fat', 'reduced fat', 'low salt'.

The National Diet and Nutrition Survey

This survey, conducted by the Department of Health (1 June 2000), sampled over 1700 young people, representative of the UK population as a whole. Their physical measurements, patterns of food consumption and levels of physical activity over a period of a week were measured. The main findings were that young people were eating insufficient amounts of fruit and vegetables to maintain a balanced diet, resulting in serious shortages of bone-strengthening minerals in both males and females, which could result in osteoporosis in later life. Lack of iron in the oldest girls suggests that anaemia is a major problem; lack of zinc contributes to an overall deterioration of health and the immune system.

The most popular foods were white bread, savoury snacks, chips, biscuits, boiled, mashed and jacket potatoes and chocolate confectionery. The most commonly consumed meats were chicken and turkey.

Salt

Intake of salt, excluding additions during cooking and at the table, were on average twice the government recommendations. Salt consumption is known to be a risk factor for increased levels of blood pressure.

Fruit and vegetables

The government guidelines are to consume at least five portions of fruit or vegetables a day. Not only are these sources of a range of vitamins and minerals, they also provide fibre and naturally occurring energy in the form of glucose. A high level of fruit and vegetable consumption is recognised as a significant protective factor against the development of heart disease and some cancers. It also assists in weight maintenance. It is essential that all children develop the habit of consuming a wide range of fruits and vegetables on a daily basis in order to maintain good health in adult life.

Vegetarians

Some 10 per cent of 15–18-year-old girls claimed to be vegetarian or vegan. Vegetarians, and vegans in particular, need to carefully balance their food intake to ensure that they do not go short of iron, vitamin B12, zinc, vitamin D and calcium. The less restricted the diet the better. However, vegetarians have a lower risk of heart disease, stroke, diabetes, gallstones, kidney stones and colon cancer; they are also less likely to become overweight or to have raised cholesterol levels.

Pregnant and breastfeeding women

Foods to avoid: do not eat soft, mould-ripened cheese, pâté, raw or partially raw eggs, undercooked meat and poultry, tuna, swordfish or marlin, liver or liver-containing foods, alcohol or more than two portions of oily fish a week.

Special diets

There will be occasions when caterers will be asked to provide some special diets or to cater for a guest with special dietary needs.

i

Further information
To find out more, contact the British Nutrition Foundation, High Holborn House, 52–54 High Holborn, London WC1V 6RQ (website: www.nutrition.org.uk) or the Nutrition Society, 10 Cambridge Court, 210 Shepherd's Bush Rd, London W6 7NJ (website: www.nutsoc.org.uk).

Table 5.10 Special diets

DIET	FOODS TO AVOID
Vegetarian and other ethical diets	Meat or fish of any type, or dishes made with or containing the products of animals Check for 'vegetarians' who occasionally eat fish and/or meat (*semi-vegetarian* or *demi-vegetarian*), do not eat milk and dairy products (*ovo-vegetarian*), do not eat eggs (*lacto-vegetarian*), do not eat any food of animal origin, including honey, dairy products, egg (*vegan* – vegetables, fruits, grains, legumes, pasta made without eggs, soya products and other products of plans are acceptable to vegans), eat only fruit, nuts and berries (*fruitarian* or *fructarian*)
Religious diets	*Muslim:* pork, meat that is not halal (slaughtered according to custom), shellfish and alcohol (even when used in cooking) *Hindu:* meat, fish or eggs (orthodox Hindus are usually strict vegetarians); less strict Hindus may eat lamb, poultry and fish but definitely not beef as cattle have a deep religious meaning (milk, however, is highly regarded) *Sikh:* beef, pork, lamb, poultry and fish may be acceptable to Sikh men; Sikh women tend to avoid all meat *Jewish:* pork, pork products, shellfish and eels, meat and milk served at the same time or cooked together; strict Jews eat only Kosher meat; milk and milk products are usually avoided at lunch and dinner (but acceptable at breakfast) *Rastafarian:* all processed foods, pork, fish without fins (eels), alcohol, coffee, tea
Therapeutic diets	*Diabetes:* dishes that are high in sugar and/or fat (low-calorie sweeteners can be used to sweeten desserts) *Low cholesterol and saturated fat:* liver, egg yolks and shellfish (which are high in cholesterol), beef, pork and lamb (which contain saturated fats), butter, cream, groundnut oil, margarine (use oils and margarines labelled high in polyunsaturated fats) *Low fat:* any food that contains fat, or has been fried or roasted *Low salt:* foods and dishes that have had salt added in cooking or processing (including smoked and cured fishes and meats, and hard cheeses), or that contain monosodium glutamate *Low residue:* wholemeal bread, brown rice and pasta, fried and fatty foods *Milk-free:* milk, butter, cheese, yoghurt and any pre-prepared foods that include milk products (check label) *Nut allergy:* nuts, blended cooking oils and margarine (since these may include nut oil; use pure oils or butter), and any dishes containing these (check label) *Gluten-free:* wheat, wholemeal, wholewheat and wheatmeal flour, wheat bran, rye, barley and oats (some doctors say oats are permitted, the Coeliac Society advises against), and any dishes made with these, including pasta, noodles, semolina, bread, pastries, some yoghurts (e.g. muesli), some cheese spreads, barley-based drinks, malted drinks, beer, some brands of mustard, proprietary sauces made with flour (use cornflour to thicken; rice, potato, corn and sage are also acceptable).

Table 5.10 gives examples of some of the special diets that a caterer may have to produce. See also the section on food allergies, below.

Today there is a body of opinion within the medical profession which suggests that a regular diet of fresh fruit and vegetables can help to eliminate a number of diseases and certain types of cancers. Also it is advisable to reduce fat intake, eat more fish, wholegrain breads, pulses and rice.

Practical steps to consider in order to achieve this are:

- accurate descriptions of dishes
- avoid general statements (i.e. 'all dishes may contain traces of nuts')

- choose suppliers that provide accurate information (i.e. ingredients labelling)
- choose and scrutinise the ingredients lists of convenience foods for any hidden components
- train staff on the content of dishes so they can provide helpful, accurate information to customers
- employ policies for segregation and prevention of cross-contamination in the kitchen.

Figure 5.9 A basic preparation area

Overweight and obesity

The challenge in the future will be to change the food culture in the UK to one that is more geared towards a healthy diet. It is now estimated that one-third of all cancers are the result of poor diet.

One of the biggest problems facing the UK and other developed countries is obesity.

Obesity

Obesity is a condition in which abnormal or excessive fat accumulation in adipose tissue impairs health. It is defined in adults as a body mass index (BMI) above 30. Obesity is one of the most visible and, until recently, most neglected public health problems. Body weight is influenced by energy intake (from food) and energy expenditure (needed for basal metabolism such as keeping the heart beating) and for physical activity. If a person regularly consumes more energy (calories) than they use, they will start to gain weight and eventually become overweight or obese. If a person regularly consumes less energy than they use they will lose weight. Extra energy is stored in the body as fat. Balancing energy intake and output to maintain a healthy weight has many benefits.

How common is overweight and obesity?

In the early 1980s, 6 per cent of men and 8 per cent of women in the UK were obese. The latest figures for Great Britain (Henderson *et al.*, 2003) show that 42 per cent of men and 32 per cent of women are overweight (i.e. have a BMI of between 25 and 30), and 25 per cent of men and 20 per cent of women are obese (BMI>30). Obesity tends to be more common among people aged 40–60 years and those from lower income groups. Today, more adults are obese than ever before. The number of obese children is also increasing. According to the Health Survey for England (Department of Health, 2002), 5.5 per cent of boys and 7.2 per cent of girls, aged 2–15 years were obese in 2002. Overall, more than one in five boys (21.8 per cent) and one in four girls (27.5 per cent) is either overweight or obese according to recent international classifications.

Obesity is now a worldwide public health problem, affecting all age and socioeconomic groups. It is the most important dietary factor in chronic diseases such as cancer, cardiovascular disease and type 2 diabetes. It is second only to smoking as a cause of cancer. People who are overweight or obese are more likely to suffer from coronary heart disease, type 2 diabetes, gallstones, osteoarthritis (of the knees), high blood pressure and some types of cancer. Obese women are more likely to have complications during and after pregnancy. The World Health Organization (WHO) has predicted that one of the consequences of the global epidemic of obesity will be 300 million people with type 2 diabetes by 2025.

It is not just a problem of excess fat, but where that fat is deposited. People who have extra weight (fat) around their middle – 'apple shaped' – are at greater risk of some of these diseases than those who have most of the extra weight around their hips and thighs – 'pear shaped'. Because the health risks of obesity are compounded by the influence of fat distribution, waist-to-hip ratios or waist circumferences are now commonly measured. In general, men are at increased risk of obesity-related diseases when their waist circumference reaches 94 cm (37 inches). For women, risks increase at 80 cm (32 inches). The risks of disease become substantially increased at 102 cm (40 inches) for men and 88 cm (35 inches) for women.

Obesity and diabetes

Obese people also have a higher risk of developing diabetes. Diabetes develops when the body cannot use glucose properly. Around 1.4 million people in the UK have been diagnosed with diabetes, of whom around 1 million have type 2 diabetes. In addition, there are a large number of people who may have unrecognised diabetes.

Eating a healthy balanced diet, taking regular physical exercise, and maintaining a healthy body weight can help to prevent or delay the onset of type 2 diabetes. People with diabetes should try to maintain a healthy weight and eat a diet that is low in fat (particularly saturated fats) and salt, but that contains plenty of fruit and vegetables (at least five portions a day), and starchy carbohydrate foods such as bread, rice and pasta (particularly wholegrain versions).

Other health concerns

Yet another future challenge for the hospitality industry is to reduce the amount of salt used in cooking. It is now well recognised that there is a link between salt and hypertension (high blood pressure). High blood

Figure 5.10 Are you a healthy weight?

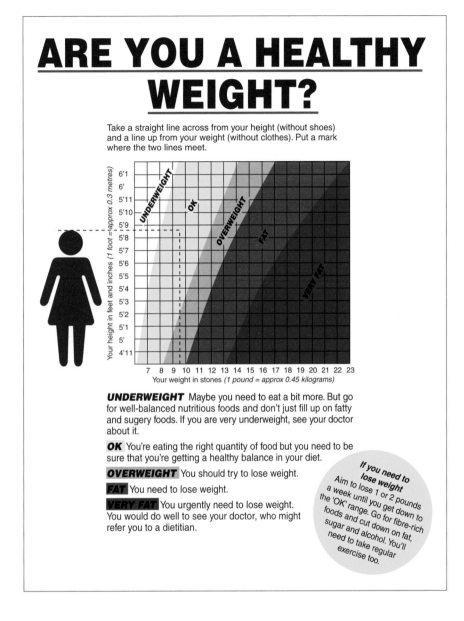

ARE YOU A HEALTHY WEIGHT?

Take a straight line across from your height (without shoes) and a line up from your weight (without clothes). Put a mark where the two lines meet.

UNDERWEIGHT Maybe you need to eat a bit more. But go for well-balanced nutritious foods and don't just fill up on fatty and sugery foods. If you are very underweight, see your doctor about it.

OK You're eating the right quantity of food but you need to be sure that you're getting a healthy balance in your diet.

OVERWEIGHT You should try to lose weight.

FAT You need to lose weight.

VERY FAT You urgently need to lose weight. You would do well to see your doctor, who might refer you to a dietitian.

If you need to lose weight Aim to lose 1 or 2 pounds a week until you get down to the 'OK' range. Go for fibre-rich foods and cut down on fat, sugar and alcohol. You'll need to take regular exercise too.

pressure often causes no symptoms but increases the risk of developing conditions such as heart disease and stroke.

Around a third of the adult population in the UK has been diagnosed with hypertension; it is most common in older people, those with a family history of the condition and in some ethnic groups.

A number of lifestyle factors can help to prevent or treat high blood pressure – for example, not smoking, being physically active, maintaining a healthy body weight, drinking alcohol in moderation (if at all), eating a balanced and varied diet that is low in fat (particularly saturated fats) and sodium (salt), and that includes low-fat dairy. A diet that is low in fat and includes low-fat dairy foods, and fruit and vegetables, has been shown to lower blood pressure in people with or without high blood pressure. This diet reduced the amount of fat, saturates and cholesterol, and increased the amount of potassium, magnesium and calcium. Reducing the amount of salt in the diet also had a beneficial effect. The best effect was achieved when both approaches were combined. This highlights the importance of improving the diet overall rather than focusing on single nutrients. Eating a healthy, balanced diet will also help to maintain a healthy body weight.

Salt and health

A recent report by the Scientific Advisory Committee on Nutrition concluded that sodium intake is an important determinant of blood pressure, in part influencing the rise of blood pressure with age. As the main source of sodium in the diet is salt (sodium chloride), it has been recommended that people in the UK try to reduce their sale intake to a maximum of 6 g per day. For most people this will mean reducing their current intake by one-third.

Salt added at the table and during cooking contributes around 10–15 per cent of our total salt intake and naturally occurring salt in foods contributes another 10–15 per cent. Traditionally, salt has been used as a preservative and flavour enhancer. On average around 75 per cent of the salt in our diet comes from processed foods such as bread and cereal products, breakfast cereals, meat products, some ready meals, smoked fish, pickles, canned vegetables, canned and packet sauces and soups, savoury snack foods, biscuits and cakes. Spreading fats and cheese also make a small contribution to intake.

The cooperation and commitment of the food and hospitality industry is, therefore, required to develop lower-salt products to help people reduce their salt intake. The FSA is working closely with the food industry to explore ways to lower the sodium content of processed foods, and a number of manufacturers and retailers have already taken action to achieve the necessary reduction. However, such activities will be successful only if there is consumer acceptance of these products. The FSA is playing its part by raising public awareness of the dangers of high blood pressure and the need to reduce the amount of salt in our diets. People can do this by using food labels to select lower-salt/sodium products and by persevering so as to adapt their palates to less salty tastes.

Potassium, calcium and magnesium

An inadequate dietary intake of potassium may increase blood pressure. A high potassium intake may, therefore, protect against developing hypertension and improve blood pressure control in patients with hypertension. There is also evidence to suggest that the effect of sodium (salt) on blood pressure may be related to the amount of potassium in the diet, and that the ratio of sodium to potassium in the diet might be more important than the absolute amount of either. Potassium is found in meat, milk, vegetables, potatoes, fruit (especially bananas) and fruit juices, bread, fish, nuts and seeds.

Studies have also suggested that ensuring an adequate amount of calcium and magnesium in the diet is important to protect against high blood pressure, as well as for general health. Sources of calcium include milk and dairy products, soft bones in canned fish, bread, pulses, green vegetables, dried fruit, nuts and seeds. Foods containing magnesium include cereals and cereal products, meat, green vegetables, milk, potatoes, nuts and seeds.

Diet and cancer

Approximately one-third of all cancers may be linked to diet.

What research tells us

Many of the early theories on the links between diet and cancer were tested in the laboratory and on animals. These provided helpful leads, but chemicals often react in quite different ways in humans than they do in animals or in a test tube. Also, it is not safe to assume that links found in animals equally apply to humans. The best information comes from studying human beings.

Types of study

Epidemiological studies look at what people eat, alongside the incidence of cancer; because dietary habits vary enormously these can produce a wealth of information on how diet may affect health.

- **Migrant studies** provide useful information on dietary and genetic factors. When Japanese people migrated to Hawaii, for example, their dietary patterns changed – and so did their risk of certain cancers. As the traditional Japanese diet has become more westernised so rates of breast and colon cancer have increased.
- **Case control studies** investigate the links that can be deduced by comparing the diets of cancer patients with similar people who do not have cancer. These tend to yield the best results when there is a big difference between the diets of those with and without cancer.
- **Cohort studies** follow the health and diet of healthy people over a long period of time to see if there is any difference in the diets of those who develop cancer and those who don't.
- **Intervention studies** track results from a particular diet or supplement, using a control group that is not given the diet or supplement. Ethically, of course, people should not be exposed to substances thought to increase the risk of cancer, so these studies are on particular nutrients thought to protect against cancer. 'Double blind' trials – when neither the researchers nor the individuals know which group they belong to – produce the most reliable results.

Table 5.11 Protective nutrients: their sources and functions

VITAMINS AND MINERALS	POSITIVE FUNCTION	SOURCES
Carotenoids These are precursors of vitamin A; they include alpha-carotene, beta-carotene, xanthophylls (the main one is lutein), lycopene and cryptoxanthin	Antioxidant	Dark-green leafy vegetables, orange vegetables and fruit *Lutein:* kale, spinach, broccoli, corn *Lycopene:* tomatoes, watermelons, pink grapefruit, guavas *Cryptoxantin:* mangoes, papayas, persimmons, red peppers, pumpkins
Folate (folic acid)	Antioxidant; may affect division of cells in the colon	Beans, green leafy vegetables, liver, nuts, wholegrain cereals
Selenium	Stimulation of detoxification enzymes	Brazil nuts, bread, eggs, fish, meat
Vitamin C (ascorbic acid)	Antioxidant	Broccoli, cabbage and other green leafy vegetables, citrus fruit, mangoes, peppers, strawberries, tomatoes
Vitamin D	May control cell growth through its effect on calcium	Sunlight
Vitamin E	Antioxidant	Nuts, seeds, vegetables oils, wheatgerm, whole grains
OTHER BIOACTIVE COMPOUNDS	POSITIVE FUNCTION	SOURCES
Allium compounds (contain sulphur)	Stimulate detoxification enzymes	Chives, garlic, onions
Flavonoids (e.g. quercetin)	Antioxidant function within the plant	Berries, broad beans, broccoli, onions, tomatoes
Isothiocyanates	Stimulate detoxifying enzymes	Broccoli, Brussels sprouts, cabbage and other brassicas
Phytoestrogens (isoflavones and lignans)	May alter steroid hormone metabolism	*Isoflavones:* beans, chickpeas, lentils, soya *Lignans:* oils seeds (e.g. flax, soya, rape), legumes and various other vegetables and fruit, particularly berries, whole grains
Plant sterols	May bind with hormones in the gut and influence hormone metabolism	Cereals, fruit, nuts, seeds, vegetables
Terpenoid (e.g. D-limonene)	Stimulate enzyme systems	Oil of lemons, oranges and other citrus fruits

Dr Clare Shaw, Royal Marsden Hospital

Some research may indicate a link between diet and cancer, while other research may provide more conclusive results. Where evidence is sufficiently strong, prestigious organisations such as the World Cancer Research Fund and the WHO publish guidance to help people make dietary changes.

Dietary influences

Studies over many years have shown a number of interesting correlations between different diets and cancers. The incidence of certain cancers, especially stomach and bowel, has increased as large-scale food processing has replaced many of the wholegrain cereals, pulses and roots in our diet with white flour and refined cereals and sugars.

Cancers of the stomach and oesophagus are much less common where the typical diet is high in cereals, tubers and starchy foods – often providing half of the dietary energy needs – but low in animal proteins (meat and dairy products). Diets in developed countries tend to be high in animal proteins, sugar and salt, but low in starches.

There is a greater incidence of stomach cancer in countries where traditionally a lot of salty foods are eaten – for example, Japan, China and Portugal.

In southern European countries, the consumption of fruit and vegetables is generally higher than in northern Europe, and the incidence of cancers of the mouth and throat, oesophagus, lung and stomach is lower in the south.

How can diet influence the development of cancer?

A damaged cell needs to replicate in order to grow into a group of cancer cells. Some substances in our diet may either encourage the replication process and promote cancer growth or slow it down, so protecting against cancer.

- **Carcinogenic agents:** These agents may directly influence DNA or protein in cells. Examples include alfatoxins, which are found in mouldy food, alcohol and certain compounds produced by some cooking and food-processing methods.
- **Tumour promoters:** Unlike carcinogens, tumour promoters do not act directly on DNA, but stimulate the genes and encourage replication. Some hormones may act in this way, and although the body produces these hormones naturally, diet can affect the level of, for example, oestrogens in the body. Other tumour promoters include alcohol and a high-fat or high-energy diet, which may promote the production of harmful substances, such as free radicals. Free radicals are thought to influence DNA disorganisation.

But, just as we may introduce harmful elements into our bodies through our diet, there are also nutrients that may protect us.

- **Protective nutrients:** Many foods contain protective substances that may reduce damage to tissues by free radicals, or potentially reduce cell growth.
- **Antioxidants:** Antioxidants are important constituents of the diet and are involved in DNA and cell maintenance and repair. They may reduce the production of free radicals, preventing early damage to cells and so reduce the chance that they will become cancerous.

Further information
To find out more about
catering for health,
contact the Health
Development Authority,
Trevelyan House, 30
Great Peter Street,
London SW1P 2HW.

Antioxidants in the diet may be in the form of vitamins or minerals, such as vitamins C and E, beta-carotene and selenium, or they may be found in flavonoids in vegetables.

- **Phytoestrogens:** Phytoestrogens have properties similar to oestrogens, but they are much weaker than the oestrogens the body itself produces. They can be divided primarily into two groups: isoflavones and lignans. Isoflavones are linked to the protein part of food and lignans to the fibre. Table 5.11 includes examples of sources of phytoestrogens.
- **Other bioactive compounds:** Many foods have functions beyond the vitamins and minerals they contain. Research is revealing that some of their chemicals and reactions may be beneficial to health. In laboratory experiments, for example, garlic extracts have killed *Heliobacter pylori*, a bacteria that can grow in the stomach and is known to increase the risk of cancer. Sulphur-containing compounds in garlic and onions may also reduce the formation of carcinogenic compounds that arise from the curing of meats.

FOOD ALLERGIES AND INTOLERANCES

Estimates by the British Allergy Foundation and the Institute for Food Research put the proportion of the population with an allergy to at least one food at between 1 and 2 per cent, and the number is said to be growing each year by 5 per cent. The FSA has recently updated the food labelling regulations to incorporate more information on packaging about the type and level of allergens in supermarket foods. It is also strongly encouraging caterers to tell customers more and more about what is in their foods.

Food intolerances can be described as an adverse reaction to food. Intolerances fall into three groups:

1 intolerance to certain foods that cause a reaction – i.e. rashes and headaches
2 inability to digest certain foods – i.e. lactose intolerance, where there is not enough of the correct enzyme to digest the lactose
3 intolerance to certain chemicals – i.e. artificial colours, flavourings (as discussed on page 174).

Further information
To find out more contact
the British Allergy
Foundation, St Bart's
Hospital, London EC1A
7BE (website:
www.allergyuk.org).
See also:
- HCIMA Technical Brief
  No. 43
- www.foodallergy.com.

Food allergies are a type of intolerance where the body's immune system sees the harmless food as harmful and therefore causes an allergic reaction. The allergic reaction that some people have to certain food items can sometimes be fatal.

Foods that may cause an allergic reaction in a very small number of people include milk and dairy products, fish, shellfish, eggs and nuts (particularly peanuts but also cashew, pecan, Brazil and walnuts). Peanuts are often commonly used in Bombay mix, peanut butter, satay sauce, nut-coated cereals, groundnut and arachide oils, salted peanuts, chopped nuts, vegetarian dishes, and salads that are a mixture of, say, nuts and fresh fruit.

The Anaphylaxis Campaign has warned caterers to be on the alert for foods containing flour made from lupin seeds as this can cause an allergic reaction similar to that of peanuts. Lupin flour is widely used as an ingredient in France, Holland and Italy because of its nutty taste, attractive yellow colour and because it is guaranteed GM free. Symptoms of anaphylactic shock include swelling of the throat and mouth, difficulty in swallowing and breathing, nausea, vomiting and unconsciousness. The fast administration of adrenaline will give relief.

Persons suffering an allergy to nuts need to know if and where they are used.

Table 5.12 Special diets for those with food allergies and intolerances

TYPE OF DIET	PROBLEMS	FOODS TO AVOID	PERMITTED FOODS
Coeliac	An allergy to gluten. Results in severe inflammation of the gastro-intestinal tract, pain and diarrhoea, and malnutrition due to inability to absorb nutrients	All products made from wheat, barley or rye, this includes bread; always check the label on all commercial products	Potatoes, rice and flours made from potatoes and rice; also cornflour, fresh fruit and vegetables
Food allergies	Individuals can suffer severe and rapid reactions to any food, which can be fatal; common allergies are to peanuts and their derivatives, sesame seeds, cashew nuts, pecan nuts, walnuts, hazelnuts, milk, fish, shellfish and eggs	Peanuts, chopped nuts, groundnut oil, satay sauce, arachide oil, peanut products and other nut products	
Low cholesterol	High levels of cholesterol circulating in the bloodstream are associated with an increased risk of cardiovascular disease	Liver, kidney, egg yolks, fatty meats, bacon, ham, pâté, fried foods, pastry, cream, full-fat milk, full-fat yoghurt, cheeses, salad dressings, biscuits, cakes	Lean meat and fish grilled or poached, fresh fruit and vegetables, low-fat milk, low-fat yoghurt, porridge, muesli
Diabetic	The body is unable to control the level of glucose in the blood	As above, plus high-sugar dishes; this can lead to comas and long-term problems such as increased risk of cardiovascular disease, blindness and kidney problems	As above plus wholemeal bread, pasta, rice, potatoes, pulses

FOOD ADDITIVES

There is an increasing trend in the UK towards 'cleaning up' recipes and using as few artificial additives or as many natural ingredients as possible. For this reason, the use of some additives (such as monosodium glutamate) is increasingly frowned upon.

Further information
To find out more about additives, contact the Food Standards Agency, Room No. 213, Whitehall Place (East Block), London SW1A 2HH (website: www.food.gov.uk).

Additives can be divided into 12 categories and, except for purely 'natural' substances, their use is subject to certain legislation.

1 **Preservatives:** natural ones include salt, sugar, alcohol and vinegar; synthetic ones are also widely used.
2 **Colouring agents:** natural, including cochineal, caramel and saffron, and many synthetic ones.
3 **Flavouring agents:** synthetic chemicals to mimic natural flavours (e.g. monosodium glutamate to give a meaty flavour to foods).
4 **Sweetening:** saccharin, sorbitol and aspartame.
5 **Emulsifying agents** (to prevent separation of salad creams, ice cream, etc.); examples are lecithin and glyceryl monostearate (GMS).
6 **Antioxidants:** to delay the onset of rancidity in fats due to exposure to air; examples are vitamin E and butylated hydroxy toluene (BHT).
7 **Flour improvers:** to strengthen the gluten in flour, such as vitamin C.
8 **Thickeners:** animal (gelatine); marine (agar-agar); vegetable (gum tragacanth – used for pastillage – and pectin; synthetic products.
9 **Humectants:** to prevent food drying out, such as glycerine (used in some icings).
10 **Polyphosphate:** injected into poultry before rigor mortis develops; it binds water to the muscle and thus prevents 'drip', giving a firmer structure to the meat.
11 **Nutrients:** vitamins and minerals added to breakfast cereals, vitamins A and D added to margarine.
12 **Miscellaneous:** anti-caking agents added to icing sugar and salt; firming agents (calcium chloride) added to tinned fruit and vegetables to prevent too much softening in the processing; mineral oils added to dried fruit to prevent stickiness.

FOOD SPOILAGE

Unless foods are preserved they deteriorate; therefore, to keep them in an edible condition it is necessary to know what causes food spoilage. In the air there are certain micro-organisms called moulds, yeasts and bacteria, which cause foods to go bad.

There are two main types of spoilage:

1 chemical – i.e. over-ripening, breakdown of protein in meat leading to oxidation and rancidity
2 microbial – i.e. micro-organisms attack the food leading to spoilage and, in some cases, food poisoning.

Microbial spoilage

Moulds

These are simple plants that appear like whiskers on foods, particularly sweet foods, meat and cheese. To grow, they require warmth, air, moisture, darkness and food; they are killed by heat and sunlight. Moulds can grow where there is too little moisture for yeasts and bacteria to grow, and will be found on jams and pickles.

Although most of the time moulds are not harmful, they do cause foods to taste musty and to be wasted. There are a couple of types of moulds that are dangerous to health, so it is best not to eat them.

Correct storage in a dry cold store prevents moulds from forming.

Not all moulds are destructive. Some are used to flavour cheese (Stilton, Roquefort) or to produce antibiotics (penicillin, streptomycin).

Yeasts

These are single-cell plants or organisms, larger than bacteria, that grow on foods containing moisture and sugar. Foods containing only a small percentage of sugar and a large percentage of liquid, such as fruit juices and syrups, are liable to ferment because of yeasts. Although they seldom cause disease, yeasts do increase food spoilage; foodstuffs should be kept under refrigeration or they may be spoiled by yeasts. Yeasts are also destroyed by heat. The ability of yeast to feed on sugar and produce alcohol is the basis of the beer- and wine-making industries. Yeasts are also used in breadmaking and other fermented goods.

Bacteria

Bacteria are minute plants, or organisms, that require moist, warm conditions and a suitable food to multiply. They spoil food by attacking it, leaving waste products, or by producing poisons in the food.

Their growth is checked by refrigeration and they are killed by heat. Certain bacterial forms (spores) are more resistant to heat than others and require higher temperatures to kill them.

Pressure cooking destroys heat-resistant bacterial spores provided the food is cooked for a sufficient length of time, because increased pressure increases the temperature; therefore heat-resistant bacterial spores do not affect canned foods as the foods are cooked under pressure in the cans. Acids are generally capable of destroying bacteria, such as vinegar in pickles.

Dehydrated foods and dry foods do not contain much moisture and, provided they are kept dry, spoilage from bacteria will not occur. If they become moist then bacteria can multiply – if dried peas are soaked and not cooked, for example, the bacteria present can begin to multiply.

Chemical spoilage

Food spoilage can occur due to other causes, such as by chemical substances called enzymes, which are produced by living cells. Fruits are ripened by the action of enzymes; they do not remain edible indefinitely because other enzymes cause the fruit to become over-ripe and spoil.

When meat and game are hung they become tender; this is caused by enzymes. To prevent enzyme activity going too far, foods must be refrigerated or heated to a temperature high enough to destroy the enzymes. Acid retards the enzyme action: lemon juice, for example, prevents the browning of bananas or apples when they are cut into slices.

KEEPING UP TO DATE

Changes are occurring constantly regarding food production and manufacture, which may affect the use of foods in the kitchen. Consumers' reaction to reports of changes published in the press or seen or heard on the TV or radio may affect demand. Similarly, information about nutritional values can affect customers' preferences and thus cause trends and affect menu selection.

It is therefore essential to be aware of these reports and when necessary to act according to government recommendations. One example of research that has affected kitchen practice has been the use of eggs. In recent years, the rise in fatalities from bacteria such as BSE and E. coli has led to renewed concern and scrutiny of food production techniques.

Recommendations and contradictions produced by dietetic research can cause trends and affect consumer habits. The use of butter and margarine is one such example.

It is essential to keep up to date through the media and adopt a common-sense attitude to the comments made, but to take action when serious recommendations are made by valid research bodies.

METHODS OF PRESERVATION

In order to preserve food, it is important to kill the micro-organisms that cause the spoilage and then store the food in an environment where it cannot be re-infected, or in conditions where deterioration is slowed down or stopped.

Foods may be preserved by:

- removing the moisture from the food – drying, dehydration
- making the food cold – chilling, freezing
- applying heat – canning, bottling
- radiation, using X- or gamma-rays
- chemical means – salting, pickling, crystallising
- vacuum packing
- smoking
- chemical
- gas storage.

Drying or dehydration

Water is needed by micro-organisms to survive and reproduce. Therefore, by removing the water in foods below a critical value (this is a value that is specific for different types of foods) spoilage is reduced. In the past, this was done by drying foods (e.g. fruits) in the sun; today many types of equipment are used, and the food is dried by the use of air at regulated temperatures and humidity.

Advantages of drying
- If kept dry, food keeps indefinitely.
- Food preserved by this method occupies less space than food preserved by other methods. Some dried foods occupy only 10 per cent of the space that would be required when fresh.
- Dried foods are easily transported and stored.
- The cost of drying and the expenses incurred in storing are not as high as those for other methods of preservation.
- There is no waste after purchase, therefore portion control and costing are simplified.

Foods preserved by drying
- Vegetables: peas, onions, beetroot, beans, carrots, lentils, cabbage, mixed vegetables, potatoes.
- Herbs, eggs, milk, coffee.
- Fruits: apples, pears, plums (prunes), apricots, figs, grapes (sultanas, raisins, currants).
- Meat, fish.

Vegetables
Many vegetables are dried; those most used are the pulse vegetables (beans, peas and lentils), which are used for soups, vegetable purées and many vegetarian dishes. Usually potatoes are cooked, mashed and then dried. The other dried vegetables are used as a vegetable (cabbage, onions).

Pulse vegetables may be soaked in water before use, then washed before being cooked. Vegetables that are dehydrated (having a lower content of water as more moisture has been extracted) are soaked in water.

Dehydrated potatoes are in powder form and are reconstituted with water, milk, or milk and water. They often have manufactured vitamin C added as dehydration results in a loss of this vitamin.

Herbs
Fresh herbs are tied into bundles and allowed to dry out in a dry place.

Fruits
Sultanas, currants and raisins are grapes that have been dried in the sun

or by hot air. Figs, plums, apricots, apples and pears are also dried by hot air. Apples are usually peeled and cut into rings or diced and then dried.

All dried fruits must be washed before use, and fruits such as prunes, figs, apricots, apples and pears are cooked in the water in which they are soaked.

Little flavour or food value is lost when drying fruits, with the exception of loss of vitamin C.

Milk

Milk is dried either by the roller or spray process. With the roller method the milk is poured onto heated rollers, which cause the water to evaporate; the resulting powder is then scraped off. This method is not widely used now as it damages the milk proteins and results in a less soluble dried product, which is more difficult to reconstitute. With the spray process the milk is sent through a fine jet as a spray into hot air, the water evaporates and the powder drops down. The temperature is controlled so that the protein in the milk is not cooked.

Milk powder may be used in place of fresh milk, mainly for economic purposes (especially skimmed milk powder), and is used for making custard and white sauce.

Eggs

Eggs are dried in the same way as milk, and although they have a food value similar to fresh eggs, dried eggs do not have the same aerating quality. When reconstituted the eggs should be used at once; if they are left in this state in the warm atmosphere of a kitchen, bacteria can multiply and food poisoning may result; although pasteurised before drying, the mixture may be contaminated in the kitchen and it is a very suitable food for the growth of bacteria. Dried eggs are mainly used in the bakery trade.

Freeze drying

This is a process of dehydration whereby food requires no preservation or refrigeration yet, when soaked in water, regains its original size and flavour. It can be applied to every kind of food. The food is frozen in a cabinet, the air is pumped out and the ice vaporised. This is called freeze drying and is the drying of frozen foods by sublimation under conditions of very low pressure. (Sublimation is the action of turning from solid to gas without passing through a liquid stage; in this case it is ice to steam without first turning to water.)

When processed in this way, food does not lose a great deal of its bulk, but it is very much lighter in weight. When water is added the food gives off its natural smell.

Preservation by chilling and freezing

At low temperatures micro-organism growth is much slower. Therefore, refrigeration is used not to kill micro-organisms but to slow down their multiplication and their enzyme action. As a result, refrigeration prolongs the life of the food but not for long periods of time and, eventually, the food will go bad. Microbial and biochemical changes that affect the flavour, texture, colour and nutritional value of foods still take place and it is important to remember that the food must not be contaminated before chilling. Refrigerators are kept at a temperature of 0–7°C (32–45°F).

The lower the temperature the food is stored at, the longer the storage life. This is because the micro-organisms become inactive around -10°C and enzymes become inactive around -18°C. Most frozen foods can be kept at -17°C (1°F) for a year and at -28°C (-18°F) for two years. Foods must be kept in deep freeze until required for use.

Cold chilled storage of fresh foods merely retards the decay of the food; it does not prevent it from eventually going bad. The aim of chilling is to slow down the rate of spoilage; the lower the chill temperature within the range -1°C (30°F) and 18°C (46°F) the slower the growth of micro-organisms and the biochemical changes that spoil the flavour, colour, texture and nutritional value of foods. Lowering the temperature to this range also reduces food poisoning hazards, although it is important to remember that the food must not be contaminated before chilling.

If food is frozen slowly, large uneven crystals are formed in the cells. The water in each cell contains the minerals that give flavour and goodness to food; if food is frozen slowly, the minerals are separated from the ice crystals, which break through the cells; on thawing, the goodness and flavour drain away. Quick-freezing (see below) is more satisfactory because small ice crystals are formed in the cells of food; so, on thawing, the goodness and flavour are retained in the cells.

Meat
- **Chilling:** meat that is chilled is kept at a temperature just above freezing point and will keep for up to one month; if the atmosphere is controlled with carbon dioxide the time can be extended to ten weeks.
- **Freezing:** imported lamb carcasses are frozen; beef carcasses are not usually frozen because, owing to the size of the carcass, it takes a long time to freeze and this causes ice crystals to form which, when thawed, affect the texture of the meat; frozen meat must be thawed before it is cooked.

Quick-freezing of raw foods and cooked foods
During the cooking and freezing process, foods undergo physical and/or chemical changes. If it is found that these changes are detrimental to the product, then recipe modification is required. The following products require some modification: sauces, casseroles, stews, cold desserts, batters, vegetables and egg dishes.

Conventional recipes normally use wheat flour for thickening, but in the cook-freeze system this will not give an acceptable final product because separation of the solids from the liquids in the sauce will occur if the product is kept in frozen storage for more than a period of several weeks. To overcome this problem it is necessary to use wheat flour in conjunction with any of a number of classically modified starches, such as tapioca starch or waxy maize starch. Many recipes prove successful with a ratio of 50 per cent wheat flour to 50 per cent modified starch.

Rapid freezing of foodstuffs can be achieved by a variety of methods using different types of equipment, for example:

- plate freezer
- blast freezer
- low-temperature immersion freezer
- still-air cold room
- spray freezer (using liquid nitrogen or carbon dioxide) – known as cryogenic freezing this is a method of freezing food by very low temperature; it also freezes food more quickly than any other method; the food to be frozen is placed on a conveyor belt and passed into an insulated freezing tunnel; the liquefied nitrogen or carbon dioxide is injected into the tunnel through a spray, and vaporises, resulting in a very rapid freezing process
- freeze flow – this is a system that freezes food without hardening it.

Foods that are frozen
A very wide variety of foods are frozen, either cooked or in an uncooked state.

- **Cooked foods:** whole cooked meals, braised meat, vol-au-vents, éclairs, cream sponges, puff pastry items.
- **Raw foods:** fillets of fish, fish fingers, poultry, peas, French beans, broad beans, spinach, sprouts, broccoli, strawberries, raspberries, blackcurrants.

With most frozen foods, cooking instructions are given; these should be followed to obtain the best results.

Fillets of fish may be thawed out before cooking; vegetables are cooked in their frozen state. Fruit is thawed before use and as it is usually frozen with sugar the fruit is served with the liquor.

Advantages of using frozen foods
- Frozen foods are ready prepared, therefore saving time and labour.
- Portion control and costing are easily assessed.
- Foods are always 'in season'.
- Storage is compact.
- Additional stocks are to hand.
- Quality is guaranteed.
- Very little vitamin C is lost from fruits and vegetables even after several months in a deep freeze.

Table 5.13 Storage of tinned foods

TYPE OF TINNED FOOD	ADVISED STORAGE TIME
Fruit	Up to 12 months
Milk	Up to 12 months
Vegetables	Up to 2 years
Meat	Up to 5 years
Fish in oil	Up to 5 years
Fish in tomato sauce	Up to 1 year

Preservation by heating

Canning and bottling

Bottled and canned food are sealed in airtight bottles or tins, and heated at a high enough temperature for a sufficient period of time to destroy harmful organisms. Spoilage does not occur over life because no micro-organisms can gain access to the food. Almost any type of food can be canned.

Dented cans that do not leak are safe to use, but blown cans – that is, those with bulges at either end – must not be used.

Tinned hams are canned at a low temperature in order to retain their flavour and avoid excessive shrinkage in the can, and therefore should be stored in a refrigerator and consumed soon after purchase. Other tinned foods are kept in a dry, cool place; Table 5.13 indicates the recommended storage time.

Foods are canned in tins of various sizes (see Table 5.14).

The advantages of canned foods are similar to those of frozen foods, but a disadvantage is that, due to the heat processing, a proportion of the vitamin C and B1 (thiamin) may be lost.

Table 5.14 Tin sizes

SIZE	APPROX. WEIGHT	USE
	142 g	Baked beans, peas
	227 g	Fruits, meats, vegetables
A1	284 g	Baked beans, soups, vegetables, meats, pilchards
14Z	397 g	Fruits, vegetables
A2	567 g	Fruits, vegetables, fruit and vegetable juices
A2½	795 g	Fruits, vegetables
A10	3079 g	Fruits, vegetables, tongues

Pasteurisation

Pasteurisation is a mild heat treatment, mainly used with milk and fruit juices. The food is taken to at least 72°C for a minimum of 15 seconds and then cooled rapidly.

In milk, over 99 per cent of the micro-organisms are killed and the rest are inactivated due to the rapid cooling and refrigerated conditions the produce is held in.

The loss in nutrients and effects on flavour and the quality of the products are minimal because the temperatures reached are not very high and are maintained for only a short period of time.

Sterilisation

This heat-treatment method employs much higher temperatures for a much longer period of time. The product is then packed in sterile containers. As a result, the product has a much longer shelf-life than its pasteurised counterpart and the cartons can be stored at ambient temperatures rather than chilled.

UHT (ultra heat treated) milk is an example of this and there is a more noticeable change in the flavour and quality of the finished product.

Preservation by salting and smoking

Salting

Micro-organisms cannot grow in high concentrations of salt. This method of preservation is used mainly to preserve meat and fish, and its advantage lies chiefly in the fact that a wider variety of dishes with different flavours can be put on the menu.

The salt added to butter and margarine, and also to cheese, acts as a preservative.

Meats

Meats that are salted or 'pickled' in a salt solution (brine) include brisket, silverside of beef, ox tongues and legs of pork.

Fish

Fish are usually smoked as well as being salted and include salmon, trout, haddock and herring. The amount of salting varies. Bloaters are salted more than kippers, and red herrings more than bloaters.

Smoking

There are two types of smoking:

1 hot smoking
2 cold smoking.

Smoking is mainly used nowadays to enhance the flavour and colour of the product, as its preservation effect is mainly limited to the surface of the product. Smoking does not allow long-term storage.

Smoke is a very complex material, with upward of 200 components that include alcohols, acids, phenolic compounds and various toxic, sometimes carcinogenic, substances. The toxic substances inhibit the growth of microbes, and the phenolics retard fat oxidation, and the whole complex imparts the characteristic flavour of burning wood to the meat, fish or vegetables.

Smoke substitutes are sometimes used in preference to real smoke to give the flavour and characteristics of traditionally smoked food. One smoke substitute is known as liquid smoke and does not contain carcinogenic substances.

The difference between smoke cooking and curing
Smoke cooking is done at higher temperatures in order to cook the meat. Smoke curing is really just smoking cured meat or sausage. Although smoking meat does provide some preservative effect, this alone is not sufficient to allow long-term storage.

The temperature of smoke when cooking meat
The temperature is very important. There are a variety of different smokes on the market, all with temperature guides; some recommend 93°C–104°C (200–220°F).

Temperature control is very important as excess heat will melt the fat and leave a dry product.

Examples of woods used for smoking
- **Alder:** the traditional wood for smoking salmon in the Pacific north-west, alder also works well with other fish. It has a light, delicate flavour.
- **Apple and cherry:** both woods produce a slightly sweet, fruity smoke that is mild enough for chicken or turkey, but capable of favouring a ham.
- **Hickory:** the king of the woods. The strong, hearty taste is perfect for pork shoulder and ribs, but also enhances any red meat or poultry.
- **Maple:** mildly smoky and sweet, maple mates well with poultry, ham and vegetables.
- **Mesquite:** great for grilling because it burns very hot, but below average for barbecuing for the same reason. Also, the smoke taste turns from tangy to bitter over an extended cooking time.
- **Oak:** if hickory is the king of barbecue woods, oak is the queen. The most versatile of hardwoods, blending well with a wide range of flavours.
- **Pecan:** burns cool and offers a subtle richness of character.
- **Grapevines:** very distinctive aroma, ideal for grilling food.

The smoking process

Before smoking commences, the raw meat or fish is either dry salted or soaked in brine. In hot countries salting is still used for the purpose of preservation, but in more temperate climates the salt is used only as a seasoning.

During smoking, weight loss occurs in the product, due to evaporation of water content from within the flesh of the meat or fish. This weight loss is essential to successful smoking. It follows that the greater the weight loss the greater the keeping qualities. Today, flavour tends to be more important than keeping qualities so it is better to create humid conditions to produce a succulent product.

Hot and cold smoking

Cold smoking flavours but does not cook the product. It is usually carried out at a temperature of between 10°C and 29°C (50–85°F). Some cold smoked products are eaten without further cooking (e.g. salmon, beef fillet, halibut and cod roe), whereas others – such as haddock, herring (kippers) and cod fillets – require a further period of cooking, although obviously not so much as a completely raw product as the cooking process has already been started.

Hot smoked products, after salting or brining, are first cold smoked to partially dry them out and to impart a smoked flavour. In the case of fish the temperature is then raised to 93–104°C (200–240°F) and the fish are then cooked. Care must be taken during the initial cold smoking to see that the temperature does not exceed 26°C (85°F) as this will harden the outside and stop further smoke penetration. Again, during hot smoking, temperatures must be monitored to see that the fish do not become overcooked. Herbs and spices may be incorporated into the smoking process.

Preservation by sugar

A high concentration of sugar prevents the growth of moulds, yeasts and bacteria. This method of preservation is applied to fruits in a variety of forms: jams, marmalades, jellies, candied, glacé and crystallised.

- Jams are prepared by cooking fruit and sugar together in the correct quantities to prevent the jam from spoiling. Too little sugar means the jam will not keep.
- Jellies, such as redcurrant jelly, are prepared by cooking the juice of the fruit with the sugar.
- Marmalade is similar to jam in preparation and preservation, citrus fruits being used in place of other fruits.
- Candied fruit is made when the peel of such fruit as orange, lemon, grapefruit and lime, and also the flesh of pineapple, are covered with hot syrup; the syrup's sugar content is increased each day until the fruit is saturated in a very heavy syrup, then it is allowed to dry slowly.

- Crystallised fruit is made following candying. It is left in fresh syrup for 24 hours and then allowed to dry slowly until crystals form on the fruit. Angelica, ginger, violet and rose petals are prepared in this way.
- Glacé fruit, usually cherries, is first candied, then dipped in fresh syrup to give a clear finish.

Figure 5.11 The pH range of some foods

Acid									Alkaline				
1	2	3	4	5	6	7	8	9	10	11	12	13	14
Strong acid			Medium acid		Weak acid		Weak alkali		Medium alkali		Strong alkaline		
Lemons Vinegar Rhubarb			Pear Bananas Carrots Tomatoes				Some mineral waters Hard water		Egg white Bicarbonate of soda				

Preservation by acids

The acidity and alkalinity of foods

The level of acidity or alkalinity of a food is measured by its pH value. The pH can range from 1 to 14, with pH7 denoting neutral (neither acid nor alkaline).

Most micro-organisms grow best at near neutral pH. Bacteria (particularly harmful ones) are less acid-tolerant than fungi, and no bacteria will grow at a pH of less than 3.5. Spoilage of high-acid foods, such as fruit, is usually caused by yeasts and moulds. Meat and fish are more susceptible to bacterial spoilage, since their pH is closer to neutral.

The pH may be lowered so that the food becomes too acidic (less than pH1.5) for any micro-organisms to grow, such as the use of vinegar in pickling. In the manufacture of yoghurt and cheese, bacteria produce lactic acid; this lowers the pH, and retards the growth of food poisoning and spoilage organisms.

Foods may be preserved in vinegar, which is acetic acid (ethanoic acid) diluted with water. In the UK, malt vinegar is most frequently used, although distilled or white wine vinegar is used for pickling white vegetables such as cocktail onions and also for rollmops (herrings).

Foods usually pickled in vinegar include gherkins, capers, onions, shallots, walnuts, red cabbage, mixed pickles and chutneys.

Preservation by chemicals

A number of chemicals in certain foods, such as sausages, meats and jams, are permitted by law, but their use is strictly controlled. (Campden preserving tablets can be used for domestic fruit bottling.)

Some of the more popular ones are:

- **sulphur dioxide and sulphites** – use in dried fruit and vegetables, sausages, fruit-based dairy products, cider, beer and wine, biscuit dough
- **sorbic acid** – soft drinks, fruit yoghurt, processed cheese
- **sodium and potassium nitrite/nitrate** – bacon, ham, cured meats, corn beef and some cheeses.

Preservation by radiation

What is irradiation?

Foods are exposed to ionising radiation, which transfers some of its energy as it passes through the food, killing the pathogenic bacteria, which would otherwise make the food unsafe to eat, or, at lower doses the spoilage bacteria, which cause food to rot. Ionising radiation is electromagnetic, like radio waves, infra-red light or ultraviolet light. It is similar to ultraviolet radiation but has a higher frequency and much greater energy. This is sufficient to protect food effectively, but not enough to make it radioactive.

Irradiation methods have other key advantages over heating, chilling and chemical preservation methods.

- Irradiation works well with frozen or heat-sensitive products, as it does not cause any significant increase in temperature.
- Packaged products can be sterilised in the final pack, thus preventing contamination.
- Irradiation has a minimal impact on the nutritional value of the food. Proteins and carbohydrates are unaffected.
- Irradiation processing is a clean technology. No chemical additives are used or residues left behind in the food, and the process does not contaminate or damage the environment.
- The chemical changes caused in the food by the ionising radiation are in general much less severe than those arising from other food-processing methods such as cooling and heating.

At present, 36 countries allow irradiation of about 30 individually specified foods. In 21 of these countries there are active commercial food irradiative plants.

The Food Labelling (Amendment) (Irradiated Food) Regulations 1990 came into force on 1 January 1991 in parallel with those regulations setting out the controls on irradiation. The regulations require all foods that have been irradiated to carry an indication of treatment using the specified words 'irradiated' or 'treated with ionising radiation'.

Preservation by gas storage

Gas storage is used in conjunction with refrigeration to preserve meat, eggs and fruit. Varying the gas composition surrounding the food increases the length of time it can be stored.

Modified atmosphere packing

This is one method of altering the gas composition surrounding the product to give extended life.

Extra carbon dioxide added to the atmosphere surrounding the foods increases the length of time they can be stored. Without the addition of gas these foods would dry out more quickly.

Vacuum packaging

There are two distinct methods in which vacuum packaging can be incorporated into kitchen procedures. The first process relates to preparation and preservation. The second is a process of cooking 'sous-vide': a process of preparation, sealing inside a pouch or bag, cooking at a low temperature, followed by rapid chilling and storage at no more than 2°C. (There is more on this in Chapter 7.)

Benefits to the caterer
- **Reduced dehydration and drip loss:** weight loss can be considerably reduced when meat is vacuum packed, and when this also cuts out the need to trim, financial benefits are significant.
- **Increased storage life:** 'use by' times can be extended on chilled items (3–5°C), as shown in Table 5.15.
- **Increased hygiene and reduced cross-contamination:** vacuum pouches provide external barriers and will ensure food is protected in a hygienic condition, unaffected by any cross-contamination after packaging.
- **Improved workflow:** in any restaurant, there will inevitably be periods of time that are quiet. To spend that time vacuum packaging is not only an excellent use of your staff but also helps to relieve the workload when staff are busy. Vacuum packaging will make optimum use of all available time by helping to even out the workload.
- **Pre-packaging:** food may be pre-portioned and vacuum packed without the pressure of time; accurate weights and a reduction of waste should be obtained. The food can be kept chilled until needed. This also allows planning to take place for banquets, and can help overcome labour shortages at weekends and during holiday periods.
- **Reduced wastage:** vacuum packaging in advance can help minimise waste.
- **Satellite kitchens:** these can readily be supplied with vacuum-packed portions, eliminating the need for preparation in several areas.
- **Bulk buying:** many foods, like meat and fish, are affected by burn or

Table 5.15 'Use by' periods for chilled items

Fresh meat	14 days
Cheese	14 days
Fruit and vegetables	7 days
Fish	7 days

dehydration in the freezer. The protective qualities of a vacuum pouch ensure this problem is eliminated.

Precautions

There are certain precautions that the chef has to be aware of when using vacuum packaging. The shelf-life of cooked foods should be kept to a minimum under chilled conditions. Cooked meats and fish should not be packed unless sous-vide techniques are used. Stock rotation must be strictly observed. All packs must be clearly labelled with the description of the contents, weight, date and 'use by' date. In the event of any pack becoming blown or leaking, the contents should immediately be opened, examined and repacked only if satisfactory. Strict hygiene, the immediate packing of foodstuffs, and accurate chill conditions are vital parts of the process.

Modified atmosphere packaging (MAP)

This is a flexible way of extending the shelf-life of many kinds of fresh foods up to two to three times the normal levels. The method involves replacing the normal surrounding or 'dead space' atmosphere within food packages with specific mixtures of gases or single gases. Its objectives are to inhibit the growth of pathogenic bacteria and moulds, and to extend the shelf-life of chilled and certain ambient food products.

Originally the system was known as controlled atmosphere packaging, and was used for the retail portioning and packaging of red meat. The method was based on what is now known as the 'date of packaging + five days' system, using an 80 per cent oxygen/20 per cent carbon dioxide gas mixture. The gases used are carbon dioxide, nitrogen and oxygen. They are natural gases like those present in the air, but for MAP they are supplied purified and free of bacteria.

- Carbon dioxide (CO_2) inhibits the growth of pathogenic bacteria at temperatures not exceeding 8°C (46.4°F) for a restricted period. CO_2 does not kill the bacteria but will restrict mould growth over long periods.
- Nitrogen has a neutral effect on foodstuffs and is used in 100 per cent strength for dried and roasted foods, dairy cakes, cream and milk powders. The gas is also used in conjunction with CO_2 as a support gas.
- Oxygen sustains basic metabolism and prevents spoilage caused by anaerobic bacteria. It is also used in MAP gas mixtures for packaging red meats, where it preserves the red colour of the meat.

MAP effectively increases the length of time certain foods can be stored in the refrigerator. The gas mixtures used vary according to the product being packaged. MAP is particularly successful with bakery products where elevated CO_2 content permits high relative humidities with negligible mould growth.

Chefs employed in large food production operations and those employed as development chefs use MAP to aid food preparation and quality. Over the next few years we are likely to see further developments in this area as the catering industry becomes more involved in using gases to aid preservation of ingredients.

Table 5.16
Recommended gas mixture percentages (%) for MAP (based on refrigeration storage)

PRODUCT	OXYGEN (%)	NITROGEN (%)	CARBON DIOXIDE (%)	SHELF–LIFE
Red meat	80	–	20	5–8 days
White fish	30	30	40	5–6 days
Fatty fish	–	40	60	5–6 days
Salmon	20	20	60	5–6 days
Poultry	–	75	25	17–18 days
Hard cheese	–	–	100	3 weeks
Bacon, cooked meats	–	65–80	20–35	3–4 days
Bread	–	30–40	60–70	3 weeks
Dairy cakes	–	100	–	3 weeks

Some references to nutrition and food science elsewhere in the book:

REFERENCES

Catering for Health: A Guide to Teaching Healthier Catering Practices is available from Food Standards Agency Publications, PO Box 367, Hayes, Middlesex UB3 1UT.

Fox, B.A. and Cameron, A.G. (1995) *Food Science, Nutrition and Health* (6th edn). Hodder Arnold.

Gaman, P.M. and Sherrington, K.B. (1998) *The Science of Food* (4th edn). Butterworth-Heinemann.

Henderson, L., Irving, K., Gregory, J. *et al.* (2003) *The National Diet and Nutrition Survey*. London: TSO.

Further information

For further information on methods of preservation refer to the following sources.

- Eating for Health (HMSO).
- Food (Control of Irradiation) Regulations 1990 (HMSO).
- Gaman, P.M. and Sherrington, K.B. (1996) The Science of Food. Pergamon.
- Guidelines on Pre-cooked Chilled Foods (HMSO).
- Kilgour, O.F.G. (1976) An Introduction to Science for Catering and Homecraft Students. Heinemann.
- Manual of Nutrition (HMSO).
- McCance and Widdowson's The Composition of Foods (HMSO).
- Education Department, Unilever Ltd, Unilever House, Blackfriars, London EC4.
- Health Education Authority, Trevelyan House, 30 Great Peter Street, London SW1P 2HW.
- Nutrition Society, 10 Cambridge Court, 210 Shepherd's Bush Road, London W6 7NJ.

TOPICS FOR DISCUSSION

1 Why is a balanced diet desirable? What do you consider to be necessary to provide a balanced diet?

2 Why do you think trends, fads and fashions occur in our eating? Discuss how you could encourage a positive approach to having healthy eating habits.

3 How has presentation of foods changed and why have these changes come about?

4 What problems are associated with certain people's diets? What specific considerations are there for the diets of children, the elderly, nursing mothers and teenagers?

5 For what reasons may the nutritional value of foods be affected? Discuss examples of how this may occur and how such effects may be prevented.

6 What are the main sources of nutritional information?

7 Do you consider TV adverts and/or programmes affect people's diets?

PART 4

PLANNING, PRODUCTION AND SERVICE

Chapter 6 KITCHEN PLANNING, EQUIPMENT, SERVICES AND ENERGY CONSERVATION

INFLUENCING FACTORS ON DESIGN

Factors that influence kitchen planning and design include:

- the size and extent of the menu and the market it serves
- services – gas, electricity and water
- labour, skill level of staff
- amount of capital expenditure, costs
- use of prepared convenience foods
- types of equipment available
- hygiene and the Food Safety Act 1990/91/95
- design and decor
- multi-usage requirements.

The size and extent of the menu

Before a kitchen is planned, the management must know its goals and objectives in relation to market strategy. In other words, what markets are you aiming at and what style of operation are you going to operate? The menu will then determine the type of equipment you will require in order to produce the products that you know from the market research the customer is going to buy. You also need to know the target numbers you intend to service.

Services

The designer must know where the services are located and how efficient use can be made of them.

Labour and skill level

What kind of people does the company intend to employ? This will have an effect on the technology and equipment to be installed. The more prepared food used, the more this will affect the overall kitchen design.

Amount of capital expenditure

Most design has to work with a detailed capital budget. Often it is not always possible to design, then worry about the cost afterwards. Finance will very often determine the overall design and acceptability.

Because space is at a premium, kitchens are generally becoming smaller. Equipment is therefore being designed to cater for this trend, becoming more modular and streamlined and generally able to fit into less space. This is seen as a cost-reduction exercise. Labour is a significant cost factor, so equipment is being designed for ease of operation, maintenance and cleaning.

Use of prepared convenience foods

A fast-food menu using prepared convenience food will influence the planning and equipping very differently than for an à la carte or cook-chill kitchen. Certain factors will have to be determined.

- Will sweets and pastries be made on the premises?
- Will there be a need for larder or butcher?
- Will fresh or frozen food, or a combination of both be used?

Types of equipment available

The type, amount and size of the equipment will depend on the type of menu being provided. The equipment must be suitably sited. When planning a kitchen, standard symbols are used that can be produced on squared paper to provide a scale design. Computer-aided design (CAD) is now often used to do this.

Hygiene and the Food Safety Act 1990/91/95

The design and construction of the kitchen must comply with the Food Safety Act 1990/91/95. The basic layout and construction should enable adequate space to be provided in all food-handling and associated areas for equipment as well as working practices, and frequent cleaning to be carried out.

Design and decor

The trend towards provision of more attractive eating places, carried to its utmost perhaps by the chain and franchise operators, has not been without its effect on kitchen planning and design. One trend has been that of bringing the kitchen area totally or partially into view, with the development of back-bar type of equipment – for example, where grills or griddles are in full public view and food is prepared on them to order.

While there will be a continuing demand for the traditional heavy-duty type of equipment found in larger hotels and restaurant kitchens, the constant need to change and update the design and decor of modern restaurants means that the equipment's life is generally shorter – reduced perhaps from ten years to seven or five, or even less – to cope with the demand for change and redevelopment.

This has resulted in the generally improved design of catering equipment with the introduction of modular units.

Multi-usage requirements

Round-the-clock requirements such as in hospitals, factories where shift work takes place, the police and armed forces, have also forced kitchen planners to consider the design of kitchens with a view to their partial use outside peak times. To this end kitchen equipment is being made more adaptable and flexible, so that whole sections can be closed down when not in use, in order to maximise savings on heating, lighting and maintenance.

KITCHEN DESIGN

Kitchens must be designed so that they can be easily managed. Managers must have easy access to the areas under their control and good visibility in the areas that have to be supervised. Large operations should work on separate work floors, for reasons of efficiency and hygiene:

- product – raw materials to finished product
- personnel – how people move within the kitchen; for example, staff working in dirty areas (areas of contamination) should not enter areas of finished product, or where blast-chilling is taking place.
- containers/equipment/utensils – equipment should, where possible, be separated out into specific process areas
- refuse – refuse must be kept separated and should not pass into other areas in order to get to its storage destination.

Figure 6.1 Kitchen design

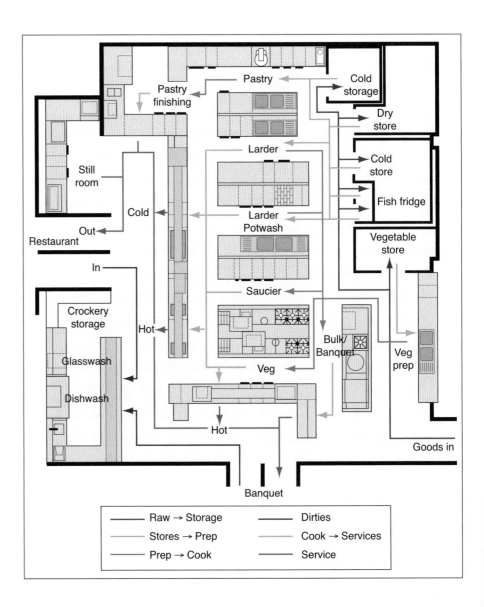

Product flows

Each section should be subdivided into high-risk and contaminated sections. High-risk food is that which, during processing, is likely to be easily contaminated.

Contaminated food is that which is contaminated on arrival before processing – for example, unprepared vegetables, raw meat.

Back-tracking or cross-over of materials and product must be avoided.

Work flow

Food preparation rooms should be planned to allow a 'work flow' whereby food is processed through the premises from the point of delivery to the point of sale or service, with the minimum of obstruction. The various processes should be separated as far as possible, and food intended for sale should not cross paths with waste food or refuse. Staff time is valuable, and a design that reduces wasteful journeys is both efficient and cost-effective.

The overall sequence of receiving, storing, preparing, holding, serving and clearing is achieved by:

- minimum movement
- minimal back-tracking
- maximum use of space
- maximum use of equipment with minimum expenditure of time and effort.

Figure 6.2 Work flow

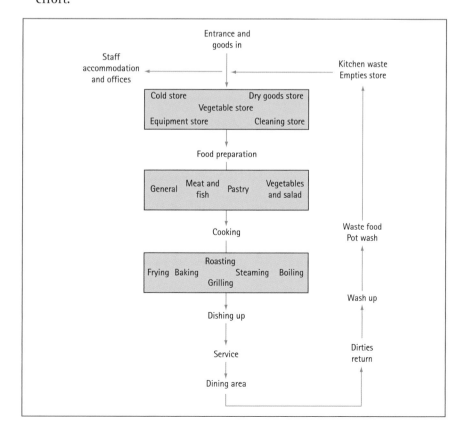

Work space

Approximately 4.2 m (15 square feet) is required per person; too little space can cause staff to work in close proximity to stoves, steamers, cutting blades, mixers, and so on, thus causing accidents. A space of 1.37 m (4.5 feet) from equipment is desirable, and aisles must be of adequate size to enable staff to move safely. The working area must be suitably lit, and ventilated with extractor fans to remove heat, fumes and smells.

Working sections

The size and style of the menu and the ability of the staff will determine the number of sections and layout that is necessary. A straight-line layout would be suitable for a snack bar, while an island layout would be more suitable for a hotel restaurant.

Access to ancillary areas

A good receiving area needs to be designed for easy receipt of supplies with nearby storage facilities suitably sited for distribution of foods to preparation and production areas.

Hygiene must be considered so that kitchen equipment can be cleaned, and all used equipment from the dining area can be cleared, cleaned and stored. Still room facilities may also be required.

Equipment

The type, amount and size of equipment will depend on the type of menu being provided. Not only should the equipment be suitably situated but the working weight is very important to enable the equipment to be used without excess fatigue. When a kitchen is being planned, standard symbols are used that can be produced on squared paper to provide a scale design. Hand-washing facilities and storage of cleaning equipment should not be omitted.

Kitchen equipment manufacturers and gas and electricity suppliers can provide details of equipment relating to output and size.

The various preparation processes require different areas depending on what food is involved. In a vegetable preparation area, water from the sinks and dirt from the vegetables are going to accumulate, and therefore adequate facilities for drainage should be provided. Pastry preparation, on the other hand, entails mainly dry processes.

Whatever the processes, there are certain basic rules that can be applied that not only make for easier working conditions but help to ensure that food hygiene regulations are complied with.

Food preparation areas

Proper design and layout of the preparation area can make a major contribution to good food hygiene. Staff generally respond to good working conditions by taking more of a pride in themselves, in their work and in their working environment.

Adequate work space must be provided for each process and every effort must be made to separate dirty and clean processes. Vegetable preparation and wash-up areas should be separate from the actual food preparation and service areas. The layout must ensure a continuous work flow in one direction in order that cross-over of foods and any cross-contamination is avoided. The staff should not hamper each other by having to cross each other's paths more than is absolutely necessary.

Actual worktop areas should be adequate in size for the preparation processes necessary, and should be so designed that the food handler has all required equipment and utensils close to hand.

Accommodation must be based on operational need. The layout of the kitchen must focus on the working and stores area, and the equipment to be employed. These areas must be designed and based on the specification of the operation.

Kitchens can be divided into sections; these must be based on the process. For example:

- **dry areas** – for storage
- **wet areas** – for fish preparation, vegetable preparation, butchery, cold preparation
- **hot wet areas** – for boiling, poaching, steaming; equipment needed will include atmospheric steamers, bratt pans, pressure steamers, steam jacketed boilers, combination oven
- **hot dry areas** – for frying, roasting, grilling; equipment needed will include cool zone fryers, salamanders, pressure fryers, induction cookers, bratt pans, halogen cookers, roasting ovens, microwave, charcoal grills, cook and hold ovens
- **dirty areas** – for refuse, pot wash areas, plate wash; equipment needed will include compactors, dishwashers, refuse storage units, glass washers, pot wash machines.

Size of kitchen and food preparation areas
Size is determined also by purpose and function.

- The operation is based on the menu and the market it is to serve.
- The design and equipment is based on the market.
- Consideration must be given to the management policy on buying raw materials. Choice will determine kitchen plans on handling raw materials.
- Prepared food will require different types of equipment and labour requirements compared to part-prepared food or raw-state ingredients.
- Prepared food examples are sous-vide products, cook-chill, cook-freeze and prepared sweets. Part-prepared food examples are peeled and cut vegetables, convenience sauces and soups, portioned fish/meat. Raw-state food examples are unprepared vegetables, meat that requires butchering, and fish requiring filleting and portioning.

Consideration must also be given to the service policy on using all-plate service or a mixture of plate and silver service or self-service, and how all this will affect the volume and type of dishwashing required.

Planning and layout of the cooking area

Because 'raw materials' enter the cooking section from the main preparation areas (vegetables, meat and fish, dry goods), this section will be designed with a view to continuing the flow movement through to the servery. To this end, roasting ovens, for example, are best sited close to the meat preparation area, and steamers adjacent to the vegetable preparation area.

Layout is not, however, just a question of equipment siting and selection, much depends on the type of management policy on use of prepared foods and the operating cycle. Clearly the cooking section should contain no through traffic lanes (used by other staff to travel from one section to another). The layout should be planned so that raw foodstuffs arrive at one point, are processed in the cooking section and then despatched to the servery. There should be a distinct progression in one direction.

As with other areas, the cooking section should be designed with a view to making maximum use of the available area and providing economy of effort in use.

Island groupings

In an island arrangement, equipment is placed back to back in the centre of the cooking area. There will need to be sufficient space to allow for this, including adequate gangways around the equipment and space to place other items along the walls.

Wall siting

An alternative arrangement involves siting equipment along walls. This arrangement is possible where travel distances are reduced, and normally occurs in smaller premises (or sections thereof).

L- or U-shaped layouts

L- or U-shaped arrangements create self-contained sections that discourage entry by non-authorised staff; they can promote efficient working, with distances reduced between work centres.

When planning the layout of the cooking section the need to allow sufficient space for access to equipment such as ovens should be borne in mind. Opening doors creates an arc that cannot be reduced, and the operator must have sufficient room for comfortable and safe access. It is also likely that trolleys will be used for loading and unloading ovens, or rolling tables drawn into position in front of the oven.

The choice of layout

Selection of equipment will be made after detailed consideration of the functions that will be carried out within the cooking area of the kitchen. The amount of equipment required will depend upon the complexity of the menus offered, the quantity of meals served, and the policy of use of materials – from the traditional kitchen organisation using only fresh vegetables and totally unprepared items, to the use of prepared foods, chilled items and frozen foods, where the kitchen consists of a regeneration unit only.

Given, however, that a certain amount of equipment is required, the planner has the choice of a number of possible layouts, within the constraints of the building shape and size, and the location of services. The most common are the island groupings, wall siting and the use of an L- or U-shaped layout and variations upon these basic themes.

Siting of equipment

The kitchen operation must work as a system. It is advisable to site items of equipment used for specific functions together. This will help increase efficiency and avoid shortcuts.

Hand basins must be sited strategically to encourage frequent hand washing in all food preparation areas. One should be in evidence at each workstation.

The kitchen environment

- **Space:** The Office, Shop and Railway Premises Act 1963, stipulates 11.32 cubic metres (400 cubic feet) per person, discounting height in excess of 3 m (10 feet).
- **Humidity:** A humid atmosphere creates side effects such as food deterioration, infestation risk, condensation on walls and slippery floors. Anything higher than 60 per cent humidity lowers productivity. Provision for the replacement of extracted air with fresh air is essential.
- **Temperature:** No higher than 20–26°C (68–79°F) is desirable for maximum working efficiency and comfort, with 16–18°C (61–64°F) in preparation areas.
- **Noise:** Conversation should be possible within 4 m (13 feet).
- **Light:** The minimum legal level in preparation areas is 20 lumens per square foot with up to 38 lumens preferable in all areas.

Ventilation systems

There are three basic types of ventilation system.

1 **Extract:** this system only removes air, thereby creating a negative pressure in the space. Outside air will come into the space wherever it can, usually through doorways, window areas or specially prepared openings. It can be used to avoid contaminants spreading to other

areas, as a negative pressure is created within the space in which the system operates

2 **Inlet:** this system is concerned only with the supply of outside air. In this case, the space is under positive pressure, with the air leaving through doorways or windows. This system is used mostly in clean spaces, thus preventing contaminants coming in from other areas. It is not a suitable system for a catering kitchen but may prove useful in areas such as storage rooms and larders, where it is desirable to prevent contaminants from reaching the foods stored.

3 **Combined:** this balances the flow of air in and out the space.

All these systems use mechanical means of moving the air – that is, by electrically driven fans. In the first two cases, the replacement and displacement air, respectively, are virtually impossible to control, and there will always be draughts, particularly when the outside air is cold.

The ideal system, although more expensive, is the combined system, where the extract and supply of air can be controlled. It is especially suitable for kitchen ventilation, where large quantities of air are required to be removed from relatively small spaces.

The best and most effective way of removing contaminants is at source. This is normally by means of a purpose-made hood over the equipment that is producing heat, grease, smells, and so on. The following conditions relating to the hood must be satisfied:

- the hood should be made of non-corrosive material and so designed that it can be cleaned easily
- it must have a condensate channel around its bottom edge
- it must overhang the equipment underneath by 230–300 mm
- it must allow a sufficient velocity of air to pass over the edge of the hood.

Ventilation requirements for kitchens

There are three basic ways of determining these requirements.

1 **Air changes:** this method involves specifying an air change rate throughout the area. This is usually between 20 and 35 air changes per hour, but this method is only an approximation and, should there be more than one hood, then it would be difficult to apportion.

2 **Air velocity:** this system involves knowing the size of the hood over the equipment and allowing a certain velocity of air over the face area. Although this is a better method than the previous one, it is very difficult to obtain the correct velocity and reliance on experience is necessary. Velocity is usually between 0.3 and 0.8 mm per second.

3 **Air volume:** the most useful method is to allow a specific volume of air for each particular piece of equipment. Table 6.1 shows the air volumes that can be used for the different types of equipment.

EQUIPMENT	CUBIC METRES PER SECOND
Ranges (unit type) approx. 1 m²	0.3
Pastry ovens	0.3
Fish friers	0.45
Grills	0.25–0.3
Boiling pans (90–135 litres)	0.3
Steamers	0.3
Sinks (sterilising)	0.25
Bains-marie	0.2
Stills boilers	0.15–0.25

It is important to note that the system will not necessarily function properly just by having the correct volume of air. Close attention must be paid to the design and installation of the hood, as indicated above, and, in addition, the trunking must (as far as possible) be constructed without sharp bends or long horizontal runs.

Special filters should be installed within the extract hood to collect contaminants, otherwise grease could build up and become a fire hazard.

Self-cleaning kitchen extracts

A system of self-cleaning ventilation equipment is available that can be adapted to operate either as a full extract system over kitchen equipment or be specially designed as part of individual items of equipment such as grills, deep-fat fryers and ovens.

The cleaning cycle is normally operated each day and requires that a supply of hot water is available to the ventilator, together with a facility for dosing with a suitable detergent. The extract fan must be switched off, an operation that, in itself, can be adapted to begin the cleaning operation.

Hot water, together with detergent, is then released into the ventilator for a predetermined period, controlled by an automatic timer. The deposits of grease and lint are washed out of the ventilator into drainage gutters, which need to be connected to the drainage system.

This timer shuts off the water supply at the end of the cleaning cycle and the ventilator is ready for reuse.

The ventilators can be fitted with automatic fire protection, which will result in baffles closing over the air inlet, shutting off the fan and operating the water supply to smother any fire.

i

Further information
For further information, consult HCIMA Technical Brief No. 30: Kitchen Ventilation.

Consultants

There are a number of specialist consultants involved in kitchen design. Consultants are often used by companies to provide independent advice and specialist knowledge. Their expertise should cover:

- equipment
- mechanical and electrical services
- food service systems and methods
- drainage
- architectural elements
- ventilation/air conditioning
- statutory legislation (Food Act, Health and Safety Act, fire regulations)
- energy conservation
- recycling
- green issues/legislation (waste management)
- refrigeration.

Consultants should provide the client with unbiased opinions and expertise not available in their company. Their aim should be to raise the standards of provision and equipment installation, while providing an efficient and effective food production operation that also takes into account staff welfare.

Maintenance

Planning and equipping a kitchen is an expensive investment, therefore to avoid any action by the Environmental Health Officer, efficient, regular cleaning and maintenance is essential. (The kitchens at the Dorchester hotel are swept during the day, given soap/detergent and water treatment after service, and any spillages cleaned up immediately. At night, contractors clean the ceilings, floors and walls.)

Kitchen design: industry trends

In most cases, throughout the industry, companies are looking to reduce labour costs while maintaining or enhancing the meal experience for the customer. Some trends in various situations are as follows.

- Hotels: greater use of buffet and self-assisted service units.
- Banqueting: move towards plated service, less traditional silver service.
- Fast food: new concepts coming onto the market, more specialised chicken and seafood courts, more choices in ethnic food.
- Roadside provision: increase in number of operations, partnerships with oil companies, basic grill menus now enhanced via factory-produced à la carte items.
- Food courts: development has slowed down; minor changes all the

time; most food courts offer an 'all day' menu. Restaurant Associates (Compass) are introducing food courts into hotels.
- Restaurants/hotels: less emphasis on luxury-end, five-star experience.
- Theme restaurants: will continue to improve and multiply.
- Hospitals: greater emphasis on bought-in freezer and chilled foods; steam cuisine; reduced amount of on-site preparation and cooking.
- Industrial: more zero-subsidy staff restaurants, increased self-service for all items; introduction of cashless systems will enable multi-tenant office buildings to offer varying subsidy levels.
- Prisons, institutions: little if any change; may follow hospitals by buying in more preprepared food; may receive foods from multi-outlet central production units, tied in with schools, meals on wheels provision, etc.
- University/colleges: greater move towards providing food courts; more snack bars and coffee shops.

Chefs and managers are often asked to assist in the design of food service systems. In these circumstances there are various issues that need to be taken into account. If possible all designs should be market led in the first place.

- Market expectations: type of customer demand (including price), type of menu, type of meal, type of establishment, 'product life' and possibility of 'product' changes, customer participation.
- Operational needs: amount of space available, expected throughput/ seat turnover, type of operation (e.g. call order, traditional).
- Amount of basic preparation: amount of regeneration, storage needs, flows of materials, people and equipment, availability of supplies, frequency of delivery, need for storage, availability of services – gas, electricity, water, waste disposal, energy costs, ventilation, extraction and induction systems.
- Type and quantity of labour to be employed: e.g. unspecialised staff using pre-prepared materials, traditional 'partie' system using basic ingredients, room for future expansion.
- Finance: objective (e.g. to make a profit, to provide a service), cost of space (£s per square metre), amount and type of finance (e.g. purchase, leasing, hire purchase), whether to use second-hand equipment, depreciation policy, life of investment.

Kitchen and restaurant areas

The calculation of the amount of space required is very complex as it is dependent on a mixture of influencing factors, including:

- volume of meals served, average time to consume a meal/product, seat turnover
- time over which the meals will be served
- size of menu

- complexity of individual menu items
- style of service (e.g. counter/plate/guéridon)
- mix of fresh and convenience food production
- number and type and size of dining facilities served by the kitchen (e.g. restaurants, floors)
- type of cooking methods to be used
- structural features of the building
- cost of floor space in the planned facility.

Kitchen equipment trends

- Refrigeration: more concentration on providing CFC-free equipment.
- Environmental: with an environmentally conscious society, energy conservation will feature higher in the development agenda; this will include heat recovery systems, recirculated air systems, improved working conditions and lighting systems.
- Cooking: more use of induction units, combination ovens, microwave and tunnel ovens.
- Servery counters: more decorative units being used.
- Dishwasher/potwash: greater economy of water, more mechanised and automated use of combination machines.
- Ventilation: moves towards integrated wash systems, recirculated air systems, integral air supply, integral fire suppression.

The general trend will be towards self-diagnostic equipment and automated service call-out. With the use of replacement components, there is less emphasis on repairs.

LINKING EQUIPMENT TO COMPUTERS

Head chefs and food and beverage managers will have PCs in their offices for jobs like recipe development, accounts, inventory and email. Electronic point of sale (EPOS) terminals in restaurant bars can interface directly with back-of-house computers. Some EPOS systems with kitchen monitor hook-ups can optimise meal preparation by telling chefs when to start cooking particular components, thus allowing all the items that make up an order to be completed at exactly the same time.

A growing range of kitchen equipment, from cookers and refrigerated storage to large ware-washing systems, come with on-board computer control, and several products can additionally be specified with extra hardware and software to permit continuous monitoring of the main equipment functions. Some appliances can also be specified with a two-way interactive link, enabling programs subject to frequent change (such as recipes) to be downloaded to the appliance from a computer directly via cable or wireless hook-up, or via modem connection to the Internet.

Further information
To find out more about water management, contact Water Training International, Burn Hall, Tollerton Road, Huby, Yorkshire YO6 1JB.

WATER MANAGEMENT

Legislation

Each country has its own laws governing the use of water. In the UK these include the Water Industry Act 1991, the Health & Safety at Work Act 1974 and the Water Supply Bylaw 1989.

The purpose of water law is to:

- discourage undue consumption of water
- prevent contamination of the water supply.

Substantial savings in water can be made through the renewal and replacement of wasteful, older water-using equipment. Self-closing taps, for example, reduce water consumption by as much as 55 per cent.

In many countries it is an offence for the owners or occupiers of buildings to intentionally or negligently allow any 'fitting to waste', or to unduly consume water. Examples:

- taps constantly dripping or left running
- overflows from storage and WC cisterns dripping
- water leaks not repaired.

There is evidence to show that the undertaking of a water-management audit can save money. Such an audit examines and quantifies possible savings.

Immediate practical action

- Water metering.
- Tap flow regulator – flow control.
- Urinals using less water.
- Shut-off devices and self closing taps.
- Automatic or programmed mains shut-off device when buildings are not in use.
- Low-flow shower heads.

EQUIPMENT DESIGN

The Food Safety (General Food Hygiene) Regulations 1995 require all articles, fittings and equipment with which food comes into contact to be kept clean and to be constructed of such materials and maintained in such condition and repair as to minimise risk of contamination, and to enable thorough cleaning and, where necessary, disinfection. Equipment must also be installed in such a way that the surrounding area is able to be cleaned.

Recommendations for equipment

The following equipment is preferable:

- tubular machinery frames
- stainless steel table legs
- drain cocks and holes instead of pockets and crevices that could trap liquid
- dials fitted to machines having adequate clearance to facilitate cleaning.

Preparation surfaces

The choice of surfaces on which food is to be prepared is vitally important. Failure to ensure a suitable material may provide a dangerous breeding ground for bacteria. Stainless steel tables are best as they do not rust, and their welded seams eliminate unwanted cracks and open joints. Sealed tubular legs are preferable to angular ones because, again, they eliminate the corners in which dirt collects. Tubular legs have often been found to provide a harbourage for pests.

Preparation surfaces should be jointless, durable, impervious, of the correct height and firm-based. They must withstand repeated cleaning at the required temperature without premature deterioration through pitting and corrosion.

Choosing cutting boards

Bear in mind the following aspects when choosing cutting boards:

- water absorbency – soft woods draw fluids into them and, with the fluids, bacteria is also drawn in
- wooden cutting boards made of hard wood, if cleaned and sterilised, are perfectly acceptable in catering premises
- resistance to stains, cleaning chemicals, heat and food acids
- toxicity – the cutting board must not give off toxic substances
- durability – the cutting board must withstand wear and tear
- cutting boards must not split or warp.

Appearances can be deceptive. Two researchers at the University of Wisconsin, Madison, USA, set out ways of decontaminating wooden kitchen surfaces and ended up finding that such surfaces are pretty good at decontaminating themselves. When working with wood from nine different species of tree and four sorts of plastic, the results were always the same. The researchers spread salmonella, listeria and E. coli bacteria over the various samples and left them for three minutes. The level of bacteria on the plastic remained the same, while the level on the wood plummeted, often by as much as 99.9 per cent. Left overnight at room temperature the bacteria on the plastic actually multiplied, while the wooden surfaces cleaned themselves so thoroughly that the researchers could not record anything from them. This is because of the porous structure of wood – previously thought to be a disadvantage in soaking up fluid with bacteria in it. Once inside, however, the bacteria sticks to the wood's fibres and are 'strangled' by one of the many noxious anti-microbial chemicals with which living trees protect themselves.

Colour coding
To avoid cross-contamination, it is important that the same equipment is not to be used for handling raw and high-risk products without being disinfected. To prevent the inadvertent use of equipment for both raw and high-risk foods, it is recommended that, where possible, different colours and shapes are used to identify products or raw materials used.

Fixing and siting of equipment

Where practicable, equipment should be mobile to facilitate its removal for cleaning – that is, castor mounted and with brakes on all the wheels.

A guide for stationary equipment
To allow for the cleaning of wall and floor surfaces, stationary equipment must be positioned:

- 500 mm from the walls
- with 250 mm clearance between the floor and underside of the equipment.

KITCHEN ORGANISATION

The purpose of efficient kitchen organisation is to produce the required quantity of food, of the best possible standard for the required number of people – on time, and by the most effective use of staff, equipment and materials.

Kitchen design and work flow

The kitchen should be designed not only to be suitable for the proposed menu(s), but also to be flexible enough to cope with any menu changes that may occur. (See also the section on kitchen design, pages 237–246.) To get ideas on effective kitchen design:

- visit existing kitchens with a critical eye
- ask staff for comments on the suitability, or otherwise, of layout, and its practicality
- seek professional advice from a number of manufacturers.

WORKING METHODS

Time and motion studies are essential for all tasks. Working in a hot environment – possibly against the clock, possibly leading to stress – it is necessary to conserve energy. A skilled craftsperson is one who completes the task in the minimum time, to the required standard and with the minimum effort.

Simplifying an operation

The objective is to make work easier; this can be achieved by simplifying the operation, eliminating unnecessary movements, combining two operations into one or improving old methods. For example, if you are peeling potatoes and you allow the peelings to drop into the container in the first place, the action of moving the peelings into the bowl and the need to clean the table could have been eliminated. This operation is simplified if, instead of a blunt knife, a good hand potato peeler is used, because it is simple and safe to use, requires less effort, can be used more quickly and requires less skill to produce a better result. If the quantity of potatoes is sufficient, then a mechanical peeler could be used, but it would be necessary to remember that the electricity used would add to the cost and that the time needed to clean a mechanical aid may lessen its work-saving value. If it takes 25 minutes to clean a potato-mashing machine that has been used to mash potatoes for 500 meals, it could be time well spent in view of the time and energy saved mashing the potatoes. It may not be considered worthwhile using the machine to mash potatoes for 20 meals, however. Factors such as this need to be taken into account.

Overcoming fatigue

Working methods may be observed in catering at many different levels, from the experienced methodical chef wiping the knife after cutting a lemon, to the complexity of the Ganymede system in a large hospital, or the carefully planned call-order unit in a fast-food operation where, because of careful thought and study, wastage of time, money and materials is reduced to a minimum. But even with the aid of mechanical devices, labour-saving equipment and the extensive use of foods that have been partially or totally prepared, people at work still become fatigued.

It is most important to stand correctly – well balanced with the weight of the body divided on to both legs, and with the feet sensibly spaced and the back reasonably straight when working for long periods in one place. Particular care is needed when lifting: stand with legs apart and bend the knees (not the back), and use the leg muscles to assist lifting. The object to be raised should be held close to the body.

It is possible to cultivate the right attitude to work, as well as good working habits. Certain jobs are repetitive, some require considerable concentration, while others cause physical strain; not all work provides equal job satisfaction. If 500 fish cakes have to be shaped, it is worthwhile setting targets to complete a certain number in a certain time. Such simple things as not counting the completed items but counting those still to be done motivates some people to greater effort. Some circumstances do not lend themselves to overcoming the physical pressures, however – for example, if 150 people require 150 omelettes then, provided the eggs are broken and seasoned and kept in bulk with the correct-size ladle for portioning, the attitude to adopt may be to try to do each omelette better and quicker than the last. If careful thought and study are given to all practical jobs, wastage of time, labour and materials can often be eliminated.

Equipment and layout

Properly planned layouts with adequate equipment, tools and materials to do the job are essential if practical work is to be carried out efficiently. If equipment is correctly placed then work will proceed smoothly in proper sequence without back-tracking or criss-crossing. Work tables, sinks and stores, and refrigerators should be within easy reach in order to eliminate unnecessary walking. Equipment should be easily available during all working times.

The storage, handling of foods, tools and utensils, and the movement of food in various stages of production needs careful study. Many people carry out practical work by instinct and often evolve the most efficient method instinctively. Nevertheless careful observation of numerous practical workers will show a great deal of time and effort wasted through bad working methods. It is necessary to arrange work so that the shortest possible distance exists between storage and the place where the items are to be used.

When arranging storage see that the most frequently used items are nearest to hand. Place heavy items where the minimum of body strain is required to move them. Keep all items in established places so that time is not lost in hunting and searching for them. Adjustable shelving can be a help in organising different storage requirements. Only after all the pre-planning of the job is complete comes the actual work itself.

Careful preparation of foods and equipment (a good mise-en-place) is essential if a busy service is to follow and is to be operated efficiently so that orders move out methodically without confusion.

The work to be done must be planned carefully so that the items requiring long preparation or cooking are started first. Where fast production is required lining up will assist efficiency. Work carried out haphazardly, without plan or organisation, obviously takes longer to do than work done according to plan. There is a sequence to work that leads to high productivity and an efficient worker should learn this sequence quickly.

KITCHEN SUPERVISION/MANAGEMENT

The organisation under different industries varies according to their specific requirements, and the names given to people doing similar jobs may also vary. Some companies or organisations will require operatives, technicians and technologists; others need craftspeople, supervisors and managers. The supervisory function of the technician, chef de partie or supervisor may be similar.

The hospitality and catering industry is made up of people with craft skills. The craftsperson is involved with food production, the chef de partie may be the supervisor, supervising a section or sections of the food production system. The head chef will have both managerial and supervisory skills and he/she will determine kitchen policies.

Supervisors are involved with the successful deployment of money, material and people. The primary role of the supervisor is to ensure that a group of people work together to achieve the goals set by the business. Managing physical and human resources to achieve customer service goals requires planning, organising, staffing, directing and controlling.

Supervisors and head chefs need to motivate people, to persuade them to act in certain ways. In the kitchen/restaurant, as in any other department, staff must first be motivated to follow procedures. This can be done in a positive way by offering rewards, or in a negative way with catering staff who do not comply with requirements. Both methods can be effective, and can be used by supervisors to achieve their goals. One of the most effective ways is for a supervisor to build a team and offer incentives for good performance. However, staff can become indifferent to repeated schemes such as 'employee of the month'. A good supervisor will attempt to introduce novelty and fun into the reward system.

The supervisory function

Certain leadership qualities are needed to enable the supervisor to carry out his or her role effectively. These qualities include the ability to:

- communicate
- initiate
- make decisions
- coordinate
- mediate
- motivate
- inspire
- organise.

Those under supervision should expect from the supervisor:

- consideration
- understanding
- respect
- consistency.

In return the supervisor can expect:

- loyalty
- respect
- cooperation.

The good supervisor is able to obtain the best from those for whom he or she has responsibility, and can also completely satisfy the management of the establishment that a good job is being done.

The job of the supervisor is essentially to be an overseer. In the catering industry the name given to the supervisor may vary: sous-chef, chef de partie, kitchen supervisor or section chef. In hospital catering the name would be sous-chef, chef de partie or kitchen supervisor. The kitchen supervisor will be responsible to the catering manager, while in hotels and restaurants a chef de partie will be responsible to the head chef. The exact details of the job will vary according to the different areas of the industry and the size of the various units, but generally the supervisory role involves three functions: technical, administrative and social.

Technical function

Culinary skills and the ability to use kitchen equipment are essential for the kitchen supervisor. Most kitchen supervisors will have worked their way up through the section or sections before reaching supervisory responsibility. The supervisor needs to be able 'to do' as well as knowing 'what to do' and 'how to do it'. It is also necessary to be able to do it well and to be able to impart some of these skills to others.

Administrative function

The supervisor or chef de partie will, in many kitchens, be involved with the menu planning, sometimes with complete responsibility for the whole menu but more usually for part of the menu, as happens with the larder chef and pastry chef. This includes the ordering of foodstuffs (which is an important aspect of the supervisor's job in a catering establishment) and, of course, accounting for and recording materials used. The administrative function includes the allocation of duties and, in all instances, basic work-study knowledge is needed to enable the supervisor to operate effectively. The supervisor's job may also include the writing of reports, particularly in situations where it is necessary to make comparisons and when new developments are being tried.

Social function

The role of the supervisor is perhaps most clearly seen in staff relationships because the supervisor has to motivate the staff under his or her responsibility. 'To motivate' could be described as the initiation of movement and action, and having got the staff moving the supervisor needs to exert control. Then, in order to achieve the required result, the staff need to be organised.

Thus the supervisor has a threefold function regarding the handling of staff – namely to organise, to motivate and to control. This is the essence of staff supervision.

Elements of supervision

The accepted areas of supervision include:

- forecasting and planning
- organising
- commanding
- coordinating
- controlling.

Each of these will be considered within the sphere of catering.

Forecasting

Before making plans it is necessary to look ahead, to foresee possible and probable outcomes, and to allow for them. For example, if the chef de partie knows that the following day is her/his assistant's day off, s/he looks ahead and plans accordingly; when the catering supervisor in the hospital knows that there is a flu epidemic and two cooks are feeling below par, he or she plans for their possible absence; if there is a spell of fine, hot weather and the cook in charge of the larder foresees a continued demand for cold foods, or when an end to the hot spell is anticipated, then the plans are modified. For the supervisor, forecasting is the good use of judgement acquired from previous knowledge and experience. For example, because many people are on holiday in August fewer meals will be needed in the office restaurant; no students are in residence at the college hostel, but a conference is being held and 60 meals are required. A motor show, bank holidays, the effects of a rail strike or a wet day, as well as less predictable situations, such as the number of customers anticipated on the opening day of a new restaurant, all need to be anticipated and planned for.

Planning

From the forecasting comes the planning: how many meals to prepare; how much to have in stock (should the forecast not have been completely accurate); how many staff will be needed; which staff and when. Are the staff capable of what is required of them? If not, the supervisor needs to plan some training. This, of course, is particularly important if new equipment is installed. Imagine an expensive item, such as a new type of oven, ruined on the day it is installed because the staff have not been instructed in its proper use; or, more likely, equipment lying idle because the supervisor may not like it, may consider it is sited wrongly, does not train staff to use it, or for some similar reason.

As can be seen from these examples it is necessary for forecasting to precede planning, and from planning we now move to organising.

Organising

In the catering industry organisational skills are applied to food, to equipment and to staff. Organising in this context consists of ensuring that what is wanted is where it is wanted, when it is wanted, in the right amount and at the right time.

Such organisation involves the supervisor in the production of duty rotas, maybe training programmes and also cleaning schedules. Consider the supervisor's part in organising an outdoor function where a wedding reception is to be held in a church hall: 250 guests require a hot meal to be served at 2 pm and in the evening a dance will be held for the guests, during which a buffet will be provided at 9 pm. The supervisor would need to organise staff to be available when required, to have their own meals and maybe to see that they have got their transport home. Calor gas stoves may be needed, and the supervisor would have to arrange for these to be serviced and for the equipment used to be cleaned after the function. The food would need to be ordered so that it arrived in time to be prepared. If decorated hams were to be used on the buffet then they would need to be ordered in time so that they could be prepared, cooked and decorated over the required period of time. If the staff have never carved hams before, instruction would need to be given; this entails organising training. Needless to say, the correct quantities of food, equipment and cleaning materials would also have to be at the right place when wanted; and if all the details of the situation were not organised properly problems could occur.

Commanding

The supervisor has to give instructions to staff on how, what, when and where; this means that orders have to be given and a certain degree of order and discipline maintained. The successful supervisor is able to do this effectively, having made certain decisions and, usually, having established the basic priorities. Explanations of why a food is prepared in a certain manner, why this amount of time is needed to dress up food, say for a buffet, why this decision is taken and not that decision, and how these explanations and orders are given, determine the effectiveness of the supervisor.

Coordinating

Coordinating is the skill required to get staff to cooperate and work together. To achieve this, the supervisor has to be interested in the staff, to deal with their queries, to listen to their problems and to be helpful. Particular attention should be paid to new staff, easing them into the work situation so that they quickly become part of the team or partie. The other area of coordination for which the supervisor has particular responsibility is in maintaining good relations with other departments. However, the important persons to consider will always be the customers – for example, the patients, the school children – who are to receive the service, and good service is dependent on cooperation between waiters and cooks, nurses and catering staff, stores staff, caretakers, teachers, suppliers, and so on. The supervisor has a crucial role to play here.

Controlling

This includes the controlling of people and products, preventing pilfering as well as improving performance; checking that staff arrive on time, do not leave before time and do not misuse time in between; checking that the product, in this case the food, is of the right standard – that is to say, of the correct quantity and quality; checking to prevent waste, and also to ensure that staff operate the portion control system correctly.

This aspect of the supervisor's function involves inspecting and requires tact; controlling may include the inspecting of the swill bin to observe the amount of waste, checking the disappearance of a quantity of food, supervising the cooking of the meat so that shrinkage is minimised and reprimanding an unpunctual member of the team.

The standards of any catering establishment are dependent on the supervisor doing his or her job efficiently, and standards are set and maintained by effective control, which is the function of the supervisor.

Responsibilities of the supervisor

Delegation

It is recognised that delegation is the root of successful supervision; in other words, by giving a certain amount of responsibility to others, the supervisor can be more effective.

The supervisor needs to be able to judge the person capable of responsibility before any delegation can take place. But then, having recognised the abilities of an employee, the supervisor who wants to develop the potential of those under his or her control must allow the person entrusted with the job to get on with it.

Motivation

Since not everyone is capable of, or wants, responsibility, the supervisor still needs to motivate those who are less ambitious. Most people are prepared to work so as to improve their standard of living, but there is also another very important motivating factor: most people wish to get satisfaction from the work they do. The supervisor must be aware of why people work and how different people achieve job satisfaction, and then be able to act upon this knowledge. A supervisor should have been on a training course to attempt to understand what motivates people as there are a number of theories that s/he can use to stimulate ideas.

Symptoms of poor motivation

There are many symptoms of poor motivation, in general terms they reveal themselves as a lack of interest in getting the job done correctly and within the required time. Although they may be indicators of poor motivation, the lack of efficiency and effectiveness could also be a result of the staff overworking, personal problems, poor work design, repetitive work, lack of discipline, interpersonal conflict, lack of training or failure of the organisation to value its staff. An employee may be highly motivated but may find the work physically impossible.

Welfare

People always work best in good working conditions and these include freedom from fear: fear of becoming unemployed, fear of failure at work, fear of discrimination. Job security and incentives, such as opportunities for promotion, bonuses, profit sharing and time for further study, encourage a good attitude to work; but as well as these tangible factors people need to feel wanted and that what they do is important. The supervisor is in an excellent position to ensure that this happens. Personal worries affect individuals' performance and can have a very strong influence on how well or how badly they work. The physical environment will naturally cause problems if, for example, the atmosphere is humid, the working situation ill-lit, too hot or too noisy, and there is constant rush and tear, and frequent major problems to be overcome. In these circumstances staff are more liable to be quick-tempered, angry and aggressive, and the supervisor needs to consider how these factors might be dealt with.

Understanding

The supervisor needs to try to understand both men and women (and to deal with both sexes fairly), to anticipate problems and build up a team spirit so as to overcome the problems. This entails always being fair when dealing with staff, and giving them encouragement. It also means that work needs to be allocated according to each individual's ability; everyone should be kept fully occupied and the working environment must be conducive to producing their best work.

Communication

Finally, and most important of all, the supervisor must be able to communicate effectively. To convey orders, instructions, information and manual skills requires the supervisor to possess the right attitude to those with whom he or she needs to communicate. The ability to convey orders and instructions in a manner that is acceptable to the one receiving them is dependent not only on the words but on the emphasis given to the words, the tone of voice, the time selected to give them and on who is present when they are given. This is a skill that supervisors need to develop. Instructions and orders can be given with authority without being authoritative.

Thus the supervisor needs technical knowledge and the ability to direct staff and to carry responsibility so as to achieve the specified targets and standards required by the organisation; this he or she is able to do by organising, coordinating, controlling and planning but, most of all, through effective communication.

Skills for effective supervision

Robert L. Katz (1974) has suggested that there are three types of skills required for effective management:

1 technical
2 people
3 conceptual.

Technical skills

These are the skills chefs, restaurant managers and the like need in order to do the job. The supervisor must be skilled in the area they are supervising because they will be required in most cases to train other staff under them. Supervisors who do not have the required skills will find it hard to gain credibility with the staff.

People skills

Supervisors are team leaders, therefore they must be sensitive to the needs of others. They must be able to communicate effectively and be able to build a team to achieve the agreed goals – listening, questioning, communicating clearly, handling conflicts, and providing support and praise when praise is due.

Conceptual skills

A supervisor must be able to think things through, especially when planning or analysing why they are not going as expected. A supervisor must be able to solve problems and make decisions. For supervisors, conceptual skills are necessary for reasonably short-term planning. Head chefs and hospitality managers require conceptual skills for long-term strategic planning.

Henry Mintzberg (1975) suggested that the supervisor has three broad roles:

1 interpersonal – people skills
2 informational – people and technical skills
3 decision making – conceptual skills.

Supervisors and ethical issues

A supervisor must be consistent when handling staff, avoiding favouritism and perceived inequity. Such inequity can rise from the amount of training or performance counselling given, from the promotion of certain employees, and from the way in which shifts are allocated. Supervisors should engage in conversation with all staff, not just a selected few, and should not single out some staff for special attention.

Ethical treatment of staff is fair treatment of staff. A good supervisor will gain respect if they are ethical.

Confidentiality is an important issue for the supervisor. Employees or customers may wish to take the supervisor into their confidence, and the supervisor must not betray this.

Micromanagement

In business management, micromanagement is a management style where a manager closely observes or controls the work of his/her employees, generally used as a pejorative term. In contrast to giving general instructions on smaller tasks while supervising larger concerns, the micromanager monitors and assesses every step.

Micromanagement may arise from internal sources, such as concern for details, increased performance pressure, or insecurity. It can also be seen as a tactic used by managers to eliminate unwanted employees, either by creating standards they cannot meet, leading to termination of employment, or by creating a stressful workplace and thus causing the employee to leave.

Regardless of the motivation, the effect may be to demotivate employees, create resentment and damage trust.

Micromanagement can also be distinguished from management by worker-to-boss ratio. At any time when there is one worker being given orders by one boss, both people are rendered useless. When a boss can do a worker's job with more efficiency than giving the orders to do the same job, this is micromanagement.

Micromanagement is a counterproductive approach to dealing with the workforce and can be costly in many areas of the business.

Identifying recruitment needs

A supervisor must be able to identify what staff are required and where they are required in order to cope with the level of business. At the same time labour costs must be kept to a minimum. The supervisor must therefore ensure adequate staffing at the lowest possible cost.

An important aspect is to be able to carefully analyse projected business in order to adopt the best staffing mix.

Job design and the allocation of duties also have to be considered; where jobs are simple and require little training, employment of casual labour can be justified. For more skilled staff, full-time employment has to be considered with investment in staff development and training.

Often the supervisor has to write job descriptions. These documents are used for a number of purposes, which include:

- deciding on the knowledge, experience and skills required to carry out the duties specified
- allowing new staff to understand the requirements of their jobs
- allowing new staff to develop accurate expectation of the jobs
- identifying training needs
- assisting in the development of recruitment strategies.

Job descriptions allow supervisors and managers to monitor performance, and to manage discipline when performance is below standard. Job descriptions assist in allowing everyone to focus on the

An example of a job description: Senior Sous Chef

Reporting to Head Chef

The Senior Sous Chef position reports to the Head Chef and is responsible for the day-to-day kitchen operation, overseeing the stores, preparation and production areas. The position involves supervising and managing the kitchen staff, with direct responsibility for rostering and scheduling production. In the absence of the Head Chef, the Senior Sous Chef will be required to take on the duties of the Head Chef and to attend Senior Management meetings in his/her absence.

Duties

- Monitor and check stores operation.
- Train new and existing staff in Health & Safety, HACCP (hazard analysis critical and control point), etc.
- Chair of the Kitchen Health and Safety Committee.
- Develop new menus and concepts together with Senior Management.
- Schedule and roster all kitchen staff.
- Maintain accurate records of staff absences.
- Maintain accurate kitchen records.
- Responsible for the overall cleanliness of the kitchen operation.
- Assist in the production of management reports.
- Establish an effective and efficient team.
- Assist with the overall establishment and monitoring of budgets.

Conditions

- Grade 3 management spine.
- Private health insurance.
- 5-day week.
- 20 days' holiday.
- Profit-share scheme after one year's service.

Personal specification: Senior Sous Chef

- Qualifications
  (i) BSc in International Culinary Arts Management or equivalent

- Experience
  (i) Five years' experience in 4- and 5-star hotel kitchens; restaurant and banqueting experience

- Skills
  (i) Proficiency in culinary arts
  (ii) Microsoft Excel, Access, Word
  (iii) Operation of inventory control software
  (iv) Written and oral communication skills
  (v) Team-building skills

- Knowledge
  (i) Current legislation in Health & Safety
  (ii) Food hygiene
  (iii) HACCP
  (iv) Risk assessment
  (v) Production systems
  (vi) Current technology

- Other attributes
  (i) Honesty
  (ii) Reliability
  (iii) Attention to detail
  (iv) Initiative
  (v) Accuracy

- Essential
  (i) Basic computer skills
  (ii) High degree of culinary skills
  (iii) Good communication skills
  (iv) Supervisory and leadership skills

- Desirable
  (i) Knowledge of employment law
  (ii) Public relations profile

precise requirements of the job and ensure that everyone is clear about their expectations.

Induction programmes

Why induction?

Every establishment should have a detailed induction system. The induction process settles new employees into their new positions. It is important for the company to make a good impression as this will influence the person's attitude to the job. The new employee needs to be aware of their responsibilities. This will include not just their day-to-day procedures but also their role in legislation, food hygiene, health and safety.

Topics for induction

- Company procedures, policies.
- Tour of establishment and facilities.
- Fire drill procedures, Health & Safety procedures.
- Reporting procedures.
- Job description explained.
- Conditions of employment.
- Emergency procedures.
- Where to go for advice or assistance.
- Equal opportunities.
- Accident reporting.
- Dismissal procedures.

During the first few weeks of employment the following topics need to be explained to the new employee:

- organisational aims and objectives
- occupational health and safety
- performance appraisal
- job description explained
- grievance procedures
- quality standards
- staff development.

Where possible, new employees should be issued with an employee handbook with information on the company. The supervisor should take time to explain the contents of this handbook. Staff retention is an important issue in the hospitality and catering industry. Supervisors have a key role in developing teams to achieve effective working relationships that value people. These can help to reduce turnover. Staff turnover is extremely costly (see box) and every attempt should be made to reduce unnecessary turnover.

The cost of staff turnover to an establishment

- Replacement costs – advertising, training, etc.
- Overtime to existing staff.
- Extra pressure on existing staff.
- Time taken to recruit staff.
- Agency costs.
- Payroll and administration costs.
- Loss of business due to insufficient staff on duty to supply the required level of service.
- Loss of business through damage to reputation.

The supervisor and performance appraisal

Supervisors manage performance informally through instructions and advice, and by providing constructive feedback. The supervisor should give praise when it is due and reprimand an employee if necessary. Informal feedback takes place on a day-to-day basis but most large organisations operate a formal appraisal system. This involves the supervisor or the manager conducting a formal interview with the employee, examining past performance and assessing opportunities for the future. Overall performance may be ranked on a performance scale. During the interview, training needs and career development are analysed to establish the employee's performance objectives and plans for achievement.

Performance appraisal forms may cover efficiency, reliability, teamwork and working relationships. In service organisations this may also include customer relations. To be more specific the job description criteria may also be included in the form. Focusing on the job description promotes discussion about what is happening in the workplace and how hurdles to ineffective performance can be overcome. Performance objectives and training plans should also relate to the job requirements.

When a supervisor conducts a performance appraisal s/he should advise the employee in advance, explaining the purpose of the appraisal. In addition, sufficient time must be allocated to the process. The following should also be taken into account:

- creating an appropriate climate for the interview
- reviewing specific job performances against specific job targets
- openly discussing issues that may have an impact on performance
- agreeing on new performance targets
- giving positive constructive feedback.

KITCHEN EQUIPMENT

Cooking equipment provides the backbone of any busy catering operation. It is the key to catering success and quality. In terms of food safety it controls the most critical step in the food production process. A mistake at the cooking stage by undercooking of raw food is likely to result in a mass food-poisoning incident.

Kitchen equipment is expensive so initial selection is important, and the following points should be considered before each item is purchased or hired.

- Overall dimensions (in relation to available space).
- Weight – can the floor support the weight?
- Fuel supply – is the existing fuel supply sufficient to take the increase?
- Drainage – where necessary, are there adequate facilities?
- Water – where necessary, is it to hand?
- Use – if it is a specialist piece of equipment for certain foods or products, will there be sufficient use to justify the expense and investment?
- Capacity – can it cook the quantities of food required efficiently?
- Time – can it cook the given quantities of food in the time available?
- Ease – is it easy for staff to handle, control and use properly?
- Maintenance – is it easy for staff to clean and maintain?
- Attachments – is it necessary to use additional equipment or attachments?
- Extraction – does it require extraction facilities for fumes or steam?
- Noise – does it have an acceptable noise level?
- Construction – is it well made, safe, hygienic and energy efficient, and are all handles, knobs and switches sturdy and heat resistant?
- Appearance – if equipment is to be on view to customers does it look good and fit in with the overall design?
- Spare parts – are they and replacement parts easily obtainable?

Kitchen equipment may be divided into three categories:

1 large equipment – ranges, steamers, boiling pans, fish-fryers, sinks, tables
2 mechanical equipment – peelers, mincers, mixers, refrigerators, dishwashers
3 utensils and small equipment – pots, pans, whisks, bowls, spoons.

Manufacturers of all kitchen equipment issue instructions on how to clean and keep their apparatus in efficient working order, and it is the responsibility of everyone using the equipment to follow these instructions (which should be displayed in a prominent place near the machines).

Arrangements should be made with the local gas board for regular checks and servicing of gas-operated equipment; similar arrangements

Further information
To find out more, see HCIMA Technical Brief No. 28, Purchasing Catering Equipment, or visit the website of the Catering Equipment Suppliers' Association (CESA): www.cesa.org.uk.

Figure 6.3 Prover

should be made with the electricity supplier. It is a good plan to keep a log book of all equipment, showing where each item is located when servicing takes place, noting any defects that arise, and instructing the fitter to sign the log book and to indicate exactly what has been done.

Legislation affecting equipment in the professional kitchen

(*This section is adapted from 'The law in your kitchen'*, Caterer and Hotelkeeper, *19 April 2006*.)
There is a large amount of legislation being imposed on professional kitchens. A great deal is concerned with how kitchen equipment is bought, operated and disposed of.

CE marking
All powered catering equipment sold in the UK and Europe must carry a small 'CE' badge. This means that the manufacturer has certified that it meets European Union safety, and in some cases performance, standards. The EU standards are among the strictest in the world and are drawn up to ensure that kitchen staff have the least possible risk of injury. Reputable brands of catering equipment bought from reputable dealers should always have the CE mark.

The regulation recognises that many kitchens have well-manufactured old equipment that predates the introduction of CE marking. That is why the legal requirement for kitchen equipment to be CE marked applies only to equipment manufactured after 1995.

When manufacturers sell kitchen equipment and offer a guarantee, it comes with conditions of servicing. Kitchen equipment is very technical, and needs a trained and accredited service engineer to keep it in working order and comply with the terms of the guarantee. If equipment breaks down and a chef calls on the guarantee for cost-free repairs, without evidence of accredited servicing the guarantee could be invalid.

When it comes to servicing and repairing kitchen equipment the law is clear. The only people who can install and maintain a gas-powered piece of kitchen equipment must be registered with the government-run safety scheme, the Council for Registered Gas Installers, generally known as CORGI registration. There are several levels of CORGI accreditation that an engineer can have. For example, a person working on a combination oven needs a different assessment from that needed to install a fryer; it is important to check that anyone servicing gas-powered equipment has the right accreditation for the equipment that they will be working on.

Health & Safety regulations
The Health & Safety Executive (HSE) makes the rules covering the safety of kitchen staff using machines or equipment. Some are guidance notes; some are law; but to go against either can result in both prosecution and compensation claims.

> **i**
> **Further information**
> For more information, visit www.hse.gov.uk.

The regulations are complex, but no chef can ignore them.

Regulations affecting ventilation systems

The important issue here is interlocking. This means that, where there is a ventilation hood over the cooking area, there is a gas supply cut-out mechanism between the cooking equipment and the ventilation hood. If the extraction fan should fail, the gas supply to the kitchen equipment will automatically be turned off.

Interlocking regulations are not retrospective, meaning that in most existing kitchens they are strongly recommended, but not mandatory.

Any new kitchen using a fan-assisted extraction system must have this interlocking gas cut-out system. If more than half the appliances are replaced in existing kitchens then an interlocking gas cut-out system must be fitted.

PUWER

PUWER stands for the Provision and Use of Work Equipment Regulations. These regulations cover how chefs use kitchen equipment and are part of a European Directive that supplements regulations under the Health and Safety at Work Act. The aim is for kitchen management to accept responsibility for the use of equipment.

PUWER regulations say that, where there is machinery in the kitchen, management should have a risk assessment carried out, provide written instructions for operating it and provide adequate training to all staff that are going to use it. Under PUWER there is a legal obligation to maintain machinery properly, and if there is a service log book with the equipment, it has to be filled in.

WEEE

Further information
To find out more, visit www.netregs.gov.uk/netr egs/legislation/380525/

This is the Waste Electrical and Electronic Equipment Directive. This EU legislation's first aim is to achieve a sustainable Europe through recycling electrical equipment. Its second is to reduce the amount of waste material that goes into landfill. Historically with catering equipment, recycling has not been a problem due to the high value of the scrap materials – mainly stainless steel – which means the equipment has a history of being recycled responsibly.

WRAS

The aim of the Water Regulations Advisory Scheme is to ensure that fittings, equipment or products that are connected to the mains supply, do not contaminate water.

Although WRAS regulations cover every industry, in commercial kitchens the main concern is the risk of contamination of pure drinking water through backflow. This is where dirty water, for whatever reason, accidentally passes back into the main water supply rather than going out to the drains. Every item of kitchen equipment that is connected to the mains must comply with the Water Supply (Water Fittings) Regulations.

Where badly contaminated water is discharged from an item of kitchen equipment, such as a dishwasher, the protection will be provided by an anti-syphonic backflow-preventing device or an air gap.

Most new equipment will come with the necessary fitting to comply with WRAS. Only engineers with a qualification to connect equipment to the water supply should fit kitchen equipment that needs a supply of water.

LARGE EQUIPMENT

Ranges and ovens

A large variety of ranges are available operated by gas, electricity, solid fuel, oil, microwave or microwave plus convection.

Oven doors should not be slammed as this is liable to cause damage.

The unnecessary or premature lighting of ovens can cause wastage of fuel, which is needless expense. This is a bad habit common in many kitchens.

When a solid-top gas range is lit, the centre ring should be removed to reduce the risk of blowback, but it should be replaced after approximately five minutes, otherwise unnecessary heat is lost.

Convection ovens

These are ovens in which a circulating current of hot air is rapidly forced around the inside of the oven by a motorised fan or blower. As a result, a more even and constant temperature is created, which allows food to be cooked successfully in any part of the oven. This means that the heat is used more efficiently, cooking temperatures can be lower, cooking times shortened and overall fuel economy achieved.

Forced air convection can be described as fast conventional cooking: conventional in that heat is applied to the surface of the food, but fast since moving air transfers its heat more rapidly than does static air. In a sealed oven, fast hot air circulation reduces evaporation loss, keeping shrinkage to a minimum, and gives the rapid change of surface texture

Figure 6.4 Central cooking range

Figure 6.5 Deck oven

Figure 6.6 Forced air convection oven

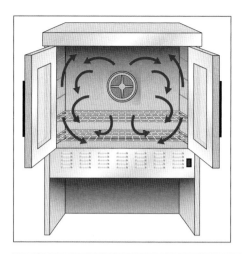

Figure 6.7 Hot air convection oven

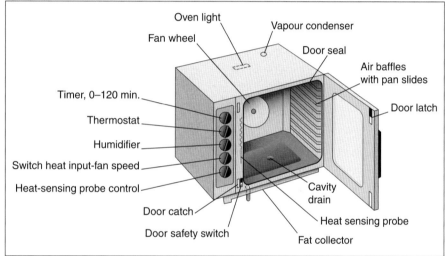

Figure 6.8 Hot air steamer oven

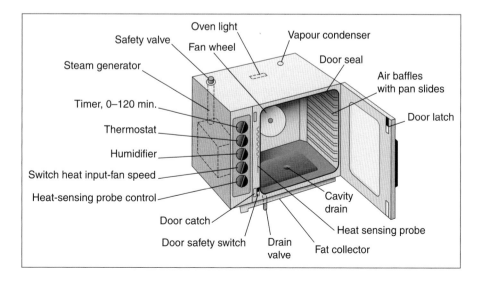

and colour that are traditionally associated with certain cooking processes.

There are four types of convection oven.

1 Where forced air circulation within the oven is accomplished by means of a motor-driven fan, the rapid air circulation ensures even temperature distribution to all parts of the oven.
2 Where low-velocity, high-volume air movement is provided by a power blower and duct system.
3 A combination of a standard oven and a forced convection oven designed to operate as either by the flick of a switch.
4 A single roll-in rack convection oven with heating element and fan housed outside the cooking area. An 18-shelf mobile oven rack makes it possible to roll the filled rack directly from the preparation area into the oven.

Combination ovens

Combination ovens (combi-ovens) have brought about a revolution in baking, roasting and steaming. There are now many varieties of combination ovens available on the market, fuelled by gas or electricity, and they are widely used in most sectors of the catering industry. They are especially used in large banqueting operations.

Ovens can be programmed easily to produce exact cooking times and the regeneration of chilled food, allowing chefs to produce consistent products every time.

The special features of combination ovens are:

- they reduce cooking times
- they are fully automatic – enable desired browning levels and exact core temperatures to be achieved
- they are self-cleaning
- a combination oven system will allow more food to be produced in less space
- energy efficiency
- increased productivity.

A new type of combination oven has now been manufactured – it is a hybrid of fridge and oven, designed for use in cook-chill food systems for banqueting or industrial catering. The chilled food is held in chill until the predetermined moment when the chilling unit switches off and the oven facility kicks in, bringing the food safely up to eating temperature.

The cooking process management system

This links the combi-oven to a PC, which monitors the cooking process to help with HACCP. The computer software monitors not just the combi-ovens, but other items of cooking equipment in the kitchen, such as pressure bratt pans, steamers and boiling kettles. The chef inputs into the software what the day's food production is to be, and the computer will

Figure 6.9 Combination oven

work out the order in which the food should be cooked and in what pieces of equipment, to deliver the food just in time for freshness.

The HACCP management part of this system can track food from goods delivery to the plate by using probes – for example, a chilled or frozen chicken can be probed to monitor and record temperatures before the cooking process so that if a problem occurs in the food cycle, the kitchen manager can check to see if there were any discrepancies in the goods storage procedures.

During the cooking the probes will record any variations to the pre-set cooking programme. This means the software system can alert the kitchen management team not just that a problem has occurred during the cooking procedure, but where it occurred.

Combination ovens: cooking profile
Example: rationale

These are pre-programmed, offering ideal procedures for cooking different meats – in particular for roasts such as leg of lamb and roast pork. The special feature of these intelligent profiles is that they detect automatically the size of the meat and the volume of the food in the cooking cabinet. In addition, with the assistance of the internal quality temperature (IQT) sensor, they also determine the exact core temperature of the food, the remaining cooking time and the current level of browning. The profiles are self-regulating – that is, they adjust the cooking processes to the size of the meat and the load of food in the cooking cabinet.

IQT sensor: rationale

The sensor is inserted into the food to facilitate the detection of the core temperature. This prevents overcooking of joints and reduces weight loss.

Alto-shaam cook and hold ovens
These ovens reduce labour and product shrinkage, provide product consistency and increase holding life for banqueting service. Two items are available, one for holding and serve, the other for regeneration and serve.

Smoking ovens
Smoking certain foods is a means of cooking, injecting different flavours and preserving (there is more on the use of smoking as a method of preservation in Chapter 5). Smoking ovens or cabinets are well insulated with controlled heating elements on which wood chips are placed (different types of wood chips give differing flavours). As the wood chips burn, the heated smoke permeates the food (fish, chicken, sausages, etc.) that is suspended in the cabinet.

Microwave ovens
Microwave cookery is a method of cooking and heating food by using high-frequency power. The energy used is the same as that which carries

Further information
To find out more, contact the Microwave Association, 3 Popham Gardens, Lower Richmond Road, Surrey TW9 4LJ (website: www.microwaveassociati on.org.uk).

the television signal from the transmitter to the receiver, but is at a higher frequency.

The waves disturb the molecules or particles of food and agitate them, thus causing friction, which has the effect of heating the food. In the conventional method of cooking, heat penetrates the food only by conduction from the outside. Food being cooked by microwave needs no fat or water, and is placed in a glass, earthenware, plastic or paper container before being put in the oven. Metal is not used as the microwaves are reflected by it.

All microwave ovens consist of a basic unit of various sizes with varying levels of power. Some feature additions to the standard models, such as automatic defrosting systems, browning elements, 'stay-hot' controls and revolving turntables.

The oven cavity has metallic walls, ceiling and floor, which reflect the microwaves. The oven door is fitted with special seals to ensure that there is minimum microwave leakage. A cut-out device automatically switches off the microwave energy when the door is opened.

Combination convection and microwave cooker

This cooker combines forced air convection and microwave, either of which can be used separately but that are normally used simultaneously, thereby giving the advantages of both systems: speed, coloration and texture of food. Traditional metal cooking pans may also be used without fear of damage to the cooker.

Figure 6.10 (a) Microwave energy being reflected off cooking cavity walls; (b) microwave energy being absorbed by food; (c) microwave energy passing through cooking container material

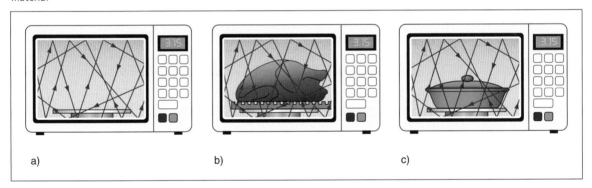

a)   b)   c)

Figure 6.11 A microwave oven

Induction cooking

Advantages of induction cooking hobs

- **Power savings:** the induction hob has a very high energy efficiency and only draws power when a pan is on the ring. Energy costs are substantially reduced.
- **Safety:** only the pan gets hot, therefore you cannot burn yourself on this type of hob.
- **Cool working environment:** as virtually all the energy is developed as heat directly in the pan very little heat escapes to the atmosphere, therefore providing a cool working environment.
- **Less extraction:** because of the cool working environment the kitchen needs much less extraction, further reducing energy bills.
- **Hygiene:** the flat ceramic top provides a wipe-clean hygienic surface that remains cool, therefore spillage will not burn onto the cooking surface.
- **No combustion gases:** unlike gas hobs, induction hobs do not emit any combustion gases and are environmentally friendly.
- **Speed of cooking:** modern induction hob designs are faster than gas hobs.

History

Traditional ranges and ovens work because the energy source – for example, electricity – causes the burners to heat up. That heat is then transferred to the pan or pot placed upon the heated surface. In this method of creating heat, it is the burner that actually cooks the food. Conversely, an induction cooktop holds a series of burners called induction coils, which are based on magnetic principles. These coils generate magnetic fields that induct a warming reaction in steel-based pots or pans; it is the cooking vessels themselves that heat the food, not the stove elements. Because of this form of heat generation, the cooktops may feel slightly warm to the touch after they are turned off, but they remain relatively cool – and thus much safer.

Temperature, speed and control are additional benefits with an induction cooktop. This type of stove heats up faster than an electric

Figure 6.12 Portable induction hob

Figure 6.13 Induction wok

i

Further information
To find out more, contact
Induced Energy Limited,
New Building,
Westminster Road,
Northamptonshire NN13
7EB (website:
www.inducedenergy.com).

range, allowing for faster cooking times – water will boil at half the time as on an electric cooking surface. Because of this reduced cooking time, energy savings can be substantial. Induction cooktops are 85–90 per cent more energy efficient than electricity-powered stoves and ovens, and use approximately half the energy of gas-sourced models.

Cleaning an induction cooktop is a breeze because the surface is flat and continuous; there are no nooks or crannies where food particles or spillovers can collect. Range-top mess is also reduced because the induction cooktops offer convenient safeguards; they turn themselves off if a pot has gone dry and, if there is a spillover, the cooking surface prevents the burning on and hardening of spilled food.

While induction cooktops will save money in the long run, there are some costly initial investments. The cooktops themselves, which range from a one-unit hotplate type to the traditional four-burner size, range in price from several hundred to several thousand pounds.

An additional expense can arise if you need to replace your current cookware. Induction cooktops induct energy only into ferrous metal-based pots and pans. If you are currently using cast iron, steel-plated or certain types of stainless steel pans, you should be able to continue to use the cookware you already own. However, you cannot cook with materials such as copper, aluminium or glass. Some makes of stainless steel pots and pans are conducive to cooking on an induction cooktop while others are not. If in doubt, test your present cookware with a magnet – if the magnet sticks to the pot, the pot will work with an induction cooktop.

Try to find an induction hob that works using normal pans. Beware of induction hobs that need special pans or do not give constant performance pan to pan.

Halogen hob

This runs on electricity, and comprises five individually controlled heat zones, each of which has four tungsten halogen lamps located under a smooth ceramic glass surface. The heat source glows red, when switched on, getting brighter as the temperature increases.

When the hob is switched on, 70 per cent of the heat is transmitted as infra-red light directly into the base of the cooking pan, the rest is from conducted heat via the ceramic glass. Ordinary pots and pans may be used on the halogen hob, but those with a flat, dark or black base absorb the heat most efficiently.

The halogen range includes a convection oven, and the halogen hob unit is also available mounted on a stand.

Steamers

There are basically three types of steaming ovens:

i

Further information
Further information can
be obtained by visiting
the website of the
Catering Equipment
Suppliers' Association
(CESA): www.cesa.org.uk.

1 atmospheric
2 pressure
3 pressureless.

Figure 6.14 Pressureless steamer

There are also combination steaming ovens: pressure/convection steam; pressureless/fully pressurised; steaming/hot air cooking; combination of hot air and steam; combination of hot air and steam with two settings.

In addition, dual-pressure steamers, switchable between low pressure and high pressure, and two pressure settings plus zero are available. Steaming ovens continue to develop, improve and become more versatile. The modern combination steamers which can be used for steaming, stewing, poaching, braising, roasting, baking, vacuum cooking, gratinating, reconstituting, blanching and defrosting, have electronic controls for easier setting and more precise time/temperature controls. The advantage of the electronic controls is that they assist in fuel efficiency. They are available in several sizes and there are many examples of their efficiency. For example, one large hotel has been quoted as saying: 'using five electrically heated combi-steamers we served 500 English breakfasts straight from the oven – no messing about with hot plates and cupboards'.

With such a wide range of models available it is increasingly important to consider carefully which model is best suited to a particular kitchen's requirements.

Large pans, boilers and fryers

Bratt pan
The bratt pan is one of the most versatile pieces of cooking equipment in the kitchen because it is possible to use it for shallow-frying, deep-frying, stewing, braising and boiling. A bratt pan can cook many items of food at one time because of its large surface area. A further advantage is that it can be tilted so that the contents can, quickly and efficiently, be poured out on completion of the cooking process. Bratt pans are heated by gas or electricity; several models are available incorporating various features to meet differing catering requirements.

Boiling pans
Many types are available in different metals – aluminium, stainless steel, etc. – in various sizes (10-, 15-, 20-, 30- and 40-litre capacity) and they

Figure 6.15 Bratt pans and boiler

Figure 6.16 Examples of deep fat fryers

may be heated by gas or electricity. As they are used for boiling or stewing large quantities of food, it is important that they do not allow the food to burn; for this reason the steam-jacket type boiler is the most suitable. Many of these are fitted with a tilting device to facilitate the emptying of the contents.

After use, the boiling pan and lid should be thoroughly washed with mild detergent solution and then rinsed well. The tilting apparatus should be greased occasionally and checked to see that it tilts easily. If gas fired, the gas jets and pilot should be inspected to ensure correct working. If a pressure gauge and safety valve are fitted these should also be checked.

Pasta cooker
This equipment is fitted with water delivery and drain taps, and can be used for the cooking of several types of pasta simultaneously. It is electrically operated.

Deep fat fryers
A deep fat fryer is one of the most extensively used items of equipment in many catering establishments. The careless worker who misuses a deep fat-fryer and spills food or fat can cause accidents and waste money.

Fryers are heated by gas or electricity and incorporate a thermostatic control in order to save fuel and prevent overheating. There is a cool zone below the source of heat into which food particles can sink without burning, thus preventing spoiling of other foods being cooked. This form of heating also saves fat.

Pressure fryers
Food is cooked in an air-tight frying vat, thus enabling it to be fried a lot faster and at a lower oil temperature.

Hot air rotary fryers
These are designed to cook batches of frozen blanched chips or battered foods without any oil in four to six minutes.

Computerised fryers are available, which may be programmed to control automatically cooking temperatures and times, on and off switches, basket lifting and product holding times. Operational information is fed from a super-sensitive probe, which is immersed in the frying medium and passes information about temperature and rates of temperature change that may be caused by: the initial fat temperature; amount of food being fried; fryer efficiency and capacity; fryer recovery rate; quantity and condition of fat; product temperature and water content.

With all the above information the fryer computes exact cooking times and an automatic signalling device indicates the end of a cooking period.

Deep fat fryers should be cleaned daily after use by following the manufacturers instructions. For example:

- turning off the heat and allowing the fat or oil to cool
- draining off and straining the fat or oil
- closing the stopcock, filling the fryer with hot water containing detergent and boiling for 10–15 minutes
- draining off the detergent water, refilling with clean water plus 1 litre of vinegar per 5 litres of water and reboiling for 10–15 minutes
- draining off the water, drying the fryer, closing the stopcock and refilling with clean fat or oil.

Hot cupboards

Commonly referred to in the trade as the hotplate, hot cupboards are used for heating plates and serving dishes, and for keeping food hot. Care should be taken to see that the amount of heat fed into the hot cupboard is controlled at a reasonable temperature. This is important, otherwise the plates and food will either be too hot or too cold, and this could obviously affect the efficiency of the service. A temperature of 60–76°C (140–169°F) is suitable for hot cupboards and a thermostat is a help in maintaining this.

Hot cupboards may be heated by steam, gas or electricity. The doors should slide easily, and occasional greasing may be necessary. The tops of most hot cupboards are used as serving counters and should be heated to a higher temperature than the inside. These tops are usually made of stainless steel and should be cleaned thoroughly after each service.

Bains-marie

Bains-marie are open wells of water used for keeping foods hot; they are available in many designs, some of which are incorporated into hot cupboards, some in serving counters, and there is a type that is fitted at the end of a cooking range. They may be heated by steam, gas or electricity, and sufficient heat to boil the water in the bain-marie should be available. Care should be taken to see that a bain-marie is never allowed to burn dry when the heat is turned on. After use the heat should be turned off, the water drained and the bain-marie cleaned inside and outside with hot detergent water, rinsed and dried. Any drain-off tap should then be closed.

Figure 6.17 Waiter at hotplate   Figure 6.18 Water bath

Food distribution equipment

In situations requiring mobile equipment (e.g. hospitals, banqueting) wheeled items are essential to facilitate service, particularly of hot foods.

Grills and salamanders

The salamander or grill heated from above by gas or electricity probably causes more wastage of fuel than any other item of kitchen equipment through being allowed to burn unnecessarily for long periods unused. Most salamanders have more than one set of heating elements or jets and it is not always necessary to have them all turned on fully.

Salamander bars and draining trays should be cleaned regularly with hot water containing a grease solvent such as soda. After rinsing they should be replaced and the salamander lit for a few minutes to dry the bars.

For under-fired grills (see Figure 6.19) to work efficiently they must be capable of cooking food quickly and should reach a high temperature 15–20 minutes after lighting; the heat should be turned off immediately after use. When the bars are cool they should be removed and washed in hot water containing a grease solvent, rinsed, dried and replaced on the grill. Care should be taken with the fire bricks if they are used for lining the grill as they are easily broken.

Contact grills

These are sometimes referred to as double-sided or infragrills and have two heating surfaces arranged facing each other. The food to be cooked is

Figure 6.19 Under-fired grill   Figure 6.20 Bar grill

placed on one surface and is then covered by the second. These grills are electrically heated and are capable of cooking certain foods very quickly, so extra care is needed, particularly when cooks are using this type of grill for the first time.

Fry plates, griddle plates

These are solid metal plates heated from below, and are used for cooking individual portions of meat, hamburgers, eggs, bacon, etc. They can be heated quickly to a high temperature and are suitable for rapid and continuous cooking. Before cooking on a griddle plate a light film of oil should be applied to the food and the griddle plate to prevent sticking. To clean griddle plates, warm them and scrape off any loose food particles; rub the metal with pumice stone or griddle stone, following the grain of the metal; clean with hot detergent water, rinse with clean hot water and wipe dry. Finally re-season (prove) the surface by lightly oiling with vegetable oil.

Griddles with zone heating are useful when demand varies during the day. These reduce energy consumption in quiet periods while allowing service to be maintained.

Mirror chromed griddles have a polished surface that gives off less radiated heat, which saves energy and makes for a more pleasant working environment.

Barbecues

Barbecues are becoming increasingly popular because it is easy to cook and serve quick, tasty food on them, and the outdoor location, smell and sizzle develop an atmosphere that many customers enjoy.

There are three main types of barbecue: traditional charcoal, gas (propane or butane) and electric. Remember that the charcoal-fired type takes about an hour before the surface is ready. With gas and electricity the barbecue is ready to cook on almost immediately.

Gas is more flexible and controllable than electricity. Propane gas is recommended because it can be used at any time of the year. Butane does not work when it is cold. Propane is, however, highly flammable and safety precautions are essential. Anyone connecting the gas container must be competent in the use of bottled gas. The supply pipe must be guarded to avoid accidental interference, and the cylinder must be placed away from the barbecue. The cylinder must be upright and stable, with the valve uppermost and securely held in position. Connections must be checked for leaks.

Sinks

Stainless steel is generally used for all purposes.

Tables

- Formica- or stainless steel-topped tables should be washed with hot detergent water then rinsed with hot water containing a sterilising agent – alternatively, some modern chemicals act as both detergent and sterilising agents. Wooden tables should not be used.
- Marble slabs should be scrubbed with hot water and rinsed. All excess moisture should be removed with a clean, dry cloth.
- No cutting or chopping should be allowed on table tops; cutting boards should be used.
- Hot pans should not be put on tables; triangles must be used to protect the table surface.
- The legs and racks or shelves of tables are cleaned with hot detergent water and then dried. Wooden table legs require scrubbing.

Butcher's or chopping block

A scraper should be used to keep the block clean. After scraping, the block should be sprinkled with a few handfuls of common salt in order to absorb any moisture that may have penetrated during the day.

Do not use water or liquids for cleaning unless absolutely necessary as water will be absorbed into the wood and cause swelling.

Storage racks

All type of racks should be emptied and scrubbed or washed periodically.

Figure 6.21 Storage rack

MECHANICAL EQUIPMENT

(The Health & Safety Executive offers two publications on catering machinery, both obtainable from HMSO.)

If a piece of mechanical equipment can save time and physical effort and still produce a good end result then it should be considered for purchase or hire. The performance of most machines can be closely controlled and is not subject to human variations, so it should be easier to obtain uniformity of production over a period of time.

The caterer is faced with two considerations:

1 the cost of the machine – installation, maintenance, depreciation and running cost
2 the possibility of increased production and a saving of labour costs.

The mechanical performance must be carefully assessed and all the manufacturer's claims as to the machine's efficiency checked thoroughly. The design should be foolproof, easy to clean and operated with minimum effort. **Before cleaning, all machines should be switched off and the plug removed from the socket.**

When a new item of equipment is installed it should be tested by a qualified fitter before being used by catering staff. The manufacturer's instructions must be displayed in a prominent place near the machine. The manufacturer's advice regarding servicing should be followed and a record book kept, showing what kind of maintenance the machine is receiving and when. The following list includes machines typically found in catering premises, which are classified as dangerous under the Provision and Use of Work Equipment Regulations 1998 (PUWER).

1 Power-driven machines:
   - worm-type mincing machines
   - rotary knife, bowl-type chopping machines
   - dough mixers
   - food mixing machines when used with attachments for mincing, slicing, chipping and any other cutting operation, or for crumbling
   - pie and tart making machines
   - vegetable slicing machines.
2 Potato peelers:
   - potatoes should be free of earth and stones before loading into the machine
   - before any potatoes are loaded, the water spray should be turned on and the abrasive plate set in motion
   - the interior should be cleaned out daily and the abrasive plate removed to ensure that small particles are not lodged below
   - the peel trap should be emptied as frequently as required.
   - the waste outlet should be kept free from obstruction.
3 Machines, whether power-driven or not:
   - circular knife slicing machines used for cutting bacon and other foods (whether similar to bacon or not)
   - potato chipping machines.

FOOD-PROCESSING EQUIPMENT

Food mixer

This is an important labour-saving, electrically operated piece of equipment used for many purposes: mixing pastry, cakes, mashing potatoes, beating egg whites, mayonnaise, cream, mincing or chopping meat and vegetables.

- It should be lubricated frequently in accordance with manufacturer's instructions.
- The motor should not be overloaded, which can be caused by obstruction to the rotary components. For example, if dried bread is being passed through the mincer attachment without sufficient care the rotary cog can become so clogged with bread that it is unable to move. If the motor is allowed to run, damage can be caused to the machine.

Figure 6.22 A hand-held liquidiser ('blitzer')

- All components, as well as the main machine, should be thoroughly washed and dried. Care should be taken to see that no rust occurs on any part. The mincer attachment knife and plates will rust if not given sufficient care.

Food-processing machines

Food processors are generally similar to vertical, high-speed cutters except that they tend to be smaller and to have a larger range of attachments. They can be used for a large number of mixing and chopping jobs but they cannot whisk or incorporate air to mixes.

Figure 6.23 Gravity slicer

Figure 6.24 Vertical, variable-speed mixers

Figure 6.25 Belt-driven food processor

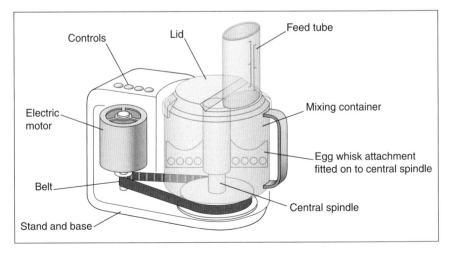

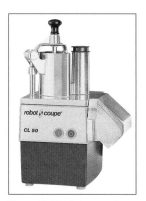

Figure 6.26 High-speed food processor

Liquidiser or blender

This is a versatile, labour-saving piece of kitchen machinery that uses a high-speed motor to drive specially designed stainless steel blades to chop, purée or blend foods efficiently and very quickly. It is also useful for making breadcrumbs. As a safety precaution food must be cooled before being liquidised.

Food slicers

Food slicers are obtainable both in manually and electrically operated versions. They are labour-saving devices, but can be dangerous if not used with care, so working instructions should be placed in a prominent position near the machine.

- Care should be taken that no material likely to damage the blades is included in the food to be sliced. It is easy for a careless worker to overlook a piece of bone that, if allowed to come into contact with the cutting blade, could cause severe damage.
- Each section in contact with food should be cleaned and dried carefully after use.
- The blade or blades should be sharpened regularly.
- Moving parts should be lubricated, but oil must not come into contact with the food.
- Extra care must be taken when blades are exposed.

Chipper

The electric chipper should be thoroughly cleaned and dried after use, particular attention being paid to those parts that come into contact with food. Care should be taken that no obstruction prevents the motor from operating at its normal speed. Moving parts should be lubricated according to the maker's instructions.

Masher (hand or electric)

The hand type should be washed immediately after use, then rinsed and dried.

The electric masher should have the removable sections and the main machine washed and dried after use, extra care being taken over those parts that come into contact with food. The same care should be taken as with electric chippers regarding obstruction and lubrication.

Ice cream makers, juicers and mixers

Ice cream and sorbet machines are available from 1-litre capacity and enable establishments to produce home-made ice cream and sorbet using fresh fruit in season or frozen and canned fruits at all times of the year.

Figure 6.27 Ice cream machine

Figure 6.28 Portable ice cream machine

Juicers and mixers can provide freshly made fruit and vegetable juices, milk shakes and cocktails.

BOILERS

Water boiling appliances for tea and coffee making

There are two main groups of water boilers: bulk boilers from which boiling water can only be drawn when all the contents have boiled, and automatic boilers, which provide a continuous flow of boiling water.

Bulk boilers
These are generally used when large quantities of boiling water are required at a given time. They should be kept scrupulously clean, covered with the correct lid to prevent anything falling in, and when not used for some time should be left filled with clean, cold water.

Automatic boilers
These boilers have automatic waterfeeds and can give freshly boiled water at intervals. It is important that the water supply is maintained efficiently, otherwise there is a danger of the boiler burning dry and being damaged.

Pressure boilers

This is the type that operates many still sets, consisting of steam heating milk boilers and a pressure boiler providing boiling water. Care should be taken with the pilot light to see that it is working efficiently. As with all gas-fired equipment it is essential that regular inspection and maintenance are carried out by registered gas fitters.

Coffee and milk heaters

Water-jacket boilers are made for the storage of hot coffee and hot milk, with draw-off taps from the storage chamber. Inner linings may be of glazed earthenware, stainless steel or heat-resistant glass. It is very important that the storage chambers are thoroughly cleaned with hot water after each use and then left full of clean, cold water. The draw-off taps should be cleaned regularly with a special brush.

REFRIGERATORS, COLD ROOMS, CHILL ROOMS, DEEP-FREEZE CABINETS AND COMPARTMENTS

Location

As adequate ventilation is vital, locate refrigeration equipment in a well-ventilated room away from:

- sources of intense heat – cookers, ovens, radiators, boilers, etc.
- direct sunlight – from window or skylights
- barriers to adequate air circulation.

In large establishments it is necessary to have refrigerated space at different temperatures. The cold rooms may be divided into separate rooms: one at a chill temperature for storing salads, fruits and certain cheeses; one for meats, poultry, game and tinned food, which have to be refrigerated; and one for deep-frozen foods. Frequently, the cold room storage is designed so that the chill room, the cold room and the deep-freeze compartment lead on from each other. Refrigerated cabinets, thermostatically controlled to various desired temperatures, are also used in large larders. Deep-freeze cabinets are used where a walk-in, deep-freeze section is not required: they maintain a temperature of -18°C (0°F). Chest-type deep-freeze cabinets require defrosting twice a year. It is important to close all refrigerator doors as quickly as possible to contain the cold air.

Hygiene precautions

Refrigeration cannot improve the quality of foodstuffs; it can only retard the natural process of deterioration. For maximum storage of food and minimum health risk:

- select the appropriate refrigerator equipment for the temperature requirement of the food
- always ensure refrigerators maintain the correct temperature for the food stored
- keep unwrapped foods, vulnerable to contamination, and flavour and odour transfer, in separate refrigerators or in airtight containers and away from products such as cream, other dairy products, partly cooked pastry, cooked meat and delicatessen foods
- do not store foods for long periods in a good, general-purpose

Figure 6.29 Refrigerated food to go

Figure 6.30 Gastronorm counter

refrigerator because a single temperature is not suitable for keeping all types of food safely and at peak condition
- never keep uncooked meat, poultry or fish in the same refrigerator, or any other food that is not in its own sealed, airtight container
- never refreeze foods that have been thawed out from frozen
- always rotate stock in refrigerator space
- clean equipment regularly and thoroughly, inside and out.

Loading

- Ensure that there is adequate capacity for maximum stock.
- Check that perishable goods are delivered in a refrigerated vehicle.
- Only fill frozen food storage cabinets with pre-frozen food.
- Never put hot or warm food in a refrigerator unless it is specially designed for rapid chilling.
- Ensure that no damage is caused to inner linings and insulation by staples or nails in packaging.
- Air must be allowed to circulate within a refrigerator to maintain the cooling effect – do not obstruct any airways.

Cleaning

- Clean thoroughly inside and out at least every two months as blocked drain lines, drip trays and air ducts will eventually lead to a breakdown.
- Switch off power.
- If possible, transfer stock to available alternative storage.
- Clean interior surfaces with lukewarm water and a mild detergent. Do not use abrasives or strongly scented cleaning agents.
- Clean exterior and dry all surfaces inside and out.
- Clear away any external dirt, dust or rubbish that might restrict the circulation of air around the condenser.
- Switch on power, check when the correct working temperature is reached, refill with stock.

Further information
Further information can be obtained from the British Refrigeration Association, Henley Road, Medmanham, Marlow, Buckinghamshire SL7 2ER (website: www.feta.co.uk/bra/).

Defrosting

This is important as it helps equipment perform efficiently and prevents a potentially damaging build-up of ice. Presence of ice on the evaporator or internal surfaces indicates the need for urgent defrosting; if the equipment is designed to defrost automatically this also indicates a fault.

Automatic defrosting may lead to a temporary rise in air temperature; this is normal and will not put food at risk.

For manual defrosting of chest freezers always follow the supplier's instructions to obtain optimum performance. Never use a hammer or any sharp instrument that could perforate cabinet linings – a plastic spatula can be used to remove stubborn ice.

Emergency measures

Signs of imminent breakdown include: unusual noises, fluctuating temperatures, frequent stopping and starting of the compressor, excessive frost build-up, absence of normal frost.

Prepare to call a competent refrigeration service engineer, but first check that:

- the power supply has not been accidentally switched off
- the electrical circuit has not been broken by a blown fuse or the triggering of an automatic circuit breaker
- there has been no unauthorised tampering with the temperature control device
- any temperature higher than recommended is not due solely to routine automatic defrosting, to the refrigerator door being left open, to overloading the equipment or to any blockage of internal passage of air
- there is no blockage of air to the condenser by rubbish, crates, cartons, etc.

If you still suspect a fault, call the engineer and be prepared to give brief details of the equipment and the fault. Keep the door of the defective cold cabinet closed as much as possible to retain cold air. Destroy any spoilt food.

Monitoring refrigeration efficiency

The Energy Technology Support Unit (ETSU) estimates that businesses could save 20–25 per cent of the energy currently consumed by refrigeration plants. Your local energy efficiency advice centre may be able to provide consultancy services at subsidised or no cost.

All types of refrigerators – walk-in, cabinet, with or without forced air circulation – should be fitted with display thermometers or chart recorders that will enable daily monitoring to check that the equipment is working correctly. Sensors that can set off available alarms must be placed in the warmest part of the cabinet.

Further information
Further information can be obtained from www.business.com/direct ory/food-and-beverages/ restaurants-and-foodservice/equipment-and-supplies/ dishwashers or www.powersourcing.com /se/dishwashingequipme nt.htm

Chilled display units include:

- multi-deck cabinets with closed doors, used for dispensing sandwiches, drinks and other foods; used if food needs to be displayed for more than four hours
- open and semi-open display cabinets where food is presented on the base of the unit and cooled by circulating cooled air
- gastronorm counters (see Figure 6.30).

Because of surrounding conditions it is unsafe to assume that refrigerated display cabinets will maintain the temperature of the food below 5°C (41°F), which is why these units should never be used to store food other than for display periods of not more than four hours.

Maintenance and servicing should be carried out regularly by qualified personnel.

DISHWASHING MACHINES

For hygienic washing-up, the generally recognised requirements are a good supply of hot water at a temperature of 60°C (140°F) for general cleansing, followed by a sterilising rinse at a temperature of 82°C (180°F) for at least one minute. Alternatively, low-temperature equipment is available that sterilises by means of a chemical: sodium hypochlorite (bleach).

Dishwashing machines take over an arduous job and save a lot of time and labour, ensuring that a good supply of clean, sterilised crockery is available.

There are three main types.

1 **Spray-type pass-through dishwashers:** the dishes are placed in racks, which slide into the machines, where they are subjected to a spray of hot detergent water at 48–60°C (118–140°F) from above and below. The racks move on to the next section where they are rinsed by a fresh hot shower at 82°C (180°F). At this temperature they are sterilised, and on passing out into the air they dry off quickly.
2 **Brush-type machines:** use revolving brushes for the scrubbing of each article in hot detergent water; the articles are then rinsed and sterilised in another compartment.

Figure 6.31 Automatic pastry roller (dough brake)

3 **Agitator water machines:** baskets of dishes are immersed in deep tanks and the cleaning is performed by the mechanical agitation of the hot detergent water. The loaded baskets are then given a sterilising rinse in another compartment.

Dishwashing machines are costly and it is essential that the manufacturer's instructions with regard to use and maintenance are followed at all times.

MISCELLANEOUS EQUIPMENT

Food waste disposers

Food waste disposers are operated by electricity and take all manner of rubbish, including bones, fat, scraps and vegetable refuse. Almost every type of rubbish and swill, with the exception of rags and tins, is finely ground, then rinsed down the drain. It is the most modern and hygienic method of waste disposal. Care should be taken by handlers not to push waste into the machine with a metal object as this can cause damage.

Other pieces of equipment that may be found in a busy kitchen include an automatic pastry roller (see Figure 6.31) and toasters.

SMALL EQUIPMENT AND UTENSILS

Small equipment and utensils are made from a variety of materials such as non-stick coated metal, iron, steel, copper, aluminium and wood.

Iron

Items of equipment used for frying, such as movable fritures and frying pans of all types, are usually made of heavy, black, wrought iron.

Frying pans are available in several shapes and many sizes. For example:

Figure 6.32 Sieves/colanders

Figure 6.33 Clockwise from top left: radish decorator, egg wedger, egg slice, parmesan grater, lemon squeezer, corer/slicer, all-purpose press, nutmeg grater, garlic shredder, cheese slice, cheese wire

Figure 6.34 All-Clad applies the science of metallurgy to the art of cooking

- omelette pans
- frying pans
- oval fish-frying pans
- pancake pans.

Baking sheets are made in various sizes, of black wrought steel. The less they are washed the less likely they are to cause food to stick. New baking sheets should be well heated in a hot oven, thoroughly wiped with a clean cloth and then lightly oiled. Before being used, baking trays should be lightly greased with a pure fat or oil. Immediately after use and while still warm they should be cleaned by scraping and dry wiping. Hot soda or detergent water should be used for washing.

Tartlet and barquette moulds and cake tins should be cared for in the same way as baking sheets.

Tinned steel

A number of items are made from this metal:

- conical strainer (chinois), used for passing sauces and gravies
- fine conical strainer, used for passing sauces and gravies
- colander, used for draining vegetables
- vegetable reheating container
- soup machine and mouli strainer, used for passing thick soups, sauces and potatoes for mash
- sieves.

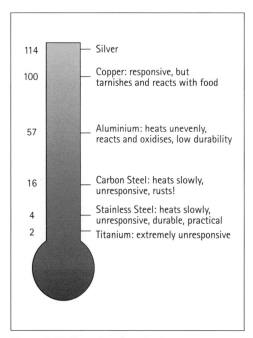

Figure 6.35 Hierarchy of conductors

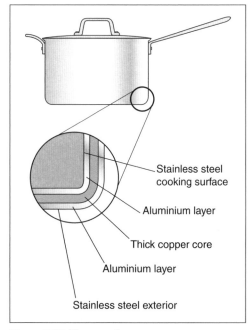

Figure 6.36 Diagram of a pan

All-Clad

All-Clad is all about the application of the science of metallurgy to the art of cooking. Each All-Clad pan is made of several layers of different metals and alloys, permanently bonded together (clad). The science lies in choosing the optimum thickness and purity of each layer, and bonding them together in the correct order to optimise:

- conductivity
- responsiveness
- non-reactivity
- consistency
- practicality
- durability.

All-Clad has taken all of these factors into account to combine the right metals of the right thickness, and put them in the right place to optimise the strengths of each of the metals.

Cooking pans

The ideal pan?
The ideal cookware would:

- heat evenly, with no hotspots, at a consistent rate
- cool evenly at a consistent rate
- be responsive to temperature changes
- not react with any foodstuffs or cleaning agents
- work equally well on any cooker type or in the oven.

No single metal or alloy meets these criteria, so the best cookware has always used layers of different metals, such as tinned copper pans.

Stainless steel
All-Clad Stainless features a magnetic grade of stainless steel on the exterior for induction compatibility. It has an aluminium core and the same high-quality stainless interior layer as all of the other All-Clad products. The total thickness is 2.7 mm with 0.38 mm interior stainless and 0.38 mm exterior stainless.

Copper Core
Copper Core is a unique new range made of 60 per cent copper bonded with both aluminium and stainless steel, with the conductivity and heat retention of copper and aluminium.

Sophisticated techniques such as infra-red thermal imaging ensure that All-Clad offers superior performance.

Aluminium

(Note: minimum use of aluminium is recommended – stainless steel (see below) is to be preferred.)
Saucepans, stockpots, sauteuses, sauté pans, braising pans, fish kettles

and large, round, deep pans and dishes of all sizes are made in cast aluminium. They are expensive, but one advantage is that the pans do not tarnish; also because of their strong, heavy construction they are suitable for many cooking processes.

A disadvantage is that in the manufacture of aluminium, which is a soft metal, other metals are added to make pans stronger. As a result certain foods can become discoloured (care should be taken when mixing white sauces and white soups). A wooden spoon should be used for mixing, then there should be no discoloration. The use of metal whisks or spoons must be avoided.

Water boiled in aluminium pans is unsuitable for tea making as it gives the tea an unpleasant colour. Red cabbage and artichokes should not be cooked in aluminium pans as they will take on a dark colour, caused by a chemical reaction.

Stainless steel

Heavy-duty stainless steel pans, incorporating an extra thick aluminium base that gives excellent heat diffusion, are available. They are suitable for all surfaces except induction hobs. Stainless steel is also used for many items of small equipment.

Figure 6.37 Non-stick pans

Figure 6.38 Mouli, potato ricer, potato mashers, pestle, mortar, wooden mushroom

Figure 6.39 Vegetable slicers (mandolins)

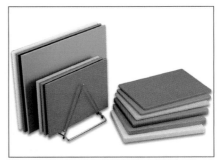

Figure 6.40 Modern cutting boards

Non-stick metal

An ever-increasing variety of kitchen utensils (saucepans, frying pans, baking and roasting tins) are available, and are suitable for certain types of kitchen operation, such as small scale or à la carte. Particular attention should be paid to the following points, otherwise the non-stick properties of the equipment will be affected:

- excessive heat should be avoided
- use plastic or wooden spatulas or spoons when using non-stick pans so that contact is not made to the surface with metal
- extra care is needed when cleaning non-stick surfaces; the use of cloth or paper is most suitable.

There are many small pieces of equipment made from metal of all types (see Figures 6.38 and 6.39).

Wood and compound materials

Cutting boards
These are an important item of kitchen equipment, which should be kept in use on all table surfaces to protect the table and the edges of cutting knives.

Wooden chopping boards
To comply with current regulations, wooden boards should not splinter or leak preservatives. They should be of close-grained hardwood, either in a thick, solid slab or separate pieces with close-fitting joints.

- Before using a new board, wash to remove any wood dust.
- After use, scrub with hot detergent water, rinse with clean water, dry as much as possible and stand on its longest end to prevent warping.
- Do not use for heavy chopping; use a chopping block instead.

Cutting boards of compound materials
There are several types available. When selecting compound cutting boards it is essential to purchase those with a non-slip surface.

- **Polyethylene:** six boards can be obtained marked in different colours along one edge. These can be kept in a special rack after washing and when not in use. This system is designed to cut down on cross-contamination by using one board exclusively for one type of food (see Figure 6.40).
- **Rubber:** cutting boards are also made of hard rubber and rubber compounds (rubber, polystyrene and clay). These are hygienic because they are solid, in one piece and should not warp, crack or absorb flavours. They are cleaned by scrubbing with hot water and then drying or passing through a dishwasher.

Figure 6.41 Examples of flameproof china dishes

Plastic cutting boards

Plastic is the most popular material for cutting boards. It has the advantage of being able to be put through a dishwasher, and can be colour coded so that high-risk foods are prepared only on the one cutting board, thereby reducing the risk of cross-contamination.

The accepted UK system is:

- **yellow** for cooked meats
- **red** for raw meats
- **white** for bread and dairy products (e.g. cheese)
- **blue** for raw fish
- **green** for salad and fruit
- **brown** for raw vegetables grown within the soil.

Rolling pins, wooden spoons and spatulas

These items should be scrubbed in hot detergent water, rinsed in clean water and dried. Rolling pins should not be scraped with a knife as this can cause the wood to splinter. Adhering paste can be removed with a cloth. Wooden spoons and spatulas are being replaced by a high-density plastic capable of withstanding very high temperatures. Wooden spoons/spatulas are considered unhygienic unless washed in a suitable sterilising solution such as sodium hypochloride solution (bleach) or a solution of Milton. Metal piping tubes are being replaced by plastic; these can be boiled and do not rust.

Wooden sieves and mandolins

When these are being cleaned, care of the wooden frame should be considered, taking into account the previous remarks. The blades of the mandolin should be kept lightly greased to prevent rust (stainless-steel mandolins with protective guards are available).

China and earthenware

Bowls and dishes in china and earthenware are useful for serving and for microwaved dishes. They should be cleaned in a dishwasher with mild detergent and rinse aid, or by hand, using the appropriate detergent for hand washing.

Materials (cloths etc.)

All materials should be washed in hot detergent water immediately after use, rinsed in hot, clean water and then dried. Tammy cloths, muslins and linen piping bags must be boiled periodically in detergent water. Kitchen cloths should be washed or changed frequently, otherwise accumulating dirt and food stains may cause cross-contamination of harmful bacteria/germs on to clean food.

Muslin may be used for straining soups and sauces.

Piping bags are made from disposable plastic and are used for piping preparations of all kinds.

Kitchen cloths:

- general purpose – for washing-up and cleaning surfaces
- tea towel (teacloth) – for drying up and general-purpose hand cloths
- bactericide wiping cloths – impregnated with bactericide to disinfect work surfaces; these cloths have a coloured pattern that fades and disappears when the bactericide is no longer effective; they should then be discarded
- oven cloths – thick cloths designed to protect the hands when removing hot items from the oven; oven cloths must only be used dry, never damp or wet, otherwise the user is likely to be burned.

Papers

- Greaseproof or silicone: for lining cake-tins, making piping bags and wrapping greasy items of food.
- Kitchen: white absorbent paper for absorbing grease from deep-fried foods and for lining trays on which cold foods are kept.
- General purpose: thick, absorbent paper for wiping and drying equipment, surfaces, food, etc.
- Towels: disposable, for drying the hands.

Foils

- Clingfilm: a thin, transparent material for wrapping sandwiches, snacks, hot and cold foods; clingfilm has the advantage of being very flexible and easy to handle and seal; due to risk of contamination, it is advisable to use a clingfilm that does not contain PVC or is plasticiser-free.
- Metal foil: a thin, pliable, silver-coloured material for wrapping and covering foods and for protecting oven-roasted joints during cooking.

ENERGY CONSERVATION AND EFFICIENCY

The emphasis in coming years for chefs and managers will be to save energy. With the rising cost of fuel, pressure will be on all operations to look at efficient ways of saving money on fuel.

Climate change

Scientists predict that global warming will cause the earth's temperature to rise by between 1.5° and 5.8°C, and sea levels by between 10 and 90 cm over the coming 100 years. This will have severe implications, such as increased rainfall and more 'severe weather events', such as storms and flooding, worldwide.

Although the climate has always changed naturally, science shows that human activity is now the cause of major change: global temperatures have risen 0.6°C over the last 140 years (since the start of the Industrial Revolution), and the rate of warming is greater than at any time since the last Ice Age. Economic 'growth' and development remains dependent on the burning of fossil fuels, whose by-products (known as 'greenhouse gases') act as insulators in the atmosphere, inhibiting the earth's natural cooling mechanism.

However, if the world reduces its dependency on the use of fossil fuels then it is possible to ensure that the rise in the earth's temperature will be minimised.

There have been a number of international conferences where nations have signed treaties agreeing to limit their production of fossil fuels. In 1997 in Kyoto, Japan, the UK agreed to lower its greenhouse gas emissions by 12.5 per cent by the years 2008–2010.

Energy consumption in the hospitality industry

Statistics issued by the Building Research Establishment (BRE) indicate that the UK's hospitality sector remains a major consumer of fossil fuels, accounting for 16 per cent of all energy used in the service sector. Its consumption of electricity and fossil fuels is greater than that in education, government or the health service. The major cost sectors for energy use are heating, air conditioning, cooking and refrigeration, lighting and production of hot water. It is estimated that most hospitality businesses could, however, save between 20 and 40 per cent of energy.

The main uses of energy are for providing catering services and hot water.

Chefs and managers have to take responsibility for energy management. Fuel tariffs have to be checked to ensure the most competitive rates are achieved. Assess the current fuel costs and identify any wastage. All staff should be trained to save fuel and monitor use.

Energy and the environment

The burning of fossil fuels to generate energy releases gases into the atmosphere. These include sulphur dioxide, which gives rise to acid rain, and carbon dioxide, which is the main contributor to the threat of global warming.

Factors to convert consumption of fuels to emissions of carbon dioxide, in kg of carbon dioxide produced per kWh of fuel used, are:

- gas – 0.21
- oil – 0.29
- electricity – 0.72.

Table 6.2 Energy efficiency measures and percentage savings

	BOILERS, CONTROLS AND HOT WATER	FOSSIL SAVING %	ELECTRICITY SAVING %	LIGHTING, CATERING AND OTHER SERVICES	FOSSIL SAVING %	ELECTRICITY SAVING %
No cost	Ensure systems come on only when, where and to the extent they are needed	1	2	Switch off lights and other equipment whenever possible Label light switches	0	0.5
	Establish a daily routine for checking control settings, especially where they may have been overridden in response to unexpected circumstances	1	1	Make maximum use of daylight Place lights where they will be most effective Clean light fittings and use translucent shades Improve the reflection of light from walls and ceilings by using pale colours	0	0.5
	Use your existing equipment effectively Check that timers, programmers, optimum start controls and weather compensation controls are set up and operating correctly	3	1	Set illumination levels to the type of activity Reduce lighting levels where possible and remove surplus lamps (but do not compromise safety)	0	0.5
	Isolate parts of systems that are not in use – for example, seasonally Remove redundant pipework during refurbishment	1	0	Provide training for catering staff about energy costs and correct use of equipment Set energy targets for meals, monitor consumption and give feedback to staff	0.2	0.2
	Ensure plant is regularly and correctly maintained	0.5	0.5	Ensure regular maintenance of cooking utensils, all appliances, burners, timers, controls and taps Badly maintained equipment wastes energy	0.2	0.2

Table 6.2 continued

	BOILERS, CONTROLS AND HOT WATER	FOSSIL SAVING %	ELECTRICITY SAVING %	LIGHTING, CATERING AND OTHER SERVICES	FOSSIL SAVING %	ELECTRICITY SAVING %
	Review hot water thermostat accuracy and temperature settings periodically Reducing temperatures will save energy – but take precautions to avoid the risk of legionnaires' disease	1	0	Ensure optimum use of hot water, ventilation and lighting in the kitchen for various times of day and night Do not use hobs or ovens for space heating Run dishwashers only on full loads	0.2	0.2
Low cost	Fit draught stripping around windows and doors Fit heavy curtains to guest and public rooms	1	0	Where fittings allow, replace 38 mm fluorescent light tubes by 26 mm type, and install electronic starters and ballasts	0	0.5
	Check boiler efficiency periodically and make improvements as required	2	0	Consider replacement of tungsten lamps (including light fittings where necessary) by compact fluorescent types	0	6
	Provide temperature and time controls for domestic hot water	1	0	Consider installation of timers, dimmers, photocells and sensors so lighting operates only when, where and to the extent needed	0	1
	Install showers and flow restrictors where possible Reduce standing losses from hot water storage by lagging pipes and tanks	2	1	Consider installation of bedroom key fobs so lights and other electrical items operate only when rooms are occupied	0	1
	Consider direct fired water heaters for hot water in place of boiler serving calorifier	3	0	When replacing catering equipment, review current developments in appliance design to select the most energy efficient	1	1

Table 6.2 continued

	BOILERS, CONTROLS AND HOT WATER	FOSSIL SAVING %	ELECTRICITY SAVING %	LIGHTING, CATERING AND OTHER SERVICES	FOSSIL SAVING %	ELECTRICITY SAVING %
	Establish a system for setting targets for energy consumption, monitoring actual consumption and assessing performance	1	2	If you have a swimming pool, provide and use a cover to reduce heat losses at night	0.5	0
	Modernise heating and ventilation plant controls	6	1	Ensure enough linen is available so that laundry equipment is run at full load	0.5	0
	Provide power factor correction, and consider load shedding to reduce maximum demand charges This will not save fuel but will reduce electricity charges	6	1	Use high-efficiency lights for all external lights, including car parking areas, controlled by timers and/or photocells	0	0.5

A typical hotel releases about 160 kg of CO_2 per square metre of floor area annually, equivalent to about 10 tonnes per bedroom.

Who benefits from energy efficiency?

- Hotel owners and management benefit because efficiently run buildings cost less to operate.
- Guests benefit because an efficiently controlled hotel satisfies their needs and leads to repeat business.
- Staff benefit through improved morale and better motivation, which in turn increase productivity.
- The environment benefits because using energy efficiently reduces adverse effects on the environment and preserves non-renewable resources for future generations.

Energy efficiency measures and percentage savings

The savings quoted in Table 6.2 are the minimum you can expect to achieve. Small percentage savings can mean appreciable cash benefits.

Services and energy

The supply of gas, electricity and water are of vital importance to the caterer. Any information required is best obtained from the appropriate local board so that it will be up to date.

> ⓘ
> **Further information**
> See HCIMA Technical Brief No. 36, or contact the Department for Environment, Food and Rural Affairs (Defra) for information about energy efficiency (see www.defra.gov.uk).

Water

Water authorities are required, by law, to provide a supply of clean, wholesome water, free from suspended matter, odour and taste, all bacteria that are likely to cause disease, and mineral matter injurious to health.

Electrical safety

All electrical products must meet safety criteria laid out in European and national regulations.

Gas

Gas is a safe fuel, but like all fuels it must be treated with respect.

What to do if you smell gas:
- Open all doors and windows.
- Check whether a gas tap has been left on, or if a pilot light has gone out. If so, turn off the appliance.
- If in doubt, turn off the gas supply at the meter and phone for emergency service.

Electricity

Electricity cannot be heard, tasted or smelled. Installed and used correctly, it is a very safe source of energy, but misused it can kill or cause serious injury. It is therefore essential that any electrical installation is undertaken by qualified engineers in accordance with British Standard 7671, and carried out by registered contractors of the National Inspection Council for Electrical Installation Contracting (NICIEC). A technical brief, 'Guide to Electric Lighting, No. 7/97', is available from HCIMA.

Comparison of fuels

Electricity and mains gas are most generally used in catering. Bottled gas (e.g. Calor) is also used in some catering operations. Before deciding on the fuel to use (if there is a choice) the following factors should be considered:

- safety
- cost
- efficiency
- storage requirements
- constancy of supply
- cleanliness and need for ventilation
- cost of equipment, installation and maintenance.

Energy conservation

At the Earth Summit in Rio de Janeiro in 1992 the UK signed an international agreement, entitled the 'Climate Change Convention', whereby it agreed that by the year 2000 the UK would reduce its fossil fuel emissions to the same levels as those of 1990. Energy conservation is not just an ethical or green issue but makes good business sense.

Table 6.3 Comparison of electricity and gas

ADVANTAGES	DISADVANTAGES
Electricity	
Clean to use, low maintenance Easily controlled, labour saving Good working atmosphere Little heat loss, no storage space required Low ventilation requirements	Time taken to heat up in a few instances Particular utensils are required for some hobs, e.g. induction More expensive than gas
Gas	
Convenient, labour saving, no smoke or dirt Special utensils not required No fuel storage required Easily controllable with immediate full heat and the flames are visible Cheaper than electricity	Some heat is lost in the kitchen. Regular cleaning required for efficient working For gas to produce heat it must burn; this requires oxygen, which is contained in the air, and as a result carbon dioxide and water are produced As a result, adequate ventilation must be provided for combustion and to ensure a satisfactory working environment

The costs of energy use in hotel and catering establishments vary widely according to the type of fuel used, the type and age of equipment, the way in which it is used and the tariff paid.

The basic principles of energy management are:

- obtain the best tariff available
- purchase the most suitable energy-efficient equipment
- reduce heat loss to a minimum
- match heat and cooling loads on environmental systems whenever possible to the demands
- maintain all equipment to optimum efficiency
- ensure that the operating periods of systems and equipment are set correctly
- use heat recovery systems
- monitor energy consumption
- train staff to be energy efficient.

Some factors to be considered in energy conservation

- Always replace equipment with low energy rating equipment, by referring to wattage and running costs.
- Ensure that all machinery is maintained at its optimum efficiency and that equipment needing regular cleaning is serviced in accordance with maintenance manual requirements. This particularly applies to filters on ventilation and on conditioning systems, refrigeration plant condensers, cooking equipment and dishwashing machines.

- When replacing equipment, it is an opportune time to review the contents of the menu, the cooking and storage methods that the menu requires. Can certain procedures be scaled down or omitted, or can alternative procedures be used?
- Check all pre-heating of equipment – overlong pre-heating wastes fuel.
- Constantly review all heating and cooking procedures.
- Is it possible to reduce operating hours?
- Regularly check ventilation systems.
- Regularly check that storage temperatures for hot water systems are not more than 65°C for central systems and 55°C for local units. Also ensure that this temperature is not less than 55°C to avoid the risk of legionnaires' disease.
- Regularly check all lighting systems; where possible use energy-efficient compact fluorescent bulbs.
- Train staff not to waste lighting or use lighting unnecessarily.

REFERENCES

Katz, R.L. (1974) 'Skills of the effective administrator', *Harvard Business Review* 52(1).

Mintzberg, H. (1975) 'The manager's job: folklore and fact', *Harvard Business Review* 74.

TOPICS FOR DISCUSSION

1 Who should be responsible for planning a kitchen?
2 Discuss the worst organised kitchen that you have seen and how it could be improved.
3 Give good and bad examples of working methods.
4 Discuss the advantages and disadvantages of the straight-shift and split-shift systems from the point of view of the staff and the employer.
5 Compile a list of all the factors that affect the good design of a kitchen. Discuss why they are necessary to enable efficiency.
6 Poor design may cause accidents in the kitchen. Discuss the ways in which accidents can be prevented.
7 Discuss the reasons why organisation of staff needs to be considered in relation to a specific menu and the factors that influence the composition of the menu.
8 Discuss the qualities that go towards being a good (a) head chef, (b) chef de partie.
9 Organisational ability is a quality that is often quoted as an essential element to being successful in the kitchen. Discuss, with examples if possible, your understanding of organisational ability regarding (a) resources, (b) staff, (c) yourself.

TOPICS FOR DISCUSSION

10 Discuss the role of supervision and relate this, if possible, to an establishment you know.

11 As an employee how do you like to be supervised?

12 What are the characteristics of a good supervisor?

13 List the essential requirements of kitchen equipment.

14 Discuss the respective advantages of a conventional oven, convection oven and a combination convection/steaming oven.

15 Compare induction cooking plates, halogen hobs and conventional cooking tops.

16 Compare copper pans and stainless-steel pans.

17 What are the benefits of the bratt pan?

18 What essential items of mechanical equipment are needed?

19 Discuss the importance of sufficient refrigeration.

20 What are the benefits of the food waste disposer or the advantages of a food compactor?

21 What is the argument for maintaining wooden chopping boards?

22 Discuss the design of equipment in relation to maintaining high standards of hygiene.

23 What factors should be considered by those designing kitchen equipment?

24 What faults, if any, do you wish to be remedied in any items of equipment?

25 What improvements could you suggest?

26 The advantages of gas or electricity for kitchen equipment.

27 How to effect economy in the consumption of energy by catering equipment.

28 Why maintenance of all services is essential.

29 How water conservation can be achieved.

30 Why hot water is more costly than cold water, and how these costs can be reduced.

31 How could the use of the sun and wind be used to reduce costs in small establishments?

32 Discuss how training could reduce wastage of water, gas and electricity.

Chapter 7 PRODUCTION SYSTEMS

A STRATEGIC AND METHODICAL APPROACH TO FOOD PRODUCTION AND SERVICE

Every chef's challenge is to ensure that the production of food (mise-en-place) is as safe, efficient, cost effective and consistent as possible. This is only possible when the chef can analyse the full process using a critical path and identify all areas of work.

There is more evidence that today's young chef has the desire to achieve great things, which in itself is very admirable, however this approach, if not tempered, is flawed and could cause frustrations when you are in a senior post within an organisation. The current desire to achieve, have the highest accolades with the biggest salary, and the best and most original food, detracts from the very foundation that supports the product that is so important to the organisation. This approach is partly driven by the media promoting the 'celebrity chef' and sometimes endorsing the taking of an 'unethical' approach in order to achieve stardom.

The 'progressive approach' is to establish a level of consistency in the building of knowledge where the trainee starts with the basics and progresses methodically, learning all areas of their craft. For example:

- health and safety
- personnel legislation
- understanding facilities in the kitchen environment
- self-motivation
- working with others
- financial acumen
- making effective decisions
- kitchen administration and organisation
- communication with others
- delegation
- the welfare of others
- conceptual skills
- recruitment and training
- understanding the market
- understanding suppliers and their relationships.

The above list identifies most of the areas that will support the food and beverage product, making it consistent and able to achieve longevity, with the capacity to maintain growth and gain the market edge. The above list does not include food production and food styles, however, nor does it cover the scientific 'wow!' and bafflement factor.

However, the above list is the essential foundation on which the food and beverage product should be based; without this foundation the product itself is prone to collapse, leading to heightened risk and ultimately placing the product/brand at risk.

Areas of 'risk'

Areas of risk include:

- heath and safety
- financial loss
- the market
- the workforce
- incorrect convergence of facilities
- suppliers
- cooking consistency.

All the above areas hold potential risks that could devalue the product/brand by making the end result inconsistent, which will lead to a fall in profits and perhaps increase staff turnover. In extreme cases, businesses in hospitality that fail do so due to one or more of the above areas not being properly managed.

QUALITY IN THE MANAGEMENT OF FOOD AND BEVERAGE PRODUCTION SYSTEMS

European Foundation for Quality Management Excellence Model (1999)

The European Foundation for Quality Management Excellence Model is a non-prescriptive framework, which recognises that there are many approaches to achieving sustainable excellence in all aspects of performance. The model is based on nine criteria. It emphasises that results for customers, people (employees) and society are achieved through leadership driving policy and strategy, people management, partnership and resources, and processes leading to business results.

Each of the nine elements shown in the model (Figure 7.1) is a criterion that can be used to appraise an organisation's progress towards total quality management. The four results criteria are concerned with what the organisation has achieved and is achieving. The five enablers criteria are concerned with how results are being achieved. The arrows shown are intended to emphasise the dynamic nature of the model. They indicate that innovation and learning help to improve the enablers and that this in turn leads to improved results. The overall objective of comprehensive self-appraisal and self-improvement is to regularly review each of the nine criteria and, thereafter, to adopt relevant improvement strategies.

Figure 7.1 European Foundation for Quality Management Excellence Model

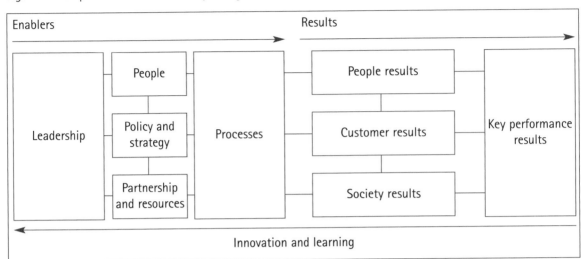

British Standard EN ISO 9002: 1994

The British Standard scheme was introduced in 1979 with the aim of providing a method for organisations to assess the suitability of their suppliers' products. The scheme aimed to rationalise the many schemes of supplier assessment used by various purchasing firms and organisations.

The British Standard Quality Award BS EN ISO 9002: 1994, is a quality kitemark (standard or benchmark) in the fitness for purpose and safety in use sense, in the service provided and/or the products designed and constructed to satisfy the customer's needs. It is concerned primarily with evidence of systematic processes that are employed within an operation and which can demonstrate that there is a link between customer demand and the services and products on offer.

BS EN ISO 9002 identifies the systems, procedures and criteria that ensure that a product or service meets a customer's requirements. The key elements in quality management for most organisations in the hotel and catering (hospitality) industry include:

- management responsibility – policy, objectives, identification of key personnel
- quality system procedures – all functions must be covered
- auditing the system – it must be audited internally
- quality in marketing – honest promotional activities
- material control and traceability – supplies must be traceable
- non-conformity – ensuring that faulty products/service do not reach the customer
- corrective action – identifying reasons for faults, and subsequently implementing measures to correct them and records of the faults and measures, written and kept

- after-sales service – procedures for monitoring quality of after-sales service
- documentation and records – records of checks and inspections, action taken, audit reports
- personnel and training – identification of needs, provision and verification of training
- product safety and liability – procedures for handling, storing and processing materials (for example, foods).

BS EN ISO 9002 can be important to food service operations for two reasons. First, when purchasing goods and services, BS EN ISO 9002 indicates that a supplier operates a quality system of a high standard. Second, food service operators, such as contract caterers, may find that they will not be considered as potential tenderers if they have not achieved BS EN ISO 9002. Additionally, BS EN ISO 9002 may even provide useful evidence that due diligence had been exercised – for example, in the event of a food service operation being prosecuted under the Food Safety Act 1990.

In an increasingly competitive marketplace, and with increasing uniformity between operations, the level of service provided and its quality become ever more important. It is the front-line members of staff that offer this service – their training and development are crucial to the successful running of an operation. Total quality management (TQM) offers a framework by which members of staff are given the scope to treat guests as individuals, and thereby offer superior service.

However, the costs involved in attaining the standard can be high, and therefore the introduction of BS EN ISO 9002 needs to be carefully assessed before implementation takes place. On the other hand, the reviews from many of the organisations moving towards BS EN ISO 9002 have suggested that it is cost-effective.

PROBLEMS

Food production systems, such as cook-chill, cook-freeze and sous-vide, have been introduced into certain areas of catering in order to increase efficiency and productivity; changes have been made to maximise the utilisation of equipment and to maintain high levels of output and viability.

The particular problems of the catering industry are as follows.

- **Staff:** unattractive work conditions, limited numbers of skilled staff, mobility of labour.
- **Food:** high cost, wastage.
- **Equipment:** high cost of replacement and maintenance, under-usage.
- **Energy:** wasteful high-cost traditional systems, availability.
- **Overheads:** wage increases, payments to National Insurance.

ⓘ

Further information
Further information on quality matters can be obtained from the following sources.

- European Foundation for Quality Management, Brussels Representative Office, Avenue des Pleiades 15, 1200 Brussels, Belgium (website: www.efqm.org).
- The complete documents on BS EN ISO 9002: 1994 are available from the British Standards Institution, Linford Wood, Milton Keynes MK14 6LE (website: www.bsi-global.com).
- East, J. (1993) Managing Quality in the Catering Industry. Croner Publications.
- HCIMA Technical Brief No. 20/98, 'BS EN ISO 9002: 1994' (HCIMA, 1998).

- **Space:** most kitchens and services must be adequate for comfortable working while using space efficiently; space is very costly.

The solution to these problems comes in the form of centralisation of production, using the skilled staff available to prepare and cook in bulk and then to distribute to finishing kitchens, which are smaller in size, employing semi-skilled and unskilled labour.

Cook-freeze and cook-chill systems have been developed to meet these requirements, each system having advantages over the other depending on the size and nature of the overall operation. For example, cook-freeze is not adaptable to very small units or to haute cuisine. Cook-chill can be adapted to any type of unit but cannot take advantage of seasonal, cheaper commodities.

Sous-vide, which is a method of working under vacuum-sealing, ice-water bath chilling and chilled storage, has also been developed as a production system.

Many catering operations face problems because of the growing shortage of skilled catering staff and the ever-increasing turnover of employees:

- it is essential that skilled staff are more fully utilised and given improved working conditions
- certain catering tasks require deskilling so as to be carried out by a greater proportion of unskilled staff
- better benefits and conditions of employment must be provided for fewer key staff in order to reduce levels of staff turnover and enhance job satisfaction.

Assured safe catering

This is a system developed for and with caterers to control food safety problems. It is based upon some of the principles of hazard analysis and critical control point (HACCP), and involves looking at the catering operation step by step – from the selection of ingredients right through to the service of food to the customer. With careful analysis of each step of the catering operation anything that may affect the safety of the food is identified. The caterer can then determine when and how to control that hazard. Assured safe catering helps prevent safety problems by careful planning in easy steps.

HYGIENE OF FOOD PRODUCTION SYSTEMS

Hygiene committees

It is generally recognised that one of the principal concerns of food production for caterers is to ensure that the food is safe when consumed.

Figure 7.2 The process of
food hygiene management
for production

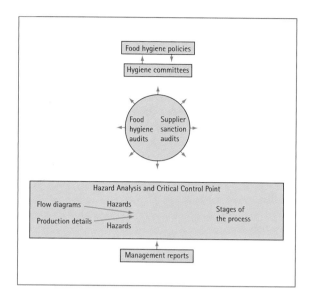

The need for special attention to be given to food hygiene is now well
recognised. This involves everyone, whether directly or indirectly
involved with food handling. In order for both to focus attention on the
subject it is advisable for large caterers to set up hygiene committees.
These should comprise those with an immediate responsibility for
maintaining hygiene standards, quality control and training personnel, as
well as representatives from all sections of the food production line,
including food service personnel.

It is advisable that staff be seconded to the committee for a set period
of time (a maximum of two years), in order to encourage others in the
organisation to show an interest. The objective is to set the pace in food
hygiene standards. It can be useful from time to time to invite specialist
speakers to talk on hygiene subjects relating to the industry – for
example, cleaning, equipment and transportation.

Figure 7.3 Elements of
production

Food	Preparation	Cooking	Holding	Regeneration	Presentation
Fresh	Weigh/measure	Blanche	Chill	Regithermic	Bain marie
Fresh cooked	Clean/open	Warm	Sous vide	Microwave	Service flats
Fresh prepared	Chop/cut	Simmer	Freeze	Convection	Plates
Canned	Combine/mix	Boil	Tray	Traditional	Trays
Frozen	Blend	Steam	Hot cupboard		Vending
Chilled	Shape/coat	Grill	Cold cupboard		Buffet
Vaccum	Form	Sauté			Trolley
Dehydrated		Brown			Dishes
Smoked		Bake			
Salted		Roast			
Crystallized		Fry			
Acidified		Microwave			
Pasteurized					
Bottled					
UHT					

Foods in ◄─────────────────── Process ──────────────────► Output

Food safety legislation

The Food Hygiene (England) Regulations 2005 give effect to the EU Regulations and came into force on 1 January 2006. Article 5 of the Regulations states that:

> Food business operators shall put into place, implement and maintain a permanent procedure based on the principles of hazard analysis critical control points (HACCP).

Table 7.1 Example of a HACCP control chart

PROCESS STEPS	HAZARDS	CONTROLS	CRITICAL LIMIT	MONITORING	CORRECTIVE ACTION
Purchase	Contamination, pathogens, mould or foreign bodies present	Approved supplier			Change supplier
Transport and delivery	Multiplication of harmful bacteria	Refrigerated vehicles		Check delivery vehicles, date marks, temperatures	Reject if >8°C or out of date
Refrigerate	Bacterial growth; further contamination – bacteria, chemicals, etc.	Store below 5°C, separate raw and cooked foods; stock rotation	Food below 5°C	Check and record temperature twice a day; check date marks	Discard if signs of spoilage or past date mark
Prepare	Bacterial growth; further contamination	No more than 30 minutes in 'danger zone'; good personal hygiene; clean equipment and hygienic premises		Supervisor to audit at regular intervals; visual checks; cleaning schedules	Discard if >8°C for 6 hours
Cook	Survival of harmful bacteria	Thorough cooking	75°C	Check and record temperature/time	Continue cooking to 75°C
Prepare for service	Multiplication; contamination	No more than 20 minutes in 'danger zone'	2 hours	Supervisor to audit at regular intervals	Discard if >8°C for 2 hours
Chill	Multiplication; contamination	Blast chiller	90 minutes to below 10°C	Supervisor to audit at regular intervals	Discard if >20°C for 2 hours
Refrigerate	Multiplication; contamination	Store below 5°C; separate raw and ready-to-eat foods	8°C for 4 hours	Check and record temperature twice a day	Discard if >8°C for 4 hours
Reheat	Survival	Reheat to 75°C in centre	75°C (82°C in Scotland)	Check and record temperature of each batch	Continue reheating to 75°C

Figure 7.4 The seven
principles of HACCP

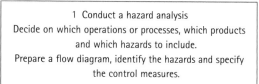

1 Conduct a hazard analysis
Decide on which operations or processes, which products
and which hazards to include.
Prepare a flow diagram, identify the hazards and specify
the control measures.

2 Determine the critical control points (CCPs)
Control measures must be used to prevent, eliminate or
reduce a hazard to an acceptable level.

3 Establish critical limits
Must be measurable, e.g. temperature, time, pH, weight
and size of food.
Set a target limit and a critical limit; the difference
between the two is called the tolerance.

4 Establish a system to monitor control of each CCP
What are the critical limits, how, where and when the
monitoring should be undertaken, and who is
responsible for monitoring.

5 Establish corrective actions when monitoring indicates a
particular CCP is not under control.
Deal with any affected product, and bring the CCP and the
process back under control.

6 Establish procedures for verification to confirm that the
HACCP system is working effectively
Validation – obtain evidence that the CCPs and critical
limits are effective.
Verification – ensure that the flow diagram remains valid,
hazards controlled, monitoring is satisfactory, and
corrective action has been or will be taken.

7 Establish documentation and records concerning all
procedures appropriate to these principles and their
application
This will be proportionate to the size and type of business.
Documentation is necessary to demonstrate that food
safety is being managed. Managers need records when
auditing and they will need to be available for
enforcement officers and external auditors.

Food handlers must receive adequate instruction and/or training in food hygiene to enable them to handle food safely.

Those responsible for the HACCP-based procedures in the business must have enough relevant knowledge and understanding to ensure the procedures are operated effectively.

The procedures will need to show the environmental health officer that there is effective food safety management in place. This includes the following elements.

- Identifying risks to food safety that might be present or occur within your business. (What can go wrong and where?)
- Controls have been put in place that deal with these risks. (What can I do about it?)
- Controls are carried out. If something goes wrong everyone is clear what to do about it and does it. (What is acceptable? How can I check? What can I do about it?)
- The procedures are kept up to date. (How do I confirm this is still working?)
- Documents and records are kept that show the procedure is working and reviewed. (What documents and records do I need?)

One of the benefits of having a HACCP system is that it is useful in demonstrating 'due diligence'.

Notes

- A 'team' of people responsible for the HACCP system must be identified and trained. In a small business, one person may be responsible.
- When deciding which hazards are significant, their reduction to acceptable levels must be essential to the production of 'safe food' (e.g. poor temperature control or prolonged holding in the danger zone could result in food-poisoning bacteria multiplying to large numbers). Not cooking food thoroughly could result in the survival of food-poisoning bacteria.
- Food safety training and effective supervision must take place, and staff training records must be kept.
- Physical or chemical hazards could occur at any stage in the process.

A practical example
Cooking
The cooking of the fresh chicken, which can then be held hot prior to service, or chilled and refrigerated:

- **hazard** – pathogenic bacteria present in raw poultry
- **control** – the chicken must be cooked thoroughly to 75°C to kill all pathogens
- **monitor** – check the temperature in the thickest parts (thigh and leg

Figure 7.5 Flow diagram
for cooking a fresh chicken

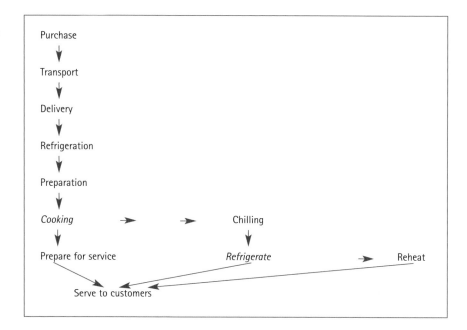

joint) using visual check that the juices run clear and/or a temperature
probe
- **hot holding** – chicken must be kept above 63°C (use temperature probe
  to check)
- **chill and refrigerate** – chill to below 10°C within 90 minutes and place
  in refrigerator
- **documentation** – temperatures measured and recorded; hot holding
  equipment checked and maintained; must be hot when food placed in
  it; record details of any corrective action.

Cold storage
The cold storage of the cooked chicken in the refrigerator after cooking
and chilling:

- **hazard** – multiplication of salmonella or campylobacter in the cooked
  chicken
- **control** – store below 5°C in refrigerator
- **monitor** – check temperature of the food (not fridge temperature) is
  below 5°C
- **corrective action** – if food has been above 8°C for more than four
  hours, it should be thrown away; the reason should be investigated
  and the problem put right
- **documentation** – temperatures measured and recorded twice a day;
  record details of any corrective action.

Table 7.2 Pros and cons of HACCP

REASONS FOR HACCP	ADVERSE CONSEQUENCES
Necessary to comply with EU legislation	More likely to infringe food safety legislation
Helps demonstrate due diligence	Reduced confidence in management from
Action is taken before serious problems occur	outside bodies (more frequent inspections)
Food safety is integrated into recipe	More likely to produce unsafe food
development and menu planning	Risk of civil action
All staff involved in carrying out controls	More food is wasted
Generates a food safety culture	Food handlers do not recognise their
Risks are reduced	involvement and responsibilities
Internationally recognised	

Food hygiene audits

Food hygiene audits are intended to scrutinise the food production operation with a view to recording deficiencies and areas for improvement, or simply to monitor performance at a certain point. These may be linked to any quality assurance criteria.

The approach to the audit may vary but it generally involves a suitably qualified person carrying out an in-depth inspection of both premises, plant and food production practices. There should be a report-back procedure to management, with observations where necessary and any recommendations.

Caterers can change their techniques of operation for various reasons, without being aware of any hazards that are introduced, and it is very easy for staff who are familiar with the production plant to fail to see problem areas that are emerging. It may be that staff are beginning to be lax in connection with a certain task. It could be that maintenance is required to parts of the building. Similarly, equipment may need attention. Day-to-day familiarity with the work and the operation often means that those closest to it simply do not notice problems and therefore a hygiene audit is one way of bringing in someone who can look critically, to the extent of picking up any problem areas or practices.

The frequency of these audits will vary. High-intensity production will justify more frequent audits. It is important that whatever emerges from the in-depth inspections must be properly recorded and brought to the attention of the appropriate people: either the management or individual food handlers, or both. Management must in turn ensure that the hygiene audit is acted upon, otherwise there is little value in the exercise.

Standards of hygiene

To ensure safe hygienic standards in any system the following points are crucial.

Refrigeration
Efficient refrigeration and temperature control are essential otherwise

there is a danger of deterioration in structure, quality, appearance and nutritional value. Any rise in temperature will encourage the growth of micro-organisms and lead to poor-quality food, which may need to be destroyed.

It is vital that accurate temperature control and monitoring are carried out throughout the cook-freeze, blast-freeze, storage and regeneration process to ensure that food is always held at acceptable and safe temperatures.

Devices used to measure temperature (see Figure 7.5) include:

- hand-held probes, which provide a digital readout for random checking at all stages
- audible alarms, fitted inside cold stores to warn of rises in temperature
- temperature gauges, which give a visible reading of the temperature.

Production

In order to ensure that high-quality, palatable food is produced at all times it is essential that working conditions are maintained to the highest possible standards, as laid down in the HMSO publication *Clean Catering* (ISBN 011 320 4833). For example:

- stringent personal hygiene precautions against infection of the food
- all working surfaces and utensils thoroughly cleaned to minimise spread of bacteria
- clean equipment and utensils separated from used items awaiting cleaning
- separation of raw and cooked foods at all times
- strict control of cooking times and temperatures
- staff training in food hygiene
- consultation with medical and public health officers when planning food production systems.

Equipment

The equipment used will vary according to the size of the operation, but if food is batch-cooked then convection ovens, steaming ovens, bratt pans, jacketed boiling pans, tilting kettles, and so on, may be used.

Figure 7.6 A selection of temperature measuring devices

Further information
For further information, visit the British Institute of Cleaning Science's website at www.bics.org.uk.

Certain oven models are available in which a set of racks can be assembled with food and wheeled in for cooking.

The main difference between cook-freeze and cook-chill is the degree of refrigeration and the length of storage life. Other than these differences the information given in this chapter relates to both systems. (For details of cook-freeze, see page 327.)

We will now take a closer look at some of the methods of food production highlighted in Table 7.3.

COOK-CHILL

Cook-chill is a catering system based on the normal preparation and cooking of food followed by rapid chilling storage in controlled low-temperature conditions above freezing point – 0–3°C (32–37°F) – and subsequently reheating immediately before consumption. The chilled food is regenerated in finishing kitchens, which require low capital investment and minimum staff. Almost any food can be cook-chilled provided that the correct methods are used during the preparation.

The cook-chill system is used in volume catering, in hospitals, schools and in social services. It is also used for banquets, in conference and exhibition catering, in vending machines where meals are dispensed to the customer, and in factories, hospitals and services outside of main meal times.

Table 7.3 Methods of food production

NO.	METHOD	DESCRIPTION
1	Conventional	Term used to describe production utilising mainly fresh foods and traditional cooking methods
2	Convenience	Method of production utilising mainly convenience foods
3	Call order	Method where food is cooked to order either from customer (as in cafeterias) or from waiter; production area often open to customer area
4	Continuous flow	Method involving production-line approach where different parts of the production process may be separated (e.g. fast food)
5	Centralised	Production not directly linked to service; foods are 'held' and distributed to separate service areas
6	Cook-chill	Food production storage and regeneration method utilising principle of low temperature control to preserve the qualities of processed foods
7	Cook-freeze	Production, storage and regeneration method utilising principle of freezing to control and preserve the qualities of processed foods; requires special processes to assist freezing
8	Sous-vide	Method of production, storage and regeneration utilising principle of sealed vacuum to control and preserve the quality of processed foods
9	Assembly kitchen	A system based on accepting and incorporating the latest technological development in the manufacturing and conservation of food products

Foods suitable for the cook-chill process

- **Meats:** All meat, poultry, game and offal can be cook-chilled. Meat dishes that need to be sliced, such as striploin of beef, are cooked, rapidly chilled, sliced and packaged for storage. The regeneration temperature must reach 70°C (158°F) in the centre of the produce for two minutes. Therefore, it is not possible to serve undercooked meats.
- **Fish:** All precooked fish dishes are suitable for cook-chilling.
- **Egg dishes:** Omelettes and scrambled eggs are now commonly used in this process, especially on airlines. Omelettes are now manufactured by companies that are able to supply the airline with the chilled product. The quality of the end product has greatly improved and continues to do so as more and more money is invested in product development.
- **Soups and sauces:** Most soups and sauces can now be chilled successfully. Those with a high fat or egg yolk content do need a certain amount of recipe modification to prevent separation on regeneration.
- **Desserts:** There are a large number of desserts that chill well, especially the cold variety. Developments continue with hot sweets, especially those that require a hot base and a separate topping.

Recipe modification

Successful production of chilled food does require a certain amount of recipe modification. These modifications may have to be introduced during the preparation or cooking or both.

- **Battered fish:** The batter should be made thicker, using a mixture with a higher fat content. This type of batter does not easily break away from the fish and will give a crisper end product.
- **Stewed/braised items:** Cut meat into smaller portions to avoid undue thickness. Flour-based sauces must be thoroughly cooked otherwise they will continue to thicken during regeneration.
- **Scrambled eggs:** Cook until the egg begins to scramble, remove from heat and allow the product to continue to cook to a soft consistency. Chill immediately in shallow dishes and stir during chilling.
- **Creamed and mashed potatoes:** More liquid is added than normal, giving a loose and less dense product. This assists the chilling and regeneration stages as the potato absorbs more liquid when chilled.

The purpose of chilling food

The purpose of chilling food is to prolong its storage life. Under normal temperature conditions, food deteriorates rapidly through the action of micro-organisms and enzymic and chemical reactions. A reduction in the storage temperature inhibits the multiplication of bacteria and other micro-organisms, and slows down the chemical and enzymic reactions.

At normal refrigeration temperatures reactions are still taking place but at a much slower rate, and at frozen food storage temperatures – -20°C (24°F) approximately – all reactions nearly cease. A temperature of 0–3°C (32–37°F) does not give a storage life comparable to frozen food, but it does produce a good product.

It is generally accepted that, even where high standards of fast chilling practice are used and consistent refrigerated storage maintained, product quality may be acceptable for only a few days (including the day of production and consumption). The storage temperature of 0−3°C (32−37°F) is of extreme importance to ensure both full protection of the food from microbiological growth and the maintenance of maximum nutritional values in the food. It is generally accepted that a temperature of 10°C (50°F) should be regarded as the critical safety limit for the storage of refrigerated food. Above that temperature, growth of micro-organisms may render the food dangerous to health.

In a properly designed and operated cook-chill system, cooked and prepared food will be rapidly cooled down to 0−3°C (32−37°F) as soon as possible after cooking and portioning, and then stored between these temperatures throughout storage and distribution until required for reheating and service. Food prepared through the cook-chill system should be portioned and transferred to a blast chiller unit within 30 minutes. This will reduce the risk of the food remaining at warm incubation temperatures, and prevent the risk of contamination and loss of food quality.

The cook-chill process

- The food should be cooked sufficiently to ensure destruction of any pathogenic micro-organisms.
- The chilling process must begin as soon as possible after completion of the cooking and portioning processes, within 30 minutes of leaving the cooker. The food should be chilled to 3°C (37°F) within a period of 90 minutes. Most pathogenic organisms will not grow below 7°C (45°F), while a temperature below 3°C (37°F) is required to reduce growth of spoilage organisms and to achieve the required storage life. However, slow growth of spoilage organisms does take place at these temperatures and for this reason storage life cannot be greater than five days.
- The food should be stored at a temperature of 0−3°C (32−37°F).
- The chilled food should be distributed under such controlled conditions that any rise in temperature of the food during distribution is kept to a minimum.
- For both safety and palatability the reheating (regeneration) of the food should follow immediately upon the removal of the food from chilled conditions and should raise the temperature to a level of at least 70°C (158°F).
- The food should be consumed as soon as possible and not more than two hours after reheating. Food not intended for reheating should be

consumed as soon as convenient and within two hours of removal from storage. It is essential that unconsumed reheated food is discarded.

• A temperature of 10°C (50°F) should be regarded as the critical safety limit for chilled food. Should the temperature of the chilled food rise above this level during storage or distribution, the food concerned should be discarded.

Cook-chill is generally planned within a purpose-designed, comprehensive, new central production unit to give small-, medium- or large-scale production along predefined flow lines, incorporating traditional catering/chilling/post-chilling packaging and storage for delivery to finishing kitchens. Within an existing kitchen, where existing equipment is retained with possible minor additions and modifications, chilling/post-chilling packaging and additional storage for cooked chilled food are added.

Finishing kitchens

These can consist of purpose-built regeneration equipment plus refrigerated storage. Additional equipment, such as a chip fryer, boiling table and pressure steamer for chips, sauces, custard, vegetables, and so on, can be added if required, to give greater flexibility.

Where chilled food is produced to supply a service on the same premises, it is recommended that the meals should be supplied, stored and regenerated by exactly the same method as used for operations where the production unit and finishing kitchens are separated by some distance.

Failure to adhere to just one procedure could result in disorganised production and reduced productivity. Once a decision is taken to sever production from service this method should be followed throughout the system.

Distribution of cook-chill

Distribution of the chilled food is an important part of the cook-chill operation. Fluctuations in storage temperature can affect the palatability and texture of food, and lead to microbiological dangers that require the food to be discarded. The distribution method chosen must ensure that the required temperature of below 3°C (37°F) is maintained throughout the period of transport. Should the temperature of the food exceed 5°C (41°F) during distribution the food ought to be consumed within 12 hours; if the temperature exceeds 10°C (50°F) it should be discarded (Department of Health guidelines). Because of this, refrigeration during distribution is to be encouraged in many circumstances.

In some cases the cook-chill production unit can also act as a centralised kitchen and distribution point. Food is regenerated in an area adjacent to the cook-chill production area, and heat retention or insulated boxes are used for distribution. During transportation and service the food must not be allowed to fall below 62.8°C (145°F).

Know the legal requirements

Contravention of the Food Safety Act 1990, the amendment regulations and lack of due diligence can be very costly if legal action is taken and proved against the caterer or food manufacturer. The labelling of food products, recording of temperatures, maintenance of hygiene standards and promotion of staff training is essential in defence of due diligence. For this defence to be successful, the caterer must convince the court that all the requirements under the law have been complied with and that the accepted customs and practices of the profession have been carried out. It is also of paramount importance that a caterer records that these systems have been adhered to by the submission of documentary evidence.

Avoiding the dangers of cook-chill

It is essential to:

- maintain and record the correct temperatures
- maintain high standards of hygiene
- use fresh, high-quality ingredients, avoiding raw materials that may contain excessive numbers of micro-organisms.

Deliveries
All food purchased must be of prime quality and stored correctly under the required temperatures.

Preparation
All food must be prepared quickly under the appropriate conditions avoiding any possible cross-contamination and at the correct temperature.

Initial cooking and processing
During the cooking process the centre of the food must reach a temperature of at least 70°C (158°F); preferably this temperature should reach 75°F or even 80°C (167–177°F) to achieve a greater safety margin.

Portioning
This should take place under appropriate conditions in a controlled environment, which is maintained to the highest hygiene standards. The depth of the food should be no more than approximately 5 cm (2 inches). The containers must be labelled with the date of cooking, number of portions and reheating instructions.

Chilling
All food must be chilled within 30 minutes of cooking and reduced to a temperature of 0–3°C (32–37°F) within 90 minutes.

Figure 7.7 Production unit: planning for cook-chill

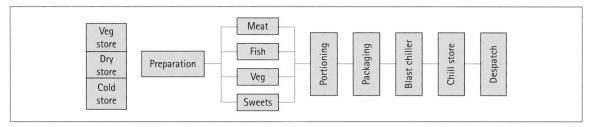

Portioning after chilling

In some cook-chill systems the food is chilled in multi-portion containers then plated before reheating. The portioning process should be carried out in a controlled environment within 30 minutes of the food leaving the chilled store and before reheating commences at a temperature of 10°C (50°F). It is then transported under chilled conditions to the desired location – for example, the hospital ward – where it is reheated to at least 70°C (158°F) but preferably 80°C (177°F) on the plate on which it is to be served.

Storage

All chilled cooked food must be stored in its own special refrigeration area. Never store cooked chilled food under the same conditions as fresh products. Always monitor the temperature of the product regularly.

Reheating

All cook-chill food must be reheated as quickly as possible to a minimum temperature of 70°C (158°F), ideally 75°C (167°F) but preferably 80°C (177°F).

Storage and quality of cook-chill foods

It has been found that, during the storage period before reheating and consumption, certain products deteriorate in quality.

- The flavour of certain meat dishes – in particular white meats, veal and poultry – deteriorates after three days.
- Chilled meats without sauces can develop acidic tastes.
- Fatty foods tend to develop 'off' flavours due to the fat oxidising.
- Fish dishes deteriorate more rapidly than meat dishes.
- Dishes containing meat tend to develop a 'flat' taste, and if spices have been used these can dominate the flavour of the meat by the end of the chilled storage period.
- Vegetables in general may discolour and develop a strong flavour.
- Dishes that contain large amounts of starch may taste stale after the chilled storage time.

Containers

The choice of containers must protect and in some cases enhance the

Figure 7.8 A delivery temperature recorder, which gives a printout of data

Figure 7.9 Testing food with a hand-held thermometer

quality of the product at all stages, it must assist in the rapid chilling, safe storage and effective reheating. Therefore the container must be:

- sturdy – to withstand chilling, handling and reheating
- safe – not made of a substance that will cause harmful substances to develop in the food, nor react with the food to cause discolouring or spoilage
- have an easy-to-remove lid – without damaging contents or causing spillage
- attractive – to enhance the appearance of the product
- airtight and watertight – so that moisture, flavours or odours do not penetrate the food or escape during storage and transportation.

There are various types of container available.

Single-portion containers

These can be of cardboard laminated with plastic, aluminium foil (unsuitable for microwave heating), plastic compounds or stainless steel and ceramic, which are durable and reusable (stainless steel is, however, unsuitable for microwave ovens).

Multi-portion containers

These can be of strong plastic compounds, stainless steel, ceramic or aluminium foil. Gastronorm containers are shown in Figure 7.11.

Figure 7.10 A central monitoring alarm unit and an example of the areas it covers

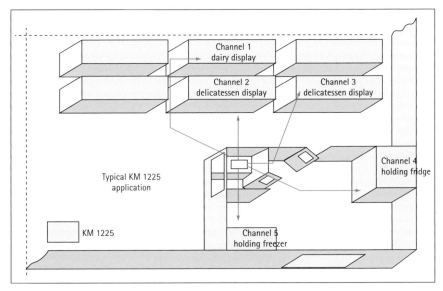

Labelling

Labels must stick securely to containers and be easy to apply, clearly identifying the product. Colour coding is sometimes used to help identify the different day of production. For example:

Figure 7.11 Module sizes for gastronorm containers

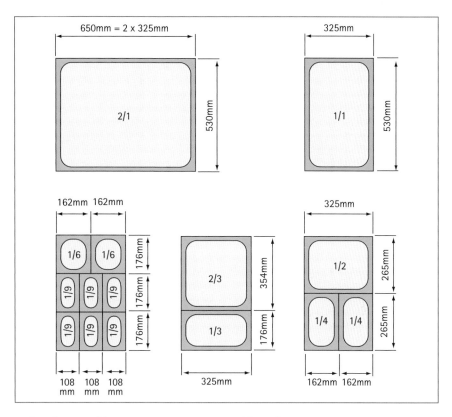

- Sunday – white
- Monday – red
- Tuesday – yellow
- Wednesday – blue
- Thursday – orange
- Friday – green
- Saturday – purple.

Chilling equipment

Only specially purpose-built and designed equipment can take the temperature of cooked food down to safe levels fast enough.

Blast chillers or air blast chillers

These use rapidly moving cold air to chill the food evenly and rapidly. Some models have temperature probes so that the temperature of the food being chilled can be checked without opening the door.

Cryogenic batch chillers

These use liquid nitrogen at a temperature of $-196°C$ ($-321°F$); this is sprayed into the chilling cabinet containing the warm food. In the warmer temperature of the cabinet, the liquid nitrogen turns to super-cold gas, absorbing the heat from the food as it does so. Fans move the cold gas over and around the food. Once the gas has become warm it is removed from the cabinet. Some equipment uses carbon dioxide instead of nitrogen.

Figure 7.12 Labelling system

MONDAY *Lunes - Lundi*	TUESDAY *Martes - Mardi*	WEDNESDAY *Miercoles - Mercredi*
Item: _____ Prep Date: ___ Time: ___ ☐AM ☐PM Shelf Life: ___ ☐Shifts ☐Fresh Daily Use By: ___ ☐4 PM ☐Close Emp: ___	Item: _____ Prep Date: ___ Time: ___ ☐AM ☐PM Shelf Life: ___ ☐Shifts ☐Fresh Daily Use By: ___ ☐4 PM ☐Close Emp: ___	Item: _____ Prep Date: ___ Time: ___ ☐AM ☐PM Shelf Life: ___ ☐Shifts ☐Fresh Daily Use By: ___ ☐4 PM ☐Close Emp: ___
THURSDAY *Jueves - Juedi*	FRIDAY *Viernes - Vendredi*	SATURDAY *Sabado - Samedi*
Item: _____ Prep Date: ___ Time: ___ ☐AM ☐PM Shelf Life: ___ ☐Shifts ☐Fresh Daily Use By: ___ ☐4 PM ☐Close Emp: ___	Item: _____ Prep Date: ___ Time: ___ ☐AM ☐PM Shelf Life: ___ ☐Shifts ☐Fresh Daily Use By: ___ ☐4 PM ☐Close Emp: ___	Item: _____ Prep Date: ___ Time: ___ ☐AM ☐PM Shelf Life: ___ ☐Shifts ☐Fresh Daily Use By: ___ ☐4 PM ☐Close Emp: ___
SUNDAY *Domingo - Dimanche*		
Item: _____ Prep Date: ___ Time: ___ ☐AM ☐PM Shelf Life: ___ ☐Shifts ☐Fresh Daily Use By: ___ ☐4 PM ☐Close Emp: ___		

Reheating equipment

The caterer has the following choice of equipment for regenerating cook-chill products.

- **Combination ovens:** These are ideally suited for bulk production and can be used with steam, which is very effective in producing quality products.
- **Steamers:** These may be used for certain foods, especially vegetables.
- **Microwave ovens:** These are used for small amounts of food.
- **Infra-red ovens:** These may be used for small or large quantities of food.

Points to remember to ensure a satisfactory product

- Time and temperature are crucial.

Figure 7.13 A blast chiller

- The food should not wait longer than 30 minutes to be chilled.
- The food should not be above 3°C (38°F) at the end of the chilling time. A higher temperature may be due to the food being packed too deep in the containers; the food may have been covered; there may be a malfunction in the equipment.
- Food should not be stored beyond its 'use by' date.
- The temperature of the food rising above 3°C (38°F) during transportation should be avoided. This may be due to: the journey taking too long using unrefrigerated transport; the refrigerated van not operating correctly; the insulated box (if used) not being precooled, or the lid not properly fitted. Whatever the cause, it must be recorded and the appropriate persons informed. If the temperature has not risen above 10°C (50°F) and the food is going to be served within 12 hours, the food may be allowed through. This will obviously depend on the type of food. Outside of these limits it should be discarded. If in doubt, throw it out.
- Food should not be overcooked after reheating. This may be due to the food being heated too long or the temperature being too high, or faulty equipment being used.

Figure 7.14 Refrigeration for cook-chill catering

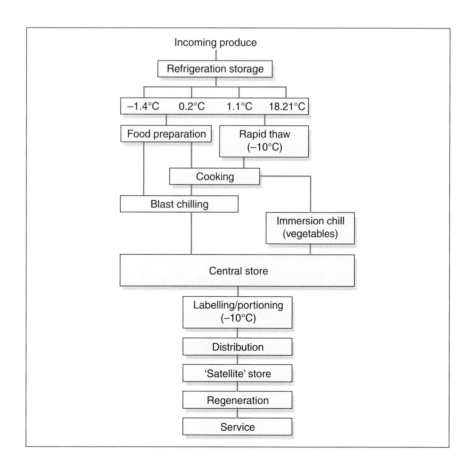

Further information
For further information, contact the Chilled Food Association, PO Box 14811 London NW10 9ZR (website: www.chilledfood.org).

- Avoid food not reaching 70°C (158°F) within the 30 minutes allowed for reheating. This may be due to: the label information not being followed correctly; the label information not being correct; the lid being taken off when it should have been left on; faulty equipment. If the food temperature is unsafe, throw it away.
- Avoid damaged containers. This may be due to: mishandling during transportation; badly stacked storage containers.
- Observe high standards of personal hygiene and kitchen hygiene, to avoid product contamination or cross-contamination.
- Portions must be controlled when filling packages in order to: ensure efficient stock control; control costs; ensure that sufficient food is delivered to regenerating/finishing kitchens. Check that the standard regeneration procedures are safe to use.
- Food containers must be sealed correctly before storage in order to: protect the food from airborne contamination; enhance the presentation of dishes; prevent the evaporation of moisture when heated; reduce the dehydration effects chilling has on food; avoid finishing products being tampered with.

Table 7.4 Characteristics of cook-chill and fast-food systems

	COOK-CHILL	FAST FOOD
Types of equipment	Flexible, general purpose	Single purpose Single function
Design of process	Functional	Product flow
Set-up time	Variable	Long
Workers	Variously skilled, partie system, limited flexibility	Low skill Flexible
Inventories for start of process	Vary, depending on 'foods in' required Limited in time by planning and forecasting Limited by preplanning and forecasting	High to meet potential demand
Holding inventory	Five days max. Level forecasted	Ten mins max. Level controlled
Lot sizes	Small to large (multiples of ten)	Individual
Production time	Variable depending on menu requirements	Short or constant
Product range	Fairly wide but within constraints of three- or four-course meals, lunch or dinner	Very restricted
System structure	Stock/customer/operation	Stock/queue/operation
Capacity	Variable	Highly variable
Scheduling	Externally orientated	Externally orientated

- All food products must be labelled correctly before storage to: identify the product and the day of production by the colour coding and 'eat-by' date; facilitate stock control; maintain stock rotation; enable visitors such as environmental health officers to check that the food safety laws have been and are being complied with; ensure that quality tracking can be carried out.
- Ensure that older stock is consumed before the new.
- Ensure the security of storage areas against unauthorised access in order to: prevent pilferage or damage by unauthorised persons; prevent unnecessary opening of store doors, which could destabilise storage temperature and thus may affect the temperature of the product, rendering it unsafe.

Comparison of cook-chill and fast-food systems

The characteristics of each system are listed in Table 7.4.

COOK-FREEZE

Cook-freeze is a specialised food production and distribution system that allows caterers to take advantage of the longer life through blast freezing at -18 to $-20°C$ ($0°$ to $-32°F$) and stored at that temperature until required for resale or consumption for up to three to six months. Blast freezers have increasingly been introduced with success into catering operations. The ability to freeze cooked dishes and prepared foods, as distinct from the storage of chilled foods in a refrigerator or already frozen commodities in a deep-freeze, allows a caterer to make more productive use of kitchen staff. It also enables economies to be introduced into the staffing of dining rooms and restaurants.

The cook-freeze process

Cook-freeze uses a production system similar to that used in cook-chill. The recipes used have to be modified, enabling products to be freezer-stable, and modified starches are used in sauces so that, on reheating and regeneration, the sauce does not separate. Blast freezers are used in place of blast chillers. The freezing must be carried out very rapidly to retain freshness and to accelerate temperature loss through the latent heat barrier, thus preventing the formation of large ice crystals and rupturing of the cells.

Blast freezing takes place when low-temperature air is passed over food at high speed, reducing food in batches to a temperature of at least $-20°C$ ($-4°F$) within 90 minutes. Blast freezers can hold from 20 to 400 kg (40–800 lb) per batch, the larger models being designed for trolley operation.

Preparation of food

The production menu for a month is drawn up and the total quantities of different foods required calculated. Supplies are then ordered, with special attention given to their being:

- of high quality
- delivered so that they can immediately be prepared and cooked without any possibility of deteriorating during an enforced period of storage before being processed.

The dishes included in the menu must be cooked to the highest standards, with rigid attention to quality control and to hygiene. Deep-freeze temperatures prevent the multiplication of micro-organisms but do not destroy them. If, therefore, a dish were contaminated before being frozen, consumers would be put at risk months later when the food was prepared for consumption. The exact adjustment of recipes to produce the best result when the food is subsequently thawed and reheated is still in process of being worked out by chefs, using numerous variations of the basic system. The single change needed in cookery recipes involving sauces is the selection of an appropriate type of starch capable of resisting the effect of freezing. Normal starches will produce a curdled effect when subsequently thawed and reheated.

In order to achieve rapid freezing with a quick reduction of temperature to $-18°C$ ($0°F$) or below, the cooked food must be carefully portioned (close attention being paid to the attainment of uniform portion size). Portions, each placed into a disposable aluminium foil container, may conveniently be placed into aluminium foil trays holding from six to ten portions each, sealed and carefully labelled with their description and date of preparation.

Freezing

The food thus divided into portions and arranged in trays is immediately frozen. An effective procedure is to place the trays on racks in a blast-freezing tunnel and expose them to a vigorous flow of cold air until the cooked items are frozen solid and the temperature reduced to at least $-5°C$ ($23°F$). The quality of the final product is to a significant degree dependent on the rapidity with which the temperature of hot cooked food at, say, $80°C$ ($176°F$) is reduced to below freezing. The capacity of the blast freezer should be designed to achieve this reduction in temperature within a period of 60–90 minutes.

Storage of frozen items

Once the food items are frozen they must at once be put into a deep-freeze store maintained at $-18°C$ ($0°F$). For a catering operation involving several dining rooms and cafeterias, some of which may be situated at some distance from the kitchen and frozen store, four weeks' supply of cooked dishes held at low temperature allows full use to be made of the facilities.

Transport of frozen items to the point of service

If satisfactory quality is to be maintained, it is important to keep food, frozen in the cooked state, frozen until immediately prior to its being served. It should therefore be transported in insulated containers to peripheral or finishing kitchens, if such are to be used, where it will be reheated.

If frozen dishes are to be used in outside catering, provision should be available for transporting them in refrigerated transport and, if necessary, a subsidiary deep-freeze store should be provided for them on arrival.

The reheating of frozen cooked portions

In any catering system in which a blast-freezing tunnel has been installed to freeze pre-cooked food, previously portioned and packed in metal foil or other individual containers, it is obviously rational to install equipment that is particularly designed for the purpose of reheating the items ready to be served. The blast-freezing system is effective because it is, in design, an especially powerful form of forced convection heat exchanger arranged to extract heat. It follows that an equally appropriate system for replacing heat is the use of a forced convection oven, especially for the reception of trays of frozen portions. Where such an oven is equipped with an efficient thermostat and adequate control of the air circulation system, standardised setting times for the controls can be laid down for the regeneration of the various types of dishes that need to be reheated.

Quality control

Adequate control of bacterial contamination and growth, which are hazards in any kitchen, can be achieved by a survey of the initial installation by a qualified analyst, and regular checks taken on every batch of food cooked. Very large kitchens employ a full-time food technologist/microbiologist. In smaller operations the occasional services of a microbiologist from the public health authority should be used.

How freezing affects different foods

Meat, poultry and fish

The tendency for the fat in meat to oxidise and go rancid, even in frozen storage, means that lean meat is better than fatty meat for freezing. Chicken fat contains a natural antioxidant (vitamin E), and this will react to prevent rancidity occurring.

Fresh meat must always be used for cook-freeze dishes. Never use meat that has previously been frozen. This is because each time meat is thawed, even in cool conditions, there is a chance for food-poisoning bacteria to multiply.

Some loss of flavour in fish is unavoidable and any surfaces left exposed can suffer from oxidation, thus producing a rancid taste.

Deep-fried fish in batter has to be modified so that the batter does not peel off as a result of the freezing process. The batter should be made thicker or with a higher fat content.

Freezing does not stop the enzyme activity in the meat, poultry or fish that makes the fat present in the flesh go rancid. This particularly affects the unsaturated fats that are present in pork, poultry and fish. These items should therefore not be stored frozen for longer than two to three months. It is advisable therefore to trim off all fat before processing these items.

Fruit and vegetables

When fruit and vegetables turn brown, it is because of the action of enzymes present. These enzymes cause discoloration and gradually destroy the nutritive value of the fruit. Refrigeration slows this process down, and freezing will further slow it down but not stop it completely. Therefore, fruit and vegetables should be blanched or completely cooked prior to freezing, which will stop the enzymic processes.

The freezing process also has a softening effect on the texture of fruit and vegetables. This is acceptable for hard fruits such as apples, unripened pears and so on; it is not, however, suitable for soft fruits such as strawberries. Fruits like these are suitable for freezing only if they are later to be used as a filling or in a sauce, but not for decorative purposes.

Only exceptionally fresh vegetables should be used for freezing. Avoid bruised vegetables, which may produce the development of 'off' flavours. Blanch the vegetables to inactivate the enzymes, but avoid over-blanching, otherwise the vegetables will be overcooked. Blanch if possible in high-pressure steamers as this will help reduce vitamin C loss.

Recipe modification

Generally, recipes have to be modified for the cook-freeze process.

Sauces, batters, thickened soups, stews and gravies will break down and separate unless the flour used in the recipes has an addition of waxy starch. Colflo and Purity 69 are two commercially manufactured starches used in cook-freeze recipes.

Jellies and other products containing gelatine are unsuitable because they develop a granular structure in the cook-freeze process, unless the recipe is modified with stabilisers.

Packaging

Packaging is a very important consideration as it affects the storage and regeneration of the product. Containers must protect the food against oxidation during storage and allow for freezing and reheating. The containers must be:

- watertight
- disposable or reusable
- non-tainting
- equipped with tight-fitting lids.

Packaging materials

There are a number of packaging materials available, which include plastic compounds, aluminium foil and cardboard plastic laminates. These are available as single-portion packs, complete meal packs and bulk packs.

Choosing the container

Various factors affect your choice of container.

- **Menu choice:** single packs provide the greatest flexibility.
- **Food value:** the overheating of complete meal packs, or the edges of bulk packs, will damage the nutritional value.
- **Storage space:** large bulk packs make the best use of space.
- **Handling time:** after cooking, bulk packs are the quickest and easiest to fill, whereas complete packs are more difficult to fill. Bulk packs do, however, have to be portioned at the time of service and are therefore more time-consuming than if single packs are used.
- **Quality of the food:** freezing time is obviously affected by the depth of the food; therefore bulk packs, where the food is relatively deep, may not survive the freezing process as well as single-portion packs. Bulk packs also rely on trained service staff to present the food attractively and portion it accurately. Regeneration instructions can be complex if complete meal packs contain different food components that, in theory, may require different lengths of reheating time.

Freezing equipment

Specialist equipment is required in order to reduce the temperature of the food to the required storage temperature of -18°C (0°F).

- **Air blast freezers or blast freezers:** These take approximately 75–90 minutes to freeze food, depending on how it is packaged. Extremely cold air – between $-32°C$ and $-40°C$ ($-26°F$ and $-40°F$) – is blown by fans over the cooked food. The warm air is constantly removed and recirculated through the heat exchange unit to lower its temperature. In the larger cook-freeze units the food is pushed in on a trolley at one end and then wheeled out at the other end frozen.
- **Cryogenic freezers:** These use liquid nitrogen with the freezing time taking on average 25 minutes, depending on the food being frozen, provided the food is left uncovered. Liquid nitrogen at $-196°C$ ($-321°F$) is sprayed into the freezing chamber. Fans circulate the nitrogen so that the foods freeze evenly. The warm gas is pumped out of the cabinet as more cold nitrogen is pumped in. Some freezers used liquid carbon dioxide.
- **Plate freezers and tunnel freezers:** These are used in food manufacturing and are less likely to be used in catering.

Transportation and distribution

Cook-freeze meals have to be delivered to finishing kitchens at the same temperature as they were held in storage. For short distances, insulated containers are used. These are cooled down before use. However, it is safer and more efficient to use refrigerated vans.

Finishing kitchen equipment

Thawing cabinets are similar to a forced air convection oven, but use a temperature of 10°C (50°F).

- **Rapid thawing cabinet**: These are used to defrost containers of frozen meals before they are placed in the oven; this has the effect of halving the reheating time. The temperature of the food is brought from −20°C to 3°C (−4°F to 37°F) in approximately four hours, under safe conditions. Warming is kept at a steady controlled rate by a process of alternating low-volume heat with refrigeration.
- **Combination ovens**: These are suitable for large quantities of food.
- **Microwave ovens**: These are suitable only for small amounts of food.
- **Dual-purpose ovens**: These are microwave ovens that have a second heat source – for example, an infra-red grill – and a defrost control that switches the microwave power on and off.

Forced air convection ovens
These are suitable for large quantities of food.

Preparation
- Make sure that all preparation and cooking areas are clean and that the equipment is in working order.
- Never use previously frozen food.
- Avoid any delay between preparation and cooking.

Cooking
- Check on the cooking process for the food to ensure that it takes account of the overall effect on flavour, texture and nutritional value.
- Always use temperature probes to check that the centre of the food has reached a safe temperature before the final cooking is complete.

Portioning and packaging
- Make sure all areas are clean and hygienically safe.
- Ensure that all packaging is ready and that it is of the correct size and material.
- All reusable containers must be cleaned and sterilised thoroughly.
- Make sure that all assistants who portion and package wear food-handling gloves.
- Make sure that all general equipment used in this area is sterilised.
- Accurately portion the food according to the recipe.

- Do not pack the food to a depth greater than 5 cm (2 inches). For food that is to be microwaved the depth should be less.
- Portions must be controlled when filling in order to: standardise costs, control costs, facilitate stores control, assist in food service, standardise the thawing and reheating process, allow the sealing to be properly completed.
- Food containers must be sealed correctly before storage in order to: prevent spoilage due to contact with the cold air, prevent spillage prior to freezing, allow for safe stacking, helping to prevent damage to containers.
- Cover the food before blast freezing.
- Check and record the temperature of the food.

Labelling
- Label all food correctly.
- Ensure labels have the right information which should include: production date, 'use by' date, name of dish, description of contents, storage life, number of portions, instructions for reheating/regenerating – including type of oven, temperature, time, and whether lid should be on or off.
- Correct labelling will: accurately identify the contents of the container, enable quick and efficient stock-taking, indicate important information regarding the packaging, date and the 'use by' date, give information on the number of portions contained in the package.

Freezing
- Check all fast freezers are ready for use.
- Freezing should be done immediately after cooking.
- The foods must be frozen below −5°C (23°F) within 90 minutes.
- There must be at least 2 cm (0.75 inches) air space between layers of containers in the freezer.
- Immediately after freezing the food must be transported to the deep-freeze storage.

Storing
- Store the food at the correct deep-freeze storage temperature of -20°C to −30°C (24°F to −22°F) and at least below −18°C (0°F).
- Monitor deep freezer temperatures at all times and keep accurate records.
- Maintain the stock control rotation; keep all stock record systems up to date.
- Store the food in the accepted manner on shelves and racks above the floor, away from the door and with enough space around to allow the cold air to circulate.
- Always wear protective clothing when entering the deep freeze store.
- Destroy any foods that have passed their 'use by' date.
- It is important to monitor and record food temperatures regularly in

order to: prevent contamination from incorrect storage conditions, ensure flavour and texture is maintained.
- Stock rotation procedures must be followed in order to: prevent damage or decay to stock, ensure that older stock is used before new stock.
- Storage areas must be secured from unauthorised access in order to: prevent pilferage or damage by unauthorised persons, prevent injury to unauthorised persons, prevent unnecessary opening of store doors, which would destabilise the temperature.

Distribution
- Maintain freezer temperatures during distribution.
- DHSS guidelines state that if the food is going to be regenerated within 24 hours, the permissible temperature range is between 0° and −18°C (32° and 0°F). Otherwise the temperature must be kept below −18°C (0°F).
- All documentation and control systems for checking delivery should be followed and implemented carefully.

Regeneration
- Check that the work area is ready for operation.
- Remove products from deep freeze for regeneration; check the labels.
- Make sure equipment is at the correct temperature and in working order.
- Follow the regeneration instructions on the label.
- The foods must be reheated to at least 70°C (158°F) but to 75–80°C (167–177°F) immediately before service. Check temperature has been reached by using a sterilised calibrated temperature probe.
- Serve the food as soon as possible after regeneration.
- Food that has not been eaten within two hours should be thrown away. Food that has been allowed to cool must never be reheated.

General
- To avoid separated sauces, the recipe must be modified correctly using the appropriate starches.
- Meat and fish will taste rancid if badly prepared or kept for too long a storage period.
- Soggy, coated food will occur if the lid is not removed when regenerating.
- A backlog of food for freezing will occur with poor production planning.
- Freezer burn occurs due to badly packaged food or when food is stored for too long.
- Standards of personal hygiene and kitchen temperature are of paramount importance to maintain a clean and safe product.

Figure 7.15 Speed of
freezing and crystal
formation

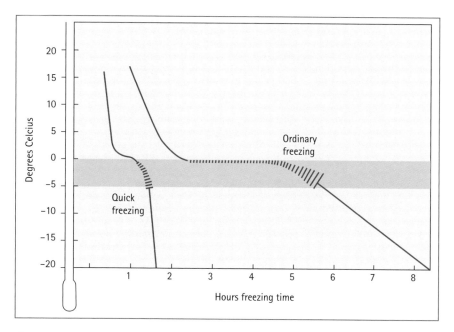

OVERALL BENEFITS OF COOK-CHILL/COOK-FREEZE

To the employer:

- portion control and reduced waste
- no over-production
- central purchasing with bulk-buying discounts
- full utilisation of equipment
- full utilisation of staff time
- overall savings in staff
- savings on equipment, space and fuel
- fewer staff with better conditions – no unsociable hours, no weekend work, no overtime
- simplified, less frequent delivery to units
- solves problem of moving hot foods (EC regulations forbid the movement of hot foods unless the temperature is maintained over 65°C (149°F); maintaining 65°C is regarded as very difficult to achieve and high temperatures inevitably will be harmful to foods).
  To the customer:
- increased variety and selection
- improved quality, with standards maintained
- more nutritious foods
- services can be maintained at all times, regardless of staff absences.

Advantages of cook–freeze over cook–chill

- Seasonal purchasing provides considerable savings.
- Delivery to units will be far less frequent.

- Long-term planning of production and menus becomes possible.
- Less dependence on price fluctuations.
- More suitable for vending machines incorporating microwave.

Advantages of cook-chill over cook-freeze

- Regeneration systems are simpler – infra-red and steam convection ovens are mostly used and only 12 minutes is required to reheat all foods perfectly.
- Thawing time is eliminated.
- Smaller capacity storage is required: three to four days' supply as opposed to up to 120 days.
- Chiller storage is cheaper to install and run than freezer storage.
- Blast chillers are cheaper to install and run than blast freezers.
- Cooking techniques are unaltered (additives and revised recipes are needed for freezing).
- All foods can be chilled so the range of dishes is wider (some foods cannot be frozen). Cooked eggs, steaks and sauces such as hollandaise can be chilled (after some recipe modification where necessary).
- No system is too small to adapt to cook-chill.

VACUUM COOKING (SOUS-VIDE)

i

Further information
To find out more, visit www.julabo-sous-vide.de.

This is a form of cook-chill, using a combination of vacuum sealing in plastic pouches, cooking by steam and then rapidly chilling in an ice-water bath, as this most effective way of chilling. The objective is to rationalise kitchen procedures without having a detrimental effect on the quality of the individual dishes.

The process

- Individual portions of prepared food are first placed in special plastic pouches. The food can be fish, poultry, meats, vegetables and so on, to which seasoning, a garnish, sauce, stock, wine, flavouring, vegetables, herbs and/or spices can be added.
- The pouches of food are then placed in a vacuum-packaging machine, which evacuates all the air and tightly seals the pouch.
- The pouches are next cooked by steam. This is usually in a special oven equipped with a steam control programme, which controls the injection of steam into the oven, to give steam cooking at an oven temperature below 100°C (212°F). Each food item has its own ideal cooking time and temperature.
- When cooked, the pouches are rapidly cooled down to 3°C (37°F), usually in an iced water chiller, or an air blast chiller for larger operations.

Figure 7.16 Vacuum packer

- The pouches are then labelled and stored in a holding refrigerator at an optimum temperature of 3°C (37°F).
- When required for service the pouches are regenerated in boiling water or a steam combination oven until the required temperature is reached, then cut open and the food presented.

Vacuum pressures are as important as the cooking temperatures with regard to weight loss and heat absorption. The highest temperature used in sous-vide cooking is 100°C (212°F) and 1000 millibars is the minimum amount of vacuum pressure used.

As there is no oxidation or discoloration involved, this method is ideal for conserving fruits, such as apples and pears (e.g. pears in red wine, fruits in syrup). When preparing meats in sauces the meat is pre-blanched then added to the completed sauce.

Sous-vide is a combination of vacuum sealing, tightly controlled en papillotte cooking and rapid chilling, which can be used by almost any type of catering operation.

Advantages

- Long shelf-life, up to 21 days, refrigerated.
- Ability to produce meals in advance means better deployment of staff and skills.
- Vacuum-packed foods can be mixed in cold store without risk of cross-contamination.
- Reduced labour costs at point of service.
- Beneficial cooking effects on certain foods, especially moulded items and pâtés. Reduces weight loss on meat joints.
- Full flavour and texture is retained as food cooks in its own juices.
- Economises on ingredients (less butter, marinade, etc.).
- Makes pre-cooking a possibility for à la carte menus.

- Inexpensive regeneration.
- Allows a small operation to set up bulk production.
- Facilitates portion control and uniformity of standards.
- Has a tenderising effect on tougher cuts of meat and matures game without dehydration.

Disadvantages

- Extra cost of vacuum pouches and vacuum-packing machine.
- Unsuitable for meats (e.g. fillet steak) and vegetables that absorb colour.
- All portions in a batch must be identically sized to ensure even results.
- Most dishes require twice the conventional cooking time.
- Unsuitable for large joints as chilling time exceeds 90 minutes.
- Complete meals (meat and two vegetables) not feasible; meat component needs to be cooked and stored in separate bags.
- Extremely tight management and hygienic controls are imperative.
- Potentially adverse customer reaction ('boil-in-the-bag' syndrome).

Points to remember

- High standards of kitchen hygiene and personnel hygiene must be observed.
- Prime-quality ingredients should be used.
- All aspects of the Food Safety Act 1990 must be adhered to.
- Where possible, sous-vide should operate in a temperature-controlled environment.
- All the basic principles of cook-chill apply to sous-vide.

CENTRALISED PRODUCTION

Why centralise?

Reasons for considering centralised production units are as follows.

- **Labour:** reduction of kitchen preparation staff in end units.
- **Food cost:** greater control over waste and portion sizes; competitive purchasing through bulk buying.
- **Equipment:** intensive central use of heavy equipment reduces commitment in individual units.
- **Product:** more control on product quality.
- **Labour strategy:** staff are employed at regular times (9 am to 5 pm), which can eliminate or lessen the difficulty of obtaining staff who will work shifts.

When considering a centralised production system it is essential that a detailed financial appraisal is produced and then looked at carefully, as each establishment has its own considerations. No general rule can be given as profitability depends on the product, the size of each unit, the number of units and the method of preserving food.

Design

Centralised production systems can be designed in two ways:

1 using existing catering (operations) unit and modifying, etc.
2 purpose-built.

Types of unit

Centralised production units are grouped into four types:

1 units preparing fresh cooked foods, which are then despatched
2 cook-freeze – food is partly prepared or cooked, then frozen and regenerated when required
3 cook-chill – food is cooked, then chilled and regenerated when required
4 sous-vide – food is sealed in a special casing, vacuum-sealed, cooked and chilled.

Food production and preparation

The profitability of the production system depends largely upon the content of the end-unit menus.

Meat
Careful purchasing is essential and the menu must be planned carefully.

- The cut of meat required must be clearly specified in order to produce the exact dishes.
- Strict portion control must be adhered to.
- Trimmings/by-products must be fully utilised: meat trimmings for cottage/shepherd's pie, bones for stock.

Vegetable preparation
Because of increasing labour costs and difficulty in obtaining staff, a number of establishments now purchase prepared potatoes, that are washed, peeled and in some cases shaped; prepared root vegetables; topped and tailed French beans; and ready-prepared salads.

Reception and delivery

It is desirable to have two loading bays: one for receiving and one for delivery. They should be adjacent to the relevant store to facilitate loading. The receiving bay should be adjacent to the prime goods store for purchased meat, vegetables, and so on, and the delivery bay near to the finished goods stores that contain items ready to go out to their end units.

Staff

Apart from a butcher, some of the staff may not be highly skilled. The various processes involved in meat production can be divided as follows and staff trained for each procedure.

- **Machine operators:** staff operating dicing machines, mincing machines, hamburger machines, to a strict procedure.
- **Trimmers:** staff who are taught to trim carcasses and prime cuts.
- **Packers:** pack goods into foil cans, operate vacuum-packing machines, and label or pack finished goods into containers; caterers will have to consider if it is economically viable to have a butchery or whether to buy in prepared meats (this very much depends upon the range of menu).

Frequently, staff who are employed to carry out specific functions within a centralised kitchen may not have catering qualifications but will be trained by the organisation.

Method of operation

There are two types of operation:

1 weekly production
2 daily total run.

Forecasts obtained from the end unit determine the quantity of the production run. This prepares items of a particular type on one occasion only. As soon as the run is completed the next run is then scheduled. The main advantage of this type of production is in the comparative ease with which a control system may be installed and operated.

A disadvantage is that, in the event of an error in production scheduling, it is wasteful and costly to organise a further production run of small volume. Another disadvantage is that the method leads to the building-up of stocks, both finished and unfinished, thereby affecting the profitability of the operation.

A daily total run is based upon the needs or items required by the end-unit. A disadvantage is that the forecast gap is shorter, so the end units are not able to provide accurate requisitions.

Purchasing

Any organisation depending for its existence on the economics of bulk purchasing must pay particular attention to the process of buying.

The following are the main objectives of the buyer.

- Quality and price of goods must be equalled with the size of purchase order.
- All purchase specifications must be met.
- Buying practice must supplement a policy of minimum stock holding.

Transport

The distribution of goods, routing and the maintenance of vehicles are very important to a centralised production operation. The usual practice is for transport to be under the control of a senior manager, who also has the complicated job of batching up deliveries (normally weekly or bi-weekly). It is important that the senior manager has considerable administrative skill in order to prevent errors occurring.

Centralised production very often means that production is separated from the food service by distance, time, or both. An example is in hospital wards; here there are satellite kitchens or regeneration kitchens. Other examples exist in aircraft catering and banqueting. Banqueting houses that use cook-chill either purchase from their own production unit or an independent company.

Fast food

Fast food is characterised by a smooth operation. The principal control adopted is 'door time': $3\frac{1}{2}$ minutes is the control average, $1\frac{1}{2}$ minutes queuing and 1 minute serving. Capital costs are high for production equipment. The menu range is narrow, with the equipment often being specially developed to do one job. This is essentially one cell or family of related parts of one product.

Increases in volume required are met by increasing the speed of foods through the system. This is achieved by increasing labour and by duplicating the same cell. Workers are multi-functional but often of low skill. Staffing can be applied to a number of parts, depending on volume of throughput. This type of staffing can give high job satisfaction (although short term), similar to the rotation of chefs through the partie system.

This operation comes nearer to the continuous flow ideal and is often quoted as a classic just-in-time (JIT) system.

The principles of manufacturing exist in both fast food and cook-chill systems. Other systems, such as cook-freeze and sous-vide, will take on a variety of cells relating to different parts of the meal. The fast-food system is primarily based upon one-cell systems. All systems use variations in the number of workers to control costs.

Small centralised operations

There are some very good examples of smaller centralised operations to be seen now in the catering industry. The purpose of installation is to provide ready-prepared goods that may be served to banquets or supplied to grills/coffee shops.

The preparation of the food takes place during the kitchen 'slack' period, principally after the luncheon service. The made-up items are put into polythene bags, which contain from one to six portions. The packed items are marked with the date of packing, and the name of the item, and then blast frozen prior to storage. They are kept in store from three to six months, and moved on a first-in, first-out basis. Some items have limited storage time so careful checking of dates is an important factor to consider. Refrigerators in the outlets are stocked up daily from the central code store.

When an item is ordered it is reheated by a simple boiling process operated by a timer. The cooked items are placed on the plate, with the garnish and vegetables being added separately. There are also, of course, many other refinements: carefully calculated production schedules and coloured photographs of the dishes to guide presentation, for example.

Ganymede dri-heat

This is a method of keeping foods either hot or cold. It is used in some hospitals as it ensures that the food that reaches the patients is in the same fresh condition as it was when it left the kitchens.

A metal disc or pellet is electrically heated or cooled, and placed in a special container under the plate. The container is designed to allow air to circulate round the pellet so that the food is maintained at the correct service temperature.

This is used in conjunction with conveyor belts and special service counters, and helps to provide a better and quicker food service.

Microsteam technology

Used for food production in hospitals and schools, microsteam is a fast, healthy cooking system, which maintains the freshness of food using steam cooking. It enables nutritious meals to be available in minutes without the need for full kitchen back-up.

It works with a broad range of raw ingredients, from fresh vegetables to chicken and seafood. The vacuum-packed polymer packaging allows cooking to near perfection, resulting in maximum flavour and minimal nutritional loss.

Microsteam is a unique value-control system that regulates the pressure throughout the cooking process. As soon as the pack goes into the microwave, energy waves create steam from the water in the raw ingredients, which gradually builds up in the container. The pack expands as it cooks, which is where the smart valve comes in – releasing the pressure gradually so that it stays at just the right level to cook the food perfectly. Each dish is ready in just a few minutes, with no preparation time involved.

The most important point about microsteaming is that it's not about reheating pre-cooked food: it's about cooking the freshest ingredients from raw – from chicken to couscous, fish to fresh vegetables. Steam cooking has long been recognised as one of the healthiest ways to prepare food, keeping nutritional loss to a minimum, and retaining much more vitamin C and chlorophyll than traditional or cook-chill methods.

The microsteam system is space saving. It reduces the need for bulky equipment. It allows kitchen systems to be simplified. If packages are kept sealed they will retain their heat at 75°C for 20 minutes.

With this system it is easier to manage the bulk production and cooking of fresh vegetables and other items for large-scale banqueting and industry events. The technology can also be used for vending machines, is suitable for people working off-peak hours, for airports, call centres, trains and any environment where it's difficult to have full kitchen back-up.

The scheme has been trialled by the NHS Better Hospital Food Programme, with favourable results – not just in terms of health benefits but also because it means patients and doctors are no longer restricted to set meal times.

IN-FLIGHT CATERING

In-flight catering is one of the most extensive food production operations within the catering industry (see Figure 7.17). Some in-flight caterers may produce up to 36,000 meals a day during the peak season. This section describes a typical system that would be used by many in-flight caterers throughout the world. Caterers involved in large-scale production are able to learn from the in-flight production system – in particular, the production planning process, production scheduling and the production systems.

Basic principles of the design of in-flight food production kitchens

Factors that will influence the design of in-flight food production kitchens are similar to those to be considered when designing other food production systems:

- the size and extent of the operations, in terms of the maximum number of flight meals to be produced
- amounts of capital expenditure costs
- policy on the use of pre-prepared products

Figure 7.17 In-flight food production flow chart

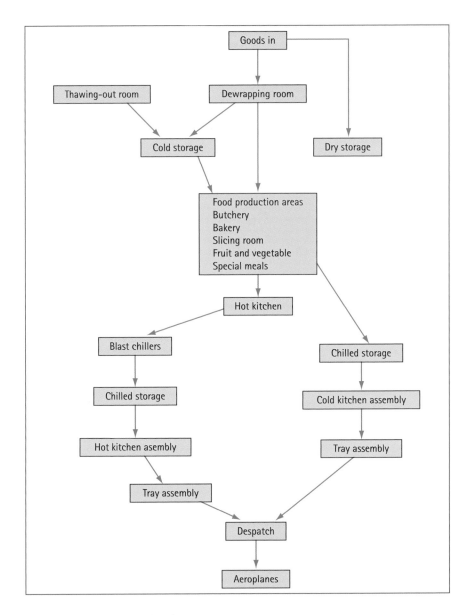

- the use of latest technology
- hygiene and food safety legislation
- the complexity of menus required by the airlines.

The flow process

Each kitchen should have a flow process chart detailing the materials (food) and labour. The chart will show the main parts of the process, demonstrating the flow of materials and labour, the transportation of products, storage and chilling. The chart will also clearly identify when the operator should temperature test and for how long.

Production planning

Good production planning for in-flight caterers involves a similar principle to JIT (just-in-time production techniques), meaning 'producing the necessary units, in the necessary quantities, at the necessary time'. This concept has in one way or another been used by large-scale caterers for some time, the difference being they have never referred to it as JIT, just good business practice. The principles of JIT are:

- stock levels kept down to the level as and when required; order in as and when needed (stockless production)
- elimination of waste
- enforced problem solving
- continuous flow manufacturing.

There is and has to be a strong emphasis on continual improvement rather than accepting the status quo.

Balancing resources and passenger needs in a production plan

To achieve the tight balance between passenger needs and resources, the following factors need to be considered.

Orders:
- from the airline
- for stock
- broken down into details
- forecasting against budgeted figures and adapting to daily changing needs.

Priority:
- sequenced into date, time aircraft is due to take off
- special meal requirements identified
- evenly balanced workload where appropriate.

Availability:
- labour
- equipment
- outsourcing of quality and consistency can be guaranteed.

Cost:
- spend from airlines
- downtime costs from excessive change-overs
- cost of subcontracting.

Overall production control

A production plan is rarely, if ever, carried out in all its details. Equipment breaks down, staff can be off sick, suppliers fail to deliver, skilled people leave the company, and so on.

The function of production control is, first, to ensure that production is maintained in line with the production plan wherever possible and, second, to respond to the things that do go wrong and rework the plan in order to get back on schedule. However, the quality and consistency of the agreed specification must always be met.

Food production managers monitor the supply and production process to ensure that there is always up-to-date information on what has been achieved, or what further actions may be necessary to maintain the production flow and to achieve an airline's desired specification. Where deviations from the production plan are spotted, corrective action is then taken to overcome any shortfalls in production.

Regular checks must be made on food availability, and alternative suppliers must be identified in cases of emergency where a designated supplier fails to deliver on time or the exact quantity required.

All food production managers and supervisors must be aware of what labour hours are available, and how the operation is performing in terms of quality and productivity.

The production system

A large-scale operation producing approximately 30,000 meals a day, supplying 200 fully catered flights, could well be dealing with over 300 food suppliers. In a typical system, all stock would be on a 48-hour holding cycle, raw materials being held for no longer than 24 hours before being used in production.

The meal requirements are given to the food production manager and despatch control department. There is often a computer link that relays all flight details and eating requirements on each flight. The manager (usually the head chef or executive chef) gives the orders to the stores department. All orders to each supplier are on computer printouts ready to be checked against a receipt of delivery.

The delivery should be systematically unrolled to avoid cross-contamination, segregating the delivery of each high-risk food – for example, poultry, meat and fish. The deliveries must be checked against the production requirements on the computer printout; if there is any discrepancy the order should be refused.

The dry goods should be brought to the dry storage area. Any cold and frozen goods should be dealt with in a separate area where they can be unwrapped. This is to prevent any cardboard boxes or external wrappings entering into the food production or cold storage areas. These goods should be transferred to colour-coded plastic boxes. Computer-printed tags can be used to identify each plastic box. The tag attached to the box will normally have the day and date contents of each box. Frozen goods then pass into purpose-built thawing rooms. Chilled products are transferred to the cold storage areas. All storage rooms must be controlled and monitored 24 hours a day. When required these items are removed into the production areas, where skilled operatives continue the production process.

Over the last few years there has been a move towards purchasing prepared and pre-prepared items; this is likely to accelerate in the future. A whole manufacturing industry has grown up around the supply of such products to other caterers. The advantage of using such products is that they provide greater cost control, reduce labour and processing costs, reduce hygiene costs and often give better standardisation, while giving the caterer greater flexibility in operations and purchasing power. Some manufacturers work directly with the airline to greater understand needs, and this avoids a lot of re-working. It is also important to ensure that the airline recruits what it needs to deliver its own customer satisfaction rather than being led by its caterer, who may want development for different reasons.

Some caterers still have their own bakery and pastry departments. Most buy in bread and bread rolls, and therefore concentrate on sweets and pastries. Again the tendency is now towards purchasing pre-prepared sweets.

FUTURE DEVELOPMENTS

Industrial food service catering

Many different food delivery systems now operate within industrial catering. These concepts are developed by contract catering companies, which have to work hard to retain old contracts and obtain new ones. Customers within these units have high expectations and demand high-quality products, mirroring what is often available on the high street. One concept that has become increasingly popular is WorldMarché (literally 'world market').

What is WorldMarché?

WorldMarché is a front-of-house, hot portable food delivery system that brings the full colour and flavour of the chef's theatre to customers. The system takes full advantage of new technological advances, allowing the chef the flexibility to use a number of different cooking methods to create innovative dishes that are freshly cooked to order fast. This concept has been developed by the Compass Group to satisfy its clients and customers better, and respond to some of the challenges set by clients in the areas of cost reduction and space saving.

Why was WorldMarché designed?

WorldMarché was designed to meet the culinary needs of an ever-changing world. Customers' lifestyles have changed and the catering industry needs to respond to this if it is going to retain and grow business. Disposable income and leisure time available to customers in

Figure 7.18 WorldMarché

Figure 7.19 WorldMarché

the western world have risen to an all-time high, and the meal experience, ingredient, and control and participation demands have risen accordingly. Customers now demand:

- a greater variety of food offers, including international cuisine
- use of fresh, quality ingredients
- food available quickly
- innovative approaches to food delivery
- value for money
- more control over what is being cooked for them as a result of clients' enhanced nutritional knowledge
- greater theatre and entertainment.

What are the benefits of WorldMarché?

For the customer:

- fresh quality food cooked to order fast
- limitless choice of dishes
- dishes cooked to customer requirements
- food created in front of the customer in a fun way, which means added theatre, participation and customer interaction
- value for money
- food ready to go.

For the contract caterer:

- simple to operate
- reduces wastage
- builds customer and client loyalty
- increases turnover and profit
- increases spending per head
- increases cooking skills
- maximises the use of labour
- reduces menu fatigue
- reduces running costs
- fits any servery
- tried and tested
- proven results.

For the client:

- WorldMarché will fit any space and fits well with client demands of occupying less space
- innovative approach that will drive sales and profit

Figure 7.20 Stir-frying using the WorldMarché system

Figure 7.21 Preparing food using the WorldMarché system

- easy to implement
- increases customer loyalty
- delivering what the customer demands
- improved customer satisfaction levels.

How does WorldMarché work?

WorldMarché comes in two sizes according to the space you have available. There is:

1 GrandMarché – larger version, and
2 MiniMarché – smaller version.

To set you up there is a starter kit for each, which is known as the WorldMarché platform. This includes vario wok, ice box with eutectic plates, silesia contact grill, dry bain-marie, extractor canopy, and so on. From here you can then mix and match to tailor the WorldMarché system to each unit's requirements. All the portable, interchangeable cookery equipment is designed to be powered from a 13-amp plug for ease of use, and the extractor system has been designed to allow you to cook in the servery without setting off the fire alarm.

With the WorldMarché system you can cook 'any food - any time - anywhere' – the options are limitless. You can create anything from traditional breakfasts through to crispy duck or Chinese noodles using the system. Every dish can be cooked fresh to order in minutes, either using the wok or silesia grill, (e.g. omelette, 20 seconds; steak, two minutes).

The system allows you to create a 'call order' menu that will sell even more of your best sellers both during and outside peak service times. The fresh food offers will fulfil those parts of the day where more revenue should be realised.

Figure 7.22 Control of hygiene in food preparation

DEPARTMENT OF HEALTH

ASSURED SAFE CATERING · CRITICAL CONTROL POINTS

Step	Hazard	Action
1 Purchase	High-risk* (ready-to-eat) foods contaminated with food-poisoning bacteria or toxins (Poisons produced by bacteria).	Buy from reputable supplier only. Specify maximum temperature at delivery.
2 Receipt of food	High-risk* (ready-to-eat) foods contaminated with food-poisoning bacteria or toxins.	Check it looks, smells and feels right. Check the temperature is right.
3 Storage	Growth of food poisoning bacteria, toxins on high-risk* (ready-to-eat) foods. Further contamination.	High-risk* foods stored at safe temperatures. Store them wrapped. Label high-risk foods with the correct 'sell by' date. Rotate stock and use by recommended date.
4 Preparation	Contamination of High-risk* (ready-to-eat) foods. Growth of food-poisoning bacteria.	Wash your hands before handling food. Limit any exposure to room temperatures during preparation. Prepare with clean equipment, and use this for high-risk* (ready-to-eat) food only. Separate cooked foods from raw foods.
5 Cooking	Survival of food-poisoning bacteria.	Cook rolled joints, chicken, and re-formed meats eg. burgers, so that the thickest part reaches at least 75°C. Sear the outside of other, solid meat cuts (eg. joints of beef, steaks) before cooking.
6 Cooling	Growth of any surviving spores or food poisoning bacteria. Production of poisons by bacteria. Contamination with food-poisoning bacteria.	Cool foods as quickly as possible. Don't leave out at room temperatures to cool, unless the cooling period is short, eg place any stews or rice, etc, in shallow trays and cool to chill temperatures quickly.
7 Hot-holding	Growth of food-poisoning bacteria. Production of poisons by bacteria.	Keep food hot, above 63°C.
8 Reheating	Survival of food-poisoning bacteria.	Reheat to above 75°C.
9 Chilled storage	Growth of food-poisoning bacteria.	Keep temperature at right level. Label high-risk ready-to-eat foods with correct date code.
10 Serving	Growth of disease-causing bacteria. Production of poisons by bacteria. Contamination.	COLD SERVICE FOODS - serve high-risk foods as soon as possible after removing from refrigerated storage to avoid them getting warm. HOT FOODS - serve high-risk foods quickly to avoid them cooling down.

A. *High-risk foods are those which may easily support the growth of food poisoning organisms and won't be cooked any further before you serve them, for example; cooked fish, meat patés, cooked egg dishes, pre-prepared dairy products that may only be re-heated.
B. Some food-poisoning bacteria can form spores which may survive cooking.

If cooling is delayed or takes a long time, these spores may grow or produce toxins (poisons). After cooking, food should be cooled quickly to prevent or reduce this. The list above is not exhaustive but shows some of the hazards likely to be present in any operation. In your catering operation you may be able to identify other hazards not listed above. If you do so make sure you control these as well.

What food offers are included in WorldMarché?

- **Hot Wok:** Oriental dishes – e.g. sizzling stir-fry with crunchy vegetables and rice or noodles; choose from Chinese, Thai or Indonesian.
- **Go East:** Aromatic dishes from India and Pakistan, using the colour and aromatic flavour of fresh spices.
- **Trad Favourites:** Classics such as 'roast meat and two veg', bangers and mash, toasties and juicy grilled steaks.
- **Fast Diner:** Fresh food fast. Choose from North American, Tex Mex, Caribbean or Fusion.
- **Smart Start:** Full English breakfast: eggs (fresh fried or scrambled to order); fast bacon that is cooked to perfection; fresh fruit; fruit dishes; yoghurts; milk on ice.
- **Trattoria:** Mediterranean foods from regions ranging from Italy to Greece – from home-cooked pasta to pizza with a wide range of mouthwatering toppings and sauces. Toasted panini of every kind.

To accompany this there are some simple 'slot in' food counter signage and point of sale materials that can be changed instantly according to the time of day and the food offer available.

What is the brand proposition?

- Any food, any time, anywhere.
- Flexible, exciting, innovative 'cooking theatre'.
- Guarantees freshness and quality – fast.

The WorldMarché food delivery system has been developed and pioneered by the Compass Group of Companies. Such concepts need constant development and innovation in order to anticipate changes in customer tastes, fashions and lifestyles.

The kitchen

The kitchen is a centre of creativity but it also creates much cost. The question is, 'How does the food and beverage manager get the cost of food preparation down to a level, or a percentage, that allows the profitable exploitation of the kitchen and the accompanying restaurant?' The answer is that the manager should know what it means to prepare traditional food in a modern, cost-saving way, making use of:

- modern cooking and regeneration equipment
- new generations of high-quality convenience-orientated, partly prepared food components
- new working methods in the kitchen.

In a traditional kitchen, whole products are prepared from scratch. This means that:

- large storage rooms are needed for raw materials

- storage rooms are needed for peeled/cooked preparations
- numerous preparation rooms are needed for meat, fish, vegetables
- various preparation tools are needed – meat saw, chopper, vegetable peeler, cutter
- traditional cooking equipment is needed – fry pan, grill, cooking pots, deep-fryer, braising pan
- a large stove top is needed for a large team.

The chef

The food and beverage manager's biggest challenge will certainly be to convince the tradition-orientated chef that the time has come to adopt new, economical ways of preparing food.

The chef will no longer mainly excel in preparing food, but will spend more time on:

- selection of the most suitable ingredients and meal components
- menu development, recipes
- controlling the correct cooking and regeneration procedures
- organising the kitchen staff.

The chef/pastry chef thus becomes the production manager, who plans, organises, supervises and personalises.

Key questions

Will future employers be able to rely on their managers' know-how to organise or reorganise food and beverage systems that will contribute to the improved economical results needed and guarantee the quality level required?

For a regeneration-on-the-plate recipe, we have to answer the following questions.

- Who makes the recipe? Which recipe? Where – work area?
- When – one, two, three days ahead, or the same day, in the morning or in the evening?
- How – with what types of product? With what type of equipment? With what type of technique?

Important points to bear in mind
Only regenerate what is needed; strictly follow recipes (measuring); produce at the right time; train young chefs in this type of food preparation.

The assembly kitchen concept

Research – quality – production – tradition – innovation. This is a system based on accepting and incorporating the latest technological developments in the manufacturing and conservation of food products. In the modern assembly kitchen, the chef does not automatically buy his ingredients. On the contrary, he will carefully choose from the 'five product types' (see the accompanying box) what is best for him by asking himself the following questions.

- Which fresh produce will I use?
- Which semi-prepared food bases will I use?
- Which finished products will I use?

The assembly kitchen still relies on skilled personnel. It requires a thorough understanding of how to switch over from the traditional labour-intensive production method to a more industrial type of production, with some of the principles of the cook-chill, cook-freeze or sous-vide production systems taken on board. It realises the existence and availability of modern kitchen equipment and new generations of high-quality convenience orientated food bases.

The five products types

1 Fresh (raw product)
- meat with bones
- vegetables, potatoes, fruits, unpeeled
- whole fish
- milk

2 Shelf-stable
- sterilised, pasteurised – vegetables, potatoes, fruits; dairy products, meat products
- dehydrated products, partly elaborated – stocks, sauces; mousses, creams, custards; bouillons, soups, purées; culinary aids

3 Frozen
- meat, fish, vegetables, potatoes, fruits
- pastry products, ice cream

4 Chilled ('fresh' products, partly prepared)
- meat or fish, boned, cut into pieces or portioned
- washed, peeled and cut vegetables, potatoes, fruits, etc.

5 Chilled (products, normally cooked and packed or sous-vide)
- meat, fish, vegetables, desserts (with or without sauce)

Thus, the concept includes:

- preparing the food component in an appropriate kitchen, respecting legislation
- arranging everything cold (even raw) on the plate
- regenerating (even cooking) on the same plate as served
- if necessary, serving the sauce.
  Success requires:
- appropriate material and equipment
- very precise preliminary preparations (mise-en-place)
- support from a well-trained team (kitchen and service staff).
  Advantages include:
- fewer staff needed for arranging
- the regeneration can be done near the consumer
- different types of plate can be regenerated at the same time
- hygiene, and consequently safety, is guaranteed
- storage rooms needed for only five types of product (see page 353)
- large preparation areas disappear
- smaller equipment is needed.
  Inconveniences include:
- very hot plates
- some additional investments required (trolleys, etc.)
- some products cannot be prepared (French fries, etc.).

A planning schedule would envisage:

- 2 days   – cooking and chilling
  - storing at 13°C (37°F) in labelled, dated gastronorm containers
- 12 hours   – arrange food on to plates
  - storage at 13°C (37°F) on trolley
- 30 mins   – taking the trolley out of storage
  - setting of regeneration equipment
  - regeneration
- 2 mins   – taking out and finishing of plates
  - sauce, garnish
  - serving
  - cleaning of equipment

The principal investments will be for:

- multi-purpose equipment, covering most of the cooking methods
- storage for dry, chilled, frozen products
- equipment to chill or freeze
- equipment to regenerate on plates, gastronorm pans.

The new-generation equipment must be:

- easy to handle
- gastronorm
- easy to clean
- easy to service.

Some references to production systems elsewhere in the book:

Kitchen hygiene 620
Hospitals, NHS 23
Food hygiene 631
Preservation 220
Equipment 265

REFERENCES

The following sources were used as the basis for this chapter.
* Food Standards Agency publications: *Safer Food Better Business* (England); *Safe Catering* (Northern Ireland); *CookSafe* (Scotland).
* Visit www.food.gov.uk for advice and information.

TOPICS FOR DISCUSSION

1 The advantages and disadvantages of the cook-chill and cook-freeze systems.
2 Essential hygiene and food safety requirements for cook-chill and cook-freeze systems.
3 The reason for quality control, temperature control and microbiological control when producing cook-chill and cook-freeze foods.
4 Types of operation suitable for using cook-chill and cook-freeze foods.
5 For and against a centralised production system, with examples.
6 The food production system and its main advantages.
7 The principles of in-flight catering.
8 Catering on board the trains travelling through the Channel Tunnel.
9 What do you consider to be the future of food production systems?

Chapter 8 MENU PLANNING, DEVELOPMENT AND STRUCTURE

EVOLUTION

Initially, menus were lists of food, in seemingly random fashion with the food being raw, prepared or cooked. Individual menus came into use early in the nineteenth century, and courses began to be formulated. For special occasions seven or so courses might be served e.g. hors d'oeuvre, soup, fish, entrée, sorbet, roast, sweet, savoury.

With the formulation of menus, artistry and flair began to influence the various ways of cooking, and dishes were created after 'the style of' (e.g. à la Francaise) and/or given the names of important people for whom they had been created (e.g. peach Melba, a simple dish of poached fresh peach, vanilla ice cream and fresh raspberry purée created by Escoffier at the Savoy for Dame Nellie Melba, the famous opera singer).

As the twentieth century advanced, and people moved and settled around the world more, so began the introduction of styles of food and service from a wide variety of nations, resulting in the number of ethnic dishes and ethnic restaurants that abound today.

Eating at work, at school, in hospitals and institutions led to a need for healthy, budget-conscious food.

Rapid air transport made it possible for foods from all corners of the globe to be available which, together with domestic and European produce, gives those who compose menus a tremendous range of choice.

ESSENTIAL CONSIDERATIONS PRIOR TO PLANNING A MENU

- **Competition:** be aware of any competition in the locality, including prices and quality. It may be wiser to produce a menu that is quite different.
- **Location:** study the area in which your establishment is situated and the potential target market of customers.

- **Analyse:** the type of people you are planning to cater for (e.g. office workers in the city requiring quick service).
- **Outdoor catering:** are there opportunities for outdoor catering or takeaway food?
- **Estimated customer spend per head:** important when catering, for example, for hospital staff and patients, children in schools, workers in industry. Whatever level of catering, a golden rule should be 'offer value for money'.
- **Modern trends in food fashions:** these should be considered alongside popular traditional dishes.
- Decide the **range of dishes** to be offered and the **pricing structure.** Price each dish separately? Or offer set two- to three-course menus? Or a combination of both?
- **Space and equipment in the kitchens** will influence the composition of the menu (e.g. avoiding overloading of deep-frying pan, salamanders and steamers).
- **Number and capability of staff:** overstretched staff can easily reduce the standard of production envisaged.
- **Availability of supplies and reliability of suppliers:** seasonal foods and storage space.
- **Food allergies** (see page 216).
- **Cost factor:** crucial if an establishment is to be profitable. Costing is essential for the success of compiling any menu. Modern computer techniques can analyse costs swiftly and on a daily basis.

TYPES OF MENU

The main types of menu in use are as follows.

- **Table d'hôte or set-price menu:** a menu forming a meal, usually of two or three courses at a set price. A choice of dishes may be offered at all courses.
- **À la carte:** a menu with all the dishes individually priced. Customers can therefore compile their own menu, which may be one, two or more courses. A true à la carte dish should be cooked to order and the customer should be prepared to wait.
- **Special party or function menus:** menus for banquets or functions of all kinds.
- **Ethnic or speciality menus:** these can be set-price menus or with dishes individually priced, specialising in the food (or religion) of a particular country or in a specialised food itself – e.g. ethnic (Chinese, Indian, kosher, African-Caribbean, Greek), speciality (steak, fish, pasta, vegetarian, pancakes).
- **Hospital menus:** these usually take the form of a menu card given to the patient the day before service so that his or her preferences can be

ticked. Both National Health Service and private hospitals cater for vegetarians and also for religious requirements.

- **Menus for people at work:** such menus vary in standard and extent from one employer to another due to company policy on the welfare of their staff and workforce. There may also be a call-order à la carte selection charged at a higher price. The food will usually be mainly British with some ethnic and vegetarian dishes. Menus may consist of soup, main course with vegetables, followed by sweets, cheese and yoghurts. According to the policy of the management and employee requirements, there will very often be a salad bar and healthy-eating dishes included on the menu. When there is a captive clientele who face the same surroundings daily and meet the same people, then no matter how long the menu cycle or how pleasant the people, or how nice the decor, boredom is bound to set in and staff then long for a change of scene. So, a chef or manager needs to vary the menu constantly to encourage customers to patronise the establishment rather than going off the premises to eat. The decor and layout of the staff restaurant plays a very important part in satisfying the customer's needs. The facilities should be relaxing and comfortable so that he or she feels that the restaurant is not a continuation of the workplace. Employees who are happy, well nourished and know that the company has their interests and welfare at heart will tend to be well motivated and work better.
- **Menus for children:** in schools there is an emphasis on healthy eating and a balanced diet, particularly in boarding schools. Those areas with children of various cultural and religious backgrounds have appropriate items available on the menu. Many establishments provide special children's menus that concentrate on favourite foods and offer suitably sized portions.

Cyclical menus

These are menus that are compiled to cover a given period of time: one month, three months, etc. They consist of a number of set menus for a particular establishment, such as an industrial catering restaurant, cafeteria, canteen, directors' dining room, hospital or college refectory. At the end of each period the menus can be used again, thus overcoming the need to keep compiling new ones. The length of the cycle is determined by management policy, by the time of the year and by the different foods available. These menus must be monitored carefully to take account of changes in customer requirements and any variations in weather conditions that are likely to affect demand for certain dishes. If cyclical menus are designed to remain in operation for long periods of time, then they must be carefully compiled so that they do not have to be changed too drastically during operation.

Advantages

- Cyclical menus save time by removing the daily or weekly task of compiling menus, although they may require slight alterations for the next period.
- When used in association with cook-freeze operations, it is possible to produce the entire number of portions of each item to last the whole cycle, having determined that the standardised recipes are correct.
- They give greater efficiency in time and labour.
- They can cut down on the number of commodities held in stock, and can assist in planning storage requirements.

Disadvantages

- When used in establishments with a captive clientele, the cycle has to be long enough so that customers do not get bored with the repetition of dishes.
- The caterer cannot easily take advantage of 'good buys' offered by suppliers on a daily or weekly basis, unless such items are required for the cyclical menu.

Pre-planned and pre-designed menus

Advantages

- Pre-planned or pre-designed menus enable the caterer to ensure that good menu planning is practised.
- Before selecting the dishes that he or she prefers, the caterer should consider what the customer likes, and the effect of these dishes upon the meal as a whole.
- Menus that are planned and costed in advance allow banqueting managers to quote prices instantly to a customer.
- Menus can be planned to take into account the availability of kitchen and service equipment, without placing unnecessary strain upon such equipment.
- The quality of food is likely to be higher if kitchen staff are preparing dishes they are familiar with and have prepared a number of times before.

Disadvantages

- Pre-planned and pre-designed menus may be too limited to appeal to a wide range of customers.
- They may reduce job satisfaction for staff who have to prepare the same menus repetitively.
- They may limit the chef's creativity and originality.

THE STRUCTURE OF MENUS

Length

The number of dishes on a menu should offer the customer an interesting and varied choice. In general, it is better to offer fewer dishes of good standard than a long list of mediocre quality.

Design

This should complement the image of the dining room and be designed to allow for changes (total or partial), which may be daily, weekly, monthly, etc. An inset for dishes of the day or of the week gives the customer added interest.

Language

Accuracy in dish description helps the customer to identify the food they wish to choose. Avoid over-elaboration and flowery choice of words. Wherever possible, use English language. If a foreign dish name is used then follow it with a simple, clear English version.

Presentation

Ensure the menu is presented in a sensible and welcoming way so that the customer is put at ease and relaxed. An offhand, brusque presentation (written or oral) can be off-putting and lower expectations of the meal.

Planning

Consider the following:

- type and size of establishment – pub, school, hospital, restaurant, etc.
- customer profile – different kinds of people have differing likes and dislikes
- special requirements – kosher, Muslim, vegetarian
- time of the year – certain dishes acceptable in summer may not be so in winter
- foods in season – are usually in good supply and reasonable in price
- special days – Christmas, Hogmanay, Shrove Tuesday, etc.
- time of day – breakfast, brunch, lunch, tea, high tea, dinner, supper, snack, special function
- price range – charge a fair price and ensure good value for money; customer satisfaction can lead to recommendation and repeat business
- number of courses
- sequence of courses
- use menu language that customers understand

- sensible nutritional balance
- no unnecessary repetition of ingredients from dish to dish
- no unnecessary repetition of flavours and colours
- be aware of the Trade Descriptions Act 1968 (see below) – 'Any person who in the course of a trade or business: applies a false trade description to any goods or supplies or offers to supply any goods to which a false trade description is applied shall be guilty of an offence.'

Menu policy: summary

- Provide a means of communication.
- Establish the essential and social needs of the customer.
- Accurately predict what the customer is likely to buy and how much he or she is going to spend.
- Purchase and prepare raw materials to pre-set standards in accordance with predictions and purchasing specifications.
- Skilfully portion and cost the product in order to keep within company profitability policy.
- Effectively control the complete operation from purchase to service on the plate.
- Customer satisfaction is all-important: remember who pays the bill.

CONSUMER PROTECTION

There is a comprehensive set of legislation concerned with protecting the consumer. This can be divided into that which is concerned with health and safety, economic protection such as weights and measures, and others that deal with unfair contract terms. Fundamentally, however, all consumer protection starts with the basic contract. If a supplier fails to supply what a consumer has contracted to purchase, the supplier may be in breach of contract. However, because breach of contract cases can be difficult to prove and expensive, the government over the years has introduced legislation to improve protection for the consumer.

The main consumer protection acts

Price Marking (Food and Drink on Premises) Order 1979

The wording and pricing of food and drink on menus and wine lists must comply with the law and be accurate. However, by offering dishes on the menu there is no legal obligation to serve the customer if he or she may cause a nuisance to other customers or because, due to demand, the dish has sold out and is 'off' the menu. But for establishments providing accommodation there is an obligation to provide refreshment providing the customer is able to pay and is in an acceptable state (e.g. sober).

Trade Descriptions Act 1968/1972

This act makes it a criminal offence to falsely describe goods or services, or to supply or offer for sale any goods or services to which a false description applies. It is also an offence to make reckless statements (i.e. statements without the knowledge to support the claims made about the goods or services). Examples of offences include describing pork as veal or frozen foods as fresh.

There are also offences under the Food and Safety Act 1990.

Sale of Goods and Services Act 1982

This act aims to ensure that goods sold are of satisfactory quality and fit for the purpose intended. This would especially apply to equipment as well as commodities. It applies to the *sale* of goods and services only. From the caterer's viewpoint this act works mainly to his or her advantage, whereas the Supply of Goods and Services Act 1982 (see below) works mainly to the customer's advantage. In essence, the act is concerned with ensuring that customers receive goods that are of satisfactory quality and are fit for the purpose.

Goods may be defined as of satisfactory quality 'if they are as fit for the purpose or purposes for which goods of that kind are commonly bought as it is reasonable to expect having regard to any description applied to them, the price (if relevant) and all the other circumstances'.

In addition to goods being of satisfactory quality they must also be fit for the purpose. This means that, if a purchaser makes known a specific purpose for their goods, then the goods should be able to satisfy that purpose.

Supply of Goods and Services Act 1982

This act is concerned with 'implied' terms in a contract.

Sale and Supply of Goods Act 1994

This is an amending act that mainly amends the Sale of Goods Act 1979.

Consumer Protection Act 1987

This act deals with three main areas: liability for defective products; consumer safety; misleading price indications. It contains recommendations in the form of a code of practice regarding a service charge. This should be incorporated in the inclusive price where practicable and indicated (e.g. 'price includes service'). Non-optional charges (e.g. cover charges or minimum charges) should be prominently displayed.

Code of Practice on Price Indications

Authorised the issue of a code of practice on prices. This covers the Code of Practice for Traders on Price Indications, and contains recommendations on service, cover and minimum charges in hotels, restaurants and similar establishments. It states:

> If your customers in hotels, restaurants or similar places must pay a non-optional charge e.g. a 'service charge':

1   incorporate the charge within the fully inclusive prices wherever practicable
2   display the fact clearly on any price list or priced menu whether displayed inside or outside (e.g. by using statements like 'all prices include service').

Do not include suggested optional sums, whether for service or any other item, in the bill presented to the customer.

The code concedes that it is not practical to include some non-optional extra charges – for example, cover charges or minimum charges – in a quoted price. In these cases the charge should be shown as prominently as other prices on any list or menu, whether displayed inside or outside.

Data Protection Act 1984

The Data Protection Act 1984 regulates the use of personal data – data being information recorded in a form in which it can be processed by equipment operating automatically in response to instructions given to it; 'personal data' being data consisting of information that relates to a living individual who can be identified from that information (or from that and other information held by the data user).

The act imposes specific duties on data users and those running computer bureaux, and gives certain rights to individuals, including employees on whom personal data is held.

Data protection principles
- Personal data information must be fairly and lawfully obtained and processed.
- Personal data can be held only if there are one or more specified and lawful purposes.
- Personal data held for any purpose or purposes shall not be used or disclosed in any manner incompatible with that purpose or purposes.
- Personal data held should be adequate, relevant and not excessive in relation to that purpose or purposes.
- Personal data should be accurate and kept up to date.
- Personal data should not be kept longer than for the purpose or purposes for which it is required.
- An individual shall be entitled
  (a) at reasonable intervals and without undue delay or expense: (i) to be informed by any data user whether he/she holds personal data of which that individual is subject; (ii) to access any such data held by a data user, and
  (b) where appropriate to have such data corrected or erased.
- Appropriate security measures should be taken against unauthorised access to, or alteration, disclosure or destruction of, personal data, and against accidental loss or destruction of personal data.

MENU COPY

Items or groups of items should bear names people recognise and understand. If a name does not give the right description, additional copy may be necessary. Descriptions can be produced carefully, helping to promote the dish and the menu. However, the description should describe the item realistically and not mislead the customer. Creating interesting descriptive copy is a skill; a good menu designer is able to illuminate menu terms and specific culinary terms, and in doing so is able to draw attention to them. Simplicity creates better understanding and endorses the communication process.

Some menus can be built around general descriptive copy featuring the history of the establishment or the local area in which the establishment is located. Descriptive copy can alternatively be based on a speciality dish that has significant cultural importance to the area or the establishment. In doing so the description may wish to feature the person responsible for creating and preparing the dish, especially if the chef is reasonably well known and has appeared on national or local television or radio. The chef may also have had his/her recipes featured in the local press. This too may be included in the menu to further create interest.

Menu copy should be set in a style of print that is easily legible and well spaced. Mixing typefaces is often done to achieve emphasis; if overdone, however, the overall concept is likely to look a mess and therefore unattractive to the eye.

Emphasis may easily be achieved by using boxes on the menu. Also the paper used and the colour of the print can be chosen with care to make certain dishes stand out.

Some common mistakes in menu copy are:

- descriptive copy is left out when it is required (confusing to the customer)
- the wrong emphasis is given
- emphasis is lost because print size and style are not correctly used
- the menu lacks creativity (boring)
- the menu is designed for the wrong market
- much-needed information is omitted
- pricing is unclear
- the menu sequence is wrong
- customers do not see valuable copy because added sheets such as 'dish of the day' or 'today's specials' cover up other parts of the menu, or obscure essential information.

Menu cover

The cover of the menu should reflect the identity or decor of the operation, and should ideally pick up the theme of the restaurant. A theme can be effective in creating the right image of the restaurant. The cover design must therefore reflect this overall image. The paper chosen must be of good quality, heavy, durable and grease-resistant.

MENU FLEXIBILITY

In times of inflation and recession, when prices rise or the amount of disposable income decreases, customer demands change and therefore menus become outdated and obsolete.

Some operations use the menu of the day on a wall board or chalk board to provide flexibility in items offered and pricing. This custom started in Paris. A neatly written wall board told customers as they entered the restaurant what was on offer that day. Some establishments change part of their menus daily or weekly, while the main core of the menu remains the same. Changes can be made on a paper insert and this can be added to the printed menu. hors d'oeuvre, side dishes, salads, desserts and beverages do not change frequently; these dishes are printed on the main copy, while the speciality dishes, which do change more frequently, are placed on the paper insert.

Nothing becomes obsolete faster to the regular customer than the same menu. Menu fatigue sets in and you begin to lose customers. Even fast-food establishments, which have a basic menu on offer year in year out, still have to create interest by adding certain new products or new recipes to existing products in order to keep interest alive. Menus should change at least every three months.

Menu engineering

One approach to sales analysis that has gained some popularity is 'menu engineering'. This is a technique of menu analysis that uses two key factors of performance in the sales of individual menu items: the popularity and the gross profit contribution of each item. The analysis results in each menu item being assigned to one of four categories (see Figure 8.1).

1 Items of high popularity and high cash gross profit contributions. These are known as **Stars**.
2 Items of high popularity but with low cash gross profit contribution. These are known as **Plough horses**.
3 Items of low popularity but with high cash gross profit contributions. These are known as **Puzzles**.
4 Items of low popularity and low cash gross profit contribution. These are the worst items on the menu, and are known as **Dogs**.

Chefs and food and beverage managers operating in a competitive environment require a knowledge of menu engineering in order to maximise business potential. The advantage of this approach is that it

Figure 8.1 Menu engineering matrix (based on Kasavana and Smith, 1982)

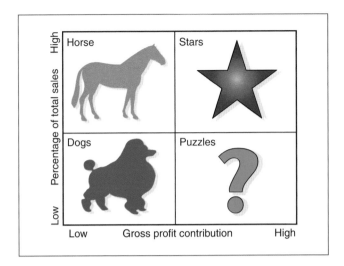

provides a simple way of graphically indicating the relative cash contribution position of individual items on a matrix, as in Figure 8.1.

There are a variety of computer-based packages that will automatically generate the categorisation, usually directly using data from electronic point of sale (EPOS) control systems. The basis for the calculations is as follows.

In order to determine the position of an item on the matrix, two things need to be calculated. These are:

1 the cash gross profit
2 the sales percentage category.

The cash gross profit category for any menu item is calculated by reference to the weighted average cash gross profit. Menu items with a cash gross profit that is the same as or higher than the average are classified as high. Those with lower than the average are classified as low cash gross profit items. The average also provides the axis separating Plough horses and Dogs from Stars and Puzzles.

The sales percentage category for an item is determined in relation to the menu average, taking into account an additional factor. With a menu consisting of ten items one might expect, all other things being equal, that each item would account for 10 per cent of the menu mix. Any item that reached at least 10 per cent of the total menu items sold would therefore be classified as enjoying high popularity. Similarly, any item that did not achieve the rightful share of 10 per cent would be categorised as having a low popularity. With this approach, half the menu items would tend to be shown as being below average in terms of their popularity. This would potentially result in frequent revision of the composition of the menu. It is for this reason that Kasavana and Smith (1982) have recommended the use of a 70 per cent formula. Under this approach, all items that reach at least 70 per cent of their rightful share of the menu mix are categorised as enjoying high popularity. For example, where a menu consists of, say, 20 items, any item that reached 3.5 per cent or more of the menu mix (70 per cent of 5 per cent) would be regarded as enjoying high popularity. While there is no convincing theoretical support for choosing the 70 per cent figure rather than some other percentage, common sense and experience tend to suggest that there is some merit in this approach.

Interpreting the categories

There is a different basic strategy that can be considered for items that fall into each of the four categories of the matrix.

- **Stars:** these are the most popular items, which may be able to yield even higher gross profit contributions by careful price increases or through cost reduction. High visibility is maintained on the menu, and standards for these dishes should be strictly controlled.
- **Plough horses:** these, again, are solid sellers, which may also be able to yield greater cash profit contributions through marginal cost reduction. Lower menu visibility than Stars is usually recommended.
- **Puzzles:** these are exactly that – puzzles. Items such as flambé dishes or a particular speciality can add an attraction in terms of drawing customers, even though the sales of these items may be low. Depending on the particular item, different strategies might be considered, ranging from accepting the current position because of the added attraction that they provide, to increasing the price further.
- **Dogs:** these are the worst items on a menu and the first reaction is to remove them. An alternative, however, is to consider adding them to another item as part of a special deal. For instance, adding them in a meal package to a Star may have the effect of lifting the sales of the Dog item and may provide a relatively low-cost way of adding special promotions to the menu.

The menu engineering methodology is designed to categorise dishes into good and poor performers. For dishes with high popularity and high contribution – Stars:

- do nothing
- modify price slightly – up or down
- promote through personal selling or menu positioning.

For dishes with high popularity and low contribution – Plough horses:

- do nothing
- increase price
- reduce dish cost – modify recipe by using cheaper commodities or reducing the portion size.

For dishes with low popularity and high contributions – Puzzles:

- do nothing
- reposition dish on menu

- reduce price
- rename dish
- promote through personal selling
- remove from menu.

For dishes with low popularity and low contribution – Dogs:

- do nothing
- replace dish
- redesign dish
- remove dish from menu.

Some potential limitations

- **Elasticity of demand:*** one of the practical difficulties with price-level adjustment is not knowing enough about the elasticity of demand. The effect of demand (number of covers) of any one change in the general level of menu prices is usually uncertain. Also, what applies to one menu item applies equally to the menu as a whole. There is an additional problem of cross-elasticity of demand, where the change in demand for one commodity is directly affected by a change in the price of another. Even less is known about the cross-elasticity of demand for individual menu items than is known about the elasticity of demand for the menu as a whole. Any benefit arising from an adjustment in the price of one item may therefore be offset by resultant changes in the demand for another item. Price-level adjustments must therefore be underpinned by a good deal of common sense, experience and knowledge of the particular circumstances of the operation.
- **Labour intensity:** in menu engineering the most critical element is cash gross profit. While this may be important, the aspect of labour intensity cannot be ignored. The cash gross profit on a flambé dish, for example, may be higher than on a more simple sweet; however, when the costs of labour are taken into account – especially at peak periods – it may well be that the more simple sweet is the more profitable overall.
- **Shelf-life:** the food cost of an item used to determine the cash gross profit may not take account of cost increases that are the result of food wastage through spoilage, especially at slack times.
- **Fluctuations in demand:** another factor is the consistency of the buying of the consumer. The approach assumes that changes can be made to promote various items and that this will be reflected in the buying behaviour of the customer. The approach will work well where the potential buying pattern of the consumer is fairly similar over long periods. However, where customers are continually changing, as for instance in the restaurant of a hotel, popularity and profitability can be affected more by changes in the nature of the customer and the

---

* Price elasticity of demand: if a price change results in a more than proportionate change in demand, demand is said to be elastic. Similarly, if the change in demand is less than proportionate, demand is inelastic. Cross-elasticity of demand describes the complementary or substitute relationship between two commodities.

resultant change in demand than as a result of the operation's attempting to manipulate the sales mix.

EXAMPLES OF DIFFERENT MENUS

Breakfast menu

Breakfast menus can be compiled from the following foods and can be offered as continental, table d'hôte, à la carte or buffet. For buffet service customers can self-serve the main items they require with assistance from counter hands. Ideally, eggs should be freshly cooked to order.

- Fruits, fruit juices, stewed fruit, yoghurts, cereals: porridge, etc.
- Eggs: fried, boiled, poached, scrambled; omelettes with bacon or tomatoes, mushrooms or sauté potatoes.
- Fish: kippers, smoked haddock, kedgeree.
- Meats (hot): fried or grilled bacon, sausages, kidneys, with tomatoes, mushrooms or sauté potatoes, potato cakes.
- Meats (cold): ham, bacon, pressed beef with sauté potatoes.
- Preserves: marmalade (orange, lemon, grapefruit, ginger), jams, honey.
- Beverages: tea, coffee, chocolate.
- Bread: rolls, croissants, brioche, toast, pancakes, waffles.

Fruit Juice – Orange, Grapefruit or Tomato
Fresh Grapefruit or Orange Segments

Stewed Fruits – Prunes, Figs or Apricots

Fresh Fruit Selection, Fresh Fruit Salad

Yoghurts

Choice of Cereals, Porridge or Mix your own Muesli

Baker's Selection

Croissant, White and Wholemeal Rolls, Continental Pastry

Your choice of White or Brown Toast

Marmalade, Preserve, Honey, Country Butter or Flora Margarine

Assorted Cold Meats and Cheese

English Breakfast Tea with Milk or Lemon

Coffee – Freshly Brewed or Decaffeinated with Milk or Cream

Hot Chocolate, Cold Milk

Chilled Ashbourne Water

Figure 8.2 Sample continental breakfast menu

A LA CARTE

FRUITS & JUICES

Fresh Orange or Grapefruit Juice £.... Large £....

Pineapple, Tomato or Prune Juice £.... Large £....

Chilled Melon £.... Stewed Prunes 3.... Half Grapefruit £....

Stewed Figs £.... Fresh fruit in Season £....

BREAKFAST FAVOURITES

Porridge or Cereal £....

Eggs, any style: One £..... Two £....

Ham, Bacon, Chipolata Sausages or Grilled Tomato £....

Omelette, Plain £.... with Ham or Cheese £....

Grilled Gammon Ham £.... Breakfast Sirloin Steak £....

A Pair of Kippers £.... Smoked Haddock with a Poached Egg £....

Pancakes with Maple Syrup £....

FROM OUR BAKERY

Croissants or Breakfast Rolls £.... Brioche £....

Assorted Danish Pastries £.... Toast £....

BEVERAGES

Tea, Coffee, Sanka, Chocolate or Milk £....

Service Charge 15%

Figure 8.3 Sample English à la carte breakfast menu

Points to consider when compiling a breakfast menu
- It is usual to offer three of the courses previously mentioned: fruit, yoghurt or cereals; fish, eggs or meat; preserves, bread, coffee or tea.
- As large a choice as possible should be offered, depending on the size of the establishment, bearing in mind that it is better to offer a smaller number of well-prepared dishes than a large number of hurriedly prepared ones.
- A choice of plain foods, such as boiled eggs or poached haddock, should be available for the person who may not require a fried breakfast.

Buffet breakfast – offers a choice of as many breakfast foods as is both practical and economic. Can be planned on a self-service basis or part self-service and assisted service (e.g. hot drinks and freshly cooked eggs).

Luncheon and dinner menus

Types of menu
- A set-price one-, two- or three-course menu with ideally a choice at each course.

Figure 8.4 Luncheon menu: staff restaurant

	MONDAY	TUESDAY	WEDNESDAY	THURSDAY	FRIDAY
Soup of the Day	Mushroom and Chive (V) (L)	Roasted Pepper (V) (L)	Parsnip and Apple (V) (L)	Chilli and Sweet Potato (V) (L)	Leek and Potato (V) (L)
Main Meal 1	Aromatic Chicken Korma served with Rice and Poppadom (H)	Toad in the Hole accompanied with Onion Gravy (H)	Roast Turkey with Bread Sauce and Cranberry (M)	Poached Lemon and Bay Leaf Chicken Breast (L)	Breaded Hake with Chips and Lemon (H)
Main Meal 2	Boiled Ham on the Bone with a Creamy Parsley Volouté (M)	Jambalaya with Chorizo, Prawns, Rice and Sweet Peppers (M)	Beef and Hoi Sin with Green Peppers and Noodles (M)	Pan-fried Lambs Livers with Redcurrant Jus (M)	Hot Chilli Con Carne with Rice and Sour Cream (H)
Vegetarian Meal	Vegetarian Cottage Pie with Garden Vegetables and a Crusted Potato Topping (M)	Pesto Roasted Vegetables with Chick Pea Couscous (M) (N)	Lightly Spiced Bean and Tomato Bruschetta (M)	Vegetable Balti with Coriander, Cumin, Mango and Turmeric (M)	Sweet Potato and Mushroom Pave with Tomato Chutney (M)
Potatoes & Vegetables	Rice or Baby Jackets Green Bean Provencale	Mashed Potato Sauté Courgettes	Roast Potatoes Vichy Carrots	Parmentier Potatoes Buttered Cabbage	Chips or New Potatoes Mushy Peas
Hot Dessert	Bread and Butter Pudding with Custard Sauce (H)	Banana Sponge with Toffee Sauce (H)	Apple and Cinnamon Crumble with Custard Sauce (H)	Pineapple Upside Down with Custard Sauce (H)	Orange Sponge with Chocolate Sauce (H)

Some of our Foods may contain GM soya or maize; please ask our staff for details.
N = Contains Nuts, L = Low Fat Content, M = Medium Fat Content, H = High Fat Content

Figure 8.5 Sample
luncheon menu

LUNCH

Galvin

Bistrot de Luxe

Entrées
Steak tartare
Soupe de poissons, rouille & croûtons
Salad of endive with Roquefort, chives & walnuts
Matjes Harengs marines, pommes à l'huile
Oak smoked salmon, fromage blanc & blini
Salad of Dorset crab, apple dressing
Half dozen Fines de Claire oysters
Salad of buffalo mozzarella & caponata
Escargots bourguignon
Parfait of foie gras & duck liver
Rillette of black boar

Plats Principles
Grilled Crottin de Chavignol, morels, peas & asparagus
Confit of organic salmon, Bayonne ham, beurre de tomate
Roast tranche of cod, crushed Jersey Royals, étuvée of leeks
Pot roast Landaise chicken, tagliatelle of asparagus & morels
Grilled calf's liver, shallots aigre-doux, lardoons & flat leaf parsley
Roast pork fillet, Bayonne ham, black pudding & caramelised apples
Roast rump of lamb, broad bean risotto
Braised veal's cheek, fresh pasta, baby spinach & Madeira sauce
Tête de Veau, sauce Ravigote

Desserts
Oeuf ê la neige
Délice of milk and dark Valhrona chocolate
Crème brûlée, coconut mousseline
Gariguette strawberries, crème Chantilly
Apricot & chocolate soufflé
Prune & Armagnac parfait
Baba au rhum
Tarte au citron
Assiette de fromages with walnut & raisin loaf

Menu Prix Fixé
Gravadlax of organic salmon or velouté of broad beans
Grilled sea trout, petits pois à la Française or Confit duck, honey & rosemary
spring cabbage
Chocolate mousse, orange jelly or Brie de Meaux & walnut bread

Figure 8.6 Sample dinner
menu

DINNER

The Grill Room at The Dorchester

Appetisers
Oak smoked wild Scottish salmon
Lobster soup with flamed Scottish lobster
Squab pigeon and spring vegetable consommé with black truffles
Crisp red mullet and spring vegetable salad with sundried tomato cream
Seared scallops with cauliflower purée, citrus vinaigrette and mimolette crisps
Foie gras and duck confit terrine with onion marmalade and toasted brioche
Caramelised endive with goats' cheese, honey and winter truffles
Ham hock ravioli with white beans, trompettes and parsley
Denham Estate venison burger with quail's egg, griottine cherries, parsnips and Port
Warm Gressingham duck salad with glazed root vegetables, chestnuts and meat juices
Baby spinach salad with cashel blue, spiced pears and walnuts

Main Courses
Roast sea bass fillet with olive oil mash, red pepper relish and aged balsamic vinegar
Dover sole grilled or pan fried with brown butter and capers
Seared tuna with fennel, cherry tomatoes and Jersey Royals
Ragoût of John Dory, lobster and mussels with crème fraîche and chives
Free-range chicken breast with creamed morels, asparagus and tarragon
New season rack of lamb with aubergine caviar, couscous and confit garlic
Roast rib of Aberdeen Angus beef with Yorkshire pudding and roast potatoes
Rabbit leg with calf's sweetbread, ceps, smoked bacon and Lyonnaise potatoes
Saffron risotto cake with stuffed tomato, grilled vegetables and Parmesan

Specialities from The Grill
Served with either hand-cut chips or olive mash, sauce béarnaise, sauce bordelaise, green
peppercorn sauce or rosemary butter
Veal chop
Rib eye steak
Calf's liver and bacon
Lobster (1 kg)

Desserts
Crisp apple tart with clotted cream and calvados
Lemon and blueberry millefeuille with blood orange sorbet
Hot ginger pudding with plums and crème fraîche sorbet
A plate of Valrhona chocolate desserts
Home-made vanilla and rhubarb yoghurt with churros
Strawberry ripple ice cream or mango sorbet
Honey roast pear with caramel sauce and cardamom custard
Iced passion fruit and bitter chocolate délice with chilli and coriander

Selection of Cheeses from the Board
***
Coffee and Petits Fours

- A list of well-varied dishes, each priced individually so that the customer can make up his/her own menu of whatever number of dishes they require.
- Buffet, which may be all cold or hot dishes, or a combination of both, either to be served or organised on a self-service basis. Depending on the time of year and location, barbecue dishes can be considered.
- Special party, which may be either: set menu with no choice; set menu with a limited choice, such as soup or melon, main course, choice of two sweets; served or self-service buffet.

Only offer the number of courses and number of dishes within each course that can be satisfactorily prepared, cooked and served.

A vegetarian menu may be offered as an alternative to or as part of the à la carte or table d'hôte menus (see Figures 8.7 and 8.8 for examples).

Tea menus

These vary considerably, depending on the type of establishment, and could include, for example:

- assorted sandwiches
- bread and butter (white, brown, fruit loaf)
- assorted jams
- scones with clotted cream, pastries, gâteaux
- tea (Indian, China, iced, fruit, herb).

VEGETARIAN MENU

Iced Cucumber Soup
(Flavoured with mint)

Avocado Waldorf
(Filled with celery & apple bound in mayonnaise, garnished with walnuts)

* * *

Vegetable Lasagne
(Layers of pasta & vegetables with melted cheese, served with salad)

Mushroom Stroganoff
(Flamed in brandy, simmered in cream with paprika & mustard, served with rice)

Chilli con Elote
(Seasonal fresh vegetables in a chilli & tomato fondue, served with rice)

Poached Eggs Elizabeth
(Set on buttered spinach, coated in a rich cream sauce)

Figure 8.7 Sample vegetarian menu 1

Friday 24th June

Crostini with Roasted Tomato & Pesto

★★★

Courgette & Coriander Soup

★★★

Red Pepper Plait
Potatoes Dauphinoise & Green Beans

★★★

Strawberry & Rhubarb Compote
or
Vegan "Ice Cream"

★★★

Coffee, Tea or Herbal Tea

Figure 8.8 Sample vegetarian menu 2

Figure 8.9 Afternoon tea table

The commercial hotels, tea rooms, public restaurants and staff dining rooms may offer simple snacks, cooked meals and high teas. For example:

- assorted sandwiches
- buttered buns, scones, cakes Scotch pancakes, waffles, sausage rolls, assorted bread and butter, various jams, toasted teacakes, scones, crumpets, buns
- eggs (boiled, poached, fried, omelettes)
- fried fish, grilled meats, roast poultry
- cold meats and salads
- assorted pastries, gâteaux
- various ices, coupes, sundaes
- tea, orange and lemon squash.

Light buffets (including cocktail parties)

Light buffets can include:

- hot savoury pastry patties of, for example, lobster, chicken, crab, salmon, mushrooms, ham
- hot chipolatas; chicken livers, wrapped in bacon and skewered
- bite-sized items – quiche and pizza, hamburgers, meatballs with savoury sauce or dip, scampi, fried fish en goujons, tartare sauce
- savoury finger toast to include any of the cold canapés; these may also be prepared on biscuits or shaped pieces of pastry
- game chips, gaufrette potatoes, fried fish balls, celery stalks spread with cheese
- sandwiches; bridge rolls, open or closed but always small
- fresh dates stuffed with cream cheese; crudités with mayonnaise and cardamom dip; tuna and chive Catherine wheels; crab claws with garlic dip; smoked salmon pin wheels; choux puffs with Camembert
- sweets (e.g. trifles, charlottes, bavarois, fruit salad, gâteaux).

Fork buffets

All food must be prepared in a way that enables it to be eaten with a fork or spoon.

Fast-food menus

Although some people are scornful of the items on this type of menu, calling them 'junk food', nevertheless their popularity and success is proven by the fact that, starting with the original McDonald's, which opened in Chicago in 1955, there are now many thousands of outlets worldwide. McDonald's offers customers a nutrition guide to its products, as well as information for diabetes sufferers.

Banquet menus

When compiling banquet menus, consider the following points.

- The food, which will possibly be for a large number of people, must be dressed in such a way that it can be served fairly quickly. Heavily garnished dishes should be avoided.
- If a large number of dishes have to be dressed at the same time, certain foods deteriorate quickly and will not stand storage, even for a short time, in a hot place.

A normal menu is used, bearing in mind the number of people involved. It is not usual to serve farinaceous dishes, eggs, stews or savouries. A luncheon menu could be drawn from the following and

Figure 8.10 Sample banquet menu

Avocado filled with cream cheese and two fruit sauces

★ ★ ★

Seafood filled fish mousse with crayfish sauce

★ ★ ★

Butter cooked fillet of beef with sliced mushrooms and tongue in Madeira sauce
A selection of market vegetables
Potatoes garnished with cream cheese

★ ★ ★

Light soft meringue topped with fruit

★ ★ ★

Coffee
Sweetmeats

would usually consist of three courses. Dinner menus, depending on the occasion, generally consist of three to five courses.

- **First course:** soup, cocktail (fruit or shellfish), hors d'oeuvre, assorted or single item, a small salad.
- **Second course:** fish, usually poached, steamed, roasted or grilled fillets with a sauce.
- **Third course:** meat, poultry or game, hot or cold, but not a stew or made-up dish; vegetables and potatoes or a salad would be served.
- **Fourth course:** if the function is being held during the asparagus season, then either hot or cold asparagus with a suitable sauce may be served as a course on its own.
- **Fifth course:** sweet, hot or cold, and/or cheese and biscuits.

The meal experience

If people have decided to eat out then it follows that there has been a conscious choice to do this in preference to some other course of action. In other words, the food service operator has attracted the customer to buy their produce instead of another product – for example, the theatre, cinema or simply staying at home. The reasons for eating out may be summarised under seven headings.

1 **Convenience:** for example, being unable to return home, as in the case of shoppers, people at work or those involved in some leisure activity.
2 **Variety:** for example, trying new experiences or as a break from home cooking.
3 **Labour:** for example, getting someone else to prepare and serve food, and wash up, or simply the impracticality of housing special events at home.
4 **Status:** for example, business lunches or people eating out because others of their socio-economic group do so.
5 **Culture/tradition:** for example, special events or because it is a way of getting to know people.
6 **Impulse:** a spur-of-the-moment decision.
7 **No choice:** for example, those in welfare, hospitals or other forms of semi- or captive markets.

People are, however, a collection of different types, as any demographic breakdown will show. While it is true that some types of food service operation might attract certain types of customer, this is by no means true all the time; for example, McDonald's is marketed to the whole population, and customers are attracted depending on their needs at the time.

The decision to eat out may also be split into two parts: first, the decision to do so for the reasons given above, and then the decision as to what type of experience is sought. It is generally agreed that there are a

Figure 8.11 Taking orders

number of factors influencing this latter decision. The factors that affect the meal experience may be summarised as follows.

- **Food and drink on offer:** this covers the range of foods, choice, availability, flexibility for special orders, and the quality of the food and drink.
- **Level of service:** depending on the needs people have at the time, the level of service sought should be appropriate to these needs. For example, a romantic night out may call for a quiet table in a top-end restaurant, whereas a group of young friends might be seeking more informal service. This factor also takes into account services such as booking and account facilities, acceptance of credit cards and the reliability of the operation's product.
- **Level of cleanliness and hygiene:** this relates to the premises, equipment and staff. Over the past decade this factor has increased in importance in customers' minds. The recent media focus on food production and the risks involved in buying food have heightened public awareness of health and hygiene aspects.
- **Perceived value for money and price:** customers have perceptions of the amount they are prepared to spend and relate these to differing types of establishment and operation. However, many people will spend more if the value gained is perceived to be greater than that obtained by spending slightly less.
- **Atmosphere of the establishment:** composed of a number of factors, such as design, decor, lighting, heating, furnishings, acoustics and noise levels, other customers, staff and the attitude of staff.

Identifying these factors is important because it considers the product from the point of view of the customer. All too often, food service operators can get caught up in the provision of food and drink, spend several thousand pounds on design, decor and equipment, but ignore the actual experience the customer might have. Untrained service staff are a good example of this problem. Operations can tend to concentrate on the core product and forget the total package. A better understanding of the customer's viewpoint or the nature of customer demand leads to a better product being developed to meet it.

MANAGING A FUNCTION

A function can be described as the service of food and drink at a specific time and place, for a given number of people at a known price.

Examples of hospitality functions include:

- social functions – weddings, anniversaries, dinner dances
- business functions – conferences, meetings, working lunches, working dinners
- social and business functions – corporate entertaining.

Sometimes functions are called banquets, however the word banquet is normally used to describe a large, formal occasion.

The variety of function events ranges from simply providing bar facilities in a conference reception area before a meeting, to the more formal occasion catering for 1500 to 2000 people. Many establishments concentrate and market themselves as specialist function caterers. The function business may be the company's sole business; on the other hand, it may be part of the product range – for example, in a hotel, you may well find rooms, restaurants, conferences facilities and banqueting.

The type of function facilities found in an establishment will also depend on the level of market for which it is catering. Function catering is found in the commercial and public sector of the hospitality industry. The types of function suites and variety of functions on offer in all establishments will often differ considerably.

Policy decisions relating to function catering are determined by a number of characteristics inherent to this type of catering. First, depending on where the establishment is located there will be a banqueting season; this is where the main business is concentrated – for example, from May to September (depending on the location) is known as the 'wedding season'.

A considerable amount of information is available to the caterer in advance of the function. This includes:

- number of guests
- price per head or cover
- menu requirement
- drink required
- type of menu.

This information allows the manager to assess the resource requirement. For example:

- staffing
- linen
- food and drink
- equipment.

The manager is then also able to assess the profit margins to be achieved. This will aid the control procedures and help to establish yardsticks against which the performance of a function may be measured.

Financial considerations

Function catering is most commonly associated with the commercially orientated sector of the hospitality industry. Gross profit margins in function catering tend to be higher than those achieved in hotel restaurants and coffee shops.

An average gross profit percentage of 65–75 per cent is usually required in function catering, depending on the type of establishment, types of customers, level of service, and so on.

The types of customers and their spending power can in most cases be determined in advance. The average spending power will comprise the cost of the meal and will generally include the beverages served during the function. Items that may not be included in the price of the meal are pre-dinner drinks, liqueurs and such like.

The financial policy will also determine the pricing structures of the different types of functions and different menus on offer. Some establishments will also make a separate charge for room hire.

The pricing structure for an establishment's function catering will be determined by its cost structure, with reference to its semi-fixed and variable costs. There are a variety of pricing structures that may be used for costing functions, the adoption of any one being determined by such factors as the type of establishment, the food and beverage product on offer, and the cost structure of the establishment.

Marketing considerations

The marketing policy of a function establishment will focus on the market the business aims to capture, and how best to promote the special characteristics of the establishment. Different marketing techniques will be used to 'sell' the establishment.

An establishment's marketing policy should contain a review relating to the competition in the area in order to keep abreast of fashions and trends in the function market. To assist in this review it is important that information and quotations are obtained from other establishments. A manager must be constantly aware of the types of products and services on offer in the marketplace. Every consideration must be given to customers' needs and matching these needs to the establishment's facilities.

In the marketing of an operation's function facilities the function manager should be aware of who is buying the 'product' in a particular organisation being contracted. Arrangements should be made to show the client the facilities, and every effort should be made to create a good impression.

The function manager should devise a marketing plan based on the marketing policy for a given period. This plan should take into account the following factors.

- **Finance:** targets of turnover, profit for a given period.
- **Productivity:** targets of productivity and performance of the banqueting function department.
- **Promotions:** general – how to increase business and how this is to be achieved; special – specially devised promotions to be launched in a given period, often aimed at different groups, clubs, etc.
- **Facilities:** focused on selling certain facilities – for example, recently refurbished.
- **Development:** the promotion of a new development or concept; the launch of new conference/seminar rooms.
- **New product lines:** launch of weekend breaks for clubs, groups, etc., with special rates.
- **Research:** ongoing market research, project research, etc.

Every organisation needs to advertise and promote its functions. There are a number of ways in which an organisation can promote the business:

- special brochures
- photographs
- press releases about functions sent to local newspapers, magazines, etc.

Brochures have to be designed carefully using professional designers, printers, and so on. The menus should be clear and easily understood, with the prices stated. All photographs must be clear and accurate; they should be in no way misleading.

Brochures or folders should ideally contain the company logo. The pack should also contain the following:

- a letter from the banqueting manager to the client
- rates and prices
- wine lists
- details of all function rooms, with size and facilities on offer
- maps
- sample menus.

Any menus included will have been carefully constructed by the chef, with predetermined gross profits, recipe specifications and purchasing specifications in mind.

Pricing

Function menus are usually pre-listed with the desired profit margins added to them. These menus will generally have a standard set of purchasing and operational specifications added to them. However, there is normally a flexible element added to it. It is not unusual for a banqueting manager to offer additions to the menu at no additional cost to the client in order to capture the business in a competitive environment.

The relationship between price and value for money is an important aspect of pricing. Value for money extends far beyond the food to be served. It takes into account the whole environment in which the food is consumed: the atmosphere, decor and surroundings of the establishment, and the level of service.

In order to be successful and to obtain a satisfactory volume of sales, pricing has to consider three basic factors.

The nature of demand for the product

First, we have to think of the elasticity of demand (this means how sensitive demand is to the effects of pricing). Menus are said to have an elastic demand when a small decrease in the price brings about a significant increase in sales, and alternatively if an increase in price brings about a decrease in sales. Menus with an inelastic demand mean that a small increase or decrease in price does not bring about any significant increase or decrease in sales.

The level of demand for the product

Most catering operations experience fluctuations in demand for their products. The change in demand affects the volume of sales, which results in the under-utilisation of premises and staff. Fluctuation in demand makes it necessary to take a flexible approach to pricing in order to increase sales. For example, at certain times of the year it may be possible to obtain deals on functions.

The level of the competition for the product

Competition is an important factor in pricing. Establishments commonly monitor the prices in competitors' establishments, recognising that customers have a choice. Monitoring competition is not just about examining price, however, but also the facilities, decor, services, and so on.

The exact method of pricing used by an establishment will depend on the exact market in which it is operating. The price itself can be a valuable selling tool and a great aid to achieving the desired volume of sales.

Every business, whatever its size, can choose to set its prices above its proper costs or at, or below, the prices of its competitors. More often establishments are forced to fix their price by the competition. This is the discipline of the marketplace. The challenge then is to get the costs below the price that has to be set. The danger here is that managers tend to subconsciously alter the costs. This happens when fixed costs such as wages, heating, and so on, are split over all the sales to arrive at the unit cost. It is always tempting then to overestimate the sales, thereby reducing the unit cost.

No one should attempt to sell anything until they have calculated the break-even point. This is the point the amount of sales (menus, portions) at a certain price have to reach to cover their variable costs and all the fixed costs. Profit only starts when the break-even point has been reached.

Pricing is as much about psychology as accounting. Establishments also need to market-research price. Too low a price, although enabling them to produce profit on paper, may fail as customers may perceive the product to be cheap and of poor quality. Some people expect to pay high prices for some goods and services.

PLANNING A FUNCTION

Collecting the function details

Customers are usually invited for a detailed view of the venue; in some establishments this will include a menu tasting. During the menu tasting the customer is encouraged to discuss their requirements; the food and beverage manager will gather this information. The customer will also be advised of the different options available. For example:

- different room layouts
- choice of menu, vegetarian or allergy requirements
- order of service
- flowers
- cloakroom requirements
- technical requirements, overhead projectors, public address system, etc.

The customer requirements are then summarised on a function sheet and divided into departmental responsibilities. The function sheet may be issued to the customer one week before the function.

Ideally, function sheets should be colour-coded for each department one week before the function. The date for confirmation of the final catering numbers is noted on the function sheet.

Internal communication procedures

Internal communication is especially important within any organisation. Frequent meetings are essential to inform staff of forthcoming events and the expected working hours for the following week. Often, more detailed and user-friendly, internal function sheets are compiled so that the key people are aware of customer requirements.

Internal function sheets should be given to the relevant staff at least one week in advance of the function. It is then up to each department to assess its own responsibilities and needs relating to the event so that the work can be planned in advance. These sheets will determine the amount of staff required for the function, and how much linen, crockery, glassware, and so on, is required.

Such decisions will have to be made taking account of the price the customer is paying and the overall budget. Final attendance numbers should be confirmed with the client at least 48 hours before the event.

An example of costs and resources

Different services provided may be priced separately (e.g. menu price may comprise internal costs). For example:

- 30 per cent – food cost
- 30 per cent – labour
- 30 per cent – operational costs (e.g. linen, cleaning, etc.)
- 10 per cent – profit.

Usually each department has its own budget to reach. Resources for each department must be deployed and used effectively in order to maximise profitability.

All revenue earned and costs are summarised on a weekly basis in the form of a weekly cost-breakdown report. This is then passed on to the control office, manager or director.

Expenditure for each function is usually controlled on a daily basis. The head chef must be aware of the total food expenditure target for each function. All costs must be controlled through the careful management of resources. Staffing needs to be kept to a minimum without compromising quality.

The importance of timing

The accurate timing of functions is vital, for the following reasons.

- Each department needs time to prepare for the function. Some departments will require more time than others. For example, the kitchen needs the most time to prepare the menu, while a technician requires only a few minutes to prepare the video playback machine.
- The timing of deliveries is most important as late deliveries can cause severe problems for the kitchen. It is also important that deliveries meet the required specification.
- In high-quality banqueting houses much of the service and presentation is finished at the last minute.
- Any delays in the function will result in hourly paid staff being paid extra time, thus pushing up costs.
- Timing can affect the smooth running of the function, and whether it is possible to turn the room around in enough time for a second function (e.g. lunch, then dinner).

The importance of communication and information

Communication and flow of information in any organisation is of paramount importance to a successful organisation.

Information needs to be broken down and allocated to the appropriate departments, and it is vital that there is two-way communication between departments. Any changes to the function must be communicated to all those concerned immediately.

Information, first, is obtained by the first point of customer contact (i.e. the event organiser, the food and beverage manager, conference and function organisation). At a later stage more specialist information is gathered by the individual department heads, using various means of communication:

- telephone
- email
- fax
- meetings.

This information is recorded in different stages:

- telephone enquiry
- bookings diary
- hire contract
- function sheet
- internal function sheet
- invoice
- feedback form
- weekly report
- thank you letter.

Information may be presented in different ways, either formally or informally.

Formal correspondence
Information relating to a client's function must be professionally presented, accurate and reflect the company's image.

Internal information
This must also be accurate and well presented so that staff are able to understand clearly what is expected of them. All instructions should be in detail, leaving nothing to chance or guesswork.

Customer information
All information relating to the needs of the customers must be recorded throughout the booking process using appropriate documentation:

- hire contract
- function sheets, and so on.

Special requirements
In small establishments the services on offer can be tailored to the needs of the customer.

- Dietary needs must be catered for.
- It is important that, if wheelchair access is required, it is made available.

- Where it is difficult to accommodate certain special requirements, the customer should be given alternatives, where possible.

Food allergies

When planning menus for a large function the chef must think of the danger of any food allergies. All waiting staff must be informed of the contents of the dishes (e.g. shellfish, gluten, peanuts).

Legal requirements

All functions must be planned within the legal framework. Consideration must be given to the welfare of staff. Provide training in health, safety and hygiene. Employees must understand the fire regulations and evacuation procedures. Training is particularly important in risk assessment, handling dangerous equipment and handling chemical products.

Companies have a legal responsibility to the customer – for example, the customer needs to be aware of the maximum number of guests permitted in the building due to fire regulations and, similarly, whether or not a licence extension or evacuation procedures in the event of a fire or bomb threat are in place.

The issuing of a contract forms a legal bond between the customer and the venue.

The event

Staff are required to familiarise themselves with the function sheets, identifying any special requirements that are needed by the organiser. Staff also require a full briefing so that they understand exactly what is required of them and to reconfirm the function details. It is important that the client feels that they are being looked after and that they can feel at ease. The function must be executed as planned, in line with the client's needs.

At the end of the function it is essential to gain feedback from the client to ensure that, if the client was not satisfied, a follow-up letter apologising or offering some compensation can be sent. This client evaluation should then be passed on to the staff.

A final calculation of the costs incurred by each department needs to be done to check the efficiency of the budget management. Invoices are then raised.

Some companies will contact the client one to three days after the function to obtain constructive feedback, using a standard evaluation form for them to fill in.

Well-organised functions that give customer satisfaction can not only be profitable but may also lead to repeat business.

Figure 8.12 Briefing staff

REFERENCES

Kasavana, M.L. and Smith, D.I. (1982) *Menu Engineering*. Haworth Press.

Some references to commodities elsewhere in the book:

Speciality restaurants	19
Transport catering	21
Computers	671
Diets	206

TOPICS FOR DISCUSSION

1. A sensible menu policy.
2. The advantages and disadvantages of a cyclical menu.
3. The advantages of using the English language in menus. When would you consider using another language?
4. The essentials of menu design and construction.
5. The various styles of buffet menus.
6. The implications of menu fatigue.
7. How would you promote your menu for a 50-seater high-street bistro in the centre of town?
8. Each member of the group to obtain a number of differing menus (e.g. breakfast, lunch, dinner, special party) from different types of catering area (e.g. school meals, industrial catering, small, medium and large hotels, and restaurants) for discussion and critique.
9. How have menus changed over the last 20 years? Discuss why they have changed.
10. What menu changes do you envisage? Explain why you think they will occur.
11. Specify the essential menu requirements, and state your reasons, for children, teenagers and senior citizens.

Chapter 9 FOOD PURCHASING, STORAGE AND CONTROL

LIAISING WITH FOOD SUPPLIERS

There are certain important factors involved in a successful working relationship with food suppliers. Both parties have responsibilities that must be carried out to ensure proper food safety and quality. Food-borne illness incidents, regardless of their cause, have an impact on the reputation of caterers, and suppliers' business will be lost. A good working relationship and knowledge of each other's responsibilities is a major help in avoiding such incidents.

Suppliers must be aware of what is expected of the product. They must also make sure that the caterer is aware of any food safety limitations associated with the product. These are usually stated on all labelling. Such statements may simply say 'keep refrigerated' or 'keep frozen', others may well include a graph or chart of the projected shelf-life at different storage temperatures. The responsibility for meeting these specifications is an important factor in a successful catering operation.

FOOD PURCHASING

The purchasing cycle is pivotal to overall business performance, and a firm purchasing policy is the initial control point of the catering business.

Once a menu is planned, a number of activities must occur to bring it into reality. One of the first and most important stages is to purchase and receive the materials needed to produce the menu items. Skilful purchasing with good receiving can do much to maximise the results of a good menu. There are six important steps to remember:

1 know the market
2 design the purchase procedures
3 determine purchasing needs
4 receive and check the goods
5 establish and use specifications
6 evaluate the purchasing task.

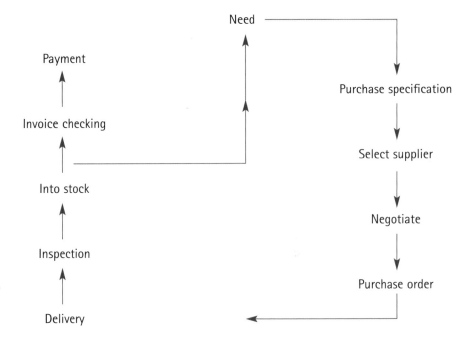

Figure 9.1 The purchasing cycle

Source: D. Drummond, Purchasing and Costing for the Hospitality Industry, 1998, Hodder Arnold.

Knowing the market

Since markets vary considerably, to do a good job of purchasing a buyer must know the characteristics of each market.

A market is a place in which ownership of a commodity changes from one person to another. This could occur using the telephone, on a street corner, in a retail or wholesale establishment, or at an auction.

It is important that a food and beverage purchaser has knowledge of the items to be purchased, such as:

- where they are grown
- seasons of production
- approximate costs
- conditions of supply and demand
- laws and regulations governing the market and the products
- marketing agents and their services
- processing
- storage requirements
- commodity and product, class and grade.

The buyer

This is the key person who makes decisions regarding quality, amounts, price and what will satisfy the customers but also make a profit. The wisdom of the buyer's decisions will be reflected in the success or failure of the operation. The buyer must not only be knowledgeable about the products, but must have the necessary skills required in dealing with sales people, suppliers and other market agents. The buyer must be prepared for hard and often aggressive negotiations.

The responsibility for buying varies from company to company according to size and management policy. Buying may be the responsibility of the chef, manager, storekeeper, buyer or buying department.

A buyer must have knowledge of the internal organisation of the company, especially the operational needs, and be able to obtain the products needed at a competitive price. Buyers must also acquaint themselves with the procedures of production and how these items are going to be used in the production operations, in order that the right item is purchased. For example, the item required may not always have to be of prime quality – for example, tomatoes for use in soups and sauces.

A buyer must also be able to make good use of market conditions. For example, if there is a glut of fresh salmon at low cost, has the organisation the facility to make use of extra salmon purchases? Is there sufficient freezer space? Can the chef make use of salmon by creating a demand on the menu?

Buying methods

These depend on the type of market and the kind of operation. Purchasing procedures are usually formal or informal. Both have advantages and disadvantages. Informal methods are suitable for casual buying, where the amount involved is not large, and speed and simplicity are desirable. Formal contracts are best for large contracts for commodities purchased over a long period of time; prices do not vary much during a year once the basic price has been established. Prices and supply tend to fluctuate more with informal methods.

Informal buying

This usually involves oral negotiations, talking directly to sales people, face to face or using the telephone. Informal methods vary according to market conditions.

Formal buying

Known as competitive buying, formal buying involves giving suppliers written specifications and quantity needs. Negotiations are normally written.

Selecting suppliers

The selecting of suppliers is an important part of the purchasing process. First, consider how a supplier will be able to meet the needs of your operation. Consider:

- price
- delivery
- quality/standards.

Information on suppliers can be obtained from other purchasers. Visits to suppliers' establishments are to be encouraged. When interviewing prospective suppliers, you need to question how reliable a supplier will be under competition and how stable under varying market conditions.

Principles of purchasing

A menu dictates an operation's needs. Based on this the buyer searches for a market that can supply the company. After the right market is located, the various products available that may meet the needs are then investigated. The right product must be obtained to meet the need and give the right quality desired by the establishment. Other factors that might affect production needs include:

- type and image of the establishment
- style of operation and system of service
- occasion for which the item is needed
- amount of storage available (dry, refrigerated or frozen)
- finance available and supply policies of the organisation
- availability, seasonality, price trends and supply.

The skill of the employees, catering assistants and chefs must also be taken into account, as well as condition and the processing method, the ability of the product to produce the item or dish required, and the storage life of the product.

Three types of need

1 **Perishable:** fresh fruit and vegetables, dairy products, meat and fish; prices and suppliers may vary; informal needs of buying are frequently used; perishables should be purchased to meet menu needs for a short period only.
2 **Staple:** supplies that are canned, bottled, dehydrated or frozen; formal or informal purchasing may be used; because items are staple and can easily be stored, bid buying is frequently used to take advantage of quantity price purchasing.
3 **Daily use needs:** daily use or contract items are delivered frequently on par stock basis; stocks are kept up to the desired level and supply is automatic; supplies may arrive daily, several times a week, weekly or less often; most items are perishable, therefore supplies must not be excessive but only sufficient to get through to the next delivery.

What quantity and quality?

Determining the quantity and quality of items to be purchased is important. This is based on operational needs. The buyer must be informed by the chef or other members of the production team of the products needed. The chef and his or her team must establish the quality and they should be required to inspect the goods on arrival. The buyer with this information then checks out the market and looks for the best quality and best price. Delivery arrangements and other factors will be handled by the buyer. In smaller establishments the chef may also be the buyer.

When considering the quantity needed, the following factors should be borne in mind:

- the number of people to be served in a given period
- the sales history
- portion sizes (this is determined from yield testing a standard portion-control list drawn up by the chef and management teams).

Buyers need to know about production, often to be able to decide how many portions a given size may yield. He or she must also understand the various yields. Cooking shrinkage may vary, causing problems in portion control and yield.

The chef must inform the buyer of quantities. The buyer must also be aware of different packaging sizes, such as jars, bottles, cans, and the yield from each package. Grades, styles, appearance, composition, varieties and quality factors must be indicated, such as:

- colour
- bruising
- texture
- irregular shape
- size
- maturity
- absence of defects.

Quality standards should be established by the chef and management team when the menu is planned. Menus and recipes may be developed using standardised recipes that relate directly to the buying procedure and standard purchasing specifications.

Buying tips

The following is a list of suggestions to assist the buyer.

- Acquire, and keep up to date, a sound knowledge of all commodities, both fresh and convenience, to be purchased.
- Be aware of the different types and qualities of each commodity that is available.
- When buying fresh commodities, be aware of part-prepared and ready-prepared items available on the market.
- Keep a sharp eye on price variations. Buy at the best price to ensure

the required quality and also an economic yield. The cheapest item may prove to be the most expensive if waste is excessive. When possible, order by number and weight. For example, 20 kg plaice could be 80 × 250 g (8 oz) plaice, 40 × 500 g (1 lb) plaice, 20 × 1 kg (2.2 lb) plaice. It could also be 20 kg total weight of various sizes and this makes efficient portion control difficult. Some suppliers (e.g. butchers, fishmongers) may offer a portion-control service by selling the required number of a given weight of certain cuts. For example, 100 × 150 g (6 oz) sirloin steaks, 25 kg (50 lb) prepared stewing beef, 200 × 100 g (4 oz) pieces of turbot fillet, 500 × 100 g (4 oz) plaice fillets.

- Organise an efficient system of ordering with copies of all orders kept for cross-checking, whether orders are given in writing, verbally or by telephone.
- Compare purchasing by retail, wholesale and contract procedures to ensure the best method is selected for your own particular organisation.
- Explore all possible suppliers: local or markets, town or country, small or large.
- Keep the number of suppliers to a minimum. At the same time have at least two suppliers for every group of commodities, when possible. The principle of having competition for the caterer's business is sound.
- Issue all orders to suppliers fairly, allowing sufficient time for the order to be implemented efficiently.
- Request price lists as frequently as possible and compare prices continually to make sure that you buy at a good market price.
- Buy perishable goods when they are in full season as this gives the best value at the cheapest price. To help with the purchasing of the correct quantities, it is useful to compile a purchasing chart for 100 covers from which items can be divided or multiplied according to requirement. An indication of quality standards can also be incorporated in a chart of this kind.
- Deliveries must all be checked against the orders given for quantity, quality and price. If any goods delivered are below an acceptable standard they must be returned, either for replacement or credit.
- Containers can account for large sums of money. Ensure that all containers are correctly stored, returned to the suppliers where possible and the proper credit given.
- All invoices must be checked for quantities and prices.
- All statements must be checked against invoices and passed swiftly to the office so that payment may be made in time to ensure maximum discount on purchases.
- Foster good relations with trade representatives because much useful up-to-date information can be gained from them.
- Keep up-to-date trade catalogues, visit trade exhibitions, survey new equipment and continually review the space, services and systems in use in order to explore possible avenues of increased efficiency.

- Organise a testing panel occasionally in order to keep up to date with new commodities and new products coming on to the market.
- Consider how computer applications can assist the operation (see Chapter 17).
- Study weekly fresh food price lists.

PORTION CONTROL

Portion control means controlling the size or quantity of food to be served to each customer. The amount of food allowed depends on the three following considerations.

1 **The type of customer or establishment:** there will obviously be a difference in the size of portions served, such as to those working in heavy industry or to female clerical workers. In a restaurant offering a three-course table d'hôte menu for £25 including salmon, the size of the portion would naturally be smaller than in a luxury restaurant charging £17.50 for the salmon on an à la carte menu.
2 **The quality of the food:** better-quality food usually yields a greater number of portions than poor-quality food: low-quality stewing beef often needs so much trimming that it is difficult to get six portions to the kilogramme, and the time and labour involved also loses money. On the other hand, good-quality stewing beef will often give eight portions to the kilo, with much less time and labour required for preparation, and more customer satisfaction.
3 **The buying price of the food:** this should correspond to the quality of the food if the person responsible for buying has bought wisely. A good buyer will ensure that the price paid for any item of food is equivalent to the quality – in other words, a good price should mean good quality, which should mean a good yield, and so help to establish sound portion control. If, on the other hand, an inefficient buyer has paid a high price for food of indifferent quality then it will be difficult to get a fair number of portions, the selling price necessary to make the required profit will be too high and customer satisfaction can be affected.

Portion control should be closely linked with the buying of the food; without a good knowledge of the food bought it is difficult to state fairly how many portions should be obtained from it. To evolve a sound system of portion control, each establishment (or type of establishment) needs individual consideration. A golden rule should be: 'a fair portion for a fair price'.

Conveniently portioned items are available, such as individual sachets of sugar, jams, sauce, salt and pepper, individual cartons of milk and cream, and individual butter and margarine portions.

Portion control equipment

There are certain items of equipment that can assist in maintaining control of the size of the portions:

- scoops, for ice cream or mashed potatoes
- ladles, for soups and sauces
- butter pat machines, regulating pats from 7 g upwards
- fruit juice glasses (75–150 g)
- soup plates or bowls (14, 16, 17, 18 cm)
- milk dispensers and tea-measuring machines
- individual pie dishes, pudding basins, moulds and coupes.

The following real-life examples demonstrate how portion control can save a great deal of money.

- It was found that 0.007 litres of milk was being lost per cup by spilling it from a jug; 32,000 cups = 5224 litres of milk lost daily; this resulted in a loss of hundreds of pounds per year.
- When an extra penny's worth of meat is served on each plate it mounts up to a loss of £3650 over the year when 1000 meals are served daily.

Portion amounts

The following is a list of the approximate number of portions obtainable from various foods.

General
- Soup: 2–3 portions to each half a litre.
- Hors-d'oeuvres: 120–180 g per portion.
- Smoked salmon: 16–20 portions to the kg when bought by the side; 20–24 portions to the kg when bought sliced.
- Shellfish cocktail: 16–20 portions per kg.
- Melon: 2–8 portions per melon, depending on the type of melon.
- Foie gras: 15–30 g per portion.
- Caviar: 15–30 g per portion.

Fish
- Plaice, cod, haddock fillet: 8 portions to the kg.
- Cod and haddock on the bone: 6 portions to the kg.
- Plaice, turbot, brill, halibut, on the bone: 4 portions to the kg.
- Herring and trout: 1 per portion (180–250 g fish).
- Mackerel and whiting: 250–360 g fish.
- Sole for main dish: 300–360 g fish.
- Sole for filleting: 500–750 g best size.
- Whitebait: 8–10 portions to the kg.
- Salmon (gutted, but including head and bone): 4–6 portions to the kg.

- Crab or lobster: 250–360 g per portion (a 500 g lobster yields about 150 g meat; a 1 kg lobster yields about 360 g meat).

Sauces
For each type, 8–12 portions to the half litre:

- hollandaise
- custard
- béarnaise
- apricot
- tomato
- jam
- any demi-glace, reduced stock or jus-lié
- chocolate.

For each type, 10–14 portions to half litre:

- apple
- cranberry
- bread.

For each type, 15–20 portions to half litre:

- tartare
- vinaigrette
- mayonnaise.

Meats
Beef:
- roast boneless – 6–8 portions per kg
- boiled or braised – 6–8 portions per kg
- stews, puddings and pies – 8–10 portions per kg
- steaks – rump – 120–250 g per one portion, sirloin – 120–250 g per one portion, tournedos – 90–120 g per one portion, fillet – 120–180 g per one portion.

Offal:
- ox liver – 8 portions to the kg
- sweetbreads – 6–8 portions to the kg
- sheep's kidneys – 2 per portion
- ox tongue – 4–6 portions per kg.

Lamb
- leg – 6–8 portions to the kg
- shoulder, boned and stuffed – 6–8 portions to the kg
- loin and best end – 6 portions to the kg
- stewing lamb – 4–6 portions to the kg
- cutlet – 90–120 g
- chop – 120–180 g.

Pork:
- leg – 8 portions to the kg
- shoulder – 6–8 portions to the kg

- loin on the bone – 6–8 portions to the kg
- pork chop – 180–250 g.

Ham:
- hot – 8–10 portions to the kg
- cold – 10–12 portions to the kg
- sausages are obtainable 12, 16 or 20 to the kg
- chipolatas yield approximately 32 or 48 to the kg
- cold meat – 16 portions to the kg
- streaky bacon – 32–40 rashers to the kg
- back bacon – 24–32 rashers to the kg.

Poultry:
- poussin – 1 portion 360 g (1 bird), 2 portions 750 g (1 bird)
- ducks and chickens – 360 g per portion
- geese and boiling fowl – 360 g per portion
- turkey – 250 g per portion.

Vegetables:
- new potatoes – 8 portions to the kg
- old potatoes – 4–6 portions to the kg
- cabbage – 6–8 portions to the kg
- turnips – 6–8 portions to the kg
- parsnips – 6–8 portions to the kg
- swedes – 6–8 portions to the kg
- Brussels sprouts – 6–8 portions to the kg
- tomatoes – 6–8 portions to the kg
- French beans – 6–8 portions to the kg
- cauliflower – 6–8 portions to the kg
- spinach – 4 portions to the kg
- peas – 4–6 portions to the kg
- runner beans – 6 portions to the kg.

METHODS OF PURCHASING

There are three main methods for buying, each depending on the size and volume of the business.

1 **The primary market:** raw materials may be purchased at the source of supply (the grower, producer or manufacturer) or from central markets such as Smithfield (meat), Nine Elms (fruit and vegetables) or Billingsgate (fish) in London. Some establishments or large organisations will have a buyer who will buy directly from the primary markets. Also, a number of smaller establishments may adopt this method for some of their needs (the chef patron may buy his fish, meat and vegetables directly from the market).

2 **The secondary market:** goods are bought wholesale from a distributor or middleman; the catering establishment will pay wholesale prices and obtain possible discounts.

3 **The tertiary market:** the retail or cash-and-carry warehouse is a method suitable for smaller companies. A current pass obtained from the warehouse is required in order to gain access. This method also requires the user to have his or her own transport. Some cash-and-carry organisations require a VAT number before they will issue an authorised card. It is important to remember that there are added costs:

   - running the vehicle and petrol used
   - the person's time for going to the warehouse.

Cash and carry is often an impersonal way of buying as there are no staff available with whom to discuss quality and prices.

Standard purchasing specifications

Standard purchasing specifications are documents that are drawn up for every commodity describing exactly what is required for the establishment. These standard purchasing specifications will assist with the formulation of standardised recipes. A watertight specification is drawn up which, once approved, will be referred to every time the item is delivered. It is a statement of various criteria related to quality, grade, weight, size and method of preparation, if required (such as washed and selected potatoes for baking). Other information given may be variety, maturity, age, colour, shape, and so on. A copy of the standard specification is often given to the supplier and the storekeeper, who are left in no doubt as to what is needed. These specifications assist in the costing and control procedures.

Commodities that can be specified include the following.

- Grown (primary): butcher's meat; fresh fish; fresh fruit and vegetables; milk and eggs.
- Manufactured (secondary): bakery goods; dairy products.
- Processed (tertiary): frozen foods including meat, fish, and fruit and vegetables; dried goods; canned goods.

It can be seen that any food product can have a specification attached to it. However, the primary specifications focus on raw materials, ensuring the quality of these commodities. Without quality at this level, a secondary or tertiary specification is useless. For example, to specify a frozen apple pie, this product would use:

- a primary specification for the apple
- a secondary specification for the pastry
- a tertiary specification for the process (freezing).

But, no matter how good the secondary or tertiary specifications, if the apples used in the beginning are not of a very high quality, the whole product will not be of a good quality.

Example of a standard purchasing specification

Tomatoes

- Commodity: round tomatoes.
- Size: 50 g (2 oz) 47–57 mm diameter.
- Quality: firm, well formed, good red colour, with stalk attached.
- Origin: Dutch, available March–November.
- Class/grade: super class A.
- Weight: 6 kg (13 lb) net per box.
- Count: 90–100 per box.
- Quote: per box/tray.
- Packaging: loose in wooden tray, covered in plastic.
- Delivery: day following order.
- Storage: temperature 10–13°C (50–55°F) at a relatively humidity of 75–80 per cent.
- Note: avoid storage with cucumbers and aubergines.

For most perishable items, rather than entering into a long-term contract, a daily or monthly quotation system is more common. This is essentially a short-term contract regularly reviewed to ensure that a competitive situation is maintained.

THE STANDARD RECIPE

The standard recipe is a written formula for producing a food item of a specified quality and quantity for use in a particular establishment. It should show the precise quantities and qualities of the ingredients, together with the sequence of preparation and service. It enables the establishment to have greater control over cost and quantity.

Objective

To predetermine the following:

- the quantities and qualities of ingredients to be used, stating the purchase specification
- the yield obtainable from a recipe
- the food cost per portion
- the nutritional value of a particular dish.

To facilitate:

- menu planning, purchasing and internal requisitioning, food preparation and production, portion control.

Extract from a purchase specification

Schedule B: Supplier's quality and preparation specification

Product: Beef and veal

General

1 All products supplied to – must comply with the provisions of the Weights and Measures Act 1976 and 1985, Trade Descriptions Act 1968/1972, Food Safety Act 1990 and any amendments that are enforced from time to time.

2 No meat from cow (including that designated as 'commercial') or bull carcasses will be supplied.

3 Cuts, joints and steaks of fresh beef are to be prepared from the chilled unfrozen carcasses or primal cuts of 'clean' steers and heifers of English, Irish or Scottish origin.* Beef of intervention storage and from imported chilled and frozen meat can also be supplied if they originated from animals that conformed to the standards of home-killed graded beef.

4 No cuts from excessively lean or fat carcasses to be supplied.

5 Unfrozen beef carcasses and primal cuts from the hindquarter must be stored at chilled temperatures for 7–10 days prior to preparation, to allow for maturation.

6 Cuts, joints and steaks of veal are to be prepared from the chilled unfrozen carcass of English or Dutch milk-fed beasts.

7 Beef and veal other than that supplied frozen must be kept chilled (below 5°C) throughout preparation, storage and distribution.

8 Prepared cuts of chilled beef and veal that are supplied frozen must be fully frozen to a temperature of not higher than -18°C by mechanical blast freezers. Meat that has not been frozen by such means cannot be supplied to –. The exception to this is stewing steak that has been frozen to much higher temperatures to allow mechanical dicing.

9 Fresh beef and veal that has been designated as frozen must be delivered by transport that has frozen storage capacity. The temperature of the meat must not reach a value of more than -10°C during distribution.

10 Meat purchased as frozen and then thawed for the preparation of joints, steaks, mince or stewing steak, must not be refrozen.

11 Prepared cuts must be wrapped and sealed in polythene bags and delivered in a rigid impervious receptacle or tray of good hygienic standard.

12 Suppliers of fresh beef and veal to – must adhere to the purchasing and supply specification of Schedule D.

* Home-killed beef to conform to the Meat and Livestock Commission (MLC) grading system.

- Outline of the quantities and quality of goods required
- Whether supplier has 'sole' status
- Incorporation of the purchase specification
- The way in which unsatisfactory goods will be treated
- The collection arrangements for returnable containers
- A disputes procedure and an indemnity clause
- Delivery arrangements and invoicing procedures
- A termination and review clause

Also the standard recipe will assist new staff in the preparation and production of standard products, which can be facilitated by photographs or drawings illustrating the finished product.

COST CONTROL

It is important to know the exact cost of each process and every item produced, so a system of cost analysis and cost information is essential. The advantages of an efficient costing system are as follows.

- It discloses the net profit made by each section of the organisation and shows the cost of each meal produced.
- It will reveal possible sources of economy and can result in a more effective use of stores, labour, materials, and so on.
- Costing provides information necessary for the formation of a sound pricing policy.
- Cost records provide and facilitate speedy quotations for all special functions, such as parties, wedding receptions, and so on.
- It enables the caterer to keep to a budget.

No one costing system will automatically suit every catering business, but the following guidelines may be helpful.

- The cooperation of all departments is essential.
- The costing system should be adapted to the business, not vice versa. If the accepted procedure in an establishment is altered to fit a costing system then there is danger of causing resentment among staff and as a result losing their cooperation.
- Clear instructions in writing must be given to staff who are required to keep records. The system must be made as simple as possible so that the amount of clerical labour required is kept to a minimum. An efficient mechanical calculator or computer should be provided to save time and labour.

To calculate the total cost of any one item or meal provided it is necessary to analyse the total expenditure under several headings. Basically the total cost of each item consists of the following three main elements.

1 **Food or materials costs:** known as variable costs because the level will vary according to the volume of business; in an operation that uses part-time or extra staff for special occasions, the money paid to these staff also comes under variable costs; by comparison, salaries and wages paid regularly to permanent staff are fixed costs.
2 **All costs of labour and overheads:** regular charges that come under the heading of fixed costs; labour costs in the majority of operations fall into two categories: direct labour cost, which is salaries and wages paid to staff such as chefs, waiters, barstaff, housekeepers, chambermaids,

and where the cost can be allocated to income from food, drink and accommodation sales; and indirect labour cost, which would include salaries and wages paid, for example, to managers, office staff and maintenance staff who work for all departments (so their labour cost should be charged to all departments). Overheads consist of rent, rates, heating, lighting and equipment.

3 **Cleaning materials:** an important group of essential items that is often overlooked when costing. There are over 60 different items that come under this heading, and approximately 24 of these may be required for an average catering establishment. These may include: brooms, brushes, buckets, cloths, drain rods, dusters, mops, sponges, squeegees, scrubbing/polishing machines, suction/vacuum cleaners, wet and wet/dry suction cleaners, scouring pads, detergents, disinfectants, dustbin powder, washing-up liquids, fly sprays, sacks, scourers, steel wool, soap, soda, and so on.

It is important to understand the cost of these materials and to ensure that an allowance is made for them under the heading of overheads.

Costing and profit

Pricing

There are several different approaches to pricing catering products and services. (There is more on pricing in Chapter 14.)

Competitive pricing

Using this method, prices are based on the prices charged by competitors for broadly similar products and services. The argument for this approach is that the consumer's choice is dependent largely upon price and that catering operations charging more than their competition price themselves out of business.

'Backward' pricing

This method bases prices on what market research indicates the consumer will be prepared and able to pay. Once the price has been determined, the cost of materials, labour and overheads is calculated in order to show a satisfactory profit. This method tends to be used by the more sophisticated operators.

Cost plus

This is the system used by many sectors of the industry. In order to arrive at the selling price, a percentage of ratio of cost price (e.g. 100 per cent) is added to cost of raw materials. This 'mark-up' should set a level that meets costs and, in commercial catering, makes a profit as well. There are variations on this cost-plus approach.

Gross profit-fixed percentage mark-up

The food cost of each dish is calculated and a fixed gross profit (e.g. 100 per cent) added. Gross profit refers to the difference between cost and selling price.

It is usual to express each element of cost as a percentage of the selling price. This enables the caterer to control profits.

Gross profit, or kitchen profit, is the difference between the cost of the food and the net selling price of the food. Net profit is the difference between the selling price of the food (sales) and total cost (of food, labour and overheads). Here is an example:

Sales – Food cost = gross profit (kitchen profit)

Sales – total cost = net profit

Food cost + gross profit = sales

Example	Food sales for 1 week	=	£25,000
	Food cost for 1 week	=	£12,000
	Labour and overheads for 1 week	=	£9,000
	Total costs for 1 week	=	£21,000
	Gross profit (kitchen profit)	=	£13,000
	Net profit	=	£4,000

Food sales – food cost   £25,000 − £12,000 = £13,000 (gross profit)

Food sales – net profit   £25,000 − £4,000 = £21,000 (total costs)

Food cost + gross profit   £12,000 + £15,000 = £25,000 (food sales)

Profit is always expressed as a percentage of the selling price.

∴ the percentage profit for the week is:

$$\frac{\text{Net profit}}{\text{Sales}} \times 100 = \frac{£4000 \times 100}{25,000} = 16\%$$

A breakdown reveals the figures shown in Table 9.1.

Table 9.1 Example breakdown

		PERCENTAGE OF SALES (%)
Food cost	£12,000	44
Labour	£6,000	25
Overheads	£3,000	18
	£21,000	
Net profit	£4,000	13
Sales	£25,000	

If the restaurant served 1000 meals then the average amount spent by each customer would be:

$$\frac{\text{Total sales £25,000}}{\text{No. of customers 1000}} = £25.00$$

As the percentage composition of sales for a month is now known, the average price of a meal for that period can be further analysed:

Average price of a meal = £25.00 = 100%

25p = 1%

which means that the customer's contribution towards:

Food cost	= 25 × 48	= £12.00
Labour	= 25 × 24	= £6.00
Overheads	= 25 × 12	= £3.00
Net profit	= 25 × 16	= £4.00
Average price of meal		= £25.00

A rule that can be applied to calculate the food cost price of a dish is: let the cost price of the dish equal 40 per cent and fix the selling price at 100 per cent.

$$\text{Cost of dish} = 400p = 40\%$$

$$\therefore \text{Selling price} = \frac{400 \times 100}{40} = £10.00$$

Selling the dish at £10, making 60 per cent gross profit above the cost price, would be known as 40 per cent food cost. For example:

Sirloin steak (250 g (8 oz))
250 g (8 oz) entrecote steak at £10.00 a kg = £2.50

$$\text{To fix the selling price at 40\% food cost} = \frac{2.50 \times 100}{40} = £6.25$$

If food costing is controlled accurately the food cost of particular items on the menu and the total expenditure on food over a given period are worked out. Finding the food costs helps to control costs, prices and profits.

An efficient food cost system will disclose bad buying and inefficient storing, and should tend to prevent waste and pilfering. This can help the caterer to run an efficient business, and enable her/him to give the customer adequate value for money.

The caterer who gives the customer value for money together with the desired type of food is well on the way to being successful.

Table of selling prices for various levels of profit on sales (e.g. Table 9.2)

- Look up pounds in lower table.
- Look up pence in upper table.
- Add results together.

Table 9.2 Gross profit table*

	Selling prices for percentage gross profit on sales								
COST	**10%**	**20%**	**30%**	**40%**	**50%**	**60%**	**70%**	**80%**	**90%**
10p	.11	.13	.14	.17	.20	.25	.33	.50	1.00
20p	.22	.25	.29	.33	.40	.50	.67	1.00	2.00
30p	.33	.38	.43	.50	.60	.75	1.00	1.50	3.00
40p	.44	.50	.57	.67	.80	1.00	1.33	2.00	4.00
50p	.56	.63	.71	.83	1.00	1.25	1.67	2.50	5.00
60p	.67	.75	.86	1.00	1.20	1.50	2.00	3.00	6.00
70p	.78	.88	1.00	1.17	1.40	1.75	2.33	2.50	7.00
80p	.89	1.00	1.14	1.33	1.60	2.00	2.67	4.00	8.00
90p	1.00	1.13	1.29	1.50	1.80	2.25	3.00	4.50	9.00
1.00	1.11	1.25	1.43	1.67	2.00	2.50	3.33	5.00	10.00
2.00	2.22	2.50	2.86	3.33	4.00	5.00	6.67	10.00	20.00
3.00	3.33	3.75	4.29	5.00	6.00	7.50	10.00	15.00	30.00
4.00	4.44	5.00	5.71	6.67	8.00	10.00	13.33	20.00	40.00
5.00	5.56	6.25	7.14	8.33	10.00	12.50	16.67	25.00	50.00
6.00	6.67	7.50	8.57	10.00	12.00	15.00	20.00	30.00	60.00
7.00	7.78	8.75	10.00	11.67	14.00	17.50	23.33	35.00	70.00
8.00	8.89	10.00	11.43	13.33	16.00	20.00	26.67	40.00	80.00
9.00	10.00	11.25	12.86	15.00	18.00	22.50	30.00	45.00	90.00
10.00	11.11	12.50	14.29	16.67	20.00	25.00	33.33	50.00	

* Gross profit (GP) is normally the surplus, after material costs have been deducted, expressed as a percentage of sales revenue. Croners Catering

Example
If a dish costs £2.80 to produce, what should its selling price be to achieve 60 per cent profit on sales?

£2.00	=	£5.00 selling price
0.80	=	£2.00 selling price
Selling price	=	£7.00
Add VAT (£7.00 × 1.175)		£1.22
Final selling price		£8.22

Table 9.3 Mark-up table*

	Selling prices for mark-up or profit on cost											
COST	33%	67%	100%	133%	167%	200%	233%	267%	300%	333%	367%	400%
10p	.13	.17	.20	.23	.27	.30	.33	.37	.40	.43	.47	.50
20p	.27	.33	.40	.47	.53	.60	.67	.73	.80	.87	.93	1.00
30p	.40	.50	.60	.70	.80	.90	1.00	1.10	1.20	1.30	1.40	1.50
40p	.53	.67	.80	.93	1.07	1.20	1.33	1.47	1.60	1.73	1.87	2.00
50p	.67	.84	1.00	1.17	1.33	1.50	1.67	1.83	2.00	2.17	2.33	2.50
60p	.80	1.00	1.20	1.40	1.60	1.80	2.00	2.20	2.40	2.60	2.80	3.00
70p	.93	1.17	1.40	1.63	1.87	2.10	2.33	2.57	2.80	3.03	3.27	3.50
80p	1.06	1.34	1.60	1.86	2.13	2.40	2.67	2.93	3.20	3.47	3.73	4.00
90p	1.20	1.50	1.80	2.10	2.40	2.70	3.00	3.30	3.60	3.90	4.20	4.50
1.00	1.33	1.67	2.00	2.33	2.67	3.00	3.33	3.66	4.00	4.33	4.66	5.00
2.00	2.67	3.33	4.00	4.67	5.34	6.00	6.67	7.33	8.00	8.67	9.33	10..
3.00	4.00	5.00	6.00	7.00	8.00	9.00	10.00	11.00	12.00	13.00	14.00	15.00
4.00	5.33	6.67	8.00	9.33	10.68	12.00	13.33	14.67	16.00	17.33	18.67	20.00
5.00	6.67	8.33	10.00	11.67	15.35	15.00	16.67	18.33	20.00	21.67	23.33	25.00

* Mark-up is the surplus expressed as a percentage of material costs (see 'gross profit', above)
Croners Catering

Use of mark-up tables (e.g. Table 9.3)
- Look up pounds in lower table.
- Look up pence in upper table.
- Add results together.

Example

If a dish costs £2.80 to produce, what should its selling price be to make a 200 per cent profit on cost?

£2.00 cost gives	=	£6.00 selling price
0.80 cost gives	=	£2.40 selling price
TOTAL		£8.40
Add VAT (£8.40 × 1.75)		£1.47
Final selling price	=	£9.87

Table 9.4 The food and beverage manager's guide to factors affecting the gross profit % (1)

AREA	CAUSES	METHOD OF DETECTION	REMEDIES
Purchasing **1 Suppliers and specifications**	Poor specifications	Not fit for job in hand with regard to size, weight, standard, quality Goods disposed of or more used than necessary	Recheck all specifications against requirements
	Supplier unable to cope with volume or standard	As above	Change supplier
	Acceptance of minimum deliveries, which are in excess of daily requirements	Food wasted (kitchen bins checked)	Agree smaller deliveries or change supplier
	Not keeping close to agreed prices or checking market prices	Check market prices and competitors	Continually monitor suppliers' price lists
	Poor response following complaints	Items not changed immediately and credit note system not responsive	Change supplier
	Poor yields	Observation and physical checks	Carry out regular yield checks and introduce standard recipes
	Poor menu planning	Poor profitability Use of high-priced items out of season	Plan menus to take advantage of seasonal items Include realistic mix of high- and low-cost items
2 Ordering	Incorrect specification, quantity or price	Delivery note, visual check, invoice check	Increase control procedures Ensure orders are placed only by authorised staff Over-ordering, resulting in over-stocking
	Stock deteriorating Stock value high	Shortage of storage space	Closely monitor levels of business and establish trends Establish stock levels for non-perishable goods Eliminate standing orders Order as frequently as purchase contract allows to ensure lower stocks

Table 9.5 The food and beverage manager's guide to factors affecting the gross profit % (2)

AREA	CAUSES	METHOD OF DETECTION	REMEDIES
Materials lost during delivery 1 Receipts short on delivery	Quantity not checked: • staff too busy • staff indifferent • staff unsuitable • staff untrained • insufficient time • staff failing to follow procedures • dishonesty • delivery times inappropriate Poor transportation of goods: • incorrect temperatures • incorrect packaging of goods • credit notes not checked	Inspection and observation of deliveries: • spot checks at delivery • unsigned delivery notes • staff shortages • observation • security checks • observation, goods arriving when stores unmanned • log temperatures of delivery vans • check condition of packaging • check credit notes	Establish procedures for checking orders on receipt of goods Constant spot checks Careful selection, training and monitoring of staff Report driver to supplier Visual checks Follow up on records
2 Change in source of supply and quantity	Inappropriate specifications issued Changes in supply standards not checked	Checking of material specifications against goods received	Establish appropriate purchase specifications
3 Poor stock rotation	Failure by staff Lack of training	Inspection and observation of storage areas and date-stamped goods Spot checks on stores Question staff on understanding of process	Establish stock rotation procedures (bin card system) Regular inspections Staff training Review stores layout
4 Hygiene	Failure of staff to carry out procedures Training update	Regular inspection of stores area	Establish procedures (HACCP) Instigate and maintain staff training

FOOD COST AND OPERATIONAL CONTROL

As food is expensive, efficient stock control levels are essential to help the profitability of the business. The main difficulties of controlling food are as follows.

- Food prices fluctuate frequently because of inflation and falls in demand and supply, through poor harvests, bad weather conditions, and so on.
- Transport costs rise due to wage demands and cost of petrol.
- Fuel costs rise, which affects food companies' and producers' costs.
- Any food subsidies imposed by governments could be removed.
- Changes occur in the amount demanded by the customer; increased

advertising increases demand; changes in taste and fashion influence demand from one product to another.
- Media focus on certain products that are labelled healthy or unhealthy will affect demand; for example butter being high in saturated fats, sunflower margarine being high in polyunsaturates.

Table 9.6 Food costings

FOOD COST (%)	TO FIND THE SELLING PRICE MULTIPLY THE COST PRICE OF THE FOOD BY:	IF THE COST PRICE OF FOOD IS £4, THE SELLING PRICE IS:	IF THE COST PRICE IS £1.20, THE SELLING PRICE IS:	GROSS PROFIT (%)
60	1.66	£6.64	£1.92	40
55	1.75	£7.00	£2.04	45
50	2	£8.00	£2.40	50
45	2.22	£8.88	£2.64	55
40	2.5	£10.00	£2.88	60
33.3	3	£12.00	£3.60	66.6

Each establishment should devise its own control system to suit its own needs. Factors that affect a control system are:

- regular changes in the menu
- menus with a large number of dishes
- dishes with a large number of ingredients
- problems in assessing customer demand
- difficulties in not adhering to or operating standardised recipes
- raw materials purchased incorrectly.

Factors assisting a control system include:

- menu remains constant (e.g. McDonald's, Harvester, Pizza Hut, Burger King)
- standardised recipes and purchasing specifications used
- menu has a limited number of dishes.
Stocktaking is therefore easier and costing more accurate.

In order to carry out a control system, food stocks must be secure, refrigerators and deep freezers should be kept locked, portion control must be accurate. A book-keeping system must be developed to monitor the daily operation.

VAT

If food and drink is sold for consumption in catering, VAT must be added and, if the turnover exceeds £60,000, the business must be registered.

Calculating VAT
Standard-rate VAT is 17.5 per cent, which has to be added to the value of any taxable sale.

VAT-inclusive price
The VAT-inclusive price may be calculated as follows:

$$\text{Net of VAT sale value £90.00}$$
$$£90 \times \frac{117.5}{100} = £105.75$$
$$\text{or, more simply,}$$
$$£90 \times 1.175 = £105.75$$

VAT-exclusive price
In order to calculate the VAT-exclusive element of a VAT-inclusive price of £105.75, it is not correct to take 17.5 per cent of the value of the inclusive selling price of £105.75 – this would result in a net price of £87.24. Instead the correct calculation is:

$$\frac{£105.75}{100 + 17.5} = £90.00$$

VAT element
In order to calculate the value of the VAT in an inclusive price of £105.75 the calculation is:

$$£105.75 \times \frac{7}{47}$$

In the hospitality and catering industry VAT is collected by the operator from the customer to be forwarded to the VAT department of Her Majesty's Customs & Excise office. This applies to all food and drink sales for consumption on the premises of businesses that have a taxable turnover of £55,000 in 12 months.

If food is sold to be taken away and consumed off the premises, it is standard-rated or zero-rated, depending on whether the food is hot.

The control cycle of daily operation

Purchasing
It is important to determine yields from the range of commodities in use, which will determine the unit costs. Yield testing indicates the number of items or portions obtained and helps to provide the information required for producing, purchasing and specification. Yield testing should not be

confused with product testing, which is concerned with the physical properties of the food (e.g. texture, flavour, quality). In reality, tests are frequently carried out that combine these objectives.

Receiving
Goods must be checked on delivery to make sure they meet the purchase specifications.

Before items are delivered, it is necessary to know what has been ordered, both the amount and quality, and when it will be delivered. This is essential so that persons requiring items will know when foods will be available, particularly perishable items, and so that, on arrival, they can be checked against the required standard. It is also helpful for the storekeeper to know when to expect the goods so that he or she can plan the working day and also inform staff awaiting the arrival of items.

The procedure for accepting deliveries is to ensure that:

- adequate storage space is available
- access to the space is clear
- temperature of goods, where appropriate, is checked
- perishable goods are checked immediately
- there is no delay in transporting items to cold storage
- all other goods are checked for quantity and quality, and stored
- any damaged items are returned
- items past their 'use by' or 'best before' dates are not accepted
- receipts or amended delivery notes record returns
- one part of the delivery note is retained
- the other part is kept by the supplier
- a credit note is provided for any goods not delivered
- should there be any discrepancies, the person making the delivery and the supplier are informed.

ORGANISATION OF CONTROL

Control in every catering organisation is crucial: in small restaurants and tea shops, in hospital kitchens and in large hotels, in contract and airline catering, in school meals – in fact, in every establishment.

The role of potential managers and managers, whether they are called food and beverage manager or assistant F&B manager, executive chef, chef de cuisine, sous chef, head chef, chef de partie, or whatever, is to organise:

- themselves
- other people
- their time
- physical resources.

An essential factor of good organisation is effective control of oneself, of those responsible to you, and of physical resources, which often includes financial control. The amount and how it is administered will vary from establishment to establishment. However, successful control applies to all aspects of catering, namely:

- purchasing of food, etc.
- security
- storage of food, etc.
- waste
- preparation of food
- energy
- production of food
- first aid
- presentation of food
- equipment
- hygiene
- maintenance
- safety
- legal aspects.

Control of resources

The effective and efficient management of resources requires knowledge and, if possible, experience. In addition, it is necessary to keep up to date. This may require attending courses on management, computing, hygiene, legislation, and so on. Membership of appropriate organisations, such as HCIMA or former student associations, can also be valuable, as is attending exhibitions and trade fairs.

How the control of resources is administered will depend partly on the systems of the organisation but also on the way the person in control operates. Apart from knowledge and experience, respect from those for whom one is responsible is earned, not given, by the way staff are handled in the situation of the job. Having earned the respect and

---

Checklist for control

Goods inwards

- Are deliveries correct in terms of quality, quantity, hygiene, temperature?

Storage

- Items issued in rotation, accurate recording.
- Correct standards of hygiene: temperature, security, minimum wastage.

Food preparation ⎫	Proper standard of
Production ⎬	hygiene and safety
Presentation	Accurate portion control
Back door	Measures to prevent pilfering
Recording ⎫	
Monitoring ⎬	Is it effective, adequate?
Checking ⎭	

cooperation of staff, a system of controls and checks needs to be operated that is smooth-running and not disruptive. Training and delegation may be required to ensure effective control and, periodically, it is essential to evaluate the system to see that the recording and monitoring are being effective.

The purpose of control is to make certain:

- that supplies of what is required are available
- that the supplies are of the right quality and quantity

Figure 9.2 Organisation of resources

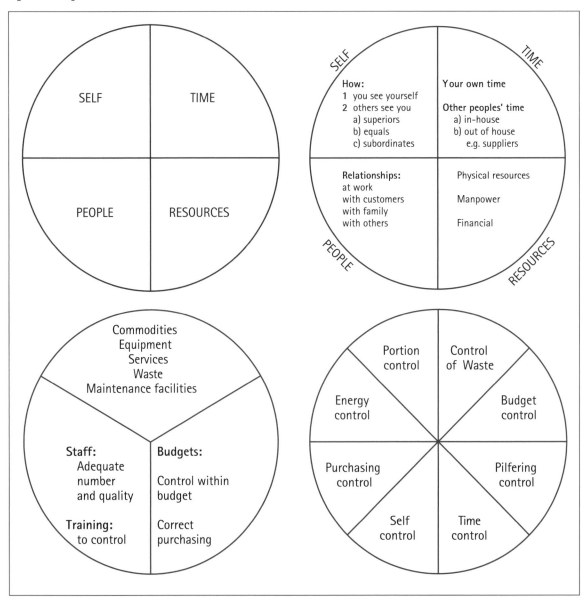

- that they are available on time
- there is the minimum of wastage
- there is no overstocking
- there is no pilfering
- that legal requirements are complied with.

Means of control

Checks need to occur spontaneously, without previous warning of the check being made, at regular intervals, which may be daily or weekly. These checks may involve one item, several items or all items. Records need to correspond with the physical items. For example, if records indicate 40 packets of sugar at 1 kilo, then those 40 x 1 kilo packets need to be seen. It is necessary to know to whom any discrepancies should be reported and what action should be taken. Therefore the policy of the establishment should be clear to all members of staff.

A system of authorisation regarding who may purchase and who may issue goods to whom, with the necessary suitable documents and records, needs to be established and inspected to see that it works satisfactorily.

The following topics, covered in other parts of this book, are essential reading:

- food purchase and control (see pages 387–393 in this chapter)
- energy conservation (Chapter 6)
- health (Chapter 5)
- legal aspects (Chapter 16)
- supervision (Chapter 13)
- computers (Chapter 17)
- hygiene (Chapter 16).

INTRODUCTION TO THE ORGANISATION OF RESOURCES

Health and safety requirements

To comply with the regulations it is essential to observe the following good practice requirements, not only because of the legal requirement but for the benefit of all who use the storage areas of the premises.
- Receiving areas must be clean and free from litter.
- Waste bins, empty return boxes, and so on, should be kept tidy and safe.
- Waste bins (rubbish and swill) must be kept with lids on, emptied frequently and kept clean.
- All storage areas must be kept clean and tidy.
- Trolleys and stacking shelves should be suitable for heavy items.

- Trolleys should not be overloaded; accidents can occur due to careless loading, such as heavy items on top of light ones.
- Lifting of heavy items should be done in a manner to prevent injury.
- Cleaning equipment and materials must be available and kept separate from food items.
- All items should be stored safely, shelves not overloaded, heavier items lower than lighter items, with suitable steps to reach higher items.
- Stores should have a wash hand basin, towel, soap and nail brush.
- Unauthorised persons should not have access to the stores or areas where goods are delivered.
- Be prepared for the unexpected; accidents can occur due to: delivery vehicles and trolley movement; breakages of containers, glass jars, etc.; undue waste left by delivery or storekeeping staff.
- Know where the first aid box is.
- Know the procedures to follow in the event of an accident.

Temperature of food on delivery

Procedures must be laid down for checking the temperature of foods on arrival at the establishment. Delivery vehicles are subject to legislation and food should be at these temperatures when delivered.

Documentation of deliveries

Goods are ordered from the supplier for the amounts required and when needed. The quality and details of the foods will have been specified by the establishment so that when delivered the goods should comply with what was ordered.

Storing and issuing

Raw materials should be stored correctly under the right conditions, temperature, etc. A method of pricing the materials must be decided, and one of the following should be adopted for charging the food to the various departments. The cost of items does not remain fixed over a period of time; over a period of one year a stores item may well have several prices. The establishment must decide which price to use:
- actual purchase price
- simple average price
- weighted average price
- inflated price (price goes up after purchase)
- standard price (fixed price).

Weighted average price example (of dried beans)

$$= 5\,\text{kg} \times 80\text{p} \qquad = \quad £4.00$$

$$10\,\text{kg} \times 100\text{p} \qquad = £10.00$$

$$\text{Total} \qquad\qquad\qquad £14.00$$

$$\therefore\ 14.00 \div 15\,\text{kg} = 93\text{p per kg} = \text{weighted average price}$$

Preparing

This is an important stage of the control cycle. The cost of the food consumed depends on two factors:

1 the number of meals produced
2 the cost per meal.

In order to control food costs we must be able to:

- control the number to be catered for
- control the food cost per meal in advance of production and service by using a system of pre-costing, using standardised recipes, indicating portion control.

Sales and volume forecasting

This is a method of predicting the volume of sales for a future period. In order to be of practical value the forecast must:

- predict the total number of covers (customers)
- predict the choice of menu items.

Therefore it is important to:

- keep a record of the numbers of each dish sold from a menu
- work out the average spent per customer
- calculate the proportion, expressed as a percentage, of each dish sold in relation to total sales.

Forecasting is done in two stages.

1 **Initial forecasting**: this is done once a week in respect of each day of the following week. It is based on sales histories, information related to advance bookings and current trends, and when this has been completed, the predicted sales are converted into the food/ingredients requirements. Purchase orders are then prepared and sent to suppliers.
2 **The final forecast**: this normally takes place the day before the actual preparation and service of the food. It must take into account the latest developments, such as the weather and any food that needs to be used up; if necessary suppliers' orders may need to be adjusted.

Sales forecasting is not a perfect method of prediction, but it does help with production planning. Sales forecasting, however, is important when used in conjunction with cyclical menu planning.

Pre-costing of dishes

This method of costing is associated with standardised recipes, which give the total cost of the dish per portion and often with a selling price.

Summary of factors that will affect the profitability of the establishment

These include:

- overcooking food resulting in portion loss
- inefficient preparation of raw materials
- poor portion control
- too much wastage, insufficient use of raw materials; left-over food not being utilised (see HCIMA Technical Brief No. 9)
- theft
- inaccurate ordering procedures
- inadequate checking procedures
- no reference mark to standardised recipes and yield factors
- insufficient research into suppliers
- inaccurate forecasting
- bad menu planning.

Food labels

A great deal of information can be obtained from a food product by looking at the label. A number of regulations control what is permissible on a food product label:

- name of food
- list of ingredients
- conditions of use – special storage conditions
- indication of durability
- name and address of the manufacturer
- instructions for use, if necessary
- average weight of contents.

Further information
To find out more about food labelling, visit www.food.gov.uk/foodlabelling.

List of ingredients

If an ingredient is dehydrated or in a concentrated form, it may be positioned in the list according to its weight before dehydration (i.e. when fresh). Similarly, reconstituted foods may be listed after reconstitution.

Water and volatile products used as ingredients must be listed in order of their weight in the finished product. Mixtures of ingredients like nuts, vegetables and herbs can be put under the heading 'in variable proportions', provided no single one dominates.

Table 9.7 List of permitted titles for additives

Acid	Emulsifying salts	Preservation
Acidity regulator	Firming agent	Propellant gas
Anti-caking agent	Flavour enhancer	Raising agent
Anti-foaming agent	Flour treatment agent	Stabiliser
Antioxidant	Gelling agent	Sweetener
Bulking agent	Glazing agent	Thickener
Colour	Humectant	
Emulsifier	Modified starch	

Table 9.8 Indication of durability*

DATE TO BE DECLARED	PERIOD OF DURABILITY
'Best before' – day/month	Within 3 months
'Best before end' – month/year	3–18 months
'Best before end' – month/year or year	18 months-plus

Minimum durability is indicated by 'best before' followed by the date up to which the food remains in first-class condition if stored correctly; the 'use by' date should be indicated by 'use by' followed by the date – day/month or, for longer periods, day/month/year; details of necessary storage conditions must be given

Table 9.9 Nutritional labelling

This must be in tabular form – for example:*	
Per serving (x.g) and per 100g	
Energy	kJ and kcal
Protein	g
Carbohydrate of which Sugars	g
Polyols	g
Starch	g
Fats of which Saturates	g
Monounsaturates	g
Polyunsaturates	g
Cholesterol	mg
Fibre	g
Sodium	g
Vitamins*	Units as appropriate
Minerals	Units as appropriate

Names of each vitamin and mineral to be given, and relevant units (e.g. vitamin C ascorbic acid 60 mg)

The naming of ingredients is important (e.g. 'fish' can be used for any species, 'fat' for any refined fat, 'sugar' for any type of sucrose).

Flavouring is identified by the word 'flavouring', the word 'natural' may be added for naturally occurring products. Additives can be listed by either the principal function they serve, followed by the name or by their E-numbers (see Table 9.7).

Food labelling is strictly governed by law, and part of the role of the Food Standards Agency (FSA) is to prevent mislabelling or misdescription of foods.

Food authenticity is all about whether a food matches its description. If you, the buyer are being deceived, then this deceit can be passed on to your customers by inaccurate wording on menus and/or incorrect answers given to customers in reply to questions about ingredients in certain dishes.

Types of misdescription

- **Health and safety:** e.g. people with an intolerance or allergy to certain foods may suffer severe or life-threatening reactions.
- **Not having the necessary composition for a legal name:** e.g. if named 'chocolate' the food must contain a certain amount of cocoa solids; a sausage must contain a certain amount of meat.
- **Substitution with cheaper ingredients:** e.g. diluting olive oil with lower-quality vegetable oil.
- **Incorrect origin:** e.g. misdescribing the meat species in a product or not declaring any other meat present; giving an incorrect county or country of origin of a food or wine.
- **Incorrect declaration of quantity:** e.g. giving the wrong amount of meat in a burger.

STOREKEEPING

A clean, orderly food store, run efficiently, is essential in any catering establishment for the following reasons.

- Stocks of food can be kept at a suitable level, so eliminating the risk of running out of any commodity.
- All food entering and leaving the stores can be properly checked; this helps to prevent wastage.
- A check can be kept on the percentage profit of each department of the establishment. (This control may be assisted by computer application, see Chapter 17, page 675.)
  A well-planned store should include the following features.
- It should be cool and face the north so that it does not have the sun shining into it.
- It must be well ventilated, vermin-proof and free from dampness

(dampness in a dry store makes it musty, and encourages bacteria to grow and tins to rust).

- It should be in a convenient position to receive goods being delivered by suppliers and also in a suitable position to issue goods to the various departments.
- A wash hand basin, soaps, nail brush and hand drier must be provided for staff; also a first-aid box.
- A good standard of hygiene is essential, therefore the walls and ceilings should be free from cracks, and either painted or tiled so as to be cleaned easily. The floor should be free from cracks and easy to wash. The junction between the wall and floor should be rounded to prevent the accumulation of dirt. A cleaning rota should clearly show daily, monthly and weekly cleaning tasks.
- Shelves should be easy to clean.
- Good lighting, both natural and artificial, is very necessary.
- A counter should be provided to keep out unauthorised persons, thus reducing the risk of pilfering.
- The storekeeper should be provided with a suitable desk.
- There should be ample, well-arranged storage space, with shelves of varying depths and separate sections for each type of food. These sections may include deep-freeze cabinets, cold rooms, refrigerators, chill rooms, vegetable bins and container stores. Space should also be provided for empty containers.
- Efficient, easy-to-clean weighing machines for large- and small-scale work should be supplied.
- Stores staff must wear clean overalls at all times, and suitable shoes to help prevent injury if a heavy item is dropped on the feet.
- Steps to help staff reach goods on high shelves and an appropriate trolley should be provided.

Store containers

Foods delivered in flimsy bags or containers should be transferred to suitable store containers. These should be easy to wash and have tight-fitting lids. Glass or plastic containers are suitable for many foods, such as spices and herbs, as they have the advantage of being transparent; therefore it is easy to see at a glance how much of the commodity is in stock.

Bulk dry goods (pulses, sugar, salt, etc.) should be stored in suitable bins with tight-fitting lids. These bins should have wheels so that they can be moved easily for cleaning. All bins should be clearly labelled or numbered.

Sacks or cases of commodities should not be stored on the floor; they should be raised on duck boards so as to permit the free circulation of air.

Some goods are delivered in containers suitable for storage and these need not be transferred. Heavy cases and jars should be stored at a convenient height to prevent any strain in lifting.

Special storage points

- Always comply with 'best before' or 'use by' dates.
- All old stock should be brought forward with each new delivery.
- Commodities with strong smells or flavours should be stored as far away as possible from those foods that readily absorb flavour; strong-smelling cheese should not be stored near eggs, for example.
- Bread should be kept in a well-ventilated container with a lid. Lack of ventilation causes condensation and encourages mould. Cakes and biscuits should be stored in airtight tins.
- Stock must be inspected regularly, particularly cereals and cereal products, to check for signs of mice or weevils.
- Tinned goods should be unpacked, inspected and stacked on shelves. When inspecting tins, the following points should be checked for: blown tins – this is where the ends of the tins bulge owing to the

Table 9.10 Temperatures and storage times for freezers

SYMBOL	MAXIMUM TEMPERATURE	SAFETY STORAGE TIME
*	-6°C (21°F)	7 days
**	-12°C (10°F)	1 month
***	-18°C (0°F)	3 months
****	-18°C (0°F)	3 months-plus

Table 9.11 Storage temperatures for frozen items of foods

Meat	-20°C to	-16°C
Fish	-20°C to	-16°C
Frozen foods	-20°C to	-16°C
Ice cream	-22°C to	-18°C

Table 9.12 Storage temperatures of refrigerated food items*

*These are temperatures that must not be exceeded; lower temperatures down to 1°C (34°F) are preferable

Cooked pies, pasties, sausage rolls	7°C
Pies containing gelatine	5°C
Milk and cream	5°C
Eggs	4°C

Table **9.13** Refrigerated products in the right cabinet

TYPE	TEMPERATURE	PRODUCTS
Refrigerator	1–4°C (34–39°F)	Cooked meats (ham, pork, beef, lamb, etc.); cooked poultry and game (chicken, turkey, duck, etc.); dairy products (milk, butter, fats, eggs, cheese); prepared salads, sandwiches
Meat cabinet	-2–0°C (28–32°F)	Fresh lamb, beef, pork, chicken, turkey, duck, etc.
Fish cabinet	-2–0°C (28–32°F)	Fresh fish (cod, plaice, haddock, skate, etc.)
Freezer	-18– -20°C (0– -4°F)	Frozen meat; poultry; vegetables; prepared meals; ice cream, etc.

formation of gases either by bacteria growing on the food or by the food attacking the tinplate; all blown tins should be thrown away as the contents are dangerous and the use of the contents may cause food poisoning; dented tins – these should be used as soon as possible, not because the dent is an indication of inferior quality but because dented tins, if left, will rust and a rusty tin will eventually puncture; the storage life of tins varies considerably and depends mainly on how the contents attack the internal coating of the tin, which may corrode and lay bare the steel.

- Due to the use of fewer preserving additives, many bottled foods now need to be refrigerated once they are opened.
- Cleaning materials often have a strong smell; therefore they should be kept in a separate store. Cleaning powders should never be stored near food.

Storage accommodation

Foods are divided into three groups for the purpose of storage: perishable foods, dry foods and frozen foods.

- **Perishable foods** include meat, poultry, game, fish, dairy produce and fats, vegetables and fruit.
- **Dry foods** include cereals, pulses, sugar, flour, etc., bread and cakes, jams, pickles and other bottled foods and canned foods (cleaning materials can also be included in this section).
- **Frozen foods** must be placed immediately into a deep freeze at a temperature of -20°C.

Storage of perishable foods

Meat and poultry
- Meat joints should be hung on hooks over a drip tray to collect any blood.

- The temperature of refrigerators should be between $-1°C$ (30°F) and $1°C$ (34°F).
- The humidity level should be approximately 90 per cent.
- Meat and poultry should ideally be stored in separate places.
- Cuts of meat may be brushed with oil or wrapped in oiled greaseproof paper, wrapped in clingfilm or vacuum packed.
- Drip trays and other trays used for meat or poultry should be cleaned daily.
- Frozen meat and poultry must be stored at between $-18°C$ and $-20°C$.

Fish

- Store in ice in a fish refrigerator or fish drainer at between $-1°C$ (30°F) and $1°C$ (34°F).
- Keep different types of fish separated.
- Smoked fish should be kept separate from fresh fish.
- Frozen fish should be stored at $-18°C$.

Vegetables

- Ideally, have a cool, dry vegetable store with racks.
- As a safety precaution do not stack sacks too high.
- Leave potatoes in sacks.
- Place root vegetables on racks.
- Store green vegetables on racks.
- Store lettuce leaves as delivered in a cool environment.
- Remove any vegetables that show signs of decay.
- Leave onions and shallots in nets or racked.
- Place cauliflower and broccoli on racks.
- Leave courgettes, peppers, avocado pears and cucumbers in delivery containers.
- Leave mushrooms in containers.

Fruit

- Soft fruits should be left in punnets and placed in refrigeration.
- Hard fruits and stone fruits are stored in the cold store.
- Do not refrigerate bananas as they will turn black. If possible hang by the stems to slow down ripening.

Eggs

- Store refrigerated at $1-4°C$.
- Keep away from other foods; their shells are porous and they can absorb strong smells.
- Keep in their delivery boxes; handle as little as possible.
- Use in rotation.

Milk and cream

- Store in the refrigerator below $5°C$.
- Partially used containers should be covered.
- Use in rotation.

Cheese and butter

- Refrigerate at a temperature below 5°C.
- Cut cheeses should be wrapped.
- Use in rotation.

Bread, etc.

- Use in rotation: first in first out.
- Store in a well-ventilated cool store.
- Avoid overstocking.
- Take care that biscuits are stacked carefully to avoid breaking.
- Frozen gâteaux should be kept frozen.
- Cakes containing cream must be refrigerated.

Sandwiches

- All sandwiches must be sold within four to 24 hours of preparation.
- They must be stored at a maximum temperature of 8°C (46°F).
- Sandwiches to be sold within four hours are not covered by this legislation.

Storage of dry goods

- Storage must be cool, well lit and well ventilated.
- Storage should be off the floor or in bins.
- Issue goods in rotation: last in last out.
- Stack items so that stock rotation is simple to operate.
- Arrange items in such a way that they can easily be checked.

Storage of ice cream and frozen goods

- Store immediately on receipt.
- Storage temperature must be $-20°C$.
- Use in rotation.
- Keep chest lid closed as much as possible.

Cleanliness and safety of storage areas

High standards of hygiene are essential in the store.
- Personnel must:
  (a) wear clean clothing
  (b) be clean in themselves
  (c) be particular with regard to hand washing
  (d) have clean hygienic habits.
- Floors must:
  (a) be kept clear
  (b) be cleaned of any spillage at once
  (c) be in good repair.
- Shelving must:

(a) be kept clean
(b) not be overloaded.
- Cleaning materials must be:
(a) kept away from foods
(b) stored with care and marked dangerous if they are dangerous chemicals.
- Windows and, where appropriate, doors must be fly- and bird-proof.
- Walls should be clean and, where any access by rodents is possible, sealed.
- Equipment such as knives, scales, etc., must be:
(a) thoroughly cleaned
(b) stored so that cross-contamination is prevented.
- Cloths for cleaning should be of the disposable type.
- Surfaces should be cleaned with an antibacterial cleaner.
- All bins should have lids and be kept covered.
- All empties should be stacked in a safe area with care.
- Waste and rubbish should not be allowed to accumulate.
- Empty bottles, waste paper, cardboard and so on should be recycled.

The cold room

A large catering establishment may have a cold room for meat, with possibly a deep-freeze compartment where supplies can be kept frozen for long periods. The best temperature for storing fresh meat and poultry (short term) is between 4° and 6°C (39–43°F) with controlled humidity (poultry is stored in a cold room). Fish should have a cold room of its own so that it does not affect other foods. Game, when plucked, is also kept in a cold room.

The chill room

A chill room keeps food cold without freezing, and is particularly suitable for those foods requiring a consistent, not too cold, temperature, such as dessert fruits, salads and cheese. Fresh fruit, salads and vegetables are best stored at a temperature of 4–6°C (39–43°F) with a humidity that will not result in loss of water from the leaves, causing them to go limp. Green vegetables should be stored in a dark area to prevent the leaves turning yellow. Certain fruits, such as peaches and avocados, are best stored at 10°C (50°F), while bananas must not be stored below 13°C (55°F) otherwise they will turn black. Dairy products (milk, cream, yoghurt and butter) are best stored at 2°C (35°F). Cheese requires differing storage temperatures according to the type of cheese and its degree of ripeness. Fats and oils are best stored at 4–7°C (39–45°F) otherwise they are liable to go rancid.

Refrigeration

Because spoilage and food-poisoning organisms multiply most rapidly in warm conditions, there is a need for refrigeration through every stage of food delivery, storage, preparation, service and, in certain situations, onward distribution. Refrigeration does not kill micro-organisms but prevents them multiplying. Many cases of food poisoning can be tracked back to failure to control food temperatures or failure to cool food properly.

Temperature control is so important that statutory measures have been extended by the Food Hygiene Regulations whereby all food must be stored at or below 8°C (46°F) and some foods at lower temperatures. Chilling at 0°–3°C (32–37°F) and freezing at −18° to −22°C (0° to 27.6°F) is the easiest and most natural way of preserving food and maintaining product quality because it:

- cuts down on wastage (reducing operating costs)
- allows a wider variety of food to be stacked
- gives flexibility in delivering, preparation and use of foods.

To maintain the quality and freshness of food, refrigeration at correct temperatures must be provided:

- at delivery
- for onward distribution
- for storage
- for preparation
- for holding, display and service.

Types of refrigeration

- Mise-en-place – these are smaller refrigerators placed near to or under specific working areas. Some types have bain-marie-style containers that allow for the storage of the many small prepared food items required in a busy à la carte kitchen.
- Separate cabinets are essential for such foods as pastry, meat and fish, and cold buffets where food is displayed for more than four hours.
- Quick chillers – as the slow cooling of cooked food can allow rapid bacterial growth, rapid chillers are available.
- Display cabinets incorporating forced circulation of chilled air.

Temperature checks

In addition to the legal requirements for food to be stored at the correct temperature, the maintenance of correct temperature display should be specified on each cabinet and should be monitored regularly, with the use of probes, thermometers, etc. Temperatures and recommended storage times are listed on page 420.

Points to note on refrigeration

- All refrigerators, cold rooms, chill rooms and deep-freeze units should be inspected and maintained regularly by qualified refrigeration engineers.

- Defrosting should take place regularly, according to the instructions issued by the manufacturers. Refrigerators usually need to be defrosted weekly; if this is not done, then the efficiency of the refrigerator is reduced.
- While a cold unit is being defrosted it should be thoroughly cleaned, including all the shelves.
- Hot foods should never be placed in a refrigerator or cold room because the steam given off can affect nearby foods.
- Peeled onions should never be kept in a cold room because their smell can taint other foods.

Vegetable store

This should be designed to store all vegetables in a cool, dry, well-ventilated room, with bins for root vegetables and racking for others. Care should be taken to see that old stocks of vegetables are used before new ones; this is important as fresh vegetables and fruits deteriorate quickly. If it is not convenient to empty root vegetables into bins they should be kept in the sack on racks off the ground.

Ordering of goods within the establishment

In a large catering establishment the stores carry a stock that, for variety and quantity, often equates to a large grocery store. Its operation is similar in many respects, the main difference being that requisitions take the place of cash. The system of internal and external accountancy must be simple but precise.

The storekeeper

The essentials that go to making a good storekeeper are:

- experience
- knowledge of how to handle, care for and organise the stock in his or her charge
- a tidy mind and sense of detail
- a quick grasp of figures
- possibly computer literate
- clear handwriting
- a liking for his or her job
- honesty.

There are many departments that draw supplies from these stores – kitchen, still room, restaurant, grill room, banqueting, floor service. A list of these departments should be given to the storekeeper, together with the signatures of the heads of departments or those who have the right to sign the requisition forms.

All requisitions must be handed to the storekeeper in time to allow the ordering and delivery of the goods on the appropriate day. Different-coloured requisitions may be used for the various departments if desired.

Duties of a storekeeper

- To keep a good standard of tidiness and cleanliness.
- To arrange proper storage space for all incoming foodstuffs.
- To keep up-to-date price lists of all commodities.
- To ensure that an ample supply of all important foodstuffs is always available.
- To check that all orders are correctly made out, and dispatched in good time.
- To check all incoming stores – quantity, quality and price.
- To keep all delivery notes, invoices, credit notes, receipts and statements efficiently filed.
- To keep a daily stores issue sheet.
- To keep a set of bin cards.
- To issue nothing without receiving a signed chit in exchange.
- To check all stock at frequent intervals.
- To see that all chargeable containers are properly kept, returned and credited – that is, all money charged for sacks, boxes, and so on, is deducted from the account.
- To obtain the best value at the lowest buying price.
- To know when foods are in or out of season.

Types of records used in stores control

Bin card

There should be an individual bin card for each item held in stock. The following details are found on the bin card:
- name of the commodity
- issuing unit
- date goods are received or issued
- from whom they are received and to whom issued
- maximum stock
- minimum stock
- quantity received
- quantity issued
- balance held in stock.

In large catering operations, the traditional bin number system has been computerised. Beverages are managed through the Fidelio Food and Beverage system. This is a fully integrated system with the following key features.

- Stock control – pricing, recipe function for cocktails, stock-take store values, variances are automated.
- Breakdowns are per outlet.

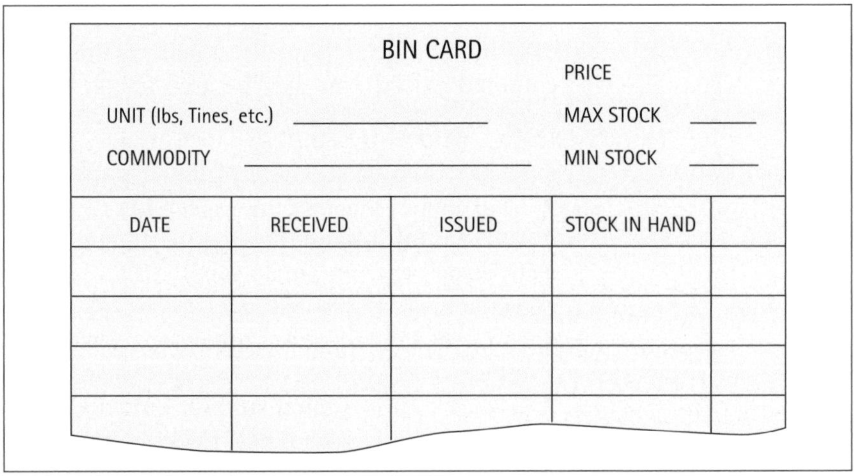

Figure 9.3 Example of a bin card

BIN CARD				PRICE	
UNIT (lbs, Tines, etc.) _____				MAX STOCK _____	
COMMODITY _____				MIN STOCK _____	
DATE	RECEIVED		ISSUED	STOCK IN HAND	

- Generates purchase orders.
- Interfaced with point of sale system (e.g. MICROS 8700, Fidelio Front Office for charging and Fidelio F&B for consumption).
- Invoice management – receiving and invoice control, invoice control is interfaced with a system (e.g. Oracle) for financial reporting.

Fidelio is one of the mainstay operating systems that is the backbone of all F&B control systems currently in use.

Stores ledger

This is usually found in the form of a loose-leaf file giving one ledger sheet to each item held in stock. The following details are found on a stores ledger sheet:

- name of commodity
- classification
- unit
- maximum stock
- minimum stock
- date of goods received or issued
- from whom they are received and to whom issued
- invoice or requisition number
- quantity received or issued and the remaining balance held in stock
- unit price
- cash value of goods received and issued, and the balancing cash total of goods held in stock.

Every time goods are received or issued the appropriate entries should be made on the necessary stores ledger sheets and bin cards. In this way the balance on the bin card should always be the same as the balance shown on the stores ledger sheet.

Example of an operation

Stores Ledger/Departmental Requisitions

- Process – Outlets do a Fidelio requisition according to the outlet par stock and forecasted two-day expected levels of trading.
- Cellarman/stores supervisor allocates the request; this entails filling orders from stock, and managing par stock levels in accordance with outgoing requisition.
- Order requests are transferred to purchase orders and communicated to supplier for delivery.
- To minimise stock-holding values, and efficiently utilise space within the property, daily deliveries have been negotiated with main suppliers.
- One supplier is usually identified from whom it is compulsory for the entire estate to purchase 99 per cent of *all* beverages.
- Monthly stock-take and variance reports are produced.
- Value of the stock for recording on the balance sheet is automatically calculated.

Figure 9.4 Example of a daily stores issue sheet

Commodity	Unit	Stock in hand	Monday In	Monday Out	Tuesday In	Tuesday Out	Wednesday In	Wednesday Out	Thursday In	Thursday Out	Friday In	Friday Out	Total purchases	Total issues	Total stock
Butter	kg	27		2						3				5	22
Flour	Sack	2		1			1					1		1	2
Olive oil	Litres	8		1						$1/2$				$1^1/2$	$6^1/2$
Spices	30g packs	8		4			6						6	4	12
Peas, tin	A10	30		6						3				9	21

_____ CANTEEN Week ending _____ No. meals served _____ Cost per meal _____

Commodity	Hand B/F	Stock received during week M	Tu	W	Th	F	Total	Stock used during week M	Tu	W	Th	F	S	Total	@*	Cost	In hand C/F
Apples, canned																	
Apples, dried Apricots, etc. – dried																	
Baking powder																	
Baked beans																	

* The cost of stock used can be checked by using two extra columns

Figure 9.5 Example of a stores ledger sheet

BIN No   DESCRIPTION   CLASSIFICATION   CODE UNIT MAXIMUM MINIMUM

Date	DETAIL	Invoice or Req. No.	QUANTITY Recvd	Balance	Issued	UNIT PRICE	VALUE Received	Balance	Issued

Figure 9.6 Example of a stores requisition sheet

DEPARTMENTAL REQUISITON BOOK									267	

Date _____   Class _____

Description	Quan.	Unit	Price per Unit	Issued if different	Quan.	Unit	Price per Unit	Code	£	

Departmental requisition book

One of these books should be issued to each department in the catering establishment that needs to draw goods from the store. These books can either be of different colours or have departmental serial numbers. Every time goods are drawn from the store a requisition must be filled out and signed by the necessary head of department – this applies whether one or 20 items are needed from the store. When the storekeeper issues the goods he or she will check them against the requisition and tick them off; at the same time the cost of each item is filled in. In this way the total expenditure over a period for a certain department can quickly be found. The following details are found on the requisition sheet:

- serial number
- issue number, if different
- name of department
- quantity of goods issued
- date
- unit
- description of goods required
- price per unit
- quantity of goods required
- cash column
- unit
- signature
- price per unit.

Order book

This is in duplicate and has to be filled in by the storekeeper every time he or she wishes to have goods delivered. Whenever goods are ordered, an order sheet must be filled in and sent to the supplier, and on receipt of the goods they should be checked against both delivery note and duplicate order sheet. All order sheets must be signed by the storekeeper. Details found on an order sheet are as follows:

- name and address of catering establishment

- description of goods to be ordered
- name and address of supplier
- date
- serial number of order sheet
- signature
- quantity of goods
- date of delivery, if specific day required.

Stock sheets

Stock should be taken at regular intervals of either one week or one month. Spot checks are advisable about every three months. The stock check should be taken where possible by an independent person, thus preventing the chance of pilfering and 'fiddling' taking place. The details found on the stock sheets are as follows:

- description of goods
- price per unit
- quantity received and issued, and balance
- cash columns.

The stock sheets will normally be printed in alphabetical order.

All fresh foodstuffs, such as meat, fish and vegetables, will be entered on the stock sheet in the normal manner, but as they are purchased and used up daily, nil stock will always be shown on their respective ledger sheets.

Commercial documents

Essential parts of the control system of any catering establishment are delivery notes, invoices, credit notes and statements.

Delivery notes

These are sent with goods supplied as a means of checking that everything ordered has been delivered. The delivery note should also be checked against the duplicate order sheet.

Invoices

These are bills sent to clients, setting out the cost of goods supplied or services rendered. An invoice should be sent on the day the goods are despatched or the services are rendered or as soon as possible afterwards. At least one copy of each invoice is made and used for posting up the books of accounts, stock records, and so on (see Figure 9.7).

Invoices contain the following information:

- name, address, telephone numbers (as a printed heading), fax numbers, of the firm supplying the goods or services
- name and address of the firm to whom the goods or services have been supplied

- the word 'invoice'
- date on which the goods or services were supplied
- particulars of the goods or services supplied, together with the prices
- a note concerning the terms of settlement, such as 'Terms: 5% per month', which means that if the person receiving the invoice settles his or her account within one month he or she may deduct 5 per cent as a discount.

Credit notes

These are advice to clients, setting out allowances made for goods returned, or adjustments made through errors of overcharging on invoices. They should also be issued when chargeable containers such as crates, boxes or sacks are returned. Credit notes are exactly the same in form as invoices except that the words 'credit note' appear in place of the word 'invoice'. To make them more easily distinguishable they are usually printed in red, whereas invoices are always printed in black. A credit note should be sent as soon as it is known that a client is entitled to the credit of a sum with which he or she has previously been charged by invoice.

Statements

These are summaries of all invoices and credit notes sent to clients during the previous accounting period (usually one month). They also show any sums owing or paid from previous accounting periods and the total amount due. A statement is usually a copy of a client's ledger account and does not contain more information than is necessary to check invoices and credit notes.

Cash discount

This is a discount allowed in consideration of prompt payment. At the end of any length of time chosen as an accounting period (such as one month) there will be some outstanding debts. In order to encourage customers to pay within a stipulated time, sellers of goods frequently offer a discount. This is called cash discount. By offering cash discount, the seller may induce his or her customer to pay more quickly, so turning debts into ready money. Cash discount varies from 1.25 to 10 per cent, depending on the seller and the time: 2.5 per cent if paid in 10 days; 1.25 per cent if paid in 28 days, for example.

Trade discount

This is discount allowed by one trader to another, a deduction from the catalogue price of goods made before arriving at the invoice price. The amount of trade discount does not therefore appear in the accounts. For example, in a catalogue of kitchen equipment, a machine listed at £250 less 20 per cent trade discount shows:

Figure 9.7 Example of an invoice and statement

```
┌─────────────────────────────────────────────────────────────┐
│  ┌───────────────────────────────────────────────────────┐  │
│  │ INVOICE                                                 │  │
│  ├───────────────────────────────────────────────────────┤  │
│  │ Phone: 0208 574 1133              No. 03957            │  │
│  │ Fax: 0208 574 1123          Vegetable Suppliers Ltd.,  │  │
│  │ Email: greend@veg.sup.ac.uk         D. Green           │  │
│  │ Website: http//www.greend.com    5 Warwick Road,       │  │
│  │ Messrs. L. Moriarty & Co.,          Southall,          │  │
│  │ 597 High Street,                    Middlesex          │  │
│  │ Ealing,                                                 │  │
│  │ London, W5                       Terms: 5% One month   │  │
│  ├───────────────────────────────────────────────────────┤  │
│  │ Your order No. 67 Dated 3rd September, 19...       £    │  │
│  ├───────────────────────────────────────────────────────┤  │
│  │ Sept 26th     10 kg Potatoes bag 6.00          6.00    │  │
│  │               5 kg Sprouts, net 8.00           2.10    │  │
│  │                                               14.00    │  │
│  └───────────────────────────────────────────────────────┘  │
│                                                               │
│  ┌───────────────────────────────────────────────────────┐  │
│  │ STATEMENT                                               │  │
│  ├───────────────────────────────────────────────────────┤  │
│  │ Phone: 0208 574 1133        Vegetable Suppliers Ltd.,  │  │
│  │ Fax: 0208 574 1123                  D. Green           │  │
│  │ Email: greend@veg.sup.ac.uk      5 Warwick Road,       │  │
│  │ Website: http//www.greend.com       Southall,          │  │
│  │ Messrs. L. Moriarty & Co.,          Middlesex          │  │
│  │ 597 High Street,                                        │  │
│  │ Ealing,                          Terms: 5% One month   │  │
│  │ London, W5                                              │  │
│  ├───────────────────────────────────────────────────────┤  │
│  │ 19...                                             £     │  │
│  │ Sept 10th     Goods                          45.90     │  │
│  │      17th     Goods                          32.41     │  │
│  │      20th     Goods                          41.30     │  │
│  │      26th     Goods                          16.15     │  │
│  │                                             135.76     │  │
│  │      28th     Returns credited                4.80     │  │
│  │                                             130.96     │  │
│  └───────────────────────────────────────────────────────┘  │
└─────────────────────────────────────────────────────────────┘
```

- catalogue price – £250
- less 20 per cent trade discount – £50
- invoice price – £200.

£200 is the amount entered in the appropriate accounts.

In the case of purchase tax on articles, discount is taken off after the tax has been deducted from list price.

Gross price is the price of an article before discount has been deducted.

Net price is the price after discount has been deducted; in some cases a price on which no discount will be allowed.

Table 9.14 Cash account

DR.	FIRST WEEK					CR.
DATE	RECEIPTS	£	DATE	PAYMENT		£
Oct 3	to lunches	400	Oct 1	by repairs		80
4	" teas	100	2	" grocer		100
5	" tax rebate	60	6	" butcher		120
				" balance c/fwd		260

DR.	SECOND WEEK					CR.
DATE	RECEIPTS	£	DATE	RECEIPTS		£
Oct	to balance b/fwd	260	Oct 8	by fishmonger		50
9	" sale of pastries	100	10	" fuel		50
11	" goods	200	11	" tax		40
			12	" balance c/fwd		360
		560				560

DR.	THIRD WEEK					CR.
DATE	RECEIPTS	£	DATE	RECEIPTS		£
Oct	To balance b/fwd	360	Oct 19	By butcher		80
15	" teas	120	21	" grocer		60
17	" pastries	110		" balance c/fwd		650
24	" goods	60				
26	" goods	80				
29	" goods	60				
		790				790

Cash account

The following are the essentials for the keeping of a simple cash account:

- all entries must be dated
- all monies received must be clearly named and entered on the left-hand or debit side of the book
- all monies paid out must also be clearly shown and entered on the right-hand or credit side of the book
- at the end of a given period – either a day, week or month or at the end of each page – the book must be balanced – that is, both sides are totalled and the difference between the two is known as the balance; if, for example, the debit side (money received) is greater than the credit side (money paid out), then a credit or right-hand side balance is shown, so that the two totals are then equal; a credit balance then means cash in hand
- a debit balance cannot occur because it is impossible to pay out more than is received.

An example is given in Table 9.14.

Example

Make out a cash account and enter the following transactions:

Oct.	1	Paid for repair to stove	£109.00
	2	Paid to grocer	200.00
	3	Received for lunches	750.00
	4	Received for teas	200.00
	5	Received tax rebate	97.84
	6	Paid to butcher	120.00
Oct.	8	paid to fishmonger	72.60
	9	Received for sale of pastries	112.90
	10	Paid for fuel	80.00
	11	Paid tax	60.00
	11	Received for goods	500.00
	12	Paid to greengrocer	112.36
Oct.	15	Received for teas	150.20
	17	Received for pastries	150.00
	19	Paid to butcher	100.80
	21	Paid to grocer	95.00
	24	Received for goods	130.00
	26	Received for goods	150.00
	29	Received for goods	140.00

General rule
- Debit – monies coming in.
- Credit – monies going out.

Statement

Received monthly, and verified by cost control, who will ensure all invoices have been accounted.

Copy of invoices and credit notes are requested from the supplier.

Cash accounting

At hotel unit level, this is not applicable unless the hotel is privately owned – in which case, a cash flow reconciliation will be used similar to the example illustrated in table 9.14.

Example as used in a large hotel

Invoice statements

- Delivery notes received and checked in loading bay against delivery and purchase order – delivery note input into Fidelio on the basis of the purchase order, discrepancies are identified to supplier and purchasing.
- Delivery note and purchase order are transferred to Food and Beverages Accounts Payable, invoice will follow.
- Invoice checked against delivery note and purchase order, discrepancies will be corrected in Fidelio, outstanding credit notes will be requested from supplier.
- Invoice control – invoice details entered to Fidelio, this closes the purchasing and delivery process.
- Information is interfaced with Oracle for recording and payment.
- Oracle will automatically pay in line with pre-agreed payment terms, regardless of input date of data.
- On completion of input, statement is considered paid even though cheque or bank transfer may not have been expedited.
- From date of input statement recorded as a cost of sale on our ledger for the month.

Some references to storage and control elsewhere in the book:

Safety	578
Each commodity	75
Costing	675
Waste	655
Hygiene	614
Computers	671
Pricing	365
Management control	520
People control	530

TOPICS FOR DISCUSSION

Food purchasing

1 A food-buying policy.
2 Is there a need for portion control?
3 The relationship between food quality and price.
4 The reasons for using standard purchasing specifications.
5 The use of standardised recipes.
6 How you would implement a cost control system.
7 The advantages of a computerised stock-keeping system.
8 How the role of the storekeeper may change in the future.

Storage and control

1 Why control of goods from receipt (delivery) to final destination (the customer) is essential.
2 What controls are needed regarding goods, staff and the preparation and service of food?
3 The need to be knowledgeable regarding the cost and quality of foods in relation to selling price.
4 The implication of setting the selling price too low, and also of setting it too high.
5 How do you consider a fair profit percentage is arrived at? Specify the establishment you have in mind.
6 What do you understand to be a 'suitable portion'? Give examples and explain your reasoning.

Chapter 10 AN OVERVIEW OF FOOD AND BEVERAGE SERVICE

WHAT IS FOOD AND BEVERAGE SERVICE?

Food and beverage service is the essential link between the menu, beverages and other services on offer in an establishment, and the customers. People working in food and beverage service are the main point of contact between customers and an establishment. It is an important role in a noble profession, with increasing national and international status. Skills and knowledge, and therefore careers, are transferable between establishments, sectors and throughout the world.

For a particular food and beverage (or food service) operation the choices of how the food and beverage service is designed, planned, undertaken and controlled are made taking into account a number of organisational variables. These include:

- customer needs
- level of customer demand
- the type and style of the food and beverage operation
- the nature of the customers (non-captive, captive or semi-captive)
- prices to be charged
- production process
- volume of demand
- volume of throughput
- space available
- availability of staff
- opening hours
- booking requirements
- payment requirements
- legal requirements.

Food and beverage service was traditionally seen as a delivery system, where only the requirements of the operation itself would determine how the service was designed, planned and controlled. More recently, however, this view has changed significantly. The customer is now seen as being central to the process and also an active participant within it. It is now also recognised that food and beverage service actually consists of two separate systems, which are operating at the same time. These are:

1 the service sequence – which is concerned with the delivery of the food and beverages to the customer (see below)
2 the customer process – which is concerned with the experience the customer undertakes (see page 442)

The service sequence

The service sequence is essentially the bridge between the production system, the beverage provision and the customer process (or experience). The service sequence consists of a number of stages, which can be summarised as:

- preparation for service
- taking food and beverage orders
- the service of food and beverages
- billing
- clearing
- dishwashing
- clearing following service.

Within these elements, there are a variety of alternative ways of achieving the service sequence.

Preparation for service

Within the service areas, there are a variety of tasks and duties that need to be carried out in order to ensure that adequate preparation has been made for the expected volume of business and the type of service that is to be provided. These activities include:

- taking and checking bookings
- checking and ensuring the cleanliness of glassware, crockery, flatware and cutlery
- dealing with linen and paper items
- undertaking housekeeping duties
- arranging and laying up the service areas
- stocking hotplates, workstations, display buffets
- setting up bars and bar areas
- arranging and laying up lounge areas
- briefing staff to ensure that they have adequate knowledge of the product and the service requirements.

Taking food and beverage orders

Taking orders from customers for the food and beverages they wish to have, takes time. The order-taking process is part of a longer process, which feeds information to the food production or bar areas, and provides information for the billing method.

Whatever type of system is used – whether manual or electronic – it will be based on one of the following three basic order-taking methods.

1 **Duplicate:** order taken and copied to supply point; copy retained by server for service and subsequent billing.

2 **Triplicate:** order taken and copied to supply point and cashier for billing, third copy retained by server for service.
3 **Service with order:** taking order and serving to order, as used in, for example, bar service or takeaway methods.

For more on computerised systems, see Chapter 17.

Within the order-taking procedure there are many opportunities for exploiting the potential for personal selling that can be carried out by service staff. Personal selling refers specifically to the ability of the staff in a food and beverage operation to contribute to the promotion of sales. This is especially important where specific promotions are being undertaken. Service staff must therefore be trained in selling and also be well briefed on special offers (see the section on the customer process, on page 442).

The service of food and beverages

The choice of service method will depend as much on the customer service specification (see page 448) as on the capability of the staff, the capacity of the operation and the equipment available. Differing service methods will also determine the speed of service and the time the customer takes to consume the meal, which in turn will have an impact on the throughput of customers.

Good food and beverage service is achieved where management continually reinforces and supports service staff in the maintenance of good standards of achievement. Additionally, the provision and maintenance of good service is primarily dependent on teamwork, not only among service staff but also among and between staff in other departments.

Billing

The various billing methods found in food service operations are as follows.

- **Bill as check:** second copy of order used as bill.
- **Separate bill:** bill made up from duplicate check and presented to customer.
- **Bill with order:** service to order and billing at same time, e.g. bar or takeaway methods.
- **Prepaid:** customer purchases ticket or card in advance, either for a specific meal or to a specific value.
- **Voucher:** customer has credit issued by third party, e.g. luncheon voucher or tourist agency voucher for either a specific meal or to a specific value.
- **No charge:** customer not paying.
- **Deferred:** refers to, for example, function-type catering where bill paid by organiser.

The actual choice of billing method will be dependent on the type and style of the operation. However, the billing system is also part of a longer process linked, first, to the order-taking method and, second, to the revenue control procedures.

Clearing

The various clearing methods found in food service operations may be summarised as follows.

- **Manual 1:** the collection and taking of soiled ware by waiting staff to dishwash area.
- **Manual 2:** the collection and sorting to trolleys by operators for transportation to dishwash area.
- **Semi-self-clear:** the placing of soiled ware by customers on strategically placed trolleys within dining area for removal by operators.
- **Self-clear:** the placing of soiled ware by customers on conveyor or conveyorised tray-collecting system for mechanical transportation to dishwash area.
- **Self-clear and strip:** the placing of soiled ware into conveyorised dishwash baskets by customer for direct entry of baskets to the dishwashing machine.

The choice of clearing method, whether manual by staff or involving customers, will be dependent not only on the type of operation but also on the nature of the demand being met.

Dishwashing

The capacity of the dishwashing system should always be greater than the operational maximum required. This is because slow dishwashing increases the amount of equipment required to be in use at a particular time, and increases the storage space required in service areas.

The various dishwashing systems are as follows.

- **Manual:** the manual washing by hand or brush machine of soiled ware.
- **Semi-automatic:** the manual loading by operators of a dishwashing machine.
- **Automatic conveyor:** the manual loading by operators of soiled ware within baskets mounted on conveyor for automatic transportation through a dishwashing machine.
- **Flight conveyor:** the manual loading by operators of soiled ware within pegs mounted on conveyor for automatic transportation through dishwasher.
- **Deferred wash:** the collection, stripping, sorting and stacking of ware by operators for dishwashing at a later stage.

Essentially, the potential volume that can be accommodated increases, as well as potential efficiency, from the manual method to the flight conveyor method, and the choice of method will be largely dependent on the scale of the operation. It is also often necessary to employ more than one method.

Further information
Further information can be obtained from www.business.com/directory/food-and-beverages/restaurants-and-foodservice/equipment-and-supplies/dishwashers or www.powersourcing.com/se/dishwashingequipment.htm

For hygienic washing-up, the generally recognised requirements are a good supply of hot water at a temperature of 60°C (140°F) for general cleansing, followed by a sterilising rinse at a temperature of 82°C (180°F) for at least one minute. Alternatively, low-temperature equipment is available that sterilises by means of a chemical, sodium hypochlorite (bleach).

Dishwashing machines take over an arduous job and save a lot of time and labour, ensuring that a good supply of clean, sterilised cutlery, crockery and glassware is available.

There are three main types of dishwasher.

1 **Spray type machines:** the dishes are placed in racks that slide into the machines, where they are subjected to a spray of hot detergent water at 48–60°C (118–140°F) from above and below. The racks then move on to the next section, where they are rinsed by a fresh hot shower at 82°C (180°F). At this temperature they are sterilised, and on passing out into the air they dry off quickly.
2 **Brush-type machines:** revolving brushes are used for the scrubbing of each article in hot detergent water; the articles are then rinsed and sterilised in another compartment.
3 **Agitator water machines:** baskets of dishes are immersed in deep tanks and the cleaning is performed by the mechanical agitation of the hot detergent water. The loaded baskets are then given a sterilising rinse in another compartment.

Dishwashing machines are costly and it is essential that the manufacturer's instructions with regard to use and maintenance are followed at all times.

Clearing following service

After the service periods, there are a variety of tasks and duties to be carried out, partly to clear from the previous service and partly to prepare for the next. The efficient management of the clearing stage can have a dramatic impact on the potential reuse of an area.

Included in this stage of the service sequence is the requirement for the management of cleaning programmes. Detailed cleaning schedules need to be developed to ensure that all cleaning activities are coordinated. These can be daily, weekly, monthly and for other periods. Alongside

Figure 10.1 Feeding people at work

these cleaning schedules, it is desirable to incorporate maintenance checks. These, together with the operation of cleaning schedules, can help to ensure that equipment and facilities are always available and in working order.

The customer process

The customer receiving the food and beverage product is required to undertake or observe certain requirements – this is the customer process. If food and beverage service is viewed only as a delivery process, then the systems and procedures of an establishment tend to be designed only from the delivery perspective. However, for food and beverage service to work well, the customer has to be seen as being central to the process.

In food and beverage operations there are five basic processes that customers undertake.

1 **Table service:** service at a laid cover. This type of service, which includes waiter service and bar counter service, is found in restaurants, cafés and in banqueting.
2 **Assisted service:** part service at a laid cover and part self-service. The customer is served part of the meal at a table and is required to obtain part through self-service from some form of display or buffet. This type of service is found in carvery-type operations and is often used for meals such as breakfast in hotels.
3 **Self-service:** self-service by the customer. The customer is required to help him or herself from a buffet or counter. This type of service can be found in cafeterias and canteens.
4 **Service at a single point:** the customer orders, pays and receives the food and beverages at a single point, for example at a counter, at a bar in licensed premises, in a fast-food operation or at a vending machine.
5 **Specialised service or service in situ:** the food and beverages are taken to where the customer is. This includes tray service in hospitals and aircraft, trolley service, home delivery, lounge and room service.

In the first four of these customer processes, the customer comes to where the food and beverage service is offered, and then the service is provided in areas primarily designed for the purpose. However, in the fifth customer process the service is provided in another location, and where the area is not primarily designed for the purpose.

A summary of the five customer processes is shown in Table 10.1, and a full listing of all food and beverage service methods is given on pages 443–445.

Figure 10.2 Salad bar

Table **10.1** Summary of the five food and beverage service customer processes

SERVICE METHOD	SERVICE AREA	ORDERING/ SELECTION	SERVICE	DINING/ CONSUMPTION	CLEARING
Table service	Customer enters and is seated	From menu	By staff to customer	At laid cover	By staff
Assisted service	Customer enters and is usually seated	From menu, buffet or passed trays	Combination of both staff and customers	Usually at laid cover	By staff
Self-service	Customer enters	Customer selects items onto tray	Customer carries	Dining area or takeaway	By staff or customers
Single-point service	Customer enters	Orders at a single point	Customer carries	Dining area or takeaway	By staff or customers
Specialised or in situ service	Where the customer is – in situ	From menu or predetermined	Brought to customer – in situ	Where served – in situ	By staff or customers

Source: Lillicrap and Cousins, 2006

Figure **10.3** Gastropub dining

FOOD AND BEVERAGE SERVICE METHODS

(This section is adapted from Lillicrap and Cousins, 2006.)
There are 15 different service methods found in the hospitality industry; these fall into the five customer process groups identified above.

- **Table service:** This is service of food and beverages to a customer at a laid cover.
- **Waiter service:**
  - **Silver/English service:** presentations and service of food to a customer by waiting staff from a food flat or dish.
  - **Family service:** main courses plated and with vegetables, placed in multi-portion dishes on tables for customers to help themselves. Any sauces are usually offered.
  - **Plated/American service:** service of pre-plated foods to customers, now widely used in many establishments and in banqueting.
  - **Butler/French service:** presentation of food individually to customers by food service staff for customers to serve themselves.
  - **Russian service:** table laid with food for customers to help themselves. (This is a modern interpretation, but may also be used to indicate Guéridon or butler service.)
  - **Guéridon service:** food served onto the customer's plate at a side table or from a trolley. May also include the preparation of salads and dressings, carving, cooking and flambé dishes,
- **Bar counter service:** Service to customers seated at a bar counter (usually U-shaped) on stools.

Figure 10.4 Fine dining

- **Assisted service:** This is a combination of table service and self-service. Commonly applied to carvery-type operations; some parts of the meal are served to seated customers, the customers collect other parts. Also used for breakfast service.
- **Buffet:** Customers select food and drink from displays or passed trays; consumption is either at tables, standing or in lounge area.
- **Self-service:** Customers serve themselves.
- **Cafeteria service:**
  - **Counter:** customers line up in a queue at a service counter and choose the menu items they require at different points. The customer places her/his items on a tray. Some establishments use a 'carousel' – a revolving stacked counter – saving space.
  - **Free flow:** selection as in a counter service. Customers move at will to random service point exiting via a payment point.
  - **Echelon:** this is a series of counters at angles to customer flow within a free-flow area, thus saving space.
  - **Supermarket:** island service points within a free-flow area.
    Note: call order cooking may also feature in some cafeterias.
- **Single-point service:** This is the service of customers at a single point where they consume on the premises or they take away.

Figure 10.5 Informal dining (brasserie)

Figure 10.6 School meals service

Figure 10.7 Fast-food service

- **Takeaway:** Customer orders are served from a single point, usually at a counter, hatch or snack stand; customer normally consumes the food off the premises although some takeaway establishments provide limited seating. This service method is commonly used for fast-food operations and also includes drive-thrus (see below), where the customer drives a vehicle past order, payment and collection points.
- **Vending:** The automatic retailing of food and beverage products.
- **Kiosks:** Service provided by outstations during peak demand in specific locations.
- **Food court:** A group of autonomous counters where customers may either order and eat, or buy from a number of counters and take away or eat in a central eating area.
- **Bar:** A selling point for the consumption of intoxicating liquor in licensed premises.
- **Specialised (or in situ) service:** Service to customers where they are located and in areas not primarily designed for service.
- **Tray service:** Service of a meal or part of a meal in a tray to the customer in situ, e.g. in hospitals or on an aircraft.

Figure 10.8 Hospital catering

- **Trolley:** Service of food and beverages from a trolley away from dining areas to customers – for instance, at their seats or desks. Used, for example, on aircraft and trains, and in offices.
- **Home delivery:** Food and beverages delivered to a customer's home or place of work (e.g. pizza delivery, meals on wheels or sandwiches to offices).
- **Lounge service:** Service of food and beverages in a lounge area (e.g. a hotel lounge).
- **Room service:** Service of food and beverages in hotel guest rooms, or in meeting rooms.
- **Drive-thru:** Customers are served food and beverages to their vehicles.
  (Note: Banquet/function catering is a term used to describe food and beverage operations that are providing service for a specific number of people at specific times in a variety of dining layouts. Service methods also vary. The term banquet/function catering therefore refers to the organisation of service rather than a specific service method.)

Figure 10.9 Outdoor
catering service

Figure 10.10 Restaurant

FOOD AND BEVERAGE SERVICE STAFF

In food and beverage establishments today, there are many different ways
of using and deploying staff. Also differing terminology is used to
describe what people do.

For food and beverage service staff the four key requirements are:

1 sound product knowledge
2 competence in technical skills
3 well-developed social skills, and
4 the ability to work as part of a team.

While there have been changes in food and beverage service, with less
emphasis on the high-level technical skills in some sectors, these four key
requirements remain for all staff. However, the emphasis on these key
requirements varies according to the type of establishment and the
particular service methods being used.

Food and beverage staff play an important role in the customer's
overall meal experience. As well as being trained in knowledge of the
product and technical service skills, service staff must be trained in
customer service skills. They must have the ability to respond to
customer needs and to observe the overall dynamics of a restaurant.
Good food and beverage staff should, through experience, be able to
anticipate the individual needs of customers and be able to read their
body language. Customers want individual attention; good service
professionals will be able to anticipate the individual needs of the
customer.

In food and beverage service most of the basic service skills required
are transferable to any type of operation. For example, carrying plates,
trays, glasses and cutlery, carving skills and beverage service skills are
broadly similar wherever they are carried out. The variation is in the
application of these skills, which is usually governed by the requirement
of the particular establishment.

Roles in food and beverage service

There are many types of job role within food and beverage service. We will now take a look at some of these.

- **Food and beverage manager:** Depending on the size of the establishment, the food and beverage manager is either responsible for the implementation of agreed policies or for contributing to the setting of catering policies. The larger the organisation the less likely the manager is to be involved in policy setting. In general, food and beverage managers are responsible for the following areas.
    - Ensuring that the required profit margins are achieved for each food and beverage service area, in each financial period.
    - Updating and compiling new wine lists according to availability of stock, current trends and customer needs.
    - Compiling, in liaison with the kitchen, menus for the various food service areas and for special occasions.
    - The purchasing of all materials, both food and beverages.
    - Ensuring that quality in relation to the price paid is maintained.
    - Determining portion size in relation to selling price.
    - Departmental training and promotions, plus the maintenance of the highest professional standards.
    - Employing and dismissing staff.
    - Holding regular meetings with section heads to ensure all areas are working effectively, efficiently and are well coordinated.
- **Restaurant manager/supervisor:** This person has overall responsibility for the organisation and administration of particular food and beverage service areas, and is also responsible for staff training duty rotas, and the maintaining of an efficient and smooth service.
- **Head waiter/maître d'hôtel/supervisor:** This person has overall charge of the staff team and is responsible for seeing that all the duties necessary for the service are carried out efficiently.
- **Station head waiter/section supervisor:** The station head waiter has

Figure 10.11 Serving wine

Figure 10.12 Bar

overall responsibility for a team of staff serving a number of sets of tables – which could be anything from four to eight in number – from one sideboard. Each set of tables under the station head waiter's control is called a station.

- **Station waiter/chef de rang:** The station waiter caries out the full range of service duties within a specific station. There may also be an assistant station waiter.
- **Waiter/server/commis de rang/busboys/busgirls:** Work under the direction of the station waiter. During the pre-preparation period, cleaning and preparatory tasks will be carried out by the commis de rang, and during the service the commis mainly fetches and carries.
- **Trainee/commis debarrasseur/apprentice:** The debarrasseur is the 'learner', having just joined the food service staff, and possibly wishing to take up food service as a career.
- **Floor service staff/chef d'étage/floor waiter:** Responsible for the service of food and beverages on the floor of a hotel.
- **Lounge staff/chef de salle:** Responsible for the service of a range of foods and beverages within the lounge areas.

- **Wine butler/wine waiter/sommelier:** Responsible for the service of all alcoholic drinks during the service of meals. This person must have a detailed knowledge of wine and be able to 'sell' it to customers.
- **Bar staff:** Responsible for the service of all alcoholic and non-alcoholic beverages.
- **Cashier:** Responsible for billing and taking payments, or making ledger account entries for a food and beverage operation.
- **Counter assistants:** Responsible, for stocking counters and serving or portioning food for customers.
- **Table clearers:** Responsible for clearing tables in seating areas where the service is not waiter service.
- **Function catering/banqueting staff:** These are staff at a variety of levels that are responsible for the organisation, administration and preparation, and service of functions. Banqueting service staff are often employed on a casual basis.

CUSTOMER SERVICE SPECIFICATION

Increasing competition within the industry has meant that the quality of the service, and the perceived value of the experience by the customers, have become the main differentiators between operations that are seeking to attract similar customers. Consequently, understanding the customer's involvement in the process, and identifying the experience they are likely to have and should expect, have become critical to the business success of food service operations.

Like the food, beverage and other product specifications, there must also be a customer service specification. For food and beverage operations the customer service specification is focused as much on identifying the procedures that need to be followed as they are on the way they are carried out. This is because food and beverage is more than a delivery system – it also requires customers to be assisted in following various procedures, such as being seated at a table, and also aims to facilitate positive interaction between staff and customers.

However, a customer service specification cannot be achieved if it does not take account of both the infrastructure supporting the specification as well as the ability to implement standards within the interactive phase. A customer service specification can be defined that takes account of a combination of the following five key characteristics.

1 **Service level:** the method of service and the extent of the individual personal attention that is given to customers.
2 **Availability of service:** e.g. the opening times, the variation in the menus, and wine and drinks lists on offer.
3 **Level of standards:** e.g. food quality, decor, equipment cost, staffing professionalism.
4 **Reliability of the service:** the extent to which the product is intended to be consistent in practice.
5 **Flexibility of the service:** the provision of alternatives, or variations in the standard product on offer.

In designing a food service operation to meet a customer service specification, care is taken to ensure the profitability of the operation by considering the efficiency of the use of resources. The following resources are used in food service operations.

- **Materials:** commodities and equipment.
- **Labour:** staffing and staff costs.
- **Facilities:** the premises and the volume of business that the premises are physically able to support.

The management of the operation must therefore take account of the effect that the level of business has on the ability of the operation to maintain the service while, at the same time, ensuring high productivity in all the resources being used.

The operation must be physically capable of supporting the customer service specification, otherwise limitations in the physical capabilities of the operation to meet the requirements of the customer service specification will always be the cause of difficulties. In addition, staff must be capable of supporting the intended customer service specification. This takes account of the technical and interpersonal skills, product knowledge and teamworking capabilities of the staff.

As well as interaction with customers, service staff also interact with staff outside of the service areas (e.g. kitchen staff, bill office staff, dispense bar staff, stillroom staff). It is important that the provision of the food and beverage product within an establishment is seen as a joint effort between all departments, with each understanding the needs of the others in order to meet customers' demands.

In order to minimise problems with customer relations, there has to be equal concern over the physical aspects of the service, the way in which the service is operated, and with the interpersonal interaction between customers and staff. Knowing what the potential for customer satisfaction is from the food and beverage product can help to ensure that there are procedures in place for dealing with any difficulties that might arise. The potential for satisfaction should already have been built in to the design of the product so that it meets the needs the customers have at the time. There is also the potential, however, for dissatisfaction. Potential dissatisfactions fall into two categories: those that are controllable by the establishment – such as scruffy, unhelpful staff, or cramped conditions – and those that are uncontrollable – such as behaviour of other customers, the weather or transport problems. Being able to identify all such possibilities provides an operation with the potential to have procedures in place to deal with them when they occur.

RESTAURANT PLANNING

When planning a restaurant there is a need to focus on the market it is aiming to attract, its customers, the theme the restaurant will take, and the type of food and service it is going to offer. In any establishment a customer's first impressions, on entering the service area, are of great importance. A customer may be gained or lost on these impressions alone. The creation of atmosphere, by the right choice of decor, furnishings and equipment, is therefore a major factor that contributes to the success of the food service operation. A careful selection of items in terms of shape, design and colour enhances the overall decor or theme, and contributes towards a feeling of total harmony. The choice of layout, furniture, the linen, tableware, small equipment and glassware will be determined by considering:

- the type of clientele expected
- the site or location
- the layout of the food and beverage service area
- the type of service offered
- the funds available.

There are many service areas behind the scenes – or what may be termed 'back of house'. These areas are usually between the kitchen and food and beverage service areas. They are important parts of the design of a food service operation, acting as the link between kitchen or food preparation areas and the restaurant or food and beverage service areas. These areas are also meeting points for staff of various departments as they carry out their duties, and therefore there must be close liaison between these various members of staff and between the departments to ensure the smooth running of the operation.

Figure 10.13 Restaurant receptionist

In general, especially in large operations, five main back-of-house service areas can be identified.

1 Stillroom (the area directly between the food production area and the food service area, where food and beverage items are prepared for the service of meals that are not catered for by the other major departments in a food service operation, such as the kitchen, larder and pastry).
2 Silver or plate room (for the storage of all metal service equipment).
3 Wash-up (usually adjacent to the stillroom area).
4 Hotplate (often called the pass, where orders are given in and collected from the food production area by service staff).
5 Spare linen store (used for paper and linen).

A well-designed layout of all these areas is important to ensure an even flow of work by the various members of staff. However, the layout itself may vary with different establishments, depending on the type of operational needs.

The general considerations for the planning of the back-of-house service areas are:

- appropriate siting, with logical layout of equipment
- ease of delivery access
- ease of service
- ensuring hygiene, health and safety requirements are met
- ease of cleaning
- sufficient storage space for service equipment and food items
- security.

The front-of-house areas are used by both customers and staff, and include:

- foodservice area(s)
- reception – the place for taking bookings, receiving customers and processing the bills
- licensed bar
- coffee lounge

Table **10.2** Examples of space allocation in different types of food and beverage service area

Restaurant and hotel dining areas (note: space allocation includes sideboards, aisles, etc.)	
Style	Space per cover (m²)
Traditional restaurant	1
Banqueting	0.9
High-class restaurants	2
(Note: for safety reasons all aisles should be 1 metre wide)	

Cafeteria – square metres per meal served/hour			
Meals	Up to 200	200–500	500+
M²	0.45–0.70	0.35–0.45	0.25–0.35

Fast-food outlets – The average overall size of most fast food outlets is currently around 1000–1500 m²

Source: adapted from Cousins et al., 2004

- customer cloakroom facilities.

The general considerations for the planning of the areas used by both customers and staff include, first, the general considerations for staff-only back-of-house areas as above, and then taking into account the consideration of:

- decor and lighting
- heating and ventilation
- noise level
- the size and shape of the areas.

In most food service operations the back-of-house and front-of-house areas are quite separate so that customers cannot see into the back-of-house areas, especially the kitchen. More recently, however, food service operations have begun to make a feature of the cooking area, which is on full view to the customer and contributes to the customer's meal experience. In this case the kitchen is a central feature with some of the cooking smells and noise going into the food service area.

Space

The amount of space required per customer depends on the type of standard expected from the style and theme of the operation. Consideration has to be given to comfort versus the maximum number of customers you are trying to fit in to the restaurant. The more 'upmarket' the restaurant, the more comfortable and spacious it should be. Examples of the space allocation for different type of food and beverage service areas are given in Table 10.2.

Table 10.3 Matching wine/drinks and foods: some general considerations

Acidity	Can be used to match, or to contrast, acidity in foods, e.g. crisp wines to match lemon or tomato, or to cut through creamy flavours.
Age	As wine ages and matures it can become delicate, with complex and intricate flavours. Stronger-tasting foods can overpower older wines. More simple foods, such as grills or roasts, tend to match better.
Oak	Heavily oaked wines can overpower more delicate foods. The more oaked the wine, the more robust and flavoursome the foods need to be.
Sweetness/dryness	Generally the wine/drinks should be sweeter than the foods or the wines/drinks will taste flat or thin. Sweet dishes need contrast for them to match well with sweeter wines (e.g. acids in sweeter foods can harmonise with the sweetness in the wines/drinks). Savoury foods with sweetness (e.g. carrots or onions) can match well with ripe, fruity wines. Blue cheeses can go well with sweet wines. Also sweeter wines can go well with salty foods.
Tannin	Tannic wines match well with red meats and semi-hard cheeses (e.g. Cheddar). Tannic wines are not good with egg dishes, and wines with high tannin content do not work well with salty foods.
Weight/body	Big, rich wines and beers go well with robust (flavoursome) meat dishes, but can overpower lighter-flavoured foods.

Table 10.4 Some possible food and wine/drink combinations

Apéritifs	The apéritif is meant to stimulate the appetite and therefore should preferably be dry. If wine will be consumed with the meal, then the apéritif selected should be a 'grape' (wine-based) rather than a 'grain' (spirit-based) apéritif, since the latter can spoil or dull the palate. Dry and medium wines and fortified wines such as dry sherries, dry vermouths and Sercial or Verdelho Madeira are all good examples of apéritifs.
Hors d'oeuvre	Sometimes combinations can be difficult because of overpowering dressings on salad items. However, Fino or Manzanilla Sherry, Sancerre, Pinot Grigio, Sauvignon Blanc or Gewürztraminer can be tried. Sometimes, depending on the dishes, the lighter reds may make a good combination with the foods. Also beers that might be considered include smoked beers and Japanese beers.
Soups	Various wines, depending on the ingredients of the soup. Also sherry or dry port or Madeira could be tried, as could traditional English ales. Consommés and lobster or crab bisque can be enhanced by adding a glass of heated sherry or Madeira before serving.
Terrines, pâtés and foie gras	Beaujolais or a light, young, red wine, rosé wines, white wines from Pinot Gris or Sauvignon Blanc grapes and also some sweet white wines, especially Sauternes or demi-sec Champagne for foie gras. Fruit beers and English porters might also be tried.
Omelettes and quiches	Difficult for wine, but an Alsatian Riesling or sylvaner could be tried, as could white beers.
Farinaceous dishes (pasta and rice)	Classically Italian red wines such as Valpolicella, Chianti, Barolo, Santa Maddalena or Lago di Caldaro. Also most lagers or IPA (India pale ale).
Fish	
Oysters, shellfish and sushi	Dry white wines: Champagne, Chablis, Muscadet, Soave and Frascati; also white (wheat) beers, Guinness or other stouts.
Smoked fish	White Rioja, German whites, white Graves, Verdicchio; smoked beers and Japanese beers
Fish dishes with sauces	Fuller white wines such as Vouvray, Montrachet or Yugoslav Riesling, rosé wines and lighter red wines; white beers.
Shallow-fried or grilled fish	Vinho Verde, Moselle, Californian Chardonnay, Australian Sémillon or Chardonnay; most lagers or IPA (India pale ale) and English porter, especially with scallops.
White meats	The type of wine/drink to serve is dependent on whether the white meat (chicken, turkey, rabbit, veal or pork) is served hot or cold.
Served hot with a sauce or savoury stuffing	Either a rosé such as Anjou, or light reds like Beaujolais, New Zealand Pinot Noir, Californian Zinfandel, Saint-Julien, Bourg and Burgundy (e.g. Passe-tout-grains) and Corbières; white beers.
Served cold	Fuller white wines such as Hocks, Gran Viña Sol, Sancerre and the rosés of Provence and Tavel; white beers.
Other meats	
Duck and goose	Big red wines that will cut through the fat, Châteauneuf-du-Pape, Hermitage, Barolo and the Australian Cabernet Shiraz; also most beers.
Roast and grilled lamb	Medoc, Saint-Emilion, Pomerol and any of the Cabernet Sauvignons; also most beers.
Roast beef and grilled steaks	Big red Burgundies, Rioja, Barolo, Dão and wines made from the Pinot Noir grape; most beers and especially flavoured beers (e.g. heather or honeydew).

Table 10.4 continued

Meat stews	Lighter reds, Zinfandel, Côtes du Rhône, Clos du Bois, Bull's Blood, Vino Nobile di Montepulciano; Belgian Abbey-style and Trappist beers, flavoured beers (e.g. heather or honeydew), darker beers.
Hare, venison and game	Reds with distinctive flavour, Côte Rôtie, Bourgeuil, Rioja, Chianti, Australian Shiraz, Californian Cabernet Sauvignon, Chilean Cabernet Sauvignon, and also fine red Burgundies and Bordeaux reds; Belgian Abbey-style and Trappist beers.
Oriental foods, Peking duck, mild curry, tandoori chicken, shish kebab	Gewürztraminer, German and Lutomer Riesling, Vinho Verde, Mateus rosé or Anjou rosé. Also most lagers and IPA (India pale ale).
Cheese	The wine from the main course is often followed through to the cheese course, although it is also worth considering the type of cheese being served.
Light, cream cheeses	Full-bodied whites, rosés and light reds; beers generally.
Strong, pungent (even smelly) and blue-veined varieties	Big reds of Bordeaux and Burgundy, or tawny, vintage or vintage-style ports and also the luscious sweet white wines, or beers generally, especially fruit beers.
Sweets and puddings	Champagne works well with sweets and puddings. Others to try are the luscious Muscats (de Beaumes-de-Venise, de Setúbal, de Frontignan, Samos), Sainte-Croix-du-Mont, Sauternes, Banyuls, Monbazillac, Tokay, wines made from late-gathered individual grapes in Germany, and also the orange muscats and speciality drinks such as Vin de Frais (fermentation of fresh strawberries), both of which can go well with chocolate. Fruit beers (which can also be especially good with chocolate), porters and Belgian-style strong golden ales can all pair well with various sweets and puddings.
Dessert (fresh fruit and nuts)	Sweet fortified wines, sherry, port, Madeira, Málaga, Marsala, Commandaria; also white beers.
Coffee	Cognac and other brandies; good aged malt whiskies; calvados, sundry liqueurs and ports; Champagne; white beers.

Source: adapted from Lillicrap and Cousins, 2006

LICENSING AND ALCOHOL

Matching food to wine/drinks

The enjoyment of food together with wine or other drinks is very much a matter of personal taste. Today there is a quite relaxed attitude: people have broken away from the very rigid approach to the marriage of food and wine/drinks. People tend to drink what they like, when they like, and tend to be much more open and honest about their wine preferences. Customers should not feel intimidated by wine waiters when they order unconventional food and wine/drink matches.

When matching foods to wines/drinks the overall the intention is to provide those that harmonise well together, each enhancing the other's performance. The combinations that prove most successful are those that please the individual. When considering possible food and wine partnerships, there are no guidelines to which there are not exceptions. However, there are some general considerations that can be taken into account when matching wine/drinks and foods (see Table 10.4).

Beers can also be offered with food, either alongside or as an alternative to wines. As with wines it is a question of trial and error to achieve harmony between particular beers and foods. Generally the considerations for the pairing of beers and foods are similar to those for matching wines with foods, and in particular taking account of acidity, sweetness/dryness, bitterness, tannin, weight and the complexity of the taste.

An overview of licensing

Under the Licensing Act 2003, a single integrated system has been introduced throughout England and Wales to regulate the sale and supply of alcohol, the provision of entertainment to the public and the provision of late-night refreshment.

Under the act there is a statutory requirement that all retail sales of alcohol must be made or authorised by a personal licence holder. In addition, all premises licensed for the sale of alcohol must have a designated premises supervisor appointed for those premises. This designated premises supervisor must be a personal licence holder.

For a business to carry out any of the following activities, a licence is required:

- the retail sale of alcohol
- supplying alcohol in club premises
- provision of regulated entertainment
- late-night refreshment.

There are two types of licence, each of which is described below.

Personal licence
A personal licence is granted to an individual and authorises that individual to sell alcohol in accordance with the terms of the premises licence relating to the place where the alcohol is being sold.

A personal licence allows a person to sell alcohol or authorise the sale of alcohol. Any sales, or authorisation of the sale of alcohol, made by a personal licence holder must be made in accordance with the terms of the premises licence relating to the premises at which the sale is taking place.

A personal licence lasts for a period of ten years. To apply for a personal licence a person must:

- be 18 years of age or above
- possess an accredited licensing qualification
- not have forfeited a personal licence in the preceding five-year period
- not have any unspent convictions for any relevant offences in England

or Wales, or for any foreign offences (these offences include theft, violence, drugs, firearms-related and drink-driving).

Premises licence

A premises licence can be granted in respect of any premises, and authorises those premises to be used for one or more of the licensable activities.

The term 'premises' can be applied to:

- any building, part of a building or open space
- moveable structures such as a beer tent, a parked vehicle such as a burger van, or vessels such as riverboats.

An application for a premises licence application may be made by:

- an individual, who must be aged 18 or over
- a company, which carries on a business involving the use of these premises for licensable activities.

In many cases, there may be more than one person entitled to apply for a premises licence. For example, the applicant could be the person actually carrying out the business, such as a pub tenant or off-licence manager, or the company that owns the property.

In the case of supermarkets, it would be the company who would apply for and hold the premises licence and not the manager of the supermarket. For smaller, owner-managed retail shops, the premises licence holder could be either the business owner or the landlord who owns the property in which the business is situated.

Internet and mail-order sales

Where sales are made over the internet, by telephone or by email order, it is not considered that they are made from the call centre or over the internet, but from the premises from which the alcohol is dispatched. Therefore, a call centre taking orders does not require a premises licence and no personal licence holder needs to be present when orders are taken. The warehouse that dispatches alcohol to customers requires both a premises licence and a designated premises supervisor.

Mandatory conditions on a premises licence

Where a premises licence authorises the supply of alcohol, the licence always includes the following two conditions.

1 No supply of alcohol can be made unless there is a designated premises supervisor appointed in respect of the premises. The designated premises supervisor must hold a current personal licence.
2 Every supply of alcohol under the premises licence must be made or authorised by a person who holds a personal licence. This means that if an individual is not a personal licence holder, that person can only sell alcohol in licensed premises if permission to do so has been given by a personal licence holder.

The role of the designated premises supervisor
Where the premises licence authorises the supply of alcohol as one of the licensable activities the premises licence holder must nominate a designated premises supervisor. This person is responsible for the day-to-day running of the premises and is the personal licence holder.

There may well be a number of personal licence holders working at premises but there can be only one designated premises supervisor at any one time. It is not possible to have more than one designated premises supervisor for any one premises.

The personal licence holder responsible for supplying alcohol or authorising the supply of alcohol by others does not have to be the designated premises supervisor.

A premises selling alcohol, which does not have a designated premises supervisor is in breach of licensing law. Any sales from such premises would constitute unauthorised licensable activity.

There is nothing to prevent the premises licence holder from also being the designated premises supervisor for those premises.

Sale and supply of alcohol to children
The sale and consumption of alcohol is rigorously controlled by law in the case of persons under the age of 18. It is the positive duty of licence holders and anyone who works in licensed premises not to sell alcohol to a person aged under 18 years of age. There is one exception, however: a 16 or 17 year old is allowed to drink beer, wine or cider with a table meal provided that an adult purchases the drink. An adult must accompany the 16 or 17 year old at the table meal.

Children on licensed premises
The law contains no general prohibition on the admission of children. The licence holder must decide whether allowing children into the premises would be appropriate for the nature and style of the business concerned.

It is an offence to allow children under the age of 16, who are not accompanied by an adult, to be present in premises:

- used exclusively or primarily for the sale of alcohol for consumption on those premises when they are open
- between midnight and 5 am
- when open and where the premises are licensed for the sale of alcohol for consumption on the premises.

The law does not prevent the admission of unaccompanied children under 16 to certain restaurants or casinos where the consumption of alcohol is secondary to activities such as dining, provided that unaccompanied children are not present after midnight. Children who are accompanied by an adult may, however, be present after midnight.

No offence is committed if the unaccompanied child is in the premises solely for the purpose of going to or coming from another place, to or from which there is no other convenient route.

It is an offence to sell alcohol to someone aged under 18 under any circumstances, regardless of where the alcohol is sold.

It is an offence for anyone under the age of 18 to purchase or attempt to purchase alcohol, or for someone over the age of 18 to purchase or attempt to purchase alcohol on behalf of someone under 18.

Licensing authorities

Under the terms of the Licensing Act 2003, the responsibility for all forms of alcohol and entertainment licensing in each geographical area in England and Wales lies with the licensing authority responsible for that particular area. A licensing authority can be any one of the following bodies:

- a District Council in England
- a County Council in England, where there are no separate districts within the county
- a County Council or County Borough in Wales
- the council of each London Borough
- the Common Council of the City of London
- the Council of the Isles of Scilly.

Licensing objectives

The governing principles of licensing law in England and Wales are called the licensing objectives. These are:

- the prevention of crime and disorder
- public safety
- the prevention of public nuisance
- the protection of children from harm.

Offences under the Licensing Act 2003

There are a number of offences under the Act, including:

- exposing alcohol for unauthorised sale
- keeping alcohol on sale for unauthorised sale
- allowing disorderly conduct on licensed premises
- sale of alcohol to a person who is drunk
- obtaining alcohol for a person who is drunk
- failure to leave licensed premises
- keeping of smuggled goods.

The nature of alcohol and how it affects the body

Alcohol is classed as a drug because, when consumed, it alters the physical, mental and emotional state of the drinker.

Where the alcohol by volume (abv) is over 0.5 per cent, the drink is classed as alcohol for the purpose of licensing law.

Strength of alcoholic drinks

The strength of an intoxicating drink depends on how much alcohol it contains. The amount of alcohol contained is expressed as percentage alcohol by volume: 'abv' for short. The formula for expressing abv on labels is: alc. % vol or % vol. So a fortified wine, such as sherry or vermouth, labelled as alc. 18% vol means that 18 per cent of any given quantity is pure alcohol.

Examples
- Whisky labelled as alc 40% vol or 40% vol means 40 per cent of any given quantity is pure alcohol. Most spirits are around 40 per cent abv.
- Wines labelled as alc 12% vol or 12% vol means that 12 per cent of any given quantity is pure alcohol. Wines vary from 8 per cent to 16 per cent abv.
- Beer labelled as alc 3.2% vol or 3.2% vol means that 3.2 per cent of any quantity is pure alcohol. Beers range from 3 per cent to 9 per cent abv. Ciders range from 3 per cent to 8.5 per cent abv.

Alcohol-free and low-alcohol drinks

To be classified as alcohol-free, a drink must contain no more than 0.05 per cent abv. To be classified as low alcohol, no more than 1.2 per cent abv. Both must be labelled accordingly.

Units of alcohol

A unit is 8 grams (g) or 10 millilitres (ml) of alcohol. Any quantity of drink that contains 8 g or 10 ml of alcohol is said to contain one unit. Half a pint of beer of 3.6 per cent abv contains about 8 g of alcohol, hence one unit. One 25 ml measure of whisky of 40 per cent abv also contains 8 g of alcohol; therefore in alcohol intake terms, half a pint of

Table 10.5 Summary of the strengths of alcoholic drinks

Not more than 0.05 per cent abv	Alcohol free; no premises or personal licence is required for sale or supply
Above 0.5 per cent abv	Legally defined as alcohol
Not more than 1.2 per cent abv	Low alcohol
More than 1.2 per cent abv	abv must be shown on the label or displayed at point of sale
1 unit of alcohol	8 g or 10 ml of alcohol

beer 3.6 per cent abv 8 g of alcohol is equivalent to one measure of whisky.

Recommended safe limits of alcohol

Moderate drinking can be beneficial to health; excessive drinking can be detrimental to health.

Recommended safe limits of alcohol, as recommended by the government and other organisations such as the Portman Group are as follows:

- men should drink no more than three to four units a day and no more than 21 units per week
- women should drink no more than two to three units a day and no more than 14 units per week.

Alcohol in the body

When drunk, alcohol is absorbed into the blood and reaches all parts of the body. Most of the alcohol is absorbed rapidly into the bloodstream. Nearly all the alcohol has to be burnt up by the liver and the rest is disposed of either in sweat or urine. A person becomes drunk because he/she drinks alcohol faster than his/her body can eliminate it, to a point where it affects the body. The amount of alcohol in the bloodstream is measured by the blood alcohol concentration (BAC). BAC varies according to a person's sex, weight, body composition and speed of drinking.

BAC is measured in milligrams (mg) of alcohol in millilitres of blood. A BAC of 80 mg of alcohol in 100 ml of blood is the level above which it is an offence to drive. This measurement has an equivalent in terms of micrograms in ml of breath (35 micrograms in 100 ml of breath). This can be measured using a breathalyser.

The amount of alcohol that gets into the bloodstream and the speed with which it does, depends on the following factors.

- **Quantity:** how many drinks a person consumes and how strong the drinks are.
- **The size of a person:** the amount of alcohol will produce a higher BAC in women than men.

Figure 10.14
Recommended weekly units

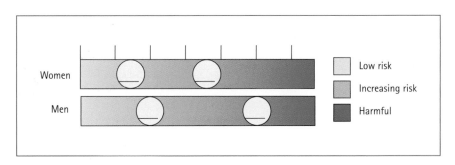

Figure 10.15 Popular drinks
and their units

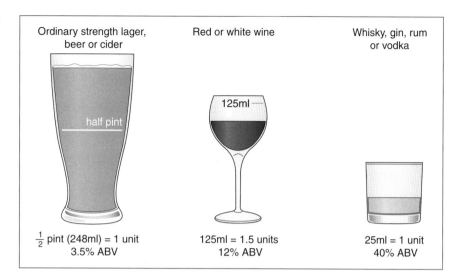

Ordinary strength lager,
beer or cider

Red or white wine

Whisky, gin, rum
or vodka

125ml

half pint

$\frac{1}{2}$ pint (248ml) = 1 unit
3.5% ABV

125ml = 1.5 units
12% ABV

25ml = 1 unit
40% ABV

Further information
Detailed information on
all aspects of food and
beverage service can be
found in Lillicrap and
Cousins (2006).

- **Food eaten:** the presence of food in the stomach slows down the rate at which alcohol enters the bloodstream.

Usually about 20 minutes after the last drink, BAC starts to fall. Some alcohol is lost through the lungs, some in the urine but most is removed by the liver as the blood circulates through it.

As a rough guide, it takes one hour to remove one unit of alcohol from the body.

What is a sensible limit?

Keep to the recommended sensible limits if you want to avoid damaging your health. As noted above, the recommended sensible limit is up to 21 units for men and up to 14 units a week for women, with one or two drink-free days (see Figure 10.15). Remember, there are times when even one or two drinks can be too much – for example, if you are going to drive or operate machinery. It can be dangerous to drink alcohol if you are taking certain types of medicine.

REFERENCES

Cousins, J., Foskett, D. and Gillespie, C. (2004) *Food and Beverage Management* (2nd edn). Pearson Education.

Lillicrap, D.R. and Cousins, J. (2006) *Food and Beverage Service* (7th edn). Hodder & Stoughton.

TOPICS FOR DISCUSSION

1   Discuss the relationship between the kitchen staff and waiting staff. Explain how good relations may be developed.
2   Discuss the merits of six different methods of service and the kind of establishment for which they would be suitable.
3   Why should food service staff be knowledgeable about the food dishes they will serve?
4   Why should the kitchen staff appreciate the role of the waiting staff?
5   Explain your reasons for what you consider to be a suitable selection for a wine/drinks list. State the kind of establishment you have in mind.
6   Discuss the following statement: 'Every chef should serve as a waiter and every waiter work as chef for a period of time.'
7   What is your opinion of the kitchen being on view to customers? What do you think is the opinion of customers?

Chapter 11 CHEMISTRY IN THE KITCHEN, AND PRODUCT DEVELOPMENT

UNDERSTANDING BASIC CHEMISTRY

Modern-day chefs are encouraged to be creative, to use their flair and imagination to create interesting and appetising dishes. An understanding of the basic chemistry of food products will help chefs in their work to produce dishes that are practically feasible. A knowledge of how ingredients perform under different conditions is also valuable in development work.

PH AND WATER

(See also page 229.)
Pure water has a pH of 7.0. Water is seldom pure, however. Rain water and distilled water sometimes contain dissolved materials. All water contains dissolved gases from the air. Distilled water has enough dissolved carbon dioxide to make it distinctly acidic. The pH of distilled water is approximately 5.5 and that of rainwater can be even lower when it washes certain industrial pollutants out of the atmosphere. This is known as acid rain.

Dissolved gases contribute to the flavour of water. The nature of water often affects the food we cook in it. For example, hard water causes difficulties when cooking pulses since magnesium and calcium interfere with tenderising these foods. Likewise an acidic cooking medium will stop dried beans from absorbing water and softening properly.

Not only is water a component of all foods, it also contributes significantly to the physical differences among foods and to the changes that foods undergo.

PROTEINS

Proteins are an important part of many foods and ingredients that a chef uses. Amino acids are the structural units of proteins. There are some 20 different amino acids found in proteins. The nature of the protein is determined both by the proportions of each amino acid and by the order in which they are arranged. A typical protein may contain 500 amino acids; this means that there can be much variation between different types of protein.

Proteins are most complex substances. For example, glucose has a simple molecular weight of 180 daltons (a dalton is a measurement of relative molecular mass, devised by John Dalton in 1808), whereas a simple amino acid such as lactoglobulin has a molecular weight of 4200. Some proteins have a molecular weight of several million.

The structure of an amino acid can affect its chemical properties. The general structure is shown in Figure 11.1.

Figure 11.1 The basic structure of an amino acid

| AMINO GROUP
(NH_2)
reacts with acid | R represents residual
part of molecule

H   R   O
\   \| //
N— C — C
/   \| \
H   H   OH | CARBONYL GROUP
(COOH)
reactions with alkali |

The majority of amino acids have only one carbonyl and amino group. They are termed neutral. If more than one amino group is present the amino acid is called basic. If more than one carbonyl group is present it is called acidic. Development chefs do not need to know about the proportion or order of the amino acids in a protein. What they should be concerned with is the shape of the protein, and how this shape can be changed.

The amino acids are held together in their long chains by what are called 'strong bonds'; these are very hard to break. To split up the proteins into amino acids requires conditions such as heating in the presence of a strong acid or by certain enzymes. The procedures in the kitchen are unlikely to break these strong bonds. Cooking has a much greater effect on what is known as secondary structure. Since proteins are long chains, they can double back on themselves to form loops. These loops are held in place by 'weak bonds' to give a secondary structure.

Protein shapes

When developing new products it is advisable to understand the shape of the protein molecule. Many of the cooking processes used by chefs will break the weak bonds and thus change the shape of the molecule. The effect of changing the shape of the protein molecule may be useful, but in some cases it may be undesirable. There are two main protein shapes: fibrous and globular.

Fibrous proteins

Fibrous proteins are insoluble, resistant to acids and alkali, and unaffected by moderate heating. They maintain their strand-like shape. They are often coiled like springs, and can be elastic or stretchy. Sometimes two or more strands are twisted together and held together by weak bonding. Fibrous proteins are generally very tough and are found in animal tissue.

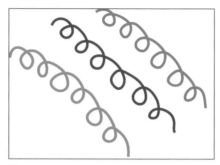

Figure 11.2 Fibrous protein

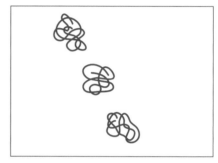

Figure 11.3 Globular protein

Globular proteins

These are usually water soluble and affected by acid and alkali. They are shaped like tiny balls with weak bonding. These proteins are not usually part of the structure of the plant or animal, but tend to be functional proteins such as enzymes or storage proteins.

Functional proteins

Proteins are made from a varying number of amino acids that are chemically different and capable of interacting and cross-linking. This can be made use of in foods for a number of functional reasons. Basic (alkaline) proteins can be used in combination with an acidic protein. At the pH of the food the basic protein will have an overall negative charge on its molecule and the acidic protein will be positive. This means the protein chains will be strongly attractive and will readily cross-link. This protein combination will be useful as a foaming agent in foods. A typical foam is produced by whipping egg white. But this foam quickly collapses if there is any fat in contact with it. These functional protein combinations are so strong that they resist the effect of fat and can be whipped up with fat in a formulation such as a creamy dessert.

Denaturing protein

It is important to understand what happens to protein when it is cooked, mixed with other ingredients or treated by different methods, such as whipping. The protein is denatured during cooking. Proteins are denatured when their properties are completely altered; the bonds that hold the protein are broken and replaced by other weak bonds not normally present, and a new shape is formed. Solubility is decreased, visibility increased; it is an irreversible change.

Proteins can be denatured in many different ways.

- Heat: normal cooking methods.
- Salting: by adding salt.
- Mechanical action: whipping egg whites.
- Enzymes: meat tenderisers.
- Acid: by adding acid, yoghurt, sour cream.

Figure 11.4 Food analysis

Effect of heat on globular proteins

We will take making an egg custard as an example. The main ingredients are milk, sugar and eggs. They are beaten together before the cooking process. As it cooks the mixture thickens. The thickening is due to the heat denaturation of the egg proteins. First, the egg albumen molecules – in this case the globular proteins – are moved about by the input of heat energy. As this movement becomes more vigorous, the weak bonds that hold the globules in place start to break up. Second, the protein chains start to unfold and may come into contact with other chains and form new weak bonds. Third, a stable three-dimensional 'mesh' of large molecules is formed. This traps many small pockets of water and limits the movement of the water. The effect is a thick, smooth texture. If the egg custard is allowed to continue cooking, the protein mesh will contract or coagulate and squeeze out the pockets of water. The custard will then curdle and resemble lumps of scrambled egg suspended in milk. This loss of water is known as syneresis. The presence of salt or acid will speed up the process of coagulation. This is evident if vinegar is added to water for poaching eggs.

Effect of heat on fibrous proteins

Although fibrous proteins do not dissolve in water they do have the capacity to attract and bind water. This is often important in meat cooking, particularly when producing chopped meat or minced products that require moisture to be added to them.

When fibrous proteins are heated they contract and squeeze out the associated water. For example, when fillet steak is cooked, the protein called myosin coagulates at 71°C (160°F). If the temperature continues to increase, the protein contracts, squeezes out much of the water associated with it, and thus becomes drier and the eating quality is impaired. For a tender, juicy fillet steak the chef would heat the steak just sufficiently to sear the outside. This will also melt any fat, acting as a lubricant and improving the overall tenderness and eating quality.

Cuts of meat can consist of large amounts of connective tissue – for example, collagen and elastin. Collagen is tough and chewy. Elastin is stretchy and heating has little effect on it except helping to produce a tougher product; meat that contains a high proportion of it is naturally tougher and therefore not usually suitable for prime cooking. Collagen will denature, becoming water soluble when heated in water. This then becomes gelatine.

Effects of acids on proteins

(See page 229 for information on pH.)
Acids play an important part in cooking procedures:

- as a component in raising agents in baking powder
- as a preservative in yoghurt
- as a tenderising agent in meats.

The citric acid in lemon juice will slow down any browning reaction on cut fruit.

Proteins can also be denatured by acids. The albumen in milk is a globular protein. In its natural state, each albumen molecule carries a negative electrical charge. Charged particles are similar to the north and

Table 11.1 Types of protein found in food

TYPE	PROTEIN	WHERE FOUND
Fibrous	Collagen	Connective tissue
Fibrous	Elastin	Connective tissue
Fibrous	Gluten	Wheat flour
Globular	Albumen	Egg white, milk
Globular	Casein	Milk
Generally globular	Enzymes	Many tissues
Fibrous	Myosin	Muscle

Figure 11.5 Acid
coagulation of milk

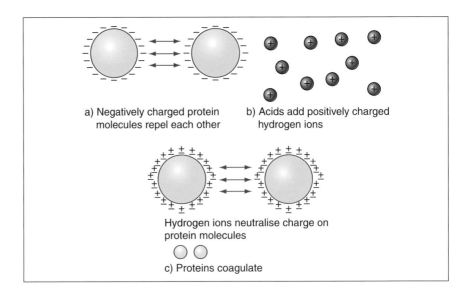

a) Negatively charged protein
molecules repel each other

b) Acids add positively charged
hydrogen ions

Hydrogen ions neutralise charge on
protein molecules

c) Proteins coagulate

south poles on magnets – that is, like repels like: whenever a negative
particle gets near another negative particle they repel each other and
remain separate.

If acid is added to milk (see Figure 11.5), then we are adding hydrogen
ions, which are very small positively charged particles. The hydrogen
ions (positively charged) are attracted to the albumen globules
(negatively charged) and the two neutralise each other. The albumen is
then electrically neutral, and any globules that come in contact stick
together or coagulate and form a mass with a gel-like, semi-solid
consistency. This process is useful in food preparation – for example, in
cheese making, yoghurt and sour cream.

Effect of mechanical action on protein

The bonds that maintain the shape of protein molecules are so weak that
we are able to break them by agitating the molecules – for example,
meringues, which are foams (relatively stable masses of air bubbles that
are pockets of gas surrounded by a thin film of water). Foams in beer are
less stable because there is no stabiliser present.

By whipping egg whites we are adding air and physically agitating the
egg white globular proteins. The mechanical stresses resulting from the
physical agitation and contact with air act to unfold the globular
proteins. The unfolded proteins associate to form a sort of mesh
reinforcement of the bubble walls. (This can be considered the culinary
equivalent of quick-setting cement.) The egg white foam is relatively
stable because it is held together by proteins, while the foam in a head of
beer quickly deflates.

Gluten gives bread dough both its elasticity and plasticity. Gluten is
formed by two proteins, gliadin and glutenin, coming together in the

presence of water; they form a tangled mass of protein molecules. During kneading, the gluten molecules are physically rearranged from a tangled mass to a series of parallel sheets. The molecules in the sheets of gluten are shaped like tiny springs and account for the stretchy nature of bread dough. The sheets of gluten act to trap the gas formed by the yeast growing in the dough, and allow the bread to rise.

ENZYMES

Enzymes are proteins that are catalysts, meaning that they speed up chemical reactions. Enzymes catalyse a wide range of chemical reactions that take place in all living things. Some enzymes are useful while others lower the quality of foods. An example of one enzyme is rennet added to milk to produce junket.

Each enzyme requires an optimum temperature in which to work. At lower temperatures they will act more slowly and at higher temperatures they will gradually be destroyed. The optimum temperature for an enzyme that comes from a mammal is often close to 37°C (98.6°F) (body temperature). Enzymes are also affected by acidity and can sometimes be controlled by changing the pH. An example of this is using lemon juice to stop the enzyme-catalysed browning of apples.

Ageing of meat: the role of enzymes

Like cheese and wine, meat benefits from a period of 'ageing', or slow chemical change, before it is consumed. The flavour improves and it becomes more tender. As lactic acid accumulates in the tissue after slaughter, it begins to break down the walls of lysosomes – the cell bodies that store protein-attacking enzymes. As a result, these enzymes will digest proteins indiscriminately. Flavour changes result from the degradation of proteins into individual amino acids, which generally have a strong flavour. It is not clear whether these same enzymes also tenderise the meat by breaking up the actin–myosin complex.

Glycogen, a carbohydrate energy reserve, is stored by animals. It is glycogen that is converted to the lactic acid required in the ageing process. Glycogen cannot be converted to carbon dioxide and water as it would be in the living animal due to the lack of oxygen, instead it is converted to lactic acid. The lactic acid lowers the pH of the muscle from about 7.0 in the living animal to 5.6 in the dead animal. The lactic acid breaks down the structures in the cells that contain enzymes capable of digesting protein. Protein muscle fibres are partly digested. As a result of these changes the meat is softer and more tender. It has been partially degraded by its own enzymes.

For these changes to occur during ageing it is necessary to have an adequate supply of glycogen in the muscle when the animal is

Table 11.2 Effect of heat on materials found in meat

MEAT MATERIAL	WHAT HAPPENS	EFFECT
Muscle protein (myosin)	Fibres shrink and lose water	Meat becomes tougher
Connective tissue (collagen)	Heat plus water causes collagen to denature	Gelatine is formed
Fat	Fat melts and acts as a lubricant	Meat seems more tender

Table 11.3 Enzyme effects on foods

FOOD	CHANGE	ENZYME SOURCE
Desirable changes		
Black tea	Oxidation similar to browning of apples	Naturally present
Beef	Tenderising during ageing	Naturally present
Bananas and apples	Conversion of starch to sugar during ripening	Naturally present
Meat	Tenderisers	Pawpaw, pineapple
Cheddar cheese	Conversion of milk to 'curds and whey'	Calves' stomach
Starch	Conversion of starch to glucose syrups	Moulds
Undesirable changes		
Fatty meats	Development of rancidity	Naturally present
Fruit jellies	Failure to set when using fresh pineapple or pawpaw	Present in fruit
Fruits and vegetables	Development of brown colour where exposed to air	Naturally present

slaughtered. If the animal is not fed or is subjected to stress before slaughter the glycogen will have been used up, and the desirable post-mortem changes will not take place.

CARBOHYDRATES

These can be sugars and non-sugars.

Carbohydrates are an extremely diverse group of substances. Simple sugars are the first products of the photosynthetic process in plants. Plants trap energy from sunlight using the green pigment called chlorophyll, and use it to produce sugars from carbon dioxide and water. In this way plants are the ultimate source of all our food. Sugars may be more or less sweet. Generally the more complex carbohydrates lack a sweet flavour. The number in Table 11.5, under 'sweetness', for simple sugars compares the relative sweetening power of a sugar to sucrose. Values greater than 100 are sweeter and values less than 100 are less sweet than an equal weight of sugar. Some substances are considerably sweeter than sugar. For example, saccharin would have a value of 3000; this means that 1 g of saccharin has the sweetening power of 300 g of sucrose.

Fructose and glucose are monosaccharides. Sucrose, maltose and lactose are disaccharides.

Complex carbohydrates are composed of long chains of sugars up to 1000 units in length.

Sugars in cooking

The first concentrated sweetener was honey. Bees produce honey from nectar (a weak solution of sucrose produced by flowers). The bees use an enzyme in their saliva to break down the sucrose into fructose and glucose, and concentrate the nectar by evaporating some of the water. Honeys can contain small amounts of other substances found in the nectar from some plants, which can be poisonous. Honey is used as a flavouring agent, sweetener and as a humectant (water-holding property).

Table 11.4 Types of carbohydrate

SUGARS	NON–SUGARS
Monosaccharides	Polysaccharides (starch)
Disaccharides	Complex polysaccharides (pectin, alginates)
Trisaccharides	
Tetrasaccharides	

Table 11.5 Simple carbohydrates found in food

NAME	SWEETNESS	OCCURRENCE IN FOODS
Fructose (fruit sugar)	170	Fruits, jams, honey
Sucrose (table sugar)	100	Many foods
Glucose (blood sugar)	70	Grapes, honeys, jams
Lactose (milk sugar)	40	Milk, milk products
Maltose (malt sugar)	30	Malt, glucose syrup

Table 11.6 Complex carbohydrates found in food

NAME	OCCURRENCE IN FOODS
Starch	Flours, potatoes, corn
Inulin	Jerusalem artichokes
Cellulose	Vegetables, wholegrain cereals
Pectin	Fruits, jams

Figure 11.6 Types of
starches

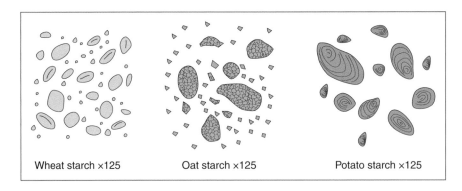

Wheat starch ×125   Oat starch ×125   Potato starch ×125

Products that contain honey stay moist longer than those made with sugar.

Sugar is also used for volume as it gives bulk to baked goods, ice creams, jams and confectionery. It assists in the leavening of some cakes by aiding the incorporation of air. Air is incorporated into cake making during the creaming process by the physical action of the sugar crystals dragging pockets of air into the fat. The size of the crystals affects the properties of the sugar. If the crystals are too large, few pockets of air will be incorporated. If too fine the sugar will dissolve rather than remain in discrete crystals. Sugar is also necessary for the action of pectin for the setting of jams and preserves.

Sugar can contribute to the colour of cooked food products by caramelisation or through the 'Maillard reaction' (browning). Both processes require high temperatures. The Maillard reaction requires the presence of sugar and protein. Both react together at relatively low temperatures, but this is significant only at above 149°C (300°F). The high temperatures required for both these reactions to occur explain why steamed foods are often blander than roasted foods. The Maillard reaction is responsible for colour and flavour in foods such as roasted meats, nuts, coffee beans, bread crusts, and so on. Lactose is more likely to participate in the Maillard reaction than some other sugars. Lactose and protein are found in milk. Thus bread brushed with milk before baking will have an attractive brown crust on removal from the oven.

The viscosity of many liquids is affected by sugar.

Complex carbohydrates

These are important in product development because they have a major influence on the texture of foods.

Starch

Starch is found in foods that come from plants. It consists of long straight or branched chains of glucose molecules. The plant makes starch as a means of storing glucose. Starch is found in seeds, roots and tubers, and stored in the form of granules or grains. The starch granules from different sources show characteristic sizes and shapes. Starch molecules in the granules are of two types. One is a long chain of glucose units called amylose, accounting for 20–30 per cent of the starch. The rest is a branched molecule, shaped rather like a bush, called amylopectin.

When starch granules are mixed with cold water, they will only absorb water and swell to a limited extent. The water cannot penetrate between the strongly attached starch chains. As the water is heated, the molecules of water move more rapidly, and thus begin to penetrate the starch grains; the water causes the grain to swell. As swelling occurs the mixture thickens. Some of the starch molecules burst out from the granule and form a tangled mass that contributes to the thickening process known as gelatinisation.

The temperature at which gelatinisation occurs depends upon the type of starch used and generally varies from 60°C (140°F) for potato starch to 83°C (181.4°F) for corn starch. As a rule large starch granules gelatinise at lower temperatures than small starch granules.

Starch grains must be separated before any heat is applied. The chef is able to do this in three ways:

1 disperse the starch in cold liquid
2 mix the starch grains with sugar
3 coat the grains with solid or melted fat, as in the making of a roux.
  The thickening capacity of starches depends on the following factors.

- The type of starch used is important. Arrowroot has a greater thickening capacity than corn or potato starch. High-amylose starches have better thickening properties because of their long chain-like molecules, which are more likely to become tangled than the compact amylopectin molecules.
- Thickening properties are changed by heat treatment. For example, the browning of flour in the oven has less thickening power because of the chemical changes caused by using this method of heating.
- Sugar decreases the thickness of starch-thickened fillings. The effect of sugar is related to its water-attracting ability; available water is reduced and this allows the starch granules to swell.
- Acid reduces the thickening power of starch. The acid breaks down the starch chains. This breakdown occurs faster if the reaction takes place at high temperature. Therefore any acid required for flavour should be added at the end of gelatinisation to minimise the acid hydrolysis of the starch.

Why modify starch?

Unmodified starches can be used in cooking but have limited use in food manufacturing – for example, in chilled and in particular frozen food. Natural waxy starch from maize will hydrate and swell rapidly but lose its viscosity on standing, producing a weak-bodied paste. Starch is modified to enhance or repress its inherent properties for a particular application – for example, to provide:

Figure 11.7 Cross-linking

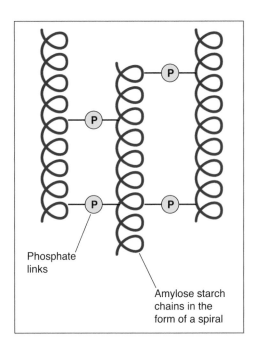

Phosphate
links

Amylose starch
chains in the
form of a spiral

- thickening
- improved binding
- improved mouth-feel
- improved stability
- gelling.

Types of starch modification

Cross-linking (or cross-binding)

Cross-linking (see Figure 11.7) is achieved by a chemical process, which places phosphate groups as bridges between starch chains. Thus, starch with a high proportion of amylose takes on the properties of one with a higher amylopectin (highly branched content).

Phosphate cross-bonded starch

Cross-linking with phosphate can be considered as spot-welding of the starch granules at random spots on the starch chains. This results in strengthening of tender starches, and cooked pastes are more viscous and heavier bodied. Of equal importance is that the modified starch is much less likely to break down due to heating, cook-chill, cook-freeze, increased acidity or agitation.

Cross-linking helps to control the texture of starch and provides considerable tolerance to the effects of heat, acid and agitation. As a result, it gives better control and improved flexibility in dealing with formulations processing and shelf life.

Other ingredients affect the swelling characteristics of starch and the final viscosity of the product being thickened. Acids disrupt the bonding (hydrogen bonding) between starch chains and allow more rapid hydration and thus swelling of the starch.

Table 11.7. Use of modified starches

STARCH	PROPERTIES	USES
Modified by acid	Low gel strength Clear Low paste viscosities	Binder To replace fat Jelly sweets
Phosphate cross-linked	High gelatinisation Temperature/heat stable	Processed foods
Stabilised	Freeze-thaw stability Reduced retrogradation High water-holding capacity	Frozen foods Cook-freeze production
Pre-gelatinised (instant or cold water swelling)	Thickens with cold water Quick hydration	Desserts Instant custard Instant mixes
Corn syrups (acid or enzyme hydrolysed starch)	Sweetening Bulking Thickening control	Frozen desserts Bakery products
High-fructose corn syrup	Very sweet	Confectionery Desserts

Unmodified starch

This will break down at lower pHs – in, for example, pickled products. Soluble solids (e.g. sugars) dissolve in water, which would be used to swell the starch, thus reducing the amount of water available and the resulting swelling of the starch. Sugar should be held back in mixing and cooking a product until the starch is completely cooked. Fats and proteins coat starch granules, delay swelling and lower the final viscosity attained.

Agitation and shearing forces extended by high-speed mixing, milling, homogenisation or pumping can damage the starch granules.

Cross-linking the starch can build in resistance to shear (agitation) as well as to higher temperatures and acidity.

Other starch modifications

- **Stabilisation:** Starches can be electrolytically charged with the same electrical charge so that the starch chains repel each other, like two north poles of magnets. This prevents starch from agglomerating and separating out.
- **Acid modification:** The starch is hydrolysed with acid but the granules stay intact, thus producing lower viscosity and clearer starch pastes.
- **Pre-gelatinisation (instant or cold water swelling starches):** The starch is gelatinised by heating with water in the normal manner, then the mixture is spray-dried. The resulting powder will produce a starch gel more or less constantly on the addition of cold water. This method is suitable for use with quick-cook products and instant desserts.

Complex carbohydrates in plant cell walls

Pectin, cellulose and hemicellulose are found in plants. Cellulose and hemicellulose form the rigid walls around each cell. Pectin is found between the cell walls and acts as a glue-like substance, which holds the cells together. All three substances contribute to the fibre in our diets. Rigid cellulose in the cell walls provides much of the crunchiness in vegetables. Cellulose is not water soluble and is not affected much by cooking. Pectins, however, can be dissolved by hot water. This is exactly what happens when vegetables are cooked and accounts for the softer texture of cooked vegetables and fruit.

Hemicellulose will dissolve in the presence of alkali. Vegetables cooked in the presence of carbonate of soda lose their structure and will become mushy if cooking is continued.

Pectins are used to set jams and jellies, and are in flan gels and commercial dessert mixes. Fruits can be divided into high-pectin and low-pectin types. The low-pectin types require the addition of pectin or may be mixed with a high-pectin fruit to allow gelling. Pectins are long chains of sugars, which form a network trapping water to form the gel.

A firm gel depends on:

- percentage of pectin
- molecular weight of the pectin
- percentage of methyl ester groups
- amount of sugar
- the pH of the mix.

Most gels are made with about 65 per cent sugar; in excess of this crystallisation will occur on the surface.

Most pectin products will not form gels until the pH is lowered to about 3.5. The firmness of the gelling increases as the pH is lowered. A pH lower than the optimum will cause a weak gel and water separation (syneresis).

Types of pectin used to develop food products
- **Rapid-set pectins:** degree of methyl group 70 per cent, forming gels with acid and sugar; optimum pH is 3.5; starts to gel on cooling to 88°C (190.4°F).
- **Slow-set pectins:** degree of methyl groups 50–70 per cent, gels with sugar and acid; pH 2.8–3.2; starts to gel at 54°C (129°F).
- **Low methoxyl pectins:** degree of methyl ester groups <30 per cent; these do not form gels with acid and sugar, but will gel in the presence of calcium ions or other polyvalent ions (milk).

Pectin is added to natural juice products to give a permanent cloudiness. Pectin is used as a stabiliser in ice cream products to prevent large crystals forming. It may also be used in mayonnaise as an emulsifying agent.

Sugar syrups

Sugar syrups are produced from starch by controlled acid/or enzyme hydrolysis. The syrups are colourless, viscous and vary in sweetness according to the level of starch breakdown. The mixture of sugars in the syrup consists of simple sugars like glucose and maltose, with varying amounts of longer-chain carbohydrates.

Table 11.8 Uses of sugar syrups

Source: modified from Proudlove, 2001

PRODUCT	USE OF SUGAR SYRUP
Bakery products	Helps produce brown crust Delays staling by holding water
Confectionery products	In boiled sweets and toffees to prevent sugar (sucrose) crystallisation

LIPIDS

Lipids include fats, oils, cholesterol and certain emulsifying agents known as phospholipids. One example is lecithin, found in egg yolk. An important feature of these materials is that they are 'hydrophobic', which means that they repel water.

Lipids are important in food production. They contribute to the eating quality of cakes, pastries and biscuits; they affect the texture of yeast products by separating the gluten layers and, in pastry making, by shortening the gluten strands.

Lipids in culinary work

- **Cooking medium:** provides heat transfer; used as a lubricant.
- **Texture:** gives goods a 'shorter texture'; provides smooth mouth-feel; aids aeration; aids moistness; provides volume in bread.
- **Emulsification:** emulsifies sauces, ice creams, etc.
- **Flavour:** provides a flavouring agent (e.g. butter, olive oil, peanut oil); acts as a solvent for some flavour components of foods.

Table 11.9 Sources of fatty acid types

TYPE OF FATTY ACID	NUMBER OF DOUBLE BONDS	WHERE FOUND
Saturated	0	Palm oil, coconut oil, butter, beef fat, mutton fat, lard
Monounsaturated	1	Olive oil, peanut oil, lard
Polyunsaturated	2 or more	Corn oil, soya bean oil, sunflower oil, walnut oil

Lipid structure

In order to use lipids effectively in food production we must know something about their behaviour, or their molecular structure. Fats and oils are triglycerides, meaning that they are comprised of three molecules of fatty acids, bonded to one molecule of glycerol:

Figure 11.8 Triglycerides

$$
\text{glycerol} \begin{cases} \text{fatty acid} - 1 \\ \text{fatty acid} - 2 \\ \text{fatty acid} - 3 \end{cases}
$$

The way fats and oils behave is affected by the nature of the fatty acid. The fatty acids consist of chains of carbon atoms that vary in length from four to about 20 carbon atoms. Molecules with short-chain fatty acids will have a lower melting point than those with long-chain fatty acids. These fatty acids may also be divided up into saturated and unsaturated groups. All fats contain a mixture of saturated and unsaturated fatty acids. The difference between a saturated fat and an unsaturated fat is based on their individual chemistry. The chains of carbon atoms that make up fatty acids may be joined together with what is known as a single bond or with a double bond (see Figure 11.9).

If the fatty acid contains no double bonds it is called a saturated fatty acid. If it contains one double bond it is monounsaturated, and if there is more than one double bond it is called polyunsaturated.

The saturated fatty acids are found in animal fats and in a few oils from tropical plants, such as palm oil and coconut oil. Olive oil is mostly monounsaturated, while sunflower, corn and peanut oils, and margarine made from these oils are highly unsaturated.

Figure 11.9 Single bonds and double bonds in fatty acids

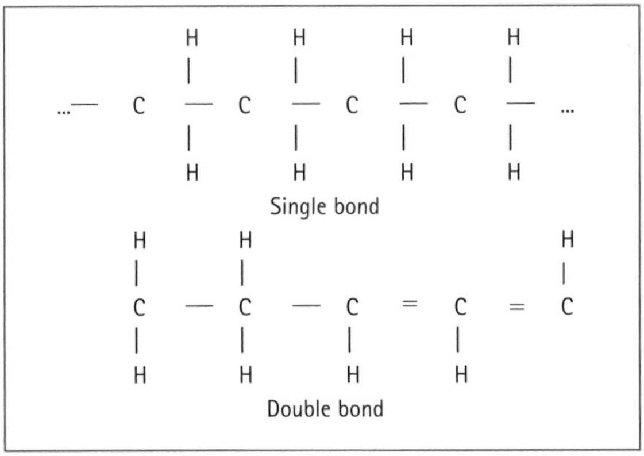

Table 11.10 Factors affecting the development of rancidity in fats

FACTOR	EFFECT
Water	Necessary for development of rancidity by hydrolysis
Heat	Speeds up most chemical reactions including development of rancidity
Lipases (enzymes that split fats)	Present in certain foods and can cause rancidity
Metal ions (iron)	Speed up development of rancidity in fats (e.g. cast iron pans)
Light	Speeds up oxidation
Salt food particles	Speed up development of rancidity

Types of fatty acids

- **Never in fats:** formic methanoic, acetic ethanoic, propionic.
- **Only found in butter:** butyric, caproic, caprillic.
- **Most common:** capric, myristic, stearic, lauric, palmitic.

Important facts in the chemistry of fats

- Most fats contain at least five different sorts of fatty acids in their make-up.
- The number of triglycerides is large.
- Oleic acid is the most important of all the fatty acids occurring in fats. Often it is more than 50 per cent of the total fatty acids in a fat, and it is always present in a fat.
- If a particular saturated acid is present, then it very often happens that the acids immediately above and below it in the fatty acid series also occur.

Spoilage of fats and oils

Fats require care to maintain quality. They may deteriorate for the following reasons.

- **Odours:** many compounds that have a strong aroma can dissolve in fats; if fats are stored in an open container they are able to absorb these odours.
- **Rancidity:** this is caused by the presence of free fatty acids, which have an unpleasant smell; for example, butyric acid accounts for the smell of rancid butter; caproic acid has a very strong smell; rancid fats are able to impart their smell to any foods they are used in or are cooked in.

One way that rancidity develops is when some of the fat molecules are split by a reaction with water that releases fatty acids and glycerol. The action involves an enzyme and is called hydrolysis.

Oxidation will also cause rancidity. This involves the reaction of unsaturated fatty acids with oxygen to release small fatty acids and other molecules that affect the flavour and aroma. The development of rancidity by hydrolysis or oxidation occurs faster under certain conditions.

Other factors can slow down the development of fat oxidation. These are known as antioxidants. They can be naturally occurring or artificial. Examples include vitamin E, ascorbic acid and certain herbs, such as sage and rosemary. Artificial antioxidants include butylated hydroxyanisole (BHA) and butylated hydroxytoluene (BHT). These are added to many commercial fats. Antioxidants only slow the development of rancidity in fats. They cannot prevent it totally.

EMULSIONS

The hydrophobic nature of fats and oils presents problems when developing recipes in attempting to make a stable dispersion of an oil and water. Emulsifiers stabilise dispersion of the immiscible liquids. The stable dispersion is called an emulsion. Emulsifiers can be proteins, plant gums or resins, starch or very small particles such as ground mustard. (Thus mustard added to a vinaigrette acts as an emulsifying agent as well as a flavouring agent.)

The type of emulsion formed by an oil–water system depends upon a number of factors:

- the composition of the oil and water phases
- the chemical nature of the emulsifying agent
- the proportions of oil and water present.

If the polar group of an emulsifier is more effectively adsorbed than the non-polar group, adsorption by the water is greater than by the oil. The extent of adsorption at a liquid surface depends upon the surface area of liquid available, and increased adsorption of emulsifier by water is favoured by the oil–water interface becoming convex towards the water, thus giving an oil–water emulsion.

The relative proportions of oil and water also help to determine which type of emulsion forms. If more oil than water is present, the water tends to form droplets and a water–oil emulsion is formed. If more water than oil is present an oil–water emulsion is favoured.

Artificial emulsifiers are added during the preparation of many emulsions. An example is GMS (glyceryl monostearate). GMS is a monoglyceride that is formed when one hydroxyl group of glycerol

Figure 11.10 GMS

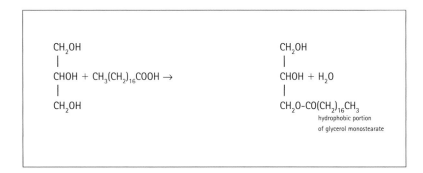

is esterified with stearic acid. An example is shown in Figure 11.10.

One part of the GMS molecule is hydrophilic because it contains hydroxyl groups, and the rest of the molecule, as indicated, is hydrophobic. When GMS is added to a water–oil emulsion the hydrophilic parts of the molecules are absorbed into the surface of the water droplets and the lipophilic parts are absorbed into the surface of the oil round drops, as shown in Figure 11.11.

Figure 11.11 Molecules of emulsifier absorbed at a water–oil interface, forming a complete protective film around a water droplet

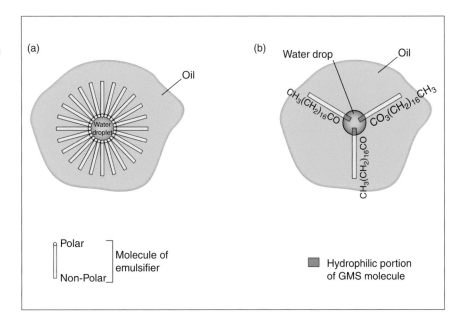

Lecithin

Lecithin is the phospholipid emulsifier found in egg yolk and is also extracted from vegetable oils. The structure of lecithin is a triglyceride of two fatty acids and phosphoric acid (see Figure 11.12).

Figure 11.12 Lecithin

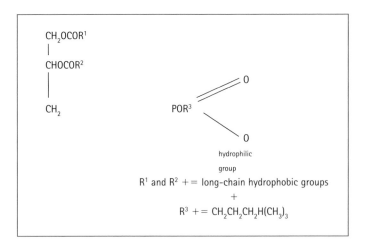

CH_2OCOR^1

$CHOCOR^2$

CH_2 POR^3

O

O

hydrophilic

group

R^1 and R^2 += long-chain hydrophobic groups

+

R^3 += $CH_2CH_2CH_2H(CH_3)_3$

In many recipes, stabilisers are added to products in addition to emulsifiers. Stabilisers are proteins, carbohydrates, starches and gums. Their function is to hold the emulsion together once it has been formed. Such substances improve the stability of emulsions, mainly by increasing their viscosity. Viscosity increases, the freedom of movement of the dispersed droplets of the emulsion is reduced, and this lessens the chance of their coming into contact and coalescing.

If you add oil or butter when making hollandaise or mayonnaise, the sauce may curdle because the lecithin has had insufficient time to coat the droplets. This can be rectified by adding the broken sauce to more egg yolks.

The most important characteristic of emulsions is that they require energy for their formation.

Table **11.11** Functions of emulsifiers

FUNCTION	MECHANISM	EXAMPLES
Emulsification	Stabilise oil in water or water in oil emulsions to prevent separation	Mayonnaise, dressings, soups (e.g. lecithin glyceryl monostearate (GMS))
Complete formation	Modify starch or protein-containing products	Starch – complexing with monoglycerides GMS to reduce staling of bread Protein – complexing with diaceyyl tartaric acid esters of monoglycerides
Fat 'crystal' modification	Modify and stabilise fat	Stops fat separating (e.g. bloom on chocolate; use sorbitan triterate as emulsifier)

Source: modified from Proudlove, 2001

Table 11.12 Functions
of emulsifiers in
particular products

FUNCTION	PRODUCT
Inhibit syneresis Repress sugar crystals	Meringues Fruit cakes Pie fillings Icings Confectionery
Anti-staling agent – retains moisture	Bread Cakes
Aid to reconstitution	Dried foods

ADDITIVES

Most food products are made from a mixture of ingredients and
additives. The main food value of the product comes from the
ingredients, which are helped to achieve their finished-product status by
the use of additives. The fewer the additives the better as, today, additives
tend to attract an adverse consumer reaction. The main ingredients of
food products came under the general headings of carbohydrates, fats
and proteins. As well as sources of these being fruit and vegetables,
meat, fish and cereals, increasingly the use of new ingredients from the
world of biotechnology will come into play (for example, xanthan gum).

What are additives?

Additives are chemicals, both synthetic and natural, that are used to give
various functional properties to foods. The additives in the quantities used
are edible but are not foods in their own right. Some additives are very
widespread in nature – for example, pectin, ascorbic acid (vitamin C) –
others come from specific sources – for example, gums from certain
seaweeds. Naturally occurring additives must be treated and controlled in
exactly the same way as synthetic ones.

Functional properties of additives

It is possible to divide additives into four main groups according to their
functional properties. Additives in a food alter either:

1 its physical characteristics
2 its sensory characteristics, such as flavour, texture and colour
3 its storage life
4 its nutritional status.

  Some additives can fulfil more than one function (e.g. thickeners such
as starch fall into groups, provide physical characteristics and give
sensory characteristics). Vitamin C is an antioxidant, but it is also a
vitamin so gives nutritional value.

Additives affecting the physical characteristics of a food

A food product may be:

- made thicker and gelled
- made more or less acid
- aerated with gas bubbles
- emulsified.

Thickening or gelling

Hydrocolloids are substances capable of holding, by various means, large quantities of water with other structures, or joined to their large molecules. Many substances have this property, including carbohydrates such as starch and pectin, many gums, and a few animal products, particularly gelatine.

Additives affecting the sensory characteristics of a food

For food to be enjoyable it must taste and smell right, feel right in the mouth, and be attractive to the eye (see the section on the sensory evaluation of food, below).

Flavours are odours and are detected by the nose. Fruit flavours are often termed essential oils (arising from the word 'essence'). Less volatile natural flavourings are extracted by solvents – for example, from dried spices. These flavourings are called oleoresins. A number of substances have been found to have the ability to enhance the flavour of other substances, and to modify or mask undesirable flavours. The best-known flavour enhancer is monosodium glutamate (MSG), which stimulates the taste buds. MSG has been used by the Chinese for generations and was found to be the main flavour component of soy sauce. The ingestion of large amounts has been known to cause sickness or dizziness.

Sugar usage has decreased and the growth of artificial sweeteners has been considerable. Saccharin has been used for many years. Aspartame is a sweetener used in soft drinks, particularly the diet varieties. It is made up of two naturally occurring amino acids: aspartic acids and phenylalanine. Unfortunately in acid drinks, over a period, it breaks down and so products using it must be less acid, with a shorter shelf life.

Colours are used to modify the appearance of a product to make it more attractive to the consumer, caramel being the most commonly used. There are 58 permitted colours.

Additives affecting the storage life of a food

Preservatives extend the storage life of a product. Preservatives help to reduce or prevent wastage of food through spoilage caused by micro-organisms. Longer shelf lives enable a greater variety of products to be kept in store.

Some common examples of preservatives

- Sorbic acid E200 – used in soft drinks.
- Benjoic acid E210 – used in soft drinks.
- Sulphur dioxide E220.
- Potassium nitrate E252 – used in curing meats.

Fats, oils and foods containing preservatives are subject, over a period of time, to the effects of oxygen in turning the product rancid. This type of rancidity is accelerated by light and by certain metals, particularly copper and iron. Antioxidants are added to foods such as these to slow down or prevent the process of rancidity, and thus extend the storage life of the product. Some antioxidants stop the chemical reactions involved in rancidity, whereas others remove oxygen from the product. Another type of rancidity – hydrolytic rancidity – is caused by the presence of water, and by some enzymes or micro-organisms. This type of rancidity – found in butter, for example – is not prevented by antioxidants.

Common antioxidants

- Ascorbic acid E300 – used in fruit drinks.
- Propyl gallate E310 – used in vegetable oils.
- Butylated hydroxyanisole E320 – used in stock cubes.

Additives affecting the nutritional status of a food

These are minerals, vitamins and protein supplements. Such substances are only legally additives when they fulfil a technological purpose – for example, ascorbic acid (vitamin C) is an antioxidant. Some nutrients must be added to foods by law – for example, vitamins A and D must be added to margarine.

Additives used by manufacturers during processing

Processing aids are additives that manufacturers use to facilitate the production of a foodstuff.

- Solvents are used to extract substances from materials – for example, fruit flavours from peels.
- Anti-caking agents are added to powders to keep them free-flowing – for example, magnesium carbonate (504) is added to ensure that salt does not cake.

Acidity control

In some cases food products and recipes need their acid level to be modified in order to be acceptable. To control the acidity of a product or recipe, a buffer is added. Many types of acids are used to increase the acidity of a product. Some common examples are:

- sodium lactate (E325) – a buffer used in preserves and confectionery
- calcium citrate (E833) – a buffer used in soft drinks, sweets and preserves
- acetic acid (E260) – vinegar used in pickles and mayonnaise
- tartaric acid (E334) – acid used in desserts and raising agents
- citric acid (E330) – widely used acid, useful in binding up traces of metal.

The use of raising agents has made possible a vast range of baked products. Sodium hydrogen carbonate (bicarbonate) and an acid such as cream of tartar (E336) or calcium hydrogen phosphate (E341) makes up the raising agents.

GUMS

Gums are used for thickening and gelling. These gums include alginates, celluloses, xanthan, pectins, carrageenans, Arabic (acacia), tragacanth and carob bean gum (also known as locust bean gum). These thicken products, gel and stabilise to prevent separation.

Alginates

Alginates are extracted from brown seaweed, where the gum occurs in the cell walls and intercellular spaces. Alginates thicken solutions to form gel films.

Alginates are complex polysaccharides built up from two main units in random order to make large molecules. The two components are mannuronic and guluronic acids, which are sugar derivatives. The long chains gel with the help of calcium ions (ca++), which bridge across at special points in the chains called 'action zones'.

Xanthan gum

Xanthan gum has a high molecular weight; it is a polysaccharide that occurs naturally on the outside of the cells (the capsule) of the bacterium *Xanthomonas Campestris*. Solutions of xanthan gum are thixotropic – that is, they become thinner when subjected to agitation or shear (e.g. shaking or stirring), but thicken again on standing. This gives excellent mouth-feel to many products and allows rapid flavour release due to shear thinning resulting from chewing. Shaking products in bottles also thins the gum, allowing easy dispersal of syrups, toppings and salad dressings.

When xanthan gum and locust bean gums are mixed at normal temperatures, a greater increase in overall viscosity occurs (synergistic effect). A gel is produced when solutions of the two are heated above 55°C and subsequently cooked. A similar synergistic effect occurs with guar gum.

Figure 11.13 Egg box model for alginate formation

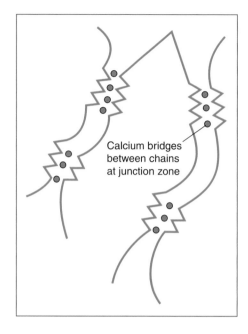

Calcium bridges between chains at junction zone

Source: modified from Proudlove, 2001

Table 11.13 Uses of gums

MAIN PROPERTY	USE	REASONS FOR USE
Thickening	Sauces, syrups, cake mixes, pie filling, soups, canned meat, ice cream	Thickens batter Moisture retention Reduces moisture absorption by pastry Temporary or delayed thickening Checks growth of ice crystals
General colloidal properties	Water ices, whipped cream, cream substitutes, stabilise edible emulsions	Checks dripping Checks separation Gives quick whipping
Drinks		Prevents 'ringing' (colours separating out on standing)
Gel formation	Milk desserts, table jellies, aerated desserts	Cold prepared

Carrageenans

These are polysaccharides produced from seaweed. Their main use is for gelling, particularly in milk-based desserts. Carrageenan reacts with the milk protein casein to make a gel, which can be used as the basis of desserts.

Table 11.14
Carboxymethyl cellulose
applications

FUNCTION	PRODUCT
Stabiliser Produce smoothness Retard ice growth Resist meeting	Ice cream Milk beverages Frozen desserts
Aid to emulsification Stabilise oil Emulsion system	Cream substitutes Salad dressings

Table 11.15 Xanthan
gum food applications

Bakery fillings	Cold make-up Produces good mouth-feel Filling not absorbed by pastry
Frozen foods	Excellent emulsion and suspension Stability and viscosity maintenance of dressings, sauces, gravies Improves freeze-thaw stability of starch-thickened products

*Source: modified from
Proudlove, 2001*

Celluloses

Cellulose on its own will not mix with water and is also indigestible, hence its value as dietary fibre. Cellulose can be modified in a number of ways to make it more soluble or dispersible in water, sometimes with added properties.

Methylcellulose is a derivative that, when mixed with water, on heating becomes thicker but thins again on cooling. It is useful when added to tomato fillings on, say, pizzas to prevent it dripping from the pizza base during cooking.

Carboxymethyl cellulose has many uses as a stabiliser to prevent water or oil separation (see Table 11.14).

THE SENSORY EVALUATION OF FOOD

The most important thing to remember when applying chemistry to food products is that the food must ultimately give pleasure to the consumer. This is dependent on appearance, flavour, smell and texture. These are assessed by our senses. Scientists use complex and expensive equipment to measure the factors in food that determine taste, aroma or tenderness. The process is based on objective assessment and is vital in product development.

When referring to our senses we are concerned with vision, hearing, smell, touch and taste. Some scientists add three more factors: temperature, pain and balance. Except for balance, all these senses are used to relay messages about the food.

Table 11.16 Examples of types of taste

TASTE	EXAMPLE
Sweet	Sugar, saccharin, aspartame, cyclamates
Salt	Sodium chloride
Bitter	Alkaloids (in caffeine)
Sour	Acids, vinegar, lemon juice
Metallic	Potassium chloride found in some salt substitutes
Soapy	Aftertaste in baking powder goodsc

Taste and smell are the most important chemical receptors and are often used with the most expensive equipment found in food laboratories. Vision and smell operate at a distance, meaning that the individual does not have to come into contact with the food in order to use these senses.

Examples of the messages that a sense tells us about food

- **Vision:** colour, freshness, size, maturity, shape, quality.
- **Smell:** freshness, character, ripeness, identification.
- **Hearing:** sizzling related to temperature, texture, crispness, crunchiness.
- **Touch:** texture, ripeness, consistency, mouth-feel.
- **Taste:** salt, sour, sweet, bitter.
- **Temperature:** hot/cold, chilled.
- **Pain:** chilli pepper.

When we eat and enjoy food the messages we receive by our senses are harmonious and form a much more complicated picture than that gained by one sense alone. Flavour is a combination of smell, taste and mouth-feel. If any one of these components is missing – for example, smell when we have a cold – the overall impact is changed.

Cooking and processing food is the use of chemical technology to create a harmonious product using colour, smell, taste, texture and mouth-feel. A knowledge of basic food ingredients and their chemistry will help the chef both develop new recipes and dishes, and give him/her a knowledge of how to correct dishes when things go wrong.

Vision

Colour has an effect on 'eye appeal', having an overall effect on the presentation of the food. The colour of food is extremely important to our enjoyment of it. People are sensitive to the colour of the food they eat and will reject food that is not considered to have the accepted colour. For example, strawberries that have been preserved in sulphite lose all their natural colour and appear white. If strawberries are to be canned or used in jam, artificial colour must be added before they are considered acceptable to eat. Colour is added to a wide range of food products to enhance attractiveness.

There is a strong link between the colour and the flavour of food. An ability to detect the flavour of food is very much connected with its colour and if the colour is unusual our sense of taste is confused. For example, if a fruit jelly is red, it is likely that the flavour detected will be that of a red-coloured fruit such as a strawberry even if the true flavour is lemon or banana.

The depth of colour in food also affects our sense of taste. We associate strong colours with strong flavour. For example, if a series of jellies all contain the same amount of given flavour, but are of different shades of the same colour, then those having a stronger colour will appear also to have a stronger flavour.

Smell

Smell is a chemical sense that acts over a distance. Chemicals are detected by their volatile compounds; this means that they must evaporate and become airborne easily. Smell receptors are located in the back of the nasal cavity, known as the olfactory area (see Figure 11.14).

The air is able to reach the olfactory area through both the nose and the mouth. Many of the characteristics associated as flavours are actually related to smell rather than taste. When we eat food, the volatile components evaporate and reach the olfactory area through the back of the throat, which connects the mouth and nasal cavity. When we have a cold, the membranes of the nasal cavity swell and prevent access to the area containing the smell receptors. We say we cannot taste, when what we actually mean is we cannot smell the food.

The sense of smell is very sensitive, it may be divided into the following basic types:

- pungent
- floral
- putrid
- peppermint
- camphoric
- ethereal
- musky.

Taste

Taste is another chemical sense, but unlike smell it does not work at a distance. The messages we receive from taste are simpler than those of smell. There are four basic tastes: salt, sweet, sour and bitter; metallic and soapy tastes may also be included.

Figure 11.14 The olfactory area

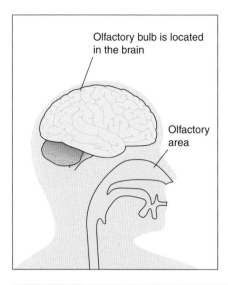

Olfactory bulb is located in the brain

Olfactory area

Table 11.17 Examples of textures encountered in food

FOOD	TEXTURE	FOOD	TEXTURE
Cheese	Solid	Sauces	Thick
	elastic		Thin
	crumbly		Lumpy
	creamy	Vegetables	Crisp
	Melted		Crunchy
	liquid		Soft
	viscous	Soups	Thick
			Thin
			Lumpy

Taste buds are located on the tongue. Babies and children have more taste buds than adults – the number decreases with age.

For a substance to give a sensation of taste it must be soluble in water. When we eat food, some of it dissolves in saliva, which contributes to the taste sensation we experience.

Our reactions to taste differ considerably. Many taste preferences are learnt in childhood. We generally are much more sensitive to bitter than to any other tastes – meaning we are able to taste smaller amounts of bitter substances than of sweet, salty or sour substances.

Taste is affected by several factors. Flavour enhancers – for example, MSG (monosodium glutamate) – increase the intensity of both salt and bitter tastes, and of 'meatiness'.

The temperature of food also affects the way we perceive taste. We are most sensitive to taste when food is between 22° and 41°C (71.6–105.8°F).

Table 11.18 The 12 ways of cooking foods

METHOD	EFFECT ON FOODS
1 Boiling	Gentle boiling helps to break down the tough fibrous structure of certain foods, which would be less tender if cooked by other methods. When boiling meats for long periods the soluble meat extracts are dissolved in the cooking liquid. Cooking must be slow to give time for the connective tissue in tough meat to be changed into soluble gelatine, so releasing the fibres and making the meat tender. If the connective tissue gelatinises too quickly the meat fibres fall apart and the meat will be tough and stringy. Gentle heat will ensure coagulation of the protein without hardening. Vegetables should be boiled for the shortest time possible otherwise their nutrient content will be reduced or lost.
2 Poaching	Helps to tenderise the fibrous structure of the food, and the raw texture of the food becomes edible by chemical action.
3 Stewing	In the slow process of cooking in gentle heat, the connective tissue in meat and poultry is converted into a gelatinous substance so that the fibres fall apart easily and become digestible. The protein is coagulated without being toughened.
4 Braising	Causes the breakdown of tissue fibre in the structure of certain foods, which softens the texture, thus making it tender and edible.
5 Steaming	The structure and texture of food is changed by chemical action and becomes edible.
6 Baking	Chemical action caused by the effect of heat on certain ingredients (e.g. yeast, baking powder) changes the raw structure of many foods (e.g. pastry, bread) to an edible texture.
7 Roasting and spit-roasting	The surface protein of the food is seared by the initial heat of the oven and improves the appearance, but not necessarily the palatability. This does not necessarily prevent the escape of the natural juices as was once thought to happen. When the food is highly browned, the oven temperature is reduced to cook the inside of the food without hardening the surface.
8 Grilling	Because of the speed of cooking there is maximum retention of nutrients and flavour because the effect of fierce heat on the surface of meat rapidly coagulates and seals the surface protein, thus helping to retain the meat juices.
9 Shallow-frying	The high temperature produces almost instant coagulation of the surface protein of the food. Some of the frying medium will be absorbed by the food being fried, which will change the nutritional content.
10 Deep-frying	Foods coated with flour, eggs, milk, breadcrumbs or a batter absorb the minimum amount of fat because the surface is sealed by the coagulation of the protein. Uncoated foods, such as chips, absorb a huge amount of fat, thus affecting their texture and nutritional content.
11 Paper bag cookery	Because the food is tightly sealed in oiled greaseproof paper or foil, no steam escapes during cooking and maximum natural flavour and nutritive value are retained.
12 Microwave cookery	A method of cooking and heating food by using high-frequency power. The microwave disturbs the molecules or particles of food and agitates them, thus causing friction, which has the effect of cooking the whole of the food. This method of cooking causes the food to become edible by the heat generated. Proteins become denatured, starches are gelatinised, with most of the moisture and flavour being retained.

Temperatures above and below this range decrease the sensitivity of the taste buds.

Touch

Touch, as referred to in connection with sensory evaluation, is mouth-feel – the way food feels in the mouth. Mouth-feel is very important when we assess or develop food products, recipes and dishes. Mouth-feel adds to a food's acceptability. Texture is a message we receive from mouth-feel. This includes consistency, chewiness, brittleness, crunchiness, astringency, and so on. These sensations add greatly to our enjoyment of food.

COOKING PROCESSES AND THEIR EFFECTS ON FOODS

There are 12 ways of cooking foods (see Table 11.18).

GENETICALLY MODIFIED FOOD

Scientists can create plants that nature itself has never created – plants that are resistant to chemicals that kill weeds (herbicides), plants that produce chemicals to kill insects (pesticides) and plants that last longer after harvesting. The methods used to produce these new crops involve the crops' genes changing or modifying. Genes are contained in the cells of all living things; they guide how living things are made and how they function.

What are genes?

Genes are the 'recipe' for all living things. They act as codes for different traits such as the size or colour of fruit. These traits are passed from one generation to the next. Genes are carried in a chemical called DNA.

DNA stands for deoxyribonucleic acid. Its secret lies in its structure – a long, ladder-like molecule that winds like a spiral staircase (see Figure 11.15). The rungs of the ladder are made up of chemicals.

Figure 11.15 The DNA ladder

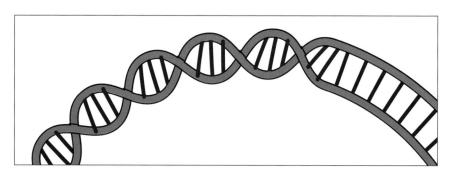

The order of the chemicals along the DNA spiral forms a code that spells out the cell's job, just like letters of the alphabet spell out the words in this book.

Chromosomes

In the nucleus (middle) of a cell there are a certain number of chromosomes. Chromosomes are packages of tightly coiled DNA. In a human the DNA in a single cell, stretched out, would be two metres long; in a whole body, this would make a hundred billion kilometres of DNA. All living things have chromosomes, though not all have the same number: humans have 46 per cell and tomatoes have 24. Half the chromosomes come from the father and half from the mother, so there are two copies of each chromosome, one from each parent.

Genes

There are many, many genes in a chromosome. Each gene is a section of the DNA spiral that is responsible for making a particular protein. Proteins determine what plants and animals look like and how they work. Seen close up, DNA looks like a double spiral.

Swapping genes

The secret of swapping genes lies in the rings of DNA called plasmids, which are found in bacteria. Plasmids seem to be nature's way of moving genes between different organisms. By cutting open the ring and putting in an extra piece of DNA – a gene – the plasmid's genetic message can be changed.

The first experiments were done in bacteria called *Esherichia coli* (E. coli). By modifying the plasmids in these E. coli cells and growing them in a petri dish, they could be turned into bacterial factories, able to make

Figure 11.16 Proteins

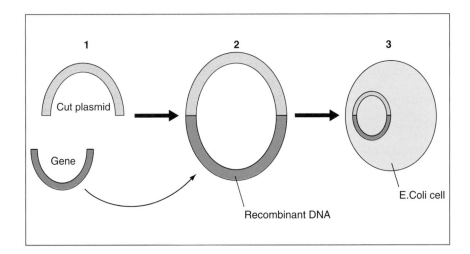

any protein. Different proteins are needed to build the different tissues of living things.

Plasmids can be cut open using enzymes. The cutting process leaves the plasmid with sticky ends. If another stretch of DNA – a gene – is added, it sticks and completes the ring. The result is called recombinant DNA. The new plasmid is then put back into the E. coli cell.

How is genetic modification done?

Now scientists are going beyond using recombinant DNA in bacteria. By adding genes or stopping existing genes working, they can create crops that resist weedkillers, plants that produce their own insecticides, or tomatoes that go soft more slowly because the gene that makes them rot has been deactivated.

The desired gene is chosen and isolated. This might be a gene that makes strawberries sweeter by producing more sugar. The gene is cut into the plasmid of a bacterium called *Agrobacterium Tumefaciens*. Cells are taken from the strawberry plants. The bacterium containing the plasmid is mixed with the strawberry cells in a dish that contains a nutrient jelly (agar) to keep the cells alive. The cells are tested to see which of them have been infected by the bacterium and have accepted the plasmid. The modified cells are encouraged to grow into plants, which are then planted in large nurseries to create more plants or seed for sale to farmers.

Some plants, including cereals, cannot be modified by the *Agrobacterium* method. To modify these plants, genes are coated onto tiny gold pellets, which are then fired, like a shot from a gun, into plant cells. Some of the genes work inside the cells to produce a modified plant.

Types of modification

The most common GM crops grown at the moment are those that resist herbicides. The second most common are the crops that can kill pests. Some crops have been given both these genes.

A bacterium called *Bacillus Thuringiensis* (Bt), which is found in the soil, produces a toxin that kills insects but is harmless to people. Putting the Bt toxin gene into maize plants allows them to make their own poison, which kills a crop pest called the corn borer.

In future, GM crops that grow in poor, dry or salty soils may be developed. This would make huge areas of worthless land productive.

Potatoes modified to contain less starch could make healthier chips because they do not absorb so much fat in the cooking. GM vegetables produced with added nutrients may help to fight off heart disease and cancer.

Effects on nature

GM plants could have unexpected effects on nature, however. The poisons intended to kill pests could damage other insects, while genes put into plants could escape in their pollen.

Laboratory experiments in the United States have shown that the Bt toxin intended to kill pests can also kill Monarch butterflies, which are harmless to crops. Recent research has shown that GM crops are leaking toxins from their roots into the soil. This affects the soil and may even produce new strains of pests.

Pollen from GM crops may be carried a long distance by wind and may cross-pollinate with wild plants or other crops. This may create odd breeds and affect organic crop farmers.

PRODUCT DEVELOPMENT

Why produce new recipes and new menus? In order to create or develop customer or consumer satisfaction it is essential to prevent menu apathy and to produce interest, enabling the discovery of new flavours and combinations. The exercise is two-fold: to satisfy both customer and management. Therefore the prime consideration is the cost of the development and the selling price. It is essential to consider the style or type of establishment and the kind of clientele for whom the changes are intended, as well as regional variations and food fashions.

The reasons for change could include:

- menu fatigue
- a need to stimulate business
- changes in clientele
- new chef and staff
- food fashion changes
- opening of a similar local establishment
- availability of supplies.

Whatever the cause, it is necessary to introduce new recipes and menus in relation to the organisation's objectives. It follows that, in every sphere of catering, whether school meals, in hospitals, speciality outlets or exclusive restaurants, recipe and menu changes may need to occur. If new developments are intended it is first essential to evaluate:

- the cost of development
- the effect the change or changes will have on the existing situation
- the ability of staff to cope
- that there is adequate equipment and suitable suppliers
- the presentation of the dishes
- the format of the menu.

Recipe development: preparation

Preparation prior to the practical aspects of producing new recipes includes the need to construct a method of recording accurate details of ingredients, their cost, quality and availability. Time needed for preparation, production and yield must also be recorded. Space should be made on the chart to specify several attempts, so that comparisons can be made and to ensure that there is adequate space for making notes.

An evaluation sheet is required so that a record is made of the opinions of the tasting panel or persons consulted. This sheet will, as appropriate, be constructed to include space for flavours, colour, texture, presentation, and so on.

Developing new ideas

The developing of new recipes is challenging, stimulating and creates new interest, but where do original ideas come from? Many are triggered by the creations of others. It is therefore particularly worthwhile to keep abreast of what is happening around us. Here are a few suggestions for doing just that.

Publishing
- *Caterer and Hotelkeeper* magazine
- Books produced by leading chefs
- Magazines, including women's magazines
- Newspaper articles
- Libraries, etc.

TV and radio
- *Masterchef* TV competition
- *Ready Steady Cook*, and similar TV programmes
- *Junior Masterchef* TV competition
- Food programmes

Contacts
- Visiting other establishments
- Competitors
- Visiting catering exhibitions
- Catering organisations, and so on
- Lectures, demonstrations

Extra care needs to be taken when introducing new recipes to patients in hospitals and nursing homes, and in the provision of meals in schools and residential establishments, to ensure that the nutritional content is suitable. Dieticians can provide advice on the dietary requirements of such people.

Communication

Information sources for recipes are available everywhere. Every kind of establishment, from the local Chinese restaurant to the five-star hotel, can present innovative ideas. Overseas travel can be influential in bringing new dishes to the UK. Department stores, exhibition centres, outdoor events, and so on, may well also stimulate ideas. The range of ingredients available from catering suppliers is immense, but local markets and supermarkets should not be ignored as sources of supply.

With new developments in mind, it is necessary to pass on these proposals to both senior management (who will be responsible for their implementation) and to fellow members of the kitchen brigade (for their constructive comments). If possible, put your ideas to the test with respected members of the catering profession with whom you are acquainted. The proposals should include estimated food costing, times to produce, labour costs, equipment and facilities needed, and details of staff training if required. Knowledge of the establishment's organisation is important so that the right person or persons are involved.

Quality of materials

The highest possible standards of ingredients should be used so that a true and valid result is available for assessment of the recipe.

Staff abilities

The staff's craft skills should be appraised in order to assess their capability in coping with innovations. Failure to do so could jeopardise the whole project. Also their cooperation in putting new ideas into practice should be sought; and encouragement given when the outcome is successful.

Equipment facilities

New recipes can affect the utilisation of existing equipment by overloading at peak times. The capacity of items such as pastry ovens, deep-fat fryers or salamanders can already be fully used. New items can affect the production of the present menu; this fact should be borne in mind so that service is not impaired.

Cooking

It goes without saying that accurate cooking is essential with any development. *Practical Cookery* gives guidance on this aspect of the project (see the 'References' section for full details of this publication).

Implementation

Having tested and arrived at the finished recipe, staff may need to practise production and presentation of the dish. This may include both small and large quantities, depending on the establishment. In all cases careful recording of all aspects of the operation can help in the smooth running of the exercise, in particular basic work study should be observed. Constructive comments should be sought from staff, in particular any problems should be discussed.

The results of such trial runs should be conveyed to senior personnel, and any problems that have been identified should be resolved.

Having validated the recipe, checked on a reliable supplier and ensured the capability of the staff, it is important that all concerned know when the dishes will be included on the menu.

Storekeepers, kitchen staff and serving staff need to be briefed, as do any other departments involved, as to the time and date of implementation.

Presentation

Of particular importance is how the customer sees the dish; when it is received it needs to appeal to the senses of sight and smell – even before taste. Consideration needs to be given early in the development of the idea to what dish or plate will be used, what will accompany it and the skill needed to serve it. Foods in some establishments are prepared and cooked in front of the customer, while some require the dish to be cooked fresh while the customer waits. Therefore, details of presentation must be recorded and, where possible, a test conducted in the actual situation.

Should the new recipe be for a food service operation that involves preparation, cooking and presentation before the customer so that all or part of this is seen by the potential consumer, then attention needs to be paid to the skills of the chef, and extra training – not only in culinary skills but also in customer-handling skills – may be needed, as well as particular attention to hygiene. These factors need to be observed at the development stage so that customer satisfaction occurs immediately.

Organisation

To implement new dishes, adequate time needs to be allowed to test and develop the recipe, to train the staff, to appraise comments and modify recipes if necessary. Staff must be briefed on the composition of the dish, particularly serving staff, as well as being told when it will be included on the menu. They need to be asked if there are any problems; if required this could be done in a written form. Senior personnel need to be informed verbally or in writing of the implementation of the new items.

Should the new dish or dishes require skills that are unfamiliar to some staff, then the workload of individuals may need to be changed so as to accommodate staff with the appropriate skill. In estimating how long it will take to implement the new dish, factors to take account of are: the skills of the staff; whether suitable equipment is available; that suppliers can produce the required ingredients in the right quantity at the desired quality at a suitable price.

Clear written instructions may need to be provided – which means the sequence in which the ingredients are to be used, with the appropriate amount (for example, 10 portions or 50 portions).

The introduction of a salad bar or sweet trolley including new dishes can affect the service of the usual dishes. If the clientele require, say, vegetarian dishes, or those with particular cultural or religious needs have special requests, then adaptations may be necessary to accommodate these in the existing set-up (see below).

In addition to obtaining feedback from staff, it is just as important, if not more so, to obtain comments from the customer or consumer.

Managing resources when developing recipes

The following points should be considered:

- the elimination of waste
- the control of materials and ingredients
- the careful use of energy
- the most effective use of time.

Ensure that a record is kept so that no resources are misused. Failure to control and monitor resources can be expensive in terms of time, materials and effort.

Specific considerations

When considering any development, it is necessary to take into account current problems and issues that may affect the outcome. It is essential to keep up to date on issues such as the BSE scare and the effect on consumers' choice or rejection of beef. The increasing use of organic foods may encourage customer demand for such foods to be used; strictly speaking, all foods are organic, but the term has become restricted to mean those grown without the use of pesticides or processed without the use of additives. There is little difference nutritionally between organic and non-organic produce. The *Manual of Nutrition* (MAFF, 1995) is a most useful reference book for information on nutrition.

Certain groups of people have restrictions on their eating habits, which must be observed when producing new recipes for them.

- **Vegetarians:** no meat, most eat no fish, most eat cheese, eggs and milk.
- **Vegans:** no food of animal origin.
- **Hindus:** no beef, mainly vegetables, no alcohol.
- **Muslims:** no pork, no alcohol, no shellfish, meat should be halal (i.e. killed according to Muslim custom).
- **Sikhs:** no beef, no alcohol, only meat killed with one blow to the head.
- **Jews:** no pork, meat must be kosher, only fish with fins and scales, meat and dairy produce not to be eaten together.
- **Rastafarians:** no animal products except milk, no canned or processed foods, no salt added, foods should be organic.

Menu design

The function of a menu is to inform potential customers what dishes are available and, as appropriate, the number of courses, the choice on the courses and the price. The wording should make clear to the kind of customer using the establishment what to expect. The menu may also be used to promote specific items, such as when an ingredient is in season, children's menus, reductions for senior citizens or served at particular times.

If printed, the type should be clear and of readable size; if handwritten, the script should be of good quality so as to create a good impression. Menus are expensive to produce, but when attractive and they fulfil the function of informing, they may enhance the reputation of the establishment and increase custom.

Further information
- Vegan Society: www.vegansociety.com
- Vegetarian Society UK Ltd: www.vegsoc.org

REFERENCES

Foskett, D., Ceserani, V. and Kinton, R. with contributions by Campbell, J. (2004) *Practical Cookery* (10th edn). London: Hodder Arnold.
MAFF (1995) *Manual of Nutrition*. London: HMSO.
Proudlove, R.K. (2001) *The Science and Technology of Foods*. Forbes Publications.

Some references to chemistry elsewhere in the book:

Nutrition	180
Preservation	220
Bacteria	636
pH	229
Hygiene	614

TOPICS FOR DISCUSSION

1. What advantages does a chef have in understanding basic food science?
2. Why product development is important to food production outlets.
3. How emulsions are formed and stabilised.
4. The effect of heat on proteins and carbohydrates.
5. Current product development in the food and catering industry.
6. How working in a product development kitchen differs from a production kitchen.

Chapter 12 PRODUCT DEVELOPMENT AND MANUFACTURING TO DELIVER CONVENIENCE IN THE KITCHEN

A FOOD MANUFACTURER'S UNDERSTANDING OF CONVENIENCE

'I would like to be seen as a modern chef of today by creating both classical and contemporary recipes and concepts, using my traditional culinary and general catering background and experience of yesterday, with today's and tomorrow's new and emerging trends and technologies.'

This quote is from Ray Lorimer FHCIMA – co-author of this chapter, classically trained chef, caterer and food logistician. Ray has 27 years'

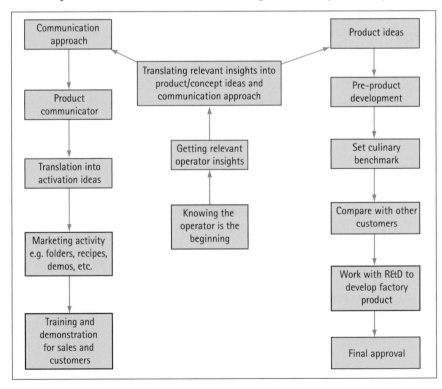

Figure 12.1 The role of chefs in concept and product development at Unilever

Further information
To find out more about the sponsor's brands and products, with recipes and other useful information, visit www.unileverfoodsolutions. co.uk.

experience in the army as master chef and catering officer and since 1992 has been one of the new breed of chefs working in the hospitality and catering industry. His comment perfectly summarises the approach to product development adopted by successful food manufacturers to help caterers and chefs in the industry grow their businesses. At Unilever Foodsolutions there are over 100 chefs with similar experience and backgrounds, working within local centres around the world.

The best convenience foods are those that are the closest match to the dishes chefs prepare from first principles in the kitchen. For this reason, food manufacturers employ professional chefs, who are not just involved in innovation and product improvements, but also carry out training and make presentations to sales and marketing teams and, critically, catering and chef customers (see Figure 12.1).

WHAT IS HAPPENING IN THE INDUSTRY?

The food market is extremely dynamic and food manufacturers look at what is happening out-of-home, on the shelves in the supermarkets, and at culinary trends across the world.

Some of the more significant areas include the following:

- **Health and vitality:** Obesity is a serious problem in Britain. The Government is trying to persuade consumers to improve their diet when eating at home and out-of-home.

  When people are deciding what to buy for home consumption, health is a prime factor, but because eating out is often a leisure activity, it is seen as an indulgence. However, health is an area which has grown between 2005 and 2006 and this growth is set to continue (see Figure 12.2).

  It is seen as especially important to educate consumers early, and one area of focus is to encourage school children to eat a balanced diet. Manufacturers produce foods that deliver against nutritional targets set by the Food Standards Agency for school meal providers.
- **Fusion cuisine:** Global travel, mass migration and the Internet have created a virtual world cookbook, where culinary traditions merge and great new food combinations are conceived. Fusion cooking is the marriage of flavours and ingredients from different parts of the globe, which come together to create a new dining experience. Convenience foods can mirror the original ingredients and give authenticity to a dish that has been prepared by chefs with little or no experience of a particular style of cooking, so that, for example, a Moroccan lamb tagine could be offered on the same menu as salmon fillets with a pesto crust.
- **Assembly cooking – homemade:** Ready meals are at one end of the convenience scale, those prepared from first principles at the other. In between comes assembly cooking, where the customer has clear

Figure 12.2 Core consumption drivers for in-home and out-of-home meals, March–August 2006

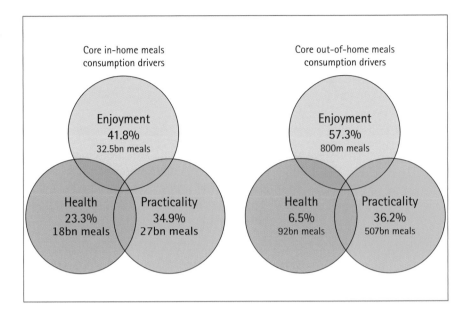

Core in-home meals consumption drivers

Enjoyment
41.8%
32.5bn meals

Health
23.3%
18bn meals

Practicality
34.9%
27bn meals

Core out-of-home meals consumption drivers

Enjoyment
57.3%
800m meals

Health
6.5%
92bn meals

Practicality
36.2%
507bn meals

Source: Worldpanel™, TNS 2006

evidence that their meal has been prepared on the premises, but the chef has used part-prepared ingredients to achieve the end result. An example would be penne pasta with tomato and mascarpone sauce, garnished with fresh herbs.

- **Increased control on waste and yield:** Preparing food from scratch generates more waste than using prepared products stating the number of portions on the pack. Convenience foods can help to reduce waste and also help chefs control portion sizes and thus meet their target gross profit. This is particularly important in kitchens where tight control on costs is critical and it helps ensure a profitable business model.
- **Hygiene and food scares:** Recently there have been a number of new regulations affecting the preparation and storage of foods, including the HACCP rules, which are having an effect on what happens in the kitchen. Regulations like these mean that chefs have to be more aware of food hygiene principles and the issues involved in, for example, handling raw foods to avoid the spread of harmful bacteria. Manufactured foods, such as a mayonnaise, can play a role in helping chefs meet these legal requirements because they have been through processes like pasteurisation, which eliminates bacteria.
- **Changing skills:** As convenience foods become more widely used, so the dynamics in the kitchen are changed. This does not mean that fewer skills are needed; it means that different skills are needed. 'Cooking smart' means classic meets contemporary. It is key that convenience foods are used in a contemporary classical manner and with fresh ingredients. It is important to highlight the assistance these products can offer to the chef in achieving daily business targets.

Classic meets contemporary recognises the chef's desire to be creative and supports that. It does, however, give some examples of the

Figure 12.3 The lower the skill level in the kitchen, and the higher the number of meals served, the greater the need for convenience products

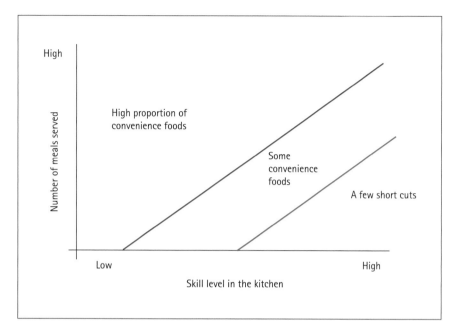

Further information
To find out more about healthy eating and food safety, visit www.foodstandards.gov. uk. It is particularly good for the latest news on legal requirements.
The Food and Drink Federation is the voice of the UK food industry. Its aim is to promote consumer confidence in the food chain. Visit www.fdf.org.uk.

costs of preparing products classically, from scratch, and makes comparisons of how the chef-developed manufactured products can provide a quality alternative within the appropriate environment.

Generally speaking, the lower the skill level in the kitchen, and the higher the number of meals served, the greater the need for convenience products (see Figure 12.3).

HOW UNILEVER FOODSOLUTIONS WORKS IN AND SUPPORTS THE INDUSTRY

Culinary and customer insight

The culinary services team at Unilever Foodsolutions is made up of fully trained, professional chefs, who work with customers in all types of catering outlets – pubs, restaurants, hotels, staff restaurants, schools and hospitals – to understand what issues in the kitchen are not being addressed by products currently on the market. This is the foundation from which to improve existing products and bring new ones to the market.

The culinary services team's roles include:

- working with hospitality businesses
- visiting chefs in individual outlets to profile and observe kitchen practices, service and equipment
- discovering ways in which convenience foods could save time and money and enhance the menu
- helping to develop the appropriate products to address industry needs.

Business structure

Unilever Foodsolutions is a global business, with branches in some 150 countries. The Unilever Group, of which Unilever Foodsolutions is a part, owns brands including Knorr, Hellmann's, Lipton and Carte d'Or. In the UK, Flora spreads, PG Tips tea and Colman's mustards are all part of the range.

Unilever Foodsolutions' success in the catering market is based on its strong customer relationships, brands, customer insight (understanding how chefs use its products and what they need), investment in innovation and the continual upgrading of its existing products.

THE CONVENIENCE CATEGORIES AND THEIR ROLE

What is a category?

Chefs categorise food by its place on the menu – as a starter, for example, or as a pudding. Food manufacturers and suppliers sub-divide these menu sections into product categories, e.g. bakery, savoury pies, ready meals, poultry products, frozen desserts and ingredients such as sauces.

Some other examples of product categories are described below.

Stocks and bouillons

Stocks and bouillons are used as the base for soups and sauces, adding flavour and depth to the dish. Manufactured products have developed over the years from a powder format into pastes and concentrates, which now account for the main part of the market.

The traditional method of making stocks by simmering bones and vegetables for several hours is problematic in a busy modern kitchen. It uses a lot of energy, there is the risk of fire if the stock is left on the hob overnight and the broth is a breeding ground for bacteria that may not all be killed off in the final cooking process.

The clamp-down on the use of bones and offal during the BSE epidemic of the 1990s brought bouillons to the fore, especially with continued legislation such as HACCP. Many chefs switched to convenience products and have remained with them ever since.

The products on the market save time and money and, with the changing skill base, can help in an ever-busy kitchen.

Soup

Soup is a very flexible dish and well-placed to deliver on the growing health options required by consumers. It can be served as a starter, as a light bite or as part of a meal deal, e.g. soup and a sandwich at an all-in-one price.

Nearly all national cuisines around the world include some form of soup:

- British, e.g. cream of watercress, leek and potato, Highland vegetable
- Continental, e.g. beef goulash, red pepper and tomato, French onion
- Russian, e.g. borscht
- Oriental, e.g. Thai vegetable, won-ton
- African, e.g. Moroccan chickpea.

Dehydrated soup has been on the market for decades. It is still the mainstay for many caterers, especially those preparing food on a large scale, for example in hospitals or staff catering. Powder technology has improved greatly over time and the dried product of today is very different from the dried product of 10 years ago.

Food manufacturers have developed a choice of formats for chefs in response to changing market trends. Soups are now available dry, in powder and roux technology granules, liquid ambient (room temperature), chilled and frozen. They are packed in cartons, poly-bottles or pouch packs.

One pack may contain enough for just one person or a larger quantity such as 25 servings. Increasingly, there is a move to single serve, which addresses wastage and portion control problems.

Convenience soup is prepared according to the instructions on the pack and enhanced to offer a chef's own touch, for example with:

- finely chopped vegetables
- a swirl of cream
- croûtons
- herbs
- flavoured oil.

Sauces

Sauces dictate the nature of a dish. The same piece of meat can be transformed into something out of the classical repertoire or something from another country's cuisine. Using different sauces, chicken breast meat, for example, can be transformed into chicken tikka masala, Jamaican jerk chicken or chicken à la king.

Food manufacturers have developed a range of sauce formats from powders, roux granules and pastes through to ready-prepared. Liquid roux merits special attention. This kitchen essential is available in the form of never-fail granules, providing a basic sauce from which many others can be created.

There are now hundreds of different varieties available, reflecting the big demand from caterers. Meat with sauce remains a popular dish with UK consumers and many of the most popular dishes eaten out of home are served with a sauce as the following top 10 (TNS Worldpanel Foodservice 2006) shows:

- pizza
- roast dinner: chicken, beef, pork or lamb with roast potatoes, vegetables, Yorkshire pudding and gravy
- steak pie, chips and peas
- lasagne with garlic bread
- chicken curry with rice
- beefburger served in a roll with chips and salad and/or vegetables
- steak and chips with a sauce, peppercorn being the most popular
- fish, fried in batter, with chips and peas or mushy peas
- shepherd's pie with chips and vegetables
- spaghetti bolognaise.

Table 12.1 Examples of classic, modern and ethnic sauces

CLASSIC	MODERN	ETHNIC
Béchamel	Pepper	Korma
Demi glace	Chilli	Tikka masala
Chasseur	Provençale	Sweet and sour
Béarnaise	Blue cheese	Cajun

Ethnic sauces, usually in paste and ready-to-use formats, helped to bring authentic ethnic dishes within the reach of classically trained chefs who had no previous experience of these culinary traditions. Before their introduction, if customers wanted, for example, an authentic Thai curry, they would be unlikely to find it outside a Thai restaurant. Now, it is commonplace in pubs and staff restaurants.

Dressings

Dressings may come in the form of powder mixes or ready-prepared products. They are packed in bulk for use in the kitchen and come in portion-packs and table-top sizes for front-of-house. Some different types of dressing are described below.

- **Mayonnaise:** Manufactured mayonnaise has always been popular with chefs, but after the outbreak of salmonella in eggs in 1988, many more stopped making their own in the kitchen, and switched to manufactured products. Pasteurisation occurs in the factory process and this kills harmful bacteria.

  Mayonnaise acts as a binding agent. It adds a moist, creamy texture to food but is deliberately neutral, letting the flavour of the other ingredients come through. Alternatively, there are flavoured mayonnaises, e.g. garlic, available which have the same useful properties as the plain variety, but also enhance the taste of the dish. There are also lighter versions containing fewer calories and less fat. It is also a great accompaniment front-of-house, to be served with salads and hot meals.

- **Vinaigrette:** The traditional combination of oil and vinegar has been

Figure 12.4 A merchandising unit for tea

given an extra lift by food manufacturers, who have introduced flavoured versions, e.g. raspberry or garlic and herbs.

- **Creamy dressings:** These complement different cuisines, e.g. American-style dishes work well with Caesar, Thousand Island and blue cheese dressings.

Front-of-house, it is good to choose brands for dressings and condiments that customers recognise and trust, e.g. Heinz Tomato Ketchup, Colman's English Mustard and Hellmann's Real Mayonnaise. This gives your customers reassurance that you are serving them their favourites. Research shows this can really help to improve the whole experience (Deep Blue Research, January 2005).

Hot beverages

Suppliers of the leading tea and coffee brands have been some of the most prodigious in terms of creating variations on a theme: square, round and pyramid teabags; latte, espresso and cappuccino coffees. This is a high margin category, where well known brands command a premium. Consumers will often be prepared to pay more for a cup of Nescafé coffee or PG Tips tea than they will for a no-name label.

For this reason, the brand manufacturers have new ways of helping caterers serve hot beverages to the consumer. In the case of tea get the basics right:

- serve piping hot
- give the consumer control over the brewing
- serve with fresh milk.

To add value:

- make the most of the communication: let consumers know what varieties and which brands you serve on your menu
- present it well: many suppliers offer merchandising front-of-house to keep it tidy (see Figure 12.4)
- don't forget the 'tea-to-go' opportunity.

Spreads

Butter is a staple in every kitchen but just as consumers are looking for lower fat, lighter spreads when preparing family meals at home, caterers should offer healthier alternatives to their customers when eating out. People like to see portions of Flora spread alongside Lurpak or Anchor butter when they come down to breakfast in a hotel, for example.

The Government push behind healthy eating will also make it even more critical for caterers, especially school meal providers, to offer healthier alternatives. The balance between consumers wanting indulgence and health means you need to offer choice.

COMMERCIAL THINKING FOR YOUR MENU

The role of convenience foods

The main reason why caterers use convenience foods is to control and reduce their kitchen costs, but there are many other benefits. Convenience foods mean:

- **a smaller kitchen team:** Caterers can offer customers an extensive choice of dishes, with only a very small team in the kitchen, if they base their menu on a high proportion of ready- or part-prepared meals. This is especially useful where staff are hard to find and skills are limited.

    However, in such circumstances the only creative outlet for catering professionals is presenting the food attractively on the plate, and there is the risk that customers will recognise the dishes as being the same as those served by other catering operators. A middle path is for chefs to combine convenience products with those prepared from first principles, to create a menu that has variety and appeal, without putting the kitchen team under impossible pressure. This is the classic meets contemporary approach described at the beginning of the chapter.

- **fewer or different skills required:** Ready-prepared dishes can be served by people without higher catering qualifications, especially if it is simply a case of defrosting, heating and serving a frozen meal. This is one extreme, but in kitchens where convenience foods are used alongside fresh ingredients, it is not a case of de-skilling so much as re-skilling. Chefs choose which dishes to prepare from first principles, and decide where to take a short cut. This requires planning and management as well as craft skills. Assembling meal components is often a good compromise where the skill base is limited.

- **better portion control:** Make up convenience foods according to the instructions on the packet and divide them as advised to give exactly the right size portion every time. Caterers can work out the exact cost of each portion and accurately calculate the necessary selling price to achieve their target gross profit.

- **less waste:** Waste is minimised or totally eradicated when caterers use convenience products. If the chef is preparing a banquet for 150, it is easy to make up 150 exact portions, with nothing left over, and in a situation where demand is sporadic, chefs can make up a portion-size quantity to order and dose accurately.

- **easy budgeting:** Convenience food prices stay the same over a long period compared with, for example, daily market pricing of fresh meat, fish and vegetables. Chefs know exactly how much the product costs today, this week or next month.

- **consistency:** The same dish can be prepared to the same standard, every day, no matter who is in the kitchen. Just follow the simple instructions.

- **uniformity:** This is important for branded hotel, restaurant and large pub operations. Using convenience food they can be sure that the same dish will be prepared to the same standard in any one of their outlets, from one end of the country to the other.
- **availability:** Popular brands of foodservice convenience foods are easily sourced through the wholesaler, cash and carry and now even a few large supermarkets.
- **functionality:** Clever convenience foods can solve a problem in the kitchen or help to make the chef's life easier. For example, single portions of ready-to-serve soup can be used for all-night hotel room service, without the need for someone to be on call in the kitchen.
- **a longer shelf-life:** Convenience foods can last months and sometimes years unopened. There is a reduced danger of running out and little or no risk of having to discard ingredients that have gone past their best.
- **value:** Using convenience products usually works out cheaper than preparing the same food from first principles, even before you take into account labour and energy costs. Why not try costing out a dish?

How to make the menu more profitable

'Cooking smart' means combining cooking from first principles with buying-in part-prepared and fully-prepared products, to create a menu that appeals to customers, stands out from competitors, and gives the operator a good return.

The right combination will vary from operation to operation, or outlet to outlet, depending on various factors, including:

- **style of operation:** A chef-patron with a fine-dining restaurant will use only a modest number of convenience products. The whole point of their operation will be to show off their skill in preparing and cooking dishes from first principles. By contrast, a less skilled outlet or chain may use a high proportion of ready-prepared foods to ensure consistent delivery of standards across all their estate, up and down the country.
- **volume:** Contract caterers handling directors' dining, where they are catering for only a small number of people at one time, will be able to prepare more dishes from first principles than a team turning out 300-plus meals a day in a busy staff restaurant. There is a fine balance between quantity and quality and the chef will manage this carefully.
- **type of customers:** A tiny minority of gourmands will probably only ever be satisfied with food prepared from first principles, but for the vast majority of the population, expectations are driven by the different situations in which they find themselves. Someone in their works' restaurant may be happy with a portion of steak pie that they know is not fully prepared from scratch, for £2.50. When they are out with their partner for a special meal and paying in excess of £15, however, they will probably expect something that has been prepared by a professional chef on the premises from first principles.

Table 12.2 Menu
calculator

G/ML	INGREDIENT	COST PER KG/LITRE	COST PER PORTION
	Total cost per portion		
	Energy/fixed costs/labour (optional)		
	Enter target gross profit (%)		
	Menu selling price, including VAT		

- **price:** Consumers have a sense of what they are willing to pay, depending on the occasion and the type of operation, e.g. they will be prepared to spend more on a long-anticipated anniversary dinner in a restaurant than they will on an impromptu meal with friends in their local pub.

It may be helpful to use a menu calculator, like Table 12.2, to work out how much to charge for a dish to make the menu more profitable. By listing the ingredients used and taking into account fixed costs like energy, it is possible to work out a total cost per portion and determine what price to sell it at in order to achieve the desired profit.

- **staff skills:** The greater the level of skill among the kitchen staff, the less dependent they are likely to be on convenience foods. However, it is rare to find a kitchen that has a full complement of skilled staff during every service and the head chef may well decide to take a few short cuts to allow more time to be spent on the dishes for which the establishment is renowned.
- **facilities:** In a tiny kitchen, convenience foods require less space for preparation than raw ingredients. In a large, well-equipped kitchen, there is the opportunity to prepare more dishes from scratch.

THE PRODUCT DEVELOPMENT PROCESS

The innovation process

There is no shortage of ideas at the beginning of bringing a new product to market, but these have to be whittled down to the ones that will really make a difference in the kitchen or for the consumer.

It is important to remember that wholesalers and cash and carries have limited space in warehouses and on delivery vehicles, so only a limited number of lines can be stocked at each depot. New products need to add value and help grow sales for the caterer and the wholesaler or cash and carry.

Food manufacturers do not want to flood the market with lots of new products, but cannot afford to sit still as consumer tastes are changing all the time. New product development has to be well thought out and timely. The ideal new product launch will address a market need based on insight and give the manufacturer a few months' lead over its competitors by being first to market.

It usually takes 12-18 months to bring a product to market and longer if new technology is included. It is estimated that some 70% of new products fail, so getting the right one is critical.

How a new product comes to market

A new product goes through a four-stage innovation process:

1 idea
2 testing
3 validation
4 launch.

Idea
The idea is not plucked out of thin air. It is based on a business opportunity that has been identified, with a clear customer benefit. Some of the areas looked at include the following:

- **consumer insight:** Companies spend thousands of pounds on market research every year. It is the bedrock for strategy and planning. Interpret it correctly and they gain a tremendous competitive advantage. Get it wrong and the company could be in serious trouble. Good market research means the business is basing its decisions on fact, rather than relying on the management team's hunches.

    Manufacturers producing convenience foods for caterers need to start with the end consumer, tracking food trends; eating habits; taste preferences – these are all vital pieces of information.
- **customer insight:** While consumer insight drives creativity in terms of new things to eat, new ways of eating at different times and in different places, customer insight takes research into the commercial

kitchen, looking into the storerooms, finding out how chefs prepare products and working out ways to make their lives easier, while matching or improving the quality of the food they serve, and recognising the different needs of a classic kitchen compared with an automated chain kitchen. Understanding needs and issues leads to developing new solutions which address the current problem.

- **sector insight:** Chefs in different types of establishment behave differently. The factors that motivate someone producing hospital meals will be very different from those that drive a restaurateur, or a caterer in a staff restaurant. How they prepare the dish will vary significantly.

  Products have to be developed with the appropriate sectors in mind. People who run busy pub kitchens, for example, may be looking for dishes that are quick to produce. Customers in a restaurant are generally prepared to wait 20 minutes for their starter to arrive, but in a pub, food ideally needs to be on the table within a quarter of an hour of the order being placed. School meals must be healthy and meet Government nutritional guidelines. Products must achieve targets for salt and fat levels, and there are bonus points for items that are fortified with added nutrients and do not contain common allergens such as gluten.

- **competitor information:** Food manufacturing is an intensely competitive business. Where possible, a company will patent an idea, but this is not always possible. For the most part, rival manufacturers are content to monitor each others' statements in the press to find out which direction their competitors are headed in.

Testing

The team refines the idea and confirms what benefits it would bring to users. Market research is then carried out to validate and refine the concept and see whether there would be enough buyers prepared to pay the appropriate estimated price for the product.

Market research is typically one of the following:

- **focus group**, where six or seven chefs review, discuss and try products, giving their feedback
- **live market test:** the product is sent out to chefs to try live in a kitchen for six to 10 weeks. They then fill in a questionnaire and are interviewed for their comments.

The chef role

At this point, the culinary services team, comprising chefs, home economists and food technicians, takes up the challenge of finding a product that fills the gap or takes advantage of the opportunity identified by the various insights into consumer and caterer behaviour. Very often, this means returning to the classic repertoire contained in Larousse or

Escoffier, but bringing it up-to-date with some of the Rhodes or Ramsay thinking.

Products are developed from first principles and the results are debated by the project team, until a preferred solution or a number of options are arrived at. This is then tested and the most suitable recipe becomes the benchmark to scale up to production.

Initial samples are produced in the kitchen to establish the technical requirements and the manufacturing needs. The product might, for example, need a special type of packaging and the team would then need to see how this might best be achieved and build it into their project time plan.

Validation

The third stage is when detailed customer feedback is required; the product and packaging are finalised, and the manufacturing options are confirmed.

The technical role

The preferred sample developed by culinary services passes to the technical team, whose job it is to translate this recipe benchmark into something that can be manufactured, packed and stored, giving chefs a quality product with a suitable shelf-life after they have opened the pack.

Products that are commonplace in the kitchen may be difficult to source and work with in the factory. Chopping and adding fresh herbs to the mix at an advanced stage of the process might be too difficult and time-consuming, for example. Instead, the technicians may find an alternative which still delivers against the target benchmark.

Most manufacturers make products on a large scale and will produce their recipes by the tonne rather than by the portion. Even so, they will be able to give a very accurate price per portion for the caterer.

The initial work will be done in the development kitchen, using the products and equipment available on the factory floor, but on a smaller scale. After many tastings and adjustments, the best product in terms of quality and value will become the bench sample. This is the version the factory has to match.

With food manufacturers becoming global players, it is quite possible that the factory will be in Europe or overseas, especially if the product is from a different food culture. It is critical to ensure that the best ingredients are used to meet the high standards a chef expects in their professional kitchen.

Trials take place in the factory and there is a detailed process of tastings, re-visiting the recipe and tasting again, until everyone is satisfied with the result: right format, right ingredients, right flavour and taste, right performance in the kitchen, right price – and, of course, a product that is safe.

The final product is approved by expert taste panels and often by chefs in the market before going out.

Packaging

Packaging plays an important part in the success of a new product. If cash and carry is a big opportunity, the pack must stand out on the shelf and be easy to understand. In this case, the designers will consider how the packs look when stacked, say, six wide and three high. If the product is geared to smaller restaurants, the pack should contain 10 portions, but for hospital meals, 100 portions would be more appropriate. There may also be a practical benefit and selling point in the type of packaging chosen, for example re-sealable sacks of rice.

Packaging must be easy-to-use in the kitchen and carry all the necessary information. Examples of information which must be included are:

- legal name and product descriptor
- product code and barcode
- ingredient list – the ingredient making up the highest percentage first, then the rest in descending order of importance
- allergens
- nutrition data per 100 g/100 ml as sold and per portion if relevant
- claims, e.g. rich in vitamin C, suitable for vegetarians
- pack size, weight or volume
- hazard warning text where applicable
- method of use and cooking instructions
- storage conditions and shelf-life, unopened and opened
- company details (name and address)
- customer service contact details.

Launch

We are now ready with our first production of the new product in the warehouse.

THE ROUTE TO MARKET

In order to bring the product to market, the supplier needs to promote it to three audiences:

1 distributors: food wholesalers and cash and carry stores
2 group operators: the major hotel, restaurant and pub groups and/or education and healthcare providers
3 independent operators: owner-managed businesses or small groups of, say, less than a dozen outlets.

Distributors

There is limited space in wholesalers' warehouses and cash and carry stores, so there needs to be a strong argument about why this product is right for the market. For every new product that is accepted, another is usually de-listed.

Figure 12.5 The route to market

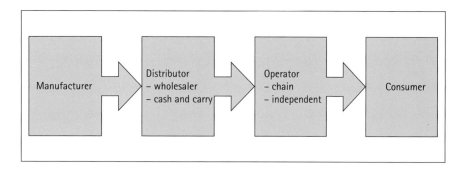

Further information
For further insight into the food distribution network, visit the Federation of Wholesale Distributors' website, www.fwd.co.uk.

New products have to appeal to distributors. They must be what their customers want and they must offer a margin for the wholesaler or cash and carry. The ideal product will sell a lot (volume), at a premium price (value), with a good return for the distributor (margin).

Distributors will ask what support the manufacturer is prepared to put behind the new product. This could be a trade press advertising campaign, which would prompt cash and carry customers to look for the product on the shelf, or it could be a tempting promotion such as a collector loyalty scheme or buy-one-get-one-free offer.

The manufacturer would usually advertise in the wholesaler's price list, which would be seen by thousands of potential customers, and there is the possibility of running a telesales activity to encourage trial, while taking orders over the telephone. Telesales operators are the people who take customer orders and they are in the perfect position to recommend the right new products to chefs.

Group operators

Food manufacturers employ national account managers to work with the purchasing departments of the bigger catering groups. National account managers understand their clients' businesses and so are able to present the benefits of existing and new products in the most appropriate way. For a hotel chain, they may focus on their suitability for banqueting, for example, and for the National Health Service, they will talk about nutrition. National account managers will also seek the advice and support of the culinary services team, presenting and demonstrating products to add value to their proposals to customers.

The food manufacturer may provide extra support. This might be point-of-sale material to drive trial and consumption with the consumer in a pub, or themed promotions in staff restaurants.

Independent operators

There are thousands of small owner-managed businesses in the catering world and it is difficult for food manufacturers to reach them. Between 20 and 25% receive industry trade magazines. These are the higher profile operators who appear in guides, attend exhibitions and are generally more involved in the industry. Food manufacturers can reach this group by advertising in the trade press; taking stands at trade shows and sponsoring national, regional and local catering and chef events. The rest are best approached via the wholesaler and cash and carry, which is why in-store promotions and price list advertising are so sought after by rival food manufacturers.

Marketing plan

The marketing of manufactured products and services is critical. Marketing has to take into account the various dynamics described above to produce a plan with the best mix of the various tools available. These include:

- trade press advertising
- PR: press and public relations
- sponsorship
- celebrity endorsement, e.g. a famous name chef; TV or film personality
- recipe booklets
- direct mail
- sampling: distributing free product samples
- on-pack promotion, e.g. collect four tokens and send off for your free gift
- sales literature and brochures
- cross promotion: buy this product at full price and get a pack of the new product for free to try
- merchandising push: sending people into cash and carry stores to arrange products in the best possible position. This usually requires a payment to the store
- cash and carry in-store promotions and sampling
- advertising in wholesalers' price lists
- trade exhibitions: stands, samples
- targeted direct mail to buyers and chefs who are likely customers
- e-advertising: banner sites and links from, for example, caterersearch.com
- website and direct e-mail.

Every product will use different things from this list, depending on the objectives.

The way of talking about the product will depend upon the type of customer. Some chefs, for example, would only consider convenience foods that provide a shortcut. They would not be in the market for a ready meal solution. On the other hand, some caterers will be more interested in the commercial return and less concerned about whether or not a dish is prepared from first principles. So long as the customer is happy, they will be satisfied. Then there are the caterers feeding students and patients, whose first thought has to be the nutritional value of the meals they serve, while being bound by very tight budgets.

The type of media used will also depend on the target audience. Traditional chefs may be best approached through print advertising and promotions, but those who have embraced new technology may be more receptive to an online campaign.

The sales role

The sales team is responsible for presenting a new product to the customer and they will have worked hand-in-hand with the marketing and culinary services departments in the run up to launch. This will include product training, combining fresh food with convenience products (classic meets contemporary) in dedicated training kitchens.

The sales team must have confidence in the product's features (its characteristics) and benefits (what it offers the caterer). They must know and understand the reasoning behind the original product idea, the decision on the final recipe and format (powder, wet, fresh, frozen, chilled), the packaging and the promotional and marketing support.

Sampling plays a key role in showing product benefits to the chef.

The role of the brand

The value of a strong and reliable brand cannot be over-estimated. If a new product is brought out under a well-loved, well-respected brand, then it starts out with reassurance and recognition of quality and trust.

Brands can work back-of-house, in the kitchen with the professional, and front-of-house, for the ultimate consumer. The brand promises reassurance and trust to both to help grow the operators' business.

TOPICS FOR DISCUSSION
1 Imagine you work in a five star hotel. How could convenience play a role in different areas: room service, banqueting, restaurant, bar? What kind of convenience products would you consider using when preparing the food?
2 Imagine you work in a staff restaurant, serving lunch to 150 workers from 12.30 – 2.00pm. What kind of convenience products would you consider using when preparing the meals?
3 How do you think skill levels will impact on convenience foods used in professional kitchens in the future? Will this mean less, more or do you think it will stay at about the current level?
4 Plot the course of a single product from idea to launch and discuss how the various departments – culinary services, marketing, sales, technical and production – work together during the process.
5 Work out the cost of preparing a portion of beef lasagne from first principles, including ingredients, labour and energy. How much would you need to charge your customer to achieve a gross profit of 65%?

PART 5 ORGANISATION AND BUSINESS DEVELOPMENT

Chapter 13 MANAGING RESOURCES

ASSESSING YOURSELF AS A MANAGER

To effectively manage people and resources it is first essential to manage oneself; to do this, it is essential to analyse oneself truthfully, assess one's weaknesses and take positive action to improve. This is necessary so that self-development improves.

'Know yourself and to yourself be true' is a maxim that assists the potential manager to develop and earn the respect of those he or she will manage. It is not easy to assess one's own personality, nor is it easy to improve or change it. The following self-analysis guide may be helpful.

- Having assessed your strengths and weaknesses, what need or needs do you require to be self-fulfilled or self-satisfied in order to develop into a successful manager? In catering, because of the variety of roles, most people's needs can be met. These include the need: to achieve; to be friendly; to show off; to be tenacious; to be free of controls; to have power; to need sympathy; to seek knowledge; to be orderly; to show care.
- Having concluded the kind of person you think you are (which may not be the same as others see you) list your qualities and your failings, and endeavour to change those you think should be changed. To be successful in achieving this it is essential to be positive and really want to improve. Be clear about the benefits of what you hope to gain. Know what you want and, when things do not go as expected, have other options and seek the advice and help of others.

Key skills for management

These include:

- self-management
- communication
- time management
- resource management
- decision making.

We will now take a closer look at some of these.

Self-management

Effective management starts with how one sees oneself, how superiors see you and how those you are responsible for see you. First and subsequent impressions are vital to successful development as a manager. First, what constitutes a good manager: what qualities, attitudes and values are desirable to form the basis from which to improve?

- Honesty and integrity.
- Orderly and of neat appearance.
- Loyalty and conscientiousness.
- Able to lead and set an example.
- Willingness and cooperativeness.
- Enthusiastic and punctual.
- Courteous and caring.

Direction

To progress it is essential to be able to clarify roles, to focus on key issues and to specify targets and standards – that is, to know in what direction you are going and how you intend to get there.

Teamwork

When working in a team it is essential to plan, to use the ideas of the team members so that you can be effective.

Actions

Actions need to be taken. Prevarication, hesitancy and lethargy do not help decision-making (see below). However, before acting, ensure that priorities are right, and use resources, manpower, finances, equipment and commodities efficiently.

Results

Analyse problems, give and receive feedback and use the information to persuade others, thus improving your own performance.

Positive balanced management

To improve performance, clear positive thinking and the ability to generate enthusiasm may be helpful. A flexible approach, sensitive to others' feelings and expectations and capable of inspiring them may well develop confidence in one's own ability.

Table **13.1** Different types of people as managers

CATEGORY OR TYPE OF PERSON		MANAGEMENT SKILLS THAT MAY NEED IMPROVING
Confident Bold Arrogant	Self-centred Authoritative Independent	May be too bossy and aggressive, needs to develop patience
Optimistic Cheerful Enthusiastic	Sociable Articulate Persuasive	May be too friendly and require greater self-discipline in difficult management situations
Relaxed Patient Laid back	Stable Passive Calm	May be unwilling to change and lacks any sense of urgency to change
Careful Neat Perfectionist	Self-disciplined Accurate Aggressive	May find difficulty in delegating, worry too much and be defensive
Agreeable Self-effacing Frustrated	Peaceful Unassuming Easily discouraged	May find leadership hard and become discouraged in difficult situations
Reserved Quiet Pessimistic	Distant Imaginative Remote	May be shy and unsociable, and not good at dealing with people
Restless Erratic Tense	Impetuous Quick Highly strung	May be seen as impatient, intolerant and aggressive, may need to learn to calm down
Independent Stubborn Argumentative	Informal Uninhibited	May be an effective delegator but unreliable and not good at making decisions

Decision making

1 Define the aim.
2 Collect the information.
3 List possible courses of action.
4 Evaluate the pros and cons, examine the consequences and make the decisions.
5 Act on the decision, monitor and review it.

First, know why a decision has been made and consider the situation and possible solutions. Evaluate how the aim will be achieved, how long it will take and what is its cost? Moreover, is it acceptable? If it is not acceptable, reconsider.

Thinking requires the following aspects to make it effective.

- **Analysing:** breaking the whole into small parts and the complex into simple elements.

- **Holistic thinking:** thinking of the entirety, the opposite to analysing.
- **Valuing:** the judgemental and critical aspect.

To make decisions fully effective it is necessary to use all three of these thought processes. Decisions based on intuition, instinct or emotion will not produce logical decision making.

Before making a decision, ensure you have the facts and then decide what to do. Value judgements are effective only if you are aware of any prejudices you have that may affect your decision, acknowledge them and learn not to be prejudiced. Also you need to know of any codes of values that are needed by the establishment, such as legal requirements, and any social behaviour codes and company procedures.

Decision-making styles

- **Autocratic:** the manager solves the problem based on the information he has.
- **Information finding:** when a manager does not have enough information or skill, he or she asks other people, then makes a decision.
- **Consultation:** the situation is explained to the group, who generate and evaluate solutions and make recommendations. The leader makes the decision.
- **Negotiation:** the group is provided with information. The group members then negotiate a solution that is acceptable.
- **Delegation:** responsibility for the decision rests with a group or an individual. The manager may guide the discussion that leads to the decision, which is then implemented.

Implementation of the decision

Having made a decision, determine clear objectives and consider what can be delegated, to whom, the time needed and whether further training is necessary. To action the decision, define it in writing, set details of progress and when to report back.

Time management

To organise oneself efficiently so as to be an effective manager requires attention to controlling one's time. Determining priorities is an essential step to this end and can be aided by producing lists and categorising jobs to be done, as well as using a diary effectively.

Time needs to be allocated for tasks such as thinking and planning, as well as using a diary effectively. A good organiser plans both for the expected and the unexpected. Be prepared for problems but allow time to prevent them if possible, and allot time for solving them.

It is important to realise that good managers need adequate-quality sleep and exercise, so as to be healthy and alert at work. Time is also needed for leisure, and self-development. Control of good eating and drinking habits may not be easy in the catering industry, but they require time to be allocated sensibly – not too long, too short or erratic.

Time is the substance life is made of; time is money, time past has gone for ever, today's newspaper is history tomorrow. You cannot buy time, but an efficient manager can organise his own time and that of those for whom he is responsible advantageously.

Unfortunately a lot of time is wasted by being punctual because others are not on time. Always be punctual and expect others to be so. Be well organised before a meeting, know what you expect from it and what others expect from you. Set objectives that are:

- clear
- attainable
- specific
- challenging
- measurable
- timed
- worthwhile.

If no time limit is stated then time could be wasted. Ideally, agree with the person the objectives that apply to them, as well as the time required to fulfil these objectives.

- Plan each day, and decide on priorities.
- Identify immediate, short-term and long-term goals, and organise office and paperwork.
- Avoid distractions, prevent interruptions.
- Delegate, make lists and delete things as they are done.
- Be organised, develop routines.
- Do important jobs when you are at your best. Set time limits and keep to them.
- Do not put off unpleasant or difficult tasks. Let others know you have a quiet time.
- Do one thing at a time and finish it if possible; plan phone calls.
- Arrange breaks; keep a notebook for ideas.
- Learn to say no, and think before acting.

Communication and information

To develop managerial skills it is important to communicate effectively with senior management and other departmental managers, and with those for whom you are responsible. It is essential to ensure that what is communicated is understood in the way it is intended. Likewise it is very important that information, suggestions, commands, decisions, requests, and so on, are clear, cannot be misconstrued and are unambiguous. Listening is an art that needs particular attention as it is a vital aspect of effective communication.

Information may be communicated by oral or visual means, depending on the establishment's policy, personal preference and the matter to be conveyed. The advantage of speech is that questions and discussions can clarify the issues immediately, and intonation and emphasis convey more accurately what is intended. While the telephone is invaluable, there is no eye contact, which makes face-to-face communication more effective. Body language conveys much to both communicators, which naturally can occur only in direct contact situations.

Written instructions, reports, and so on, have the advantage that there is tangible evidence of what is communicated. However, care must still be taken that what is written is understood by the recipient: that which is written may be clear to the person writing the instructions, but it is essential that it is specific, unambiguous and not too wordy, so that there are no misunderstandings.

Although emails are a popular modern form of communication, they also bring with them the risk of losing the value of face-to-face contact and oral skills.

Self-assessment

In order to improve performance it is desirable to review one's current situation and how to develop into the future. Appropriate others, such as colleagues in the establishment, and comparison with people in similar situations in other organisations, members of professional associations, tutors at colleges and those who have experience of management in catering, may all provide constructive advice. Keep abreast of developments by reading journals and visiting trade fairs.

Balanced organisation

Evaluate responsibilities objectively so that you understand, appreciate and can act effectively in an efficient but balanced lifestyle.

- Assess your responsibilities for: people, finance, development, administration and communication.
- People to consider are: yourself, your subordinates, your family and your department.
- Finance: your own, the department's, budgeting, authorisation of expenditure and control of expenditure.
- Development in: the organisation, the department, your own and new ideas.
- Administration may include: an office, secretary, your department, other departments and customers.
- Communication: ensure it is effective – to others and from others.

DEVELOPING TRUST AND SUPPORT WITH MANAGERS

Trust and support with one's immediate manager will simply not appear in an ad hoc fashion. For a chef this person may be the food and beverage manager or the general manager. Serious attention has to be paid to developing a communication channel with one's immediate manager in order to encourage an effective relationship that will help to achieve departmental or organisational goals. The better the communication, the more likely that the relationship will become better and more efficient.

It is important that the departmental head consults with his or her line manager on a regular basis to genuinely seek his or her views, ideas and feelings, which may improve the quality of decisions. This will stimulate better cooperation between managers.

Conflict with your immediate line manager can be very damaging. However, it is one of the main areas in which conflict can and does take place at work. Section heads may often feel dissatisfied with their line manager, perhaps in connection with pay, working conditions and the like. Another issue may be one of communication between the section head and the line manager. The section head should take time to find out about his/her line manager by discussing, observing and talking to him/her and other managers in the organisation.

It also helps if a close relationship is developed with the manager and a good understanding of all the issues the organisation is faced with. Provide the manager with ideas, give definitions of problems and your views on solutions.

A manager will generally have:

- another, or alternative, view on things
- more information on the overall picture
- advice on difficult issues
- guidance on appropriate policies
- and will be able to offer support and protection (through consultation with him or her).

The departmental head must in turn provide:

- clear documentation
- clear definition of issues
- identified courses of action and views on the various strategies available
- reasoned arguments on how/why he or she has arrived at the recommendations
- predictions about likely outcomes and contingencies if a recommendation he or she actions is unsuccessful
- information on his or her team's progress.

Your line manager is expecting you to produce results and to organise your team. This will strengthen your relationship with the line manager. Your manager will often, in turn, take a certain amount of credit for what you do well.

Consider also your own relationship with your subordinates. If the relationship works well, then what are the reasons for this? Are these relevant to establishing a working relationship with your line manager?

Assess your line manager

- Understand what she or he wants for her/himself.
- What are his or her values?

- Is she or he able to accept criticism?
- Is he or she ambitious?
- How does she or he measure herself/himself?
- Who are the people that he or she admires?
- Does the manager like open, frank discussion?
- Does the manager take risks? Or is she or he a protector?
- Is the manager an autocratic leader, expecting you to do as he or she says? Or intuitive, expecting you to follow broad, informal indications or signs?

Try to analyse why situations produce conflict or stalemate. Is it because your views differ or because you both manage the situations badly? Does this help you to decide if you have the qualities she or he values? What does your manager expect from you? Do his or her goals match yours? If not, can you live with the resulting difficulties?

Learn to understand your manager's strengths and weaknesses

- Does the manager need time and lengthy explanations?
- Is the manager good at one-to-one communication?
- Is the manager able to see essentials, and keen to resolve issues?
- Does the manager contribute to good ideas?
- Is he or she able to see practical solutions?
- Is the manager able to handle conflict, or does she or he seek to avoid it.

Once these strengths and weaknesses have been identified you should seek to complement them. You may need to modify your behaviour to ensure your relationship with him/her is legitimate, not a sellout, and can be productive – taking care not to go too far in compromising.

Analyse his or her style

- Does your manager prefer written, detailed reports? If so, you should provide them and check them thoroughly.
- He or she may prefer verbal briefings. If so, provide them but follow up with a memo.
- He or she may prefer formal meetings with itemised agendas.
- Assess the circumstances within the environment you are both working in.
- What are the pressures on you both?
- What are her or his own dealings with her or his peers and more senior managers?
- What is expected of your manager? Where does he or she look for success?
- What are the rewards for succeeding? Salary increase? Promotion? Bonus? Could this reflect on your relationship?

- How are you contributing to what she or he is trying to achieve?
- How do people view the manager in the organisation?

Making decisions

Decision making is a very important part of the management process. No matter how good you are as a section manager, how well you motivate your staff or how good your ideas, you will be judged by your manager and your staff on the quality of the decisions you make.

Quantity can be no substitute for quality. An excess of bad or short-term decisions will lead to a serious backlog of niggling problems.

Decisions are your judgement choices between alternative courses of action. To be effective, this often means keeping decision making to a minimum, but ensuring the decisions that have to be made are timed correctly, after taking into account all the facts and information at our disposal.

Managing the team and its performance in a regular series of tasks and a number of various projects involves decisions relating to routine, individuals and the team.

- Different strategies and styles of working/interaction that encourage effective working relationships with senior staff.
- Range of methods to keep the immediate manager informed and how to select an appropriate method according to a range of issues and contexts.
- The types of emerging threats and opportunities about which the manager needs to be informed, and the degree of urgency attached to this.
- How to develop and present proposals in a way that is realistic, clear and likely to influence the immediate manager's decision making positively.
- Handling disagreements positively. Assess the likely reaction from both the team and individuals.
- Avoid making decisions on impulse.
- Collect all information, not just the material that supports your view.
- Discuss decisions with more experienced senior staff, but retain responsibility for the final decision.
- Do not take premature or unnecessary decisions.

Routine decision making is often delegated by a departmental head to a junior. This encourages and develops them in the decision-making process and allows the head to concentrate on more strategic issues.

Certain decisions remain with the departmental manager:

- those that focus on overall direction
- staff resourcing
- organisation structure in the section to achieve objectives and cope with the workload

- skills, forecasting
- planning to achieve operational objectives.

Avoid using one style to deal with everything. Use 'unswerving flexibility'.

Managing projects means making hard decisions about money, materials, time and staff.

- All team members must know their roles.
- Progress must be reviewed frequently in order to spot potential problems and to note what time and resources are available.
- Continually feed back to your line manager to avoid misunderstandings or conflict if things go wrong.
- Consult experts when necessary before any emergency.
- Refer any decisions to your line manager that fall outside your sphere of authority, responsibility or flexibility. Referrals should be accompanied by a clear statement of possible choices, together with your recommendations.

Steps to effective decision making
Classify the problem
If it is generic, it is probably one of those everyday problems that has to be solved by adapting the appropriate generic rule, policy or principle. If it is extraordinary, the problem must be dealt with on its individual merits.

Define the problem
State precisely the nature of the problem and check your definition against all the observable facts. Beware the plausible but incomplete definition that does not embrace all the known facts.

Specify the conditions
Clarify exactly what the decision must accomplish. These are the so-called boundary conditions, or specifications, that must be satisfied by the solution to the problem.

Decide on the right action
Decide first of all what it is right to do rather than what is acceptable in the circumstances. Make the decision that satisfies all the specifications.

Compromise the decision
In reality there usually has to be some form of compromise, so make the best decision possible by adapting it to the circumstances.

Implement the decision
Assign the responsibility of carrying out the decision to those staff who are capable of doing so. Inform everyone who needs to know about the decision and the effects of the decision.

Review the effectiveness of the decision

The implementation process should involve feedback and monitoring. Receive reports on the results of the decision – how does the decision measure up to expectations? All positive facts should be incorporated into the classifying, defining and specifying process of making decisions.

MANAGING PEOPLE

Developing the trust and support of colleagues and team members

As individuals working within an organisation, we can achieve very little, but working within a group we are able to achieve a great deal more. Good, effective teamwork is an important feature of human behaviour and organisational performance.

Each member in a group must:

- regard themselves as being part of that group
- interact with one another
- perceive themselves as part of the group
- share the purpose of the group.

This will help build trust and support, and will result in an effective performance. Cooperation is therefore important.

People in groups will influence one another; within the group there may be a leader and/or a hierarchical system. The pressures within the group may have a major influence over the behaviour of individual members and their performance. The style of leadership within the group has an influence on the behaviour of members within the group.

Groups help shape the work pattern of organisations, and the attitudes and behaviour of members to their jobs.

Two types of team can be identified within an organisation.

- The **formal team** is the department or section created within a reorganised structure to pursue specified goals.
- The **informal team** deals with a particular situation; members have fewer fixed organisational relationships and the team is disbanded after performing its function.

Both groups have to be developed and led. Thought has to be given to relationships, and to the tasks and duties the team has to carry out.

Selecting and shaping teams to work within a department is a very important task. This is the job of the departmental head. It requires management skills. Matching each individual's talent to the task or job has to be considered. A good, developed team will be able to:

- analyse problems effectively and create useful ideas
- communicate with each other and get things done
- show good leadership, which will result in skilled operations with technical precision and ability

- evaluate logically and equate control systems.

The group will never become a team unless the personalities involved are able to relate to and communicate with one another, and value the contribution that each employee or team member makes.

The team leader has a strong influence on his or her team or brigade, and is expected to set examples that have to be followed, particularly when under pressure, dealing with conflict, personality clash, change and stress.

People's behaviour is affected by many factors. For example, individual characteristics, cultural attributes and social skills: the head must lead rather than drive, and encourage the team to practise reasonable and supportive behaviour so that any problems are dealt with in an objective way and the team's personal skills are harnessed to achieve their full potential.

Every team has to deal with:

- the egos, and the weaknesses and strengths of the individuals
- the self-appointed experts within the group
- relationships/circumstances constantly changing.

The head is able to manage the team successfully by pulling back from the task in hand. He or she must examine the processes that create efficient teamwork, finding out what it is that makes it greater than the sum of its parts. To assist this process the following attributes are necessary:

- have a consistent approach to solving problems
- take into account people's characters as well as their technical skills
- encourage supportive behaviour in the team
- create an open, healthy climate
- make time for the team to appraise its progress.

Supportive team practices

Listening skills
- Pay attention, responding positively.
- Look interested, avoid interrupting.
- Build on proposals, asking for clarity on questions.
- Summarise to check your understanding.

Cooperating
- Encourage others to give their views.
- Compliment good ideas.
- Avoid coercion and acrimony.
- Give careful consideration to different proposals.
- Offer new ideas openly.

Challenging

- Any assumptions are questioned in a reasonable manner.
- Continually refer back to the problem-solving process and aims.
- Review the progress of objectives and aims, in relation to the team and time taken.

Motivation and the team

An understanding of what motivates staff is crucial to the creation of productivity and the realisation of profits. People's needs and wants are complex and often difficult to define.

Money and status are important but they cannot be relied upon exclusively. Behavioural scientists have provided useful ways of thinking about people's needs and wants.

F.W. Taylor (1911) established a scientific management approach that involved breaking down jobs into simple but repetitive tasks, providing training, isolating individuals from distractions and each other, and paying good wages, which included bonuses for productivity over target levels.

In the short term, productive gains were significant; in the long run, these gains were less than significant as people reacted against the idea of being treated like a machine.

The scientific approach may have been discredited because some managers give too much attention to pay and too little to personal needs, and the needs of groups and teams.

Abraham Maslow (1954) concentrated on human needs, which he defined as a five-fold hierarchy.

1 **Physiological needs:** the need for food and shelter.
2 **Safety needs:** the security of home and work.
3 **Social needs:** the need for a supportive environment.
4 **Esteem needs:** gaining the respect of others.
5 **Self-fulfilment:** the need to realise one's potential.

As each goal is achieved, the next is sought. Thus, at different stages of career development, each individual has different values, depending on their progress through this 'hierarchy of needs'.

In 1959 Frederick Herzberg (see Herzberg *et al.*, 1959) added to Taylor's and Maslow's work by introducing the idea of 'hygiene factors'. If these hygiene factors are absent they will lead to dissatisfaction and will prevent effective motivation. The hygiene factors can be identified as follows.

1 The organisational policy and rules.
2 The management styles and controls.
3 Retirement and sickness policies.
4 Pay and recognition of status.

- Hygiene factors, although considered important, do not have lasting effects on motivation, as other positive motivating factors must be present.
- Money obviously plays an important role in motivation. There are a number of non-financial motivators, and these are considered to be highly important, to achieve the organisational goals.
- Most people want to achieve – those in charge of teams must recognise this and provide opportunities for others to attain levels of achievement that celebrate ability.
- People also want recognition. Praise and feedback spur people on to achieve even more.
- People generally want to move on to more challenging situations. The team should aim to challenge its members.
- Certain workers (e.g. chefs) want to practise their skill and use their intelligence to maintain interest.
- Most workers want to accept responsibility and authority.

Motivating a team

A leader must motivate his or her team, by making their work interesting, challenging and demanding. People must also know what is expected of them and what the standards are. Rewards are linked to effort and results.

Unless these factors go towards fulfilling the organisational needs and the expectations of team members, if pay and prospects within the establishment are bad, the system should be improved and performance should be recognised. Therefore, the leader should attempt to intercede on behalf of his or her staff. This, in turn, will help to increase their motivation and their commitment to the team.

For the leader to manage his or her staff effectively, it is important to get to know them well, understand their needs and aspirations, and help them achieve their personal aims.

Communication

Successful communication is vital when striving to build working relationships. Training and developing the team is about communicating. In work, the quality of our personal relationships depends on the quality of the communication system.

- The speaker must know what he or she wishes to convey.
- He or she must find visible symbols, gestures, words, body movements, to externalise the internal thoughts.
- The listener must be receptive to these visible symbols, know the language and terminology, and understand the non-verbal symbols being demonstrated.
- The listener must translate all these symbols into thought.

Communication requires a transmitter and a receiver, and therefore it is a shared responsibility. Speaking in a meeting you have several potential listeners, a memo you send to staff may have multiple copies. Many staff receive messages, commands, notices, and so on – but they don't give them. Therefore the communication system may imply only a transmitting process.

The greatest scope for quantitatively improving your communication skills is to improve your listening, observing, reading and watching abilities, as a priority over speaking and writing. The most effective transmissions are those that are able to fit into the receiving processes of the recipients.

Hearing and understanding the content of the instruction or the message is not sufficient for full communication. There has to be a match between the 'intent' and the 'effect' the instruction or message has on the individual. Breakdowns in communication can be identified by looking at the 'intent' and the 'effect' as two separate realities. Sometimes, the intent is not translated into the effect. Such breakdowns can adversely affect staff and team relationships. Good relationships depend on good communication. Awareness of the potential gap between intent and effect can help clarify and prevent any misunderstanding within the group.

By bridging the gap between intent and effect you can begin to change the culture of the working environment – the processes become self-reinforcing in a positive direction. The staff begin to respect each other in a positive framework; they listen more carefully to each other, with positive expectations, hearing the constructive intent and responding to it.

As a manager, the art is in achieving results through the team, with communication being the key to the exercise. A great deal of time will be taken up with communicating in one way or another.

Planning communication

Communication can be planned in a systematic way with clarity about the objectives and methods to be used. Not every communication needs to be planned, as many trivial or routine transmissions can go through automatic channels. The significant communication lines are those that recur frequently and/or take up a great deal of time, or that carry substantial rewards or penalties for success or failure.

First, the manager must define his or her job objectives, then he or she must identify the communication strategy to achieve these objectives.

Planning the communication will cover the subject and the method content and process.

The **content** means:
- collecting the data
- getting your thoughts in order
- formulating information.

The **process** means:
- alternative ways communication may proceed and achieve objectives.

PURPOSE OF MEETING	PREDOMINANT COMMUNICATION COMPONENT
Information exchange	Facts and opinions
Problem solving	Ideas and goal wishes
Briefing	Facts
Consultation	Opinions
Conflict resolution	Ideas and goal wishes
Morale building	Feelings and goal wishes

The **medium** can be:
- face to face – meeting, phone call, fax, email, memo.

A major factor in the quality of any communication system is the climate in which it takes place. The climate refers to the prevailing attitudes and habitual behaviours of the team within which the communication is being attempted. The degree of friendliness and/or hostility that exists between the transmitters and receivers will affect the communication outcome.

The climate for communication is greatly influenced by the leader. The leader sets the tone in the way he or she interacts with the team. Do not patronise staff as this causes resentment, which results in sullen silence or overt hostility. Being dogmatic, with a closed mind, results in others being dogmatic in return.

Accept disagreement as an interesting alternative view that is worth exploring, demonstrating how you are able to learn from it. This provides a climate of open-mindedness. Staff very often respond to the expectations communicated to them, either directly or indirectly.

Meetings

Any chef manager must ask her/himself what is the purpose of meetings, what they are trying to achieve by holding the meeting. The purpose needs to be expressed in specific terms. We are able to identify the predominant communication component in each category of meeting (see Table 13.2).

WORK–LIFE BALANCE

It is increasingly being recognised by employers of all sizes and in all industry sectors that it makes good business sense to create a better work–life balance for their workers. Where this has been successfully organised, it has resulted in increased morale and employee loyalty, better productivity and effectiveness at work, and improved adaptability in the face of change.

Research shows that, when employees are better able to integrate their needs outside work into their daily lives with no detriment to their work, there are considerable benefits to the business.

A survey of 2000 managers in the UK found that a third of them would change their jobs if they felt they could improve their work–life balance; 57 per cent of students considered achieving a balanced lifestyle and having a rewarding life outside work their top priority in their future career (DTI, 2001).

Leading the team

- Look at tomorrow's problems and issues today to detect signs of changes and pitfalls.
- Learn to adapt to change, to embrace it and turn it to positive advantage.
- Set high standards and clear objectives.
- Think clearly, allowing intuition to influence rationality.
- Create a sense of value and purpose in work, so that team members believe in what they do and do it successfully.
- Provide a positive sense of direction in order to give meaning to the lives of team members.
- Act decisively, but ensure decisions made are soundly based and not just on impulse.
- Set the right tone by your actions and beliefs, thus creating a clear, consistent and honest model to be followed.
- Choose the right time to make decisions and take action.
- Create an atmosphere of enthusiasm in which individuals are stimulated to perform well, find fulfilment, gain self-respect and play an integral role in meeting the organisation's overall goals.
- Be sensitive to individual team members' needs and their expectations.
- Define clear responsibilities and structures, so collective effort is enhanced not hindered.
- Recognise what motivates each team member and work with these motivations to achieve standards and objectives.
- Determine boundaries within which team members can work freely.

Most managers do one of the following:

- make a decision the team accepts
- 'sell' a decision before trying to have it accepted
- present decisions but respond to the team's questions
- present a tentative decision, subject to change after team input
- present problems, ask the team for input, then make a decision
- define the limits within which the team can make a decision
- chef and team make a joint decision.

MANAGING DIVERSITY

The world of work, especially the hospitality industry, is becoming more diverse. Increasing numbers of women are entering the labour force, who expect to progress to senior management; the ethnic mix is becoming wider and the population in western economies is ageing. In the case of multinational companies, domestic diversity is compounded by the diversity that is introduced through the movement of people around the globe. The mobility of labour is further encouraged by regional mechanisms such as arrangements for the free movement of people in the European Union. All these changes (and more) are affecting the nature of customers and their needs.

What is diversity?

Diversity recognises that people are different. It includes some of the more obvious and visible differences – such as gender, ethnicity, age and disability – and also the less visible differences – such as sexual orientation, background, personality and work style. Diversity management is about recognising, valuing and celebrating these differences. It is about harnessing difference to improve creativity and innovation, and is based on the belief that groups of people who bring different perspectives together will find better solutions to problems than groups of people who are the same.

Why is diversity management important?

The markets served are constantly changing (e.g. women and older people have more spending power, minority ethnic groups are an important market segment, disabled people and their carers want accessible holidays) and, in order to meet the needs of these diverse markets, the same groups need to be represented in the workforce. According to HCIMA (1999), by taking a proactive approach to diversity management the following can be achieved:

- access the best people from the widest labour pool available
- develop the creative talents of all employees
- motivate all staff
- reduce labour turnover
- improve quality and customer service.

MINIMISING INTERPERSONAL CONFLICT

Interpersonal conflict is a fact of life. It starts with children in school, who in most cases are able to resolve their disagreements quickly and often make friends again. With adults this ability to resolve conflict tends to fade away as we become older. In an organisational context a whole range of things can get in the way, which makes handling conflict even more difficult. A conflict with the manager or with colleagues can easily get entangled with issues about work and status – both of which can make it difficult to approach the problem in a rational and professional way.

- One of the skills of all front-line managers is the need to identify conflict, so that plans can be put in place to minimise it.
- Conflict arises where there are already strained relations and personality clashes between members of your team.
- Conflict often occurs in a professional kitchen when the brigade is understaffed and under pressure, especially over a long period. Pressure can also come from, for example, restaurant reviews and guides, where a chef is, say, after a Michelin star or special accolade.
- Conflicts damage working relationships and upset the team; eventually this will show in the finished product.

The chef and manager must also be aware of the insidious conflict that may be going on around them, in less obvious places. Covert conflicts are those that take place in secret, and can be very harmful. This type of conflict is often difficult to detect. A new person joining the team may have no idea that the conflict is taking place. This type of conflict will also undermine the team's performance. Such conflict may happen when a person has been passed over for promotion and has never received feedback as to why. In other words, they have been ignored. The resentment, anger and bitterness can bubble away beneath the surface.

Many conflicts start with misunderstandings or a small upset that grows and develops out of all proportion. The manager or chef should attempt to:

- stop it getting worse
- make the individuals confront their own problems
- manage the situation to avoid any escalation.

Destructive and constructive conflicts

It is important to reflect on and analyse the nature of conflict and individual attitudes to it. While conflicts can be very damaging and upsetting, there can also be some positive outcomes. Conflict can also be a learning curve that a chef or manager has to enter into; this then has to be handled properly and focused to achieve the desired outcome.
Conflict is destructive when it:

- produces name calling
- makes people feel angry and let down with each other
- causes people to close off and withdraw.

Conflict is constructive when it:

- acts as the first stage towards negotiating
- clears the air
- helps staff to talk to each other.

Some common physical reactions when we are threatened by conflict are sweaty palms, a rise in pulse rate, dry mouth, trembling.

Flight

This is an unsatisfactory way of dealing with conflict at work or, indeed, in other social situations. Much of the time, you can't just run away and, if there is no escape, it can turn into a demonstration of submission, a form of passive behaviour. Don't be so intent on pleasing others that you fail to please yourself. The emotional aftermath of submitting often results in guilt and feeling that you have let yourself down.

Examples of flight reaction and passive behaviour include:

- withdrawing eye contact, looking down, hiding behind hair
- withdrawing body language, hiding
- continual agreement.

Fight

Aggressive behaviour is equally unsatisfactory. This can be demonstrated by:

- a raised voice, clipped or sarcastic tone
- pointing a finger, clenched fist, banging the table and waving the arms
- staring and invasive eye contact – glaring
- moving closer to someone, standing up to tower over someone else
- not listening, talking so much there is no space to respond.

Why does conflict arise?

The chef/manager needs to be aware within which areas interpersonal conflict can arise in order to put strategies in place to manage it. He/she should act positively, rather than simply react to a conflict when it breaks out.

If people feel that they do not have a chance to discuss their problems and difficulties with someone this could also lead to conflict. It could also lead to:

- a breakdown in trust
- misunderstandings about standards
- failing to communicate with one another correctly
- dealing with complex personal problems that should have been passed to an expert.

Other reasons for conflict can be:

- racism, sexism, differences in opinion
- inappropriate personal habits, non-compliance with organisational norms/values
- discriminatory behaviour, working conditions
- unrealistic work expectations, personal antagonism

In some cases conflicts that arise from these issues may result in formal grievances, or even disciplinary matters. Formal procedures can often be helpful in containing conflict to a standard approach. This depersonalises it and stops the manager or chef taking it personally, converting it into a standard work-role approach that spells out who is to do what by when.

Conflict between the chef and the manager

This can be very damaging and leads to feelings of dissatisfaction. Often it may be the result of poor communication in either direction, about activities, progress results and achievements.

The main issues include:

- failing to communicate accurately or promptly – on problems, opportunities and activities
- going it alone – taking decisions that require the approval of the manager or another party
- coming up with problems rather than solutions, and neglecting to put forward proposals for action at the appropriate level of detail
- feeling hurt when ideas are rejected, instead of coming up with other proposals
- allowing some disagreements to grow without limiting the damage
- failing to do what the job requires and not meeting expectations without good reason
- balancing the expectations of the kitchen/restaurant team, and trying to live up to your manager's expectations and demands.

Therefore, there is a need to continue to find ways of improving and maintaining relationships with line managers and the team. Relationships have to be worked on, they need constant nurturing.

Turning the situation round

Here are nine steps that will help to enhance working relationships with your immediate manager.

1 Keep the manager well informed on what you and the team are doing, by means of regular progress reports that clearly identify achievements.
2 Inform him or her of problems and opportunities. Give information at the right stage.

3 Ask for advice when you need it. Use you manager as a resource.
4 Make proposals for action clearly and at the right time, giving the right level of detail.
5 Not all proposals will be accepted by your line manager. If a proposal is rejected, wait for a while, then put forward an alternative proposal.
6 Deal with disagreements with your line manager in a positive way. Avoid falling out and so damaging the relationship.
7 Continue to find ways to improve your relationship.
8 Check you have completed everything you are required to do in your job.
9 Carry out your activities positively, willingly and in a helpful way.

Sometimes there may be a member of staff who keeps calm, gets everyone listening and talking sensibly, and comes up with a reasonable compromise that gets everyone out of a hole. This person should be the chef or the manager.

REFERENCES

DTI (2001) *A Good Practice Guide for the Hospitality Industry* (produced by HCIMA's Managing Diversity Working Group in conjunction with the DTI's Work–Life Balance Team). Free copies available from DTI Publications, Tel: 0870 1502 500, Website: www.dti.gov.uk/publications.
HCIMA May 1999
Herzberg, G.F., Mausner, B. and Snydeman, B.B. (1959) *The Motivation to Work*. New York: Wiley.
Maslow, A. (1954) *Motivation and Personality*. New York: Harper & Row.
Taylor, F.W. (1911) *The Principles of Scientific Management*. New York: Harper Bros.

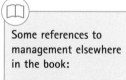

Some references to management elsewhere in the book:

TOPICS FOR DISCUSSION

1 Ways in which conflict can be resolved in a kitchen.
2 The importance of acquiring management skills when working as a head chef.
3 Why trust in the management process is important.
4 Which is more important: gaining accolades and Michelin stars or operating a successful kitchen where managers and staff feel comfortable and the product is successful?
5 The importance of developing teams.
6 Why good communication in the organisation is important.
7 What are the qualities of a good manager?
8 What does the employee expect of the manager?
9 What does the manager expect of the employee?

Chapter 14 MARKETING, SALES AND CUSTOMER CARE

MARKETING

Operating a successful business in today's competitive environment means that an establishment has to gain an advantage over its competitors. A hospitality establishment has to carefully predict customers' wants, needs and desires, and translate these into a product that people will want to purchase.

This chapter primarily focuses on promotion and selling. Marketing is necessary for the long-term survival of any business. It is not just about selling, however, it is the whole complex of business behaviour that identifies customer needs and trends in buying behaviour, and carefully monitors and interprets the business environment in which the establishment or organisation is operating. Factors include the amount of disposable income people have, the economic environment and exchange rates. There are also political factors, such as the likelihood of the introduction of a minimum wage and other legislation, such as the impact of the Food Safety Act on an establishment's hygiene costs.

Market research relies on a systematic approach, and there are a number of different approaches to researching a particular market. The SWOT analysis is a well-known example. SWOT stands for Strengths, Weaknesses, Opportunities and Threats. When a SWOT analysis is carried out it is useful to take into account the so-called '7 Ps' of marketing:

1 product
2 process
3 place
4 physical environment

5 price
6 promotion
7 people.

Strengths refer to the positive aspects of the establishment. For example:

- good reputation
- good location

- attractive environment
- comfortable restaurant.

Weaknesses could refer to:

- declining market
- lack of staff training

- lack of investment
- no parking spaces.

Opportunities could include:

- economic environment – people with high disposable incomes
- geographical – good attractive area, good parking facilities
- attractive area
- good transport links
- demographic – increasing numbers of young professional people moving into the area
- technological – availability of new equipment, good control systems available
- competition – little competition in the area.

Threats could include:

- technological – out-of-date equipment
- competition
- decline in demand for product
- geographical – area becoming run-down, poorly kept area, difficult parking
- legislation – impact of new legislation, which means more bureaucracy.

It is important for any manager to know the market, and this is done by carrying out detailed market research. Some companies will do their own market research, while others will bring in consultants. This research will assist the company in knowing the potential and current customers, the competition and the business pattern, and will bring the company closer to knowing its own product, strengths, weaknesses and specific characteristics.

Pricing

Once it is clear from the research what the business is, where the profits should be coming from and what the competition is, then decisions on pricing can be made. There are a number of different pricing policies that can be adopted.

Competitive pricing
This looks carefully at what the competition is charging and aims to price at the same level, or sometimes at a slightly lower price. It is vital that the prices charged and the cost structure are compatible.

Backward pricing
This requires an accurate estimate of what people are likely to spend in the future. The product and services are then designed to match what the market will bear – in other words, what the customer is prepared to pay for the product or service within that particular market segment.

Cost plus
This is where a set mark-up or a set percentage is added to basic costs.

This approach is reasonably high risk. For example, if the price of the raw materials rises, then a cost-plus approach will mean that the price of the product or service will also have to rise – in some cases beyond the reach of the customer. For this reason many organisations adopt the backward-pricing approach.

Marginal pricing

This takes into account the actual costs a customer incurs in using the product or service; these costs include materials and energy costs. These are the direct costs. The customer is charged just over the direct costs, and so a contribution is made to the overhead costs. Overheads such as capital, insurance and staff costs have to be incurred whether or not the customer used the product or service. This pricing is used often at weekends and off season to sell hotel rooms, in the hope that the customer will purchase other products at the realistic price.

Discounts

Discounting is used to sell hotel rooms and hospitality products. It is used to maintain customer loyalty, increase the business, to attract repeat business, increase demand in off-peak periods and to encourage the prompt settlement of accounts.

Why some restaurants fail

Location

- The basic attributes of location are missing, such as footfall, access, visibility, parking, neighbouring complementary activity. The neighbourhood profile has permanently changed but this has not been recognised by the owners/operators. For example, if office businesses have closed in an area; this means that new office populations and customers have to be generated.
- Onerous operating conditions enforced by local agencies: delivery times, dining constraints, environmental health officer checks, noise and nuisance controls. Some local authorities are strict on enforcement, which can affect trade.
- Locations with permanently high base rents and rates with large annual and five-year increases, particularly if an area is dominated by absentee institutional landlords as this drives up break-even to an unsustainable level.
- Misunderstanding and misreading of traffic flows, some ostensibly high-volume sites suffer from having mixed markets: office workers, domestic and overseas tourists, day trippers. With no one market segment strong enough to sustain business, it becomes difficult for the operator to know whom to target.

THE CATERING CYCLE

Caterers running a business should attempt to understand and apply the catering cycle principle.

Food and beverage (or food service) operations are concerned with the provision of food and a variety of beverages within business. The various elements that comprise food and beverage operations can be summarised in the catering cycle. Food and beverage operations are concerned with the following factors.

1 The markets served by the various sectors of the food service industry, and consumer needs.
2 The range and formulation of policies, and the business goals and objectives of the various operations, and how these affect the methods adopted.
3 The interpretation of demand, and decisions to be made on the food and beverages to be provided, as well as the other services.
4 The planning and design to create a convergence of facilities required for food and beverage operations, and making decisions about the plant and equipment required.
5 The development of appropriate provisioning methods to meet the needs of the production and service methods used within given operational settings.
6 Operational knowledge of technical methods and processes, and ability in the production and service processes and methods available to the food service operator, understanding the varying resource requirements (including staffing) for their operation, as well as decision-making on the appropriateness of the various processes and methods to meet operational requirements.
7 Controlling the costs of materials as well as the costs associated with the operation of production and service, and controlling the revenue.
8 The monitoring of customer satisfaction.

ASPECTS OF PROMOTION AND SELLING

Once a catering establishment has been planned, the process has to be generated whereby the buyer and seller come together. Through promotion, customers are made aware of the establishment, persuaded to make a visit and encouraged to return. Promotion is concerned with the product. This product constitutes a total package on offer, and includes some of the following concepts:

- the image of the establishment
- the prices charged
- the quality of the product and service
- the environment, facilities and services
- the style of management and staff.

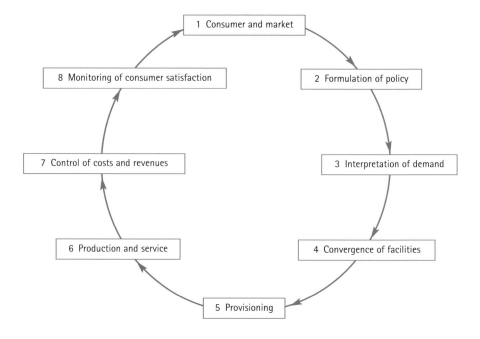

Figure 14.1 The catering cycle (Cracknell and Kaufmann, 2002)

Promotion should inform customers of the establishment, make them aware of its existence, persuade them to buy, and convince them of the image and quality of the product. This is done through:

- personal selling
- merchandising
- advertising
- public relations
- sales promotion
- agents.

Promotion is an activity that must be carefully planned and controlled. Usually, the main objective of the promotional campaign is to stimulate demand by using persuasive messages to attract new customers and past users of the establishment. Such messages must convince prospective customers that the product on offer represents good value for money.

Defining the market

The manager or chef should establish the best potential market. This will determine the type of messages to project in order to influence customer behaviour. It will also indicate the best form of media relevant to the age, sex, social class, income level and location of the target customer. It is important for these messages to emphasise the benefits of the product to the customer.

Promotion timing

Promotion timing depends on the objectives and when the decision to purchase is to be made by the customer.

Personal selling

Personal selling is done through contacts with local organisations and committees, for example, or, more directly, through senior restaurant staff talking to clients. All employees who are in contact with customers must be made aware of the importance of selling the products to increase profits and provide a satisfactory experience for the customer.

All staff must therefore gain a good knowledge of the company's products and services, and develop good social skills with an ability to promote and sell. Showing concern for customers not only makes them feel comfortable, but also promotes sales and increases the effectiveness of the establishment.

Advertising

This should convey messages that will influence consumer attitudes and behaviour favourable to the seller. Advertising should:

- increase sales immediately
- create greater public awareness of the location and existence of the establishment
- persuade the public that the product and services offer good value for money
- concentrate on the benefits of using the establishment and consuming the product
- focus on the product differences from those of competitors.

Advertising can be done via the following media:

- posters
- radio
- magazines
- television
- newspapers
- direct mail.

The selection depends on finance and desired target audience.

Direct mail
The advantages of direct mail include:

- the ability to select potential customers who are likely to buy the product – target groups can be broken down into geographical location, leisure interest and socio-economic groups, to name but a few
- the ability to express a personal message to each customer
- the ability to time the promotion
- the ability to gauge the level of response from various segments of the market and evaluate the cost-effectiveness of the exercise.

Sales promotion

Sales promotion is a day-to-day operation relating to discount offers, price reductions and special offers, such as a free bottle of wine with every meal for two. They are designed to appeal to a certain section of the market: weekend promoting, gastronomic evenings, gastronomic weekends, golfing weekends and food festivals.

Food festivals are held to promote the cuisine and beverages of a particular region or country. A themed promotion may help the business and promote sales in the following ways:

- increase sales during off-peak periods by attracting new customers
- gain publicity in local press and on local radio
- stimulate and keep the interest of regular customers.

Competing with other establishments and creating a new type of trade, such as conferences, are two other examples of sales promotion activities.

Merchandising

To be a successful caterer, it is important to have a knowledge of merchandising. The object of merchandising is to sell more and to reassure customers about the quality of what is being offered – for example, the quality of the cooking, fresh produce being used and persuading customers to return to the establishment.

Merchandising is the art of displaying products attractively in order to promote sales. This is done to great effect in supermarkets. For example, on the fresh fish counter they display a very small selection of rare or expensive fish and shellfish. This has the effect of making the fish counter interesting, drawing customers' attention and encouraging them to buy – not necessarily the specialist items, but more generally the everyday species. An example of merchandising in a fast-food restaurant is the illustrated fascia above the counter, showing what is available with the help of coloured photographs. Such a display may also be used in a luxury restaurant where a display of exotic fruits and vegetables helps to promote sales.

In a staff restaurant, tent cards and displays are used at various points on the counter to promote certain dishes. These areas are commonly known as hotspots, and are where the customer is encouraged to buy either an additional item or an item that yields a higher profit margin.

Menus and wine lists are important merchandising tools and should be at the forefront of the merchandising strategy.

The customer

First, profile the groups of customers and consider their preferences. Before you decide what you are going to display, first define:

- type of customer (age, background, social class, income groups, gender)
- the people and organisations that use your establishment
- the frequency of their custom
- their use of other catering services

- how they use their time
- how they use their disposable income.

The product

Consider the product profile; this will define the context of your merchandising policy. You must consider all aspects of the product and products, particularly those that relate to:

- the appearance of food and beverage – for example, preparing dishes in front of the customer, such as salads, grilling meat and fish or flambé dishes; this may be suitable in some situations but not others
- how customers see the service you offer
- how the product can be further developed with appearance in mind
- how the product may be promoted using posters, tent cards, illustrated menu cards, and so on.

Many of the major supermarkets can give caterers good ideas on how to develop merchandising.

What and how to display

When the marketing context has been established, the next stage is to consider how to show services and products to their best advantage and to develop aspects of them that will provide additional attractions. The caterer may like to focus on:

- the quality and freshness of ingredients
- the use of fresh flowers and fruits for display
- using a selection of finished dishes for display; this is done to great effect when displaying a choice of plated sweets on a tray
- assessing how displayed food on a self-service buffet will look after customers have taken portions from the various dishes
- how dishes deteriorate in presentation and flavour when they have been standing for too long
- assessing how the smell of cooking is an advantage or disadvantage; supermarkets often pump out the smell of freshly baked bread and this encourages people to buy bread products
- how the menu is displayed and the language that is used to describe dishes (does the layout and language encourage sales?)
- the provision of essential information about ingredients, sources of wine, vintages and prices in menus and wine lists.

Where to display

In any restaurant thought must be given to the space required for merchandising and the strategic points where a display will give maximum effect. Consider:

- customer flow
- position of check-in and cash desks
- entrances and exits
- use of lounges and bar areas
- use of displays outside restaurants (for example, in the street or windows)
- hotel bedrooms for a hotel restaurant
- the facilities of agents or business associates.

When to display

Timing is important both as an opportunity and as a means of getting the best from a merchandising project. Opportunities on many occasions present themselves at short notice and projects need not be long-lasting.

Special evening events may be held where key clients or customers are invited to sample food. Major department stores invite storecard holders to special evenings, pre-sales events or special Christmas shopping events. These account customers feel special and are encouraged to buy. If special events are to be held, the caterer must consider:

- the season
- the weather
- the event – whether it is to be local or national.

The meal experience

People who eat out do so because they want to satisfy a need. Reasons for eating out may be summarised as follows.

- For convenience – at work or near home.
- For variety – to make life more interesting.
- To avoid preparing food at home.
- Status – hosting business lunches, to feel important.
- To attend social events.
- Impulse – spur-of-the-moment decision.
- Captive market – where there is no choice (for example, hospital patients, prisoners).

People are, however, a collection of different types. While it is true that some types of food operations might attract certain types of customers, this is by no means true all the time – for example, McDonald's is marketed to the whole population and attracts customers depending on their needs at the time.

The decision to eat out may be split into two parts.

1 the decision to do so for the reasons given above
2 the decision as to what type of experience is to be undertaken.

A number of factors influence the latter decision. The factors that affect the meal experience are as follows.

- **Food and drink:** the range of foods, choice availability, flexibility of the restaurant to cope with special orders, quality of the food and drink.
- **Level of service:** depending on the needs people have at the time – the level of service must be suitable to the needs. For example, a romantic night out may call for a quiet table in a luxury restaurant, whereas a group of friends may well be seeking a more informal service. This factor also takes into account services such as booking and account facilities, acceptance of credit cards, and also the reliability of the operation's product.
- **Level of cleanliness and hygiene:** this relates to the premises, equipment and staff. These days, people are concerned about food safety and are prepared to pay for it.
- **Perceived value for money and price:** people have perceptions of the amount they are prepared to spend in different establishments, and in different operations.

Merchandising administration

Ideas have to be developed and implemented. All relevant material relating to food and drink must reflect the style and service of the product on offer.

- Descriptive terms used in menus and displays must be appropriate to the aims of the catering establishment. Accuracy and spelling is very important. Remember the menu and wine list are selling tools and should help the customer understand what you have to offer.
- All themes should be carefully researched; ambition must not exceed capability.
- Point-of-sale notices should be in keeping with the overall style of the restaurant. Wording must be positive and friendly. Notices should be presented with style and confidence.
- Avoid handwritten notices; these give a very amateurish impression of your establishment.
- Items displayed in generous quantities can assist sales. For example, when supermarkets are running special offers, they sometimes stack the product so it gives the impression that it is plentiful; this has the effect of encouraging the customer to buy not one but at least two of the items on special offer.
- Consider combined presentations: port with stilton, dessert wine with the sweet course.
- All display material must be maintained in good order, otherwise it will have the adverse effect of discouraging sales. For example, the sweet tray should be replenished. Menus and wine lists should be replaced before they become shabby.

MAKING THE MOST OF LOCAL MEDIA TO PROMOTE YOUR HOSPITALITY BUSINESS

Media habits

The proportion of people reading a national daily newspaper in Great Britain has fallen since the early 1980s. The most popular national newspaper among adults is the *Sun*. This newspaper is particularly popular among young people (15 to 24 years old). The *Daily Telegraph* and *The Times* are the most popular broadsheet newspapers, with the *Telegraph* more popular among older people. Men are more likely than women to read a newspaper, while women are more likely than men to read a magazine.

Many people also enjoy reading as a leisure activity. More daily newspapers, national and regional, are sold per person in the United Kingdom than in most other developed countries, although the proportion of people reading a national daily newspaper in Great Britain has fallen since the early 1980s.

The oldest surviving national Sunday newspaper in the world is the *Observer*, which was founded in 1791. In the year to June 1999, 60 per cent of people aged 15 and over said they read a Sunday newspaper, although readership of Sunday newspapers has declined in recent years. The most popular Sunday newspaper in 1998–99 was the *News of the World*, followed by the *Sunday Mirror* and the *Mail on Sunday*.

Table 14.1 Reading of national daily newspapers

	GREAT BRITAIN 1999/00	PERCENTAGES 2000/01
The Sun	21	20
Daily Mirror	13	12
Daily Mail	12	12
Daily Express	5	4
Daily Star	3	3
Daily Telegraph	5	5
The Times	4	3
The Guardian	2	2
The Independent	1	1
Financial Times	1	1
	54	53

Source: National Statistics website: www.statistics. gov.uk

Figure 14.2 Spending on selected reading materials by gross income quartile group, 2001/02 (UK, percentage of all spending)

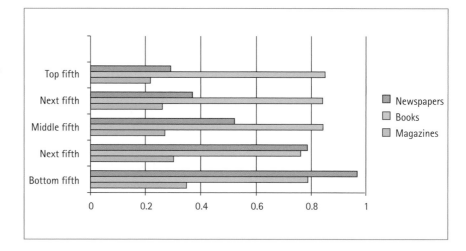

Source: National Statistics website: www.statistics. gov.uk

Reading newspapers is an important part of many people's daily routine. On an average weekday it was estimated that around 55 per cent of people aged 15 and over in the United Kingdom read a national morning newspaper in 2001 (59 per cent of men and 50 per cent of women). Over 80 per cent of adults read a regional or local newspaper every week.

There are marked variations in the spending patterns of income groups on different types of reading material. Households in the highest income group spent more than three times as much on books and magazines as on newspapers; the lowest income group spent more on newspapers than books or magazines. In 2001/02 UK households in the highest income group spent five times more on books than the lowest income group (an average of £6.29 per household per week compared with £1.17 for the lowest income group) but less than twice as much on newspapers (£2.17 and £1.45, respectively).

In Great Britain, the proportion of households with a broadband connection rose from 8 per cent to 31 per cent between April 2003 and July 2005.

Nearly nine in ten adult viewers in the United Kingdom watched television every day of the week in 2003, with nearly a quarter of viewers watching it for two to three hours a day.

Radio continues to be popular, with over 90 per cent of the total adult population tuning in at least once a week in spring 2002. Overall, men listened to the radio for a greater number of hours than women. Radio 2 was the most popular station among both men and women, followed by Radio 4 and BBC local radio. Men spend a greater proportion of their listening time than that of women tuned in to Radio Five Live, while women were more likely than men to listen to Radio 4. The BBC attracted just over half the audience share, while commercial radio stations together had just under half. According to RAJAR (Radio Joint Audience Research Limited), 14 per cent of adults in the United Kingdom said they had listened to the radio online between 23 June and 14 September 2003, compared to 10 per cent for the same period two years earlier. Online listening is most popular among the younger age groups, men and higher socio-economic groups. Regular Internet users are more than twice as likely as the average adult to listen online.

The high ownership of televisions is reflected in the amount of time spent watching TV. On average, people aged four and over in the United Kingdom spent 26 hours per week watching television and almost 19 hours listening to the radio in 1999. There are large differences between age groups. Older people watched more television than younger people, with those aged 65 and over spending twice as much time watching television as those aged 4 to 15. There were also variations across the country: those in the Scotland BBC television region spent the most time watching television – almost five hours more per week than those in the south of England BBC television region. Not only did the amount of television watched vary with age, so too did the type of programme. For example, 17 per cent of programmes watched by those aged 65 and over were news programmes, compared with 7 per cent of programmes watched by 4 to 15 year olds.

There are many opportunities available to use the media.

Remember that there are six principal 'news values' – consistent elements in virtually any news story:

- conflict, controversy or disaster
- scandal
- something that affects (especially threatens or disrupts) the community
- unusualness, novelty
- personality, character or individualism
- an event.

Get to know your local media

Make a list of all the media outlets in your area: newspapers, free sheets and radio stations. Some will be familiar to you; others can be found by looking in a reference book such as *Willings* or *Benn's* in the local library.

Compile a mailing list including the news editors of local papers, local or regional news agencies, and any other sympathetic journalist known to you. Include the names of picture editors for 'photocalls' or 'photo opportunities'. Add the news editor of the local radio station(s), as well as the producers of any programmes that may cover your activities: current affairs programmes, magazine programmes, specialist food/restaurant programmes, consumer affairs and news round-ups.

This will form the basis of your mailing list and should be kept up to date and ready to use at short notice. If your list is very short, you can type the addresses each time you send out a press release, but if you have access to a photocopier and/or a computer it is much easier to print your addresses directly on to A4 sheets of labels.

Read your local papers, listen to your local radio stations and watch television programmes. Obvious, perhaps, but too many people approach the producers of programmes they have never seen or heard, hoping for coverage.

Deadlines

When you send out a press release or ring up a newsroom, remember the journalist's deadline. Here is a rough guide to deadlines:

- weekly newspapers – two to three days before publication
- morning papers – up to 8 pm the previous day (for a major story) but usually by about 4 pm
- evening papers – 11 am the same day for the first edition
- local radio – one hour before the news bulletin
- weekly magazines – three to four days before publication.

Deadlines vary considerably and some sections of the paper close before others. It is best to ring your local newspaper and radio station and ask them to tell you their deadline.

Making contacts

There is nothing to beat having good contacts in the media. Let's assume you are starting from scratch. Compile a list of your local media as outlined above. Then ring the editor or news editor of the local paper and introduce yourself. Give him/her your work number and home number (and mobile number if you have one). *Make yourself as accessible as possible.* Ask to meet for lunch or a drink so that you can tell them what is coming up and find out what they are interested in. However, don't be too pushy. That can make you unpopular and will minimise your chances of coverage.

Each time a journalist calls you, make a note of their name, the paper or programme they represent, their direct line number, the nature of the call, and your impressions, if any. Anyone interested or sympathetic can immediately be added to your mailing list. Your 'logbook' will enable you to place the journalist the moment he/she rings you again. This will avoid your having to repeat questions like 'Which programme are you from?', which will only irritate the journalist and create an impression of inefficiency on your part. Gradually, through building up information in your logbook and by reading, listening and watching, you will be able to approach the right journalist with the right story at the right time.

Scan the newspapers carefully for names (bylines) of journalists who may be sympathetic and add them to your list. When journalists turn up at your events, make a point of chatting to them. Avoid ringing them when they are approaching their deadlines. When you do ring, get to the point quickly. Above all, when they make it clear that they are not interested in what you have to say, give up and try again next time.

How to write a press release

Press releases should be:

- neatly typed, using one-and-a-half or double spacing, with a wide margin on either side to allow the sub-editor to make notes
- written on one side of the sheet, on standard A4 paper with the logo at the top of the page; the words 'NEWS INFORMATION' or 'PRESS (or NEWS) RELEASE' should also be prominent at the top of the page
- preferably *one*, but not more than two, sides long.

Resist the temptation to go on at length in a press release.

Journalists scan press releases quickly, often throwing them in the wastepaper bin without reading them. The longer your release, the more likely it is to end up in the round file.

Even news editors in local radio stations are likely to receive several hundred press releases every day, so keep yours short! Aim to present them with a headline and opening paragraph that catch their eye and make your release stand out from the rest.

Put the address of your contact at the top of the page, including the telephone numbers of the contact at the end of your release. Put the date at the top of the first page and the words 'FOR IMMEDIATE RELEASE', unless you want to embargo it.

Type, in capital letters, a short title that summarises the context of your press release. For example, 'MICHELIN STAR CHEF TO MAKE WORLD'S BIGGEST PANCAKE'.

Keep the number of words per sentence to a maximum of 25–30, and avoid using more than three sentences per paragraph. List the items you want to include in decreasing order of importance, as the press release will be cut from the bottom up. The first paragraph should contain a summary of the whole story, so that even if all the rest is cut the first paragraph 'stands up', or makes sense on its own. The other paragraphs should provide more information in decreasing order of importance.

A good guide is to include the '5 Ws' in the first paragraph:

1. WHO – local famous chef
2. WHAT – world's largest pancake
3. WHERE – Ealing Common
4. WHEN – Tuesday 6 March 2007
5. WHY – to raise money for local hospice.

If you need to continue on to a second page, type 'mf' or 'continues' centred at the bottom of the last paragraph on page 1. Do not split a sentence between two pages. Staple the pages together. Make sure you include an abbreviated form of the heading on page two in case the pages do get separated, (e.g. 'World's largest pancake').

When you finish the press release, type 'ENDS' at the bottom of the

Figure 14.3 Chefs
merchandising own
products

last paragraph, then the name and contact number. Send out your press
release a week to ten days before the event, depending on the deadline
you are trying to meet.

Follow-up

Sending out a press release is only stage one. The follow-up to issuing a
press release is vital, but often forgotten by press officers.

A few days before the event, ring round all the newsdesks to find out
if they have received your press release. Do this in time for you to send
another one in the post. If they say they have not received it, and there is
not time to get one out in the post, fax it or deliver it by hand. When
you call make sure the exact date, time and place are in the diary.

However, once again, don't make a nuisance of yourself. If the answer
is 'No, we're not planning to cover your story', back off graciously. There
will probably be other opportunities.

A follow-up phone call will give you an opportunity to offer someone
for interview. This is particularly desirable with radio stations, as they
will often prefer someone to come in to the studio to do an interview
rather than send a reporter to the event. Make sure you are happy about
when the interview will be broadcast so that it does not damage your
chance of getting other media coverage.

Embargoes

You will probably never need to worry about embargoes, but it is worth
mentioning what they are and when they can be used. An embargo
means that you do not wish the information outlined in your press
release to be used before the exact time stated at the top of the press
release. Embargoes can be broken, so you cannot be sure that your press
release will not be printed before the stated time. Embargoes can be
useful on a few occasions. For example:

- if you want publicity for a report or book on a certain date and you
  want to give the journalist time to read it
- if you want to issue a speech in advance of an important meeting held

after the deadline of the paper, or if the journalist cannot attend for some reason

- if you are simply unable to issue the press release at a later date because you will be away; in this case make sure you include the phone number of someone who can be contacted during your absence.

Letters to the editor

The letters page of a publication is a good place to get free publicity. The letters editor is looking for punchy, articulate letters that are topical and sometimes controversial. You can write letters to local, regional and national newspapers and magazines – for example, *Caterer and Hotelkeeper*. Letters are useful for correcting inaccurate reporting of an event, but always include more information about your activities.

A letter to a letters page is a good way to flag up future events and to invite people to take part. Letters pages are not there to supply you with a free advertisement, though, so try to link your letter to something already in the news. Study the letters page and try to imitate the length and style of the letters in it. Get into a debate by writing in response to a letter that has just appeared, putting forward a different point of view.

National newspapers are unlikely to print letters about local or regional events, but will be interested in letters about national news – it is up to you to provide an angle.

Radio phone-ins

Many programmes on local radio stations are devoted wholly or partly to telephoned-in questions from the public. Queries and comments are invited on a particular topic and discussed by participants in the studio. Make a habit of listening in to phone-ins.

Once you have decided to call, jot down what you want to say. You will reach a programme assistant who will ask you what your comment or question is and she/he may arrange to call you back. Listen to the programme until the phone rings, then *switch off the radio*. If you don't, you will hear 'howlround' – a howling sound that will put you off your stride. Speak clearly, in your normal voice, to the person you wish to address. Stay on the line and don't hesitate to follow up what you have said with another point.

Telephone interviews

You may find yourself being interviewed on the telephone. *Stop and think*. Are you the best person to do the interview? If not, tell the journalist immediately. Suggest another interviewee and give the journalist their number. Then ring the person yourself to warn him/her.

When you receive a call from a newspaper journalist who wants some information, your first question should always be, 'What is your deadline?' Make a note of it and the questions they want an answer to and say you will ring back in five minutes or an hour, depending on the deadline. There is no need for you to give an immediate response and it is better to check your information and to prepare yourself with a few facts. *Always* ring back when you said you would, otherwise the journalist will never trust you again. And quite rightly.

If you are being interviewed by a newspaper journalist, choose your words carefully. They may end up in print. Don't fall into the old trap of answering yes to a question unless you are entirely happy with the sentiments expressed.

For example, a journalist might say:

> Wouldn't you say that the industry is not doing enough to tackle the skills shortage? Don't you think that government should commit more money to hospitality training.

Answer: Yes. This could end up published as:

> **Well-known chef slams government on training**
> A well-known chef said today that more public money should be committed to training and industry is not doing enough to tackle the problem of skills shortages.

Instead answer:

> No, but I would say that more is needed by industry and government to help solve the problem of skills shortages.

On and off the record

The safe rule is simply do not speak to a journalist off the record. In other words, do not say anything you would not be happy to see in print. If you know a journalist very well it can sometimes be useful to go 'off the record', but even then only to give him/her more background information about a situation. You should never say anything off the record you might later regret. It is useful to say to journalists on occasion, 'I'll talk off the record to fill you in and give you the background, and then I'll give you a comment "on the record".'

Preparing for a radio interview

Evaluate

1 Ask for details of the programme and find out what they want to know and why.
2 Anticipate the interviewer's questions. She/he will ask – who? what? where? when? why? and how? – the kind of questions the listener or viewer would want to ask.
3 Time is important. Find out when and where they will want you, how long it will last, and whether the interview will be 'live' or pre-recorded. If possible, know something about the interviewer and be

sure they know who you are. Then ring them back. Never give spontaneous interviews – create thinking time.

Investigate

4 Prepare by writing down the main points you want to get across – maximum three points – plus their supporting arguments. Check relevant facts; be sure of what you want to say, and practise with a colleague or friend.

5 Being interviewed is a one-to-one conversation with the interviewer; but remember that an audience will be listening – eavesdropping! Find out what you can about the audience – the chances are they will not be specialists in your subject, even if they're interested. Target your preparation accordingly.

Eliminate

6 Use the opportunity for maximum benefit. Whatever questions are asked be sure to say what you want to say. Use the subject of questions to make the points you want to make. Remember the time constraints: focus on the most important issues and don't get involved in the abstract or theoretical.

7 If the interview is to be 'live', find out what the first question will be. Not only will this help you to be prepared for it; it will also give you the chance to match your first answer (your most important point) with the first question.

Illustrate

8 Listen carefully to the questions and illustrate your answers with examples and anecdotes. Concentrate on the interviewer's face, make eye contact, try to look relaxed, and smile. Do not rush in to fill natural silence: that's the interviewer's job! Personalise it – don't talk about issues.

9 Don't be intimidated. You will usually know far more about the topic than the person asking the questions. The interviewer's only role is to draw you out, to help you tell your story. You are the expert but be prepared for the occasional personal question. Remember: people-based stories make powerful radio. Create 'sound pictures' to illustrate.

Orchestrate

10 Adopt a conversational and lively style, keep it brief, simple and avoid jargon. Cutting in is unattractive, but if you decide it is necessary, do it decisively or don't do it at all. Never get angry ... there could be a next time! What is the first question?

11 What you look like, the general impression you create, and how you sound, have much more impact on most people than anything you say. Looking good, even for radio, will help you *feel* good!

Public relations

Public relations is an exercise concerned with building an 'image' of the establishment in the public's mind. Public relations must create a favourable impression to present and future customers, employees and investors and, therefore, is not usually directly related to a particular product or service.

Evaluation

Evaluation is a necessary part of a promotion campaign. It is achieved by:

- monitoring the enquiries received as a result of a particular advertisement
- analysing sales figures
- measuring public awareness of a product and after promotion
- actual sales in 'test markets'.

AUTOMATIC VENDING

Vending facts and statistics

According to NOP Research, there are some 510,911 refreshment vending machines in use in the UK. Consumers spend £1.5 billion through the slots of refreshment vending machines annually. Some 8 million cups of coffee and 2 million cups of tea are vended every day. The annual wages bill of an average-size business with 50 staff could see more than £85,000 wasted in terms of time spent by employees making their own tea or coffee.

About the industry

Almost anything can be automatically vended, but the principal food and drink products are:

- hot and cold beverages
- cold drinks in bottles, cans or cartons
- confectionery and savoury snacks
- sandwiches and snack foods
- cook-chill dishes (for heating in an adjacent microwave)
- plated meals
- ice cream.

Vending operation

The vending operating company will source and site the machine for you, and be able to provide a service/maintenance contract for cleaning, filling and cash collecting, as well as any necessary maintenance.

Why vending?

- **Convenience:** vended goods are available 24 hours a day and machines can be sited just where they are wanted.
- **Time/money saving:** vending machines are not only convenient, they are time saving too. As noted above, research conducted by NOP showed that an average-size business with 50 staff could be spending more than £85,000 of its annual wages bill on time spent by employees making their own tea and coffee.
- **Hygiene:** with vending you get a clean cup every time and avoid the chore of washing up china cups or, worse still, having dirty crockery hanging around all day.
- **Recycling:** the SaveaCup scheme provides a ready way to recycle used vending cups into durable items for the office.
- **Variety:** vending machines offer a whole range of different products and beverages. Drinks vending machines can offer not just black and white coffee and tea, but can also make the drink weak or strong according to taste. Fresh brew, cappuccino and chocolate drinks are also available. Then there is confectionery, savoury snacks, ice cream, sandwiches, snack foods and meals.

Types of equipment

The main types of refreshment machine are:

- beverage – traditional or in-cup
- can or carton
- glass-fronted merchandisers for confectionery and snacks
- refrigerated food
- confectionery and ambient foods
- ice cream.

Beverage machines are available to suit all sizes of operation, from table-top machines suitable for a small office environment to fully automatic high-volume machines.

Manual dispenser-type machines are either plumbed into mains water or have a built-in water tank for filling by hand. There are two types: in-cup, where the ingredients are pre-packed in the cup, and dispenser, where customers place an empty cup under the ingredient-dispensing point.

Most dispensers are mounted on cabinets and can have payment systems fitted if required. Single product dispensers are dedicated to one drink, such as leaf tea, ground coffee, hot chocolate or cappuccino. They are sited primarily at counter service areas.

Further information
To find out more, visit the website of the Automatic Vending Association: www.ava-vending.org.

Vending equipment

The type of machine and its exact location will depend on the likely demand. Before deciding on equipment consider the following questions.

- How many people will be using the machine and during what hours?
- What products will they want?
- How much will they be prepared to pay for the drinks?
- Will there be long periods when the machine is not in use (for example, school holidays)?
- What other sources of supply are available locally? What do they charge and what do they offer?
- Where will the machine be located?
- Is it readily accessible to all those who want to use it?
- Is there a convenient supply of potable water and electricity nearby?
- Do you want users to pay by cash, token or card, or are you providing free drinks?
- What is your budget for the machine?

CUSTOMER CARE

Many staff may have the opportunity of direct contact with consumers or customers in most types of establishment. For some it will be a regular aspect of their job, for others it may be for irregular events or special occasions. Waiters/waitresses and food service personnel called upon to serve customers need to be aware of how to provide customer satisfaction.

Catering staff serving at food service counters directly to customers may be employed in canteens, refectories, dining halls, and so on, in schools, hospitals, industrial establishments, offices and other premises. Other food outlets include fast-food establishments such as crêperies, baked potato houses, McDonald's, fish and chip shops and takeaways, buffets at all kinds of functions (including outdoor catering, wedding receptions and carveries). The following information is intended to assist catering employees at all levels not only to provide customer satisfaction but to obtain job satisfaction when caring for customers. The first thing to remember is that a smile gets both the customer and you off to a good start; however, it is important to realise that excellent food served from the kitchen is only the first essential to satisfy the customer: the finest food produced for a meal can be completely spoiled if served by uncaring staff. Technical skills and technique are very important, but equally (or perhaps more) important are sincere caring attitudes and manners, with the food served in an environment that has an atmosphere that makes the customer feel at ease, wanted and welcome.

Customer care is, therefore, caring for customers. Remember:

Figure 14.4 Food cart

- put the customer first
- make them feel good
- make them feel comfortable
- make them feel important
- make them want to return to your restaurant or establishment.

It is important that you adjust your behaviour to suit certain customers and to treat all customers equally as if they were special. Give them your time and full attention. Use body language to put customers at ease.

Concentrate on:

- your appearance
- using the phone correctly
- a clean and tidy environment
- writing to customers
- answering the phone within three rings
- finding out what makes customers happy
- achieving positive results
- ensuring that what you give is what the customer wants.

The customer needs to be kept informed. You yourself should take responsibility and not pass the buck, and achieve results if people complain. You must show the customer empathy and be able to discuss things from their point of view. They expect good customer care. This is an important concept: getting customers and keeping them creates revenue (income). All other activities create costs.

Emotional factors surround the products that people buy; these include after-sales service, speed of delivery and ambience, especially in a restaurant. Customer satisfaction or dissatisfaction comes more and more from the way people are treated. Customers buy a total package. Customer care gives the caterer the opportunity to be 'special', to stand above the competition, winning customers and keeping them loyal. When a customer comes into contact with you, the caterer, your image is being exposed to the customer. The staff of the company are perceived as representing not themselves but the company that they are working for.

Customer perceptions are often emotional, idiosyncratic and sometimes irrational, often based on narrow observations. When a restaurant manager remembers a customer's name, that customer will be delighted, but if staff treat customers badly, they will be unhappy. Often customers will then react in a way that makes staff unhappy, thus affecting the business. If staff make the customers happy they will respond in kind:

Happy staff ↔ Happy customers
↓
Good profits

Staff can benefit from good customer care training. Dealing with people is a highly complex skill; we train people to use complicated machinery but we do not often consider training staff to deal with the most complex machinery of all: the human being.

The caterer must first:

- set standards for customer care
- measure performance
- set up training schemes
- reward accordingly.

Staff must know:

- what the company stands for, what its mission is
- what behaviour the company values highly
- that cutting costs is not more important than customer care
- that all guarantees must be honoured
- that the restaurant or establishment is in business to keep the customer happy
- that happy customers can lead to repeat business and recommendations to friends and colleagues.

HOW TO WIN COMMITMENT FROM STAFF

Staff will be happier and feel more committed by:

- good leadership
- avoiding unnecessary stress (remove the causes, if they are under your control)
- knowing the fundamental importance of the customer; seek ideas from your staff on how to improve customer care
- receiving good customer care training
- building pride in their work performance
- having their training reinforced periodically.

Training aspects in customer care

When you are training staff the following points can be used as a guide.

- Identify what the staff should know in caring for the customer.
- Know what the customer may ask them.
- Know what's on the menu and the composition of the dishes.
- Know what the special dishes of the day are.
- Know what the chef's specialities are.

Examples of good customer-care phrases you may hear in a restaurant or service area include:

- 'I'll take care of that for you right away.'

- 'I'll go and get it for you myself.'
- 'Is there anything else I can help you with?'
- 'I'll be glad to help you.'
- 'I don't know, but I'll find out now. Please take a seat for a moment.'
- 'I'm sorry to hear about that. Let's find out what went wrong and I'll put it right.'
- 'I'm sorry for the delay. I'll check with the kitchen to see how long your order will be.'

Good communication within the organisation assists in the development of customer care. It is important that the staff are constantly kept informed of what is going on otherwise they will feel that they are not part of the organisation. They must have a sense of 'ownership' or responsibility, since well-motivated staff are good for the organisation and will assist in the progressive development of the business, helping to avoid the 'it's not my job' attitude.

If staff are expected to work hygienically and treat the customer well, you must likewise treat the staff with respect and care for their well-being. Good staff welfare aids the process of customer care.
Staff must have good, clean changing rooms, washing and/or showering facilities, quality facilities for refreshments, and medical provision.

Staff, too, must treat each other with respect, cooperating and supporting each other. Good team spirit will ultimately rub off on the customer. Remember that behaviour begets behaviour, so if one member of staff treats another badly, they in turn may treat the customer badly.

Customer care is a team game. It is about all the staff working towards the same aim: getting the customers on their side.

Define standards of performance

The starting point is a clear analysis of what should happen at each of the points of contact that a customer might have with the restaurant. It can become a checklist, as in the following example.

- A customer enters the restaurant or service area:
  (a) the entrance should be clean and tidy
  (b) the doors could be marked 'welcome'.
- The customer is then greeted by the head waiter, restaurant manager or receptionist:
  (a) the reception area is clean and tidy, perhaps decorated with fresh flowers
  (b) menu sample and drinks list on display
  (c) all staff smartly dressed and well groomed
  (d) staff smile when greeting customers
  (e) if possible head waiter, restaurant manager or receptionist use customer's name
  (f) customer is escorted to the table, assisted into the seating position

(g) if there is any delay, staff apologise and explanation is given to the customer

(h) waiter introduces him/herself to the customer.

- At the end of the meal, head waiter or restaurant manager escorts customer to the door, smiles and exchanges pleasantries: 'good day'/'good night'.

When defining standards of performance, use numbers: for example, answer the phone within three rings; if there is a delay, update the caller every 20 seconds with 'Sorry, the line is still engaged, do you still wish to hold?'

Staff must have a sense of identity with the company or organisation. McDonald's, for example, has a 700-page *Operations and Training Manual*, which explains every stage of the cooking process and the correct behaviour to be used when dealing with customers.

Disney requires all new staff to go through an induction programme called 'Traditions', which explains about Walt Disney, the characters, what it is like to work at Disneyland, and their role. It stresses that all visitors are not 'customers' but 'guests', so they must be treated that way. Although on most days there will be more than half a million 'guests', they must be dealt with as individuals not as a crowd. These individuals look to the staff to help them enjoy their day; staff therefore have a crucial role to play. Disney explains to all its staff that they:

- are part of showbusiness
- are performers in a live show
- must make sure that nothing spoils the perfect picture the guests see
- must make a clear distinction between 'on stage' and 'off stage' – off stage they are able to relax, on stage they must play the perfect role; they must never be seen 'with their mask off'.

It may be said that caterers, too, are part of showbusiness, that waiters are performers in a live show. TGI Friday's restaurants have further developed this concept, and waiters and food service staff are interviewed on the basis of their personality. They become actors as part of a large

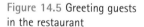
Figure 14.5 Greeting guests in the restaurant

show. Traditionally waiters that perform flambé dishes 'live' in front of a customer show off their flair and skill. Such staff develop a sense of importance and pride in their job.

Measure and monitor performance

The defined standards of performance must be monitored and measured. You need to measure success in terms of your promises to customers. Measuring the right thing helps staff understand what is important to customers and how to act accordingly.

Staff who look after customers and provide the service and care they expect, deserve reward. Good positive feedback to staff is important. You may:

- just say 'well done', which goes a long way
- make a payment of a bonus
- give an increment on their annual pay increase
- give a promotion.

Continuing customer care

Keep in touch with customers through mailshots, advertising, and so on (see page 545).

Customer care skills

Attitude and behaviour
If a customer is rude or aggressive to a waiter (e.g. blames a waiter for the chef's mistake), the waiter should not be rude or aggressive in return. If the waiter can remain calm and use his/her skills of patience, the customer will often apologise for their anger. Behaviour is a choice; you should select the behaviour that is appropriate to the customer.

When dealing with customers, behaviour should be:

- professional
- understanding – customers in a restaurant want a service and are paying for it; learn to understand their needs
- patient – learn to be patient with all customers
- enthusiastic – it can be contagious
- confident – it can increase a potential customer's trust in you
- welcoming – it can satisfy a customer's basic human desire to feel liked and be approved of
- helpful – customers warm to helpful staff
- polite – good manners are always welcomed
- caring – make each customer feel special.

Appearance
Remember, you never get a second chance to make a first impression.

What you wear and how you look is part of how potential customers judge your organisation. You are part of the company's image.

Body language
Body language includes:

- how you dress
- posture
- your distance from others
- stance
- how you sit

- facial expressions
- movements
- eye contact
- gestures
- eye movements.

Body language includes unconscious signals that tell us what people really think/feel. If someone is telling a lie, for instance, their body language will usually give them away. By focusing on other people's body language you can discover their true feeling towards you and what they think of what you are saying. It has a clear value in business situations and is therefore very important in customer care.

Learn to:

- look for what is important
- recognise other people so you are able to 'read' them better
- recognise how to use body language
- control it and use it to your advantage, so that you give the right positive message to people.

Remember that body language is universal but does mean different things in different cultures.

Signs and meanings
A gesture doesn't always reveal exactly how a person is thinking. For example, arms folded may mean that:

- they are being defensive about something
- they are cold
- they are comfortable.

Some gestures are open, expansive and positive. For example, leaning forward with open palms facing upwards shows interest, acceptance and a welcoming attitude, while leaning backwards, arms folded, head down says closed, defensive and negative, uninterested, rejection.

Using plenty of gestures usually indicates warmth, enthusiasm and emotion, while using gestures sparsely may indicate that a person is cold, reserved and logical.

Distance
Each person has around them an area that they regard as their personal space. Beware of intruding into a customer's personal space. Although some customers may regard it as friendliness, you may make others feel uncomfortable.

Placing people at a table for a meeting or for lunch or dinner is an art. The way people sit round a table, sends messages.

- Formal meeting: people sit opposite each other.
- Teamwork: sitting people side by side is stressful.

Eyes

Eye contact should be used as a way of acknowledging customers, making them feel welcome and as the foundation of building a good relationship. Eye contact should be used to show the customer you are listening.

Ears

Really listening is the highest form of courtesy.

- Look at the customer.
- Ignore any negative thoughts you have about them.
- Lean towards them.
- Think at the pace they are talking.
- Listen to every word.
- Try not to interrupt.
- Use facial expressions and body language to show you understand.
- Stick to the subject.
- Use their name wherever possible.

Greeting people

If you are already dealing with another customer in the restaurant acknowledge the new customer and reassure them that you will help them as soon as possible. Try to greet people with a smile that is genuine. You may even get one in return – after all, smiles are free! Remember that good manners are important.

Use people's names, it holds their attention, and demonstrates recognition and respect. Their name is probably the most important word in the world to them. Always use their surname until they give permission for you to use their first name.

Asking the customer questions will demonstrate:

- you have properly understood what they want
- you have time for them to talk
- interest on your part
- that you feel the customer is important
- you are able to find out how they feel
- you can keep control of the conversation
- you can understand their needs, their complaints
- you know how to make them feel better.

'Stroking'

This is defined as giving any kind of attention. Humans need 'stroking'. A prolonged absence of it can cause serious adverse effects. How good a customer feels about your restaurant or catering establishment is directly connected to the amount and types of 'strokes' (attention) they have received.

Stroking can be both positive or negative, it can be physical, verbal and non-verbal. Some examples of positive stroking include:

- greetings
- compliments
- laughing.

Some examples of negative stroking include:

- unpleasant greeting
- adverse criticism
- pushing
- swearing
- sarcastic remarks
- snatching
- absence of praise
- unpleasant hand gestures.

Pacing

Pacing is speaking in a way that is compatible with your customers. Match their speed, tone and volume. Do not talk above their heads.

Assertiveness

Remember that customers are human beings; you may have to handle them when they shout at you, interrupt you, are rude to you, criticise you or blame you for something you have not done. The answer is for you to be assertive, standing up for your rights.

Being assertive means:

- stating your views while showing that you understand their views
- enhancing yourself without diminishing them
- speaking calmly, sincerely and steadily.

Advantages of assertive behaviour

There are some advantages to be gained.

- It gives you greater self-confidence.
- You will be treating others as equals, recognising the abilities and limitations of others, rather than regarding them as superiors.
- It gives greater self-responsibility.
- It gives greater self-control; your mind is concentrated on achieving the behaviour you want.
- It can produce a win-win situation; opinions on both sides are given a fair hearing, so each side feels it has 'won'.

Telephone

A badly handled telephone call can destroy the effect of good advertising. Remember: when using the telephone, give all your attention to the customer; get their name, write it down and use it. Take note of all the other details the customer is wanting. Listen and use your voice correctly. Summarise what you have agreed with the customer at the end of the conversation.

How to handle customer complaints

Here are some statistics on complaints and customer satisfaction:

- 96 per cent of dissatisfied customers do not go back and complain, but they do tell between 7 and 11 other people how bad your restaurant or service is
- 13 per cent will tell at least 20 other people
- 90 per cent will never return to your restaurant
- it costs roughly five times as much to attract a new customer as it does to keep an existing one.

Therefore, encourage customers to complain on the spot. If they are unhappy about anything that is served to them, they should be encouraged to inform the member of staff who served them. This will give the establishment the opportunity to rectify the fault immediately. Ask them about their eating experience; this information will be vital for future planning. Treat any customer who complains well; offer them a free drink or a free meal. Make the complainant your ambassador. Show them empathy, use the appropriate body language, show concern, sympathise. Always apologise. If you handle the complaint well you will make the customer feel important. Remember:

Don't:

- say 'it's not my fault'
- say 'you're the fifth today to complain about that'
- interrupt – it will only add to their wrath
- jump to conclusions
- accept responsibility until you are sure it's your firm's fault
- be patronising
- argue
- lose your temper
- blame others.

Do:

- show empathy and use appropriate body language (e.g. show concern on your face, nod)
- use their name, when possible

Customer care
↓
Happy customers
↓
Profit
↓
Jobs

- shut up and listen, and use body language to show that you are listening (e.g. use eye contact)
- take notes
- let them make their case, they will lose their head of steam
- ask questions to clarify the details
- recapitulate; confirm with them that you've got it right.
- sympathise (regardless of where the blame lies)
- gather together your version of the facts before replying
- phone back if necessary – on time!
- apologise profusely if your company is at fault
- tell them what you propose to do
- give them alternatives to choose from, if your company is at fault
- offer more than the bare minimum (e.g. make some concession on 'future business')
- get their full agreement that this will resolve the issue
- make sure that it is done properly and that they are kept fully informed
- contact them very soon afterwards to make sure that they are happy
- see it as an opportunity to cement the relationship and encourage more business.

If you handle a customer complaint well, you will make the customer feel important. They will want to praise your company to their friends. Then they may well be prepared to deal with you again. So ask open questions to discover their future wants. For example:

- 'How often do you come to this establishment?' and 'How often do you order this from the menu'?
- 'How do you think your requirements will change in the future?'
- 'What will you be looking for then?' and 'What other services or meal items will you be looking for in the future?'

REFERENCES

Cracknell, H.L. and Kaufmann, R.J. (2002) *Practical Professional Catering Management.* Thomson Learning Vocational.

Figure 14.6 Let them make their case

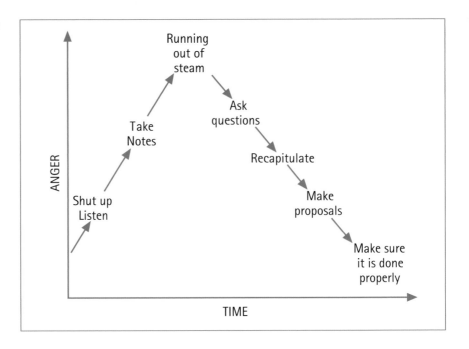

Some references to marketing elsewhere in the book:

Menu planning   356
Computer use   677

TOPICS FOR DISCUSSION

1   Your ideas for promoting a 100-seat industrial catering restaurant in an office block.
2   Examples of advertising.
3   What you understand by good public relations.
4   The advantages of cafeteria service.
5   The popularity of takeaways and what you think the changes will be in takeaway services in the future.
6   When is the use of vending machines worthwhile? Discuss where and how.
7   Can advertising increase sales? Explain how it could be used for a restaurant or any food service facility.
8   Making contact with local media to promote your business.

Chapter 15 HEALTH, SAFETY AND SECURITY

SICKNESS AND ACCIDENTS IN THE WORKPLACE

Sickness absence costs the UK economy approximately £400–500 per employee each year. Over 200 people die in accidents at work each year. Accidents can happen in any workplace (see the section on accidents, which starts on page 595).

If an employee works on a computer, they may be at risk of:

- eye and eyesight problems
- epilepsy
- upper limb pain and discomfort
- fatigue and stress.

Stress and accidents are currently the two biggest causes of absence from work.

You can report an accident at work by:

- email
- telephone
- fax
- letter.

The average number of days taken as sick leave each year in the UK is approximately 30 million.

Table 15.1 Significant factors for the catering industry

CAUSE	IMPORTANCE	SIGNIFICANT FACTOR
Slips, trips	30 per cent but 75 per cent of all major injuries	88 per cent due to slippery floors due to spillage not cleared up, wet floors and buckets etc. in passage ways and uneven floors
Handling	29 per cent	33.3 per cent due to lifting pans, trays, etc.; 33.3 per cent to handling sharp objects (e.g. knives); 33.3 per cent awkward lifts from low ovens or high positions
Exposure to hazardous substances, hot surfaces, steam	16 per cent	61 per cent from splashes; 13 per cent from hot objects. Causes: poor maintenance 28 per cent of cases; steam from ovens/steamer 23 per cent; carrying hot liquids 16 per cent; misuse of cleaning materials 14 per cent; cleaning flat fryers 14 per cent; equipment failure 12 per cent; horseplay 4 per cent; hot surfaces 1 per cent
Struck by moving articles including hand tools	10 per cent	33.3 per cent most probably from knives; 25 per cent from falling articles; one-tenth from assault
Walking into objects	4 per cent	75 per cent of cases involved walking into a fixed as opposed to a moveable object
Machinery	3 per cent	Slicers 30 per cent; mixers 16 per cent; vegetable cutting machines 9 per cent; vegetable slicing, mincing and grating attachments 10 per cent; pie and tart machines 4 per cent; dough mixer, dough moulder, mincing machine, dishwasher 2 per cent
Falls	1.8 per cent	75 per cent falls from low height (but half of the major injuries occurred on stairs)
Fire and explosion	1.6 per cent	80 per cent during manually igniting gas fire appliances, mainly ovens
Electric shock	0.5 per cent	25 per cent due to poor maintenance; 25 per cent trolley involved; 25 per cent unsafe switching and unplugging (75 per cent of these in wet conditions); 25 per cent poor maintenance
Transporter	3 per cent	50 per cent involved lift trucks

Health and safety targets

By 2010 it is the intention to reduce:

- the number of working days lost to injury and ill health at work by 30 per cent.
- by 10 per cent the number of fatal and major accidents at the workplace
- cases of work-related ill heath by 20 per cent.

Reportable major injuries

- Fracture other than finger, thumb or toe
- Amputation
- Dislocation of hip, knee or spine
- Loss of sight (temporary or permanent)
- Chemical or hot metal burn to the eye or any penetration to the eye
- Injury from electric shock or burn leading to unconsciousness or requiring resuscitation or admittance to hospital for more than 24 hours
- Any other injury leading to hypothermia, heat-induced illness or unconsciousness, or requiring resuscitation or admittance to hospital for more than 24 hours
- Unconsciousness caused by asphyxia or exposure to a harmful substance or biological agent
- Acute illness requiring medical treatment, or loss of consciousness from absorption by inhalation, ingestion or through the skin
- Acute illness requiring medical treatment where there is reason to believe that this resulted from exposure to a biological agent or its toxins or infected material

RIDDOR (Reporting Injuries, Diseases and Dangerous Occurrences)

RIDDOR regulations came into effect in 1996 and require work-related accidents, diseases and dangerous occurrences to be reported by employers to the Incident Contact Centre, Caerphilly Business Park, Caerphilly CF83 3GG. Records must be kept of each occurrence.

Examples of reportable diseases include certain poisons, dermatitis, skin cancer, lung diseases such as occupational asthma, infections such as hepatitis, tuberculosis, anthrax and tetanus.

An example of a dangerous occurrence could be an overloaded electric circuit causing a major fire.

'Three-day injuries' are not major but cause the employee to be absent for more than three days consecutively (not counting the day of the injury, but including days they would not normally be at work).

Managing absence

Managing employee absence doesn't have to be difficult or complicated.

- Tell your employees what they can expect from you to help them return to work, as far as your business permits.
- Make sure they understand their own contractual duties to you, including what procedures you require for absences from work.

It is important to have a fair and consistent approach to return to work and for you, your employees and their representatives, to be honest and able to trust each other at every step of the process. The sooner you take positive action together, the more likely it will be that your sick employees can return to work successfully and get on with the job of helping you build your business.

For small employers, an instance of an employee being off work for more than 14 days is likely to be rare, but when it does happen there are considerable benefits from working in partnership with your employees, their trades union or other employee representatives, to help those off sick return to work as soon as they are able.

By doing this you will:

- keep valued staff and avoid unnecessary recruitment and training costs
- keep your business productive and, where your sick employee has built up a loyal client base, keep this as a source of income
- reduce unnecessary overheads, such as saving on lost wages and sick pay costs
- help meet your legal duties and avoid discriminating against disabled workers
- maintain and improve workplace relations by working in partnership with your employees and their workforce representatives.

Enforcement and support

In most catering businesses, health and safety law is enforced by environmental health officers (EHOs) employed by the local authority.

CONTROL OF SUBSTANCES HAZARDOUS TO HEALTH (COSHH)

The Control of Substances Hazardous to Health Regulations 1999 (COSHH) state that:

> ... an employer shall not carry on any work which is liable to expose any employees to any substance hazardous to health unless he has made a suitable and sufficient assessment of the risks created by work to the health of these employees.

Nature of the hazard

When considering carrying out your legal obligations under the COSHH Regulations all areas should be surveyed in order to ascertain the chemicals and substances used. Table 15.2 presents a list of areas and the likely chemicals and substances to be found in them.

COSHH Register

A COSHH register should be kept by the manager for all substances used

Table 15.2 Work areas, and the chemicals and substances likely to be found in them

AREA	CHEMICALS AND SUBSTANCES
Kitchen	Cleaning chemicals including alkalis and acids, detergents, sanitisers, descalers Chemicals associated with burnishing, possibly some oils associated with machines Pest-control chemicals, insecticides and rodenticides
Restaurant	Cleaning chemicals, polishes, fuel for flame lamps including methylated spirits, LPG
Bar	Beer line cleaner, glass-washing detergent and sanitisers
Housekeeping	Cleaning chemicals including detergents, sanitisers, descalants, polishes, carpet-cleaning products, floor-care products
Maintenance	Cleaning chemicals, adhesives, solvents, paint, LPG, salts for water softening etc., paint stripper, varnishes etc.
Offices	Correction fluid, thinners, solvents, methylated spirits, toner for photocopier, duplicating fluids and chemicals, polishes

in the establishment. Technical data sheets should be attached to the completed COSHH assessment sheet.

Substances dangerous to health are labelled 'very toxic', 'toxic', 'harmful', 'irritant' or 'corrosive'. While only a small number of such chemicals are used in catering for cleaning, it is necessary to be aware of the regulations introduced in 1989 and the symbols used on products.

Principles

Those persons using such substances must be made aware of their correct use and proper dilution, where appropriate, and must wear protection: goggles, gloves and face masks as appropriate. Eye goggles should be worn when using oven cleaners, gloves when hands may come into contact with any chemical cleaner, and face masks when using grease-cutting and oven degreasers.

It is essential that staff are trained to take precautions and not to take risks.

What does COSHH require?

The basic principles of occupational hygiene underlie the COSHH Regulations.

- Assess the risk to health arising from work and what precautions are needed.
- Introduce appropriate measures to prevent or control the risk.
- Ensure that control measures are used and that equipment is properly maintained and procedures observed.
- Where necessary, monitor the exposure of the workers and carry out an appropriate form of surveillance of their health.
- Inform, instruct and train employees about the risks and the precautions to be taken.

Rules for using chemicals
- Always follow the maker's instructions.
- Always store in original containers. Decanting a chemical means you may lose its name and classification.
- Keep lids tightly closed.
- Do not store in direct sunlight, near heat or naked flames.
- Read the labels. Know the product and its risk.
- Never mix chemicals.
- Know the first-aid procedure.
- Always add product to water, not water to product.
- Dispose of empty drums immediately.
- Dispose of waste chemical solutions safely.
- Wear the correct safety equipment.

OTHER LEGISLATION

Every year in the UK 1000 people are killed at work, a million people suffer injuries, and 23 million working days are lost annually because of industrial injury and disease. As catering is one of the largest employers of labour the catering industry is substantially affected by accidents at work.

In 1974 the Health and Safety at Work Act was passed with two main aims:

1 to extend the coverage and protection of the law to all employers and employees
2 to increase awareness of safety among those at work, both employers and employees.

The law imposes a general duty on an employer 'to ensure so far as is reasonably practicable, the health, safety and welfare at work of all his employees'. The law also imposes a duty on every employee while at work to:

- take reasonable care for the health and safety of himself or herself and of other persons who may be affected by his or her acts or omissions at work
- cooperate with his or her employer so far as is necessary to meet or comply with any requirement concerning health and safety
- not interfere with, or misuse, anything provided in the interests of health, safety or welfare.

It can clearly be seen that both health and safety at work is everybody's responsibility. Furthermore, the Act protects the members of the public who may be affected by the activities of those at work.

Penalties are provided by the Act, which include improvement notices, prohibition notices and criminal prosecution. The Health & Safety

Executive was set up to enforce the law, and the Health & Safety Commission issues codes of conduct and acts as an adviser.

Responsibilities of the employer

The employer's responsibilities are to:

- provide and maintain premises and equipment that are safe and without risk to health
- provide supervision, information and training
- issue a written statement of 'safety policy' to employees, to include general policy with respect to the health and safety at work of employees, the role of the organisation in ensuring the policy is carried out, how the policy will be made effective.
- consult with employees' safety representative and establish a Safety Committee.

The Workplace (Health, Safety and Welfare) Regulations 1992 require indoor workplace temperatures to be reasonable, with effective and suitable ventilation provided.

Working in extreme temperatures can cause considerable stress on staff, which could result in conditions such as hypothermia or heat exhaustion. Before these injuries occur, staff may become tired and listless, and reduced concentration could make them more prone to accidents such as cuts and burns.

SAFETY REGULATIONS

As from 1993 six health and safety at work regulations have come into force.

1 Management of Health and Safety at Work Regulations 1992:
- risk assessment
- control of hazardous substances
- training.
2 Work Place (Health, Safety and Welfare) Regulations 1992:
- floors to be of suitable construction
- floors free from hazardous articles or substances
- steps taken to avoid slips, trips and falls.
3 Manual Handling Operation Regulations 1992:
- reducing incorrect handling of loads
- preventing hazardous handling.
4 Fire Precautions in Places of Work:
- means of fire-fighting
- evacuation procedures
- raising the alarm.
5 Provision and Use of Work Equipment:

Figure 15.1 Business protection

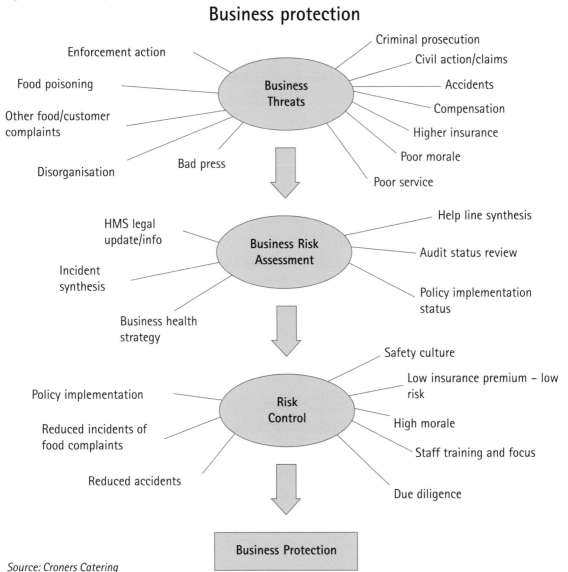

Business protection

Source: Croners Catering

- ensure correct usage
- properly maintained
- training given.
6 Health and Safety (Display Screen Equipment):
- to see that staff using visual display units have a suitable workplace and take regular breaks.

Risk assessment and reduction

Management of health and safety

The duties of employers, as specified by the Management of Health and Safety at Work Regulations 1999, are listed below. Employers have a duty under these regulations to carry out risk assessments and COSHH assessments.

Hazard

Means anything that can cause harm (e.g. chemicals, electricity, working from ladders).

Risk

Is the chance high or low, that somebody will be harmed by the hazard?

Managing risk

Managing risk is not a complicated procedure. To start with, a health and safety policy must be in place for the business.

Involve employees

These are people most at risk of having accidents, or experiencing ill health, and they also know the most about the jobs they do so are in the best position to help managers develop safe systems of work that are effective in practice. An actively engaged workforce is one of the foundations that support good health and safety. It ensures that all those involved with a work activity, both managers and workers, are participating in assessing risks.

Assessing risk

Assessing risk is the key to effective health and safety in the workplace. This means nothing more than a careful examination of what, in your work, could cause harm to people, so that you can weigh up whether you have taken enough precautions or should do more to prevent harm.

Five steps to assessing risk

1 Look for hazards – the things that could cause harm.
2 Decide who might be harmed, and how.
3 Evaluate the risks and decide whether the existing precautions are adequate, or whether more should be done.
4 Write down your findings so you have a record that you can check back against.
5 Regularly review your assessment, and revise it if necessary.

The prevention of accidents and food poisoning in catering establishments is essential; therefore it is necessary to assess the situation and decide what action is to be taken. Risk assessment can be divided into four areas, as follows.

1 Minimal risk – safe conditions with safety measures in place.
2 Some risk – acceptable risk, however attention must be given to ensure safety measures operate.
3 Significant risk – where safety measures are not fully in operation (also includes food most likely to cause food poisoning). Requires immediate action.
4 Dangerous risk – operations of process or equipment to stop immediately. The system of equipment to be completely checked and recommended after clearance.

To operate an assessment of risks the following points should be considered:

- assess the risks
- determine preventative measures
- decide who carries out safety inspections
- decide frequency of inspection
- determine methods of reporting back and to whom
- detail how to ensure inspections are effective
- see that on-the-job training in safety is related to the job.

The purpose of the exercise of assessing the possibility of risks and hazards is to prevent accidents. First, it is necessary to monitor the situation, to have regular and spasmodic checks to see that the standards set are being complied with. However, should an incident occur, it is essential that an investigation is made as to the cause or causes, and any defects in the system remedied at once. Immediate action is required to prevent further accidents. All personnel need to be trained to be actively aware of the possible hazards and risks, and to take positive action to prevent accidents occurring.

The workplace

The highest number of accidents occurring in catering premises are due to persons falling, slipping or tripping (see Table 15.1). Therefore, floor surfaces must be of a suitable construction to reduce this risk. A major reason for the high incidence of this kind of accident is that water and grease are likely to be spilt, and the combination of these substances is treacherous and makes the floor surface slippery. For this reason any spillage must be cleaned immediately and warning notices put in place, where appropriate, highlighting the danger of the slippery surface. Ideally a member of staff should stand guard until the hazard is cleared.

Another cause of falls is the placing of articles on the floor in corridors, passageways or between stoves and tables. Persons carrying trays and containers have their vision obstructed and items on the floor may not be visible; the fall may occur onto a hot stove and the item being carried may be hot. These falls can have severe consequences. The solution is to ensure that nothing is left on the floor that may cause a hazard. If it is necessary to have articles temporarily on the floor, then it is desirable that they are guarded so as to prevent accidents.

Kitchen personnel should be trained to think and act in a safe manner so as to avoid this kind of accident.

Managing health and safety

Employers must have appropriate arrangements in place (recorded where there are five or more employees) for maintaining a safe workplace. These should cover the usual management functions of:

- planning
- organisation
- control
- monitoring
- review.

The aim is to reduce risk and secure a progressive improvement in health and safety performance.

Health and safety information for employees

All employees, including trainees, must be provided with information on the particular risks they face, what to do in the event of a fire or other general emergency situation, and the preventative and protective measures designed to ensure their health and safety, including the identity of staff that would assist in the event of an evacuation. The information must be capable of being understood by those for whom it is intended.

Employees' duties
Employees have a duty to use correctly all work items provided by the employer in accordance with the training and instructions they have received to enable them to use the items safely.

Employees must immediately inform their employer, or person responsible for health and safety, of any work situation that might present a serious and imminent danger. Also employees should report any shortcomings in the health and safety protection arrangements in the company.

Consultation with employees
Safety Representatives and Safety Committees Regulations 1997
The employer is required to consult employee representatives in health and safety matters. The recognised trades union must notify the employer in writing of the names of the appointed persons who are the safety representatives.

The functions of a safety representative include:

- investigating potential hazards and dangerous occurrences in the workplace
- examining the cause of accidents, investigating complaints by any employee on health and safety issues
- making representations to the employer on general matters affecting the health, safety or welfare at work of employees
- attending health and safety meetings.

Safety committees

If two or more safety representatives make a request in writing for a committee, the employer must set up one within three months, after consultation with those who made the request.

Manual handling

The incorrect handling of heavy and awkward loads causes accidents, which can result in staff being off work for some time. Figure 15.2 shows how to lift heavy items in the correct way. The safest way to lift items is to bend at the knees rather than bending the back. Strain and damage can be reduced if two people do the lifting rather that one.

Handling checklist

- When goods are moved on trolleys, trucks or any wheeled vehicles, they should be loaded carefully (not overloaded) and in a manner that enables the handler to see where they are going.
- In stores, it is essential that heavy items are stacked at the bottom and that steps are used with care.
- Particular care is needed when large pots are moved containing liquid, especially hot liquid. They should not be filled to the brim.
- A warning sign that equipment handles, lids etc. can be hot should be

Figure 15.2 How to lift correctly

given; this can be indicated by a small sprinkle of flour or something similar.

- Extra care is needed when taking a tray from the oven or salamander so that the tray does not burn someone else.

Provision and Use of Work Equipment Regulations 1998 (PUWER)

'Work equipment' covers work machinery such as food processors, slicers, ovens, knives, and so on. These Regulations place duties on employers to ensure that work equipment is suitable for its intended use, and is maintained in efficient working order and in good repair, and that adequate information, instruction and training on the use and maintenance of the equipment and any associated hazards is given to employees.

Work equipment that possesses a specific risk must be used only by designated persons who have received relevant training. The Regulations' 'specific' requirements cover dangerous machinery parts, protection against certain hazards (i.e. falling objects, ejected components, overheating), the provision of certain stop and emergency stop controls, isolation from energy sources, stability and lighting, and markings and warnings.

PUWER 1998 replaces the list of prescribed dangerous machines as contained in the Prescribed Dangerous Machines Order 1964.

Need for signage

Following risk assessment under the Management of Health and Safety at Work Regulations 1992, safety signage should only be implemented to control a hazard when all other methods to reduce the risk to employees have been exhausted. Safety signs must not take the place of other risk-control methods and should significantly decrease the likelihood of an accident occurring.

The employer has a duty to:

- provide and maintain any safety sign
- give employees clear information on unfamiliar signs
- give employees instructions and training in the meaning of the signs and what to do in connection with them.

There are two main types of signage:

1 permanent – used for prohibitions, warnings and mandatory requirements, identifying emergency escape routes, first-aid facilities and fire-fighting equipment
2 occasional – including acoustic signals like fire alarms, and illuminated signs (such as fire escape signs) that operate with emergency lighting systems.

Figure 15.3 Prohibition sign

Figure 15.4 Warning sign

Prohibition signs

Such signs prohibit behaviour that is likely to increase or cause danger. They are round with a red circular band and crossbar, featuring a black pictogram on a white background. (Red should cover at least 35 per cent of the area of the sign.) Examples include 'No Entry' and 'No Exit' signs.

Safety signs

The display and use of safety signs and other means – such as hand and acoustic signals and marking of pipework – for communicating general and specific warnings about hazards and dangers, reminders and prohibitions, as well as matters relating to road traffic in the workplace and fire safety, are dealt with in the Health and Safety (Safety Signs and Signals) Regulations 1996.

Mandatory signs

These give warning of hazard or danger, and describe a behaviour. They take the form of a blue circle with a white pictogram. (Blue should take up at least 50 per cent of the area of the sign.) Examples include:

- for all fire doors, 'Fire Door – Keep Closed'
- for chemical dosing areas, 'Wear Gloves', 'Eye Protection Must Be Worn'
- for dangerous machinery, 'Guards Must Be In Position Before Starting'.

Emergency escape/first-aid signs

These are of a rectangular or square shape, with a white pictogram on a green background. (Green should take up at least 40 per cent of the area of the sign.)

Other signs

- Emergency eye wash stations: sign featuring 'Emergency Eye Wash'.
- For dangerous machinery, if applicable, sign featuring 'Emergency Stop Push Button'.

Figure 15.5 Mandatory signs

Personal protective equipment (PPE)

The Personal Protective Equipment at Work Regulations 1992 came into effect on 1 January 1993 and apply to all equipment designed to be worn or held by persons to protect them from one or more risks (e.g. uniforms, clothing required for hygiene purposes). The provision of equipment and clothing – for example, chefs' whites, safety shoes, eye protection goggles – which is intended to be worn or held by a person at work, as protection against risks to health and safety, is covered by the Personal Protective Equipment at Work Regulations 1992. The Health and Safety (Miscellaneous Amendments) Regulations 2002 added various points of detail on the provision of PPE, and instruction and training.

Information, instruction and training

Suitable information, instruction and training – including, where appropriate, demonstrations in the wearing of PPE – must be provided to guide employees on the proper use of PPE, how to correctly fit and wear it, its limitations, care and replacement. Managers and supervisors must

Figure 15.6 Emergency/ escape and first-aid signs

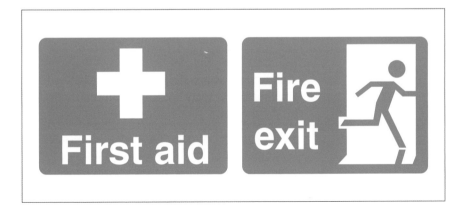

also be aware of why PPE is being used and how it should be used. Information and instruction on the use of PPE must be kept available to them.

Health and Safety (Safety Signs and Signals) Regulations 1996

On 1 April 1996 these regulations completely revoked the previous Safety Signs and Signals Regulations 1986. They aim to standardise safety signing across the European Union, so that wherever such signs are seen, they will have the same meaning. (The labelling of dangerous substances and most machinery is not covered by these regulations.)

Due to the hazardous nature of some of the work in kitchens, it is necessary to assess the risks to employees. Provision of protective clothing and footwear, properly maintained, is essential to safety. Suitable storage, such as lockers, needs to be available for the storage of personal clothing.

Items such as oven cloths and heatproof gloves need to be provided and maintained, or replaced so that they are safe to use.

First-aid equipment must be readily available and replenished when necessary. There must be one trained first-aider for every 50 employees.

Kitchen equipment

All equipment should be safe and used correctly, properly maintained and not misused.

- Tables must be strong, easily cleaned for hygiene reasons and never sat on.
- Bratt pans and tilting pans should not be able to be accidentally tilted.
- Fat fryers must not have their thermostats tampered with and must never be over-filled.
- Only step ladders should be used for reaching items stored on high shelves, not standing on boxes or a chair.
- Electrical equipment must be given special attention, particularly that listed under the Dangerous Machines Order 1964:
- worm-type mincing machines
- rotary bowl choppers
- mixing machines
- slicing/shredding machines
- chipping/chopping machines.

Only trained people (over 18) are allowed to use and clean such machines, and warning signs and instruction in their use must be sited by the machine. (For more on electrical safety, go to: www.sgs.co.uk.)

- Gas equipment must have instructions for igniting any piece of gas equipment and these should be followed. In the event of a gas leak or problems with pilot lights, maintenance personnel or the gas equipment suppliers should be contacted immediately.

- Maintenance should be regular to ensure correct function and safety of all gas and electrical equipment. This includes checking seals on microwave ovens.
- Extraction systems should function correctly, and particular care is needed to see that they are cleaned regularly as fat is liable to accumulate.
- Walk-in refrigerators and deep freezers must have a door that is operable from the inside.
- Records of staff trained in the use of equipment and records of maintenance need to be kept.

Computers and other display screen equipment

The employer and the person in control of the workplace, if this is different (e.g. because the user is employed by an agency or contractor, or is self-employed), must take steps to reduce the risks to health of these using a computer for work purposes under the Health and Safety (Display Screen Equipment) Regulations 1992.

The Health and Safety (Miscellaneous Amendments) Regulations 2002 widened the scope of the regulations to require all computers and other display screen workstations to meet health and safety specifications.

Electricity at work

The Electricity at Work Regulations 1989 introduced new fixed installation and portable appliance requirements, extending the general duties of the Health and Safety at Work Act 1974 to cover all workplaces and work activities.

All electrical equipment, both fixed and portable, must be maintained to ensure safety under the regulations.

The design, installation, operation, use and maintenance of all electrical systems and equipment in the workplace are covered by the Electricity at Work Regulations 1989. A whole range of specific and detailed health and safety requirements are laid down that both employers and the self-employed must have regard to.

- The design, installation and maintenance of electrical systems and equipment are carried out only by competent people.
- Equipment is suited to the job and the conditions in which it is used.
- The maker's instructions on the safe use and maintenance of equipment are followed.
- Employees use equipment safely, having been given the appropriate supervision, guidance and training, and report any faults or problems.

Arrangements are also important for checking the safety of electrical equipment at appropriate intervals, such as every six or twelve months, or at longer intervals depending on the equipment and the use to which it is put.

HEALTH AND SAFETY TRAINING

Health and safety training is a vital, moral and legal requirement upon all employers no matter what their business activity. All staff must be aware of occupational hazards and systems developed to reduce risks and prevent accidents.

Developing a positive safety culture

It is important to develop within the organisation a safety culture to maintain health and safety, to save time and money in preventing accidents and decreased time off work. Achieving this requires time and effort to create a caring, committed and well-organised management that understands the benefits of good health and safety practice. Knowledgeable staff who understand their responsibilities and duties also contribute positively to the business.

The safety policy is the essential basic foundation on which to build. Once this policy has been developed, control of workplace hazards is possible, and this involves getting systems and procedures under way. This is a vital part of staff training.

Periodic review of systems will be necessary to further develop health and safety, which constantly changes. Reviews should be actioned on a regular basis: when workplace systems change, when new equipment is installed, and so on.

Staff facilities and welfare

The welfare of all employees at a place of work is the responsibility of the employer. Facilities should be provided that are both safe and beneficial. These include:

- sufficient working space (minimum 11 cubic metres (14.4 cubic yards) per person)
- easy evacuation in an emergency
- floors and exit routes non-slip and in good repair
- proper ventilation
- temperature comfortable (normally 16°C (61°F) and never below 13°C (55°F), except when foods are to be kept cold)
- system of maintenance put into practice
- system of cleaning in operation
- quick disposal of waste, so that is does not accumulate
- safe and non-obstructed loading and unloading bays
- provision of adequate toilets, working facilities, drinking water
- changing facilities and accommodation for outdoor clothes, separate for men and women
- provision of a rest room, to include a non-smoking area.

Enforcement policy

Enforcement officers may:

- offer information and advice, face to face and in writing, that may include a warning that you are failing to comply with the law
- serve improvement and prohibition notices, withdraw approvals, vary licence conditions or exemptions, issue formal cautions (England and Wales only)
- prosecute (or report to the Procurator Fiscal with a view to prosecution in Scotland).

As noted above, the HSC strategy statement sets out the 'first ever' targets for Britain's health and safety system. These are, by 2010 to reduce by:

- 30 per cent the number of working days lost per 1000 workers from work-related injury and ill health
- 10 per cent the incidence rate of fatal and major injuries
- 20 per cent the cases of work-related ill health.

Enforcement of legislation

Health and safety inspectors and local authority inspectors (environmental health officers) have the authority to enforce legal requirements. They are empowered to:

- issue a prohibition notice that immediately prevents further business until remedial action has been taken
- issue an improvement notice whereby action must be taken within a stated time, to an employee, employer or supplier
- prosecute any person breaking the Act; this can be instead of or in addition to serving a notice and may lead to a substantial fine or prison
- seize, render harmless or destroy anything that the inspector considers to be the cause of imminent danger.

Environmental health officers

The environmental health officer has two main functions: one is to enforce the law; the other aspect of the job is to act as an adviser and educator in the areas of food hygiene and catering premises. Here his or her function is to improve the existing standards of hygiene and to advise how this may be achieved. Frequently, health education programmes are organised by environmental health officers; these may include talks and free literature. If in doubt about any matter concerning food hygiene, pests, premises or legal aspects, the environmental health officer is there to be consulted.

OCCUPATIONAL HEALTH

Occupational health means keeping oneself free from illnesses associated with conditions at work. Work-related illnesses are a major health problem in the UK today. Hazards at work may or may not be obvious. For example:

- exposure limits – many substances and environments established under COSHH regulations, exposure limits may be exceeded accidentally
- susceptibility to illness – this can vary from person to person.

Symptoms of illness

These may not appear for many years after the original contract – for example, in the case of asbestos causing asbestosis.

Action should be taken to protect employees from hazards at work. For example:

- assessments should be made and records kept of any hazards employees may face
- trained professionals should be employed to eliminate or reduce potential hazards
- safety policies should be designed to minimise the health risk to employees
- special equipment should be used to help shield employees from danger.

The employee must display the right attitude and action to safeguard their own health and safety while at work. She or he should cooperate with occupational health and safety programmes as these are designed to identify and control occupational health hazards.

Safety programmes

Training and information
Such programmes instruct staff in how to handle materials safely, use equipment correctly and detect symptoms of illness.

Medical examinations
Some problems can be detected early and before they become serious. Employees should have regular check-ups. This will depend on their age and position within the organisation.

Early treatment
If any unusual symptoms appear, the employee should inform their line manager, then report to the health and safety officer and seek medical advice. Early investigation and treatment can be most effective.

Monitoring illness patterns

Health professionals, such as occupational health nurses, record cases of illness, take samples from contaminated areas and keep medical records.

Self-protection

Always keep a healthy frame of mind. Never assume that 'it can't happen to me' – it can! The way to help prevent illness and accidents is to take proper precautions every day you work. Treat hazardous substances and working conditions with respect. Never cut corners to get work done faster. Follow the company's health and safety policies regarding exposure limits, clean-up procedures, protective equipment, smoking, and so on. Be aware of hazards that might exist at work. For example:

- acids
- dust
- alkalis
- noise
- asbestos
- solvents
- fumes
- paints
- resins.

Take care with substances that you use or that are used around you at work. Know the generic name of all chemicals. Check whether any substances can enter the body – for example, by inhaling, swallowing or via skin contact.

Where exposure limits have been established, stick to them. Know what the potential risks are and report any health problems that are noticed. Watch for dangerous conditions that may affect your health. These include noise, heat, radiation and vibrations, as well as leaks, spills, malfunctions in protective equipment and poor safety practices on the part of colleagues. Report any unsafe or suspicious conditions to your line manager.

Implementing a programme

Implementing health and safety measures doesn't have to be expensive, time consuming or complicated. In fact, safer and more efficient working practices can save money and greatly improve working conditions for your employees.

If you have five or more employees you will need to write down your health and safety policy. This sets out how you manage health and safety in your organisation. It needn't be overly complicated, but should be something that is meaningful and useful to you and your staff.

ACCIDENTS

It is essential that people working in the kitchen are capable of using the tools and equipment in a manner that will harm neither themselves nor those with whom they work. Moreover, they should be aware of the causes of accidents and be able to deal with any that occur.

Accidents may be caused in various ways:

- excessive haste – the golden rule of the kitchen is 'never run'; this may be difficult to observe during a very busy service but excessive haste causes people to take chances, which inevitably lead to mishaps
- distraction – accidents may be caused by not concentrating on the job in hand, through lack of interest, personal worry or distraction by someone else; the mind must always be kept on the work so as to reduce the likelihood of accidents
- failure to apply safety rules.

Accident prevention

It is the responsibility of everyone to observe the safety rules; in this way a great deal of pain and loss of time can be avoided.

It isn't difficult to keep your employees safe and healthy in the workplace. This will keep your profits where they belong: as profits for your company, not money paid out to cover avoidable staff absences due to ill health or injury.

When trying to establish the common causes of accidents and ill health at work, consider the following questions. They may help clarify the issues.

- What are the chances of people slipping or tripping at work?
- Do people work with, or come into contact with, asbestos?
- Do people work with hazardous substances?
- Do people perform work at height and, if so, is it done safely?
- Do people suffer from sprains, strains and pains?
- Do people use computers or other display screen equipment?
- Is your workplace noisy?
- Are employees exposed to vibration?
- How safe is electricity in your workplace?
- Do people know how to select and use your work equipment?
- What maintenance and building work takes place?
- What are the risks from transport in your workplace?
- Do you know the risks associated with pressure systems?
- Do you know how to prevent fire or explosion?
- Do you know where harmful radiation occurs?
- Are employees feeling stressed by work?
- What do you do if there's an accident at work?

Prevention of cuts and scratches

Knives
These should never be misused and the following rules should always be observed.

- The correct knife should be used for the appropriate job.

Figure 15.7 Sample in-house record of accidents and dangerous occurrences

Full name of injured person:			
Occupation:		Supervisor:	
Time of accident:	Date of accident:	Time of report:	Date of report:
Nature of injury or condition:			
Details of hospitalisation:			
Extent of injury (after medical attention):			
Place of accident or dangerous occurrence:			
Injured person's evidence of what happened (include equipment/items/or other persons): Use separate sheets if necessary			
Witness evidence (1):		Witness evidence (2):	
Supervisor's recommendations:			
Date:	Supervisor's signature: This form must be sent to the company health and safety officer		

- Knives must always be sharp and clean; a blunt knife is more likely to cause a cut because excessive pressure has to be used.
- Handles should be free from grease.
- The points must be held downwards.
- Knives should be placed flat on the board or table so that the blade is not exposed upwards.
- Knives should be wiped clean, holding the edge away from the hands.
- Do not put knives in a washing-up sink.

Choppers

These should be kept sharp and clean. Care should be taken that no other knives, saws, hooks or suchlike can be struck by the chopper, which could cause them to fly into the air. This also applies when using a large knife for chopping.

Cutting blades on machines

Guards should always be in place when the machine is in use; they should not be tampered with nor should hands or fingers be inserted past the guards. Before the guards are removed for cleaning, the blade or blades must have stopped revolving.

When the guard is removed for cleaning, the blade should not be left unattended in case someone should put a hand on it by accident. If the machine is electrically operated the plug should, when possible, be removed.

Cuts from meat and fish bones

Jagged bones can cause cuts, which may turn septic, particularly fish bones and the bones of a calf's head that has been opened to remove the brain. Cuts of this nature, however slight, should never be neglected. Frozen meat should not be boned out until it is completely thawed because it is difficult to handle: the hands become very cold and the knife slips easily.

Prevention of burns and scalds

A burn is caused by dry heat and a scald by wet heat. Both burns and scalds can be very painful and have serious effects, so certain precautions should be taken to prevent them.

- Sleeves of jackets and overalls should be rolled down and aprons worn at a sensible length so as to give adequate protection.
- A good, thick dry cloth or gloves are most important for handling hot utensils. A cloth should never be used wet on hot objects and is best folded to give greater protection. It should not be used if thin, torn or with holes.
- Trays containing hot liquid, such as roast gravy, should be handled carefully, one hand on the side and the other on the end of the tray so as to balance it.
- A hot pan brought out of the oven should have something white, such as a little flour, placed on the handle and lid as a warning that it is hot. This should be done as soon as the pan is taken out of the oven.
- Handles of pans should not protrude over the edge of the stove as the pan may be knocked off the stove.
- Large full pans should be carried correctly: when there is only one handle the forearm should run along the full length of the handle and the other hand should be used to balance the pan where the handle joins the pan. This should prevent the contents from spilling.
- Certain foods require extra care when heat is applied to them – as, for example, when a cold liquid is added to a hot roux or when adding

cold water to boiling sugar for making caramel. Extra care should always be taken when boiling sugar.
- Frying, especially deep frying, needs careful attention. When shallow or deep frying fish, for example, put the fish into the pan away from the person so that any splashes will do no harm. With deep frying, fritures should be moved with care and if possible only when the fat is cool. Fritures should not be more than two-thirds full. Wet foods should be drained and dried before being placed in the fat, and when foods are tipped out of the frying basket a spider should be to hand. Should the fat in the friture bubble over on to a gas stove then the gas taps should be turned off immediately. Fire blankets and fire extinguishers should be provided in every kitchen, conveniently sited ready for use.
- Steam causes scalds just as hot liquids do. It is important to be certain that before steamers are opened the steam is turned off and that when the steamer door is opened no one is in the way of the escaping steam. The steamer should be in proper working condition; the drain hole should always be clear. The door should not be opened immediately the steam is turned off – it is better to wait for about half a minute before doing so.
- Scalds can also be caused by splashing when passing liquids through conical strainers; it is wise to keep the face well back so as to avoid getting splashed. This also applies when hot liquids are poured into containers.

Emptying and cleaning fryers

Lack of care during the emptying and cleaning of fryers is a major cause of accidents. Hazards include:

- fire
- burns from hot oil
- contact with hot surfaces
- fumes from boiling cleaning chemicals
- danger of chemicals overflowing
- eye injuries from splashes
- strains and sprains while lifting and moving containers of oil.

Procedure for draining
- Switch off appliance.
- Drain only when oil is cool.
- Do not drain until oil is below 40°C.
- Follow any instructions. Remove debris.
- Clean and dry.
- Ensure that the drain-off tap cannot be turned on accidentally.
- If appropriate, eye protection should be worn.

Machinery

Accidents are easily caused by misuse of machines. The following rules should always be put into practice.

- The machine should be in correct running order before use.
- The controls of the machine should be operated by the person using the machine. If two people are involved there is the danger that a misunderstanding can occur and the machine be switched on when the other person does not expect it.
- Machine attachments should be correctly assembled and only the correct tools used to force food through mincers.
- When mixing machines are being used the hands should not be placed inside the bowl until the blades, whisk or hook have stopped revolving. Failure to observe this rule may result in a broken arm or severe cut.
- Electrical plugs should be removed from electric machines when they are being cleaned so they cannot be switched on accidentally.

The Gas Safety (Installation and Use) Regulations require employers to maintain gas appliances; this is distinctly separate from the duty of a landlord to maintain gas appliances in let properties. It is vital that all gas equipment, and in particular Calor gas equipment, is properly and regularly serviced and adjusted. For this reason, an agreement should be in place with a properly qualified gas installer or maintenance company.

Gas explosions

The risk of explosion from gas is considerable. To avoid this occurring it is necessary to ensure that the gas is properly lit. On ranges with a pilot on the oven it is important to see that the main jet has ignited from the pilot. If the regulo is low, sometimes the gas does not light at once – the gas collects and an explosion occurs. When lighting the tops of solid-top ranges it is wise to place the centre ring back for a few minutes after the stove is lit because the gas may go out – gas then collects and an explosion can occur.

Kitchen equipment

On 1 January 1996 a significant European Union directive concerning the design and installation of gas-fuelled catering equipment became mandatory. All gas appliances sold after that date, new or secondhand, must be fitted with a fuel cut-out mechanism should the main pilot light be extinguished. Equipment will be withdrawn from the marketplace if it does not comply. This gas directive joins other European laws that have come into effect and are strict guidelines or explicit instructions. These rules set out safe practice on topics as diverse as electromagnetic compatibility, pressure in systems and the surface temperature of oven doors. They accompany the six sets of UK Health and Safety at Work Regulations (1992), which came into force in 1993, the legislation that

Blowtorch danger highlighted

At its December 1999 meeting, the Health and Safety in Hospitality Liaison Committee heard of an incident involving a glass blowtorch of the sort used to caramelise crème brûlée (as opposed to glazing the brown sugar under a grill). B.G. Prichard, Health and Safety Enforcement Officer for Ceredigion, drew the Committee's attention to the 'danger that familiarity breeds contempt resulting in staff ignoring the significant risks involved in the use, storage and handling of this [now commonplace] equipment'.

In spite of instructions on the gas canister stating that it should not be exposed to temperatures exceeding 50°C, the blowtorch had been left on or near the solid-top gas cooker. The top blew off, gas escaped and there was an explosion. The glass roof of the kitchen was blown off, and the heavy wooden doors ripped from their hinges. Fortunately no one was injured. For several days the kitchen was out of use.

It transpired that the blowtorch had been used to light the oven, apparently a not uncommon practice in kitchens – and, evidently, an extremely dangerous one.

implements European Union directives on Health and Safety at Work. These regulations have developed changes in the manufacture of existing equipment.

Electrical equipment is mostly covered by a non-binding European Union directive: the Low Voltage Directive. This was approved by the European Union's members in February 1973, and was passed into UK Health and Safety law in 1989, in the form of the Low Voltage Electrical Equipment Safety Regulations.

Interlocking devices: see page 609.

Floors

Accidents are also caused by grease and water being spilled on floors and not being cleaned up. It is most important that floors are always kept clean and clear; pots, pans and suchlike should never be left on the floor, nor should oven doors be left open, because anyone carrying something large may not see the door or anything on the floor, and trip over.

Many people strain themselves by incorrectly lifting or attempting to lift items that are too heavy (see Figure 15.2 for guidance). Large stock pots, forequarters and hindquarters of beef, for example, should be lifted with care. Particular attention should be paid to the hooks in the meat so that they do not injure anyone.

On no account should liquids be placed in containers on shelves above eye level, especially when hot. They may be pulled down by someone else.

Safe kitchens are those that are well lit and well ventilated, and where the staff take precautions to prevent accidents happening. When accidents do happen, however, it is necessary to know something about first aid (dealt with in the following section).

Further information
Further information can be obtained from the Royal Society for the Prevention of Accidents (RoSPA) (website: www.hse.gov.uk) or the Health & Safety Executive (website: www.hse.gov.uk).

FIRST AID

When people at work suffer injuries or fall ill, it is important that they receive immediate attention and that, in serious cases, an ambulance is called.

The arrangements for providing first aid in the workplace are set out in the Health and Safety (First Aid) Regulations 1981. First aiders and facilities should be available to give immediate assistance to casualties with both common injuries or illness.

As the term implies, first aid is the immediate treatment given on the spot to a person who has been injured or is ill. Since 1982 it has been a legal requirement that adequate first-aid equipment, facilities and personnel to give first aid are provided at work. If the injury is serious the injured person should be treated by a doctor or nurse as soon as possible.

First-aid equipment

A first-aid box, as a minimum, should contain:

- a card giving general first aid guidance
- 20 individually wrapped, sterile, adhesive, waterproof dressings of various sizes
- 25 g (1 oz) cotton wool packs
- a dozen safety pins
- two triangular bandages
- two sterile eye pads, with attachment
- four medium-sized sterile unmedicated dressings
- two large sterile unmedicated dressings
- two extra large sterile unmedicated dressings
- tweezers
- scissors
- report book to record all injuries.

First-aid boxes must be easily identifiable and accessible in the work

Figure 15.8 First-aid kit

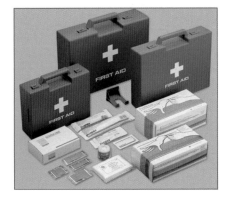

area. They should be in the charge of a responsible person, checked regularly and refilled when necessary.

All establishments must have first-aid equipment and employees qualified in first aid. Large establishments usually have medical staff such as a nurse and a first-aid room. The room should include a bed or couch, blankets, chairs, a table, sink with hot and cold water, towels, tissues and a first-aid box. Hooks for clothing and a mirror should be provided. Small establishments should have members of staff trained in first aid and in possession of a certificate. After a period of three years trained first-aid staff must update their training to remain certificated.

All catering workers and students are recommended to attend a first-aid course run by St John Ambulance, St Andrew's Ambulance Association or the British Red Cross Society.

First-aid treatment

Shock
The signs of shock are faintness, sickness, clammy skin and a pale face. Shock should be treated by keeping the person comfortable, lying down and warm. Cover the person with a blanket or clothing, but do not apply hot water bottles.

Fainting
Fainting may occur after a long period of standing in a hot, badly ventilated kitchen. The signs of an impending faint are whiteness, giddiness and sweating. A faint should be treated by raising the legs slightly above the level of the head and, when the person recovers consciousness, putting them in the fresh air for a while and making sure that they have not incurred any injury in fainting.

Cuts
All cuts should be covered immediately with a waterproof dressing, after the skin round the cut has been washed. When there is considerable bleeding it should be stopped as soon as possible. Bleeding may be controlled by direct pressure, by bandaging firmly on the cut. It may be possible to stop bleeding from a cut artery by pressing the artery with the thumb against the underlying bone; such pressure may be applied while a dressing or bandage is being prepared for application, but not for more than 15 minutes.

Nose bleeds
Sit the person down with their head forward, and loosen their clothing round the neck and chest. Ask them to breathe through their mouth and to pinch the soft part of their nose. After ten minutes release the pressure. Warn the person not to blow their nose for several hours. If the bleeding has not stopped continue for a further ten minutes. If the

Further information
Further information on first aid and emergency treatments can be obtained from the St John Ambulance Association, 27 St John's Lane, London EC1M 4BU (website: www.sja.org.uk).

bleeding has not stopped then, or recurs in 30 minutes, obtain medical assistance.

Fractures

A person suffering from broken bones should not be moved until the injured part has been secured so that it cannot move. Medical assistance should be obtained.

Burns and scalds

Place the injured part gently under slowly running water or immerse in cool water, keeping it there for at least ten minutes or until the pain ceases. If serious, the burn or scald should then be covered with a clean cloth or dressing (preferably sterile) and the person sent immediately to hospital.

Do not use adhesive dressings, apply lotions or ointments, or break blisters.

Electric shock

Switch off the current. If this is not possible, free the person by using a dry insulating material such as cloth, wood or rubber, taking care not to use the bare hands otherwise the electric shock may be transmitted. If breathing has stopped, give artificial respiration and send for a doctor. Treat any burns as above.

Gassing

Do not let the gassed person walk, but carry them into the fresh air. If breathing has stopped apply artificial respiration and send for a doctor.

Artificial respiration

There are several methods of artificial respiration. The most effective is mouth to mouth (or mouth to nose) and this method can be used by almost all age groups and in almost all circumstances.

It is stressed that we would recommend all students complete a first-aid course.

FIRE PRECAUTIONS

Fire safety

Every employer has an explicit duty for the safety of his or her employees in the event of a fire. The Regulatory Reform Fire Safety Order 2005 places a greater focus on fire prevention. It places responsibility for the fire safety of the occupants of premises and people who might be affected by fire, on a defined responsible person, usually the employer.

The responsible person must:

- make sure that the fire precautions, where reasonably practicable, ensure the safety of all employees and others in the building

Fire precautions

- Identified hazards must be removed or reduced so far as is reasonable. All persons must be protected from the risk of fire and the likelihood of a fire spreading.
- All escape routes must be safe and used effectively.
- Means for fighting fires must be available on the premises.
- Means of detecting a fire on the premises and giving warning in case of fire on the premises must be available.
- Arrangements must be in place for action to be taken in the event of a fire on the premises, including the instruction and training of employees.
- All precautions provided must be installed and maintained by a competent person.

- make an assessment of the risk of and from fire in the establishment; special consideration must be given to dangerous chemicals or substances, and the risks that these pose if a fire occurs
- review the preventative and protective measures.

Fire safety requires constant vigilance to reduce the risk of a fire, using the provision of detection and alarm systems, and well-practised emergency and evacuation procedures in the event of a fire.

A fire requires heat, fuel and oxygen (see the section on 'the fire triangle', below, and Figure 15.9). Without any one of these elements there is no fire. Methods of extinguishing fires concentrate on cooling (as in a water extinguisher or fire hose) or depriving the fire of oxygen (as in an extinguisher that uses foam or powder to smoother it).

Although businesses no longer need a fire certificate, the fire and rescue authorities will continue to inspect premises and ensure adequate fire precautions are in place. They will also wish to be satisfied that the risk assessment is comprehensive, relevant and up to date.

Fire risk assessment

A fire risk assessment will help determine the chances of a fire occurring and the dangers from fire that your workplace possesses for the people who use it. The assessment method suggested shares the same approach as that used in general health and safety legislation, and can be carried out either as part of a more general risk assessment or as a separate exercise.

A risk assessment is not a theoretical exercise. However, much work can be done on paper from the knowledge you, your employees or their representatives have of the workplace. A tour of the workplace will be needed to confirm, amend or add detail to your initial views.

For fire risk assessments there are five steps that you need to take.

1 Identify potential fire hazards in the workplace.

Figure 15.9 The fire triangle

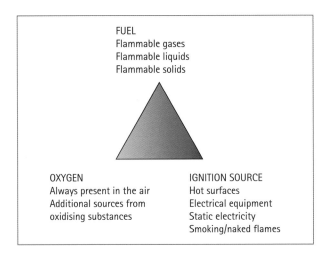

FUEL
Flammable gases
Flammable liquids
Flammable solids

OXYGEN
Always present in the air
Additional sources from
oxidising substances

IGNITION SOURCE
Hot surfaces
Electrical equipment
Static electricity
Smoking/naked flames

2 Decide who (e.g. employees, visitors) might be in danger in the event of a fire, in the workplace or while trying to escape from it, and note their location.

3 Evaluate the risks arising from the hazards and decide whether your existing fire precautions are adequate or whether more should be done to get rid of the hazard or to control the risks (e.g. by improving fire precautions).

4 Record your findings and details of the action you took as a result. Tell your employees about your findings.

5 Keep the assessment under review and revise it when necessary.

The fire triangle

As noted above, for a fire to start, three things are needed:

1 a source of ignition (heat)
2 fuel
3 oxygen.

If any one of these is missing, a fire cannot start. Taking steps to avoid the three coming together will therefore reduce the chances of a fire occurring.

Once a fire starts it can grow very quickly and spread from one source of fuel to another. As it grows, the amount of heat it gives off will increase and this can cause other fuels to self-ignite.

Fire detection and fire warning

You need to have an effective means of detecting any outbreak of fire and for warning people in your workplace quickly enough so that they can escape to a safe place before the fire is likely to make escape routes unusable.

In small workplaces where a fire is unlikely to cut off the means of escape (open-air areas and single-storey buildings where all exits are visible and the distances to be travelled are small), it is likely that any fire will quickly be detected by the people present and a shout of 'Fire!' may be all that is needed.

In larger workplaces, particularly multi-storey premises, an electrical fire warning system with manually operated call points is likely to be the minimum needed. In unoccupied areas, where a fire could start and develop to the extent that escape routes may become affected before it is discovered, it is likely that a form of automatic fire detection will also be necessary.

Means of fighting fire

You need to have enough fire-fighting equipment in place for your employees to use, without exposing themselves to danger, to extinguish a fire in its early stages. The equipment must be suitable to the risks, and appropriate staff will need training and instruction in its proper use.

In small premises, having one or two portable extinguishers in an obvious location may be all that is required. In larger or more complex premises, a greater number of portable extinguishers, strategically sited throughout the premises, are likely to be the minimum required. Means of fighting fire may need to be considered.

Lighting of escape routes

All escape routes, including external ones, must have sufficient lighting for people to see their way out safely. Emergency escape lighting may be needed if areas of the workplace are without natural daylight or are used at night.

Fire-fighting equipment

Portable fire extinguishers

Portable fire extinguishers enable suitably trained people to tackle a fire in its early stages, if they can do so without putting themselves in danger.

When you are deciding on the types of extinguisher to provide, you should consider the nature of the materials likely to be found in your workplace.

Fires are classified in accordance with British Standard EN 2 as follows.

- Class A – fires involving solid materials where combustion normally takes place with the formation of glowing embers.
- Class B – fires involving liquids or liquefiable solids.
- Class C – fires involving gases.

Figure 15.10 Fire-fighting

- Class D – fires involving metals.
- Class F – fires involving cooking oils or fats.

Class A and B fires

Class A fires involve solid materials, usually of organic matter such as wood, paper, and so on. They can be dealt with using water, foam or multi-purpose powder extinguishers, with water and foam considered the most suitable.

Class B fires involve liquids or liquefiable solids such as paints, oils or fats. It would be appropriate to provide extinguishers of foam (including multi-purpose aqueous film-forming foam (AFFF) carbon dioxide, halon or dry powder types). Carbon dioxide extinguishers are also suitable for a fire involving electrical equipment.

The fire extinguishers currently available for dealing with Class A or Class B fires should not be used on cooking oil or fat fires.

Class C fires

Dry powder extinguishers may be used on Class C fires. However, you need to consider the circumstances for their use and combine this with action such as stopping the leak to remove the risk of a subsequent explosion from the build-up of unburnt gas.

Types of portable fire extinguisher

The fire-fighting extinguishing medium in portable extinguishers is expelled by internal pressure, either permanently stored or by means of a gas cartridge. Generally, portable fire extinguishers can be divided into five categories according to the extinguishing medium they contain:

1 water
2 foam
3 powder
4 carbon dioxide
5 vaporising liquids, including halons.

Some fire extinguishers can be used on more than one type of fire. For instance, AFFF extinguishers can be used on both Class A fires and Class B fires. Your fire equipment supplier will be able to advise you.

The most useful form of fire-fighting equipment for general fire risks is the water-type extinguisher or hose reel. One such extinguisher should be provided for approximately each 200 square metres of floor space, with a minimum of one per floor. If each floor has a hose reel, which is known to be in working order and of sufficient length for the floor it serves, there may be no need for water-type extinguishers to be provided.

Areas of special risk involving the use of oil, fats or electrical equipment may need carbon dioxide, dry powder or other types of extinguisher (see above). If you are not sure what to provide in any given circumstances, your local fire authority will be able to advise you.

Fire extinguishers should conform to a recognised standard such as British Standards EN 3 for new ones and British Standard 5423 for existing ones. For extra assurance, you should look for the British

Figure 15.11 Fire blanket

Standard Kitemark, the British Approvals for Fire Equipment (BAFE) mark or the Loss Prevention Council Certification Board (LPCB) mark.

Fire extinguishers may be colour-coded to indicate their type. Previously, the entire body of the extinguisher has been colour-coded, but British Standard EN 3: Part 5 (which came into effect on 1 January 1997) requires that all new fire extinguisher bodies should be red.

Hose reels

Where hose reels are provided, they should be located where they are conspicuous and always accessible, such as in corridors.

Fire-extinguishing systems

Sprinkler systems

In smaller workplaces, portable fire extinguishers will probably be sufficient to tackle small fires. However, in more complex buildings, or where it is necessary to protect the means of escape and/or the property or contents of the building, it may be necessary to consider a sprinkler system.

Sprinkler systems are traditionally acknowledged as an efficient means of protecting buildings against extensive damage from fire. They are also now acknowledged as an effective means of reducing the risk to life from fire.

A note on fire legislation: interlocking

Any completely new kitchen built after September 2002 must have interlocking in the ventilation system, and any replacement, new installation or modification to existing ventilation systems must incorporate interlocking. (Interlocking describes the mechanical link between sensors in the extraction system and the main valve of the gas supply to cooking equipment. Should the carbon monoxide level in the ventilation system go up, the interlocker will turn off.)

Gas safety

The Gas Safety (Installation and Use) Regulations 1998 require any work to a gas fitting or gas storage vessel to be carried out by a competent person. This includes installing, reconnecting, maintaining, servicing, adjusting, disconnecting, repairing and purging the equipment of gas or air.

Competence to install, repair and maintain gas appliances

Whether a contractor or in-house employee is asked to do the work, they must be CORGI registered and the operative must have a valid certificate of competence that covers the particular type of gas work to be carried out.

SECURITY IN CATERING

Security in catering premises is a major concern, especially with the increasing rise in crime due to fraud. All establishments should endeavour to reduce the risk of temptation. Eliminating or reducing cash handling is one measure that should be encouraged. The use of credit and debit cards, while costing a small amount in charges, reduces cash handling, thus minimising risk.

Encouraging the payment of employees through cheque or bank transfer instead of by cash, means that payrolls do not have to be collected and distributed. Other such measures could include notices that no money is kept in the premises or that safes are protected by time-delay locks. Strict stock control can reduce stock levels, thereby reducing temptation and the problems of control.

A great deal of crime is of an opportunist nature. Large-scale crime is generally well planned. Reducing the amount of information available to the criminal reduces the ability for the thief to plan and thus commit the crime.

In order for a business to function it is often necessary to have cash. In order to deprive the potential criminal of knowledge make sure that only the staff that need to know actually have any information about this. For example, never have a regular routine for 'banking'. Regular and spot-check stock taking is another valuable system to identify crime.

However, in order to carry out your business efficiently it is impossible to remove all temptation. Therefore all equipment – for example, computers, fax machines, photocopiers – should be security marked.

It is important to prevent the thief entering the premises. Reception staff need to be trained to identify suspicious individuals. Everyone reporting to reception should be asked to sign in and, if they are a legitimate visitor, be given a security badge. All contract workers should be registered and given security badges; they may be restricted to working in certain areas.

A good security system should also be in force at the back door, with everyone delivering goods reporting to the security officer. Good lighting is also important for security reasons. Supervisors and managers should carry out regular checks of all areas.

Some companies write into employee contracts the 'right to search', so that searches can be carried out from time to time as a deterrent against theft. However, it is not legal to force a person to submit to a search even if they have signed a contract to that effect. However, by refusing to submit to a search they may be in breach of their employment contract.

Close-circuit television (CCTV) cameras are also used as a deterrent against crime.

Prevention of crime should be the main objective. With regard to staff the first step is to appoint honest staff by taking up references from previous employers.

The Health and Safety at Work Regulations now require employers to conduct a risk assessment with regard to the safety of staff in the catering business. Where staff constantly come into close contact with strangers, it is advisable to train them in anti-aggression techniques, which include the early recognition of volatile situations and how to defuse them. At the same time staff should be trained not to approach people who could pose a physical threat to them.

Staff who handle money should be trained in simple anti-fraud measures such as checking bank notes, checking signatures on plastic cards, and so on.

Security measures also include leaving lights on in some areas that can be seen by passers-by, as well as locking doors, windows and suchlike. Making sure that any suspicious person does not re-enter the building is also essential.

Each business will have its own type of risk. Over time, staff become familiar with the risks.

Security systems of all types should be carefully selected according to the needs of the business. Before buying into any security system agreements, seek advice from an independent security expert, who will assess the needs of the establishment. Insurance companies will have stipulated criteria to be fulfilled before they will insure the business.

Management of a security system

As with other operations a security system needs to be managed. This involves:

- developing a security policy for the establishment to cover security threats, bomb alerts, theft by customers or by employees, policy regarding prosecution
- establishing resources to cover the cost of security staff, whether in-house or contract
- developing procedures for security risk assessment, dealing with breaches of security
- understanding the legal implications of, for example, vicarious liability for false arrest or imprisonment
- seeking a proper balance between the often conflicting demands of security and safety.

The main security risks in the hotel and catering industry

- Theft: customers' property, employers' property (particularly food, drink, equipment), employees' property.
- Burglary: theft with trespass of customers' property, employers' property, employees' property.

- Robbery: theft with assault, e.g. banking cash, collecting cash.
- Fraud: false claims for damage; counterfeit currency; stolen credit cards.
- Assault: fights between customers, while staff banking/collecting cash.
- Vandalism: malicious damage to property by customers, by intruders, by employees.
- Arson: setting fire to property.
- Undesirables: drug traffickers, prostitutes.
- Terrorism: bombs, telephone bomb threats.

CATERING SAFETY MANAGEMENT: A SUMMARY

Managers must think positively about how they can sustain and improve safety if they are to comply with legislation and minimise the risk of incidents occurring. Accidents often happen because of acts or omissions by management rather than staff neglect.

The Management of Health and Safety at Work Regulations 1999 provide the basis for safety management requirements. This legislation requires:

- all involved in safety to think positively
- competence to be established
- risk assessment to be undertaken
- implementation of effective control.

Measures to reduce risk include:

- staff training on hazard awareness and control in the workplace.

Safety management involves identifying the hazards in a business and tailoring controls through physical measures, safe systems of work, the safety policy and staff training.

TOPICS FOR DISCUSSION

1 Discuss the causes of accidents and how they may be prevented. Are some people accident prone, others naturally clumsy and others lacking in common sense? If so, how can they be 'educated' to be safe workers?
2 Do notices regarding safety have any effect? How best may people employed in the kitchen be made aware of hazards, thus making a potentially dangerous environment much safer?
3 Attendance at a first-aid course could be made obligatory for every catering employee. Do you think this would be sensible? If you do, or do not, explain why?
4 Discuss what training and the procedures following training, should be provided for every person being employed in a catering establishment. Does training reduce accidents, fires, and so on?
5 What provision should be made for the welfare of catering staff? Discuss this, bearing in mind costs and the fact that in the industry many employees are casual or part-time.
6 Discuss the hazards that should be prevented in the kitchen.
7 Discuss the relationship between the caterer and the environmental health officer.
8 Discuss accident prevention and the responsibilities of the worker and the employer.
9 Is ample provision made for first aid?
10 What fire precautions and appropriate systems are in place for fire prevention?
11 Explain how fire extinguishers are recognised for their appropriate use.
12 How can premises be made secure and stealing be prevented?
13 If you find temperatures and food hygiene legislation complex, discuss how it could be simplified.
14 Discuss the relationship between knowing the law and implementing it.

Chapter 16 HYGIENE AND FOOD LEGISLATION

WHY IS HYGIENE IMPORTANT?

Hygiene is the science and practice of preserving health and is one of the most important subjects for all persons working in the hotel and catering industry to study, understand and practise in their everyday working lives. The subject is broken down into three areas – personal, kitchen and food hygiene – all of which are of equal importance.

PERSONAL HYGIENE

Personal cleanliness

Germs or bacteria are to be found in and on the body and can be transferred onto anything with which the body comes in contact. For this reason, personal cleanliness is essential to prevent germs getting onto food. Self-respect is necessary in every food-handler because a pride in one's appearance promotes a high standard of cleanliness and physical fitness. Persons suffering from ill-health or who are not clean about themselves should not handle food.

Bathing
It is essential to take a bath or a shower every day (or at least two or three times a week), otherwise germs can be transferred onto clothes and so onto food, particularly in warm weather.

Hands
Hands must be washed thoroughly and frequently, particularly after using the toilet, before commencing work and during the handling of food. They should be washed in hot water, with the aid of a nail brush and bactericidal soap. This can be dispensed from a fixed container, in liquid or gel form, and is preferable to bar soap, which can accumulate germs when passed from hand to hand. After washing, hands should be rinsed and dried on a clean towel, suitable paper towel or by hot-air drier. Hands and fingernails can be a great source of danger if not kept clean, as they can so easily transfer harmful bacteria to food.

Figure 16.1 Drying hands on a paper towel

Figure 16.2 Hygiene standards being observed in good production and service

Rings (except for a plain wedding band), watches and jewellery should not be worn where food is handled. Particles of food may be caught under the ring, and germs could multiply there until they are transferred onto food.

Watches should not be worn because some foodstuffs have to be plunged into plenty of water. In any case, the steam in a kitchen is likely to ruin watches that are not waterproofed.

Jewellery in general should not be worn since it may fall off into food, unbeknown to the wearer; small sleepers for pierced ears are, however, permissible.

Fingernails

These should always be kept clean and short as dirt can easily lodge under the nails and be dislodged when, for example, making pastry, so introducing bacteria into food. Nails should be cleaned with a nail brush; nail varnish should not be worn.

Hair

Hair should be washed regularly and kept covered where food is being handled. Hair that is not cared for is likely to come out or shed dandruff, which may fall into food. Men's hair should be kept short as it is easier to keep clean; it also looks neater. Women's hair should be covered as much as possible. Both men's and women's hair can be kept in place using a hair net. The hair should never be scratched, combed or touched in the kitchen, as germs could be transferred via the hands to the food.

Nose

The nose should not be touched when food is being handled. If a handkerchief is used, the hands should be washed afterwards. Ideally, paper handkerchiefs should be used and then destroyed, and the hands washed afterwards. The nose is an area where there are vast numbers of harmful bacteria; it is therefore very important that neither food, people nor working surfaces are sneezed over, so spreading germs.

Mouth

There are many germs in the area of the mouth, therefore the mouth or lips should not be touched by the hands or utensils that may come into contact with food. No cooking utensils should be used for tasting food, nor should fingers be used for this purpose as germs may be transferred to the food. A clean teaspoon should be used for tasting, and washed well afterwards.

Coughing over foods and working areas should be avoided as germs are spread long distances if not trapped in a handkerchief.

Ears
The ear cavities should not be touched while in the kitchen as, again, germs can be transferred.

Teeth
Sound teeth are essential to good health. They should be kept clean, and visits to the dentist should be regular so that teeth can be kept in good repair.

Feet
As food handlers are standing for many hours, care of the feet is important. They should be washed regularly, and the toenails kept short and clean. Tired feet can cause general fatigue, which leads to carelessness, and this results in a lowering of standards of hygiene.

Cuts, burns and sores
It is particularly important to keep all cuts, burns, scratches and similar openings of the skin covered with a waterproof dressing. Where the skin is septic (as with certain cuts, spots, sores and carbuncles) there are vast numbers of harmful bacteria that must not be permitted to get onto food; in most cases people suffering in this way should not handle food.

Personal habits checklist

- Avoid touching hair, ears, nose, mouth and spots when preparing food.
- Never use a handkerchief – use disposable tissues.
- Do not sneeze or cough over food.
- Do not bite your nails.
- Use utensils to handle food whenever possible, not your fingers.

Always wash hands after:

- visiting the toilet
- blowing your nose
- handling money
- disposing of rubbish
- cleaning.

Cosmetics

Cosmetics, if used by food handlers, should be used in moderation, but ideally their use should be discouraged. Cosmetics should not be put on in the kitchen and the hands should be washed well after applying them; they should be put on clean skin, not used to cover up dirt.

Figure 16.3 Sample newspaper reports of hygiene breaches

Smoking chef fined after health check

A chef carried on smoking as he cut up meat in front of a health investigator, a court heard this week.

The senior environmental officer said that a cat was allowed to walk around while food was being prepared and that staff were wearing dirty overalls.

On a later visit he found the chef smoking a cigarette as he chopped up chicken.

TV pub 'revolting'

A picturesque pub featured in a BBC programme was fined a total of £6,750 yesterday for food hygiene breaches. The magistrate hearing the case described the kitchen as 'absolutely revolting'.

Smoking

Smoking must never take place where there is food, because when a cigarette is taken from the mouth, germs from the mouth can be transferred to the fingers and so on to food. When the cigarette is put down, the end that has been in the mouth can transfer germs to work surfaces. Ash on food is most objectionable and it should be remembered that smoking where there is food is an offence against the law.

Spitting

Spitting should never occur, because germs can be spread by this objectionable habit.

Clothing and cloths

Clean whites (protective clothing) and clean underclothes should be worn at all times. Dirty clothes enable germs to multiply and if dirty clothing comes into contact with food the food may be contaminated. Cloths used for holding hot dishes should also be kept clean as cloths are used in many ways, such as wiping knives, and wiping dishes and pans. All such uses could convey germs onto food.

Outdoor clothing, and other clothing that has been taken off before wearing whites, should be kept in a locker, away from the kitchen.

General health and fitness

The maintenance of good health is essential to prevent the introduction of germs into the kitchen. To keep physically fit, adequate rest, exercise, fresh air and a wholesome diet are essential.

Figure 16.4 Poisoned any good customers lately?

Sleep and relaxation

Persons employed in the kitchen require adequate sleep and relaxation as they are on the move all the time, often in a hot atmosphere where the tempo of work may be very fast. Frequently, the hours are long or extended over a long period of time, as with split duty, or they may be extended into the night. In off-duty periods it may be wise to obtain some relaxation and rest rather than spend all the time energetically. The amount of sleep and rest required depends on each person's needs –the variation between one person and the next is considerable.

Exercise and fresh air

People working in conditions of nervous tension, rush, heat and odd hours need a change of environment and particularly fresh air. Swimming, or walking or cycling in the country may be suitable ways of obtaining both exercise and fresh air.

Wholesome food and pure water

A well-balanced diet, correctly cooked, and pure water will assist in keeping kitchen personnel fit. The habit of 'picking' (eating small pieces of food while working) is bad; it spoils the appetite and does not allow the stomach to rest.

Meals should be taken regularly; long periods without food are also bad for the stomach. Pure water is ideal for replacing liquid lost in perspiring in a hot kitchen, or soft drinks may be taken to replace some of the salt as well as the fluid lost in sweating.

Kitchen clothing

It is most important that people working in the kitchen should wear suitable clothing and footwear. Suitable clothing must be:

- protective
- washable
- light in weight and comfortable
- strong
- absorbent.

Protective
Clothes worn in the kitchen must protect the body from excessive heat. For this reason chef's jackets are double-breasted and have long sleeves; these protect the chest and arms from the heat of the stove and prevent hot foods or liquids burning or scalding the body.

Aprons
These are designed to protect the body from being scalded or burned and particularly to protect the legs from any liquids that may be spilled; for this reason the apron should be of sufficient length to protect the legs.

Chefs' hats
This is designed to enable air to circulate on top of the head and thus keep the head cooler. The main purpose of the hat is to prevent loose hairs from dropping into food and to absorb perspiration on the forehead. The use of lightweight disposable hats is both acceptable and suitable.

Washable
The clothing should be of an easily washable material as many changes of clothing are required. White clothing is readily seen to be soiled when it needs to be changed and there is a tendency to work more cleanly when wearing 'whites'. Chefs' trousers of blue and white check are a practical colour but also require frequent changing.

Light and comfortable
Clothing must be light in weight and comfortable, not tight. Heavy clothing would be uncomfortable and a heavy hat in the heat of the kitchen would cause headaches.

Strong
Clothes worn in the kitchen must be strong to withstand hard wear and frequent washing.

Absorbent
Working over a hot stove causes people to perspire; the perspiration will not evaporate in an inadequately ventilated atmosphere and so underclothes made from absorbent material, such as cotton, should be worn. The hat absorbs perspiration and the neckerchief is used to prevent perspiration from running down the body, for wiping the face and also to protect the neck, which is easily affected by draughts.

Footwear
This should be stout and kept in good repair so as to protect and support the feet. As the kitchen staff are on their feet for many hours, boots (for men) and clogs (for men and women) give added support and will be found most satisfactory.

Table 16.1 Hygienic
practice in the kitchen

ESSENTIALS	AWARENESS
Personal cleanliness and dress	The organisation's policy on food hygiene
Hand washing	
The need to report infections and cover cuts	Personal hygiene
	Cross-contamination and food storage
No smoking, eating or drinking in food rooms	Waste disposal, cleaning and disinfection
The need for temperature control (i.e. keeping food either hot or cold)	Awareness of pests
Keeping surfaces clean	

Modern industrial safety shoes with steel toecaps are to be encouraged. Sandals, training shoes and suchlike offer insufficient protection from the spillage of hot liquids.

Summary of personal hygiene

The practice of clean habits in the kitchen is the only way to achieve a satisfactory standard of hygiene. These habits are as follows:

- hands must be washed frequently and always after using the toilet; food should be handled as little as possible
- bathing must occur frequently
- hair must be kept clean and covered in the kitchen; it should not be combed or handled near food
- the nose and mouth should not be touched with the hands
- cough and sneeze into a handkerchief, not over food; people with colds should not be in contact with food
- jewellery, rings and watches should not be worn
- smoking and spitting must not occur where there is food
- cuts and burns should be covered with a waterproof dressing
- clean clothing should be worn at all times and only clean cloths used
- foods should be tasted with a clean spoon
- tables should not be sat on
- only healthy people should handle food.

KITCHEN HYGIENE

Hygiene scores

Local authority health departments will become empowered to issue a star rating based on standards in premises that enforcement officers inspect. In the USA, restaurants have to publish the results of their food hygiene and health and safety audits alongside their menus.

Cleaning and disinfection

Cleaning can be defined as the application of energy to remove dirt, grease and other soiling. Cleaning is essential to food safety as well as being a legal requirement for food businesses.

The need for cleaning

Figure 16.5 Making sure premises are clean (a)

- It reduces the risk of food spoilage and food poisoning.
- It removes materials and food that could provide harbour and nourishment for pests.
- It helps the prompt identification of pest infestation.
- It prevents the physical contamination of food.
- It assists in maintaining a comfortable working environment that is safe and attractive, assisting in promoting economical and effective working methods.
- It reduces the risk of accidents to customers and staff affected by the work.
- It promotes a quality image to customers.
- It assists in reducing maintenance costs and reduces damage to equipment.

If cleaning is not carried out or is ineffective, various problems can arise stemming from the loss of product quality, leading to:

Figure 16.6 Making sure premises are clean (b)

- customer complaints
- loss of reputation
- food poisoning and food-borne disease
- loss of sales
- legal action
- increase in food waste
- contaminated and tainted food
- corrosion and premature replacement of equipment
- incorrect use of chemicals, which could damage equipment, floors, walls and food-preparation surfaces.

Understanding cleaning

Cleaning requires energy. This consists of:

- physical energy – provided by manual labour (e.g. scrubbing)
- mechanical energy – provided by machines (e.g. floor scrubbers)
- turbulence – used with liquids; often used for cleaning certain types of equipment in place (e.g. beer lines in pubs)
- thermal energy – provided by hot water or steam

- chemical energy – provided by detergents.

Usually, a combination of two or more forms of energy is used.

Cleaning equipment and systems

These include:

- cleaning in place, which has to be done in the case of certain types of equipment, such as beer lines in a pub
- sinks and tanks
- cloths, brushes, mops and buckets
- mechanical aids such as vacuum cleaners, dishwashers and low-pressure jet washers, which may be used in combination with a foam for cleaning walls and other surfaces in high-risk areas.

Cleaning checklist

'Clean as you go': this protects food from contamination, bacteria ,and chemicals, and physically deters pests.

Use hot water with detergent or a sanitiser to break down grease and remove dirt.

Rubbish should be disposed of frequently.

Disinfectants

The process of disinfection reduces pathogenic bacteria, but not spores or toxins, to levels that are neither harmful to human health nor to the quality of food. Disinfection may be carried out using:

- heat, preferably moist heat at a temperature above 82°C (180°F)
- steam
- chemicals, either separately or in combination.

Figure 16.7 Vacuuming

Figure 16.8 Cleaning trolley

What to disinfect

Surfaces where the levels of bacteria present may have an adverse effect on the quality or safety of food should be disinfected regularly.

Examples of surfaces
- **Direct food contact surfaces:** such as chopping boards, knives, work surfaces, mixing bowls, serving dishes and slicing machines.
- **Hand contact surfaces:** such as taps, door handles, oven doors, refrigerator doors, light switches, telephones.
- **Hands:** disinfection achieved by bactericidal soap, alcohol-based disinfectant.
- **Cleaning materials and equipment:** mops, cleaning cloths, scrapers, brushes.

Disinfection needs to be carried out carefully to ensure that it is successful and safe.

All chemicals in kitchens and food premises must be food-safe. Manufacturers' instructions must always be followed. Careless use of chemicals can be dangerous. After use all detergent must be well rinsed from food surfaces before disinfecting them, otherwise the disinfectant will not be able to work properly. A number of cleaning substances are regarded as hazardous to health. Therefore, a number of precautions have to be taken to control their use.

- First, read the label and identify the substance and its potential hazards.
- Second, use only the right substance for the appropriate job.
- Third, check to see if any protective clothing is required.

It is good industrial hygiene practice:

- not to eat, drink or smoke when using chemicals
- to use protective clothing as appropriate
- to wash hands and exposed skin after using chemicals.

Always use a fresh solution of disinfectant every time a new cleaning task is carried out. Do not top up existing solutions. Mops and cloths should not be soaked in disinfectant solutions for long periods, as the solution will weaken and may allow bacteria to grow. The disinfectant must be allowed to remain on the surface for the contact time recommended by the manufacturer. Always cleanse thoroughly, unless the manufacturer's instructions state that rinsing is unnecessary.

Six basic steps for cleaning and disinfection

1 **Pre-clean:** removal of loose soil by wiping, scraping, rinsing or soaking.
2 **Main clean:** loosening the remaining soil by use of detergents.
3 **Intermediate rinse:** removal of soil and chemicals.

4 **Disinfection:** reduction of the remaining bacteria to a safe level.
5 **Final rinse:** removal of the disinfectant.
6 **Drying:** natural (e.g. air drying); physical (e.g. using disposable paper towels or a clean dry cloth).

If soiling is light, the pre-clean may be combined with the main clean. Disinfection may not be necessary on all surfaces; when disinfectants are used, disinfection may be incorporated in the main clean using a chemical sanitiser. This creates a four-stage process: pre-clean; main clean; disinfection; rinse and dry.

Some types of equipment need to be completely or partly dismantled to allow satisfactory cleaning. Electrical safety must be checked before machines are cleaned.

Cleaning schedules

It is important for every kitchen and food premises to have a cleaning schedule. Cleaning schedules communicate standards and ensure that cleaning is carried out and managed effectively. A cleaning schedule should include:

- all items and surfaces to be cleaned
- the persons responsible for carrying out the tasks
- when the cleaning must be done
- the methods of cleaning and standards required
- the time required for each cleaning process
- the chemicals, materials and equipment needed
- the safety precautions to be taken, and the protective clothing and equipment to be worn, such as goggles and gloves
- the signature of the person who carries out the task
- the signature confirming that the work has been checked.

The cleaning process must be monitored regularly and inspected to ensure that the schedule is being followed, in order to maintain standards. Checking should include the use of rapid bacterial tests or swabbing.

Figure 16.9 Spot-testing for bacteria

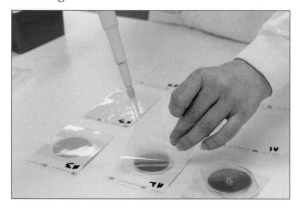

Technical terms

- **Bactericide:** a substance that destroys bacteria.
- **Cleaning:** the removal of soil, food residue, dirt, grease and other foreign matter.
- **Detergent:** a chemical or mix of chemicals that help(s) to remove grease and food particles so that surfaces are prepared for the action of disinfectants.
- **Disinfectant:** a chemical, or heat in the form of water or steam, used for disinfection.
- **Disinfection:** the reduction of micro-organisms to a level that will not lead to harmful contamination or the rapid spoilage of food. The term usually refers to the treatment of surfaces or premises, but may also be applied to aspects of personal hygiene, such as disinfecting the skin.
- **Sanitiser:** a chemical used for cleaning and disinfecting surfaces and equipment.
- **Sterilisation:** a process that kills all micro-organisms.

Neglect in the care and cleaning of any part of the premises and equipment could lead to a risk of food infection. Kitchen hygiene is of very great importance to:

- those who work in the kitchen, because clean working conditions are more agreeable to work in than dirty conditions
- the owners, because custom should increase when the public know the kitchen is clean
- the customer – no one should want to eat food prepared in a dirty kitchen.

Cleaning materials and equipment

To maintain a hygienic working environment a wide range of materials and equipment is needed. These are some of the items that need to budgeted for, ordered, stored and issued:

- brooms
- buckets
- brushes
- cloths
- dusters
- dustbin powder
- dustbins
- floor cleaner
- mops
- fly spray
- sponges
- oven cleaner
- squeegee
- plastic sacks
- scrubbing machine
- scouring powder
- wet suction cleaner
- soap
- dry suction cleaner
- steel wool
- ammonia
- washing powder
- disinfectant.

Further information
To find out more, see
HCIMA Technical Brief:
Kitchen Ventilation.

Kitchen premises

Ventilation

Adequate ventilation must be provided so that fumes from stoves are taken out of the kitchen, and stale air in the stores, larder and still-room is extracted. This is usually effected by erecting hoods over stoves and using extractor fans.

Hoods and fans must be kept clean; grease and dirt are drawn up by the fan and, if they accumulate, can drop onto food. Windows used for ventilation should be screened to prevent the entry of dust, insects and birds. Good ventilation facilitates the evaporation of sweat from the body, which keeps one cool.

Lighting

Good lighting is necessary so that people working in the kitchen do not strain their eyes. Natural lighting is preferable to artificial lighting. Good lighting is also necessary to enable staff to see into corners so that the kitchen can be cleaned properly.

Plumbing

Adequate supplies of hot and cold water must be available for keeping the kitchen clean, for cleaning food and equipment, and for staff use. For certain cleaning hot water is essential, and the means of heating water must be capable of meeting the requirements of the establishment.

There must be hand-washing and drying facilities, and suitable provision of toilets, which must not be in direct contact with any rooms in which food is prepared or stored.

Hand-washing facilities (separate from food-preparation sinks) must also be available in the kitchen, with a suitable means of drying the hands (hot-air drier or paper towels).

Further information
To find out more, see
HCIMA Technical Brief
No. 3/96.

Cleaning of toilets and sinks

Toilets must never be cleaned by food handlers. Sinks and hand basins should be cleaned and thoroughly rinsed.

Floors

Kitchen floors have to withstand a considerable amount of wear and tear, therefore they must be:

- capable of being cleaned easily
- even
- smooth, but not slippery
- without cracks or open joints
- impervious (non-absorbent).

Quarry tile, vinyl sheet or epoxy resin floors, properly laid, are suitable for kitchens since they fulfil the above requirements.

Thorough cleaning is essential: floors are swept, washed with hot detergent water and then dried. This can be done by machine or by hand,

and should be carried out at least once a day. As a safety precaution, suitable warning signs should be used to alert staff if the floor is wet.

Walls

Walls should be strong, smooth, impervious, washable and light in colour. The join between the wall and floor should be rounded for ease of cleaning. Suitable wall surfaces include ceramic tiles, heat-resistant plastic sheeting, stainless-steel sheeting, and resin-bonded fibreglass.

Clean with hot detergent water and dry. This will probably be done monthly, but the frequency will depend on circumstances.

Ceilings

Ceilings must be free from cracks and flaking. They should not be able to harbour dirt.

Doors and windows

Doors and windows should fit correctly and be clean. The glass should be clean inside and out so as to admit maximum light.

Food lifts

Lifts should be kept very clean and no particles of food should be allowed to accumulate as lift shafts are ideal places for rats, mice and insects to gain access to kitchens.

Hygiene of kitchen equipment

Kitchen equipment should be so designed that it can be:

- cleaned easily
- readily inspected to see that it is clean.

Failure to maintain equipment and utensils hygienically and in good repair may cause food poisoning. Manufacturers' instructions must always be followed. Material used in the construction of equipment must be:

- hard, so that it does not absorb food particles
- smooth, so as to be cleaned easily
- resistant to rust
- resistant to chipping.

Containers, pipes and equipment made from toxic materials, such as lead and zinc, should not be in direct contact with food or drink, or be allowed to wear excessively; copper pans that need retinning on the inside will expose harmful copper to food. Food must be protected from lubricants.

Easily cleaned equipment is free from unnecessary ridges, screws, ornamentation, dents, crevices or inside square corners, and has large smooth areas. Articles of equipment that are difficult to clean (e.g. mincers, sieves and strainers) are items where particles of food can lodge so allowing germs to multiply and contaminate food when the utensil is next used.

Routine cleaning of materials

- **Metals:** as a rule all metal equipment should be cleaned immediately after use.
- **Portable items:** remove food particles and grease. Wash by immersion in hot detergent water. Thoroughly clean with a hard bristle brush or soak until this is possible. Rinse in water at 77°C (171°F), by immersing in the water in wire racks.
- **Fixed items:** remove all food and grease with a stiff brush or soak with a wet cloth, using hot detergent water. Thoroughly clean with hot detergent water. Rinse with clean water, disinfect and dry with a clean cloth.
- **Abrasives:** should be used only in moderation as their constant scratching of the surface makes it more difficult to clean the article next time.
- **Marble:** scrub with a bristle brush and hot water and detergent, then sanitise and leave to dry.
- **Wood:** scrub with a bristle brush and hot detergent water, rinse and dry.
- **Plastic:** wash in reasonably hot water.
- **China/earthenware:** avoid extremes of heat and do not clean with an abrasive. Wash in hot water, disinfect or sanitise, and leave to dry.
- **Stainless steel:** stainless steel is easy to clean. Soak in hot detergent water. Clean with a brush, sanitise, rinse and leave to dry.
- **Tin:** tin that is used to line pots and pans should be soaked, washed in detergent water then immersed in very hot water (82°C) and dried. Tinned utensils, where thin sheet steel has a thin coating of tin, must be thoroughly dried, otherwise they are likely to rust.
- **Zinc:** This is used to coat storage bins of galvanised iron and should not be cleaned with a hard abrasive.
- **Vitreous enamel:** clean with a damp cloth and dry. Avoid using abrasives.
- **Equipment requiring particular care in cleaning** (e.g. sieves, conical strainers, mincers and graters): extra attention must be paid to these items, because food particles clog the holes. The holes can be cleaned by using the force of the water from the tap, by using a bristle brush and by moving the article, particularly a sieve, up and down in the sink, so causing water to pass through the mesh. Whisks must be thoroughly cleaned where the wires cross at the end opposite the handle as food can lodge between the wires. The handle of the whisk must also be kept clean. The use of detergents/sanitisers is recommended.
- **Saws and choppers/mandolins:** these items should be cleaned in hot detergent water, dried and greased slightly.

- **Tammy cloths, muslins and piping bags:** after use they should be emptied and food particles scraped out, scrubbed carefully and boiled. They should then be rinsed and allowed to dry. Certain piping bags made of plastic should be washed in very hot water and dried. Nylon piping bags should not be boiled.

Cleaning of large electrical equipment (ovens, mincers, mixers, choppers, slicers)

1 Switch off the machine and remove the electric plug.
2 Remove particles of food with a cloth, palette knife, needle or brush as appropriate.
3 Thoroughly clean with hand-hot detergent water all removable and fixed parts. Pay particular attention to threads and plates with holes in mincers. Disinfect using a sanitiser or equivalent.
4 Rinse thoroughly.
5 Dry and reassemble.
6 While cleaning, see that exposed blades are not left uncovered or unguarded, and that the guards are replaced when cleaning is complete.
7 Any specific maker's instructions should be observed.
8 Test that the machine is properly assembled by plugging in and switching on.

All equipment, once cleaned, should be stored properly.

Washing up

The correct cleaning of all equipment used for the serving and cooking of food is of vital importance to prevent the multiplication of bacteria. This cleaning may be divided into the pan wash (plonge) or scullery, and the china wash-up.

Scullery

Figure 16.10 Cleaning the kitchen equipment

For the effective washing up of pots and pans and other kitchen equipment the following method of work should be observed:

- pans should be scraped and all food particles placed in a bin
- hot pans should be allowed to cool before being plunged into water
- pans that have food stuck to them should be allowed to soak (pans used for starchy foods, such as porridge and potatoes, are best soaked in cold water)
- frying pans should be thoroughly wiped with a clean cloth; they should not be washed unless absolutely necessary
- trays and tins used for pastry work should be thoroughly cleaned with a clean dry cloth, while warm
- pots, pans and other equipment should be washed and cleaned with a stiff brush, steel wool or similar article, in hot detergent water

Further information can be obtained from:
- www.business.com/ directory/food-and- beverages/restaurants -and-foodservice/ equipment-and- supplies/dishwashers
- www.powersourcing. com/se/dishwashingeq uipment.htm
- British Cleaning Council, PO Box 1328, Kidderminster DY11 5ZJ Tel: 01562 851129 (website: www.britishcleaningco uncil.org).

- pan scrubbers are electrically driven with a hydraulic or flexible drive transmission; brush-type heads can be varied to suit differing surfaces or types of soiling; pan scrubbers can either be wall mounted near the pot wash or free standing mounted on mobile dollies to assist with equipment cleaning
- the washing-up water must be changed frequently; it must be kept both clean and hot
- the cleaned items should be rinsed in very hot clean water to sterilise
- pans that have been sterilised (minimum temperature 82°C (180°F)) dry quickly; if it has not been possible to rinse in very hot water they should be dried with a clean cloth
- equipment should be stored on clean racks; pans should be stacked upside down.

China wash-up

The washing up of crockery and cutlery may be done by hand or machine.

Hand washing
- Remove scraps from plates with a scraper or by hand.
- Wash in water containing a detergent as hot as the hands can bear (whether gloves are worn or not).
- Place utensils in wire baskets and immerse them into water thermostatically controlled at 82°C (180°F) for at least two minutes.
- The hot utensils will air-dry without the use of a drying cloth.
- Both the washing and sterilising water must be kept clean and at the correct temperature.

Machine washing up

There are several types of machine that wash and sterilise crockery. In the more modern versions, the detergent is automatically fed in as the machine operates continuously.

To be effective the temperature of the water must be high enough to kill any harmful bacteria and the articles passing through the machine must be subjected to the water for sufficient time to enable the detergent water to cleanse all the items thoroughly. The detergent used must be of the correct amount and strength to be effective. Alternatively, low-temperature equipment is available that sterilises by means of a chemical: sodium hypochlorite (bleach).

Where brushes are used they must be kept free from food particles.

Kitchen energy distribution systems

A system of this type operates from stainless-steel housings (known as 'raceways'), which are fastened to walls, floors or ceilings, or may be island mounted. Inside the raceways are runs of electrical bus-bars or bus-wires and plumbing pipes. At intervals appropriate for the kitchen

Further information can be obtained from the Building Design and Construction Services Directory at www.buildingdesign.co.uk.

equipment served are switch or valve sockets, electrical, gas, water, steam, and so on. Connecting flexible cords and pipes from the kitchen equipment plug into the sockets and are designed to hang clear of the floor; they are smooth-plastic coated for easy cleaning. To gain maximum advantage from this idea – in terms of hygiene, safety, flexibility, and ease of cleaning and maintenance – most of the kitchen equipment is mounted on castors.

Periodic cleaning is carried out by pulling the equipment out from the wall or island, unplugging all the services then moving the equipment away on its castors to give free access to all wall and floor surfaces as well as the backs and sides of equipment.

FOOD HYGIENE

The Food Safety Act 1990 includes:

- increased powers for environmental health officers
- provision of training for food operatives
- registration of food premises with the local authority
- the defence of 'due diligence' (if the person in charge of a catering operation can show that he or she took all reasonable precautions to avoid committing an offence then this can be used in defending any presentation under the Food Safety Act 1990/95). (See the accompanying box on this.)

Provision of safe food

This is a management responsibility. In order to provide safe food a safety control system should be implemented. The HACCP approach provides a means of ensuring the provision of safe food for customers. (HACCP stands for Hazard Analysis Critical Control Point and is the cornerstone of maintaining hygiene standards.) From January 2006, a documented HACCP system is a legal requirement for every size of food business.

Hazard analysis identifies all the factors that could lead to hazards for the consumer: all ingredients, stages in the processing of foods, environmental features and human factors that could lead to unsafe food being served.

Critical control points (CCPs) are the points at which control is essential to reduce the risk of potential hazards actually *becoming* hazardous, as demonstrated in the following examples.

- Is the food delivered at the correct temperature?
- Is the food stored and displayed at the correct temperature?
- Is cross-contamination prevented as far as possible?
- Are cleaning schedules in place for equipment?

Due diligence defence

Every food handler, whether they prepare, manufacture, serve or transport the food, has a responsibility to make sure that it is safe to eat. If the food is found to be unfit to eat, the person responsible can be prosecuted unless he or she can prove they took all responsible precautions – that he or she exercised all due diligence to avoid causing the offence. This defence can be established if a food handler can prove that it was the fault of another person, or someone that they trusted carried out all the necessary checks, that he or she had no reason to believe that their omission or action that they had taken would result in an offence.

Due diligence can be claimed if a caterer was supplied with ready-prepared meals that, after consumption, caused food poisoning. The caterer would have to prove that he or she had taken all reasonable precautions to avoid the situation occurring by carrying out all the necessary checks on the method of production and by obtaining details of storage and transportation temperatures of the food before delivery.

Written records that show dates and the types of checks made are very important and would form a crucial part of the evidence.

Food safety is achieved provided you:

* keep yourself clean
* keep the workplace clean
* wear suitable clean clothing
* protect food from contamination
* store, prepare, serve and display food at the correct temperature
* inform your manager if you have an illness
* do not work with food if you have food-poisoning symptoms.

You will then have complied with the Food Safety Act 1990.

* Are personnel correctly trained and hygienic in their working practices?

Once the hazard and the CCPs have been identified, then methods of monitoring and controlling them must be implemented. Every person must be trained in the awareness of food hygiene and the control of the identified control points.

The most succulent, mouth-watering dish into which has gone all the skill and art of the world's best chefs, using the finest possible ingredients, may look, taste and smell superb, yet be unsafe – even dangerous – to eat because of harmful bacteria and other micro-organisms. It is of the utmost importance that everyone who handles food, or who works in a place where food is handled, should know that food must be both clean and safe. Hygiene is the study of health and the prevention of disease, and because of the dangers of food poisoning, hygiene requires particular attention from everyone in the catering industry.

There are germs everywhere, particularly in and on our bodies; some of these germs, if transferred to food, can cause illness and in some cases death. These germs are so small that they cannot be seen by the naked eye, so food that looks clean and does not smell or taste bad may be dangerous to eat if harmful germs have contaminated it and multiplied.

It is the duty of every person concerned with food to prevent contamination of food by germs, and to prevent these germs or bacteria from multiplying.

Food handlers must be familiar with the Food Hygiene Regulations (see below), but no matter how much is written or read about food hygiene the practice of hygienic habits by people who handle food is the only route to safe food.

Further information
For further information, refer to the Food Standards Agency's website at www.food.gov.uk.

The Food Labelling Regulations 1996 and the Food Labelling (Amendments) Regulations 2005

There were two major changes when the amendment was issued. First, compound ingredients that make up more than 2 per cent of a product need to be broken down and labelled. (Previously, if the compound ingredient was less than 25 per cent of the finished product, it did not need to be broken down.) Second, the law places more emphasis on the labelling of allergens; it also enforces new laws in the risk assessment of allergens and on the labelling of them on-pack. For example, defensive labelling such as 'may contain peanuts' is no longer allowed – the supplier must have sufficient controls in place to prevent contamination.

Food safety (general food hygiene)

Butchers' Shops Amendment Regulations 2000
Following the Pennington Group Report proposals (after the outbreak of E. coli food poisoning in Lanarkshire in 1996) a licensing scheme for butchers was introduced. Although the scheme applies only to butchers, it is likely that a similar requirement will be placed on caterers in the future. The regulations came into force on 1 May 2000. Supermarket meat departments and butchers now have to obtain a licence to trade issued by the local environmental health department.

The Food Labelling Regulations 1984 and the Food Labelling (Amendment) Regulations 1999
These regulations mainly affect manufacturers of food but caterers and retailers are required to comply with the requirements, most notably those relating to the labelling of genetically modified (GM) soya or maize ingredients.

There are a number of basic elements to food labelling.

- The name of the food and the list of ingredients.
- An indication of shelf life (minimum durability) or, in the case of food that, in terms of microbiology, may have a short shelf life and therefore may become an immediate danger to human health, a 'use by' date.
- Special storage conditions.
- Conditions of use.
- Name and address of the manufacturer, packer or seller.

The main shelf life indicators are 'use by', or 'best before' or 'best before end' followed by the date to which the food might be considered to remain safe with good quality and fitness. Any required storage conditions would have been properly observed. Expected shelf lives and indicators to be used are as follows.

- Highly perishable, which may become a danger to health – 'use by' plus day, month and year.
- Three months or less – 'best before' day and month only.
- Three to 18 months – 'best before' plus day, month and year, or 'best before end' plus month and year.
- More than 18 months – 'best before' plus month and year, or 'best before end' and year only.

There are a number of exempt foods, including uncut fresh vegetables or high-alcohol drinks.

It is an offence to sell foods whose 'use by' dates have expired or to alter such dates once applied.

The Bread and Flour Regulations 1998
The principal effect of these regulations is to:

- continue to require the fortification of most flour with certain minerals and vitamins
- prohibit the use of flour improvers in wholemeal bread, with the exception of vitamin C (ascorbic acid)
- require that flour improvers are indicated in the list of ingredients of all pre-packed bread and on a label ticket or notice displayed with non-pre-packed bread
- prohibit use of the name 'wheatmeal' in the labelling or advertising of all sales of bread and flour
- prescribe names by which flour may be sold, including 'wholemeal', 'self-raising'
- require the name of any bread made from flour derived from wheat to include the words 'wholemeal', 'brown', 'wheatgerm', 'white', 'soda' or 'aerated' as appropriate
- list the additives permitted to be used in bread and flour.

Catering establishments making their own bread are not exempt from these regulations.

FOOD POISONING

Cases of food poisoning are on the increase and highly under-reported at up to 3 million a year. A large number of these cases could be prevented very easily.

Figure 16.11 Extract from a newspaper report on food poisoning

E. coli puts ten in hospital

TEN people were in hospital last night after an E. coli outbreak.

Two cases have been confirmed and up to 16 are suspected. One of these involves a boy of ten.

Health authorities are investigating a link with a supermarket. Yesterday the store closed its delicatessen counter and fresh fruit and vegetable stand. Customers have been asked to return all meat, dairy and fresh produce bought there since 1 November.

E. coli is a potentially fatal gastro-intestinal infection passed on from contaminated food.

Last night an NHS spokesman said none of those in hospital was dangerously ill.

Food poisoning can result from:

- ignorance of the rules of hygiene
- carelessness, thoughtlessness or neglect
- poor standards of equipment or facilities to maintain hygienic standards
- accident.

Figure 16.12 Testing for food poisoning

Figure 16.13 plated by handler wearing plastic gloves

Food poisoning can be prevented by:

- high standards of personal hygiene
- attention to physical fitness
- maintaining good working conditions
- maintaining equipment in good repair and in clean condition
- adequate provision of cleaning facilities and cleaning equipment
- correct storage of foodstuffs at the right temperature
- correct reheating of food
- quick cooling of foods prior to storage
- protection of food from vermin and insects
- hygienic washing-up procedure
- food handlers knowing how food poisoning is caused
- food handlers carrying out correct procedures to prevent food poisoning.

What is food poisoning?

Food poisoning is an illness acquired from eating contaminated food. This usually means contaminated with bacteria, viruses or a chemical, e.g. from a poisonous plant or an actual physical item that carries infection. It can be characterised by stomach pains and diarrhoea, and sometimes vomiting, generally developing within 1–36 hours after eating affected foods.

Causes of food poisoning

Food poisoning results when harmful foods are eaten, contaminated by:

- chemicals that entered foods accidentally during the growth, preparation or cooking of the food (e.g. from pesticides and cleaning fluids)
- germs (harmful bacteria) that have entered the food from humans, animals or other sources and the bacteria themselves, or the toxins (poisons) produced in the food by certain bacteria have caused the foods to be harmful; by far the greatest number of cases of food poisoning are caused by harmful bacteria
- bacteria and viruses that have come from people, animal, insects, raw food, rubbish, dust, water and the air; the bacteria or toxins (poisons) produced in the food by certain bacteria have caused the food to become harmful.

Contamination can also come from physical items (e.g. dirty clothing or touching the food).

Bacterial food poisoning

Food contaminated by bacteria (germs) is by far the most common cause of food poisoning. Cross-contamination is when bacteria are transferred from contaminated to uncontaminated foods via hands, boards, knives, surfaces, and so on.

To prevent the transfer of bacteria by cross-contamination, the following points should be observed:

- ensure food is obtained from reliable sources
- handle foods as little as possible; when practicable use tongs, palette knives, disposable plastic gloves, and so on
- ensure utensils and work surfaces are clean and sanitised
- use cloths impregnated with a bactericide that fades in colour when no longer effective
- pay particular attention when handling raw poultry, meat and fish
- wash raw fruits and vegetables
- clean methodically and as frequently as necessary; clean as you go
- keep foods covered as much as possible
- have boards and knives coloured for particular foods – for example, red for raw meat, blue for raw fish, yellow for cooked meat (see below and Figure 16.19)
- take particular care in the thorough reheating of made-up dishes.

Cross-contamination

To avoid cross-contamination it is important that the same equipment is not used for handling raw meat and milk products without being disinfected. To prevent the inadvertent use of equipment for raw and high-risk foods it is recommended that, where possible, different colours and shapes are used to identify products:

- yellow – food preparation areas
- green – food and beverage service
- blue – general purpose
- red – toilet areas.

For cutting boards and knives, the following colour coding is used:

- white – dairy products
- grey – bread
- green – fruit
- brown – vegetables

- red – raw meat
- yellow – cooked meat
- blue – raw fish.

Bacteria are minute, single-celled organisms that can be seen only under a microscope. They are everywhere in our surroundings and, as most bacteria cannot move by themselves, are transferred to something by coming into direct contact with it.

Some bacteria form spores that can withstand high temperatures for long periods of time and on return to favourable conditions germinate into normal bacteria again, which then multiply. Some bacteria produce toxins outside their cells so that they mix with the food; the food itself is then poisonous and symptoms of food poisoning follow within a few hours.

Figure 16.14 Germometer

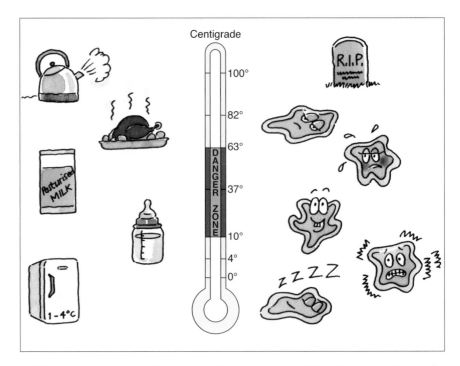

Other bacteria cause food poisoning by virtue of the large numbers of bacteria in food entering the digestive system, multiplying further and setting up an infection.

Certain bacteria produce toxins that are resistant to heat; foods in which such toxins have been produced may still cause illness, even if the food is heated to boiling point and boiled for half an hour. Some bacteria will grow in the absence of air (anaerobes), others need it (aerobes).

Bacteria multiply by dividing in two, under suitable conditions, once every 10–20 minutes. Therefore one bacterium could multiply in 10 to 12 hours to between 500 million and 1000 million bacteria.

Not all bacteria are harmful. Some are useful, such as those used in cheese production. Some cause food spoilage, such as the souring of milk.

Some bacteria that are conveyed by food cause food-borne diseases. With bacterial food poisoning the bacteria multiply *in* the food, but bacteria that cause food-borne disease use food as a means of transmission, with little or no growth in the food.

Typhoid and paratyphoid are diseases caused by harmful bacteria carried in food or water. Scarlet fever, tuberculosis and dysentery may be caused by drinking milk that has not been pasteurised.

The time between eating the contaminated food (ingestion) to the beginning of the symptoms of the illness (onset) depends on the type of bacteria that has caused the illness.

For the multiplication of bacteria certain conditions are necessary:

- food must be of the right kind

- moisture must be adequate
- temperature must be suitable
- time must pass.

Food

Most foods are easily contaminated; those less likely to cause food poisoning have a high concentration of vinegar, sugar or salt, or are preserved in some special way (see page 220).

The following foods are particularly susceptible to the growth of bacteria because of their composition:

- stock, sauces, gravies, soups
- eggs and egg products
- meat and meat products (sausages, pies, cold meats)
- all foods that are handled
- all foods that are reheated (e.g. cooked rice)
- milk and milk products.

Foods high in protein are very susceptible. Extra care must be taken to prevent them from being contaminated. The bacterium *Campylobacter* causes symptoms similar to salmonella food poisoning and can be present in unpasteurised milk and undercooked chicken.

To prevent diseases being spread by food and water the following measures should be taken:

- water supplies must be purified
- milk and meat products should be pasteurised or otherwise heat treated
- carriers should be excluded from food preparation rooms.

Temperature

Food poisoning bacteria multiply rapidly at body temperature, 37°C (98.6°F). They grow between temperatures of 5°C and 63°C. This is a similar heat to a badly ventilated kitchen and for this reason foods should not be kept in the kitchen – they should be kept in the larder or refrigerator. Lukewarm water offers an ideal heat for bacteria to grow in. Washing up must not take place in warm water as bacteria are not killed and the conditions are ideal for their growth, therefore pots and pans, crockery and cutlery may become contaminated. Hot water must be used for washing up.

Boiling water will kill bacteria in a few seconds, but to destroy toxins it is necessary to boil for half an hour. To kill the most heat-resistant spores, four to five hours' boiling is required. It is important to remember that it is necessary not only to heat foods to a sufficiently high temperature but also for a sufficient length of time to be sure of safe food. Extra care should be taken in warm weather to store foods at low temperatures and to reheat thoroughly foods that cannot be boiled.

Bacteria are not killed by cold although they multiply very slowly at very low temperatures; in a deep freeze they lie dormant for long periods.

If foods have been contaminated before being made cold, on raising the temperature the bacteria will multiply. Foods that have been taken out of the refrigerator, kept in a warm kitchen and returned to the refrigerator for use later on may well be contaminated with a higher level of infection.

Moisture

Bacteria require moisture for growth – they cannot multiply on dry food. Ideal foods for their growth are jellies with meats, custards, creams, sauces, and so on.

Time

As already noted, under ideal conditions one bacterium divides into two every 10–20 minutes; in six to seven hours millions of bacteria will have been produced. Small numbers of bacteria may have little effect, but in a comparatively short time sufficient numbers can be produced to cause food poisoning. Particular care therefore is required with foods stored overnight, especially if adequate refrigerated space is not available.

Types of food-poisoning bacteria

The commonest food-poisoning bacteria are:

- the salmonella group (causing food poisoning because of large numbers of bacteria in the food)
- *Staphylococcus aureus* (causing food poisoning due to poison (toxin) production in the food)
- *Clostridium perfringens* (causing food poisoning due to large numbers of bacteria-producing toxins in the intestines).

Figure 16.15 Germs multiplying on moist foods in a warm temperature over time

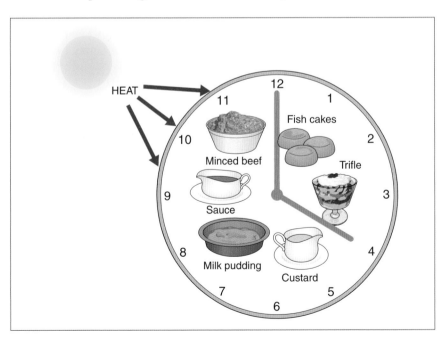

We will now take a closer look at each of these, and at some other food-poisoning bacteria.

Salmonella group
- **Incubation period:** 12–36 hours
- **Symptoms:** fever, headache, diarrhoea, vomiting
- **Prevention:** thorough cooking, correct storage

These bacteria can be present in the intestines of animals or human beings; they are excreted and anything coming into contact directly or indirectly with the excreta may be contaminated (raw meat at the slaughterhouse or the unwashed hands of an infected person). Infected excreta from human beings or animals may contaminate rivers and water to be used for drinking purposes, although chlorination of water is very effective in killing harmful bacteria.

Salmonella infection is the result of human beings or animals eating food contaminated by salmonella-infected excreta originating from human beings or animals, so completing a chain of infection. For example, when flies land on the excreta of a dog that has eaten infected dog meat and the flies then go on to food, if that food is then left out in warm conditions for a time, the people who eat the contaminated food could well suffer from food poisoning.

Figure 16.16 Foods contaminated by salmonella organisms if uncooked or lightly cooked may result in food poisoning

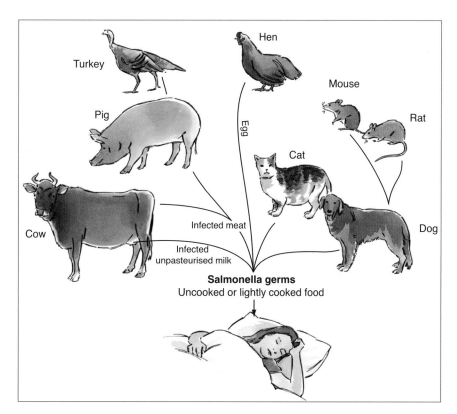

The foods most commonly affected by the salmonella group are poultry, meat and eggs (rarely processed egg products or duck eggs, although some hens' eggs have been found to be infected with salmonella). Contamination can be caused by:

Figure 16.17 Danger temperature at which germs can multiply

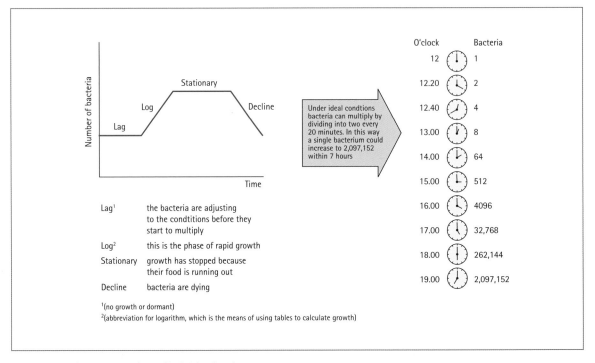

Figure 16.18 Reports on salmonella food poisoning

Food poisoning hits conference

Doctors attending a conference on diabetes at the weekend were struck down with food poisoning, believed to be salmonella.

Four hundred clinicians, nurses and health specialists had eaten cold meats, meat pies, seafood and salad at Friday lunchtime.

That evening two of the delegates were admitted to the casualty department with severe vomiting and diarrhoea. The next day a further 23 people with suspected salmonella poisoning were admitted to the hospital.

By Saturday evening 35 people had been seen, some at neighbouring hospitals and 80 people had reported symptoms of food poisoning.

VIPs food poison alert

More than 150 VIPs at two banquets in the city of London are suspected victims of food poisoning.

Salmonella is believed to be the cause and suspicion has centred on a cheese and egg savoury – Canape Roquefort – which was on both menus.

Figure 16.19 Using separate chopping boards for different foods will help to prevent cross-contamination

- insects and vermin, because salmonella is spread by droppings, feet, hairs, and so on
- the food itself (as, very occasionally, with duck eggs)
- cross-contamination (if a chicken is eviscerated on a board and the board is not properly cleaned before another food (such as cold meat) is cut on the board
- the food being infected by a human being who has the disease or who is a carrier (a person who does not suffer from food poisoning but who carries higher than normal infections and passes on the germs to others).

Preparation of mayonnaise using raw eggs is a common practice but one that is fraught with danger. The problem is that raw eggs can contain salmonella bacteria. To avoid the consequent high risk of food poisoning, the Department of Health (DoH) issued guidelines stating that unpasteurised eggs should not be used for preparing mayonnaise. Using raw egg products can be both unwise and costly. It is not illegal to use raw eggs to prepare mayonnaise, but the chances of food poisoning are high. In view of the DoH guidelines, a commercial kitchen using unpasteurised raw eggs would need to be able to show a sophisticated checking system to avoid the use of contaminated eggs and/or the use of some other factor (such as acidity) to control any food-poisoning bacteria. Without being able to demonstrate this, it is difficult, if not impossible, to rely upon a defence of due diligence. The usual catering kitchen is very unlikely to have the equipment, skills and controls available to make these checks in order to satisfy the defence. The message for caterers is either to use bought-in commercially prepared mayonnaise, or to use pasteurised eggs. The alternatives are probably too expensive to contemplate.

Staphylococcus aureus
- **Incubation period:** 2–6 hours
- **Symptoms:** severe vomiting
- **Prevention:** personal hygiene, exclusion of carriers

These germs are present on human hands and other parts of the skin, or sores, spots, and so on, and in the nose and throat.

Foods affected by *Staphylococcus aureus* include those that have been handled, where the hands have been infected from the nose or throat, cuts, etc. Brawn, pressed beef, pies and custards are foods frequently contaminated in this way (either by food handlers or airborne infection) because they are ideal foods for the multiplication of the bacterium.

Clostridium perfringens

- **Incubation period:** 8–22 hours
- **Symptoms:** diarrhoea, severe stomach cramp, little if any vomiting
- **Prevention:** thorough cooking and rapid cooling, prevention of cross-contamination

These bacteria are distributed from the intestines of humans and animals, and are found in the soil. Foods affected by *Clostridium perfringens* include raw meat, which is the main source of these bacteria, the spores of which survive light cooking.

Bacillus cereus

- **Incubation period:** 1–5 hours (common type)
- **Symptoms:** vomiting, diarrhoea
- **Prevention:** thorough cooking of rice; avoid cooking and storing rice in bulk, especially at ambient temperatures

Bacillus cereus is found in soil where vegetables and cereals, like rice, may grow. Long, moist storage of warm cooked food, especially rice, allows the spores to germinate into bacteria, which multiply and produce toxins.

Escherichia coli (E. coli)

- **Incubation period:** 10–72 hours
- **Symptoms:** vomiting, diarrhoea (kidney failure and death with certain strains)
- **Prevention:** good personal hygiene, thorough cooking, avoiding cross-contamination from raw to cooked food, proper temperature control

Found in the intestinal flora of man and animals, E. coli is usually an indicator of faecal contamination of food or water. However, certain strains are known to be pathogenic and produce an enterotoxin in the

Figure 16.20 Temperature control (a): checking chilled temperature

Figure 16.21 Temperature control (b): checking temperature after heating

Figure 16.22 News reports on E. coli and salmonella poisoning

US DELI BEHIND BIGGEST E COLI OUTBREAK

A DELICATESSEN'S potato salad is the suspected cause of one of the biggest-ever outbreaks of E. coli poisoning.

The salad was sold over the counter and also served at more than 300 parties cat...

£½m food victim

A RETIRED Army captain left brain damaged after contracting salmonella at a regimental Christmas dinner in 1990 was awarded £571,695 in damages and costs yesterday.

Thomas Maguire fo...

Food bug hits holiday Britons

MORE than 90 British holidaymakers have been struck down with salmonella poisoning at a resort on Majorca.

Tour operator Sunworld...

Salmonella is suspected as guests fall ill

Boy, 12, poisoned by cheese

A SCHOOLBOY was seriously ill in hospital last night suffering from the deadly E.coli infection.

The 12-year-old fell ill after eating an English-made gourmet cheese.

He was rushed to hospital in Bristol from his Somerset home after his family doctor was called. It

BY ANTHONY MITCHELL

was then discovered that he had eaten a Caerphilly cheese containing chives made near his home.

Last night, environmental health inspectors were set to tour specialist cheese shops and wholesalers ordering them to remove from their

shelves all cheeses made by Duckett and Co, of Walnut Tree Farm, Wedmore, Somerset.

The small cheese producer was being searched by health inspectors to trace the origins of the bacteria.

Duckett's cheeses are also used by maturers and other cheesemakers, so the

whole English cheese industry could come to a near halt during the investigation.

The Health Department said: "Among the cheeses we are appealing for retailers to stop selling is one known as Tornegus. We are also asking inspectors to sample Caerphilly and Wedmore cheeses "

intestine that results in symptoms of abdominal pain and diarrhoea. One group of pathogenic E. coli is responsible for severe infantile diarrhoea and another group causes travellers' diarrhoea. E. coli has been recorded at temperatures as low as 4°C.

Found in human sewage water and raw meat, the onset period can be between 10 and 72 hours, but usually occurs within 12 to 24 hours. Symptoms are abdominal pain, fever, diarrhoea and vomiting for one to three days.

Outbreaks of E. coli occurred in Scotland in 1997, originating from a butcher selling raw and cooked meat. They resulted in 20 deaths.

Others

Clostridium botulinum is another type of bacterium that causes food poisoning, but it is rare in the UK.

Campylobacter bacteria are a common cause of diarrhoea in the UK. Large numbers are not required to cause illness; poultry and meats are the main foods infected but adequate cooking will kill the bacteria.

Listeria bacteria are aerobic, non-sporing organisms that can cause serious food-borne disease, particularly in the elderly, the chronically sick or babies. These bacteria are found in soil, vegetables and animal feed. They are killed by correct cooking but grow at refrigeration temperatures and in mildly acidic conditions such as that found in soft cheeses where lactic acid is present.

Figure 16.23 How food poisoning may be caused

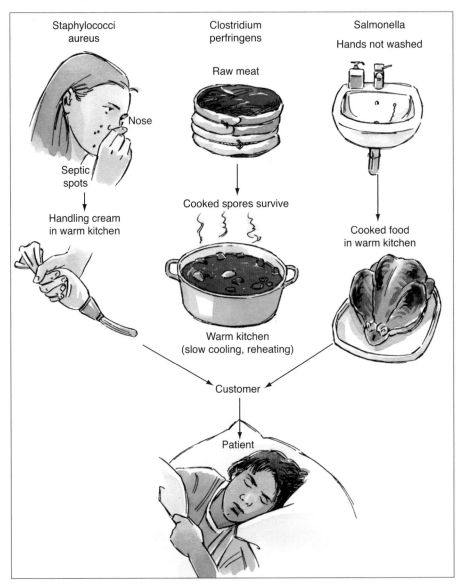

Further information
To find out more, refer
to HCIMA Technical Brief
No. 23/96, The Thawing
of Raw Poultry and
Game.

There is particular concern over contamination of pre-packed salads and chilled raw chicken. Although it is unlikely that a small number of organisms would cause any harm to healthy people, the bacteria can cause illness in vulnerable groups, infecting babies in the womb, elderly people and the sick.

Sources of infection

Food-poisoning bacteria live in:

- the soil (bacillus cereus, clostridium perfringens, listeria)
- humans – intestines, nose, throat, skin, cuts, sores, spots, and so on (staphylococcus)
- animals, insects and birds – intestines, skin, and so on (salmonella, campylobacter, E. coli)

Bovine spongiform encephalopathy (BSE) and Variant Creutzfeldt-Jakob disease (vCJD)

In 1985 the first incident of a new disease of the brain was identified in a cow, although it was not until 1986 that this was formally recognised by the authorities. In 1990 and again in 1993, when the BSE outbreak had reached its peak, the Chief Medical Officer assured the British public that beef was safe to eat. But in 1995 the first case of vCJD was diagnosed, and the British Government and the EU took a series of actions which meant that as from 1996 no cattle over the age of 30 months were allowed to enter the food chain. Exports of British beef were banned.

From November 2000 butchers' shops selling cooked and raw products are breaking the law if they do not have a licence from the local authority. Butchers are charged an annual inspection fee, which provides an authorised officer from the local council to make a full compliance audit of the business. The officer will examine compliance with the Food Safety (General Food Hygiene) Regulations 1995.

Prevention of food poisoning from bacteria

To prevent food poisoning everyone concerned with food must:

- prevent bacteria from multiplying
- prevent bacteria from spreading from place to place
- destroy harmful bacteria.

This means that harmful bacteria must be isolated, the chain of infection broken and conditions favourable to their growth eliminated. (The conditions favourable to their growth – heat, time, moisture and a suitable food on which to grow – are explained on pages 636–641). It is also necessary to prevent harmful bacteria being brought into premises or getting on to food. This is achieved by a high standard of hygiene of personnel, premises, equipment and food handling.

Foods requiring special attention to avoid food poisoning

Meat
- All made-up dishes, such as cottage pie, need extra care. They must be very thoroughly cooked.
- Reheated meat dishes must be thoroughly reheated.
- Poultry that is drawn in the kitchen should be cleaned carefully; boards, tables and knives must be thoroughly cleaned and sanitised afterwards, otherwise there is a danger of contamination from excreta.
- Meat should be handled as little as possible. Minced and cut-up meats are more likely to become contaminated because of infection from the food handler. Boned and rolled joints require extra care in cooking as inside surfaces may have been contaminated.
- Sausages should be cooked right through.
- Tinned hams are lightly cooked, therefore they must be stored in a refrigerator.

Fish
Fish is usually washed, cooked and eaten fresh, and is not often a cause of food poisoning except in reheated fish dishes. Care must be taken to reheat thoroughly such dishes as fish cakes, fish pie and coquilles de poisson.

Some shellfish, such as oysters and mussels, have caused food poisoning because they have been bred in water that has been polluted by sewage. They are now purified before being sold. All shellfish should be used fresh. If you buy them alive, there is no doubt as to their freshness.

Eggs
Both hens' and ducks' eggs have been implicated in causing food poisoning, and DoH guidelines now suggest that it would be prudent to avoid eating raw eggs or uncooked foods made from them, such as home-made mayonnaise, home-made mousses and suchlike. If dried eggs are used they should be reconstituted and used right away, not left in this condition in a warm kitchen as they may have been contaminated during or after processing. Bulk liquid egg undergoes pasteurisation but may be contaminated after the container is opened. Hollandaise sauce, which is made with eggs, is an example of a food that should not be kept in a warm kitchen for long.

Milk dishes
When used in custards, trifles and puddings, unless eaten soon after preparation, milk should be treated with care. Two hours is the maximum for keeping, then it should be discarded.

Watercress and other green salad

Watercress must be thoroughly washed as it grows in water that could be contaminated by animals. All green salads and other foods eaten raw should be washed well.

Synthetic cream

Synthetic cream can be a cause of food poisoning if allowed to remain in warm conditions for long periods. It is easily contaminated by handling and from the air. Particular care is required in the handling and holding at the correct temperature of soups, sauces and gravies because bacteria multiply rapidly in these foods.

Reheated foods

In the interests of economy a sound knowledge of handling left-over food is necessary. Many tasty dishes can be prepared, but care must always be taken to see that the food is thoroughly and carefully reheated. If care is not taken then food poisoning can result. Only sound food should be used: 'if in doubt, throw it out'.

Surplus prepared food

Some caterers, as a matter of policy and in the interests of safety, dispose of all unused prepared foods after set times, and always at the end of service. While this may be an ideal solution for some, for many it is not an option. In practical terms all reasonable steps must be taken to avoid overproduction. Caterers and consumers are most vulnerable when surplus prepared food is offered for consumption again. The best way of reducing the problem of what to do with surplus prepared food is to tighten the production planning process, and so reduce the amount of surplus prepared food.

Surplus prepared foods include:

- items displayed but not sold during a meal service
- overproduction.

Surplus food should be considered fit for consumption only if, after normal preparation and display, it has not suffered excessive handling or prolonged exposure at serving temperatures above 8°C (46°F) and has been returned to and kept in chilled storage at or below 5°C (41°F).

Surplus hot food to be served again hot must be cooled as rapidly as possible and kept at or below 5°C (41°F) until it is to be reheated for service. It must then be reheated thoroughly to temperatures in excess of 75°C (167°F) and subsequently kept above 63°C (145°F) until served. *Food should only be re-heated once.*

Surplus hot food cooled rapidly and kept at or below 5°C (41°F) can be served as cold food over the following 48 hours. Roast joints to be used for sandwiches and salads should be sliced, cooled and kept at or below 5°C (41°F) until required for service.

Care must be taken at all stages to avoid introducing contamination.

Examples of how this can occur are by slicing joints of meat on unsanitised chopping boards or using dirty knives or utensils.

Partially used products on display, such as coleslaw, should not be 'topped up' with fresh. A replacement container should be used.

The assessment of safety should consider whether the surplus food was likely to have been subject to poor temperature control or contamination during handling or display. These issues should be critical to any decision on reuse.

Procedures
- Surplus food should be sorted into its various categories and placed under refrigeration as quickly as possible.
- It is desirable to use a blast chiller to cool hot food rapidly.
- Examine items in each category for damage and possible signs of contamination. Special attention should be given to short-life products particularly those that support bacterial growth – particularly meat, fish, poultry and egg dishes, rice, pasta, mousses and fresh-cream products.
- Examine perishable items such as bread rolls, biscuits and fresh fruit for obvious signs of damage or contamination, and dispose of any suspect foods.
- Items returned to cold storage must be carefully covered and stored separately from fresh and raw foods to avoid possible risks of cross-contamination.
- Comply with any relevant 'use by' or date codes.

Responsibilities
It is the responsibility of management to develop and implement:

- a firm policy detailing procedures for dealing with surplus prepared products – this must be available for inspection and reviewed regularly
- relevant staff must be fully trained in these procedures and made aware of the potential hazards involved; the necessary controls must be in place at critical points
- all surplus prepared food must be clearly labelled showing the date of production and the 'use by' date before it is returned to cold storage.

Safety first
When deciding whether or not to use 'left-overs', again: 'if in doubt, throw it out'.

Further reading
- Food Hygiene (England) Regulations 2006
- *Industry Guide to Good Hygiene Practice: Catering Guide*, Chadwick House Group Ltd, Chadwick Court, 15 Hatfields, London SE1 8DJ Tel: 020 7827 5882
- *Managing Hygiene* (1999) HCIMA

- Hazard Analysis and Critical Control Points (HACCP), HCIMA Technical Brief No. 5
- Preventing Food Poisoning, HCIMA Technical Brief No. 12
- Cooling Cooked Joints of Meat, HCIMA Technical Brief No. 14
- Food Safety (General Food Hygiene) Regulations 1995, HCIMA Technical Brief No. 21
- HCMP Technical Brief No. 9/2000

Chemical and metallic food poisoning

Residues of drugs, pesticides and fertilisers may be present in raw materials. Pesticides sprayed onto fruit and vegetables just prior to harvesting may result in cumulative toxic effects. Two outbreaks of chemical food poisoning in 1991 resulted from the contamination of watermelons and cucumbers with the pesticide Aldicarb. In 1995 warnings were issued regarding the need to peel carrots.

Chemicals can enter foodstuffs by leakage, spillage or other accidents during processing or preparation. Chemical food additives have to undergo rigorous tests before they are allowed to be used and are usually harmless.

Certain plants themselves are poisonous, such as some fungi, rhubarb leaves and the parts of potatoes that are exposed to the sun above the surface of the soil.

Chemical poisoning may also occur because of the waste, such as mercury compounds, polluting river water used for drinking or food production. Several metals are toxic and if ingested in sufficient quantities can give rise to food poisoning. The symptoms, mainly vomiting and abdominal pain, usually develop within an hour. Diarrhoea may also occur. Metals may be absorbed by growing crops or contaminate food during processing.

Acid foods should not be cooked or stored in equipment containing any of the following metals.

- **Antimony:** used in the enamel coating of equipment. Under certain conditions antimony poisoning can occur.
- **Cadmium:** used extensively for plating utensils and fittings for electric cookers and refrigeration apparatus. It is attacked by some acids, including fruit and wines. Foods, such as meat, placed directly on refrigerator shelves containing cadmium may become poisonous.
- **Lead:** a very poisonous metal if ingested. Fruit and leafy vegetables can become contaminated by lead through airborne lead from petrol and incinerators.
- **Tin and iron:** most cans used for the storage of food are constructed of tin-plated iron sheet. Occasionally, due to prolonged storage, certain acid foods, such as pineapples, rhubarb, strawberries, citrus fruits and tomatoes, react with the tin plate and hydrogen gas is produced. Iron

and tin are absorbed by the food, which may become unfit for human consumption.

- **Zinc:** used in the galvanising of metals. Galvanised equipment should not be used in direct contact with food, particularly acid foods.
- **Aluminium:** there has been for some time some concern over the use of aluminium in kitchens. Some evidence exists that there is a link between pre-senile dementia and aluminium.
- **Copper:** copper pans should be correctly tinned and never used for storing foods, particularly acid foods, as the food could dissolve harmful amounts of copper.

Prevention of chemical food poisoning
Chemical food poisoning can be prevented by:

- using correctly maintained and suitable kitchen utensils
- obtaining food from reliable sources (i.e. sources that employ good farming practices)
- care in the use of substance hazardous to health (e.g. rat poison).

As regards the latter, a number of precautions have to be taken to control their use:

- read the label and identify the substance and its potential hazards
- use only the right substance for the appropriate job
- check to see if any protective clothing is required
- label containers correctly.

Kitchen hygiene and food poisoning

Infection can be spread by:

- humans – coughing, sneezing, by the hands, etc.
- animals, insects, birds – droppings, hair, etc.
- inanimate objects – towels, dishcloths, knives, boards, etc.

Humans
People who are feeling ill, suffering from vomiting, diarrhoea, sore throat or head cold must not handle food.

As soon as a person becomes aware that he or she is suffering from, or is a carrier of, typhoid or paratyphoid fever, or salmonella or staphylococcal infection likely to cause food poisoning or dysentery, the person responsible for the premises must be informed. He or she must then inform the Medical Officer for Health. Standards of personal hygiene should be high at all times (see the section on personal cleanliness on page 614.

Animals
When pests have access to food, warmth and shelter they thrive. Kitchen and food stores provide all these conditions and, therefore, are very

Figure 16.24 Pests

appealing environments to pests. Pests including vermin, insects, domestic animals and birds can cause damage, disease and distress, ruin reputations and lead to prosecution.

Rats and mice
Rats and mice are a dangerous source of food infection because they carry harmful bacteria on themselves and in their droppings. Rats infest sewers and drains and, since excreta is a main source of food-poisoning bacteria, it is therefore possible for any surface touched by rats to be contaminated.

Rats and mice frequent warm, dark corners and are found in lift shafts, meter cupboards, lofts, openings in walls where pipes enter, under low shelves and on high shelves. They enter premises through any holes, defective drains, open doorways and in sacks of foodstuffs.

Signs to look for are droppings, smears, holes, runways, gnawing marks, grease marks on skirting boards and above pipes, claw marks, damage to stock and also rat odour.

Rats spoil ten times as much food as they eat, and there are at least as many rats as human beings. They are very prolific, averaging ten babies per litter and six litters per year, so that under ideal conditions it is theoretically possible for one pair of rats to increase to 350 million in three years.

If premises become infested with rats or mice the environmental health inspector or a pest control contractor should be contacted.

Further information
To find out more, refer
to HCIMA Technical Brief
No. 35, Pest Control.

Insect infestation

House flies are the foremost of the insects that spread infection. Flies alight on filth and contaminate their legs, wings and bodies with harmful bacteria, and deposit these on the next object on which they settle; this may well be food. They also contaminate food with their excreta and saliva.

Cockroaches like warm, moist, dark places. They leave their droppings and a liquid that gives off a nauseating odour. They can carry harmful bacteria on their bodies and deposit them on anything with which they come into contact.

Silverfish are small silver-coloured insects that feed on starchy foods (among other things); they are found on moist surfaces. They thrive in badly ventilated areas, so improving ventilation will help to control them.

Beetles are found in warm places and can also carry harmful germs from place to place.

Insects are destroyed using an insecticide, and it is usual to employ people familiar with this work. The British Pest Control Association (website: www.bpca.org.uk) has a list of member companies.

Cats and dogs

Domestic pets should not be permitted in kitchens or on food premises as they carry harmful bacteria on their coats and are not always clean in their habits. They may also introduce fleas and should not be allowed to enter places where food is prepared.

Birds

Entry of birds through windows should be prevented as food and surfaces on which food is prepared may be contaminated by droppings and food-poisoning bacteria.

Dust

Dust contains bacteria, therefore it should not be allowed to settle on food or surfaces used for food. Kitchen premises should be kept clean so that no dust can accumulate. Hands should be cleaned after handling dirty vegetables.

Pest control

The best methods of controlling pests are through maintaining high hygiene standards including:

- the food premises to be kept clean and in good repair
- food stocks to be inspected and rotated regularly
- windows and other openings to the outside environment to be fitted with insect-proof screens in food rooms
- no food scraps to be left lying around
- dustbins and swill bins to be covered with tight-fitting lids and emptied regularly, especially in summer

- it is also good practice to employ a pest control contractor to regularly inspect the site and give advice.

To control flies, the best method is to eliminate their breeding place, As they breed in rubbish and in warm, moist places, dustbins in summer are ideal breeding grounds; correct control and disposal of waste is paramount. Other ways to control flies are to:

- screen windows to keep flies out of kitchens
- install ultra-violet electrical fly-killers (see Figure 16.25)
- use sprays to kill them (only where there is no food present)
- employ a pest control contractor.

Figure 16.25 Fly catcher: electrical equipment to attract, kill and collect winged insects

This is what happens when a fly lands on your food

- Flies can't eat solid food, so to soften it up they vomit on it.
- Then they stamp the vomit in until it's a liquid, usually stamping in a few germs for good measure.
- Then when it's good and runny they suck it all back again, probably dropping some excrement at the same time.
- And then, when they've finished eating, it's your turn.

Control and disposal of waste

Waste material is a potential threat to food safety because it is a source of contamination that can provide food for a variety of pests. There is a 'duty of care' under the Environmental Protection Act 1990 that makes the catering organisation responsible for its waste. It is a legal requirement to use licensed waste contractors, who must issue the caterer with a 'waste transfer notice'. Any special waste might need dealing with separately (e.g. chemicals, flammable substances, potentially infectious material).

There is also a legal requirement that attempts to deal with the reduction of packaging. Large businesses must register with the Environmental Protection Agency and make efforts to reduce the amount of packaging they generate as waste.

Figure 16.26 Recycling

Most establishments will have an area for 'pure' or unusable waste in dustbins. Provisions in such an area can be provided for accumulating recyclables, bearing in mind the need for safety and hygiene.

Recycling

Separation of green, brown and clear glass and paper from cardboard and plastic is necessary. Regular collections by reliable collectors are essential, and a member of staff needs to be responsible for storage, tidiness and correct usage by staff members, as well as the disposal of all materials salvaged.

The object is to reduce the unusable waste to a minimum, to utilise all that can be recycled or used. Management need to:

- provide facilities for storage
- organise collections on the premises
- educate and encourage staff to use the facilities correctly
- control the situation
- have the salvaged materials collected regularly (this entails the regular inspection of the 'waste' area and, if necessary, the remedying of any misuse)
- control the financial aspect and keep staff informed of the success of recycling, especially if any charities benefit from it.

Staff should be made aware that recycling:

- is economically necessary
- is environmentally sensible
- creates a good image of the establishment in the community.

The Environment Protection (Duty of Care) Regulations 1991

These regulations create four main responsibilities for the producers of waste.

1 To prevent any other person committing the offences of disposing of 'controlled waste' or treating or storing it: without a waste management licence; or breaking the conditions of a licence; or in a manner likely to cause pollution or harm to health.
2 To prevent the escape of waste – that is, to contain it.
3 To ensure that, if the waste is transferred, it goes only to an 'authorised person' or to a person for 'authorised transport purposes'.
4 When waste is transferred, to make sure that there is also transferred a written description of the waste that is good enough to enable the person receiving it: to avoid committing an offence; to comply with the law to prevent the escape of waste.

Waste can be divided into the following groups.

- **Dry non-food waste:** this comes mainly from packaging wood, cardboard and plastic, some of which can be sorted for resale. Cardboard and paper can be compacted by a waste compactor machine.
- **Dry food waste:** this can either be (a) disposed of at source in a waste disposal unit, which grinds the waste into small particles, mixed with water and flushed into the drainage system, or (b) stored in galvanised-steel bins with close-fitting lids for disposal to swill collectors. The Disease of Animals (Waste Food) Order 1973 requires all swill collectors to be licensed by the local authority. The operator will arrange for cleaned and sterile bins to be delivered and collected on a regular basis.
- **Unsavoury or offensive food waste:** this should be disposed of immediately, where possible using a waste disposal unit.
- **Waste cooking oils and fats:** large quantities have a resale value, small quantities can be absorbed into dry food waste.
- **Bulky waste:** this can be disposed of by either (a) incineration (only by using specific equipment or in isolated areas) or (b) by compaction. The advantages of compaction are: small, compact bulks easier to handle; less accessibility to pests; saving in refuse-collection charges, which are often calculated by volume.

The refuse site should be a clean and easy-to-clean area with a water supply for washing down, and adequate drainage. The site should be well lit and well ventilated.

For general internal rubbish, plastic- or paper-lined bins that can be destroyed with the rubbish are preferable to other types of bin. As noted above, the Environmental Protection Act 1990 imposes a 'duty of care' on anyone who produces, imports, carries, keeps, treats or disposes of 'controlled' waste (see below). As far as the catering industry is concerned the effect of the Act is to ensure that all waste is stored correctly by the producers and disposed of correctly by registered carriers and that transfer notes accompany the waste. In most cases, waste is removed by local authorities, who are registered carriers. The local authorities arrange for annual 'transfer notes' but it is the responsibility of the 'producer' to ensure that transfer notes are produced and kept.

Where private contractors are used to remove any waste the producer, (e.g. restaurant) must check that the carrier is authorised and that proper transfer notes accompany the waste. Transfer notes have to be kept for two years and may be inspected by the waste inspection authority (usually the local authority).

Controlled waste

Controlled waste includes items such as:

- left-over, unwanted foodstuffs, beverages
- kitchen waste

- used oils and fats
- unwanted containers, such as bottles, cans, boxes, wrapping materials
- used paper, such as napkins and tablecloths
- broken items, such as crockery, utensils, furniture
- anything else that is disposed of as waste.

Keeping waste safe
All waste holders (e.g. restaurants, hotels) must act to keep waste safe against:

- corrosion or wear of the waste containers
- accidental spilling or leaking, whether caused by accident, the weather, scavenging by animals, or by people.

Waste disposal
In considering proper disposal of waste the producer should ask questions such as:

- Does the waste need special containers, made of special materials, to prevent escape or exposure to air?
- Can it be mixed safely with other waste?
- Can it be safely crushed and transferred from one vehicle to another?
- Can it be safely incinerated?
- Can it be buried safely in a landfill site?

FOOD HYGIENE REGULATIONS

These regulations should be known and complied with by all people involved in the handling of food. A copy of the full regulations can be obtained from HMSO and an abstract can be obtained that gives the main points of the full regulations.

The main addition to the Food Hygiene Regulations 1995 are as follows.

- All food premises need to be registered and, where meat, eggs, dairy and fish products are involved, the premises need to be approved by the local authority rather than just registered. Any changes to the premises need to be documented and fed into the local authority.
- All food businesses need to have a documented version of HACCP (covered on page 310).

These points are reproduced in the accompanying box.

The Food Hygiene (England) Regulations 2006

Proprietors of food premises are required ...

1 To operate hygienically:
   (a) analyse food hazards
   (b) identify where hazards may occur
   (c) decide which points are critical to food safety
   (d) implement control and monitoring procedures, review periodically and change when necessary.
2 Premises must be kept clean and in good repair:
   (a) designed to permit good hygiene practices
   (b) adequate washbasins, toilets and cleaning disinfecting facilities
   (c) satisfactory standards of lighting and ventilation.
3 Walls, floors and food-contact surfaces must be easy to clean and, where necessary, to disinfect.
4 Conveyance and containers used for transporting food must be kept clean and in good repair.
5 Food equipment must be kept clean and in good repair.
6 Food waste and refuse must not be accumulated in food rooms. Adequate provision must be made for its storage and removal.
7 An adequate supply of drinking water must be provided
8 Food handlers must:
   (a) keep themselves clean
   (b) wear suitable clean and, where appropriate, protective clothing
   (c) if they know or suspect they are carrying a food-borne disease, or have an infected cut or skin condition, advise their manager
   (d) not be allowed to work if they are likely to contaminate food.
9 Food, including raw materials, must be fit for human consumption, and stored and protected to minimise risk of contamination.
10 Food handlers must be trained and supervised in food hygiene matters.
11 Offences are punishable on conviction:
   (a) fines of up to £5000 for each offence
   (b) in serious cases, up to two years in prison;
   (c) unlimited fines.

Equipment

This must be kept clean and in good condition.

Personal requirements

- All parts of the person liable to come into contact with food must be kept as clean as possible.
- All clothing must be kept as clean as possible.
- All cuts and abrasions must be covered with a waterproof dressing.

- Spitting is forbidden.
- Smoking is forbidden in a food room or where there is food.
- As soon as a person is aware that s/he is suffering from or is a carrier of such infections as typhoid, paratyphoid, dysentery, salmonella or staphylococcal infection s/he must notify her/his employer, who must notify the Medical Officer for Health.

Requirements for food premises

Toilets

- These must be clean, well lit and well ventilated.
- No food room shall contain or directly communicate with a toilet.
- A notice requesting people to wash their hands after using the toilet must be displayed in a prominent place.
- The ventilation of the soil drainage must not be in a food room.
- The water supply to a food room and toilet is permitted only through an efficient flushing cistern.

Washing facilities

- Hand basins and an adequate supply of hot water must be provided.
- Supplies of soap and hand-drying facilities must be available by the hand basins.

Other facilities

- First aid: bandages and waterproof dressings must be provided in a readily accessible position.
- Lockers: enough storage space must be available for outdoor clothes.
- Lighting and ventilation: food rooms must be suitably lit and ventilated.
- Sleeping rooms: rooms in which food is prepared must not be slept in. Sleeping rooms must not be adjacent to a food room.
- Refuse: refuse must not be allowed to accumulate in a food room. Waste bins must be lidded.
- Buildings: the structure of food rooms must be kept in good repair to enable them to be cleaned and to prevent entry of rats, mice, etc.

Food storage temperatures

- Storage: foods should not be placed in a yard lower than 0.5 m (18 inches) unless properly protected.

Penalties

Any person guilty of an offence shall be liable to a heavy fine and/or a term of imprisonment. Under the latest Food Safety Act, unhygienic premises can be closed down by a local authority immediately, on the advice of the environmental health officer.

The environmental health officer, when visiting premises, will probably check for:

- grease in ventilation ducts and on canopies
- long-standing dirt in less accessible areas
- cracked or chipped equipment
- provision for staff toilets and clothing
- 'now wash your hands' notice
- adequate and correct storage of food (cooked food stored above raw food if there is not separate refrigerated provision)
- correct storage temperature of foodstuffs
- signs of pests and how they are prevented
- any hazards
- cleaning, training records and proper supervision.

Checklist for catering establishments

- Entrances and exits unobstructed.
- Fire doors undamaged and in operating position.
- Escape routes clearly indicated.
- Fire-fighting equipment visible and accessible.
- Lighting good.
- Suitable supply of hot and cold water.
- Good ventilation.
- Separate hand-washing basin.
- Soap, nail-brush (if provided) and towels by basin.
- Floors in good repair, clean and dry.
- Equipment operating correctly.
- Guards on machines.
- All surfaces undamaged and clean.
- Staff trained to use machines.
- Notice concerning use of machine close to it.
- Suitable protective clothing worn.
- Food, equipment and cleaning materials stored properly.
- Rubbish bins covered and emptied regularly.
- Staff work in accordance with safety guidelines.
- Documented HACCP system.
- Premises are registered.

Source: based on Food Safety Act 1990; Food Safety (General Food Hygiene) Regulations 1995; Food Safety (Temperature Control) Regulations 1995; Food Premises (Registration) Regulations 1997; Food Hygiene (England) Regulations 2006

The Food Hygiene (England) Regulations 2006

These regulations came into force on 1 January 2006 and replace the Food Safety (Temperature Control) Regulations 2005.

Foods that may be subject to microbiological multiplication must be held at no more than 8°C (46°F) or above 63°C (145°C). (However, it is good practice to store such food at 5°C or less.) There are a few exceptions, which include food on display (this can be displayed for up to four hours) and low-risk and preserved foods, which can be stored at ambient temperatures. Manufacturers can vary upward the 8°C (46°F) ceiling if there is a scientific basis to do so.

Food that is to be served hot should be held at over 63°C (145°C).

Food reheated in Scotland must retain a temperature of 82°C (180°F) unless this will adversely affect the food.

This requires that any food that is likely to support the growth of pathogens, micro-organisms or the formation of toxins must be kept at or below 8°C (46°F). In other words, high-risk foods – those that are ready for consumption without further heat treatment – must be stored under temperature control. The exceptions include food that has been cooked or reheated or is for service on display for sale and needs to be kept hot. It also applies to food where there is no health risk if it is kept at ambient temperature. Any preserved foods, including dehydrated, canned foods or perhaps where sugar or vinegar is added, fall into this category, provided that the containers have not been opened. If the containers of such foods are open it may be necessary to store the food using temperature control.

Foods that require ripening or maturing, such as cheese, may be kept outside temperature control – however, once the process has been completed they should then be refrigerated.

Care should be taken with ambient ingredients that may need to be refrigerated once opened.

Delivery vehicles must be refrigerated during transportation of chilled goods.

The regulations do not cover cooking times and temperatures, however the Food Standards Agency (FSA) gives parameters for core temperatures for food to control food safety:

- 60°C for 45 minutes
- 65°C for 10 minutes
- 70°C for 30 seconds
- 80°C for 6 seconds.

As noted above, once food has been cooked or reheated, the core temperature must be kept at 63°C or above. Such situations apply to food that is:

- waiting service or despatch
- in transit to serving point
- on display on a servery, buffet, carvery or counter.

For hot food, a single period outside temperature control is allowed as long as it is no longer than two hours. Exception is made for foods served warm (e.g. hollandaise sauce). This may be kept for no more than two hours and any remaining must be discarded. For cold food (that stored at less than 8°C) a single period of four hours outside the temperature control is permitted.

After cooking, food should be reduced to 8°C or less as quickly as possible to avoid illness. It is good practice to reheat food to a core temperature of 70°C for two minutes.

Practical implications of the Temperature Control Regulations

- On receipt of deliveries goods should be cooled to the proper temperature as soon as possible.
- To account for defrost cycle or breakdown of refrigeration an allowance of 2°C (3°F) is permitted.
- A maximum time of two hours for cold food preparation in the kitchen is tolerated provided there is no more than 2°C (3°F) rise above the 5°C (41°F) or 8°C (46°F) specified temperature.
- Food intended to be served hot at 63°C (115°F) or above can be held at a temperature below 63°C (115°F) but for no more than two hours.
- Exception is made for foods served warm (e.g. hollandaise sauce). They may be kept for no more than two hours and any remaining must be discarded.
- Food intended to be served cold 5°C (41°F) or 8°C (46°F) may be held at a higher temperature but for no longer than four hours; it must then be brought back to 5°C (41°F) or 8°C (46°F).
- Displayed foods (sweet trolley, cheese board, self-service display, 'counter display with assisted service') need not be maintained at the required temperature provided display time is kept to a minimum and does not exceed four hours.

Recommended reading
To find out more see HCIMA Technical Brief No. 21/95, Food Safety, and HCIMA Technical Brief No. 33, Food Safety, Temperature Control.

Registration of premises
Under the Food Premises (Registration) Regulations 1991, as amended by the Food Premises (Registration) Amendment Regulations 1993, all existing food premises in England, Wales and Scotland, have to register with their local authority. Anyone starting a new food business must register 28 days before doing so. It is an offence not to be registered.

TAKING SERVICES FORWARD

Training

Catering establishments have a general obligation to supervise, instruct and provide training in food hygiene commensurate with their

Table 16.2 A guide to the training of individuals in food handling

CATEGORY OF STAFF	ESSENTIALS OF FOOD HYGIENE	HYGIENE AWARENESS INSTRUCTION	FORMAL TRAINING LEVEL	FORMAL TRAINING LEVEL 2 AND/OR 3
A Storekeeper Waiting staff Bar staff Catering assistants	Yes, before starting work	Yes, within 4 weeks (8 weeks for part-time staff)	No	No
B Chefs Cooks Supervisors Food preparation assistants	Yes, before starting work	Yes, within 4 weeks or 3 months for part-timers	Yes	No
C Managers Supervisors	Yes, before starting work	Yes, within 4 weeks	Yes, within 3 months	Yes, but only good practice not essential

employees' responsibilities. Details with regard to how much training is required are not specified in the regulations. However, the HMSO *Industry Guide to Catering* provides guidance on training that can be taken as a general standard to comply with the legislation.

The HMSO guide suggests three categories of food handler, all of which need training.

- Category A – support and front-of-house staff, including storekeeper, waiter/waitress, bar staff, counter staff, servery assistant, cellar person.
- Category B – those involved in the preparation of high-risk (unwrapped) foods, including chefs, cooks, catering supervisors, kitchen assistants and bar staff who prepare food.
- Category C – managers or supervisors who may handle food, including all such persons based on site.

Before any food handler starts work they must be given written and verbal instructions in the essentials of food hygiene.

The second stage of training is hygiene awareness instruction.

Formal training
Formal food hygiene training as suggested by the *Industry Guide*, going beyond essentials and awareness, is recommended to comply with the law.

Formal training beyond essentials and awareness
Level 1
The overall aim of this training is to provide a firm foundation of basic knowledge in the following disciplines:

- food poisoning micro-organisms – sources and types together with simple microbiology
- common food hazards – physical, chemical and microbiological
- personal hygiene – responsibilities
- pest prevention and control
- cleaning and disinfection
- food storage and preparation including temperature control
- legal requirements.

The duration of such a course is suggested to be at least six hours.

Level 2

This is more advanced training than level 1 and should cover more detail especially about management and food safety monitoring systems. Recommended duration is at least 36 hours. This is known as the intermediate level.

Level 3

This would be aimed at the most advanced food hygiene training and would provide management with the ability to manage and evaluate hygiene systems such as HACCP and Assured Safe Catering.

Recommended duration of training is at least 36 hours. This is known as Advanced Hygiene for Managers, and is an essential qualification for those who wish to train employees in essential food hygiene. It is also strongly advised that those who wish to deliver essential hygiene training take a trainer skills qualification as well.

(May 2002 saw the first reading of the EU food hygiene regulations; a significant change was made to the rule on training. Food business operators should ensure that food handlers are regularly supervised and annually undergo appropriate training by experts of food hygiene as well as general legislation on protection of health and prevention of infection.)

Management responsibilities

Managers must be familiar with:

- the Food Safety Act 1990
- the Food Hygiene Regulations 2005
- Hazard Analysis Critical Control Point (HACCP).

HACCP enables:

- evaluation of the operation
- the location of possible points of contamination
- the determining of the severity of the hazard
- staff to take preventative measures to protect against a food-borne illness outbreak.

It is an assessment of all the hazards associated with each step of a catering organisation. Staff need to know the hazards, the degree of risk involved and that they can apply the controls that have been introduced to reduce and eliminate the risk.

Food hygiene training areas

- Knowledge of temperature control and recording of temperatures.
- Personal cleanliness.
- Awareness of current legislation.
- Cross-contamination.
- Protective clothing.
- Bacteria triangle.
- Promote and maintain a high sense of awareness to food hygiene and safety.
- Ensure products are stored at correct temperature.
- The frequency at which the taking and recording of temperature readings are carried out.
- Any unfit food disposed of.

A summary of food hygiene practice

Dangers to food
- Chemical (copper, lead, etc.).
- Plant (toadstools).
- Bacteria (cause of most cases of food poisoning).

Bacteria
- Almost everywhere; not all are harmful.
- Must be magnified 500–1000 times to be seen.
- Under ideal conditions, they multiply by dividing in two every 20 minutes.

Sources of food-poisoning bacteria
- Human – nose, throat, excreta, spots, cuts, etc.
- Animal – excreta.
- Foodstuffs – meat, eggs, milk, from animal carriers.

Method of spread of bacteria
- Human – coughs, sneezes, hands.
- Animals – excreta (rats, mice, cows, pets, etc.), infected carcasses.
- Other means – equipment, china, towels.

Factors essential for bacterial growth
- Suitable temperature, time.
- Enough moisture; suitable food.

Methods of control of bacterial growth
- Heat: sterilisation, using high temperatures to kill all micro-organisms; pasteurisation using lower temperatures to kill harmful bacteria only; cooking.
- Cold: refrigeration at 3–5°C (37–41°F) stops growth of food-poisoning bacteria and retards growth of other micro-organisms; deep freeze at –18°C (0°F) stops growth of all micro-organisms.

Foods commonly causing food poisoning
- Poultry, made-up meat dishes, trifles, custards, synthetic cream, sauces, left-over foods.

Common causes of food poisoning
- Food prepared too far in advance, storage at ambient temperature.
- Inadequate cooling, inadequate reheating.
- Contamination of processed food, undercooking.
- Inadequate thawing, cross-contamination.
- Improper warm holding, infected food handlers.

Food poisoning prevention
- Comply with the rules of hygiene.
- Take care and thought.
- Ensure that high standards of cleanliness are applied to premises and equipment.
- Prevent accidents.

Specific points to be applied
- High standards of personal hygiene.
- Attention to physical fitness.
- Maintaining good working conditions.
- Maintaining equipment in good repair and clean.
- Use separate equipment and knives for cooked and uncooked foods.
- Ample provision of cleaning facilities and equipment.
- Correct storage of foods at the right temperature.
- Safe reheating of foods.
- Quick cooking of foods prior to storage.
- Protection of foods from vermin and insects.
- Hygienic washing-up procedure.
- Food handlers knowing how food poisoning is caused.

THE FOOD STANDARDS AGENCY

On 1 April 2000 the Food Standards Agency (FSA) took over UK responsibility for food safety and food quality from the DoH and the Ministry of Agriculture, Fisheries and Food (MAFF, now DEFRA), and the equivalent organisations in Wales, Northern Ireland and Scotland.

The FSA was established by the Food Standard Act 1999. The Agency's main objective is:

> ... to protect public health from risks which may raise in connection with the consumption of foods, and otherwise to protect the interests of consumers in relation to food.

As such, the FSA has assumed the UK Government's responsibilities relating to:

- the implementation of legislation on food safety, hygiene, composition and labelling
- diet and nutrition issues, and related consumer labelling.

Agency priorities

These include:

- better communication, with a commitment to working in an open way
- putting the consumer first
- promoting healthy and safe eating
- developing a food chain strategy from farm to fork, including the provision of advice on food safety and quality
- improving research and surveillance
- strengthening links with local authority enforcement services to improve the effectiveness and consistency of food law enforcement.

Agency structure

A 14-member board is responsible for the strategic direction of the Agency. The board's role is to ensure that the FSA fulfils its legal obligations, and takes proper account of scientific advice in the interest of consumers. Board members have a wide range of experience, and have been appointed to act in the public interest.

SOME DEFINITIONS

- **Antibiotic:** drug used to destroy pathogenic bacteria within human or animals bodies.
- **Antiseptic:** substance that prevents the growth of bacteria and moulds, specifically on or in the human body.
- **Bactericide:** substance that destroys bacteria.
- **Carrier:** person who harbours, and may transmit, pathogenic organisms without showing signs of illness.
- **Cleaning:** removal of soil, food residues, dirt, grease and other objectionable matter.

Further information
- Royal Society for the Promotion of Health (website: www.rsph.org.uk)
- Royal Institute of Public Health and Hygiene (website: www.riphh.org.uk)
- Institution of Environmental Health Officers, Chadwick House, Rushworth Street, London SE1 0QT
- Local Environmental Health Departments
- Health & Safety Executive, Rose Court, 2 Southwark Bridge, London SE1 9HS
- National Institute for Health and Clinical Excellence (website: www.nice.org.uk)
- Royal Society of Health, 38A St George's Drive, London SW1V 4BH
- Food Hygiene Bureau Ltd (website: www.foodhygienebureau.org.uk)
- Chartered Institute of Environmental Health (website: www.cieh.org.uk)

- **Contamination:** occurrence of any objectionable matter in food.
- **Danger zone of bacterial growth:** temperature range within which multiplication of pathogenic bacteria is possible (from 5°–63°C).
- **First-aid materials:** suitable and sufficient bandages and dressings, including waterproof dressings and antiseptic. All dressings to be individually wrapped.
- **Food handling:** any operation in the production, preparation, processing, packaging, storage, transport, distribution and sale of food.
- **Gastroenteritis:** inflammation of the stomach and intestinal tract that normally results in diarrhoea.
- **Germicide:** agent used for killing micro-organisms.
- **Incubation period:** period between infection and the first signs of illness.
- **Mildew:** type of fungus similar to mould.
- **Moulds:** microscopic organisms (fungi) that may appear as woolly patches on food.
- **Pathogen:** disease-producing organism.
- **Pesticide:** chemical used to kill pests.
- **Residual insecticide:** long-lasting insecticide applied in such a way that it remains active for a considerable period of time.
- **Sanitiser:** chemical agent used for cleansing and disinfecting surfaces and equipment.
- **Spores:** resistant resting phase of bacteria, protecting them against adverse conditions such as high temperatures.
- **Sterile:** free from all living organisms.
- **Sterilisation:** process that destroys all living organisms.
- **Steriliser:** chemical used to destroy all living organisms.
- **Toxins:** poisons produced by pathogens.
- **Viruses:** microscopic pathogens that multiply in the living cells of their host.
- **Wholesome food:** sound food, fit for human consumption.

Some references to commodities elsewhere in the book:

TOPICS FOR DISCUSSION

1 The implications of the Food Hygiene (England) Regulations 2006 for the catering industry.
2 The importance of regular food hygiene training for all staff.
3 The advantages and disadvantages of the Food Standards Agency.
4 The importance of good and accurate record keeping as a preparation to prove 'due diligence'.
5 Why should waste disposal and recycling occur in every establishment?
6 Explain how food should be stored hygienically.
7 Does personal hygiene matter? Discuss this topic.
8 Why is a system of recording necessary to maintain higher standards of hygiene?
9 Discuss the food hygiene regulations. Do you consider there are any omissions? If so what are they?

Chapter 17 INFORMATION AND COMMUNICATION TECHNOLOGY IN THE HOSPITALITY INDUSTRY

INFORMATION AND COMMUNICATION TECHNOLOGY IN SOCIETY

Today information technology is everywhere we look and, when added to the potential of powerful communication technology, the possibilities of how it can be used are endless. Almost everything we do or use comes into contact with information and communication technology (ICT) at some point in its development or delivery.

Most equipment, whether obviously – as in the case of computer terminals – or less so – as in the case of the microprocessor at the core of the latest piece of kitchen equipment – has computing technology at its heart, and the widespread availability of the Internet via high-speed connections has revolutionised how we communicate with each other. Add to this the latest developments in mobile and wireless technology (WiFi) and we have the basis for whole new ways in how we operate, both for business and leisure purposes.

From a business perspective the most valuable commodity for effective and efficient operation is reliable, up-to-date information – hence the need for computers and the benefits they provide in information storage, manipulation and communication.

The hospitality industry consists of mainly small to medium-sized enterprises, many privately owned and managed. Back in the early 1960s the hospitality industry in the form of the large catering company J. Lyons provided the first application of computers as a business tool. Since then their use has dramatically expanded and today the availability of cheap and powerful computers and low-cost access to the Internet are within the reach of even the smallest business.

COMPUTER OPERATIONS IN THE CATERING INDUSTRY

Most catering businesses find that the use of general-purpose computing systems, usually a basic personal computer (PC) with generic software installed, provides them with substantial advantages in respect of access to general information sources via the Internet, specific data about the financial operation and forecasting of the business, or at the most basic level help in the production of routine text- and graphics-based materials such as menus and rotas through an easily set up and operated solution (even for novice users). They are frequently linked together through networks, especially in medium-sized and larger establishments, and when used in this way offer a resource-efficient and effective way of distributing data resources and equipment.

Specialist packages

Specialist computer software packages, designed especially for managing hospitality industry-focused tasks, are readily available over a wide price range (reflecting functionality and capacity). The most commonly found are:

- reservation systems
- electronic point of sale (EPOS) systems
- food and beverage management systems
- property management systems.

Reservations systems
There are four principle types of system in use.

1 **Single property-based system:** this will usually be part of a property management system (PMS) (see below). These deal with the recording of accommodation sales for a single property.
2 For hotels that belong or are affiliated to a group, **central reservation systems** (CRSs) are run by the group or on its behalf by consortia. These provide a single point of contact for a prospective guest and ensure that sales are maximised. Increasingly these systems are directly linked with the individual property's reservations system, but in some

cases there remains a manual transfer of data between the systems at the individual property.

3 **Global distribution systems** (GDSs) are based on airline reservations systems; these in turn are linked to the CRS and travel agents (and sometimes other large users), and thus allow direct selling and reservation of accommodation to take place.

4 Currently there are a number of agencies offering the industry the opportunity to market hotels on the **World Wide Web** (www). These systems also offer the facility to make direct reservations of hotel accommodation. The benefit of this approach is that it is available to anyone having access to the Internet (see below).

Property management systems

A property management system (PMS) is the name given to the sort of system found in hotels, which manages reservations and guest billing. There are a wide range of PMSs available; these range from simple systems to cover basic reservations and billing, to sophisticated systems with many additional facilities, which through appropriate interfaces are able to monitor and control all activities within a hotel.

This means that, in small hotels, the PMS can simply look after reservations and guest billing; in large hotels it is usually used as a top-level system, and data and reports from other systems – such as event management, point of sale, food and beverage management, telephone management, security systems and in-room guest services – will be incorporated into their own billing and reporting systems. Increasingly frequently, PMSs feature an interface into central reservation systems and direct online booking services via the Internet.

Data regarding past guests stored in these systems (the guest history) are regarded as a valuable asset by the business and frequently used as the basis for sophisticated sales and marketing operations, allowing hotels to target potential guests whose preferences are known. These data are also valuable in building up information to support forecasting in respect of future patterns of business, which in turn allows effective room rates and discounts to be calculated. This information provides the basis for yield management systems, which are increasingly being used by larger establishments. The introduction of yield management (YM) techniques allows the business to maximise the financial return from bedroom sales; although the technique is not in itself computer based, the use of a computer package with electronic access to guest data statistics greatly simplifies the operation and improves the effectiveness of the YM process.

Electronic point of sale (EPOS) systems

These are used for recording the details of transactions. At the simplest level they take the form of a single cash register with a processor, memory and printer usually supplied in a single case. Although relatively simple to use they offer greatly enhanced facilities over traditional non-computerised systems, not the least of which is detailed information about how items are performing in respect of sales volume. Typical facilities offered include multiple total storing to enable sales to be analysed as required by the end user, price look-up – which enables the user to press a key labelled with the name of a dish or a drink and the correct price will be added to the transaction – and multi-level pricing to cope with special offers or 'happy hour' arrangements.

The most sophisticated systems offer a large range of features and usually consist of a number of machines linked together (networked) in restaurant, kitchen and bar, and also sometimes linked to a central computer. These large systems offer an extremely sophisticated control process, which reduces work for staff and supplies detailed information about the business to management. For example, orders keyed in by bar staff when a guest arrives in a restaurant may be transferred to the restaurant account, giving the guest one consolidated account at the end of the meal. Waiting staff entering the guest's order, often via a touch-screen terminal, into the system will find that it will automatically print out in the correct preparation department, saving a great deal of time and work. As this process goes on the guest account is automatically prepared ready for printing and presentation at the end of the meal.

With this type of system all orders to kitchen and bar are printed and show the time the order was processed; they also eliminate errors and cancel out the likelihood of arguments between staff due to badly hand-written checks. As the account is developed by the system as the meal progresses there is no danger that items will be omitted from the bill or be incorrectly charged, as happens, not infrequently, with manual systems, thus simplifying the control systems that need to be in place.

Management reports are very comprehensive, giving such details as sales of each dish or drink item. Sales breakdown by each outlet, by each member of staff and for each session are also easy to obtain. Most systems will give the profit on each item sold and may also be linked to stock-control systems. When waiting staff are responsible for their own guest bills the system will not allow them to log off duty until all accounts are cleared and the cash paid in to a central point.

Information of this type, intelligently used, can assist the management of the business to ensure maximum effectiveness.

Stock-control systems

At the simplest level these systems allow the user to enter stock received and issued, extract details of consumption and calculate the value of stock in hand. More sophisticated systems provide these basic facilities as well as a considerable range of other features such as details of suppliers, automatic issue of orders when stocks drop to a predefined level, detailed records of issues and current prices of all stock items.

Stock control is relatively easy to operate on bar stock, but dealing with food items, especially fresh foods, is far more complex as food items are rarely used in the quantities in which they are supplied, and there is a wide range of measurements in use, which require accurate conversion tables. There is also the need to allow for and deal effectively with wastage. If we take what at first glance may seem the relatively simple stock item of fresh eggs – these may be supplied by the dozen or a multiple of a dozen, or by the case or multiple or fraction of case or, in some cases, by the tray or multiple of a tray. They may be used in recipes as single eggs or by weight in ounces or grams or by volume by the fluid ounce or by the pint or litre. Recipes calling for just egg yolk or egg white, or different quantities of each, may further compound this. In this example further complications may be introduced by the use of pasteurised egg and dried egg in certain recipes.

Food and beverage management systems

Food and beverage management systems take the concept of stock control one stage further. They add a control framework that, when correctly implemented, gives greatly improved levels of management control. With this type of system a database is created of all recipes in use in the business, together with a further database containing the ingredients used to support those dishes.

Typical information stored about each ingredient is:

- ingredient code
- ingredient name
- ingredient description
- category
- purchase unit
- unit of use
- unit of measure
- content weight
- price
- supplier(s)
- tax rate
- shelf life
- re-order level
- percentage usable.

Typical information stored about each recipe is:

- recipe code
- quantity of production
- selling unit
- tax code
- re-order level
- profit required (per cent).

For each ingredient in a recipe:

- ingredient code
- ingredient unit of measure.

Using this information as a base it is possible for kitchen staff to order goods from the stores by recipe, to automatically scale for the quantity required and effectively cost those dishes. The system will then give the required selling price to achieve the required profit.

Food and beverage management systems, because of their cost and complexity, still tend to be used by large-scale users, particularly where tight control of costs and adherence to pre-set budgets is important – for example, large-production cook-chill units and hospitals. Add-on modules allow for differing user requirements such as cyclic menus and nutritional analysis.

Comprehensive reporting is offered, which gives a high level of management information and thus control. For example, it is easy to check purchase levels and to trace high-cost ingredients. These systems are frequently linked to point of sale systems to take the control process one stage further.

Menu engineering

This technique utilises the computer modelling of data and was originally developed in the USA. The system holds data about the sales volume, costs and profits of each dish on the menu. By changing the ratio of the areas it is possible, in theory, to create a menu offering the optimum balance between popularity and maximum profit. The technique can be carried out with pencil and paper, but is far more effective when using a computer system. Using such a system to build up reliable stores of trading information it becomes possible over a period of time to develop a 'computer model' of the performance of each of the dishes on the menu. This type of activity is frequently carried out using a 'model' created on a spreadsheet, such as Microsoft Excel, rather than in a stand-alone commercial package.

Dietary analysis

As they become more selective about what they eat, customers require more dietary information about the dishes on menus. Dietary analysis works from large databases of dietary information and will give details of the composition of individual foods or complete dishes at the touch of a button. Again, there is a range of systems available – from simple ones that give a relatively crude breakdown, which may be suitable for the basic information required by the average restaurant guest, to the more complex, which are linked to government food tables and give extremely accurate and comprehensive data (these are suitable for calculating detailed nutritional profiles).

Simple dietary analysis systems are often available as add-on modules to food and beverage management systems, while the more comprehensive systems are usually available as 'stand-alones' from specialist suppliers.

Event management systems

Targeted at hotels and conference centres these systems are designed to deal with all the elements of taking a booking and managing one-off events, such as conferences, meetings, weddings and banquets. The range of facilities that they offer vary, but one would expect to find a booking diary together with a comprehensive costing and billing section. Many systems have modules that allow the allocation of equipment to specific events, thus ensuring that it is not possible to inadvertently double-book equipment. The costing of food from pre-designed menus is another feature commonly found. Modules that allow the physical planning of the room layout on the screen are also available with some products. In some cases these also have the ability to give graphic views of how the room will appear from specific angles. As with any modern computer management system, comprehensive management reporting is a major feature.

Generic software

This is the term given to software that we use to support the operation of a business, but that does not have a purpose that is unique to any specific industry. The most common types found are: word processing, spreadsheets, databases, presentation tools and Internet browsers. When buying business PCs these systems are often supplied with the computer as added-value items. When purchasing independently there is a wide range of systems across a wide price band and offering a great variety of facilities. The best known and most widely used is Microsoft Office, which is offered in a number of versions.

THE INTERNET AND MARKETING

The merging of information technology and communications is having – and will in the future continue to have – a significant impact on society, the way we live our lives and certainly how we conduct our businesses. The most obvious manifestation of this is the Internet – a global network of networks. This worldwide network of computers allows anyone connected to it access to a virtually limitless database of information and almost instantaneous communication with anyone else connected.

For most businesses the Internet is used to send and receive e-mail and to access information via the www. (Technically, the Internet is the name of the system and the www is the software of its most popular element.)

For most business users the most practical method is to be connected via a high-capacity, high-speed connection known as broadband; this gives an always-on link. These are provided by a range of suppliers, which offer a variety of physical connection possibilities, including wireless links, and a range of services including email and websites that exist to provide a connection to the Internet for users; each service provider offers alternative add-on facilities and will make a charge for its services.

Most computers are now supplied with Internet-ready software and all that is necessary is to choose your connection method and supplier. To use the web a piece of software called a web browser is required. This allows you to move around the Internet once you are connected. The best known is Microsoft Explorer, which is included as part of Microsoft Windows. The other main browser, Netscape, is available free as part of the Netscape Communicator package, which can be downloaded directly from the Internet.

The web is made up of websites. It is possible to visit any website and view its contents. In addition to text and graphics, many sites offer video images and sound files. It is possible for anyone to set up a website, but most small business users contract this out to a specialist company, which will maintain and monitor the site on their behalf.

Websites have become an important marketing and promotional tool for businesses, and the hospitality industry is no exception. The major area of impact within hospitality is the selling and reservation of hotel accommodation. Many hotels now have their own websites, which act as an electronic brochure and also usually offer the opportunity to reserve accommodation. This is already having an impact on global distribution companies and travel agents, and the way they do business. Many restaurants and other catering operations are also using websites as a valuable means of promotion.

By setting up its own page on the web a business can have, for a relatively low cost, a versatile promotional tool that can be used for a variety of purposes, such as marketing and direct selling. A web presence allows the smallest operator to compete with the largest company in terms of attracting business – an important consideration in an industry with a large percentage of small operations.

While marketing currently provides the major use of the Internet for the catering industry it should not be forgotten that it also offers an unrivalled source of information on current developments and legislation, particularly useful in the food and catering technology areas. Increasingly, new information on major developments is being published on the Internet in addition to the more traditional forms of distribution.

Figure 17.1 An Internet café

Professional bodies and trade associations operate websites for their members, giving access to impressive data sources targeted at the industry. For all hospitality industry businesses the potential offered by the Internet is unlimited – it can provide them with access to a vast range of global data and expertise that can be used in the operation of the business.

COMPUTERS AND HOSPITALITY MANAGEMENT

As can be seen from the foregoing, computers are a valuable tool in the management of a business. Correctly operated and controlled they are virtually indispensable to the well-run business that wishes to keep one step ahead of the competition. However, the best of systems will give maximum effectiveness only if well managed and if management make effective use of the information the systems provide. The management of computers ideally needs to focus on two general areas: first, the selection, set-up and day-to-day operation of the equipment and, second, the application of management information obtained from the systems.

Management structure

In large hospitality businesses, especially large hotels, there may be a member of the management team, usually known as the systems manager, with responsibility for the operation of all IT systems within the business. Reporting to the general manager or chief accountant, this role is usually at head of department level. The post holder must understand the operation of the business thoroughly, and have a good all-round knowledge of applied information technology. In addition to being responsible for the smooth operation of the IT systems on a day-to-day basis the systems manager will also be responsible for the selection and updating of systems, the training of new and existing staff for the IT systems in use, and compliance with all relevant legislation. In smaller businesses, these responsibilities will usually be taken over by the manager or owner of the business, or by an assistant manager or departmental heads. Whatever the structure that is in place, it is important that management ensure that all members of staff are aware of their responsibilities in respect of the use of IT. In some cases it may be a criminal offence if systems are not correctly implemented and controlled. In any case, poor management of IT systems and the information they are able to provide will ensure that the business is not benefiting from its investment.

Choice of systems

The costs involved in setting up and running the computer over its lifetime will be far more expensive than the purchase price. When considering the computerisation of an element of the business it is good practice to remember that computers are good at repetitive tasks with large volumes of data to process. They can provide information to help you make effective decisions but they cannot in themselves take decisions for you.

The first task is to identify the areas of the business that could potentially benefit from computerisation. The most effective way to do this is to undertake a feasibility study of the existing task(s) involved to identify exactly what happens and what volume of activity takes place. On reviewing this process it may prove that you need only revise the existing systems and that a computer is not strictly necessary. If the decision is to go ahead then you must identify what information the system must provide for the management of the business. From this it is fairly easy to identify what data must go into the system to give that information as output. For example, if you expect a stock-control system to advise you when to re-order it must hold details of minimum stock levels. Once you have identified these features, together with volume and critical operational constraints such as speed, types of printer and methods of output, you are ready to go shopping.

The software, which will actually carry out the task required, is the most important element to consider. Apart from a detailed checklist drawn up on the above principles, when choosing software a purchaser will need to consider the following issues.

- Does the software cover all the major requirements of the system specification?
- What hardware configuration is required? Relative costs?
- Is costly supporting equipment or software required?
- Does the software cover all the detailed requirements of the system specification?
- What are the performance standards required (i.e. speed, capacity, number of users)?
- What level of customisation is possible?
- Is the product supported by regular updates? What are the costs of this?
- System expandability?
- How easy is it to use?
- What is the available level of support?
- Supplier background and expertise?
- Financial arrangement available?

While the hardware must at minimum be capable of running the required software, you should spend as much as possible on the processor and internal memory, known as random access memory (RAM), and external memory, the hard disk. Memory capacity especially is relatively low cost if specified at the time of purchase. Software takes more space with every upgrade or development, and a system running at capacity is generally unhappy, will run slowly and give problems in operation.

An import consideration, even today when systems are vastly more reliable than those of the early days, is that of system back-up. In short, what happens in the event of a failure? Questions to ask include the following.

- Is the system critical to the running of the business?
- For how long can I continue to operate without the system running?

The answers will provide the context in which to fully consider your hardware back-up requirements. For example, the answers for a business-critical reservation and billing system would almost certainly be very different to those for a stock-control system. Both are business critical, but of the two only the reservation and billing system could cause major financial damage to the business if unavailable for more than a very short time. Similarly, the geographic location of the business has a part to play: the power back-up required for a city-centre operation that rarely suffers mains supply failures will be very different to that needed in a rural location suffering from more frequent supply problems.

The following questions cover some of the areas a prospective purchaser will need to consider when purchasing equipment (hardware).

- Is the speed of performance adequate?
- Is the memory capacity adequate?
- What is the physical size and space requirement?
- Can the equipment be expanded to meet increased software demands?
- Reliability/back-up support?
- Ease of use/ergonomics?
- Comparative operating costs?
- Maintenance support?

Sources of supply

If considering a straightforward system for general office use, using generic business software, then it may initially appear cost effective to purchase from the direct mail suppliers who advertise in most computing magazines, or from one of the large specialist discount stores. Through large buying capacity such outlets are often able to offer attractive financial deals. Some caution is required, however, as generally a level of pre-knowledge is expected (even if not stated) and levels of user support are often more in line with the needs of a hobbyist user than that of a business that is relying on the systems. Some of these large suppliers offer support for the business user so may be worth considering where the systems are non-critical to the operation of the business. Alternatively, a number of independent training firms have become established offering short courses relating to the more popular software packages.

In most cases a specialist dealer/distributor will offer a higher level of personalised support, but this comes at a cost. For a non-technical user it is often much more cost effective in the long term to build up a relationship with a good local dealer who will get to know individual requirements and can offer good – although, it should be noted, not always impartial – advice.

Specialist companies supply most catering IT systems. Frequently these companies provide a complete service including hardware, software, installation and training. Again although not offering impartial advice they will be only too happy to discuss your specification and advise accordingly. Prices, facilities and range of services provided vary widely and it is essential to shop around. Normally with these large 'turnkey' systems (so called because, at least in theory, they do all the work, leaving you only to turn the key to switch the system on) once the decision is made the business is committed to the supplying company for the life of the system, so it is important that all factors are considered before completing the purchase.

For impartial advice it is possible to use the services of a consultant. For a fee they will investigate possible solutions for a specific problem or task, then offer or recommend a number of systems from which to choose. It is important to bear two things in mind when dealing with consultants:

1 they must be impartial – that is, not taking commission from hardware or software suppliers
2 the final choice of system will be left to the establishment.

Consultants can be extremely useful, but are no substitute for, and cannot make up for, a lack of knowledge of information technology and of its application to a business on the part of the user.

Operation

Once the business has selected and purchased a system, it will need to ensure maximum effectiveness from the investment. A computer system must give a competitive edge. No matter how well matched the system is to the needs of the business this will happen only if the systems are correctly implemented and operated.

The strategic concerns of operating computers will of course rest with the management of the business, but it is also important that management ensure that all users understand their contribution to the effective operation of the system. For example, a stock-control system will not give the correct information in its reports if the storekeeper is careless when entering delivery notes and invoices. It should be ensured that all members of staff using the systems or preparing data for entry to the systems are correctly trained, that working conditions are comfortable and comply with legislation, and that regular monitoring of system performance takes place.

System reporting

Most software systems available today have extremely comprehensive reporting facilities. In addition, many systems also have a built-in report generator to allow the user to develop reports that suit their own operation. With the high levels of compatibility found today, it is possible to export data from specialist systems into spreadsheets and databases for further analysis. While a business will expect a system to give reports on the level of activity and performance against agreed targets, the area where a computer system can really help to give competitive advantage is in the strategic development of the business. Businesses frequently export performance data from their operational systems (e.g. point of sale, food and beverage management) and use these data for the basis of computer modelling for forecasting future business performance.

LEGISLATION

This is an area that rapidly expanded from the mid-1980s, reflecting the increasing use of IT and the corresponding need to offer legal protection to suppliers, users and people on whom data are held in computers.

The principle areas for legislation, which have a major impact on the way that information technology is used in businesses, are data protection, health and safety, and copyright protection.

The Data Protection Act 1998 updated and expanded the scope of the original act of 1984. The Act defines the basic principles that must be followed if anyone wishes to store data about living identifiable individuals on a computer system. It gives the person whose data is stored right of access to the data and lays down principles for secure storage of the data. The Act makes it an offence to hold personal data, as defined in the Act, unless the holder is registered with the Data Protection Registrar.

The Screen Display (VDU) Regulations 1992 lay down very strict guidelines about the way computers are operated and the environment in which they are located. For example, there should not be glare from windows or artificial light, and the working environment must be ergonomically correct to ensure that there are no long-term health hazards for staff using the systems. The legislation also covers the actual design of the appearance of the software on the screen and states that training must take place on a regular basis. It covers issues in respect of extended use by an operative, which includes such issues as regular eye tests. The Management of Health & Safety at Work Regulations (amended 1992) also lay down specific conditions that must be followed when expectant mothers operate VDUs. This area of legislation is currently under review.

The Copyright Design and Patent Act of 1988 protects the copyright of the software owner. Amongst its provisions, this law makes it an offence to buy a piece of software for use on a single computer and then load it on further computers without additional payment.

There is also the Computer Misuse Act 1990, which makes it a criminal offence to access a computer without permission or to corrupt data stored in a computer. As more and more computers are now becoming linked, so that remote access is common, this piece of legislation will become of more benefit to smaller businesses.

FUTURE DEVELOPMENTS

Catering was the first industry to make commercial use of computing. It is increasingly important that users within the industry, whatever the size of their business, make use of applied information technology if they wish to remain effective and gain a lead over their competitors.

Computing is a fast-advancing area of technology and it is perhaps unwise to look too far into the future at where developments may take us. It seems certain that the integration of computer systems will lead to a single point of data capture and more effective use of the data once captured. The increasingly common use of computers as communication links – for example, to external suppliers using electronic data exchange – and the widespread use of the Internet will continue to have a significant impact on the way we do business.

Impact on how guests select hotels, restaurants and catering services will undoubtedly continue to be influenced by electronic promotion and access. Similarly, we will see much wider availability of access to electronic data sources, particularly in hotel guestrooms.

FURTHER READING

O'Connor, P. (2004) *Using Computers in Hospitality* (3rd edn). London: Thomson Learning.

TOPICS FOR DISCUSSION

1 Computers are used in business because they have the capability to reduce costs and improve efficiency. Identify six ways in which a computer can help reduce costs or improve efficiency in a typical catering business.

2 Discuss the advantages and disadvantages of using generic software to support the operation of routine business functions.

3 The ability to enable computers to communicate with each other easily – e.g. networking, the Internet and the added functionality of mobile communication (WiFi) – has fundamentally changed the way in which we use computing technology.

4 Take a catering business with which you are familiar and consider:
   - how it currently uses computers to support its business
   - how it is influenced by communications technology
   - what improvements could be made through better use of communications technology.

5 The Internet has had a significant impact on the way hotels market their product and take reservations. Using a suitable Internet search engine, investigate current developments in this area and consider what further changes we might expect to see over the next five years.

6 You are given the responsibility of purchasing a new stock-control package for your business. Consider the options available to you and list the steps that you would take to ensure that you arrive at the best product to support your needs.

7 Legislation now plays a major role in the way we use computers. Consider the implications of the Data Protection Act and identify the limitations and controls it places on the ways in which we can use customer data.

APPENDIX 1: USEFUL WEBSITES

Ask a Chef – www.askachef.com
BBC Food Pages – www.bbc.co.uk/food
Beverage Net – www.beveragenet.net
British Cleaning Council – www.britishcleaningcouncil.org
British Dietetic Association – www.bda.uk.com
British Hospitality Association – www.bha-online.org.uk
British Institute of Inkeeping – www.bii.org
British Nutrition Foundation – www.nutrition.org.uk
British Standards – www.bsi-global.com or www.bsi-uk.com
Caterer and Hotelkeeper – www.caterersearch.com
Catering Net – www.cateringnet.co.uk
Chartered Institute of Environmental Health – www.cieh.org
ehotelier.com – www.ehotelier.com
Food Standards Agency – www.food.gov.uk
Foodservice World – www.foodserviceworld.com
Foodservice.com – www.foodservice.com
Hospitality Net – hospitalitynet.org
Hotel and Catering, International Management Association – www.hcima.org.uk
Induced Energy Limited – www.inducedenergy.com
Industry Guide to Hygiene Practice – archive.food.gov.uk/dept_health/pdf/catsec.pdf
Into Wine – www.intowine.com
Meat and Livestock Commission – www.mlc.org.uk
RIDDOR Incident Contact Centre – www.riddor.gov.uk
Royal Institute of Public Health – www.riph.org
Royal Society for the Promotion of Health – www.rsph.org
UK Food Law – www.fst.rdg.ac.uk/foodlaw
Unilever – www.unilever.co.uk
Webtender (online bartender) – www.webtender.com
Wine and Dine E-zine – dine-online.co.uk
The Wine Line – www.the-wine-line.com
Wine Spectator – winespectator.com
Wine.com – www.wine.com
Yahoo! food websites – www.yahoo.co.uk/society_and_culture/food_and_drink

APPENDIX 2: LEGISLATION

Asylum and Immigration Act 1996
Bread and Flour Regulations 1988
Butchers Shops Amendment Regulation 2000
Children and Young Persons (Protection from Tobacco) Act 1991
Computer Misuse Act 1988
Consumer Protection Act 1987
Contracts of Employment Act 1972
Dangerous Machines Order 1964
Data Protection Act 1984
Data Protection Act 1998
Disability Discrimination Act 1995
Electricity at Work Regulations 1989
Employment Consolidation Act 1978
Employment Protections Act 1975
Employment Rights Act 1996
Equal Pay Act 1970
Fire Precautions (Workplace) Amendment 1999
Fire Precautions (Workplace) Regulations 1997
Fixed Term (Prevention of Less Favourable Treatment) Regulations 2002
Food Act 1991
Food Hygiene Regulation 1990
Food Hygiene (England) Regulations 2006
Food Labelling Amendment Regulations 1999
Food Labelling Regulations 1984
Food Premises (Registration) Amendment 1993
Food Premises (Registration) Regulations 1991
Food Safety (General Food Hygiene) Regulations 1995
Food Safety (Temperature Control) Regulations 1995
Food Safety Act 1990
Food Standards Act 1999
Gas Safety (Installation and Use) Regulations 1998
Health and Safety (Safety Signs and Signals) Regulations 1996
Health and Safety at Work Act 1974
Human Rights Act 1998
Hygiene and the Food Safety Act 1990/91
Licensing (Restaurant Meals) Act 1987
Licensing Act 1964
Part Time Workers Regulations 2000
Personal Protection Equipment at Work Regulations 1992
Price Marking (Food and Drink on Premises) Order 1979
Redundancy Payments Act 1965
Rehabilitation of Offenders Act 1974
Reporting Injuries Diseases and Dangerous Occurrences 1996

Sale and Supply of Goods Act 1994
Sale of Goods Act 1979
Screen Display (VDU) Regulations 1992
Sex Discrimination Act 1975
Supply of Goods and Services Act 1982
Trade Union and Labour Regulations Act 1974
Trade Union and Labour Relations Consolidation Act 1992
Trade Union Reform and Employment Rights Act 1993
Wages Act 1986
Water Industry Act 1991
Water Supply By Law 1989
Weights and Measures Act Intoxicating Liquor Order 1988
Working Time Regulations 1998

BIBLIOGRAPHY

British Hospitality Association (2004/5) *British Hospitality: Trends and Statistics*. BHA.

Cousins, J., Foskett, D. and Gillespie, C. (2004) *Food and Beverage Management* (2nd edn). Pearson Education.

Cracknell, H.L. and Kaufmann, R.J. (2002) *Practical Professional Catering Management*. Thomson Learning Vocational.

Croner's Catering (ongoing) Wolters Kluwer UK (see http://www.croner.co.uk/productDetails/category/managing_org/hospitality/product/Catering).

Department of Health and Social Security (DHSS) (1972) *Clean Catering*. London: HMSO (out of print).

Drummond, D. (1998) *Purchasing and Costing for the Hospitality Industry*. Hodder & Stoughton (out of print).

Ghazala, S. (ed.) (1998) *Sous Vide and Cook Chill Processing for the Food Industry*. Kluwer Academic/Plenum Publishers (Chapman & Hall Food Science Series).

Lean, M.E.J. (2006) *Fox and Cameron's Food Science, Nutrition and Health* (7th edn). Hodder Arnold.

Lillicrap, D.R. and Cousins, J. (2006) *Food and Beverage Service* (7th edn). Hodder & Stoughton.

Mintel (2004) *Eating Out Habits – UK* (see www.mintel.com).

Mintel (2005a) *Eating Out Review – UK* (see www.mintel.com).

Mintel (2005b) *The Food Market – UK* (see www.mintel.com).

Mintel (2006) *Eating Out – Ten Year Trends – UK* (see www.mintel.com).

MSN Encarta (2006) Microsoft (see http://encarta.msn.com/).

Newman, C. (2003) 'Sealed, signed and delivered!', in *Art Culinaire*, Winter.

Proudlove, R.K. (2001) *The Science and Technology of Foods*. Forbes Publications.

Shaw, C. (2005) *The Power of Food: Cancer – Food, Facts and Recipes*. Hamlyn.

Tunsey, G. and Worsley, A. (1995) *The Food System*. Earthscan Publications.

Whitbread Market Research, see www.mbdltd.co.uk.

INDEX

ELECTRONIC END USER SINGLE USE LICENCE AGREEMENT

FOR **Ceserani and Kinton's The Theory of Catering 11th edition CD-ROM Student Version** software published by Hodder and Stoughton Limited (HS) under its Hodder Arnold imprint.

NOTICE TO USER:
THIS IS A CONTRACT. BY INSTALLING THIS SOFTWARE YOU AND OTHERS TO WHOM YOU ALLOW ACCESS TO THE SOFTWARE ACCEPT ALL THE TERMS AND CONDITIONS OF THIS AGREEMENT.

This End User Single Use Licence Agreement accompanies the **Ceserani and Kinton's The Theory of Catering 11th edition CD-ROM Student Version** software (the Software) and shall also apply to any upgrades, modified versions or updates of the Software licensed to you by HS. Please read this Agreement carefully. Upon installing this software you will be asked to accept this Agreement and continue to install or, if you do not wish to accept this Agreement, to decline this Agreement, in which case you will not be able to use the Software.

Upon your acceptance of this Agreement, HS grants to you a non-exclusive, non-transferable licence to install, run and use the Software, subject to the following:

1. Use of the Software. **You may only install a single copy of the Software onto the hard disk or other storage device of only one computer.** If the computer is linked to a local area network then it must be installed in such a way so that the Software cannot be accessed by other computers on the same network. You may make a single back-up copy of the Software (which must be deleted or destroyed on expiry or termination of this Agreement). Except for that single back-up copy, you may not make or distribute any copies of the Software, or use it in any way not specified in this Agreement.

2. Copyright. The Software is owned by HS and its authors and suppliers, and is protected by Copyright Law. Except as stated above, this Agreement does not grant you any intellectual property rights in the Software or in the contents of **Ceserani and Kinton's The Theory of Catering 11th edition CD-ROM** as sold. All moral rights of artists and all other contributors to the Software are hereby asserted.

3. Restrictions. You assume full responsibility for the use of the Software and agree to use the Software legally and responsibly. You agree that you or any other person within or acting on behalf of the purchasing institution shall NOT: use or copy the Software otherwise than as specified in clause 1; transfer, distribute, rent, loan, lease, sub-lease or otherwise deal in the Software or any part of it; alter, adapt, merge, modify or translate the whole or any part of the Software for any purpose; or permit the whole or any part of the Software to be combined with or incorporated in any other product or program. You agree not to reverse engineer, decompile, disassemble or otherwise attempt to discover the source code of the Software. You may not alter or modify the installer program or any other part of the Software or create a new installer for the Software.

4. No Warranty. The Software is being delivered to you AS IS and HS makes no warranty as to its use or performance except that the Software will perform substantially as specified. HS AND ITS AUTHORS AND SUPPLIERS DO NOT AND CANNOT GIVE ANY WARRANTY REGARDING THE PERFORMANCE OR RESULTS

YOU MAY OBTAIN BY USING THE SOFTWARE OR ACCOMPANYING OR DERIVED DOCUMENTATION. HS AND ITS AUTHORS AND SUPPLIERS MAKE NO WARRANTIES, EXPRESS OR IMPLIED, AS TO NON-INFRINGEMENT OF THIRD PARTY RIGHTS, THE CONTENT OF THE SOFTWARE, MERCHANTABILITY, OR FITNESS FOR ANY PARTICULAR PURPOSE. IN NO EVENT WILL HS OR ITS AUTHORS OR SUPPLIERS BE LIABLE TO YOU FOR ANY CONSEQUENTIAL, INCIDENTAL, SPECIAL OR OTHER DAMAGES, OR FOR ANY CLAIM BY ANY THIRD PARTY (INCLUDING PERSONS WITH WHOM YOU HAVE USED THE SOFTWARE TO PROVIDE LEARNING SUPPORT) ARISING OUT OF YOUR INSTALLATION OR USE OF THE SOFTWARE.

5. Entire liability. HS's entire liability, and your sole remedy for a breach of the warranty given under Clause 4, is (a) the replacement of the Software not meeting the above limited warranty and which is returned by you within 90 days of purchase; or (b) if HS or its distributors are unable to deliver a replacement copy of the Software you may terminate this Agreement by returning the Software within 90 days of purchase and your money will be refunded. All other liabilities of HS including, without limitation, indirect, consequential and economic loss and loss of profits, together with all warranties, are hereby excluded to the fullest extent permitted by law.

6. Governing Law and General Provisions. This Agreement shall be governed by the laws of England and any actions arising shall be brought before the courts of England. If any part of this Agreement is found void and unenforceable, it will not affect the validity of the balance of the Agreement, which shall remain wholly valid and enforceable according to its terms. All rights not specifically licensed to you under this Agreement are reserved to HS. This Agreement shall automatically terminate upon failure by you to comply with its terms. This Agreement is the entire and only agreement between the parties relating to its subject matter. It supersedes any and all previous agreements and understandings (whether written or oral) relating to its subject matter and may only be amended in writing, signed on behalf of both parties.

Copyright © 2007 Hodder and Stoughton Ltd. All rights reserved.